Sheffield Hallam University
Learning and IT Services
Adsetts Centre City Campus
Sheffield   S1 1WB

102 095 976 2

KT-445-679

e the last dat

AN INTRODUCTION TO
QUALITATIVE
RESEARCH

SHEFFIELD HALLAM UNIVERSITY
LEARNING CENTRE
WITHDRAWN FROM STOCK

SAGE has been part of the global academic community since 1965, supporting high quality research and learning that transforms society and our understanding of individuals, groups, and cultures. SAGE is the independent, innovative, natural home for authors, editors and societies who share our commitment and passion for the social sciences.

Find out more at: **www.sagepublications.com**

Connect, Debate, Engage on Methodspace

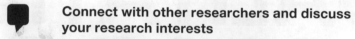 **Connect with other researchers and discuss your research interests**

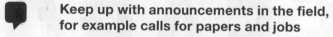 **Keep up with announcements in the field, for example calls for papers and jobs**

 **Discover and review resources**

 **Engage with featured content such as key articles, podcasts and videos**

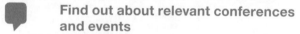 **Find out about relevant conferences and events**

Methodspace
Connecting the Research Community

brought to you by

SAGE

www.methodspace.com

AN INTRODUCTION TO
QUALITATIVE
RESEARCH
UWE FLICK

EDITION 5

Los Angeles | London | New Delhi
Singapore | Washington DC

Los Angeles | London | New Delhi
Singapore | Washington DC

SAGE Publications Ltd
1 Oliver's Yard
55 City Road
London EC1Y 1SP

SAGE Publications Inc.
2455 Teller Road
Thousand Oaks, California 91320

SAGE Publications India Pvt Ltd
B 1/I 1 Mohan Cooperative Industrial Area
Mathura Road
New Delhi 110 044

SAGE Publications Asia-Pacific Pte Ltd
3 Church Street
#10-04 Samsung Hub
Singapore 049483

Editor: Katie Metzler
Development editor: Amy Jarrold
Production editor: Ian Antcliff
Copyeditor: Neville Hankins
Proofreader: Rose James
Indexer: David Rudeforth
Marketing manager: Ben Griffin-Sherwood
Cover design: Shaun Mercier
Typeset by: C&M Digitals (P) Ltd, Chennai, India
Printed in Great Britain by Ashford Colour Press
Ltd, Gosport, Hants

© Uwe Flick 2014

First edition published 1998. Second edition published 2002. Third
edition first published 2006. Fourth edition first published 2009. This
edition published 2014.

© Originally published as *Qualitative Forschung* in the 'rowohlts
enzyklopädie' series. © 2007 Rowohlt Taschenbuch Verlag GmbH,
Reinbek bei Hamburg

Apart from any fair dealing for the purposes of research or private
study, or criticism or review, as permitted under the Copyright,
Designs and Patents Act, 1988, this publication may be reproduced,
stored or transmitted in any form, or by any means, only with the prior
permission in writing of the publishers, or in the case of reprographic
reproduction, in accordance with the terms of licences issued by the
Copyright Licensing Agency. Enquiries concerning reproduction
outside those terms should be sent to the publishers.

Library of Congress Control Number: 2013942397

British Library Cataloguing in Publication data

A catalogue record for this book is available from
the British Library

SHEFFIELD HALLAM UNIVERSITY
ADSETTS LEARNING CENTRE
300.72
FL

ISBN 978-1-4462-6778-3
ISBN 978-1-4462-6779-0 (pbk)

FSC
www.fsc.org
MIX
Paper from
responsible sources
FSC™ C013985

Brief Contents

Contents

List of Boxes

List of Figures

List of Tables

List of Case Studies

About the Author

Uwe Flick is Professor of Qualitative Research in Social Science and Education at the Free University of Berlin, Germany. He is a trained psychologist and sociologist and received his PhD from the Free University of Berlin in 1988 and his Habilitation from the Technical University of Berlin in 1994. He has been Professor of Qualitative Research at Alice Salomon University of Applied Sciences in Berlin, Germany and at the University of Vienna, Austria, where he continues to work as Guest-Professor. Previously, he was Adjunct Professor at the Memorial University of Newfoundland in St. John's, Canada; a Lecturer in research methodology at the Free University of Berlin; a Reader and Assistant Professor in qualitative methods and evaluation at the Technical University of Berlin; and Associate Professor and Head of the Department of Medical Sociology at the Hannover Medical School. He has held visiting appointments at the London School of Economics, the Ecole des Hautes Etudes en Sciences Sociales in Paris, at Cambridge University (UK), University of Lisbon (Portugal), Institute of Higher Studies in Vienna, in Italy and Sweden, and at the School of Psychology at Massey University, Auckland (New Zealand). His main research interests are qualitative methods, social representations in the fields of individual and public health, vulnerability in fields like youth homelessness or migration, and technological change in everyday life. He is the author of *Designing Qualitative Research* (London: Sage, 2007) and *Managing Quality in Qualitative Research* (London: Sage, 2007) and editor of *The SAGE Qualitative Research Kit* (London: Sage, 2007), *A Companion to Qualitative Research* (London: Sage, 2004), *Psychology of the Social* (Cambridge: Cambridge University Press, 1998), *Quality of Life and Health: Concepts, Methods and Applications* (Berlin: Blackwell Science, 1995), and *La perception quotidienne de la Santé et la Maladie: Théories subjectives et Représentations sociales* (Paris: L'Harmattan, 1993). As his most recent publications, he wrote *Introducing Research Methodology: A Beginner's Guide to Doing a Research Project* (London: Sage, 2011) and edited *The SAGE Handbook of Qualitative Data Analysis* (London: Sage, 2014).

SAGE

AN INTRODUCTION TO
QUALITATIVE RESEARCH

Book Home | **Instructor Resources** | **Student Resources**

Author: Uwe Flick

Pub Date: January 2014

Pages: 608

Learn more about this book

Book Home

Welcome to the companion website for the fifth edition of *An Introduction to Qualitative Research* by Uwe Flick. This website offers both lecturers and students a wealth of further resources designed to accompany your study of the book.

About the Book

In the new edition of his bestselling book, Uwe Flick introduces all of the main theoretical approaches to qualitative research, and provides unmatched coverage of the full range of qualitative methods now available to researchers. Organised around the process of doing qualitative research, the book guides you through ethics, research design, data collection, and data analysis.

In this fifth edition, you will find:

- A new chapter outlining methodological approaches to qualitative research

- New introductory sections at the beginning of each of the book's 7 parts, which prepare the ground and define key terms

- Lots of new practical examples which show you how to carry out all aspects of a qualitative research project

- New exercises which give you a chance to test your understanding of what you've read

This new edition will continue to ensure that *An Introduction to Qualitative Research* remains an essential introductory text for all students of qualitative research.

Instructor Resources

This site is password protected 🔒

Please read the information to your right. To access the site, click on the sign in button on the right hand side below.

The following resources are available to lecturers:

- **PowerPoint presentations** for each chapter to aid your teaching.

First-time Users

Many of the materials on the instructor site, are only available to Faculty and Administrative Staff at Higher Education Institutions who have been approved to request Review Copies by SAGE.

To create an account, please click here. In order to be approved, you must provide your institution and the course that you are or will be teaching. Once you have created an account and you have been validated as a faculty member, you will be able to access the instructor site.

Please note: Validation usually takes approximately 24-48 hours to be completed.

If you have any questions, please contact SAGE Customer Service at +44 (0) 20 7 324 8500 from 8:30 am to 5:00 pm.

Returning Users

If you already have an account with SAGE, log in using the email address and password created when registering with SAGE.

Sign In ▶

Publisher's Acknowledgements

The publishers would like to extend their warmest thanks to the following individuals for their invaluable feedback on the fourth edition and the shaping of the fifth edition.

Professor Tania Aspland, Head Education NSW/ACT, Australian Catholic University

Dr Alexander John Bridger, Senior Lecturer in Psychology, University of Huddersfield

Peter Gates, Centre for Research in Mathematics Education, University of Nottingham

Monique Hennink, PhD, Associate Professor, Emory University

Dr Yassaman Imani, Hertfordshire Business School, University of Hertfordshire

Sheila Katz, Assistant Professor of Sociology, Sonoma State University

Eula Miller, Senior Lecturer, Department of Nursing, Manchester Metropolitan University

Mr Edd Pitt, Lecturer in HE & Academic Practice, University of Kent

Sandra Spickard Prettyman, Associate Professor, University of Akron

Linnea L. Rademaker, PhD, Graduate School Dissertation Chair, Northcentral University

Dr. Susan Redman, University of Dundee, School of Nursing and Nursing and Midwifery

Ms Clarissa Sammut Scerri, Assistant Lecturer/PhD Candidate, Counselling Psychologist and Family Therapist, Dept of Family Studies, University of Malta

Preface to the Fifth Edition

Qualitative research continues to be in an ongoing process of proliferation with new approaches and methods appearing and with being taken up as a core part of the curriculum in more and more disciplines. New and older perspectives in qualitative research can be seen in sociology, psychology, anthropology, nursing, engineering, cultural studies, and so on.

One result of such developments is that the available literature in qualitative research is constantly growing: new books on qualitative research are published and new journals are started and filled with methodological papers on, and results of, qualitative research. Another result is that qualitative research is in danger of falling apart into different fields of research and methodological discussions and that in the process core principles and ideas of qualitative research across these different fields could be omitted.

To keep up with such developments and to integrate experiences with using the book in teaching, the fifth edition of *An Introduction to Qualitative Research* has been revised, updated, and expanded in several ways throughout. Major updates have given the book a different focus on several levels.

First of all, it has a stronger focus on giving (first) orientations in the field. Therefore some chapters have been moved in the book and now concentrate on introducing a part (e.g., Chapter 15 on verbal data) and the following chapters rather than summarize a number of chapters at the end of a part. A new chapter (Chapter 4, "Approaches to Qualitative Research") has been added for the purpose of better orientation. The Glossary supports the aspect of orientation.

Second, there is now a stronger focus on integrative presentations. For example, there is one chapter where narrative data are discussed focusing on collecting narrative data as well as on how to analyze them (see Chapter 18). The treatment of data in grounded theory is now integrated into one chapter (see Chapter 25). The chapter on triangulation (see Chapter 14) is now integrated into the part on research design. The former extra chapter on approaches of online research is now integrated into the other chapters—for example, you will find sections about online interviewing in the interview chapter (see Chapter 16). The same applies to online focus groups (see Chapter 17) and virtual ethnography (see Chapter 20). A final chapter about the current state of the art and the future of qualitative research (Chapter 31) attempts to integrate the diversity presented throughout the book.

Third, there is now a stronger focus on how-to-do aspects in qualitative research. For example, you will find the section on writing field notes in the chapter on observation and ethnography (see Chapter 20). Several new approaches have been integrated into the book (e.g., thematic analysis in Chapter 26) and the variety in doing specific approaches (e.g., discourse analysis) is now taken into account (see Chapter 27). And finally, the approach of the book takes into account that qualitative research practice basically rests on collecting three sorts of data: *verbal data* (such as interviews, focus groups, and narratives, see Chapters 15–18), *data beyond talk* (such as observation, documents, and visual data, see Chapters 19–22), or *naturally occurring data* (such as conversations and discourses, see Chapter 27).

Fourth, the literature has been updated and new approaches, works, and authors have been integrated. New examples and case studies have been added to better illustrate how qualitative research is done.

Since the publication of the first edition of this book, several areas of qualitative research have developed further, which has made some revisions again necessary. Research ethics is an issue that attracts growing attention and has to be developed and specified for qualitative research. The combination of qualitative and quantitative research is *en vogue* as a topic. The Internet has become a field of research and a tool to do research at the same time. Documents are data in their own right. These are some of the current trends in qualitative research, which made revision of the book a challenge.

Uwe Flick
Berlin

PART 1
Framework

Contents

Part 1 is designed to provide a framework for doing qualitative research and to help you understand the subsequent parts of this book. Chapter 1 serves as a guide to the book, introducing its major parts. It also outlines why **qualitative research** has become particularly relevant in the last decades of the twentieth century and at the beginning of the twenty-first century.

Part 1 begins with an overview of the backgrounds of qualitative research. It then introduces you to the essential features of qualitative research (in general, Chapter 2). Chapter 3 outlines the relationship between qualitative and quantitative research and the possibilities and pitfalls of combining both approaches. Chapter 4 maps out which approaches make up the field of qualitative research (and will be presented in more detail in this book). Chapter 5 outlines the ethical issues concerning qualitative research. Together, these chapters offer a background to assist the use of qualitative research methods, which are outlined and discussed in greater detail later in the book.

1

Guide to This Book

-CHAPTER OBJECTIVES-

This chapter is designed to help you

* appreciate the organization of this book;
* locate the discussions of various aspects of qualitative research;
* identify which chapters to use for various purposes.

The Approach of This Book

This book starts from the premise that qualitative research works, above all, with text. Methods for collecting information—interviews or observations—produce data, which are transformed into texts by recording and transcription. Methods of interpretation start from these texts. Different routes lead towards the texts at the center of the research and away from them. Very briefly, the qualitative research process can be represented as a path from *theory to text* and as another path from *text back to theory*. The intersection of the two paths is the collection of verbal or visual data and their interpretation in a specific research design.

This book has been written for two groups of readers: newcomers, new to qualitative research and, perhaps, to research in general; and experienced researchers. For newcomers, mostly undergraduate and graduate students, the book is conceived as a basic introduction to the principles and practices of qualitative research, the theoretical and epistemological background, and the most important methods. Experienced researchers working in the field may use this book as a sort of toolkit while facing the practical issues and problems in the day-to-day business of qualitative research.

Qualitative research has established itself in many social sciences, in psychology, in education, in nursing, and the like. As either a novice to the field or as an experienced researcher, you can use a great variety of specific methods, each of which starts from different premises and pursues different aims. Each method in qualitative research is based on a specific understanding of its object. However, qualitative methods should not be regarded independently of the research process and the issue under study. They are embedded in the research process and are, therefore, best understood and described using a process-oriented perspective. Thus a presentation of the different steps in the process of qualitative research is the central concern of the book. The most important methods for collecting and interpreting data and for assessing and presenting results are presented within the process-oriented framework. This should give you an overview of the field of qualitative research, of concrete methodological alternatives, and of their claims, applications, and limits. This is designed to help you to choose the most appropriate methodological strategy with respect to your research question and issues.

The Structure of the Book

The book has seven parts, which aim at unfolding the process of qualitative research through its major stages. Each of the central parts, Parts 3–6, begins with an overview chapter (e.g., an introduction to research design) and then develops the main issues relevant in this area (e.g., research questions or sampling).

Part 1 sets out the *framework* of doing qualitative research as discussed in Chapters 2–5:

- *Chapter 2* examines the fundamental questions of qualitative research. For this purpose, the current relevance of qualitative research is outlined against the background of recent trends in society and in social sciences. Some essential features of qualitative research in distinction from quantitative approaches are presented. To allow you to see qualitative research and methods in their context, a brief overview of the history of qualitative research in the United States and Europe is given.
- *Chapter 3* develops the relation between qualitative and quantitative research. Here, I take several points of reference for spelling out the possible links of qualitative and quantitative research. In the end, you will find some guiding questions for assessing the appropriateness of qualitative and quantitative research. This chapter allows you to identify various approaches and then decide which one is best for your research.
- *Chapter 4* provides, by way of orientation, an overview of the field of qualitative research. It outlines schools of qualitative research and discusses recent and future trends in qualitative research in different contexts.

- *Chapter 5* focuses on a different framework for qualitative research—research ethics. The ethics of qualitative research deserves special attention, as you will come much closer to privacy issues and the day-to-day life of your participants. Reflection and sensitivity to privacy are essential before launching a qualitative study. At the same time, general discussions about research ethics often miss the special needs and problems of qualitative research. After reading this chapter, you should know the importance of a code of ethics before beginning your research as well as the need for ethics committees. Whether research is ethical or not depends as much on practical decisions in the field.

After setting out the framework of qualitative research, I focus on the process of a qualitative study. Part 2 addresses *theory in qualitative research*:

- *Chapter 6* introduces the use of the literature—theoretical, methodological, and empirical—in a qualitative study. It outlines the use of and the finding of such resources while doing your study and while writing about it.
- *Chapter 7* considers first two theoretical debates that are currently very strong in qualitative research: (1) the debate concerning positivism and constructionism, which informs a great deal of qualitative research, in how to understand the issues of research, in how to conceive the research process, and in how to use qualitative methods; and (2) that over feminism and gender studies. Then it presents several theoretical positions underlying qualitative research. Symbolic interactionism, ethnomethodology, and structuralist approaches are presented as paradigmatic approaches for their basic assumptions and recent developments. From these discussions, the list of essential features of qualitative research given in Chapter 2 is completed.
- *Chapter 8* continues the discussions raised in Chapter 7, as well as outlining the epistemological background of constructionist qualitative research using text as empirical material.

In Part 3 on *research design* we come to the more practical issues of how to plan qualitative research:

- *Chapter 9* offers an overview of practical issues of how to design qualitative research. It also covers the basic designs in qualitative research and addresses the possibilities of doing qualitative research online.
- *Chapter 10* outlines the qualitative research process and shows that the single steps are linked much closer with each other than in the clear-cut step-by-step process in quantitative research.
- *Chapter 11* addresses the relevance of a well-defined research question for conducting research and how to arrive at such a research question.
- *Chapter 12* is about how to enter a field and how to get in touch with the participants of your study.
- *Chapter 13* covers the topic of sampling—how to select your participants or groups of participants, situations, and so on.
- *Chapter 14* addresses triangulation as an issue of designing qualitative research in a more complex way. Triangulation means to combine several methodological approaches in one study and in one design. This principle is outlined as triangulation in action, covering several design issues in referring to concrete examples.

Part 4 introduces one of the major strategies of collecting data. *Verbal data* are produced in interviews, narratives, and focus groups:

- *Chapter 15* gives an orienting overview of the methods for collecting verbal data. It is intended to support you in making your decision between the different ways outlined in Part 4 by comparing the methods and by developing a checklist for such a decision.
- *Chapter 16* presents a range of interviews, which are characterized by using a set of open-ended questions to stimulate the participants' answers. Some of these interviews, like the focused interview, are used for very different purposes, whereas others, like the expert interview, have a more specific field of application. Online interviewing is discussed as an alternative to face-to-face interviews.
- *Chapter 17* explores ways of collecting verbal data in a group of participants. Focus groups are currently very prominent in some areas, while group discussions have a longer tradition. Both are based on the stimulation of discussions, whereas group interviews are more about answering questions. The chapter also identifies the potential and limitations of online focus groups.
- *Chapter 18* outlines a different strategy leading to verbal data. Here the central step is the stimulation of narratives (i.e., overall narratives of life histories or more focused narratives of specific situations). These narratives are stimulated in specially designed interviews—the narrative interview in the first and the episodic interview in the second alternative. Joint narratives want to make a group of people tell a story as a common activity. This chapter takes an integrative approach to narrative research in action and covers also the specific ways of analysis developed for narrative research.

Part 5 examines alternatives of collecting qualitative *data beyond talk*. Observation and visual data, as well as documents, have become important in qualitative research:

- *Chapter 19* maps out the area of data beyond talk. This overview will help you decide when to choose which sort of data and method and what the advantages and problems of each method are.
- *Chapter 20* deals with non-participant and participant observation in the field. It also focuses on ethnography. Here observation and other data collection strategies (interviewing, using documents, etc.) are employed to complement observation itself. The chapter also covers virtual ethnography and addresses issues of documentation in ethnography, in particular how to work with field notes.
- *Chapter 21* focuses on visual data and on selecting, analyzing, studying, and using media like photos, film, and video as data.
- *Chapter 22* explores the construction and analysis of documents in qualitative research including online documents like websites.

The central parts of the book so far concentrate on the collection and production of data. Part 6 deals with *analyzing qualitative data*—how to develop theoretically relevant insights from these data and the text produced with them. For this purpose, qualitative methods for analyzing data are the focus of this part:

- *Chapter 23* gives an orienting overview of the approaches to analyzing text and other material in qualitative research. Again, you will find a comparison of the different approaches and a checklist, both of which should help you to select the appropriate method for analyzing your material and advance from your data to theoretically relevant findings.
- *Chapter 24* discusses data management and transcription in qualitative research in detail, both in their technical and in their general aspects and with examples.
- *Chapter 25* covers methods using coding and categories as tools for analyzing text. This chapter unfolds a specific research perspective in an integrative way. It describes grounded theory research as an exemplar for coding strategies, which are embedded in a more general research program. The chapter shows how analysis in this research perspective works when its elements are brought together.
- *Chapter 26* introduces other ways of coding data, in particular thematic coding and qualitative content analysis.
- *Chapter 27* continues with approaches that are more interested in how something is said and not just in what is said, and focus on naturally occurring data. Conversation analysis looks at how a conversation in everyday life or in an institutional context works, and which methods people use to communicate in any form of context. Discourse and genre analyses have developed this approach further in different directions. Hermeneutics examines texts with a combination of content and formal orientations.
- *Chapter 28* discusses the use of software for qualitative data analysis. Principles and examples of the most important software are presented. This chapter should help you to decide whether to use software for your analysis and which package.

Part 7 goes back to context and methodology and addresses issues of *grounding and writing* qualitative research and ends with an *outlook*:

- *Chapter 29* discusses first the use of traditional quality criteria in qualitative research and their limits. It also informs about alternative criteria, which have been developed for qualitative research or for specific approaches. It shows why answering the question of the quality of qualitative research is currently a major expectation from outside of the discipline and a need for improving the research practice at the same time. In its second half, this chapter explores ways of answering the question of quality in qualitative research beyond the formulation of criteria. Instead, strategies of quality management and, of answering the question of indication, are discussed for this purpose.
- *Chapter 30* addresses issues of writing qualitative research—reporting the results to an audience and the influences of the way of writing on the findings of research. The chapter concludes with a look at new forms of writing about qualitative research.
- *Chapter 31*, finally, provides a summary of the book and outlines an outlook of future developments in qualitative research.

Special Features of the Book

I have included several features to make this book more useful for learning qualitative research and while conducting a qualitative study. You will find them throughout the following chapters.

Chapter Objectives

The beginning of every chapter is designed to orient you towards the body of the chapter. Each of these first sections consists of two parts: first, there is an overview of the issues covered in the chapter; and, second, you will find a list of chapter objectives, which define what you should have learnt and know after reading the chapter. These should guide you through the chapter and help you to find topics again after reading the chapter or the whole book.

Boxes

Major issues are presented in boxes. These boxes have various functions: some summarize the central steps of a method, some give practical advice, and some list example questions (for interview methods, for example). They should structure the text, so that it will be easier to keep an orientation while reading it.

Case Studies

Case studies found throughout the text examine methods and prominent researchers' applications of them. The collections of case studies showcase the practice of principles on special occasions. They are designed to help you think about how things are done in qualitative research, and about which problems or questions come to mind while reading the case studies and the like. Many of the case studies come from published research of key figures in qualitative research. Others come from my own research and in several of them you will meet the same research projects which have been used before to illustrate a different issue.

Checklists

Checklists appear in all chapters, and particularly in Chapters 9, 15, 19, and 23. Many of the checklists offer a guide to decision-making processes for selecting methods and lists for checking the correctness of a decision.

Tables

In Chapters 9, 15, 19, and 23, you will also find tables comparing the methods described in detail in the previous chapters. These tables take a comparative perspective on a single method that permits its strengths and weaknesses to be seen in the light of other methods. This is a particular feature of this book and is intended again to help you to select the "right" method for your research issue.

Key Questions

The methods, which are presented here, are evaluated at the end of their presentation by a list of key questions (e.g., what are the limitations of the method?). These key questions arise repeatedly and should make orientation and assessment of each method easier.

Cross-referencing

Cross-referencing offers the linking of specific methods or methodological problems. This facilitates the placing of information into context.

Key Points

At the end of each chapter, you will find a list of key points summarizing the chapter's most important points.

Exercises

The exercises at the end of a chapter act as a review in assessing other people's research and planning future research.

Further Reading

At the end of a chapter, the list of references offers an opportunity to extend the knowledge presented in the chapter.

Glossary

A glossary of relevant terms has been included at the end of the book. Terms included are highlighted in blue when they appear in the text for the first time.

Companion Website

This book now has a companion website, which provides most of the literature needed for working with the exercises at the end of the chapter, answers to the questions in the exercises and links to online resources for each chapter.

How to Use This Book

There are several ways you can use this book, depending on your field specialty and experience in qualitative research. The first way of reading the book is from the beginning to the end, as it guides you through the steps of planning and setting up a research project. These steps lead you from, at the outset, getting the necessary background knowledge, then through designing and conducting research, to issues of quality assessment and writing about your research.

In the event that you use this book as a reference tool, the following list highlights areas of interest:

- Theoretical background knowledge about qualitative research is found in Chapters 2–8, which offer an overview and the philosophical underpinnings.
- Methodological issues of planning and conceiving qualitative research are explained in Part 3, where questions of designing qualitative research are discussed. Part 7 refers to this conceptual level when examining the quality issues in research.
- Issues of how to plan qualitative research are presented on a practical level in Part 3, where you will find suggestions for how to sample, how to formulate a research question, or how to enter a field.
- Parts 4–6 reveal practical issues relevant for doing qualitative research where a range of methods is described in detail.

2
Qualitative Research: Why and How to Do It

┌─CHAPTER OBJECTIVES─

This chapter is designed to help you

- understand the main characteristics of qualitative research against the background of its history and background;
- identify common features of qualitative research;
- see why qualitative research is pertinent and necessary in contemporary social research.

The Relevance of Qualitative Research

Why use qualitative research? Is there any particular need for such an approach in the current situation? As a first step, I outline why interest in qualitative research has grown considerably over the last few decades. Due to a development that has become known as the pluralization of life worlds, qualitative research is of specific relevance to the study of social relations. This phrase, associated with what Habermas terms the "new obscurity" (Habermas 1996), seeks to capture the growing "individualisation of ways of living and biographical patterns" (Beck 1992), and the dissolution of "old" social inequalities into the new diversity of milieus, subcultures, lifestyles, and ways of living.

This pluralization requires on the part of social researchers a new sensitivity to the empirical study of issues. Advocates of postmodernism have argued that the era of big narratives and theories is over: locally, temporally, and situationally limited narratives are now required. In this context, the following statement by Blumer becomes relevant once again, with fresh implications: "The initial position of the social scientist and the psychologist is practically always one of lack of familiarity with what is actually taking place in the sphere of life chosen for study" (1969, p. 33).

Rapid social change and the resulting diversification of life worlds increasingly confront social researchers with new social contexts and perspectives. As a result, their traditional deductive methodologies—deriving research questions and hypotheses from theoretical models and testing them against empirical evidence—are failing, due to the differentiation of objects. Instead of starting from theories and then testing them, research is increasingly forced to make use of inductive strategies: in the process, "sensitizing concepts" are required for approaching the social contexts to be studied. But here, theories are developed from empirical studies. Thus knowledge and practice are studied as *local* knowledge and practices (Geertz 1983).

Research Questions as a Starting Point

The main reason for using qualitative research should be that a research question *requires* the use of this sort of approach and not a different one. Let us illustrate this with an example (we will come back to this in more detail in Chapter 11). In an ongoing research project we address the following problem. Addiction to drugs and alcohol is the third most frequent mental illness. Young Russian-speaking migrants in Germany are reported to often have particularly strong patterns of alcohol and drug consumption. Thus they have a high risk of drug-associated diseases. At the same time, they are a target group which is largely under- or unserved by existing health services. This study pursues the question of how Russian-speaking migrants perceive their use of substance and possible consecutive diseases, such as hepatitis, and how they cope with them. Of particular interest are conditions of their utilization of professional help and their connected expectations and experiences, and why they may refrain from utilization.

Why should qualitative research be used for such a study? This is an example of a pluralization of life worlds mentioned above. Our knowledge about this life world (migration, Russian background, addiction) is too limited for starting from a hypothesis to test in our research. Instead we need sensitizing concepts for exploring and understanding this life world and the individual (and social) biographical processes that have led to the current situation of our participants. This social group is for several reasons a "hard-to-reach" group (which will fall out of more general studies and may refuse to fill in a questionnaire, for example). For understanding how and why the participants with hepatitis make use of social and health services or refrain from using these services, we need to understand their personal experiences with the health system, the meanings they link to such experiences, and the discourses and practices concerning these issues in their contexts. Thus we approach the issue and our target group by using qualitative methods—interviews and participant observations, for example (see Chapters 16 and 20 for details).

Limitations of Quantitative Research

Beyond the general developments and examples like the one outlined above, the limitations of quantitative approaches have always been taken as a starting point for developing more general reasons why qualitative research should be used. Traditionally, psychology and social sciences have taken the natural sciences and their exactness as a model, paying particular attention to developing quantitative and standardized methods. Guiding principles of research and of planning research have been used for the following purposes: to clearly isolate causes and effects; to properly operationalize theoretical relations; to measure and to quantify phenomena; to create research designs allowing the generalization of findings; and to formulate general laws. For example, random samples of populations are selected in order to conduct a survey representative of that population. *General statements* are made as independently as possible about the concrete cases that have been studied. *Observed phenomena* are classified according to their frequency and distribution. In order to classify causal relations and their validity as clearly as possible, the conditions under which the phenomena and relations under study occur are controlled as far as possible. Studies are designed in such a way that the researcher's (as well as the interviewer's, observer's, and so on) influence can be excluded as far as possible. This should guarantee the objectivity of the study, whereby the subjective views of the researcher as well as those of the individuals under study are largely eliminated. General obligatory standards for carrying out and evaluating empirical social research have been formulated. Procedures such as how to construct a questionnaire, how to design an experiment, and how to statistically analyze data have become increasingly refined.

For a long time, psychological research has almost exclusively used experimental designs. These have produced vast quantities of data and results, which demonstrate and test psychological relations of variables and the conditions under which they are valid. For the reasons mentioned above, for a long time empirical social research was mainly based on standardized surveys. The aim was to document and analyze the frequency and distribution of social phenomena in the population (e.g., certain attitudes). To a lesser extent, standards and procedures of quantitative research have been examined fundamentally in order to clarify the research objects and questions they are appropriate to or not.

Negative results abound when the targets previously mentioned are balanced. Some time ago Weber (1919) proclaimed that the sciences' task is the disenchantment of the world by providing analysis and explanations through the research they do. Bonß and Hartmann (1985) have stated the increasing disenchantment of the sciences—their methods and their findings. In the case of the social sciences, the low degree of applicability of results and the problems of connecting them to theory and societal developments are taken as indicators of this disenchantment. Less widely than expected—and above all in a very different way—the findings of social research have found their way into political and everyday contexts. Utilization research (Beck and Bonß 1989) has demonstrated that scientific findings are not carried over into political and institutional practices as much as expected. When they are taken up, they are obviously reinterpreted and picked to pieces. "Science no longer produces 'absolute truths,' which can uncritically be adopted. It furnishes limited offers for interpretation, which reach further than everyday theories but can be used in practice comparatively flexibly" (Beck and Bonß 1989, p. 31). In summary, the ideals of objectivity of sciences and their findings are largely disenchanted because of the problems just stated.

It has also become clear that social science results are rarely used in everyday life. In order to meet methodological standards, their investigations and findings often remain too far removed from everyday questions and problems. On the other hand, analyses of research practice have demonstrated that the (abstract) ideals of objectivity formulated by methodologists can only be met in part in conducting concrete research. Despite all the methodological controls, influences from specific interests and social and cultural backgrounds are difficult to avoid in research and its findings. These factors influence the formulation of research questions and hypotheses as well as the interpretation of data and relations.

Finally, the disenchantment that Bonß and Hartmann discussed has consequences for what kind of knowledge the social sciences or psychology can strive for and above all are able to produce:

> On the condition of the disenchantment of ideals of objectivism, we can no longer unreflectively start from the notion of objectively true sentences. What remains is the possibility of statements which are related to subjects and situations, and which a sociologically articulated concept of knowledge would have to establish. (1985, p. 21)

To formulate such subject- and situation-related statements, which are empirically well founded, is a goal that can be attained with qualitative research.

Essential Features

The central ideas guiding qualitative research are different from those in quantitative research. The essential features of qualitative research (Box 2.1) are the correct choice of appropriate methods and theories (see Chapter 7); the recognition and analysis of different perspectives; the researchers' reflections on their research as part of the process of knowledge production ('reflexivity'); and the variety of approaches and methods.

BOX 2.1

A Preliminary List of Qualitative Research Features

- Appropriateness of methods and theories
- Perspectives of the participants and their diversity
- Reflexivity of the researcher and the research
- Variety of approaches and methods in qualitative research

Appropriateness of Methods and Theories

Scientific disciplines have used defining methodological standards to distinguish themselves from other disciplines. Examples include the use of experiments as the method of psychology or of survey research as the key method of sociology. As a scientific discipline becomes established, its methods become the point of reference for deciding the suitability of ideas and issues for empirical investigations. This has sometimes led to suggestions to refrain from studying those phenomena to which the usual methods—experimentation, say, or surveys—cannot be applied. For example, it may be that variables cannot be effectively identified or isolated, in which case experimental design will not be applicable.

Of course it makes sense to reflect on whether a research question can be studied empirically (see Chapter 11). Most phenomena cannot be explained in isolation—a result of their complexity in reality. If all empirical studies were exclusively designed according to the model of clear cause–effect relations, all complex objects would have to be excluded. Sometimes it is suggested that, in the case of complex and rare phenomena, the best solution is simply not to study them. A second solution is to take contextual conditions into account in complex quantitative research designs (e.g., multi-level analyses) and to understand complex models empirically and statistically. The necessary methodological abstraction makes it more difficult to reintroduce findings in the everyday situation under study. The basic problem—the study can only show what the underlying model of reality represents—is not solved in this way.

Another way to study complex issues with qualitative research is to design methods that are sufficiently open to the complexity of a study's subject. In such cases the object under study is the determining factor for choosing a method and not the other way round. Here objects are not reduced to single variables: rather, they are represented in their entirety in their everyday context. Thus the fields of study are not artificial situations in the laboratory but the practices and interactions of the subjects in everyday life. Exceptional situations and people are frequently studied in this way (see Chapter 13). In order to do justice to the diversity of everyday life, methods are characterized by openness towards their objects, which may be guaranteed in various ways (see Chapters 16–22).

The goal of research then is less to test what is already known (e.g., theories already formulated in advance): rather it is to discover and explore the new and to develop empirically grounded theories. Here the validity of the study does not exclusively follow abstract academic criteria of science as in quantitative research: rather it is assessed with reference to the object under study. Thus qualitative research's central criteria depend on whether findings are grounded in empirical material or whether the methods are appropriately selected and applied, as well as the relevance of findings and the reflexivity of proceedings (see Chapter 29).

Perspectives of the Participants

The example of mental disorders allows us to explain another feature of qualitative research. Epidemiological studies show the frequency of schizophrenia in the population and furthermore how its distribution varies: in lower social classes, serious mental disorders like schizophrenia occur much more frequently than in higher classes. Such a correlation was found by Hollingshead and Redlich (1958) in the 1950s and has been confirmed repeatedly since then. However, the direction of the correlation could not be clarified. Do the conditions of living in a lower social class promote the occurrence and outbreak of mental disorders? Or do people with mental problems slide into the lower classes?

Moreover, these findings do not tell us anything about what it means to live with mental illness. Neither is the subjective meaning of this illness (or of health) for those directly concerned made clear, nor is the diversity of perspectives on the illness in their context grasped. What is the subjective meaning of schizophrenia for the patient, and what is it for his or her relatives? How do the various people involved deal with the disease in their day-to-day lives? What has led to the outbreak of the disease in the course of the patient's life, and what has made it a chronic disease? How did earlier treatments influence the patient's life? Which ideas, goals, and routines guide the concrete handling of this case?

Qualitative research on a topic like mental illness concentrates on questions like these. It demonstrates the variety of perspectives (those of the patient, of his or her relatives, of professionals) on the object and starts from the subjective and social meanings related to it. Qualitative researchers study participants' knowledge and practices. They analyze interactions about and ways of dealing with mental illness in a particular field. Interrelations are described in the concrete context of the case and explained in relation to it. Qualitative research takes into account that viewpoints and practices in the field are different because of the different subjective perspectives and social backgrounds related to them.

Reflexivity of the Researcher and the Research

Unlike quantitative research, qualitative methods take the researcher's communication with the field and its members as an explicit part of knowledge instead of deeming it an intervening variable. The subjectivity of the researcher *and* of those being studied becomes part of the research process. Researchers' reflections on their actions and observations in the field, their impressions, irritations, feelings, and so on, become data in their own right, forming part of the interpretation, and are documented in research diaries or context protocols (see Chapter 24).

Variety of Approaches and Methods

Qualitative research is not based on a unified theoretical and methodological concept. Various theoretical approaches and their methods characterize the discussions and the research practice. Subjective viewpoints are a first starting point. A second string of research studies the making and course of interactions, while a third seeks to reconstruct the structures of the social field and the latent meaning of practices (see Chapter 7 for more details). This variety of approaches results from different developmental lines in the history of qualitative research, which evolved partly in parallel and partly in sequence.

A Brief History of Qualitative Research

Why does it make sense to turn to the history of qualitative research at this point? Historical backgrounds of current methods and their diversity may explain this diversity and allow locating the single approach in the wider field of qualitative research. Such a look at the historical developments that happened in several contexts at the same time but in different ways may help to develop an understanding of why there are now different understandings of qualitative research, which manifest in varying concepts of epistemology, of methods, of data, and of research in general.

Here only a brief and rather cursory overview of the history of qualitative research can be given. Psychology and social sciences in general have a long tradition of using qualitative methods. In psychology, Wundt (1928) used methods of description and *verstehen* in his folk psychology alongside the experimental methods of his general psychology. Roughly at the same time, an argument between a more monographic conception of science and an empirical and statistical approach began in German sociology (Bonß 1982, p. 106). Monographic science was oriented towards induction and case studies and not so much towards using empirical or statistical methods systematically. Rather than doing representative studies referring to society as a whole, case studies were the empirical basis for analyzing a social problem in detail. In American sociology, biographical methods, case studies, and descriptive methods were central for a long time (until the 1940s). This can be demonstrated by the importance of Thomas and Znaniecki's study *The Polish Peasant in Europe and America* (1918–1920) and, more generally, with the influence of the Chicago School in sociology.

During the further establishment of both sciences, however, increasingly "hard," experimental, standardizing, and quantifying approaches have asserted themselves against "soft" understanding, open, and qualitative descriptive strategies. It was not until the 1960s that in American sociology the critique of standardized, quantifying social research became relevant again (Cicourel 1964; Glaser and Strauss 1967). This critique was taken up in the 1970s in German discussions. Finally, this led to a renaissance of qualitative research in the social sciences and also (with some delay) in psychology (Banister et al. 1994; Willig and Stainton-Rogers 2007). The developments and discussions in the United States and for example in Germany not only took place at different times, but also are marked by differing phases.

The United States

Denzin and Lincoln (2005b, pp. 14–20; 2011, p. 3) identify eight moments of qualitative research, as follows. The *traditional period* ranges from the early twentieth century to World War II. It is related to the research of Malinowski (1916) in ethnography and the Chicago School in sociology. During this period, qualitative research was interested in the other—the foreign or the strange—and in its more or less objective description and interpretation. For example, foreign cultures interested ethnography and a society's outsiders interested sociology.

The *modernist phase* lasts until the 1970s and is marked by attempts to formalize qualitative research. For this purpose, more and more textbooks were published in the United States. The attitude of this kind of research is still alive in the tradition of for example *Boys in White* by Becker et al. (1961), the *Discovery of Grounded Theory* by Glaser and Strauss (1967), Strauss (1987), and Strauss and Corbin (1990) as well as in Miles and Huberman (1994).

Blurred genres (Geertz 1983) characterize the developments up to the mid 1980s. Various theoretical models and understandings of the objects and methods stand side by side, from which researchers can choose and compare "alternative paradigms," such as symbolic interactionism, ethnomethodology, phenomenology, semiotics, or feminism (see also Guba 1990; Jacob 1987; see here Chapter 6).

In the mid 1980s, the *crisis of representation* discussions in artificial intelligence (Winograd and Flores 1986) and ethnography (Clifford and Marcus 1986) impact qualitative research as a whole. This makes the process of displaying knowledge and findings a substantial part of the research process. Qualitative research now becomes recognized as a continuous process of constructing versions of reality. After all, the version of themselves that people present in an interview does not necessarily correspond to the version they would have given to a different researcher with a different research question: researchers, who interpret the interview and present it as part of their findings, produce a new version of the whole. Readers of a book, article, or report interpret the researchers' version differently. This means that further versions of the event emerge. Specific interests brought to the reading in each case play a central part. In this context, the evaluation of research and findings becomes a central topic in methodological discussions. This raises the question of whether traditional criteria are still valid and, if not, which other standards should be applied for assessing qualitative research (see here Chapter 29).

The situation in the 1990s is seen by Denzin and Lincoln as the *fifth moment*: narratives have replaced theories, or theories are read as narratives. But here (as in postmodernism in general) we learn about the end of grand narratives like Marxism or Parson's systems theory (Parsons and Shils 1951): the accent is shifted towards theories and narratives that fit specific, delimited, local, historical situations, and problems. Experimental writing includes approaches like autoethnographies (see Ellis, Adams, and Bochner 2011 for an overview), instead of theories, and tales from the field were the outcome of qualitative research (see Chapter 30 for more details on these approaches of writing about research).

The next stage (*sixth moment*) is characterized by postexperimental writing and linking issues of qualitative research to democratic policies. Denzin and Lincoln (2000b, p. 17) mention: "Fictional ethnographies, ethnographic poetry and multimedia texts are today taken for granted. Postexperimental writers seek to connect their writings to the needs of a free democratic society."

The *seventh moment* is characterized by further establishing qualitative research through various new journals such as *Qualitative Inquiry* or *Qualitative Research*.

Denzin and Lincoln's *eighth moment* in the development of qualitative research focused on the rise of evidence-based practice as the new criterion of relevance for social science and on the new conservatism in the United States. "Evidence-based" refers to a rather narrow understanding of which kind of research produces results that can be relevant for informing practices, for example, in medicine, nursing, or social work. According to this understanding, research designs have to be based on using a control group and randomized selection and allocation of participants in the study group and the control group. If this is taken as the only relevant social research type, qualitative research is difficult to locate in this context. Denzin and Giardina (2006) discuss this development in connection with a more general new conservatism in the United States in research politics but also in social welfare policy.

Denzin and Lincoln's outline of its history is often taken as a general reference for the development of qualitative research. However, as Alasuutari (2004) mentions, such a general "progress narrative" (p. 599) may obscure the fact that qualitative research has become a globalized phenomenon with different developments in various contexts. Thus he proposes a spatial, rather than temporal, view on the development of qualitative research. Therefore I will complement Denzin and Lincoln's outline of a history of qualitative research by a sketch of the development of qualitative research in one particular region, namely German-speaking areas.

German-Speaking Areas

In Germany, Habermas (1967) first recognized that a "different" tradition and discussion of research was developing in American sociology related to names like Goffman, Garfinkel, and Cicourel. After the translation of Cicourel's (1964) methodological critique, a series of anthologies imported contributions from the American discussions. This has made basic texts on ethnomethodology or symbolic interactionism available for German discussions.

From the same period, the model of the research process created by Glaser and Strauss (1967) has attracted much attention. Discussions are motivated by the aim to do more justice to the objects of research than is possible in quantitative research, as Hoffmann-Riem's (1980) argument for the principle of openness demonstrates. Kleining (1982, p. 233) has argued that it is necessary to understand the object of research as a preliminary until the end of the research, because the object "will present itself in its true colors only at the end."

Discussions concerning naturalistic sociology (Schatzmann and Strauss 1973) and appropriate methods are determined by a similar assumption (initially implicit and, later, also explicit). Application of the principle of openness and the rules that Kleining proposes (e.g., to postpone a theoretical formulation of the research object) enables the researcher to avoid constituting the object by the very methods used for studying it. It then becomes possible "to take everyday life first and always again in the way it presents itself in each case" (Grathoff 1978; quoted in Hoffmann-Riem 1980, p. 362, who ends her article with this quotation).

At the end of the 1970s, a broader and more original discussion began in Germany, which no longer relied exclusively on the translation of American literature. This discussion dealt with interviews, how to apply and how to analyze them, and with methodological questions that have stimulated extensive research (see Flick, Kardorff, and Steinke 2004a for an overview). The main question for this period was whether these developments should be seen as a fashion, a trend, or a new beginning.

At the beginning of the 1980s, two original methods were crucial to the development of qualitative research in Germany: the narrative interview by Schütze (1977; Rosenthal and Fischer-Rosenthal 2004; see here Chapter 18) and objective hermeneutics by Oevermann, Allert, Konau, and Krambeck (1979; see also Reichertz 2004; Wernet 2014; see Chapter 27). These methods no longer represented simply an import of American developments (as had been the case in applying participant observation or interviews). Both methods have stimulated extensive research practice, mainly in biographical research (for overviews see Bertaux 1981; Rosenthal 2004). But at least as crucial as the results obtained from these methodologies has been their influence in the general discussion of qualitative methods.

In the mid 1980s, problems of validity and the generalizability of findings obtained with qualitative methods attracted broader attention. Related questions of presentation and the transparency of results were discussed. The quantity and, above all, the unstructured nature of the data required the use of computers in qualitative research too (Fielding and Lee 1991; Gibbs 2007; Kelle 1995; 2004; Richards and Richards 1998; Weitzman and Miles 1995), leading to the development of software programs like ATLAS.ti and MAXQDA.

Finally, in the 1990s the first textbooks or introductions on the background of the discussions in the German-speaking area were published. At that time also a number of specialized journals in qualitative research were established (e.g., ZQF (*Zeitschrift für Qualitative Forschung*), *Sozialer Sinn*, but also *FQS*, which was founded in Germany).

Using Table 2.1, we may contrast the lines of development in the United States and in Germany. In Germany, we find increasing methodological consolidation complemented by a concentration on procedural questions in a growing research practice in the country. In the United States, on the other hand, recent developments are characterized by a trend to question the apparent certainties provided by methods. The role of presentation in the research process, the crisis of representation, and the relativity of what is presented have been stressed, this has made the attempts to formalize and canonize methods (canonization) rather secondary. In American qualitative research the "correct" application of procedures of interviewing or interpretation has tended to count for less than the "practices and politics of interpretation" (Denzin 2000). Qualitative research therefore becomes, or is linked still more strongly with, a specific attitude based on the researcher's openness and reflexivity.

TABLE 2.1 Phases in the History of Qualitative Research

United States	Germany
Traditional period (1900 to 1945)	Early studies (end of nineteenth and early twentieth centuries)
Modernist phase (1945 to the 1970s)	Phase of import (early 1970s)
Blurred genres (until the mid 1980s)	Beginning of original discussions (late 1970s)
Crisis of representation (since the mid 1980s)	Developing original methods (1970s and 1980s)
Fifth moment (the 1990s)	Consolidation and procedural questions (late 1980s and 1990s)
Sixth moment (postexperimental writing)	Research practice (since the 1980s)
Seventh moment (establishing qualitative research through successful journals, 2000 to 2004)	Methodological proliferation and technological developments (since the 1990s)
Eighth moment (the future and new challenges – since 2005)	Establishing qualitative research (journals, book series, scientific societies–since the 1990s)

Qualitative Research at the End of Modernity

At the beginning of this chapter, some changes to the potential objectives were mentioned in order to show the relevance of qualitative research. Recent diagnoses in the sciences result in more reasons to turn to qualitative research. In his discussion of the "hidden agenda of modernity," Toulmin (1990) explains in great detail why he believes modern science is dysfunctional. He sees four tendencies for empirical social research in philosophy and science as a way forward:

- a return to the oral traditions—carried out by empirical studies in philosophy, linguistics, literature, and the social sciences by studying narratives, language, and communication;
- a return to the particular—carried out by empirical studies with the aim "not only to concentrate on abstract and universal questions but to treat again specific, concrete problems which do not arise generally but occur in specific types of situations" (p. 190);
- a return to the local—studied by systems of knowledge, practices, and experiences in the context of those (local) traditions and ways of living in which they are embedded, instead of assuming and attempting to test their universal validity;
- a return to the timely—problems are studied and solutions to be developed in their temporal or historical context and to describe them in this context and explain them from it.

Qualitative research is oriented towards analyzing concrete cases in their temporal and local particularity and starting from people's expressions and activities in their local contexts. Therefore, qualitative research is in a position to design ways for social sciences, psychology, and other fields to make concrete the tendencies that Toulmin mentions, to transform them into research programs, and to maintain the necessary flexibility towards their objects and tasks:

> Like buildings on a human scale, our intellectual and social procedures will do what we need in the years ahead, only if we take care to avoid irrelevant or excessive stability, and keep them operating in ways that are adaptable to unforeseen—or even unforeseeable—situations and functions. (1990, p. 186)

Concrete suggestions and methods for realizing such programs of research are outlined in the following chapters.

Landmarks in Qualitative Research

Knowledge about qualitative research is helpful in two ways. It can provide the starting point and basis for doing your own empirical study, for example, in the context of a thesis or later as a professional in sociology, education, social work, etc. And it is also necessary for understanding and assessing existing qualitative research. For both purposes, Box 2.2 offers a number of guideline questions, which allow a basic assessment of research (in the planning of your own or in reading other researchers' studies).

┌─ BOX 2.2 ─┐

Guideline Questions for an Orientation in the Field of Qualitative Research

1 What is the issue and what is the research question of a specific study?
2 How is the study planned; which design is applied or constructed?
3 How adequate is qualitative research as an approach for this study?
4 Is the way the study is done ethically sound?
5 What is the theoretical perspective of the study?
6 Does the presentation of results and of the ways they were produced make transparent for the reader how the results came about and how the researchers proceeded?
7 How appropriate are the design and methods to the issue under study?
8 Are there any claims of generalization made and how are they fulfilled?

These guideline questions can be asked regardless of the specific qualitative methodology that has been used. They can be applied to the various methodological alternatives.

KEY POINTS

- Qualitative research has, for several reasons, a special relevance for contemporary research in many fields.
- Quantitative methods and qualitative research methods both have limitations.
- Qualitative research exhibits a variety of approaches.
- There are common features among the different approaches in qualitative research.
- Within qualitative research, different schools and trends may be distinguished by their research perspectives.
- Qualitative research has developed over time and there are differing developments in different areas (e.g., the United States and Germany).

Exercise 2.1

Locate a qualitative study, (e.g., Joffe and Bettega 2003), read it, and answer the following questions:

1 How are essential features listed at the beginning of this chapter relevant to the example you chose?
2 How appropriate are the methods and approaches applied in this study to the issue under study?

1 If you plan your own study, reflect why qualitative research is adequate for the study.
2 Discuss the reasons for or against using quantitative methods in your study.

—Further Reading—

These references extend the short overview given here of the American and German discussions:

Denzin, N. and Lincoln, Y.S. (eds.) (2011) *The SAGE Handbook of Qualitative Research* (4th edn). London: Sage.

Flick, U. (2005) "Qualitative Research in Sociology in Germany and the US—State of the Art, Differences and Developments" [47 paragraphs]. *Forum Qualitative Sozialforschung/Forum: Qualitative Social Research*, 6(3), Art. 23, http://nbn-resolving.de/urn:nbn:de:0114-fqs0503230.

Flick, U. (ed.) (2007a) *The SAGE Qualitative Research Kit* (8 vols.). London: Sage.

Flick, U. (ed.) (2014a) *The SAGE Handbook of Qualitative Data Analysis*. London: Sage.

Flick, U., Kardorff, E.v. and Steinke, l. (eds.) (2004) *A Companion to Qualitative Research*. London: Sage.

3
Qualitative and Quantitative Research

─CHAPTER OBJECTIVES─

This chapter is designed to help you

- understand the distinctiveness of, respectively, qualitative and quantitative research;
- understand what options are available if you wish to combine qualitative and quantitative research;
- recognize what to take into account when alternative research methods are combined.

Relations of Qualitative and Quantitative Research

In many cases, qualitative methods were developed in the context of a critique of quantitative methods and research strategies (e.g., Cicourel 1964). The debates about the "right" understanding of science are not yet settled (see Becker 1996). However, in both domains a broad research practice has now developed. This speaks for itself, regardless of the fact that there is good and bad research on both sides.

The relations of qualitative and quantitative research may be examined on different levels, including:

- epistemology (and epistemological incompatibilities) and methodology;
- research designs combining or integrating the use of qualitative and quantitative data and/or methods;
- research methods that are both qualitative and quantitative;
- the linking of findings from qualitative and quantitative research;
- generalization of findings;
- assessment of the quality of research—applying quantitative criteria to qualitative research or vice versa.

Stressing the Incompatibilities

On the level of epistemology and methodology, discussions often center on the different ways of relating qualitative and quantitative research. A first relation is to stress the incompatibilities of qualitative and quantitative research in terms of epistemological and methodological principles (e.g., Becker 1996) or of goals and aims to pursue with research in general. This tension is often related to that between different theoretical positions (e.g., positivism versus constructionism or post-positivism). Sometimes these incompatibilities are referred to as different paradigms and both camps are seen as engaged in a paradigm war (e.g., Lincoln and Guba 1985).

Defining Fields of Application

One resolution of this problem is to see the research strategies as separate but parallel, with their applicability dependent on the issue and the research question. The researcher who wants to know something about the subjective experience of a chronic mental illness should conduct biographical interviews with some patients and analyze them in great detail. The researcher who wants to find out something about the frequency and distribution of such diseases in the population should run an epidemiological study on this topic. For the first question, qualitative methods are appropriate, for the second quantitative methods are suitable; each method refrains from entering the territory of the other.

CASE STUDY 3.1

Studies of Adolescents' Health Behavior

As the following examples may illustrate, a topic can be studied by using either quantitative or qualitative research. Here the health behavior of adolescents is the issue of each study. We use these examples for illustrating when quantitative approaches are used and when qualitative research is necessary.

FRAMEWORK

The "Health Behavior in Social Context" Study of the World Health Organization (WHO)

In the "Health Behavior in Social Context" (HBSC) study, children and adolescents from 36 countries were studied in a survey, using a standardized questionnaire, concerning their health status and behavior. This research was conducted in order to produce a health report for the young generation. In Germany, for example, this survey has been run repeatedly since 1993—most recently in 2006 (see Hurrelmann, Klocke, Melzer, and Ravens-Sieberer 2003; Richter, Hurrelmann, Klocke, Melzer, and Ravens-Sieberer 2008). Hurrelmann et al. (2003, p. 2) have described the aims of this study as follows:

> In this youth health survey, several questions shall be answered: descriptive questions about physical, mental and social health and about the health behavior; in the focus is the question, how far health relevant life styles are linked to subjective health; and how far personal and social risk and protective factors can be identified for the prevention of health problems together with their subjective representation in physical and in mental respects.

For this study in Germany, adolescents aged 11, 13, and 15 years were approached in schools. For the international study, a representative sample was selected comprising about 23,000 adolescents in different areas of Germany. For the German study, a subsample of 5,650 adolescents was drawn randomly from this sample. This subsample were asked to answer a questionnaire about their subjective health, risks of accidents and violence, the use of substances (tobacco, drugs, and alcohol), eating, physical activity, peer and family, and school. The research question for this study resulted from the interest in developing a representative overview of the health situation and the health-relevant behavior of the adolescents in Germany and in comparison to other countries.

Health on the Street—Homeless Adolescents

A different approach to a similar topic is provided by our second example. The study just discussed has provided a good overview of the health situation of the average youth in Germany and other countries. However, such a broad study cannot focus on particular (mainly very small and hard-to-reach) subgroups. Reasons for this include the use of random sampling and also the fact that access to the participants was via schools. Adolescents living on the street, who rarely attend any schools, if at all, were not represented in such a sample. For analyzing the specific situation and the health behavior and knowledge of this group, a different approach is required.

Accordingly, in our second example (see Flick and Röhnsch 2007), homeless adolescents were selected purposefully at their specific meeting points and hangouts and asked for interviews. Participants were aged between 14 and 20 and had no (regular) housing. To gain a more comprehensive understanding of their health knowledge and behavior under the conditions on "the street," we interviewed them and also followed

(Continued)

(Continued)

them through phases of their everyday lives, using participant observation. The topics of the interviews were similar to those of our first example above, with additional questions about the specific situation of living on the street and about how the participants entered street life.

In both the above examples, the health and the social situation of adolescents were studied—either of the youth in Germany in general or of a specific subgroup with particularly stressful conditions of living. In both cases, the results should be useful for helping to prevent health problems in the target groups and to improve the design of services for them.

Dominance of Quantitative over Qualitative Research

The view that quantitative research is the dominant form can still be found in some quantitative research textbooks and in some areas of research practice. This is the case, for example, where an exploratory study with open interviews precedes the collection of data with questionnaires, but the first step and its results are seen as only preliminary. Arguments such as using a representative sample are often used for substantiating the claim that only quantitative data lead to results in the actual sense of the word, whereas qualitative data play a more illustrative part. Statements in the open interviews are then tested and "explained" by their confirmation and frequency in the questionnaire data.

Superiority of Qualitative over Quantitative Research

The more radical position (foregrounding qualitative research) is taken more seldom. Oevermann, Allert, Konau, and Krambeck (1979, p. 352) for example argued that quantitative methods are merely research economic shortcuts of the data generating process: only qualitative methods, according to Oevermann et al., particularly the objective hermeneutics Oevermann developed (see Chapter 27), are able to provide the actual scientific explanations of facts. Kleining (1982) holds that qualitative methods can live very well without the later use of quantitative methods, whereas quantitative methods need qualitative methods for explaining the relations they find. In sociology, Cicourel (1981) sees qualitative methods as being especially appropriate for answering micro questions and quantitative methods for answering macro questions. McKinlay (1995), however, makes it clear that in public health qualitative methods rather than quantitative methods lead to relevant results at the level of socio-political topics and relations due to their complexity. Thus, reasons for the superiority of qualitative research are located both on the level of the research program and at the level of the appropriateness to the issue under study.

Linking Qualitative and Quantitative Research in One Design

Qualitative and quantitative methods can be brought together in the *design* of one study in different ways.

Integration of Qualitative and Quantitative Research

Four types of designs for integrating both approaches in one design have been outlined by Miles and Huberman (1994, p. 41), as in Figure 3.1.

In the first design, both strategies are pursued in parallel. Continuous observation of the field provides a basis on which, in a survey, the several waves are related or from which these waves are derived and shaped in the second design. The third combination begins with a qualitative method, a semi-structured interview that is followed by a questionnaire study as an intermediate step before the results from both steps are deepened and assessed in a second qualitative phase. In the fourth design, a complementary field study adds more depth to the results of a survey in the first step and is followed by an experimental intervention in the field for testing the results of the first two steps. (For similar suggestions of mixed designs, see Creswell 2008; Patton 2002.)

Sequencing Qualitative and Quantitative Research

A study may include qualitative and quantitative approaches in different phases of the research process. Barton and Lazarsfeld (1955), for example, suggest using

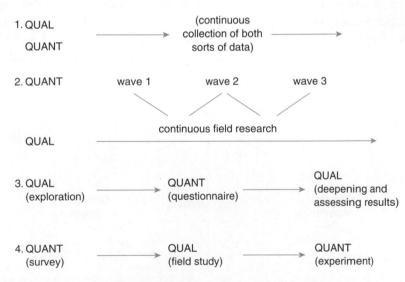

FIGURE 3.1   Research Designs for the Integration of Qualitative and Quantitative Research

Source: Adapted from Miles and Huberman (1994, p. 41)

qualitative research for developing hypotheses, which afterwards will be tested by quantitative approaches. In their argumentation, they focus not only on the limitations of qualitative research (compared to quantitative), but also explicitly see the strength of qualitative research in the exploration of the phenomenon under study. According to this argument, the two areas of research are located at different stages of the research process.

Triangulation of Qualitative and Quantitative Research

Triangulation (see Chapters 14 and 29) may refer to two situations: (1) using several qualitative methods in combination (see Flick 1992; 2004a); and (2) combining qualitative and quantitative methods. In the latter case, the different methodological perspectives complement each other in the study of an issue: the two methods are conceived in terms of the complementary compensation of the weaknesses and blind spots of each single method. The insight (which is gradually becoming established) "that qualitative and quantitative methods should be viewed as complementary rather than as rival camps" (Jick 1983, p. 135) forms the background of such a conception. Note that the different methods remain autonomous, operating side by side, and their meeting point is the issue under study. And finally, none of the methods combined is seen as either superior or preliminary. Whether or not the methods are used at the same time or one after the other is less relevant compared to the fact that they are seen as equal in their role in the project.

Some practical issues are linked to these combinations of different methods in the design of one study (e.g., on which level the triangulation is concretely applied). Two alternatives can be distinguished. Triangulation of qualitative and quantitative research can focus the single case. The same people are interviewed and fill in a questionnaire. Their answers in both are compared to each other, put together, and

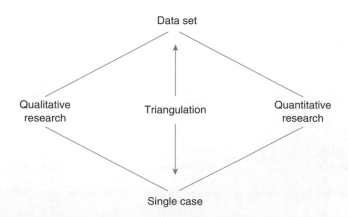

FIGURE 3.2   Levels of Triangulation of Qualitative and Quantitative Research

FRAMEWORK

referred to each other in the analysis. Sampling decisions are taken in two steps (see Chapter 13). The same people are included in both parts of the study, but in a second step it has to be decided which participants of the survey study are selected for the interviews. But a link can be established on the level of the data set as well. The answers to the questionnaires are analyzed for their frequency and distribution across the whole sample. Then the answers in the interviews are analyzed and compared, and, for example, a typology is developed. Then the distribution of the questionnaire answers and the typology are linked and compared (see Figure 3.2 and Flick 2007b).

CASE STUDY 3.2

Cancer Patients' Relatives

In this case, the authors combined qualitative and quantitative methods to study a currently relevant issue in the health area. Both authors work in the area of rehabilitation.

Schönberger and Kardorff (2004) study the challenges, burdens, and achievements of cancer patients' relatives in a combination of a questionnaire study with two waves of surveys (189 and 148 relatives and 192 patients) and a number of case studies (17, of which 7 are presented in more detail). The research questions for both parts of the study are characterized as follows:

> On the background of the existing research, we have focused on the experience of burdens, on individual and partnership coping, on integration in networks, and the evaluation of the services in the system of rehabilitation. The social scientific hermeneutic part of the study aimed at discovering structure-theoretical generalizations. (2004, p. 25)

In addition, the authors conducted 25 expert interviews in the hospitals involved in the study and 8 expert interviews in after-care institutions. The participants for the case studies were selected from the sample for the survey. Criteria for selecting a couple for a case study were: they shared a flat; the partner should not suffer from a severe illness; and the ill partner should be in a rehabilitation clinic or after-care center at the time of the first data collection (2004, p. 95). Furthermore, contrasting cases to this sample were included: people living by themselves, couples with both partners being ill, or cases in which the patient's partner had died more than a year ago.

The quantitative data were first analyzed using several factor analyses and then in relation to the research question. In the presentation of the questionnaire results, "a link to the case studies is made, if their structural features match findings from the questionnaire" (2004, p. 87), or "if they show exceptions or a deviance."

All in all, the authors highlight the gains of differentiation due to the combination of survey and case studies:

> Thus, the case studies not only allow for a differentiation and a deeper understanding of the relatives' response patterns to the questionnaire. Their special relevance

(Continued)

(Continued)

is that analyzing them made it possible to discover the links between subjective meaning making (in the illness narratives) as well as the decisions and coping strategies that were reported and the latent meaning structures. Going beyond the psychological coping concepts, it became clear that it were less the personality traits or single factors, which make it easy or difficult to stabilize a critical life situation. Above all, the structural moments and the learned capacities to integrate the situational elements in one's own biography and in the one shared with the partner were important. (2004, p. 202)

This study can be seen as an example for combining qualitative and quantitative methods (and data), in which both approaches were applied consequently and with their own logic. They provide different aspects in the findings. The authors also show how the case studies can add substantial dimensions to the questionnaire study. Unfortunately, the authors do not refer to those findings from the questionnaires which were helpful in understanding the single cases or what the relevance of the quantitative finding was for the qualitative results.

Combining Qualitative and Quantitative Data

On the level of data, the combination of approaches may be oriented to transforming qualitative data into quantitative data and vice versa. Here are a few examples.

Transformation of Qualitative Data into Quantitative Data

Successive attempts have been made to quantify statements of open or narrative interviews. Observations can also be analyzed in terms of their frequency. The frequencies in each category can be specified and compared. Several statistical methods for calculating such data are available. Hopf (1982) criticizes a tendency among qualitative researchers to try to convince their audiences by an argumentation based on quantitative logic (e.g., "five of seven interviewees have said …"; "the majority of the answers focused …") rather than looking for a theoretically grounded interpretation and presentation of findings. Such a tendency is implicit in the transformation of qualitative data into quasi-quantitative findings. Moreover, this is sometimes a move from qualitative research logic to a quantitative way of thinking. Nevertheless it can be informative that a specific statement (attitude, type, etc.) could be found in more than just one participant or in female and male participants or just for one gender. Then it may also be helpful to present figures linked to types and subgroups, even in a table. But it is important not to make this the dominant logic of analyzing the data and presenting the findings.

Transformation of Quantitative Data into Qualitative Data

The inverse transformation is normally more difficult. It is difficult to disclose each answer's context in a questionnaire. If this task is attempted then it is achieved by the explicit use of additional methods such as complementary interviews for a part of the sample. Whereas analyzing the frequency of certain answers in interviews may provide additional insights for these interviews, the additional explanation of why certain patterns of answering can be found in large numbers in questionnaires requires the collection and involvement of new sorts of data (e.g., interviews and field observations).

Combining Qualitative and Quantitative Methods

There are only a few examples of studies using methodological procedures that fully integrate qualitative and quantitative strategies. Many questionnaires include open-ended or free text questions. This is, in some contexts, already defined as qualitative research, although hardly any methodological principle of qualitative research is taken aboard with these questions. Again, this is not an explicit combination of both forms of research but rather an attempt to pick up a trend.

For the realm of analyzing qualitative data, Kuckartz (1995) describes a procedure of first- and second-order coding in which dimensional analyses lead to the definition of variables and values, which can be used for a classification and quantification. Roller, Mathes, and Eckert (1995) present a method called *hermeneutic classificatory content analysis*, which integrates ideas and procedures of objective hermeneutics (see Chapter 27) into basically a quantitative content analysis. Following a similar direction is the transfer of data analyzed with a program like ATLAS.ti into SPSS and statistical analyses. In these attempts, the relation of classification and interpretation remains rather unclear. To develop really integrated qualitative/quantitative methods of data collection or data analysis remains an unsolved problem.

Linking Qualitative and Quantitative Results

More often, combinations of both approaches are established by linking the results of qualitative and quantitative research in the same project or different projects, either one after the other or at the same time. An example can be combining the results of a survey and an interview study. This combination can be pursued with different aims:

- to obtain knowledge about the issue of the study which is broader than the single approach provided; or
- to mutually validate the findings of both approaches.

Three kinds of outcomes of this combination (see Kelle and Erzberger 2004) may result:

1 qualitative and quantitative results converge, mutually confirm, and support the same conclusions;
2 both results focus on different aspects of an issue (e.g., subjective meanings of a specific illness and its social distribution in the population), but are complementary to each other and lead to a fuller picture;
3 qualitative and quantitative results are divergent or contradictory.

The outcomes are helpful if the interest in combining qualitative and quantitative research has a focus to know more about the issue. The third case (and perhaps the second) needs a theoretical interpretation or explanation of the divergence and contradictions. Combining both approaches in the third case (and maybe the second) offers both valid findings and their limits. For a greater discussion on the problematic notion of validation through different methodologies, consult the literature on triangulation (see Chapter 14 and 29 and Flick 1992; 2007b).

Research Evaluation and Generalization

A common means of combining qualitative and quantitative research occurs when the research model of quantitative research (see Chapter 10) is applied to qualitative research. For example, the question of sampling (see Chapter 13) is seen as basically a numeric problem, as in the following question, often asked by students: "How many cases do I need to be able to make a scientific statement?" Here quantitative logic is applied to qualitative research.

Another implicit combination of qualitative and quantitative research is to apply the quality criteria of one area to the other. Qualitative research is often criticized for not meeting the quality standards of quantitative research (see Chapter 29), without taking into account that these criteria do not fit qualitative research's principles and practices. In the other direction, the same problem is given, but this is relatively seldom the case.

With respect to the problem of generalization of qualitative research, you will find quite often a third form of implicit combination of qualitative and quantitative research. Then it is forgotten that to generalize findings of a study based on a limited number of interviews in a representative survey is just one form of generalization. This numerical generalization is not necessarily the right one, as many qualitative studies aim at developing new insights and theories. The more relevant question is how to generalize qualitative findings on a solid theoretical background. It is not so much the number of cases that are studied, but rather the quality of sampling decisions on which the generalization depends. Relevant questions here are "which cases?" rather than "how many?" and "what do the cases represent or what were they selected for?" Thus, the question of generalization in qualitative research is less closely linked to quantification than it is sometimes assumed.

Mixed-Methods Research

In the recent literature you will find many publications addressing the relations, the combination, or the distinctiveness of qualitative research. Before we focus on the special aspects of qualitative research and methods in the following chapters, I want to give here a brief overview of the qualitative–quantitative debates and versions of combining both. This should help you to locate qualitative research in this broader field and also to get a clearer picture of the strengths and features of qualitative research.

Bryman (1992) identifies 11 ways of integrating quantitative and qualitative research. The logic of triangulation (1) means, to him, checking for examples of qualitative against quantitative results. Qualitative research can support quantitative research (2) and vice versa (3); both are combined in or provide a more general picture of the issue under study (4). Structural features are analyzed with quantitative methods and processual aspects with qualitative approaches (5). The perspective of the researchers drives quantitative approaches, while qualitative research emphasizes the viewpoints of the subjective (6). According to Bryman, the problem of generality (7) can be solved for qualitative research by adding quantitative findings, whereas qualitative findings (8) may facilitate the interpretation of relationships between variables in quantitative data sets. The relationship between micro and macro levels in a substantial area (9) can be clarified by combining qualitative and quantitative research, which can be appropriate in different stages of the research process (10). Finally, there are hybrid forms (11) that use qualitative research in quasi-experimental designs (see Bryman 1992, pp. 59–61).

In addition, there are publications on the integration of qualitative and quantitative methods about mixed methodologies (Tashakkori and Teddlie 2003a; 2010), but also about triangulation of qualitative and quantitative methods (Flick 2007b; Kelle and Erzberger 2004). The terms already show that different claims are made with these approaches. Mixed-methodology approaches are interested in a pragmatic combination of qualitative and quantitative research. This offers an end to the paradigm wars of earlier times. The approach is declared to be "a third methodological movement" (Tashakkori and Teddlie 2003b, p. ix). Quantitative research and methods are seen as the first movement, qualitative research as the second. The goals of a methodological discussion here are to clarify the "nomenclature," questions of design and applications of mixed-methodology research, and of inferences in this context. From a methodological point of view, a paradigmatic foundation of mixed-methodology research is the aim. Using the concept of paradigms in this context, however, indicates that the authors start from two approaches, both of them closed, that can be differentiated, combined, or rejected, without reflecting the concrete methodological problems of combining them.

The claims for mixed-methodology research are outlined as follows:

> We proposed that a truly mixed approach methodology (a) would incorporate multiple approaches in all stages of the study (i.e., problem identification, data collection, data analysis, and final inferences) and (b) would include a transformation of the data and their analysis through another approach. (Tashakkori and Teddlie 2003b, p. xi)

These claims are very strong, especially if we take the transformation of data and analyses (qualitative in quantitative and vice versa) into account (see below). In the last few years the following definition of mixed-methods research has been widely accepted:

> Mixed methods is the type of research in which a researcher or a team of researchers combines elements of qualitative and quantitative research approaches (e.g. use of qualitative and quantitative viewpoints, data collection, analysis, inference techniques) for the broad purposes of breadth and depth of understanding and corroboration. (Johnson, Onwuegbuzie, and Turner, 2007, p. 123)

Methods' Appropriateness as a Point of Reference

The debate over the relationship between qualitative and quantitative research, which was originally oriented to epistemological and philosophical standpoints, has increasingly moved towards questions of research practice such as the appropriateness of each approach. Wilson (1982) states that for the relation of both methodological traditions, "qualitative and quantitative approaches are complementary rather than competitive methods [and the] use of a particular method … rather must be based on the nature of the actual research problem at hand" (p. 501). Authors like McKinlay (1993; 1995) and Baum (1995) argue in a similar direction in the field of public health research. The suggestion is that rather than fundamental considerations determining the decision for or against qualitative or for or against quantitative methods, this decision should be determined by the appropriateness of the method for the issue under study and the research questions. Bauer and Gaskell (2000), for example, stress that it is more the degree of formalization and standardization which distinguishes the two approaches than the juxtaposition of words and numbers.

The problems involved in combining qualitative and quantitative research nevertheless have not yet been solved in a satisfying way. Attempts to integrate both approaches often end up in a one-after-the-other (with different preferences), a side-by-side (with various degrees of independence of both strategies), or a dominance (also with different preferences) approach. The integration is often restricted to the level of the research design—a combination of various methods with different degrees of interrelations among them. However, the differences between the two ways of research concerning appropriate designs (see Chapter 9) and appropriate forms of assessing the procedures, data, and results (see Chapter 29) continue to exist. The question of how to take these differences into account in the combination of both strategies needs further discussion.

There are some guiding questions for assessing examples of combining qualitative and quantitative research, as follows:

• Are both approaches given equal weight—in, for example, (1) the plan of the project, (2) the relevance of the results, and (3) judging the quality of the research?

- Are both approaches merely applied separately or are they really related to each other? For example, many studies use qualitative and quantitative methods rather independently, and, in the end, the integration of both parts refers purely to comparing the results of both.
- What is the logical relation between the two? Are they only sequenced, and how? Or are they really integrated in a multi-methods design?
- What are the criteria used for evaluating the research *all in all*? Is there a domination of a traditional view of validation or are both forms of research evaluated by appropriate criteria?

Answering these questions and taking their implications into account enables the development of sensitive designs of using qualitative and quantitative research in a pragmatic and reflexive way.

Checklist for Deciding between Using Qualitative or Quantitative Research

When deciding whether and how to use and combine qualitative and quantitative methods, the questions listed below may be used to provide clarification:

- Is the issue you study, together with its features, your major points of reference for such a decision?
- Which theoretical approaches have implications for selecting your methodological approaches?
- What role does your concrete research question play in defining how you focus your issue conceptually and how you cover it empirically?
- Is your methodological decision between qualitative and quantitative methods and designs derived from the points of reference just mentioned in this checklist?
- Have you taken your available resources into account (time, your own methodological knowledge, and competencies)?

These questions can be used to inform the planning of your own study and also for assessing the studies of other researchers.

KEY POINTS

- The linking of qualitative and quantitative research is a topic that attracts much attention.
- The combination of qualitative and quantitative research may occur on various levels.
- The combination is not merely a pragmatic issue; it requires critical reflection.
- The central point of reference is the *appropriateness* of the methods to the issue under study.

Exercise 3.1

Take the example of Nicca, Fierz, Happ, Moody, and Spirig (2012) for reflecting on and answering the following questions:

1 Considering the different ways of combining qualitative and quantitative research, which way was chosen here?
2 How adequate was the combination of qualitative and quantitative methods for this study? Explain your view.

Exercise 3.2

1 Identify an issue in your own research in which a combination of qualitative and quantitative research could be helpful and `outline the potential benefits.
2 Identify the problems you might face in applying a combination of qualitative and quantitative approaches in your research.

Further Reading

Here are some pragmatic and thoughtful works about ways and problems in linking both kinds of research:

Bryman, A. (2007) "Barriers to Integrating Quantitative and Qualitative Research," *Journal of Mixed Methods Research*, 1(1): 8–22.

Flick, U. (1992) "Triangulation Revisited: Strategy of or Alternative to Validation of Qualitative Data," *Journal for the Theory of Social Behavior*, 22: 175–197.

Flick, U. (2007b) *Managing Quality in Qualitative Research* (Book 8 of the SAGE Qualitative Research Kit). London: Sage.

Flick, U., Garms-Homolová, V., Herrmann, W.J., Kuck, J. and Röhnsch, G. (2012b) "'I Can't Prescribe Something Just Because Someone Asks for It ...': Using Mixed Methods in the Framework of Triangulation," *Journal of Mixed Methods Research*, 6(2), 97–110.

Kelle, U. and Erzberger, C. (2004) "Quantitative and Qualitative Methods: No Confrontation," in U. Flick, E.v. Kardorff and I. Steinke (eds.), *A Companion to Qualitative Research*. London: Sage. pp. 172–177.

Tashakkori, A. and Teddlie, Ch. (eds.) (2010) *Handbook of Mixed Methods in Social & Behavioral Research* (2nd edn). Thousand Oaks, CA: Sage.

4

Approaches to Qualitative Research

CHAPTER OBJECTIVES

This chapter is designed to help you

- develop your awareness of the variety of qualitative research;
- locate examples of studies in the field of qualitative research;
- provide a context for understanding the issues discussed in subsequent chapters.

This chapter explores the variety of ways of doing qualitative research on two levels: (1) by discussing major research programs; and (2) by way of orientation, introducing the central methods of data collection and analysis. In addition, the chapter seeks to establish how some major methodological issues are relevant across all methodological approaches. This overview should help to provide a context in which to place the practical steps and methodological alternatives that will be discussed in subsequent chapters.

Research Programs in Qualitative Research

In this book, several approaches to qualitative research are introduced. At some points, specific approaches are discussed in more detail for the purpose of outlining a more general problem in qualitative research. For example, in the chapter on sampling (see Chapter 13) the grounded theory approach to sampling is discussed in some detail in order to highlight general principles of qualitative research beyond grounded theory. For broadening the approach, the major research programs subsequently discussed in this book are introduced here.

Grounded Theory

This approach was developed in the 1960s by Barney Glaser and Anselm Strauss (Glaser and Strauss 1967). The basic idea behind this approach is that theories should be developed from empirical material and its analysis. Theories should be "grounded" in such material. For making the analytic process as fruitful as possible, grounded theory researchers use a very open approach to their field of study. Although researchers should be knowledgeable about existing theories about the issue and field under study, theories are not (according to this approach) the starting point of the research, but rather the endpoint.

In the empirical process, data collection is very much a pragmatic issue—all sorts of methods and data can be employed for understanding the phenomenon. While observation and ethnography (see Chapter 20) were the dominant approaches in the early days of qualitative research, other data (like interviews or documents) are used now as well. The selection of material will depend on the decision about which cases seem to be most fruitful for further developing the theory from the empirical material. More explicit suggestions are made on how to analyze the data (see the coding procedures of open, axial, and selective coding discussed in Chapter 25).

In current qualitative research the grounded theory approach remains highly influential. It has been further developed by researchers such as Kathy Charmaz, Juliet Corbin, Tony Bryant, Robert Thornberg, and others (see Bryant and Charmaz 2007a; 2007b; Thornberg and Charmaz 2014). The major outcomes of research using this approach are theories about specific phenomena in certain fields. An example might be a theory for explaining, say, how dying in hospitals is "organized" in specific communicative processes, which include some information and exclude other information at the same time (see Glaser and Strauss 1965a). We will return to that example at some points.

Ethnomethodology; Conversation and Discourse Analysis

The approach of ethnomethodology was also founded in 1960s, by Harold Garfinkel (1967) and others. The aim here, in contrast to that of grounded theory, is not so much to develop a theory of a phenomenon. Ethnomethodology is interested in analyzing the methods people use for organizing their everyday lives in a meaningful and orderly way—how they make everyday life work. The basic approach is to observe parts of mundane or institutional routines, for example, how the admittance of a psychiatric patient to a mental hospital is organized, which steps this process runs through, etc.

A stronger focus has been placed on analyzing verbal interactions—conversations—in everyday talk (e.g., telephone calls) or institutional or professional conversations (e.g., counseling interactions). In the meantime, conversation analysis has become a major research program of its own within qualitative research (see ten Have 1999 or Bergmann 2004a). Conversation analysis considers formal aspects of talk—such as turn taking between speakers in conversation and which rules can be identified in such a process. Data are collected by recording examples of such conversations using audio or video devices. Explicit methods for data collection (like interviews) are not used here (see Toerien 2014).

The concentration on formal aspects of research issues has been criticized and has thus led to the development of the more rounded approach of discourse analysis (see, e.g., Willig 2014a). Here, the focus is again on how something is talked about, but more emphasis is given to the *contents* of this talk. At the same time, the kind of discourse studied here includes not only spoken words, but also media discourses and their content and impact on the everyday life treatment of issues (e.g., media discourse about migration). In discourse analysis, methods such as interviewing are also used for collecting data. Discourse analysis is now a very important research program in current qualitative research; ethnomethodology and conversation analysis are also very active approaches. We will return to these approaches at several points of our further discussion in this book.

Narrative Studies

A third approach in qualitative research focuses in various ways on narratives. In narrative studies (see Czarniawska 2004), either existing narratives are collected and analyzed, or they are produced for research purposes in specific forms of interviews. A major background assumption is that narrative is a way of knowing and remembering events and processes (in our own personal history) as well as a way of communicating about issues (telling stories about events and processes).

For qualitative research, narratives are relevant in two ways. First, how to design a situation in which a narrative can be unfolded in an interview which is not inhibiting or influencing the story that is presented (see the narrative interview as an example for making this work, Chapter 18)? Second, how to analyze narratives that come from such a specific interview or are part of other forms of interviews—when participants start to tell a story while answering questions, for example—or come from other sources (see Chapter 18 and Esin, Fathi, and Squire 2014).

A prominent way of using narratives for studying issues such as migration, for example, is to collect biographical data such as life histories in narrative interviews and to develop typologies of migration experiences by comparing the narratives resulting from several interviews. Narrative approaches are prominent in several local (German, Polish, and Anglo-Saxon traditions, for example) and disciplinary contexts (sociology, psychology, and the like).

Ethnography

The fourth approach does not focus exclusively on talk and reports about activities and events. Ethnography is driven by the interest of *being there* (e.g., Borneman and Hammoudi 2009) and observing events and processes while they occur. The basic method is participant observation—the researchers become part of the field for some time and observe what is going on. In most cases, data collection will include talking to members in the field or collecting and analyzing documents. Participation means that the research goes on for some time, during which researchers move through the field and join activities and take notes about what they see and hear. This methodological approach was first developed in social and cultural anthropology for exploring foreign cultures.

Today, ethnographies are also used for analyzing processes and phenomena in the researchers' own cultures. Here again we find ethnographies of everyday life processes as well as in institutional contexts (see Gubrium and Holstein 2014). In many examples ethnography is more a matter of research *attitude* (i.e., being open towards the field and collecting any sorts of data for understanding it) rather than a method. In some cases, ethnographies take researchers' own experiences as focus (for such autoethnographies see Ellis et al. 2011), but the majority of ethnographic studies (see Atkinson, Coffey, Delamont, Lofland, and Lofland 2001 for an overview) focus on issues and practices from the viewpoint of other people's experience. Ethnography is a very prominent approach in qualitative research in different local and disciplinary contexts.

Although it formed the major approach in the beginning of grounded theory research, current ethnography does not necessarily pursue the aim of developing a theory. The aim is rather to produce very detailed and careful descriptions of a field and of an issue under study (see Chapter 20). However, a central part of ethnography is the writing about the field and facts that have been observed (see Chapter 30).

Hermeneutic Approaches

Whereas many of the approaches mentioned above focus on the detailed description of events and processes or on subjective accounts given by interviewees, some approaches go beyond this. Hermeneutic approaches are interested in analyzing structural causes of practices or statements—like an unconscious conflict as the cause of a Freudian slip. For this purpose, hermeneutics, for example, analyses statements in an interaction on several levels for finding out what the backgrounds of a statement are (see Wernet 2014 and Chapter 27). While in the early days of hermeneutic research, explicit data collection—in an interview, for example—was avoided in favor of recording naturally occurring interactions (in a family at the dinner table, for example), the range of data used in hermeneutic analyses has been extended. It now includes interview data as well as images, documents, art, and all sorts of practices. We find hermeneutic traditions in German sociology but also in other contexts—in Anglo-Saxon psychology (see Willig 2014b), for example.

As this short overview of approaches in qualitative research shows, we find various conceptualizations of qualitative research. At the same time this overview should show that there are overlaps between these approaches—ethnography or narrative analysis, for example, can be used for developing grounded theories. The early grounded theory studies (e.g., Glaser and Strauss's (1965a) study of dying in hospitals, which will be outlined in several cases studies in this book, see Chapters 13 and 25) methodologically built on ethnographic methods like participant observation (see Chapter 20). Charmaz and Mitchell (2001) discuss how grounded theory can be used in current ethnographies for going beyond descriptions.

But ethnography and narrative analysis are also used for other purposes, such as producing descriptions or typologies. (For example, see Hermanns' (1984) study on career development of engineers and the typologies he developed; see Case Study 18.2 in Chapter 18.) Finally, grounded theory research or discourse analysis can build on various approaches in collecting data. Thus a brief overview of the major methods in qualitative research will follow next.

Major Methods and Types of Data

In its development, qualitative research has undergone a proliferation of the methodological approaches that are used to collect data (as later chapters of this book will show in greater detail). However, on a basic level, there are three major methods in qualitative research for collecting data.

Talk as Data

A large part of qualitative research is based on using talk. We find three basic approaches. The first is to do single interviews with the participants of a study. Most interviews are based mainly on questions the interviewee is expected to answer, although they give room for other forms of response. For example, the interviewees can include spontaneous stories or examples they recount while answering a question (see Chapters 16 and 18).

The second approach is to elicit narratives in a single interview, for example, to ask the interviewees to recount their life histories after a specific event (a diagnosis, for example). Then questions and answers are not the aim of the main part of the interview in order to give the narrative the chance to develop, instead they will be postponed to the end of the interview (see Chapter 18). There are interview forms which combine both (question and narratives, e.g., the episodic interview, see Chapter 18) and interview forms addressing specific target groups, for example, experts.

The third approach to verbal data is to ask questions or stimulate discussions in groups—doing focus groups, for example (see Chapter 17). All these data have to be documented by recording them and transcribing—turning them into texts that can be analyzed.

Data beyond Talk

Observations are the focus of the second central methodological approach in data collection. Observations can include the researchers' participation in the field and in activities that are going on there. Observation can also be realized without the researchers' involvement with the field (non-participant observation). Ethnography is a wider approach that contextualizes observations in processes of participation (see Chapter 20), talking to people in the field, analyzing documents, and writing about what has been watched. Finally, observation is increasingly conducted by using technology—like video, film, or photos as the medium for recording data (see Chapter 21). Where such technology is not used, the medium for documenting what was observed is field notes written by the researchers during or after field contacts (see Chapter 20).

Using Existing Data

In many cases, researchers do not *produce* data, but instead *use* existing data for the analysis. All sorts of documents (records, files, school essays, journal articles) are used in qualitative research (see Chapter 22). Here questions arise about which documents fit the research question and design, which one to select out of a wider range of available documents, and what the quality is of these documents. Often text and paper are the features of the documents, but increasingly we find visual data like photos, films, and videos that were not produced for the research but used in it.

As we may see, we again have overlaps between the various forms of data—videos can be documents produced in a family's history for documenting weddings, birthdays, and so on. They can also be produced for research purposes, the researchers videotaping a family event for their research. Other methods can be used as stand-alone methods or be part of other methods—the interview can be the only method in a study or be part of an ethnography. Data can also be produced or come from the Internet, like doing online interviews or focus groups or analyzing virtual documents like websites.

Analyzing Data

Whether the data have been produced for the research (e.g., in interviews) or existing data are used, we can find two basic approaches to analyzing them, namely, (1) coding and categorizing and (2) investigating data in context.

Coding and Categorizing

The first approach is to develop and use categories for analyzing data—statements from interviews are identified and labeled by giving them a category. This process is called coding. Several methods are available for use in the field; categories can be developed either during the analysis or defined beforehand. One method has been developed most prominently in grounded theory research, although we find further developments from that starting point (see Thornberg and Charmaz 2014; see Chapter 25). An alternative is the major principle of qualitative content analysis (see Schreier 2014, see Chapter 26). For supporting coding and categorizing, a number of software programs (ATLAS.ti, MAXQDA, NVivo, see Chapter 28) have been developed. The core principle of coding and categorizing is that parts of the data (e.g., a statement) are taken out of their context and grouped with other bits of data (similar statements) and put in relations—categories, subcategories, etc. This is applied not only to statements, but also to extracts of observations or documents. It is also relevant for analyzing visual and virtual data like photos or Internet data.

Text in Context

The second group of approaches in qualitative data analysis takes the context of the data more strongly into account. When analyzing a narrative or a conversation, the development of the whole entity is considered as a relevant feature of what is analyzed. Therefore, conversation analysis, objective hermeneutics, and narrative studies proceed along the development of the whole case—a conversation or a narrative (see Chapters 27 and 25). This principle can also be applied to visual material or virtual data.

Again, combinations of both approaches can be found as well as further proliferations of methods (see Flick 2014b for an overview of the field).

General Issues

The overview above should provide an initial orientation in the field of qualitative research and the alternative research programs in the first step, and the methodological alternatives that are available in the second step. Which alternative should be used in the end in one's own research will depend on what is under study and what is intended to be found out. Whichever alternative you decide for on the level of the research program, you will be confronted with two sets of general issues in making your research work.

The first set is about planning your research. You will have to define a research question, design your research, and plan the project step by step. You will need to decide which cases you should use for your research (i.e., make sampling decisions) and gain access to the field where you want to do your research. These are general issues for all sorts of qualitative research and will be outlined in more detail in Part 3 of this book in the chapters addressing issues of research design.

At same time you will be confronted with a second set of general issues. You should ask and answer questions about the quality of your research and about how to present your research and findings to the audiences you want to reach with them. Again this applies to all forms of qualitative research, no matter which types of data you use and in which research program your data collection and analysis is embedded.

Checklist for Locating a Study in the Field

The questions in the checklist below might be helpful for the purpose of locating a study in the landscape of qualitative research:

1 How far does an existing study fit into one of the research programs mentioned in this chapter?
2 What is the basic methodological orientation used in this study?
3 Which sorts of data have been used in this study?

These questions can be applied to locating other researchers' existing studies in the field of qualitative research. To some extent, you may use the questions by applying them to the plan of your own study by asking where it might fit in the field.

KEY POINTS

- Qualitative research is an umbrella term which covers a number of research programs with different aims and procedures.
- In addition, the field of qualitative research consists of a variety of methods that have been developed over the course of its history.
- At the same time, methods of data collection can be summarized in three larger groups (talk as data, data beyond talk, and existing) mainly according to the data they produce.
- Methods for analyzing data have also been following two basic principles (coding and categorizing and text in context according to which they can be subsumed).
- Finally, a number of general issues of doing qualitative research apply for all the alternatives outlined here.

Exercise 4.1

1 Find a study which is based on a grounded theory approach (e.g., Neill 2010) and one based on discourse analysis (e.g., Paulson and Willig 2008) and compare them for their major similarities and differences.
2 Take the example of Flick, Garms-Homolová, and Röhnsch (2010) and consider which of the research programs and methods mentioned in this chapter apply to it.

Further Reading

These texts go further into the details of the trends and developments mentioned here for qualitative research:

Denzin, N. and Lincoln, Y.S. (eds.) (2011) *The SAGE Handbook of Qualitative Research* (4th edn). London: Sage.

Flick, U. (ed.) (2007a) *The SAGE Qualitative Research Kit* (8 vols.). London: Sage.

Flick, U. (2014b) "Mapping the Field", in U. Flick (ed.) *The SAGE Handbook of Qualitative Data Analysis.* London: Sage. pp. 3–18.

Flick, U., Kardorff, E.v. and Steinke, I. (eds.) (2004) *A Companion to Qualitative Research.* London: Sage.

Knoblauch, H., Flick, U. and Maeder, Ch. (eds.) (2005) "The State of the Art of Qualitative Research in Europe," *Forum Qualitative Sozialforschung/Forum: Qualitative Social Research*, 6(3), September, www.qualitative-research.net/fqs/fqs-e/inhalt3-05-e.htm.

5

Ethics of Qualitative Research

─ CHAPTER OBJECTIVES ─

This chapter is designed to help you

- understand the ethical issues involved in qualitative research;
- develop your sensitivity to the ethics of qualitative research;
- recognize that there is no simple solution to these issues;
- design and conduct (qualitative) research in an ethical framework.

In many domains, research has become an issue of ethics. Questions of how to protect the interests of those who are ready to take part in a study, together with scandals referring to manipulated data, have repeatedly drawn research ethics to the foreground. Codes of ethics have been developed in several disciplines and in several countries for the same discipline. In many contexts, especially in medical research, ethics committees have been established. Sometimes, their emphasis is on protecting all participants in the research process. In some countries, it is more the sensitivity of the research for vulnerable groups or for ethnic diversity, which is the focus of the ethics committee. This chapter outlines some of the problems concerning research ethics in qualitative research.

The Need for Ethics in Research

Among the general public, a sensitivity for ethical issues in research has grown due to scandals. The misuse of captives for research and experiments by doctors during the Nazi period in Germany are particularly horrifying examples, which led to the development of ethical codes for research. Past and recent cases of research fraud have led the German research councils to develop rules of good practice, which must be adopted by every university or institute applying for research funding. The growing sensitivity for ethical issues in research over the years has led to the formulation of a large number of codes of ethics and the establishment of ethics committees in many areas.

As is typical in ethics, there are tensions between the demands of (1) formulating general rules (as in codes of ethics, for example), (2) establishing institutions of control (like ethics committees, for example) and (3) taking into account the principles in day-to-day practices in the field and in the process of research. As we will see, ethics are often difficult to turn into clear-cut solutions and clarifications. Rather, researchers face ethical issues in every stage of the research process.

Definitions of Research Ethics

Ethical issues are relevant to research in general. They are especially relevant in medical and nursing research. There we find the following definition or research ethics, which can be applied to other research areas too:

> Research ethics addresses the question, which ethically relevant influences the researchers' interventions could bear on the people with or about whom the researchers do their research. In addition, it is concerned with the procedures that should be applied for protecting those who participate in the research, if this seems necessary. (Schnell and Heinritz 2006, p. 17)

In addition, Schnell and Heinritz (2006, pp. 21–24), working in the context of health sciences, have developed a set of principles specifically concerning the ethics of research. Their eight principles are listed in Box 5.1.

BOX 5.1

Principles of Research Ethics

1 Researchers have to be able to justify why research about their issue is necessary at all.
2 Researchers must be able to explain what the aim of their research is and under which circumstances subjects participate in it.

(Continued)

(Continued)

3 Researchers must be able to explicate the methodological procedures in their projects.

4 Researchers must be able to estimate whether their research acts will have ethically relevant positive or negative consequences for the participants.

5 The researchers must assess the possible violations and damages arising from doing their project—and be able to do so *before* they begin the project.

6 The researchers have to take steps to prevent violations and damages identified according to principle 5 above.

7 The researchers must not make false statements about the usefulness of their research.

8 The researchers have to respect the current regulations of data protection. (See Schnell and Heinritz 2006, pp. 21–24.)

Codes of Ethics

Codes of ethics are formulated to regulate the relations of researchers to the people and fields they intend to study. Principles of research ethics require that researchers avoid harming participants involved in the process by respecting and taking into account their needs and interests. Here are a few examples of codes of ethics found on the Internet:

- The British Psychological Society (BPS) has published a Code of Conduct, Ethical Principles, and Guidelines (http://www.bps.org.uk/sites/default/files/documents/code_of_ethics_and_conduct.pdf)
- The British Sociological Association (BSA) has formulated a Statement of Ethical Practice (http://www.britsoc.co.uk/media/27107/StatementofEthicalPractice.pdf)
- The American Sociological Association (ASA) refers to its Code of Ethics (http://asanet.org/about/ethics.cfm)
- The Social Research Association (SRA) has formulated Ethical Guidelines (http://the-sra.org.uk/sra_resources/research-ethics/
- The German Sociological Association (GSA) has developed a Code of Ethics (http://www.soziologie.de/en/gsa/code-of-ethics.html

These codes of ethics require that research should be based on informed consent (i.e., the study's participants have agreed to partake on the basis of information given to them by the researchers). They also require that the research should avoid harming the participants; this requirement includes the need to avoid invading their privacy or deceiving them about the research's aims.

In this context Murphy and Dingwall speak of "ethical theory," which they see as linked to four principles:

- *Non-maleficence*—researchers should avoid harming participants.
- *Beneficence*—research on human subjects should produce some positive and identifiable benefit rather than simply be carried out for its own sake.

- *Autonomy or self-determination*—research participants' values and decisions should be respected.
- *Justice*—all people should be treated equally. (2001, p. 339)

Consider, for example, the Code of Ethics of the GSA. The need to reduce the risk to participants of having any damage or disadvantage is formulated as follows:

> Persons, who are observed, questioned or who are involved in some other way in investigations, for example in connection with the analysis of personal documents, shall not be subject to any disadvantages or dangers as a result of the research. All risks that exceed what is normal in everyday life must be explained to the parties concerned. The anonymity of interviewees or informants must be protected. (Ethik-Kodex 1993: I B5)

The principles of informed consent and of voluntary participation in studies are fixed as follows:

> A general rule for participation in sociological investigations is that it is voluntary and that it takes place on the basis of the fullest possible information about the goals and methods of the particular piece of research. The principle of informed consent cannot always be applied in practice, for instance if comprehensive pre-information would distort the results of the research in an unjustifiable way. In such cases an attempt must be made to use other possible modes of informed consent. (Ethik-Kodex 1993: I B2)

At the level of abstraction found in such general rules, Murphy and Dingwall see a consensus in the application of the ethical principles. They see the problems rather on the level of the research practice. From their background of ethnographic research (see Chapter 20), Murphy and Dingwall identify two major problems mentioned in the literature about experiences with such codes and principles in the research practice:

> First, ethical codes that are not method-sensitive may constrain research unnecessarily and inappropriately. Secondly, and just as importantly, the ritualistic observation of these codes may not give real protection to research participants but actually increase the risk of harm by blunting ethnographers' sensitivities to the method-specific issues which do arise. (2001, p. 340)

As these authors show with many examples, a strict orientation in general rules of research ethics is difficult in areas like ethnographic research and does not necessarily solve the ethical dilemmas in this field. For example, if a number of homeless adolescents are observed for their health behavior in their everyday life in public places (see Flick and Röhnsch 2007), one will repeatedly come across situations in which they meet other adolescents briefly and by chance and communicate with them. For those adolescents, who are the focus of the study, it is possible to obtain their informed consent about taking part in the research. For the other adolescents who pass by occasionally, it will be impossible to obtain this consent. Maybe trying to obtain this consent would destroy the situation under observation. The principle of informed consent, which is basic to all codes of ethics, can be applied only in a limited way in this example. It shows how ethics codices as a solution for ethical problems have their limitations in the field during ethnography. Other authors have discussed in detail the special ethical problems in action research (Williamson and Prosser 2002), in qualitative online research (see Chapters 9, 16, and 20 and Mann and Stewart 2000, Ch. 3), or in feminist research (Mauthner, Birch, Jessop, and Miller 2002).

CASE STUDY 5.1

Covert Observation of Homosexual Practices

In the 1960s, Humphreys (1975) conducted an observational study of the sexual behavior of homosexuals. This study led to a debate on the ethical problems of observations in this and comparable fields which continued for a long time, because it made visible the dilemmas of non-participant observation (see Chapter 20).

Humphreys observed in public toilets, which were meeting places in the homosexual subculture. As homosexuality was still illegal at that time, toilets offered one of the few possibilities for clandestine meetings. This study is an example of observation without participation, because Humphreys conducted his observation explicitly from the position of sociological voyeur, not as a member of the observed events and not accepted as an observer. In order to do this Humphreys took the role of somebody (the "watch queen") whose job it was to ensure that no strangers approached the events. In this role, he could observe all that was happening without being perceived as interfering and without having to take part in the events:

> Outwardly I took on the role of a voyeur, a role which is excellently suitable for sociologists and which is the only role of a watchdog, which is not of a manifest sexual nature. ... In the role of the watch-queen-voyeur, I could freely move in the room, walk from window to window and observe everything without my subjects becoming suspicious and without disturbing the activities in any other way. (Humphreys 1973, p. 258)

After covertly observing the practices in the field, Humphreys then went on to collect participants' car license numbers and used this information to obtain their names and addresses. He used this information to invite a sample of these members to take part in an interview survey.

Humphreys used unethical strategies to disclose participants' personal information in what was originally an anonymous event. At the same time, he did much to keep his own identity and role as a researcher concealed by conducting covert observation in his watch-queen role. Each aspect of such conduct is unethical in itself—keeping the research participants uninformed about the research and violating the privacy and secrecy of the participants.

The ethical dilemmas of observation are described here in three respects. Researchers must find a way into the field of interest. They want to observe in a way that influences the flow of events as little as possible; and in sanctioned, forbidden, criminal, or dangerous activities in particular, the problem arises of how to observe them without the researcher becoming an accomplice. Therefore, this example was and still is discussed with some emphasis on the context of research ethics. This example is prominent in particular for the ethical issues linked to it and which can be demonstrated with it. But at the same time, it shows the dilemmas of finding and taking a role in observation.

Ethics Committees

Ethics committees have been established in many areas. In order to ensure ethical standards, the committees examine the research design and methods before they can be applied. In these fields, good ethical practice in research is then based on two conditions: that the researchers will conduct their research in accordance with ethical codes; and that research proposals have been reviewed by ethics committees for their ethical soundness. Reviews of ethical soundness will focus on three aspects (see Allmark 2002, p. 9): scientific quality; the welfare of participants; and respect for the dignity and rights of participants. Below we consider each in turn.

Scientific Quality

According to this criterion, any research which is only duplicating existing research, or which does not have the quality to contribute new knowledge to the existing knowledge, can be seen as unethical (see, e.g., Department of Health 2001).

In such a notion, there is already a source for conflict. For judging the quality of research, the members of the ethics committee should have the necessary knowledge for assessing a research proposal on a methodological level. This often means the members of the committees should be researchers themselves or at least some of the members. If you talk for a while with researchers about their experiences with ethics committees and with proposals submitted to them, you will hear many stories about how a research proposal was rejected because the members did not understand its premise. Or because they had a methodological background different from that of the applicant or that they simply disliked the research and rejected it for scientific rather than ethical reasons.

These stories reveal a problem with ethics committees: there are a variety of reasons why a committee may decide to reject or block a research proposal, not always based on ethical ones.

Welfare of Participants

Welfare in this context is often linked to weighing the risks (for the participants) against the benefits (of new knowledge and insights about a problem or of finding a new solution to an existing problem). Again, we find a difficulty here: weighing the risks and benefits is often relative rather than absolute and clear.

Dignity and Rights of the Participants

The dignity and rights of the participants are linked to consent given by the participant, to sufficient and adequate information provided as a basis for giving that consent, and that the consent is given voluntarily (Allmark 2002, p. 13). Beyond this, researchers need to guarantee participants' confidentiality: that information about them will be used only in such a way that it is impossible for other people to identify the participants or for any institution to use it against the interest of the participant.

The ethics committees review and canonize these general principles (for a detailed discussion of such principles see Hopf 2004b; Murphy and Dingwall 2001). The next section considers why these principles are not necessarily a clear-cut answer to ethical questions but more an orientation about how to act ethically in the research process.

How to Act Ethically

Northway (2002, p. 3) outlines the overall ethical involvement of any research: "However, all aspects of the research process, from deciding upon the topic through to identifying a sample, conducting the research and disseminating the findings, have ethical implications." You will be confronted with ethical issues at every step of the research. The way you enter a field and address and select your participants raises the issue of how you inform your participants and who you inform about your research, its purposes, and your expectations.

Informed Consent

Informed consent is defined as follows:

> The term *informed consent* implies that subjects know and understand the risks and benefits of participation in the research. They must also understand their participation is completely voluntary. (Flynn and Goldsmith 2013, p. 10)

When we take the principle of informed consent as a precondition for participation, we find in the literature the following criteria:

- The consent should be given by someone competent to do so.
- The person giving the consent should be adequately informed.
- The consent is given voluntarily. (Allmark 2002, p. 13)

This should not be too difficult to realize if you, for example, want to interview middle-class, middle-aged people with a similar educational level as your researchers have. Then you can inform them, and they may reflect and decide to consent or not (see Box 5.2 for an example of a document you might use for obtaining informed consent).

BOX 5.2

Agreement about Informed Consent and Data Protection in Interviews

Agreement about Data Protection for Scientific Interviews

- Participation in the interview is voluntary. It has the following purpose

[Issue of the study: …]

- Responsible for doing the interview and analyzing it are:

Interviewer: ……………………..

[Name of the institution: …………………………….]

Supervisor of the project:

[Name ……………………..]

[Name and address of the institution: …………………………………………]

The responsible persons will ensure that all data will be treated confidentially and only for the purpose agreed upon herewith:

- The interviewee agrees that the interview will be recorded and scientifically analyzed. After finishing the recording he or she can ask for erasing single parts of the interview from the recording.
- For assuring data protection, the following agreements are made (please delete what is not accepted):

☞ The material will be processed according to the following agreement about data protection:

Recording

1 The recording of the interview will be stored in a locked cabinet and in password-protected storage media by the interviewers or supervisors and erased after the end of the study or after two years at the latest.
2 Only the interviewer and the members of the project team will have access to the recording for analyzing the data.

(Continued)

(Continued)

3 In addition the recording can be used for teaching purposes. All participants in the seminar will be obliged to maintain the data protection.

Analysis and archiving

1 For the analysis, the recording will be transcribed. Names and locations mentioned by the interviewee will be anonymized in the transcript as far as necessary.
2 In publications, it is guaranteed that identification of the interviewee will not be possible.

The interviewer or the supervisor of the project holds the copyright for the interviews.
The interviewee may take back his or her declaration of consent completely or in parts within 14 days.

[Location, date]: ....

Interviewer: ....   Interviewee: ....

In case of an oral agreement

I confirm that I have informed the interviewee about the purpose of the data collection, explained the details of this agreement about data protection, and obtained his or her agreement.

[Location, date]: ....   Interviewer: ....

But what if you want to study people who are not (seen as) competent to understand and decide, say younger children (as in the case of Allmark 2002) or very old people with dementia or people with mental health problems? These people are referred to in this context as a vulnerable population. Then you may ask another person to give you the consent as a substitute: children's parents, family members, or responsible medical personnel in the case of an elderly or ill person. Does this meet the criterion of informed consent? You could easily find other examples in which you have to decide how far you can deviate from the general principle without ignoring it.

CASE STUDY 5.2

Collecting Data from a Vulnerable Group of Older People

Wolfram Herrmann did his PhD in the context of a larger study on residents' sleep disorders in nursing homes. His study focused on the residents' subjective perceptions of the issue of sleep, their subjective explanation of why they did not sleep well, and on how they deal with this problem (see Herrmann and Flick 2012). He interviewed 30 residents in 5 nursing homes and used the episodic interview as a method of data collection. The research was approved by the ethics committee of a large medical university in Berlin. Ethical issues concerned how to obtain the informed consent of the potential interviewees, how to find out whether they were (still) able to give such consent, and to give an interview. As a large part of the nursing home population in Germany suffers from cognitive restrictions, the participants had to be selected according to criteria as to whether they were oriented in "person and place" for being included in the interviews. To ignore such a selection criterion would have meant conducting interviews with people unable to give informed consent, while applying it would exclude a major group of residents (and potential interviewees) beforehand. Taking such a criterion seriously may produce limitations for applying the results to the target group in general (nursing home residents), while ignoring the criterion may make the quality of the data questionable not only on an ethical but also on a methodological level. Being confronted with the need to apply such a selection criterion may also produce an ethical dilemma in the step of sampling (see Chapter 13).

Avoiding Harm to Participants in Collecting Data

Collecting your data may present you with another ethical problem. If you are interested in how people live and cope with a chronic illness, for example, the planned interview questions may confront people with the severity of their illness or the lack of prospects in their future life. This may in some cases produce an internal crisis for these people. Is it ethically correct to take this risk for the sake of your research? This is discussed more generally as the ethical principle of "respect for the person," which "incorporates at least two ethical convictions: first, individuals should be treated as autonomous agents, and second, persons with diminished autonomy are entitled to protection" (The Belmont Report, 1979, quoted by Flynn and Goldsmith 2013, p. 63).

Anonymization is another challenge to deal with in data collection. In an interview, for example, you should try to avoid mentioning concrete information about the interviewee or other persons mentioned. If such information is given in the interview, you will have to take care to anonymize such information in the transcription or before using it in reports. You should also reflect on how comprehensively you need to collect data about the individual participant. Is it always necessary to collect whole life histories for answering your specific research questions? Could a more economic approach provide the data you need and pay more respect to the participants' privacy at the same time? For example, is it necessary to have the participants recount their life history from beginning to end (as in the narrative interview, see Chapter 18)? Or would recounting specific situations in which the issue under study became relevant (as in the episodic interview, see Chapter 18) also provide the information needed for the research but intrude less into the participants' privacy?

Studying a Vulnerable Group of Younger People

If we now return to the example already mentioned in Chapter 2, some ethical issues relevant to that study illustrate the general problems of ethically sound research. As mentioned above, the study addresses the health problems of a group of young, adult, Russian-speaking migrants and in particular their experiences with health services in Germany. First the design of the study: the instruments for data collection and the information given to possible participants were presented to our university's ethics committee for approval. This implied that such information had to be produced for all possible groups of participants—in this case the migrants themselves—who should be interviewed, and service providers, who should also be interviewed. We also needed to produce information sheets for institutions which could support us in gaining access (see Chapter 12) to our participants (e.g., social services, meeting points, drop-in centers, etc.). For participants who might be younger than 18 years it was necessary to obtain their parents' consent if possible. We had also to define the rules of data protection in the process, for example, in transcription etc. As some of the interviews would require translators, we also needed to define the rules of data protection for this step. For the case where participants were not willing to sign an agreement like the one in Box 5.2, we had to find a way of documenting that they had given their informed consent before the interviews.

Ethical dilemmas here arise from the need to find solutions for cases in which the usual maximum rules of ethically sound research cannot be applied—for example, because the participant is unwilling to sign a form of informed consent, but is ready to be interviewed and important for the study.

Specific needs for reflecting research ethics arise in the context of online research. Gaiser and Schreiner (2009, p. 14) have formulated several questions to consider from an ethical point of view if, for example, you are collecting your data online:

- Can participant security be guaranteed? Anonymity? Protection of the data?
- Can someone ever really be anonymous online? And if not, how might this impact the overall study design?
- Can someone "see" a participant's information, when he or she participates?
- Can someone unassociated with the study access data on a hard drive?
- Should there be an informed consent to participate? If so, how might online security issues impact the informed consent?

This list shows how general issues of research ethics are relevant for online, as well as traditional, research.

Doing Justice to Participants in Analyzing Data

In analyzing and writing about your data, you will make certain judgments (e.g., a specific person can be allocated to specific coping behaviors while other persons are allocated to other types of coping skills). If your participants read this, they may find it embarrassing to be compared (and equated) to other people and they may also see themselves in a different way. Beyond such discrepancies in classifying oneself and being classified, "doing justice to participants in analyzing data" means that interpretations are really grounded in the data (e.g., interview statements). Also they should not include judgments on a personal level and should not make the participants subject to a diagnostic assessment (of their personality, for example). The general issues of ethics in using qualitative data and their analysis are discussed by Mertens (2014) and Wertz, Charmaz, McMullen, Josselson, Anderson, and McSpadden (2011).

Confidentiality in Writing about Your Research

The issue of confidentiality or anonymity may become problematic when you do research with several members of a specific setting. When you interview several people in the same company, or several members of a family, the need for confidentiality is not just in relation to a public outside this setting. Readers of your report should not be able to identify which company or which persons took part in your research. For this purpose, encrypt the specific details (names, addresses, company names, etc.), to protect identities. Try to guarantee that colleagues cannot identify participants from information about the study. For example, when interviewing children, you may often find that parents want to know what their children said in the interview. To avoid this problem, you should inform the parents right at the beginning of your research that this is not possible (see Allmark 2002, p. 17). Finally, it is very important that you store your data (i.e., recordings and transcripts) in a safe and completely secure container, so that no one will be able to access these data, who is not meant to (see Lüders 2004b).

The Problems of Context in Qualitative Data and Research

Generally, the data of qualitative research produce more context information about a single participant than quantitative research. Usually it is impossible to identify a participant from a survey and the statistical/numerical data published across numerous cases. When you study a single case or a limited number of cases in well-defined fields and use excerpts from life histories in your publication, it is much easier to identify the "real" person from the contextual information included in such a quotation.

CASE STUDY 5.4

Interaction as an Ethically Sensitive Subject of Research

This example will show that also a specific research topic can require a specific ethical sensitiveness. Maijalla, Astedt-Kurki, and Paavilainen (2002) completed a study using grounded theory (see Chapters 10 and 25) with families. They studied the interaction

(Continued)

(Continued)

between the caregiver and a family expecting a child with an abnormality. The families involved in the study were in a state of crisis after receiving the information that their child might be born with a deformity or might not survive.

Doing research with families in such a situation first of all comes with the ethical dilemma of whether it is justified to additionally confront them with their situation by asking questions about it. Thus, participation in the study may cause some harm for the family or single members.

The authors interviewed parents from 18 families in that situation and with 22 caregivers who interacted with these families. The interviews were tape recorded and, for ethical reasons, there was no videotaping used to document the data. Potential participants received a letter stating the study's intentions and modalities of confidentiality. Consent of participation was given in written form.

As this research was carried out in the context of nursing research, an ethical issue was how to separate the roles of researcher and caregiver. It had to be clarified that the purpose of the interview was to collect data, not to work with the participants on the situation and the ways of coping with it. However, it was necessary to keep an eye on the participants' well-being during and after the interview, as the issue produced a distressing situation. Thus, the role of the caregiver became part of the arrangement again in some cases.

Researchers did justice to the participants' viewpoints during the analysis period. To support this, each researcher wrote a research diary, and research supervision was given. The transcription of the interviews was done by a professional "who signed a written commitment to secrecy and who was experienced in dealing with confidential data" (2002, p. 30). In reporting their findings, the authors took care that the formulations were general enough to protect the anonymity of their informants (2002, p. 31).

This example showed how during the different stages of the research process ethical issues came up and also how the authors tried to cope with them. Maybe the problems were more urgent here as the families were in crisis and became part of this study due to this crisis. But most of the ethical issues can be transferred to other issues of qualitative research.

Qualitative Research Ethics—Necessary for Better Research

Qualitative research is often planned to be very open to, and adaptable to, what happens in the field. Methods here are less canonized than in quantitative research. This makes reviews by ethics committees more difficult: it is, for example, difficult to foresee what sorts of data will be collected in an ethnographic study. It also sometimes makes it difficult to ask for the consent of those being researched when observations are done in open spaces like marketplaces, train stations, and the like.

This openness sometimes leads to a rather comprehensive approach in data collection ("Please tell me the story of your life and everything that may be important for my research …") instead of a clearly focused (and limited) set of questions or things to observe. Therefore, it may be helpful to reflect on a rather economic approach to the field, which means only collecting those data and aspects that are really necessary to answer the research question.

Research ethics are an important issue in planning and doing your research. It is often not possible to find easy and very general solutions to the problems and dilemmas. This has a lot to do with reflection and sensitiveness. Thinking about ethical dilemmas, however, should not prevent you from doing your research, but should help you to do it in a more reflective way and to take your participants' perspective on a different level. Seek to consider the participants' role and think from their perspective how it would be for you to do what you expect them to do in your research. This may be a good starting point for reflecting on the ethical issues linked to your specific research.

Checklist for Taking Ethical Issues into Account

In pursuing your own qualitative study, the following questions will help to ensure that you conduct it in an ethically sound way:

1 How will you put the principle of informed consent into practice?
2 How will you inform all participants that take part in a study or are involved in it?
3 How will you ensure that the participants do not suffer any disadvantages or damages from the study or from taking part in it?
4 How will you guarantee the voluntariness of the participation?
5 How will you organize the anonymization of the data and the issues of data protection in the study?
6 Have you checked your method of proceeding against the relevant ethical code(s)?
7 If so, which problems became evident here?
8 Is a statement from an ethics committee necessary for your study and, if so, have you obtained it?
9 What is the novelty in the expected results which justifies doing your project?

These questions can be applied to the planning of your own study and in a similar way to the evaluation of other researchers' existing studies.

┌─ **KEY POINTS** ──┐

- Finding solutions to ethical dilemmas is essential to legitimate research.
- In qualitative research, ethical dilemmas are sometimes particularly difficult to solve.
- Codes of ethics regulate the treatment of ethical issues generally. Ethics committees can be important in assessing research proposals and the rights and interests of the participants.

(Continued)

└───┘

(Continued)

- The dynamics of ethical dilemmas reveal themselves in the field and in the contact with people or institutions.
- Many ethical dilemmas arise from the need to weigh the research interest (better knowledge, new solutions for existing problems, and the like) against the interest of participants (confidentiality, avoidance of any harm, and the like).

Exercise 5.1

1 Take a qualitative study (like Taylor 2012) and determine whether the author(s) addressed ethical issues. How did they deal with them? What other issues of research ethics might be expected in such a study?
2 What are the ethical issues relevant to that study (even if they are not mentioned by the author(s))?

Exercise 5.2

In your own course of study, identify and debate the ethical issues, establish guidelines, and create a plan for participants.

Further Reading

The following texts give a good overview of the discussion of ethical issues for qualitative research:

Hopf, C. (2004b) "Research Ethics and Qualitative Research," in U. Flick, E.v. Kardorff and I. Steinke (eds.), *A Companion to Qualitative Research*. London: Sage. pp. 334–339.

Mertens, D.M. and Ginsberg, P.E. (eds.) (2009) *Handbook of Social Research Ethics*. Thousand Oaks, CA: Sage.

Murphy, E. and Dingwall, R. (2001) "The Ethics of Ethnography," in P. Atkinson, A. Coffey, S. Delamont, J. Lofland and L. Lofland (eds.), *Handbook of Ethnography*. London: Sage. pp. 339–351.

Taylor, S. (2012) "'One Participant Said …': The Implications of Quotations from Biographical Talk," *Qualitative Research*, 12: 388–401.

PART 2
Theory in Qualitative Research

Contents

In Part 1, we looked for a framework for doing qualitative research or a qualitative study. As we saw in Chapter 2, qualitative research is centrally concerned with the production and analysis of texts, such as transcripts of interviews or field notes and other analytic materials. We turn now to the first part of the overall journey of a qualitative research project.

In particular, we consider ways of using theories and the existing literature in qualitative research. This is in order to dispel the prejudice, sometimes encountered, that qualitative researchers should stay away from reading the existing body of research literature or from reading the methodology literature and theories about the research topic (Chapter 6).

We then consider the major theoretical perspectives underpinning qualitative research. These theoretical perspectives can be seen as the **background theories** of qualitative research. Each of them contains assumptions about the nature of realities, how to address an issue conceptually, and how to plan research (Chapter 7). In this chapter, we will also encounter two influential discussions in qualitative research. The first concerns positivism and constructivism as a basic epistemological assumption; the second focuses on the impact of feminist positions on qualitative research in general.

The discussion concerning positivism and constructivism will be developed a little more in the final chapter of this part (Chapter 8). There, we will consider questions concerning the epistemological background of using text in qualitative research and address the basic processes in constructing and understanding texts.

Part 2 as a whole sets the epistemological and theoretical ground for the more practical parts of the book in which you will learn more about how to do qualitative research.

6
Using the Existing Literature

CHAPTER OBJECTIVES

This chapter is designed to help you

- comprehend the relevance of the existing literature for planning your own research;
- understand the need to draw on the methodological literature as well as the existing substantive research and theoretical literature in your area;
- familiarize yourself with ways of finding the relevant literature.

How and When to Use the Literature

Sometimes one encounters the idea that qualitative research need not start from a review of the existing literature or even that it should simply avoid that step at the beginning. Such views stem from the fact that qualitative research is closely linked to the idea of discovering new fields and exploring areas that are new to the world of science and to research. Thus many guides to qualitative research do not include any chapter dedicated to the use of the existing literature when making a study.

However, it is rather naive to think there are still new fields to explore, where nothing ever has been published before. This may have been the case at the beginning of qualitative research, when anthropologists could sail off to explore uncharted islands. Maybe this was the case when social research (as a systematic enterprise) started to carry out the first studies among immigrant subcultures. But in the twenty-first century, after more than a century of social research and decades of rediscovering qualitative research, you will have more and more trouble finding a completely undiscovered field. Not everything has been researched, certainly, but almost everything you want to research is likely at least to connect with an existing, neighboring field.

The lack in textbooks of chapters devoted to the use of the literature may stem from a very early statement about grounded theory research. In their introduction to the *Discovery of Grounded Theory* Glaser and Strauss (1967) suggested (see Chapter 8) that researchers should start collecting and analyzing data without looking at the existing literature in the field. *Tabula rasa* was the mantra—a point that was often used later on as an argument against claims that qualitative research was scientific.

In this chapter, I will suggest that you should use several forms of literature in a qualitative study, including:

- the theoretical literature about the topic of your study;
- the empirical literature about earlier research in the field of your study or similar fields;
- the methodological literature about how to do your research and how to use the methods you chose;
- the theoretical and empirical literature to contextualize, compare, and generalize your findings.

How to Use the Theoretical Literature

In any area of research, you should familiarize yourself with the literature in your field. What are the existing writings about the social situation in a field in which you want to do interviews or make observations? What is known, for example, about the people that you want to interview? For instance, if you want to do a study with cancer patients, the question here is not necessarily what is known about the individuals you want to interview: rather, it is a question of what is known about people living in a similar situation; what is a regular career for persons with that specific cancer; how often does it occur; and so on? Are there any explanatory models about the causes and consequences of this specific disease?

In a quantitative study, you would take the existing literature about the issue of your study, derive hypotheses from it, and then test those hypotheses. In qualitative research, however, you would not do this. Instead, you use insights and information coming from the existing literature as context knowledge, which you use to see statements and observations in your research in their context. Or you use it to understand the differences in your study before and after its initial discovery process. Reviewing the theoretical literature in your area of research should help you answer questions such as:

- What is already known about this issue in particular, or the area in general?
- Which theories are used and discussed in this area?
- Which concepts are used or debated?
- What are the theoretical or methodological debates or controversies in this field?
- What questions remain?
- What has not yet been studied?

When Glaser and Strauss wrote their book *Discovery of Grounded Theory* in the 1960s, there was widespread dissatisfaction with the development of theory in the social sciences. Social scientists wanted to find overall grand theories, like the systems theories of Talcott Parsons (e.g., Parsons and Shils 1951). Though such theories were originally meant to explain more or less everything, they ended up explaining almost nothing on the level of everyday phenomena. In this situation, a need for theories closer to mundane or practically relevant issues arose, which should be answered by the empirically based theories developed in the research of grounded theory researchers.

Now the situation is quite different. The era of the overall grand theories has ended, and there are a wide variety of models and explanatory approaches for detailed problems. The trend is more towards diversification than to unification and a lot of these rather limited theories and models might be helpful for analyzing empirical material in related areas.

How to Use Theories

Let us take an example to illustrate this. For example, say you want to study the social representation of skin cancer in middle-class women in a certain part of the United Kingdom. In the context of such a research question, we can distinguish different forms of relevant theories. First, there are theories explaining the issue under study (take for instance medical or psychological theories of skin cancer in our example). They may inform you about the state of the art of scientific knowledge and about the forms of skin cancer and their reoccurrences. These theories may also inform you about possible reasons for such a disease, about ways of treating it, and finally about ways of dealing with it (e.g., treatment, coping, the likelihood of success of treatments, and so on).

This forms a part of the theoretical context that you should read in the literature. When your focus is especially on people and this disease in the United Kingdom, it might be interesting, again, to know how the issue of skin cancer is specifically relevant in the United Kingdom. So, you might try to find press coverage of this disease, the normal or special distribution and frequency of the disease in this country, and so on. To find this information, you will need to read the theoretical literature. The theories subject to this literature are called substantive theories.

The second form of theory that is relevant for your research in this example is the theory of social representation (see also Chapter 7). It gives you an idea that there are different forms of knowledge among lay people in different groups. It also provides you with ideas about how such knowledge is developed, transformed, and transmitted. This will give you a theoretical framework for conceptualizing your study.

When you focus in your study on the middle class, you will probably start from a notion of social classes, social inequality, and the distribution of privileges and disadvantages in society. This again forms a background theory for conceiving your study. When you focus on women as the target group of your study, you may also have a gender focus in your study, starting from the idea of gender differences in experience, ways of living, or knowing. Maybe you have an explicitly feminist perspective in your study (see also Chapter 7). Call these theories context theories for your research.

Finally, you may decide to use a specific methodology, say episodic interviews (see Chapter 18), to show how social representations have developed along the life course of your interviewees. This method comes with a specific theoretical conception of the issues that can be studied with it. This theory focuses, for example, on biographical information: what is a normal biography; what makes an individual's life course a deviation or a special case? It also starts from an assumption about how memory is organized. Conceptual or semantic and biographical or episodic memory and knowledge are distinguished (see Chapter 18 for details). This method comes with a lot of theoretical knowledge about how to design the situation of data collection so that the data are as rich as possible and so on. Here again, theory, which will be helpful to know, becomes relevant.

How to Use the Empirical Literature

Before you start your own empirical research, it might be helpful to find out whether there has been any other research in that or a similar area. You should search systematically for other studies in your field. They can be fruitful in inspiring you—what to do in your own research, how to design your research, what to ask in an interview, and so on. If the research is a good example, you can use it to orient your own approach; if it is a bad example, it can alert you on how not to proceed or which mistakes to avoid! In the main, you should read the empirical literature to see how other people in your area work, what has been studied, what has been focused on, and what has been left out. If it is an area where much research is going on, it might be helpful to know on which level the research concentrates and its results.

Reviewing the empirical literature in your area of research should help you to answer such questions as:

- What are the methodological traditions or controversies here?
- Are there any contradictory results and findings you could take as a starting point?

- Are there any debates about approaches and results in this area of research?
- Do any surprising findings exist in this field which call for a new study?

Strauss and Corbin (1998, pp. 49–52) have identified several ways of using the literature:

1 Concepts from the literature can be a source for making comparisons in data you have collected.
2 To be familiar with the relevant literature can enhance sensitivity to subtle nuances in data.
3 Published descriptive materials can give accurate descriptions of reality helpful for understanding your own material.
4 Existing philosophical and theoretical knowledge can inspire you and give you an orientation in the field and material.
5 The literature can be a secondary source of data—for example, quotations from interviews in articles may complement your own materials.
6 The literature can be used beforehand to formulate questions that help you as a springboard in early interviews and observations.
7 The literature may stimulate questions while you analyze your material.
8 Areas for theoretical sampling (see Chapter 13) can be suggested by the literature.
9 The literature can be used for confirming findings or can be overcome by your findings.

These nine points refer to publications from scientific writing, research, and methodology (called the technical literature by Strauss and Corbin). Non-technical literature, like letters, biographies, and all sorts of documents (see Chapter 22), can be used as primary data in their own right or for supplementing other forms of data (like interviews).

How to Use the Methodological Literature

Before you decide to use a specific method for your study, I recommend that you read the relevant methodological literature. If, for example, you want to use focus groups (see Chapter 17) in a qualitative study, familiarize yourself with a detailed overview of the current state of qualitative research. You can obtain this overview by reading a textbook or an introduction to the field. Also look through some of the relevant journals and see what has been published there in the last couple of years. Then you should identify the relevant publications about your method of choice by reading a special book, some chapters about it, and prior research examples using this method. The first step will allow you to take your decision for a specific method in the context of existing alternatives and of knowledge about them. The second step will prepare you for the more technical steps of planning to use the method and to avoid problems and mistakes mentioned in the literature. Both will help you give a detailed and concise account of why and how you used your method in your study, when you write your report later on, and so on.

Reviewing the methodological literature in your area of research should help you to answer such questions as:

- What are the methodological traditions, alternatives, or controversies here?
- Are there any contradictory ways of using the methods, which you could take as a starting point?
- Are there any debates about methodological approaches or of how to use them?
- Are there any canonizations of rule about how to use a specific method?

For example, if you decide to use a grounded theory approach (see Chapters 10, 13, and 25) for your research, it may be helpful to read about the two versions developed by Strauss and Corbin (1998) and Glaser (1992). If you want to use discourse analysis, it may be necessary to read about the different versions (e.g., Parker 2004a, Potter and Wetherell 1998, or Willig 2003; see Chapter 27) to see the distinctions, alternatives, and strengths or weaknesses of one approach over the other.

In reading and writing about your method, a review of the methodological literature in that area will help you and the readers of your research report to see your approach and findings in a wider context.

How to Use the Literature When Writing about Your Study

As may be appreciated from the above list suggested by Strauss and Corbin and from the discussion earlier in this chapter, it is important to use the literature during the writing of your study (see Chapter 30). Here the existing literature becomes relevant for grounding your argumentation, for showing that your findings are in concordance with the existing research, that your findings go beyond or contradict existing research.

In more extensive reports—or a thesis, for example—there should be a literature review. Hart gives a concise definition about a literature review's contents:

> The selection of available documents (both published and unpublished) on the topic, which contain information, ideas, data, and evidence written from a particular standpoint to fulfill certain aims or express certain views on the nature of the topic and how it is to be investigated, and the effective evaluation of these documents in relation to the research being proposed. (1998, p. 13)

You should demonstrate through the way you present the literature used in your study that you did a skilful search into the existing literature. Also it should be evident that you have a good command of the subject area and that you understand the issues, the methods you use, the state of the art of research in your field, and so on.

Where to Search the Literature

In general, the question of where to search for the relevant literature will depend on the topic of your study. You can basically look for books, for journal articles, and for material on the Internet. There are some advisory books available on this topic (Fink 2009; Machi and McEvoy 2012) and also papers available on the Internet (De Montfort University 2008; Harvard 2007). If you are looking for books, you may start using the websites of amazon.com or books.google.com to get a first orientation. You can then or in addition look at library catalogues (the OPAC of your university and databases like Scopus, Google Scholar, and the British Library's database of journal articles) or, even better, at copac.ac.uk, which includes 70 of the major university libraries in the United Kingdom and the British Library and the US Library of Congress. Another online portal to many libraries is Worldcat (www.worldcat.org/). If you look for journal articles you can go to wok.mimas.ac.uk or directly to the web of knowledge (http://apps.webofknowledge.com). There you will find journal articles from a wide range of areas, but you can also confine your research to specific databases. In particular in medical or health-related areas, PubMed (www.ncbi.nlm.nih.gov/pubmed/) is a much more specific database, which covers most of these areas.

The same applies with some online publication services organized by publishing houses such as Sage. At online.sagepub.com you can search all the journals published by this publisher, read the abstracts, and get the exact reference dates for free. If you need to read the whole article, you have to be a subscriber to the service or the journal, or buy the article from the home page, or see whether your library has subscribed to the journal that published the article.

How to Search the Literature

To find the literature you should first define and reflect on your research question (see Chapter 11), so that you can decide what you are looking for. If your research topic is for example "Homeless Adolescents Coping with Chronic Illness," you have several areas implied for which you will need to find the literature: "homelessness," "chronic illness," "coping," "adolescents." You can search for each of these areas. For that you will have to define keywords. If you take these areas as keywords, maybe you will find an overwhelming amount of literature. For example, for the keyword "homelessness" my research in the web of knowledge produced almost 3,700 titles. When I added "adolescence" as a keyword the results came down to 36; once I changed the second keyword to "adolescent" I received 260 results. Adding a third keyword ("chronic illness") led to 1 result; when you use "illness" as the third keyword, you will have 20 hits. This example shows several things at the same time. It is important to have the right keywords; often you will need combinations of them. Sometimes keywords (or combinations) are too narrow, so you should look for wider terms or use truncated terms (like "adoles*" instead of "adolescence" or "adolescent"). It also may be helpful to reflect on what synonyms could be used for your keywords in addition or as an alternative. It may also be necessary or helpful to combine the above strategies for search literature (books on amazon.com plus journals on the web of knowledge and in the database of publishers like Sage). It may be helpful to consult the literature about how to look for literature which goes into more detail than I can within the context of this book. Examples are mentioned above and at the end of this chapter.

Also you should make use of the theoretical, methodological, and empirical literature referring to your topic, area, and approach. This will help you to see what your material has to offer in a wider context, inform you about how to do your research, and tell you what problems to avoid. The Internet offers many supporting services to help you along the way to finding the literature. In the end, a good review of the literature will be a substantial part of your research report.

Checklist for Literature Reviews

For assessing your literature review for an empirical project in social research, the questions in the checklist below might be helpful:

1 How fully does your literature review cover the issues of your study?
2 Is your literature review up to date?
3 How systematic is your review of the literature?
4 Does it cover the most important theories, concepts, and definitions?
5 Does your review cover the most relevant studies in your field of research and about your issue?
6 Have you documented how and where you searched for the literature?
7 Have you handled quotations and sources carefully?
8 Have you summarized, or synthesized, the literature you found?

KEY POINTS

- In qualitative research, the use of the existing literature has become increasingly necessary.
- There are several points in the research process where the use of the literature can prove helpful or even necessary.
- In planning research, in analyzing materials, and in writing about findings, make use of the existing literature about other research, theories, and the methods you use in your study.

Exercise 6.1

Locate a qualitative study (e.g., Flick et al. 2010), read it, and answer the following questions:

1 To what extent did the authors deal with the existing literature about their field of research?
2 At which points in the publication did the authors use or refer to the existing literature?

If you are planning your own study, use the ways of finding the literature mentioned above. Seek to find the relevant literature for planning and doing your study.

—Further Reading—

Literature Search

The first book below is the most comprehensive overview of how to do a literature search for your research, where to look, and how to proceed; the following article is written for nursing but can be useful orientation for other areas as well:

Hart, C. (2001) *Doing a Literature Search*. London: Sage.
Harvard, L. (2007) "How to Conduct an Effective and Valid Literature Search." This is an extended version of the article published in *Nursing Times*, 103: 45, 32–33, available at: www.nursingtimes. net/nursing-practice/217252.article.

Literature Reviews

In the following books you will find the most comprehensive overviews of how to do a literature review for your study, which pitfalls to avoid, and how to write about what you found. The suggestions in the third reference are more up to date.

Fink, A. (2009) *Conducting Research Literature Reviews: From the Internet to Paper* (3rd edn). London: Sage.
Hart, C. (1998) *Doing a Literature Review*. London: Sage.
De Montfort University (September 2008) "How to Undertake a Literature Search and Review: For Dissertations and Final Year Projects," Department of Library Services (www.library.dmu. ac.uk/Images/Howto/LiteratureSearch.pdf).

7
Theories Underlying Qualitative Research

┌─CHAPTER OBJECTIVES─┐

This chapter is designed to help you

- understand the major background theories in qualitative research;
- acknowledge the common and distinctive features of these theories;
- understand the differences between positivism and constructivism;
- consider the contribution of feminist theories to qualitative research.

Below we will examine some theories widely used in qualitative research. First, however, we consider positivism, a theoretical position widely cited in the literature for the purpose of contrast. The distinction between positivism and constructivism underlies the epistemological discussion of qualitative research quite widely. As Oakley (1999) shows, it is often linked to the context of feminism in qualitative research, too.

Positivism

Positivism as an epistemological program goes back to Auguste Comte, who emphasized that sciences should avoid speculative and metaphysical approaches: rather, they concentrate on studying the observable facts ("positiva"). Emile Durkheim emphasized that social facts exist outside the individual awareness and in collective representations. Positivism as an epistemological program is characteristic of the natural sciences. Thus in the social sciences, and particularly in qualitative research, it is commonly used as a negative foil from which to distinguish one's own qualitative research approach.

Bryman (2004, p.11) summarizes the assumptions of positivism as follows:

(1) only phenomena and knowledge confirmed by the senses can be warranted as knowledge (phenomenalism);
(2) theories are used to generate hypotheses that can be tested and allow explanations of laws to be assessed (deductivism);
(3) knowledge can be produced by collecting facts that provide the basis for laws (inductivism);
(4) science can and must be conducted in a way that is value free and thus objective; and
(5) there is a clear distinction between scientific and normative statements.

Positivism is often associated with realism. Both assume that there is a world out there (an external reality) separate from our descriptions of it. They assume too that the social and natural sciences can and should apply the same principles to collecting and analyzing data.

The consequence of such a position is that social research is often committed to ideals of measurement and objectivity, rather than reconstruction and interpretation. Thus the research situation is conceived as independent from the individual researchers who collect and analyze the data, so that the "facts" (to use a positivist term) above can be collected in an objective way. Therefore, research situations are standardized as far as possible for this purpose. On this view, research should strive for *representativeness* in what is studied—therefore random sampling often is the ideal.

As discussed in Chapter 2, this understanding of research is not suitable for all research issues. Qualitative research and its principles (see Chapter 2 and below) have been developed to a large extent in distinction to the principles of positivism and their consequences for research just outlined. For example, if you are interested in studying how people cope with a biographical experience like losing a partner due to a lethal disease, it will be difficult to transfer such a research interest into measurement and a standardized research situation. If you want to understand such an experience from the viewpoint of your research participant, you will need to set up an open research situation in which you will apply methods (like a narrative interview, see Chapter 18) for exploring the experiences. On both sides—the interviewee's and the researcher's—interpretation and reconstruction will be a part of data collection and later in analyzing them as well. It will be difficult to find your participants by random sampling and the idea of (statistical) representativeness will miss the point here. This example may illustrate why qualitative research has been developed and discussed often in implicit or explicit distinction to positivism.

However, researchers' deployment of the word "positivism" as a contrastive has been criticized: as Hammersley (1995, p. 2) notes, "all one can reasonably infer from unexplicated usage of the word 'positivism' in the social research literature is that the writer disapproves of whatever he or she is referring to."

In the next step we consider alternative understandings of research and knowledge, which come closer to what qualitative research is about.

Constructionism

A contrasting position is that of social constructionism (or constructivism) (see also Chapter 8). A number of programs with different starting points are subsumed under these labels. What is common to all constructionist approaches is that they examine the relationship to reality by dealing with constructive processes. Examples of constructions can be found on different levels:

1   In the tradition of Piaget, cognition, perception of the world, and knowledge about it are seen as constructs. Radical constructivism (Glasersfeld 1995) takes this thought to the point where every form of cognition—because of the neurobiological processes involved—has direct access only to images of the world and of reality, but not directly to the world or to reality.
2   Social constructivism in the tradition of Schütz (1962), Berger and Luckmann (1966), and Gergen (1985; 1999) inquires after the social conventions, perception, and knowledge in everyday life.
3   Constructivist sociology of science in the tradition of Fleck, Trenn, and Merton (1979), the present-day "laboratory-constructivist" research (Knorr-Cetina 1981), seeks to establish how social, historical, local, pragmatic, and other factors influence scientific discovery in such a way that scientific facts may be regarded as social constructs ("local products").

Constructionism is not a unified program. Rather, it is developing in parallel fashion in a number of disciplines: psychology, sociology, philosophy, neurobiology, psychiatry, and information science. It informs a lot of qualitative research programs with the approach that the realities we study are social products of the actors, of interactions, and institutions.

Construction of Knowledge

Taking three main authors, we may clarify how the genesis of knowledge and its functions may be described from a constructionist viewpoint. Schütz (1962, p. 5) starts from the following premise: "All our knowledge of the world, in common-sense as well as in scientific thinking, involves constructs, i.e., a set of abstractions, generalizations, formalizations and idealizations, specific to the relevant level of thought organization." Schütz sees every form of knowledge as constructed by selection and structuring. The individual forms differ according to the degree of structuring and idealization, and this depends on their functions. The constructions will be more concrete as the basis of everyday action or more abstract as a model in the construction of scientific theories. Schütz enumerates different processes which have in common the assumption that the formation of knowledge of the world is not to be understood as the simple portrayal of given facts, but that the contents are constructed in a process of active production.

This interpretation is developed further in radical constructivism. The "core theses" of this position are formulated by Glasersfeld (1992, p. 30) as follows:

1 What we call "knowledge" in no sense represents a world that presumably exists beyond our contact with it. ... Constructivism, like pragmatism, leads to a modified concept of cognition/knowledge. Accordingly, knowledge is related to the way in which we organize our experiential world.

2 Radical constructivism in *no sense* denies an external reality.

3 Radical constructivism agrees with Berkeley that it would be unreasonable to confirm the existence of something that cannot (at some point) be perceived.

4 Radical constructivism adopts Vico's fundamental idea that human knowledge is a human construct.

5 Constructivism abandons the claim that cognition is "true" in the sense that it reflects objective reality. Instead, it only requires knowledge to be *viable* in the sense that it should *fit* into the experiential world of the one who knows.

Experiences are structured and understood through concepts and contexts, which are constructed by this subject. Whether the picture that is formed in this way is true or correct cannot be determined. But its quality may be assessed through its *viability*: that is, the extent to which the picture or model permits the subject to find its way and to act in the world. Here an important point of orientation is the question of how the "construction of concepts" functions (Glasersfeld 1995, pp. 76–88).

For social constructionism, the processes of social interchange in the genesis of knowledge take on a special significance, especially the concepts that are used. Accordingly, Gergen formulates the following:

assumptions for a social constructionism: The terms by which we account for the world and ourselves are not dictated by the stipulated objects of such accounts. ... The terms and forms by which we achieve understanding of the world and ourselves are social artifacts, products of historically and culturally situated interchanges among people. ... The degree to which a given account of the world or self is sustained across time is not dependent on the objective validity of the account but on the vicissitudes of social processes. ... Language derives its significance in human affairs from the way in which it functions within patterns of relationship. (1994, pp. 49–50)

In these assumptions, Gergen highlights that terms for analyzing the world are formulated by researchers: they do not simply stem from what is analyzed with them.

He highlights that these terms are constructed in communicative processes among people and may change over time. The construction of terminology is both a linguistic and a social phenomenon: language itself plays a central role in setting up the terms used by researchers but they are also influenced by their use in relationships.

Knowledge is constructed in processes of social interchange; it is based on the role of language in such relationships; and, above all, it has social functions. The eventualities of the social processes involved have an influence on what will survive as a valid or useful explanation. Research acts are also part of the social construction of what we can address and find in social research. And the acts of writing contribute to this social construction of worlds under study. These issues and the variety of approaches in the broader field of constructionism will be spelled out in more detail for qualitative research in Chapter 8.

Feminism

Another challenge to positivism as the epistemological program of social research has come from feminism. More than a research perspective, feminist research began as a fundamental critique of social science and research in general. The research focused on the ignorance of women's life situation and of male dominance.

Feminism as an Epistemological Challenge and Approach in Qualitative Research

As Gergen (2008, p. 282) outlines, feminist research is not necessarily linked to using qualitative methods: in psychology, for example, the majority of feminist research studies in the United States is quantitative. However, feminist research has often been characterized by using qualitative research methods in order to open up more to women's voices and needs in general. A classical study in this context is the book *In a Different Voice* by Gilligan (1982). A second example is Smith's (1978) "K is Mentally Ill." As Gergen (2008) also outlines, grounded theory research (see Chapter 25) is a very prominent methodological approach for analyzing the actors' views based on interviews. But Gergen also shows in her overview that all of the most prominent qualitative research traditions play a role in feminist research: she mentions ethnography (see Chapter 20), ethnomethodology (see above), discourse analysis (see Chapter 27), and narrative research (see Chapter 18), for example.

Mies (1983) outlines reasons why feminist research is more linked to qualitative than quantitative research. Quantitative research often ignores the voices of women, turns them into objects, and they are often studied in a value-neutral way rather than researched specifically *as women*. Qualitative research allows women's voices to be heard and goals realized. According to Ussher (1999, p. 99), feminist research is focused on a "critical analysis of gender relationships in research and theory … an appreciation of the moral and political dimensions of research … and the recognition of the need for social change to improve the lives of women."

This leads not only to defining an issue of research (gender inequalities, for example), but to challenging the way research is done on different levels. Skeggs (2001) and Smith (2002) outline a feminist understanding of ethnography on the level of data collection as well as analysis and representation of findings (and the voices of the participants). Ussher (1999) uses health psychology to address specific issues within feminist qualitative research. Kitzinger (2004) presents an approach of feminist conversation analysis in order to analyze voices in their interactional context. Wilkinson (1999) discusses focus groups as a feminist methodology. Maynard (1998) again challenges the close link of feminist and qualitative research, asking why, for example, a combination of qualitative and quantitative research should be incompatible with the framework of feminist research.

Olesen (2011, p. 131) gives a very comprehensive overview of how feminist qualitative research relates to the general field of qualitative research and what the specific approaches and contributions have been. Here we find as approaches, for example, studies interested in globalization or using standpoint theories for understanding the specific situation between gender inequality. She also discusses a number of critical trends, for example, "indigenizing feminist research." Particularly instructive is the list of "continuing issues" of feminist discourse about methods and research. Here we find the problematization of the roles of researcher and participants or of concepts such as experience. As "enduring concerns" of feminist critique of social research, Olesen discusses such concepts as bias, objectivity, reflexivity, and validity and mentions the specific ethics in feminist research. This range of discussions, only mentioned here, shows the vitality of feminist methodological discussions.

These discussions in feminism constitute not just challenges and contributions to the methodological discussion in the field of qualitative research: feminist qualitative research has further developed as a distinct approach of doing qualitative research—in psychology (see Gergen 2008) and in social sciences in general (see Olesen 2011 for an overview). In addition, feminist research has contributed several specialized fields such as gender studies and queer studies.

Gender Studies

Gildemeister (2004) discusses gender studies as a step beyond feminist and women's studies as a program. Here:

> it is consistently pointed out … that gender is a social category, and that it is always, in some fundamental way, a question of social relationships. For this reason the focus is no longer made to deal with difference as a matter of substance or essence, but on analyzing gender relationships under aspects of their hierarchical arrangement and social inequality. (p. 123)

Gender in this context is seen either as a structural category or as a social construct. The first is more interested in social inequality resulting from gender (differences), the latter more in doing gender (West and Zimmerman 1991) and how social distinctions of genders are constructed in everyday and institutional practices. For example, the study of transsexuality has become a special approach to show how normality is constructed interactionally and can be deconstructed by analyzing the breakdown of such normality:

> The *interactional* deep structure in the social construction of gender has been particularly well illustrated by trans-sexual research. ... This type of research investigates, at the breakdown point of normality, how bi-sexuality is constructed in everyday practice and methodologically, because in the change from one gender to the other the processes involved in "doing gender" can be analyzed as if in slow motion. (Gildemeister 2004, p. 126)

Feminist researchers have contributed to reflection on qualitative methods by developing a research program for studying issues of gender, gender relations, inequality, and neglect of diversity. This program is developed on levels of epistemology, methodology, and research methods at the same time and has a valuable influence on qualitative research in general.

Queer Studies

One step further goes the approach of queer studies (see Plummer 2011). The use of 'queer' here is explained by Halperin:

> Queer is by definition whatever is at odds with the normal, the legitimate, the dominant. There is nothing in particular to which it necessarily refers. (1995, p. 62)

Following theorists like Judith Butler, queer theory and research challenge the "heterosexual/homosexual binary and the sex/gender split", de-center identity, and reveal or shun all normalizing strategies (Plummer 2011, p. 201) and the like. We also find an outline of a queer methodology including a textual turn and subversive ethnography, with a strong focus on "performing gender and ethnographic performance" (pp. 202–203).

Seen together, these approaches have developed a strong impact on conceptualizations of the self, of the roles of the researchers and the participants, and on the diversification of qualitative research perspectives and methodologies. In the next step, we will address the major research perspectives that define the field of qualitative research in a theoretical and methodological way.

Research Perspectives

As outlined in Chapter 2, "qualitative research" is an umbrella heading covering various research approaches. These differ in their theoretical assumptions, in the way they understand their object, and in their methodological focus. Generally speaking, these approaches are based on three basic positions: namely, symbolic interactionism; ethnomethodology; and structuralist or psychoanalytic positions. The tradition of symbolic interactionism is concerned with studying subjective meanings and individual meaning making. Ethnomethodology is interested in routines of everyday life and their production. Structuralist or psychoanalytic positions start from processes of psychological or social unconsciousness.

It is possible to distinguish approaches that foreground the "subject's viewpoint" from those seeking descriptions of given (everyday, institutional, or more generally social) milieus. Additionally, one can find strategies either interested in how social order is produced (e.g., ethnomethodological analyses of language), or oriented towards reconstructing deep structures that generate action and meaning through psychoanalysis or objective hermeneutics.

These positions conceptualize in different ways how the subjects under study—their experiences, actions, and interactions—relate to the context in which they are studied.

Symbolic Interactionism

In the first perspective, the empirical starting point is the subjective meaning that individuals attribute to their activities and their environments. These research approaches refer to the tradition of symbolic interactionism:

> The name of this line of sociological and sociopsychological research was coined in 1938 by Herbert Blumer (1938). Its focus is processes of interaction – social action that is characterised by an immediately reciprocal orientation – and the investigations of these processes are based on a particular concept of interaction, which stresses the symbolic character of social actions. (Joas 1987, p. 84)

As Joas has shown, this position has been developed from the philosophical tradition of American pragmatism. Generally, it represents the understanding of theory and method in the Chicago School (W.I. Thomas, Robert Park, Charles Horton Cooley, or George Herbert Mead) in American sociology. In general, this approach plays a central role in qualitative research, both recently and historically. Sociologists such as Anselm Strauss, Barney Glaser, Norman K. Denzin, Howard Becker, and others directly refer to this position; Blumer's (1969) work on the "methodological position of symbolic interactionism" had a major influence on the methodological discussions of the 1970s.

Basic Assumptions

What are the basic assumptions of this approach? Blumer summarizes the starting points of symbolic interactionism as "three simple premises":

The first premise is that human beings act toward things on the basis of the meanings that the things have for them. … The second premise is that the meaning of such things is derived from, or arises out of, the social interaction that one has with one's fellows. The third premise is that these meanings are handled in, and modified through, an interpretative process used by the person in dealing with the things he encounters. (1969, p. 2)

What does this mean for the research situation? The consequence is that the different ways in which individuals invest objects, events, experiences, and so on with meaning form the central starting point for research in this approach. The reconstruction of such subjective viewpoints becomes the instrument for analyzing social worlds. Another central assumption is formulated in the so-called Thomas theorem, which further grounds the methodological principle[1] just mentioned:

Thomas's theorem claim[s] that when a person defines a situation as real, this situation is real in its consequences, leads directly to the fundamental methodological principle of symbolic interactionism: researchers have to see the world from the angle of the subjects they study. (Stryker 1976, p. 259)

CASE STUDY 7.1

Professionals' Perspectives of Clients

In a study of the health problems of homeless adolescents and their use of health and social services (see Flick and Röhnsch 2007) we not only interviewed the adolescents, but also wanted to find out how the professionals in services perceive and describe this target group and its problems. We took a theoretical perspective developed from symbolic interactions called "social problems work" (see Flick 2011; Holstein and Miller 1993) and interviewed the professionals in expert interviews (see Chapter 16). In these interviews with the professionals, we found three patterns of how they represent the adolescents and their dealing with their diseases:

1 *Ignorance.* The adolescents seem not to take their diseases seriously because of their lack of knowledge and wrong perceptions. The adolescents cannot allocate symptoms to diseases and avoid contact with medical experts as their own ignorance serves for a subjective relief.

2 *Disease as turning point.* Two social workers mention that for some of the adolescents the disease is a turning point for critically reflecting on their current way of living. In particular, hospital stays can increase the sensibility for health issues and lead to avoiding certain risks (like alcohol and drugs). Changing the way of living then leads to a partial withdrawal from street life.

3 *Utilization.* Some physicians and social workers mention how adolescents seek help for their diseases. First they contact their peers, who send them to the doctor, and give advice and practical help (e.g., putting on a bandage). This peer support is seen as ambivalent by the experts, because the adolescents, as medical lay persons, are not

> skilled at exercising these (self-)treatments, which might intensify health problems
> due to informal help. The theoretical relevance of this finding for the main issue of our
> study comes from the symbolic interactionist first perspective and the Thomas theorem
> discussed above: how the professionals approach their potential clients will depend on
> these concepts as well as the cases in which they do not see much perspective in work-
> ing with these clients.

From this basic assumption, the methodological imperative is drawn to reconstruct the subject's viewpoint in different respects. The first is in the form of
subjective theories, used by people to explain the world—or at least a certain
area of objects as part of this world—for themselves. Thus there is a voluminous
research literature on subjective theories of health and illness (for overviews see,
e.g., Flick 2003), on subjective theories in education, and in counseling actions.
The second is in the form of autobiographical narratives, biographical trajectories
that are reconstructed from the perspective of the subjects. It is important that
these should give access to the temporal and local contexts, reconstructed from
the narrator's point of view.

Recent Developments in Sociology: Interpretive Interactionism

In recent years, Denzin has argued from a position that starts from symbolic interactionism but integrates several alternative, more recent, perspectives. Here we find
phenomenological considerations (following Heidegger), structuralist ways of thinking (Foucault), feminist and postmodern critiques of science, the approach of "thick
descriptions" (Geertz 1973), and that of concepts from literature.[2]

Denzin delimits this approach in two respects. It "should only be used when the
researcher wants to examine the relationship between personal troubles (e.g., wife-
battering or alcoholism), and the public policies and public institutions that have
been created to address those personal problems" (1989a, p. 10). Furthermore,
Denzin restricts the perspective taken when he repeatedly emphasizes that the
processes being studied should be understood biographically and necessarily interpreted from this angle (e.g., 1989a, pp. 19–24).

Recent Developments in Psychology: Subjective
Theories as Research Program

The aim of analyzing subjective viewpoints is pursued most consistently in the
framework of research on subjective theories. Here, the starting point is that individuals in everyday life, like scientists, develop theories on how the world and their
own activities function. They apply and test these theories in their activities and

revise them if necessary. Assumptions in such theories are organized in an interdependent way. They possess an argumentative structure corresponding to the structure of statements in scientific theories. This type of research seeks to reconstruct these subjective theories. For this purpose, a specific interview method has been developed (see Chapter 16 for the semi-standardized interview). In order to reconstruct subjective theories as close as possible to the subject's point of view, special methods for a (communicative) validation of the reconstructed theory have been created (see Chapter 29).

For example, in an earlier study, I analyzed the subjective theories of counselors about trust in their relations to clients (Flick 1989). These subjective theories were reconstructed in interviews and included assumptions about positive and negative influences on and consequences of trust in relations as well as definitions and examples. The focus here was strongly laid on the subjective views of the counselors.

The concentration on the subjects' points of view and on the meaning they attribute to experiences and events, as well as the orientation towards the meaning of objects, activities, and events, inform a large part of qualitative research. Combining subject-oriented research with symbolic interactionism, as has been done here, certainly cannot be done without reservations. For example, the reference to symbolic interactionism in recent research on subjective theories usually remains rather implicit. Also, other research perspectives arise out of the traditions of Blumer and Denzin, which are more interested in interactions than in subjective viewpoints (e.g., the contributions to Denzin 1993). For such interactionist studies, however, it remains essential to focus the subjective meanings of objects for the participants in interactions. With regard to methods, this approach mainly uses different forms of interviews (see Chapters 16 and 18) and participant observation (see Chapter 20). These two positions—the study of subjective viewpoints and the theoretical background of symbolic interactionism—mark one pole in the field of qualitative research.

Ethnomethodology

The concern of interactionism with subjects' viewpoints produces serious limitations. An approach that seeks to overcome these, theoretically and methodologically, is provided in the form of ethnomethodology. Harold Garfinkel is the founder of this school. It addresses the question of how people produce social reality in and through interactive processes. Its central concern is with the study of the methods used by members to produce reality in everyday life.[3] Garfinkel defines the research interests related to ethnomethodology as follows:

> Ethnomethodological studies analyze everyday activities as members' methods for making those same activities visibly-rational-and-reportable-for-all-practical-purposes, i.e., "accountable," as organizations of commonplace everyday activities. The reflexivity of that phenomenon is a singular feature of practical actions, of practical circumstances, of common sense knowledge of social structures, and of practical sociological reasoning. (1967, p. vii)

The interest in everyday activities, in their execution and beyond—in the constitution of a locally oriented context of interaction in which activities are carried out—characterizes the ethnomethodological research program in general. This research program has been realized mainly in the empirical researches of conversation analysis (see Chapter 27).

Basic Assumptions

What are the basic assumptions of this approach? The premises of ethnomethodology and conversation analysis are encapsulated in three basic assumptions by Heritage:

> (1) Interaction is structurally organized; (2) contributions of interaction are both context shaped and context renewing; and (3) thus two properties inhere in the *details* of interaction so that no order of detail in conversational interaction can be dismissed *a priori* as disorderly, accidental, or irrelevant. (1985, p. 1)

Interaction is produced in a well-ordered way. The context is the framework of interaction that is produced in and through interaction at the same time. Decisions as to what is relevant to members in social interaction can only be made through an analysis of that interaction and not a priori taken for granted. The focus is not the subjective meaning for the participants of an interaction and its contents, but how this interaction is organized. The research topic becomes the study of the routines of everyday life rather than the outstanding events consciously perceived and invested with meaning.

In order to uncover the methods through which interaction is organized, researchers seek to adopt an attitude of *ethnomethodological indifference* (Garfinkel and Sacks 1970). They should abstain from any a priori interpretation as well as from adopting the perspectives of the actors or one of the actors. From the perspective of ethnomethodology, context plays a key role wherever interaction occurs. Wolff, Knauth, and Leichtl illustrate that very clearly:

> The fundamental starting point of an ethnomethodological ... proceeding is to regard any event as constituted through the production efforts of the members on the spot. This is the case not only for the actual facts in the interaction, as for example the unwinding of question–answer sequences, but also for realizing so-called macro-facts, like the institutional context of a conversation. (1988, p. 10)

Let us take an example to illustrate this a little more. According to such a notion, a counseling conversation becomes what it is (and different from other types of conversation) through the members' efforts in creating this situation. Thus, we are concerned not with the researcher's a priori definition of the situation. Rather, we are interested in the members' conversational contributions: it is through the turn-by-turn organization of the talk that the conversation is constituted as a consultation. The institutional context, however, is also made relevant in the conversation and constituted in (and through) the members' contributions. Only the specific practices of the counselor and the client turn a conversation into a consultation and, moreover, one in a specific context (e.g., in a "socio-psychiatric service").

Recent Developments of Ethnomethodology: Studies of Work

Ethnomethodological research has focused more and more on the increasingly formal analysis of conversations. Since the 1980s the second main focus on the "studies of work" has been the analysis of work processes (see Bergmann 2004a; Garfinkel 1986). Here, processes of work are studied in a broad sense and particularly in the context of scientific work in laboratories or, for example, how mathematicians construct proofs (Livingston 1986).

In these studies, various methods for describing work processes as exactly as possible are used. Among these, conversation analysis is but one approach. The scope is enlarged from studying interactive practices to a concern with the "embodied knowledge" that emerges in such practices as well as in their results (Bergmann 2004a). These studies contribute to the wider context of recent research on the sociology of scientific knowledge (see Knorr-Cetina and Mulkay 1983). In general, the sociology of scientific knowledge has been developed from the tradition of ethnomethodology.

Recent Developments in Psychology: Discourse Analysis

Starting from conversation analysis and laboratory studies, a program of "discourse analysis" has been developed in British social psychology (see Harré 1998; Potter and Wetherell 1998). Here psychological phenomena such as cognition or memory are studied by analyzing relevant discourses concerned with certain topics. These discourses range from everyday conversations to texts in the media. The stress lies on communicative and constructive processes in interactions.

The methodological starting point is to analyze the interpretive repertoires that the participants of certain discourses use to produce a specific version of reality: "Interpretive repertoires are broadly discernible clusters of terms, descriptions, and figures of speech often assembled around metaphors or vivid images. They can be thought of as the building blocks used for manufacturing versions of actions, self, and social structures in talk" (Potter and Wetherell 1998, pp. 146–147). The contents and procedures of cognitive processes are reconstructed from such discourses as well as the ways in which social or collective memories are constructed and mediated.

For example, Willig (2014a) analyzed interviews with people engaged in extreme sports and identified a number of discourses in the ways they talked about their activities. Among them are discourses of addiction and of a dual self, which elucidate how the participants position themselves in their activities and which other contexts influence their engagements.

In these approaches, the perspective remains restricted to describing the *how* in the making of social reality. Ethnomethodological analyses often provide impressively exact descriptions of how social interaction is organized. They frequently enable typologies of conversational forms to be developed. However, the aspect of subjective ascription of meaning remains rather neglected, as does the question of what role pre-existing contexts such as specific cultures play in the construction of social practices.

Structuralist Models

Qualitative research can be based on a third type of theoretical approach. A common feature of this is—although with various degrees of emphasis—that cultural systems of meaning are assumed to somehow frame the perception and construction of subjective and social reality.

Basic Assumptions

Here a distinction is made between the surface of experience and activity, on the one hand, and the deep structures of activities, on the other. While the surface is accessible to the participant subject, the deep structures are not accessible to everyday individual reflections. The surface is associated with intentions and the subjective meaning related to actions, whereas deep structures are understood as generating activities. Deep structures like these are contained in cultural models (D'Andrade 1987), in interpretive patterns and latent structures of meaning (Reichertz 2004), and finally in those latent structures that remain unconscious according to psychoanalysis (König 2004). Psychoanalysis attempts to reveal the unconscious both in society and in the research process. Analyzing this process and the relation of the researcher to those who are interviewed or observed helps to reveal how the "societal production of unconsciousness" (Erdheim 1984) works. For these analyses, the implicit and explicit rules of action are of special importance. For objective hermeneutics, which is taken here as an example of the other approaches mentioned, it is argued:

> On the basis of rules, which may be reconstructed, texts of interaction constitute the *objective meaning structures*. These objective meaning structures represent the *latent structures* of sense of the interaction itself. These objective meaning structures of texts of interaction, prototypes of objective social structures in general, are reality (and exist) analytically (even if not empirically) independent of the concrete intentional representation of the meanings of the interaction on the part of the subjects participating in the interaction. (Oevermann et al. 1979, p. 379)

In order to reconstruct rules and structures, various methodological procedures for analyzing "objective" (i.e., non-subjective) meanings are applied. One will find linguistic analyses to extrapolate cultural models, strictly sequential analyses of expressions and activities to uncover their objective structure of meanings, and the researcher's "evenly suspended attention" in the psychoanalytical process of interpretation.

In particular, objective hermeneutics, following Oevermann et al. (1979), has attracted wide attention. It has stimulated voluminous research in German-speaking areas (see Chapter 27). However, there is an unsolved problem in the theoretical basics of the approach: that is, the unclear relation of acting subjects to the structures to be extrapolated. Lüders and Reichertz (1986, p. 95), for example, criticize the metaphysics of structures which are seen virtually as "autonomously acting structures."

Other problems include the naive equation of text and world ("the world as text") and the assumption that, if analyses were pursued far enough, they would lead to the structures that generate the activities of the case under study. This assumption derives from the structuralist background of Oevermann et al.'s approach (see Chapter 27 and Wernet 2014 for examples).

Recent Developments in Social Sciences: Poststructuralism

After Derrida (1990), such structuralist assumptions have been questioned. Lincoln and Denzin (2000, p. 1051), for example, ask whether the text produced for the purposes of interpretation, as well as the text formulated as a result of the interpretation, corresponds not just to the interests (of research or whatever) of the interpreter. How far does it correspond also to the interests of those being studied and forming a topic in the text? According to this view, texts are neither the world per se nor an objective representation of parts of this world. Rather they result from the interests of those who produced the text as well as of those who read it. Different readers resolve the vagueness and ambiguity that every text contains in different ways, depending on the perspectives they bring to the particular text. On the basis of this background, the reservations formulated about objective hermeneutics' conception of structure—that "between the surface and deep structures of language use … in objective hermeneutics there is a methodological 'hiatus', which at best can be closed by teaching and treating the method as art" (Bonß 1995, p. 38)—become yet more relevant.

Recent Developments in Psychology: Social Representations

What remains unclear in structuralist approaches is the relation between implicit social knowledge and individual knowledge and actions. To answer this question, one might take up a research program in social psychology engaging in the study of the "social representation" of objects (e.g., scientific theories on cultural objects and processes of change: for an overview see Flick 1998). Such a program would address the problem of how such socially and culturally shared knowledge influences individual ways of perception, experience, and action. A social representation is understood as:

a system of values, ideas and practices with a twofold function: first to establish an order which will enable individuals to orient themselves in their material and social world and to master it; and secondly to enable communication to take place among the members of a community by providing them with a code for social exchange and a code for naming and classifying unambiguously the various aspects of their world and their individual and group history. (Moscovici 1973, p. xvii)

This approach is increasingly used as a theoretical framework for qualitative studies that deal with the social construction of such phenomena as health and illness, madness, or technological change in everyday life. For example, we studied the representations of health and ageing held by members of professional groups (general practitioners and nurses). We wanted to find out how these representations differ between the groups—thus are social representations and not individual ones—and how they influence their work and attitude towards elder patients.

Here again, social rules deriving from social knowledge about each topic are studied without being conceived as a reality *sui generis*. From a methodological point of view, different forms of interviews (see Chapter 16) and participant observation (see Chapter 20) are used.

Rivalry of Paradigms or Triangulation of Perspectives

The different perspectives in qualitative research and their specific starting points may be schematized as in Figure 7.1. In the first perspective, you would start from the subjects involved in a situation under study and from the meanings that this situation has for them. You would then reconstruct the situational context, the interactions with other members, and, as far as possible, the social and cultural meanings step by step from these subjective meanings. As the example of counseling shows, in this perspective the meaning and the course of the event "counseling" are reconstructed from the subjective viewpoint (e.g., a subjective theory of counseling). If possible, the cultural meaning of the situation "counseling" is disclosed on this path.

In the second perspective, you would start from the interaction in counseling and study the discourse (of helping, on certain problems, and so on). Here you would treat participants' subjective meanings as less interesting than the way in which the conversation is formally organized as a consultation and how participants mutually allocate their roles as members. Cultural and social contexts outside the interaction only become relevant in the context of how they are produced or continued in the conversation.

In the third perspective you would ask which implicit or unconscious rules govern the explicit actions in the situation and also which latent or unconscious structures generate activities. The main focus here is on the relevant culture and the structures and rules it offers the individuals in and for situations. Subjective views and interactive perspectives are especially relevant as means to expose or reconstruct structures.

Beyond such juxtapositions for clarifying the perspectives, there are two ways of responding to different perspectives of research. First, you could adopt a single position

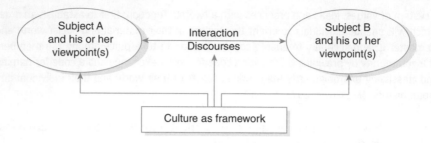

FIGURE 7.1 Research Perspectives in Qualitative Research

and its perspective on the phenomenon under study as the "one and only" and critically reject the other perspectives. This kind of demarcation has determined methodological discussion for a long time. In the American discussion, different positions have been formalized into paradigms and then juxtaposed in terms of competing paradigms or even "paradigm wars" (see Guba and Lincoln 1998, p. 218).

Alternatively, you can understand different theoretical perspectives as different ways of accessing the phenomenon under study. Any perspective may be examined as to which part of the phenomenon it illuminates and which part remains excluded. Starting from this understanding, different research perspectives may be combined and supplemented. Such a triangulation of perspectives (Flick 1992; 2004a) enlarges the focus on the phenomenon under study, for example, by reconstructing the participants' viewpoints and then analyzing afterwards the development of shared situations in interactions.

Common Features of the Different Positions

Despite differences of perspective, the following points are common to the various theoretical positions (see Table 7.1):

- *Verstehen as epistemological principle.* Qualitative research aims at understanding the phenomenon or event under study from the interior. It is the view of one subject or of different subjects, the course of social situations (conversations, discourse, processes of work), or the cultural or social rules relevant for a situation, which you would try to understand. How you put this understanding into methodological terms, and which in particular of the above aspects you focus on, depend on the theoretical position underpinning your research.
- *Reconstructing cases as starting point.* A second feature common to the different positions is that the single case is analyzed more or less consistently before comparative or general statements are made. For instance, first, the single subjective theory, the single conversation and its course, or the single case is reconstructed. Later other case studies and their results are used in comparison to develop a typology (of the different subjective theories, of the different courses of conversations, of the different case structures). What you will understand in each case as "case"—an individual and his or her viewpoints, a locally and temporally delimited interaction, or a specific social or cultural context in which an event unfolds—depends on the theoretical position you use to study the material.

THEORY IN QUALITATIVE RESEARCH

- *Construction of reality as basis.* The reconstructed cases or typologies contain various levels of construction of reality. Subjects with their views on a certain phenomenon construe a part of their reality; in conversations and discourses, phenomena are interactively produced and thus reality is constructed; latent structures of sense and related rules contribute to the construction of social situations with the activities they generate. Therefore, the reality studied by qualitative research is not a given reality, but is constructed by different "actors": which actor is regarded as crucial for this construction depends on the theoretical position taken to study this process of construction.
- *Text as empirical material.* In the process of reconstructing a case, you will produce texts on which you carry out your actual empirical analyses. The view of the subjects is reconstructed as their subjective theories or is formulated this way; the course of an interaction is recorded and transcribed; reconstruction of latent structures of meaning can only be formulated from texts given in the necessary detail. In all these cases, texts are the basis of reconstruction and interpretation. What status the text is given depends on the theoretical position of the study.

TABLE 7.1 Theoretical Positions in Qualitative Research

	Subjects' points of view	Making of social realities	Cultural framing of social realities
Traditional theoretical background	Symbolic interactionism	Ethnomethodology	Structuralism, psychoanalysis
Recent developments in social sciences	Interpretive interactionism	Studies of work	Poststructuralism
Recent developments in psychology	Research program "subjective theories"	Discursive psychology	Social representations
Common features	• *Verstehen* as epistemological principle • Reconstructing cases as starting point • Construction of reality as basis • Text as empirical material		

The list of features of qualitative research discussed in Chapter 2 may now be completed as in Box 7.1.

BOX 7.1

Features of Qualitative Research: Completed List

- **Appropriateness of methods and theories**
- **Perspectives of the participants and their diversity**
- **Reflexivity of the researcher and the research**
- **Variety of approaches and methods in qualitative research**
- *Verstehen* **as epistemological principle**
- **Reconstructing cases as starting point**
- **Construction of reality as basis**
- **Text as empirical material**

So far, I have outlined the major current research perspectives in terms of their theoretical background assumptions. The remaining part of this chapter addresses a different point of reference for theoretical discussions in qualitative research.

Guideline Questions for Locating Procedures in Theoretical Frameworks

When you plan your empirical social research project it is helpful to confront the following questions:

1 On which epistemological and theoretical foundations will you base your study?
2 How do you take these backgrounds into account in your study?
3 How do you take the participants' viewpoints into account, and how do you incorporate them in the research, in the data, and in their analysis?
4 Which methodological consequences follow for your study if you start from a constructivist epistemology and how do you put these consequences into concrete terms?
5 How do the methods you chose fit the epistemological assumptions the study is based on?

These guideline questions may also be used for assessing other researchers' studies.

KEY POINTS

- The theory of qualitative research is characterized by three perspectives, each with distinctive implications for the research methods to be used.
- These perspectives may be characterized in terms of basic assumptions and recent developments.
- We can draw some common features from these research perspectives.
- Feminism provides a theoretical framework that challenges research in two ways. It challenges (1) the routines and normalities of everyday life and (2) the ways in which research is practiced.
- The distinction between positivism and constructionism highlights the differences between qualitative research and natural sciences (and those social sciences which are created according to the model of natural sciences).

Exercise 7.1

1. Locate a published study (e.g., Flick and Röhnsch 2007) and identify which of the research perspectives discussed in this chapter correspond to the orientation of the researcher.
2. Reflect on your own study. Which of the issues in this chapter are relevant for it?

Further Reading

The following works inform the discussions mentioned at the beginning of this chapter.

Positivism and Constructionism

Flick, U. (2004b) "Constructivism," in U. Flick, E.v. Kardorff, and I. Steinke (eds.), *A Companion to Qualitative Research.* London: Sage. pp. 88–94.

Feminism

Gildemeister, R. (2004) "Gender Studies," in U. Flick, E.v. Kardorff and I. Steinke (eds.), *A Companion to Qualitative Research.* London: Sage. pp. 123–128.

Olesen, V. (2011) "Feminist Qualitative Research in the Millennium's First Decade," in N. Denzin and Y. Lincoln (eds.), *The SAGE Handbook of Qualitative Research* (4th edn). Thousand Oaks, CA: Sage. pp. 129–146.

The next two references give overviews of the more traditional positions discussed here:

Blumer, H. (1969) *Symbolic Interactionism: Perspective and Method.* Berkeley, CA: University of California Press.

Garfinkel, H. (1967) *Studies in Ethnomethodology.* Englewood Cliffs, NJ: Prentice Hall.

The following references represent more recent developments:

Denzin, N.K. (1989a) *Interpretative Interactionism.* London: Sage.

Denzin, N.K. (2004b) "Symbolic Interactionism," in U. Flick, E.v. Kardorff and I. Steinke (eds.), *A Companion to Qualitative Research.* London: Sage. pp. 81–87.

Flick, U. (ed.) (1998) *Psychology of the Social. Representations in Knowledge and Language.* Cambridge: Cambridge University Press.

Maxwell, J. and Chmiel, M. (2014a) "Notes Toward a Theory of Qualitative Data Analysis," in U. Flick (ed.), *The SAGE Handbook of Qualitative Data Analysis.* London: Sage. pp. 21–34.

Reichertz, J. (2004) "Objective Hermeneutics and Hermeneutic Sociology of Knowledge," in U. Flick, E.v. Kardorff and I. Steinke (eds.), *A Companion to Qualitative Research.* London: Sage. pp. 290–295.

Notes

1 One starting point is the symbolic interactionist assumption: "One has to get inside of the defining process of the actor in order to understand his action" (Blumer 1969, p. 16).

2 "Epiphany" as (in James Joyce's sense) "a moment of problematic experience that illuminates personal characteristics, and often signifies a turning point in a person's life" (Denzin 1989a, p. 141).

3 Bergmann holds to the general approach and the research interests linked to it: "Ethnomethodology characterizes the methodology used by members of a society for proceeding activities, which simply makes the social reality and order which is taken as given and for granted for the actors.

Social reality is understood by Garfinkel as a procedural reality, i.e., a reality which is produced locally (there and then, in the course of the action), endogenously (i.e., from the interior of the situation), audio visually (i.e., in hearing and speaking, perceiving and acting) in the interaction by the participants. The aim of ethnomethodology is to grasp the 'how,' i.e., the methods of this production of social reality in detail. It asks, for example, how the members of a family interact in such a way that they can be perceived as a family" (1980, p. 39).

8

Texts as Data in Qualitative Research

┌─ CHAPTER OBJECTIVES ───┐

This chapter is designed to help you

- understand that there is no simple "one-to-one" relationship between (1) the social realities under study and (2) their representation in texts;
- recognize that qualitative research involves various processes of social construction;
- appreciate the usefulness of the concept of mimesis for describing these processes;
- apply this insight to a prominent form of qualitative research.

└──┘

In the previous chapter, I argued that (1) *verstehen*, (2) reference to cases, (3) construction of reality, and (4) the use of texts as empirical material are common features of qualitative research across different theoretical positions. From these features, various questions emerge:

- How can we understand the process of constructing social reality? How can this construction be identified in the phenomenon under study? How is this phenomenon constructed in the process of studying it (e.g., by the way methods conceive it)?

- How is reality represented or produced in the case that is constructed for the research? How is it reconstructed in a specific way by using a specific method, for example?
- What is the relationship between text and realities?

This chapter will outline these relations and seek to answer these questions.

Text and Realities

In qualitative research, texts serve three purposes: they represent (1) the essential data on which findings are based; (2) the basis of interpretations; and (3) the central medium for presenting and communicating findings. Either interviews comprise the data, which are transformed into transcripts (i.e., texts), and interpretations of them are produced afterwards (in observations, field notes are often the textual database), or research starts from recording natural conversations and situations to arrive at transcriptions and interpretations. In each case, you will find *text* as the result of the data collection and as the instrument for interpretation.

If qualitative research relies on understanding social realities through the interpretation of texts, two questions become especially relevant: what happens in the translation of reality into text; and what happens in the retranslation of texts into reality (or in the process of inferring realities from texts)? In the latter process, text is substituted for what is studied. As soon as the researcher has collected the data and made a text out of them, this text is used as a substitute for the reality under study in the further process. Originally, biographies were studied; now narratives produced through interviews are also available for interpretation. Of such narratives there remains only what the recording has "caught" and what is documented by the chosen method of transcription. The text produced in this way is the basis of further interpretations and the findings so derived (checking back to the acoustic recordings is as unusual as checking back to the subjects interviewed or observed). It is often difficult to establish how much this text reproduces of the original issue (e.g., of a biography).

The social sciences, which have necessarily become textual sciences relying on texts as ways of fixing and objectifying their findings, need to pay more attention to these kinds of questions. The rarely mentioned question of the production of *new* realities (e.g., life as narrative) through generating and interpreting data as texts and texts as data requires further discussion.

Text as World Making: First-Degree and Second-Degree Constructions

That the relation of text and reality cannot be reduced to a simple representation of given facts has long been discussed in various contexts as a "crisis of representation" questioning the idea of objective knowledge. In the discussion around the question of how far the world can be represented in computer systems or cognitive systems, Winograd and Flores (1986) express strong doubts about this simple idea of representation. They question the idea that there is objective knowledge about an issue that can be implemented in computer programs, for example, independent of subjectivity and interpretation.

Starting from debates in ethnography (e.g., Clifford and Marcus 1986), this crisis in fact represents for qualitative research a *double* crisis—of representation and of legitimation. In terms of the crisis of representation (the consequence of the linguistic turn in the social sciences), it is doubted that social researchers can "directly capture lived experience. Such experience, it has been argued, is created in the social text written by the researcher. This is the crisis of representation. ... It makes the direct link between experience and text problematic" (Denzin and Lincoln 2000b, p. 17). And if, as this "crisis of representation" argument stresses, we never have direct access to experience itself, but only subjective versions of our research participants that are then created as results in the process of writing a social text about the participants' experiences, research faces a second crisis: can we still assess the "validity, generalizabilty, and reliability" (p. 17) of findings when we cannot directly access experience? And what does this mean for the legitimation of scientific knowledge as a representation of participants' experiences? (See Chapter 30.)

The crucial point in these discussions is how far we are still able to suppose a reality existing outside subjective or socially shared viewpoints and on which we can validate its "representation" in texts or other products of research. The several varieties of social constructivism or constructionism (see Flick 2004b for a short overview) reject such suppositions. Rather, they start from, first, the idea that the participants actively produce realities and objects through the meanings they ascribe to certain events and, second, the view that social research cannot escape this ascription of meanings if it wants to deal with social realities. Questions that arise in this context are: What do the social subjects take for real themselves and *how*? What are the conditions of such a holding-for-real? Under what conditions do researchers hold the things they observe this way for real?

Thus, the points of departure for research are ideas—the ideas of social events, of things or facts which we meet in a social field under study—and the way in which these ideas communicate with one another (i.e., compete, conflict, and succeed are shared and taken for real).

Social Constructions as Starting Points

Schütz has argued that facts become relevant only through their selection and interpretation:

> Strictly speaking, there are no such things as facts, pure and simple. All facts are from the outset facts selected from a universal context by the activities of our mind. They are, therefore, always interpreted facts, either facts looked at as detached from their context by an artificial abstraction or facts considered in their particular setting. In either case, they carry their interpretational inner and outer horizons. (1962, p. 5)

Here we can draw parallels with Goodman (1978). For Goodman, the world is socially constructed through different forms of knowledge—from everyday knowledge to science and art as different "ways of world making." According to Goodman (and Schütz), social research is an analysis of such ways of world making and the constructive efforts of the participants in their everyday lives. On a practical level, this means that, for qualitative research, it should focus the concepts and interpretations used by its participants in their everyday lives. For example, if we want to understand why existing health services are utilized or avoided by a specific social group with a specific disease, we should first find out what the subjective representations of these services and maybe also of this disease are before we simply count how many utilizers or non-utilizers exist, and relate this "fact" to the number of ill persons who could be utilizers.

A central idea in this context is the distinction Schütz makes between first-degree constructions and second-degree constructions. According to Schütz, "the constructs of the social sciences are, so to speak, constructs of the second degree, that is, constructs of the constructs made by the actors on the social scene." The actors' constructs are first-degree constructs, according to Schütz. Thus he emphasizes that scientific knowledge (second-degree constructions) is always based on actors' everyday knowledge (first-degree constructions).

In this sense, Schütz holds that "the exploration of the general principles according to which man [sic] in daily life organizes his experiences, and especially those of the social world, is the first task of the methodology of the social sciences" (1962, p. 59). In our example, the ill persons' concepts of illness and of the services would be first-degree constructions, while the typologies developed by the researchers from analyzing these concepts are second-degree constructions.

According to this distinction, everyday perception and knowledge are the basis for social scientists to develop a more formalized and generalized "version of the world" (Goodman 1978). Correspondingly, according to Schütz's argument (1962, pp. 208–210), there are multiple realities of which the world of science is only one and is organized partly according to the same principles of everyday life and partly according to other principles.

In particular, social science research is confronted with the problem that it encounters the world only through those versions of this world that subjects construct through interaction. Scientific knowledge and presentations of inter-relations include various processes of constructing reality. Both everyday subjective constructions on the part of those who are studied and scientific (i.e., more or less codified) constructions on the part of the researchers in collecting, treating, and interpreting data and in the presentation of findings are involved (see Figure 8.1).

In these constructions, taken-for-granted relations are translated: everyday experience into knowledge by those who are studied; reports of those experiences or events, and activities into texts, by the researchers. How can these processes of translation be made more concrete?

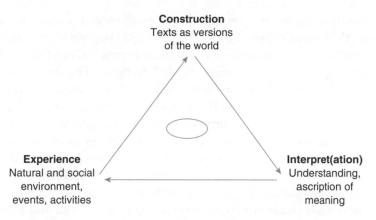

FIGURE 8.1 Understanding between Construction and Interpretation

World Making in the Text: Mimesis

To answer this question, we will borrow from aesthetics and literary sciences (see Iser 1993) the concept of mimesis. This can provide insights for a social science based on texts. Mimesis refers to the transformation of natural worlds into symbolic worlds, for example, how nature is represented in the arts, such as a painting or a theater play. Thus it was understood as the "imitation of nature." A succinct example of mimesis, and one used repeatedly, would be the presentation of natural or social relations in literary or dramatic texts or on the stage: "In this interpretation, mimesis characterizes the act of producing a symbolic world, which encompasses both practical and theoretical elements" (Gebauer and Wulf 1995, p. 3).

However, interest in this concept now goes beyond presentations in literary texts or in the theater. Recent discussions treat mimesis as a general principle with which to map out understanding of the world and of texts:

> The individual "assimilates" himself or herself to the world via mimetic processes. Mimesis makes it possible for individuals to step out of themselves, to draw the outer world into their inner world, and to lend expression to their interiority. It produces an otherwise unattainable proximity to objects and is thus a necessary condition of understanding. (Gebauer and Wulf 1995, pp. 2–3)

When these considerations are applied to qualitative research (and to the texts used within such research), mimetic elements can be identified in the following respects:

- in the transformation of experience into narratives, reports, and so on regarding the part of the persons being studied;
- in the construction of texts on this basis and in the interpretation of such constructions on the part of the researchers;
- finally, when such interpretations are fed back into everyday contexts, for example, in reading the presentations of these findings.

For analyzing the mimetic processes in the construction and interpretation of social science texts, the considerations of Ricoeur (1981; 1984) offer a fruitful starting point. For literary texts, Ricoeur has separated the mimetic process "playfully yet seriously" into the three steps of mimesis$_1$, mimesis$_2$, and mimesis$_3$. The first step (mimesis$_1$) refers to prior knowledge about the issue. The second step (mimesis$_2$) refers to how the issue is represented in a text by the writer or storyteller, whereas the third step (mimesis$_3$) refers to the readers' interpretation of the text (the story, for example)

Reading and understanding texts become active processes of producing reality, which involve not only the author of (in our case social science) texts, but also those for whom they are written and who read them. Transferred to qualitative research, this means that in the production of texts (on a certain subject, an interaction, or an event) the person who reads and interprets the written text is as involved in the construction of reality as the person who writes the text. According to Ricoeur's understanding of mimesis, three forms of mimesis may be distinguished in a social science based on texts:

- Everyday and scientific interpretations are always based on a preconception of human activity and of social or natural events, *mimesis$_1$*:

  Whatever may be the status of these stories which somehow are prior to the narration we may give them, our mere use of the word "story" (taken in this pre-narrative sense) testifies to our pre-understanding that action is human to the extent it characterizes a life story that deserves to be told. Mimesis$_1$ is that pre-understanding of what human action is, of its semantics, its symbolism, its temporality. From this pre-understanding, which is common to poets and their readers, arises fiction, and with fiction comes the second form of mimesis which is textual and literary. (Ricoeur 1981, p. 20)

- The mimetic transformation in "processing" experiences of social or natural environments into texts—whether in everyday narratives recounted for other people, in documents, or in producing texts for research purposes—should be understood as a process of construction, that is, *mimesis$_2$*: "Such is the realm of mimesis$_2$ between the antecedence and the descendance of the text. At this level mimesis may be defined as the configuration of action" (1981, p. 25).
- The mimetic transformation of texts in understanding occurs through processes of interpretation, that is, *mimesis$_3$*—in the everyday understanding of narratives, documents, books, newspapers, and so on, just as in the scientific interpretations of such narratives, research documents (protocols, transcripts, and so on), or scientific texts: "Mimesis$_3$ marks the intersection of the world of text and the world of the hearer or reader" (1981, p. 26).

Ricoeur brings this process consisting of the three forms of mimesis together in the step of reading and understanding a text:

  Hermeneutics, however, is concerned with reconstructing the entire arc of operations by which practical experience provides itself with works, authors, and readers. … It will appear as a corollary, at the end of this analysis, that the reader is that operator *par excellence* who takes up through doing something—the act of reading—the unity of the traversal from mimesis$_1$ to mimesis$_3$ by way of mimesis$_2$. (1984, p. 53)

According to this view (formulated by Ricoeur in dealing with literary texts), mimetic processes can be located in social science understanding as the interplay of

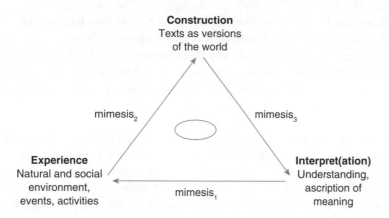

Construction
Texts as versions
of the world

mimesis$_2$ mimesis$_3$

Experience
Natural and social
environment,
events, activities

Interpret(ation)
Understanding,
ascription of
meaning

mimesis$_1$

FIGURE 8.2   Process of Mimesis

construction and interpretation of experiences (Figure 8.2). Mimesis includes the passage from pre-understanding to interpretation. The process is executed in the act of construction and interpretation as well as in the act of understanding. Understanding, as an active process of construction, involves the one who understands. According to this conception of mimesis, this process is not limited to access to literary texts but extends to understanding as a whole and thus also to understanding as a concept of knowledge in the framework of social science research. Gebauer and Wulf (1995) clarified this in their more general discussion of mimesis. They refer to Goodman's (1978) theory of the different ways of world making and the resulting versions of the world as the outcome of knowledge:

> Knowing in terms of this model is a matter of invention: modes of organisation "are not found in the world but *built into a world*". Understanding is creative. With the aid of Goodman's theory of world making, mimesis can be rehabilitated in opposition to a tradition that rigidly deprived it of the creative element – and that itself rests on false presuppositions. The isolated object of knowledge, the assumption of a world existing outside codification systems, the idea that truth is the correspondence between statements and an extralinguistic world, the postulate that thought can be traced back to an origin. Nothing of this theory remains intact after Goodman's critique: worlds are made "*from other worlds*". (Gebauer and Wulf 1995, p. 17)

Thus Gebauer and Wulf discuss mimesis in terms of the construction of knowledge in general. Ricoeur uses it to analyze processes of understanding literature in a particular way, without invoking the narrow and strict idea of representation of given worlds in texts and without the narrow concept of reality and truth.[1]

Mimesis: Biography and Narrative

For further clarification, we can now apply this idea of the mimetic process to a common procedure in qualitative research. A large part of research practice concentrates on reconstructing life stories or biographies in interviews (see Chapter 18). The starting point is to assume that a narrative is the appropriate form of presenting biographical experience (for more details see Chapters 18). In this context, Ricoeur maintains "the thesis of a narrative or pre-narrative quality of experience as such" (1981, p. 20). For the mimetic relation between life stories and narratives, Bruner highlights:

> that the mimesis between life so-called and narrative is a two-way affair. ... Narrative imitates life, life imitates narrative. "Life" in this sense is the same kind of construction of the human imagination as "a narrative" is. It is constructed by human beings through active ratiocination, by the same kind of ratiocination through which we construct narratives. When someone tells you his life ... it is always a cognitive achievement rather than a through the clear-crystal recital of something univocally given. In the end, it is a narrative achievement. There is no such thing psychologically as "life itself". At very least, it is a selective achievement of memory recall; beyond that, recounting one's life is an interpretive feat. (1987, pp. 12–13)

This means that a biographical narrative of one's own life is not a representation of factual processes. It becomes a mimetic presentation of experiences, which are constructed in the form of a narrative for this purpose—in the interview. The narrative, in general, provides a framework in which experiences may be located, presented, and evaluated—in short, in which they are lived. The issue studied by qualitative research (here) is already constructed and interpreted in everyday life in the form in which it wants to study it (i.e., as a narrative). In the situation of the interview, this everyday way of interpreting and constructing is used to transform these experiences into a symbolic world—social science and its texts. The experiences are then reinterpreted from this world: "In mimetic reference, an interpretation is made from the perspective of a symbolically produced world of a prior (but not necessarily existing) world, which itself has already been subject to interpretation. Mimesis construes anew already construed worlds" (Gebauer and Wulf 1995, p. 317).

In the reconstruction of a life from a specific research question, a version of the experiences is constructed and interpreted. To what extent life and experiences really have taken place in the reported form cannot be verified in this way. But it is possible to ascertain which constructions the narrating subject presents of both and which versions evolve in the research situation. When it comes to the presentation of the findings of this reconstruction, these experiences and the world in which they have been made will be presented and seen in a specific way—for example, in (new) theory with claims to validity: "Mimetic action involves the intention of displaying a symbolically produced world in such a way that it will be perceived as a specific world" (Gebauer and Wulf 1995, p. 317). Mimesis becomes relevant at the intersections of the world symbolically generated in research and the world of everyday life or the contexts that research is empirically investigating: "Mimesis is by nature intermediary, stretched between a symbolically produced world and another one" (1995, p. 317).

Following the views of several of the authors mentioned here, mimesis avoids those problems which led the concept of representation into crisis and into becoming an illusion.[2] Mimesis can be transferred from the context of literary presentation and understanding and used as a concept in the social sciences, which takes into account that the things to be understood are always presented on different levels. Mimetic processes can be identified in the processing of experiences in everyday practices, in interviews, and through these in the construction of versions of the world that are textualized and textualizable (i.e., accessible for social science, as well as in the production of texts for research purposes). In mimetic processes, versions of the world are produced which may be understood and interpreted in social research.

For this conceptualization of social research, Ricoeur's differentiation of various forms of mimesis is helpful as it highlights the processes involved in understanding the processes of interpretation involved in reading a text or in making sense of an event. Ricoeur's concepts allow avoiding an over-simplistic concept of representations of facts in texts or objective knowledge, which has been the issue of the debates about a crisis of representation mentioned in the beginning of this chapter. Schütz's distinction between everyday and scientific constructions elucidates that scientific knowledge in social sciences is always based on everyday knowledge in the field and on the constructions held by the participants. Scientific knowledge then becomes another version of the world in the terminology of Goodman. It is not per se superior to knowledge in the field.

Seen this way, Ricoeur and Schütz may further contribute to the framework claimed by Goodman involving different versions of the world constructed in everyday, artistic, and scientific ways. Combining these three thinkers' perspectives allows the researcher to avoid the illusions and crises, which are critically discussed for the idea of representation, while not disregarding the constructive elements in the process of representation and presentation as well as in the process of understanding.

CASE STUDY 8.1

Mimesis in the Social Construction of Self and Technology

I have studied the social representation of technology and how it became integrated into everyday life and how it changed it (see Flick 1995). The study included several groups (information engineers, social scientists, and teachers) in three contexts (France, East and West Germany). Individuals from these groups were asked to tell stories about the first encounter with technology they remember. These stories not only were representations of events, but also revealed ways in which the storytellers see themselves in relation to technology.

In these stories, mimetic processes of constructing reality, self, and technology can be found. For example, information engineers tell a story showing successful ways of managing

(Continued)

(Continued)

technical activities (e.g., successfully mending a broken hi-fi) or their *active mastering* of machines (e.g., learning to drive a big truck as a little boy). Social scientists' stories deal with *failures because of the device* or using *toys* as more or less passive experiences, while teachers tell how they *observed relatives handling technologies* (e.g., grandfather chopping wood or uncle working with a circular saw).

In all groups, we find narratives of situations showing the role of technology in the family. While these narratives are related to a *decision for a technical profession* in the case of the information engineers, consequences are contrary in the case of the other groups. For example, a female information engineer tells how she decided to become an information engineer against her father's wishes and the climate in the family that she felt to be anti-technology, while a teacher talks about his father's expectations that he should choose a technical profession, which he had to disappoint.

The topics that are common for interviewees from West Germany may be located along the dimension of *acting* with technology *versus observing* others doing this, while stories of East German interviewees move along the dimension of *mastering and failure* and around the background topic of *family and technology*. Together with this last topic, French interviewees tell stories that can be filled in the dimension of *success versus failure*. As general topical lines for all the stories, we can note the dimension *success–activity–failure* and the background topic of *family* and *technology*.

To use this concept in describing the process of social construction of objects, processes, and so on, researchers could look at what people say when they are asked to tell their first encounter with technology, for example. The relevant questions then are: What kind of version of that encounter do they construct? In what kind of context do they put this experience? What kinds of social processes or changes do they mention about that occasion or try to explain for the researcher or for themselves by this encounter of human beings and technology?

Referring again to the narratives presented above, mimetic aspects can be found on the one hand in the interviewees' retrospective interpretations of their own relations to technology as actively shaping, successfully acting, or failing. On the other hand, relations to their families are interpreted and used to reconstruct and contextualize one's own access to technology.

Technology becomes here an interpretative instrument for the self-images (for or against technology) as well as for a specific social relation—one's own family background. At first glance, this may seem circular, though it should rather be understood as two sides of the same coin. Contexts are used for embedding specific objects or experiences, and these objects or experiences are also used to understand and interpret these contexts. Both self-image and social relation become instruments to interpret one's own relation to technology, at least in situations of first experience. Technology serves for interpreting and constructing a part of one's own experiences and social contacts, as these are used to interpret one's own encounter with technology.

Mimetic interpretations are twofold: on the one hand, embedding technology-related experiences in social and self-related contexts underlines the subjective construction of technology as a social phenomenon; on the other hand, technology is used to interpret or to anchor social and autobiographical experiences (mimesis$_1$ according to Ricoeur). Technology here is the topic or medium through which these situations are retrospectively

> reconstructed. The situations are starting points for retrospectively anchoring the new aspects of technology as phenomena. In this retrospective anchoring, as well as in the social distribution and differentiation between the social groups and cultural contexts, the social representation of technology becomes evident.

Qualitative research, as mentioned in Chapter 7, is interested in understanding issues that are studied. A variety of methods have been developed from making this understanding work empirically. Qualitative researchers always are confronted with the construction of reality in the field they study—concepts held by participants, stories told about an issue, everyday or institutional routines of dealing with an issue, and so on. Experiences are not simply mirrored in narratives or in the social science texts produced about them. The idea of mirroring reality in presentation, research, and text has resulted in crisis. It may be replaced by the multi-stage circle of mimesis according to Ricoeur, taking into account the constructions of those who take part in the scientific understanding (i.e., the individual being studied, the author of the texts on him or her, and their reader). The difference between everyday and scientific understanding in qualitative research lies in its methodological organization in the research process, which the following chapters will deal with in greater detail.

Checklist for Reflecting on Relations between Text and Social World in Qualitative Data

The checklist below is designed to give you an orientation for locating your data in an epistemological way:

1 What are subjective concepts of your issue in the field you study?
2 Who is involved in constructing the data you use in your research?
3 How do the methods you employ shape the issue of your study?
4 What is your own understanding of the issue of your research?
5 How are your findings based on the participants' understandings of the issue?

KEY POINTS

- Texts form the basic material of most of qualitative research.
- The production of texts in the research process is a special case of the social construction of reality.
- World making and mimesis are two useful concepts for describing the process of social construction of text and realities.

(Continued)

(Continued)

- Ricoeur's model of three forms of mimesis describes the process of social construction step by step.
- Narratives about biographies are examples of such constructions in which mimesis plays a central role.

Exercise 8.1

1 Explain the difference between a first-degree and second-degree construction of a biographical interview, for example, in the study of Taylor (2012).
2 Describe the three forms of mimesis, using a single example.

Further Reading

The epistemological position that is briefly outlined here is based on the final four references listed below and is detailed further and put into empirical terms in the first:

Flick, U. (1995) "Social Representations," in R. Harré, J. Smith and L. Van Langenhove (eds.), *Rethinking Psychology*. London: Sage. pp. 70–96.

Gebauer, G. and Wulf, C. (1995) *Mimesis: Culture, Art, Society*. Berkeley, CA: University of California Press.

Goodman, N. (1978) *Ways of Worldmaking*. Indianapolis, IN: Hackett.

Ricoeur, P. (1984) *Time and Narrative*, Vol. 1. Chicago, IL: University of Chicago Press.

Schütz, A. (1962) *Collected Papers*, Vol. 1. The Hague: Nijhoff.

Notes

1 "Mimesis in this sense is ahead of our concepts of reference, the real and truth. It engenders a need as yet unfilled to think more" (Ricoeur 1981, p. 31).
2 "Mimesis, which seems to me less shut in, less locked up, and richer in polysemy, hence more mobile and more mobilizing for a sortie out of the representative illusion" (Ricoeur 1981, p. 15).

THEORY IN QUALITATIVE RESEARCH

PART 3
Research Design

Contents

Part 3 will introduce you to various aspects of the research process, which can be summarized under research planning and creating a research design. These aspects can also be seen as stages of planning a study, which become relevant one after the other. In the first chapter of this part, an introductory overview of research design issues is provided as a framework for the following discussion of details (Chapter 9), so that you should be prepared for the subsequent stages—encountering fields, people, and the collection of data. We will focus next on those stages of the research process prior to collecting and analyzing data. We will compare the different models of the research process used in quantitative and in qualitative research (Chapter 10) for framing the proceeding of a research project. Then we consider the relevance and practical problems of formulating a good research question as a major step at the beginning of every empirical study (Chapter 11).

As you will see, entering the research field is not merely a technical problem. Problems and strategies for this next step are outlined in

Chapter 12. Once you have found your entreé, you will have to decide whom or what to select and include in your study: sampling in qualitative research again is different from standard practices in quantitative research. Models and pitfalls for this subsequent step are discussed next (Chapter 13). In the final chapter of this part (Chapter 14), a more systematic and methodology-oriented approach in making use of different sorts of data and ways of collecting them is outlined. In using triangulation as a research strategy, we can integrate several methodological approaches and different sorts of data in a systematic research design for understanding what we study in a more comprehensive way.

The chapters in this part deal with several issues that are in fact closely interlinked. The initial chapter on design sets out a framework for the subsequent chapters. The other chapters go into more detail concerning certain aspects of this framework. Although you may read the chapters one after the other, in the end they should help you to develop an *integrated* understanding of their issues, which sees them as parallel issues rather than in a strict linear sense.

9
Designing Qualitative Research

CONTENTS

CHAPTER OBJECTIVES

This chapter is designed to help you

- recognize the basic components that influence the construction of a research design;
- recognize the most important basic designs in qualitative research;
- appreciate that you can combine some of these basic designs in your own study;
- compare the basic designs of qualitative research and distinguish their strengths and weaknesses;
- understand the design you select in the context of the research process and of the other stages of your research plan;
- understand the advantages and limitations of using the Internet in your study.

How to Plan and Construct Designs in Qualitative Research

Generally speaking, the phrase "research design" concerns issues of how to plan a study. For example: How should you set up the data collection and analysis? How should you select empirical "material" (situations, cases, persons, etc.) so that you can answer your research questions and achieve this within the time available for you using the available means? Ragin has provided a comprehensive definition of research design:

> Research design is a plan for collecting and analyzing evidence that will make it possible for the investigator to answer whatever questions he or she has posed. The design of an investigation touches almost all aspects of the research, from the minute details of data collection to the selection of the techniques of data analysis. (1994, p. 191)

Mostly, the issue of research design in qualitative research is addressed in two respects. Basic models of qualitative research designs are defined and the researchers may choose between these for their concrete study (e.g., Creswell 2008). Or else the components from which a concrete research design is put together are listed and discussed (e.g., Maxwell 2005; 2012).

If you construct a concrete research design for your study, you should consider the following components (see also Flick 2007c):

- the goals of the study;
- the theoretical framework;
- its concrete questions;
- the selection of empirical material;
- the methodological procedures;
- the degree of standardization and control;
- the generalization goals; and
- the temporal, personal, and material resources available.

The process of qualitative research represents a sequence of decisions. When you launch a research project, you can make a choice between a number of alternatives at various points in the process—from questions to data collection and analysis and ultimately to presentation of results. In these decisions, you will set up the design of your study in a dual sense: a design you planned in advance is translated into concrete procedures or else, while in process, the design is constituted and modified by virtue of the decisions in favor of particular alternatives.

Goals of the Study

You can use a qualitative study to pursue a number of different goals. The approach of grounded theory development in accordance with the model of Glaser and Strauss (1967; see Chapter 25) often provides a general orientation. In this context, I suggest that the requirement of theory development is an excessive burden for many types

RESEARCH DESIGN

of qualitative studies. In a graduate thesis with a very limited time budget, for example, this goal can be as unrealistic as it is incompatible with the intentions of many of those who commission qualitative research projects. Here what is required are detailed descriptions or evaluations of current practice. In the case of a study that seeks to provide an exact description of sequences of events in institutional or everyday practice, some of the methodological tools of Glaser and Strauss (e.g., theoretical sampling) may be applied, though they do not necessarily have to be. There are different types of objectives for qualitative studies that you can pursue: they include description, sometimes testing of hypotheses, and theory development.

At the level of objectives, Maxwell (2005, p. 16) makes a further distinction. He distinguishes between studies that pursue primarily personal goals (e.g., a graduate thesis or dissertation), those that pursue practical goals (discovering if and how a particular program or product functions), and those that pursue research goals (and are more concerned with developing general knowledge of a particular subject).

Formulation of the Research Questions

In a qualitative investigation, the research question is one of the decisive factors in its success or failure. As we will see in Chapter 11, the way in which research questions are formulated exerts a strong influence on the design of the study. Questions must be formulated as clearly and unambiguously as possible, and this must happen as early as possible in the life of the project. In the course of the project, however, questions become more and more concrete, more focused, and they are also narrowed and revised.

Maxwell (2005, p. 66) holds a different viewpoint: he argues that questions should be less the starting point but more the result of the formulation of a research design. Consequently, questions may be viewed or classified according to the extent to which they are suited for confirmation of existing assumptions (for instance, in the sense of hypotheses) or whether they aim at new discoveries or permit this.

Research questions are sometimes kept too broad; the problem then is that they provide almost no guidance in the planning and implementation of a study. But they may also be kept too narrow and thereby miss the target of investigation or block rather than promote new discoveries. Questions should be formulated in such a way that (in the context of the planned study and using the available resources) they are capable of actually being answered. Maxwell (2005), with an eye on research design, distinguishes between generalizing and particularizing questions, together with questions that focus on distinctions, and those that focus on the description of processes.

Goals of Generalization and Presentation

If you set up a research design, I recommend that you take into account what the goals of generalization are in your study (see also Chapter 29). Is your goal to do a detailed analysis with as many facets as possible, or is it a comparison or a typology of different cases, situations, and individuals, and so on? In comparative studies, the question of the principal dimensions, according to which particular phenomena are to be compared, arises. If your study is restricted to one or very few comparative dimensions based on some theory or on the research questions, this will avoid the possible compulsion to consider all possible dimensions and include cases from a large number of groups and contexts.

In my experience, it is important to assess somewhat critically the extent to which classic demographic dimensions need to be considered in every study. Do the phenomena being studied and the research question really require a comparison according to gender, age, town or country, east or west, and so on? If you have to consider all these dimensions, then you have to include a number of cases for each of the manifestations. Then very soon you will need such a large number of cases that you can no longer handle them within a project that is limited in time and personnel. Therefore, in my experience it is preferable to clarify which of these dimensions is the decisive one for your study. Studies with a sensibly limited claim to generalization are not only easier to manage but also, as a rule, more meaningful.

In qualitative research, a distinction must be made between numerical and theoretical generalization. A very small number of projects claim either to want or to be able to draw conclusions from the cases investigated about a particular population. What is more informative is the question of the theoretical generalization of the results. Here the number of individuals or situations studied is less decisive than the differences between cases involved (maximal variation) or the theoretical scope of the case interpretations. To increase the theoretical generalization, the use of different methods (triangulation) for the investigation of a small number of cases is often more informative than the use of one method for the largest possible number of cases. If you intend to develop a typology, for example, it is necessary not only to use the target selection of cases, but also to include counterexamples and to undertake case contrasts in addition to case comparisons.

Finally, you should consider what presentation goals you have with a qualitative study: Is your empirical material the basis for writing an essay, or rather for a narrative presentation that would give it more of an illustrative function? Or is it a matter of providing a systematization of the variation found in the cases investigated?

Degree of Standardization and Control

Miles and Huberman (1994, pp. 16–18) have distinguished between tight and loose research designs. They see indications of both variations in concrete cases according to the research question and conditions. Narrowly restricted questions and strictly determined selection procedures determine tight research designs. The degree of openness in the field of investigation and the empirical material remains relatively limited. The authors see these designs as appropriate when researchers lack experience of qualitative research, when the research operates on the basis of narrowly defined constructs, or when it is restricted to the investigation of particular relationships in familiar contexts. In such cases, they see loose designs as a detour to the desired result. Tighter designs make it easier to decide what data or which parts of the data are relevant and irrelevant to the investigation. They also make it easier, for example, to compare and summarize data from different interviews or observations.

Loose designs are characterized by somewhat broadly defined concepts and have, in the first instance, little in the way of fixed methodological procedures. Miles and Huberman see this type of design as appropriate when a large measure of experience is available of research in different fields, when new fields are being investigated and the theoretical constructs and concepts are relatively undeveloped. This second variant is clearly oriented to the methodological suggestions of Glaser and Strauss (1967) that are characterized, for example, in their handling of theoretical sampling by great openness and flexibility.

Even though qualitative research often sees itself as indebted to the principle of openness, I think it is sensible for many questions and projects to consider what degree of control is necessary. To what extent must there be constancy in the contextual conditions in which the comparative differences between two groups are manifested (see above)? What degree of control or comparability should be provided in conditions under which the various interviews in a study are carried out?

Selection: Sampling and Formation of Groups for Comparison

Selection decisions in qualitative research focus on people or situations, from which data are collected, and on extracts from the material collected, from which novel interpretations are made or results are presented as examples (see Chapter 13). This theoretical sampling is considered the royal way for qualitative studies. Frequently, however, other selection strategies are more appropriate if the goal is not to develop a theory but rather the evaluation of institutional practice.

One essential component of the decision about data selection (in comparative investigations) is the formation of groups for comparison. Here you should clarify at what level the comparisons are to be made: between individuals, situations, institutions, or phenomena? Accordingly, the selection should be made in such a way that several cases are always included in a single group for comparison.

Resources

One factor is frequently undervalued in the development of a research design. The available resources like time, personnel, technical support, competencies, experience, and so on are very important factors. Research proposals are frequently based on an unrealistic relationship between the planned tasks and the personnel resources (realistically) requested.

For realistic project planning, I recommend making a calculation of the activities involved which assumes, for example, that an interview of around 90 minutes will need as much time again for locating interview partners, organizing appointments, and travel. With regard to the calculation of time for transcribing interviews, the estimates will diverge depending on the precision of the system of transcription in place (see Chapter 24). Morse (1998, pp. 81–82) suggests that for transcribers who write quickly, the length of the tape containing the interview recording should be multiplied by a factor of four. If checking the finished transcript against the tape is also included, the length of the tape should be multiplied by a total of six. For the complete calculation of the project she advises doubling the time allowed for unforeseen difficulties and "catastrophes." If you plan a project that will work with transcribed interviews, you should use a high-quality recording device for the recordings. A special player with a foot-operated switch is essential for transcription.

Marshall and Rossman (2006, pp. 177–198) offer sample plans for how to calculate the time parameters of empirical projects. The time you will need for data interpretation is difficult to calculate. If you decide to use computers and programs such as ATLAS.ti and MAXQDA (see Chapter 28) for data interpretation, then you have to include sufficient time for technical preparation (installation, removal of errors, induction of team members in the use of the program, and so on) in your project plan. In the process of approving a project, the amount of equipment approved is sometimes reduced and so additional methodological stages, such as an additional group for comparison or phase of data collection, may be required. At this stage, if not before, it becomes essential that you check the relationship between tasks and resources, and you should consider shortcut strategies in the methodological procedures, if necessary.

Research designs may ultimately be described as the means for achieving the goals of the research. They link theoretical frameworks, questions, research, generalization, and presentational goals with the methods used and resources available under the focus of goal achievement. Their realization is the result of decisions reached in the research process. Figure 9.1 summarizes again the influential factors and decisions which determine the concrete formulation of the research design.

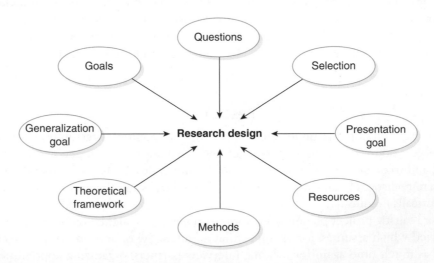

FIGURE 9.1 Components of Qualitative Research Design

Shortcut Strategies

Many of the qualitative methods in current use are connected with a high degree of precision and an equally high investment of time. In data collection, I mention the narrative interview (see Chapter 18), transcription (see Chapter 24), and interpretation (e.g., the procedures of objective hermeneutics and theoretical coding), the latter two requiring a great deal of time (see Chapters 25 and 27). In externally funded projects and commissioned research and also in graduate theses this need for time is often confronted with a very tight deadline within which the research questions have to be answered.

The term shortcut strategies refers to (justifiable) deviations from the maximum requirements of precision and completeness of such methods. For instance, for interviews with experts, you will have to consider that your interviewees will be under considerable pressure for time and you should take that into account when planning your interview. Sometimes (see Strauss 1987, p. 266) it is suggested that only parts of interviews should be transcribed, and only as precisely as is actually required by the questions of the particular investigation. The non-transcribed sections of interviews can be kept within the research process, for instance by means of summaries or lists of topics to be transcribed if necessary. Open coding (see Chapter 25) often leads to an excessive quantity of codes or categories. It has often proved useful to draw up lists of priorities related to the research questions that make it possible to select and reduce the categories. The same may be said of the selection of textual contexts, based on the research question, which are required to undergo a process of intensive interpretation.

Online Qualitative Research

Qualitative research has been affected by contemporary digital and technological revolutions. Computers are used to analyze qualitative data (see Chapter 28); tape recorders, mini-disc recorders, and MP3 recorders are used for recording interviews and focus groups (see Chapter 24). You can use the Internet to find the literature (see Chapter 6) and to publish your results (see Chapter 30).

Beyond the area of research, the Internet has become a part of everyday life for many people. In developed countries, most people are familiar with the Internet or at least know of it and what we can do with it. Due to the vast media coverage of the Internet and the possibilities of using and misusing it, most people have at least a rough idea about it. Many people have Internet access at home and many professional activities and routines have integrated the use of the Internet. Finally, the number of people using e-mail as a form of communication is growing continually across social groups. Nevertheless, we should not forget that not everyone has access to the Internet or wants to have access to it.

Given the widespread use of this medium, it is no surprise that the Internet has been discovered as an object of research and also as a tool to use for research. I want here to introduce you to some ways of using the Internet for qualitative research, show some advantages and possibilities of using it, but also show some limitations of research based on Internet methods.

The Internet as an Object of Research

As the rather vague formulations in the previous paragraph may have shown, there is still a need to study who is really using the Internet and who is not. Also, there is still a need to develop knowledge about how different people use the Internet and how this varies across social groups (e.g., across age, social class, education, or gender). For such research, you can carry out traditional projects of media use and audience research. For example, you may interview potential or real users of the Internet about their experiences and practices with it. Methods can be standardized or open-ended interviews or focus groups.

You can also do (participant) observations in Internet cafés to analyze how people use computers and the Internet, or you can do conversation analyses of how people use the Net collaboratively (e.g., analyzing children's talk in front of the screen in a computer class at school). Mitra and Cohen (1999) see the analysis of the numbers and experiences of users as the first approach to studying the Internet and the analysis of the text exchanged by users as the second. Common to such projects is that they use qualitative methods in a traditional way. Here, the Internet is only an object that people talk about or use in your study, but it is not in itself part of the study (as a methodological tool). Marotzki (2003, pp. 151–152) outlines three basic research focuses in Internet research: offline we study (in interviews, for example) how users deal with the Internet in their life world; online–offline we analyze how the Internet has changed societal, institutional, or private areas of living (also by using interviews); online we study communication in the Net in virtual communities by using interaction analysis, which means to advance into the realm of qualitative online research.

Preconditions of Qualitative Online Research

If you want to do your research online, some preconditions should be met. First, you should be able to use a computer not only as a luxurious typewriter, but in a more comprehensive way. You should also have some experience using computers, software and applications ('apps'). Also, you should have regular access to the Internet, you should feel at home working online, and you should be (or become) familiar with the different forms of online communication like e-mail, chatrooms, mailing lists, social networking sites, and blogs. I cannot give an introduction to the technical side of Internet research, but you can find easy-to-understand introductions to this special field (e.g., Kozinets, Dalbec, and Earley 2014; Mann and Stewart 2000; Marotzki, Holze, and Verständig 2014; Salmons 2010).

For doing an online study you should consider whether your research is an issue that you can best or only study by using qualitative online research. For example, if you are interested in the social construction of an illness in online discussion groups, you should analyze their communications or interview the members of such groups, and this can be done most easily if you address them online.

Following these two preconditions, a third becomes evident. The prospective participants of your study should have access to the Internet and they should be accessible via the Internet. If you want to study why people decide to stop using the Internet, you will have to find other ways of accessing your prospective participants and you should not plan your study as an online study.

Another precondition is that you should learn about the methods of qualitative research in general before you apply them to Internet research.

Transferring Qualitative Research and Methods to the Internet

The use of qualitative research on the Web is expanding rapidly (see Kozinets et al. 2014; Marotzki et al. 2014). Many qualitative methods are now used online as well. We find forms of online interviewing, the use of online focus groups, participant observation, virtual ethnography, and studies of interaction and traces of interaction (Bergmann and Meier 2004; Kozinets et al. 2014). Some of these methods can be transferred to and applied in Internet research more easily and using them online provides new options (e.g., of reaching interviewees over large distances); some of them and some of the principles of qualitative research can be transferred to the Web only with modification.

We can discuss the advantages and problems of online qualitative methods against the background of what will be said in later chapters about the methods (e.g., interviewing, see Chapters 16 and 18) as such. I will end with some more general reflections on research design and ethics (see also Chapter 5) in online research. The guiding questions will be: how can the various qualitative methods be transferred to Internet research; which modifications are necessary; and what are the benefits and costs of such a transfer (compared to their traditional offline use)?

Perspectives and Limits of Qualitative Online Research

Transferring qualitative research to the realm of the Internet is a challenge for many approaches. How do you adapt the methods and approaches? How do you adapt concepts of participation, sampling, and analysis to this field? At first sight, using the Internet for your study makes many things easier. You can reach distant people with your interview without traveling, you save time and money for transcription, you can access existing groups interested in a topic, you can maintain the anonymity of your participants more easily, you can access all sorts of documents right from your desk and computer.

At the same time, exchanging e-mails is different from asking questions and receiving answers face to face. The many people accessible on the Web do not necessarily wait to become part of your study. Problems of authenticity and contextualization result from the anonymity of participants. Websites disappear or change and so on. Because of these technical problems, you should reflect on your issue of research and whether it really indicates using the Internet for answering your research questions.

Beyond technical problems, ethical considerations (see Chapter 5) are relevant in Internet research, too. Mann and Stewart (2000, Chapter 3) have presented an ethical framework for Internet research in greater detail. This framework refers to issues such as that you should collect data only for one specific and legitimate purpose and that they should be guarded against any form of misuse, loss, disclosure, unauthorized access, and similar risks. People should know about which personal data are stored and used and should have access to them. Informed consent in interviewing but also in ethnographic studies should be obtained, which can be difficult if your target group is not clearly defined and your contact is based on e-mail addresses and nicknames. Anonymity of the participants should be guaranteed and maintained during the research and in using the material. People should know that a researcher records their chats. This also means that simply lurking (reading and copying chatroom exchanges) is not legitimate. There are several forms of "netiquettes" for the different areas of Internet use, and researchers should know them and act according to them (see Mann and Stewart 2000 for details and Kozinets et al. 2014).

If these ethical issues are taken into account and if the technical problems can be managed in a sufficient way for your research project, it can be fruitful and helpful. Academic interest in the Internet as a culture and as a cultural product has led to more development on the methodological level. The development of qualitative Internet research will develop further in the future.

Online Research in Times of Web 2.0

After a phase of implementing some of the most prominent qualitative methods as online methods in the early years of the new millennium, a set of new developments has changed forms of communication in the Web again, starting around 2005. These developments are often referred to as "Web 2.0." New forms of communicating (blogs, for example) and of social networking sites (such as Facebook, YouTube, or Twitter) have become public and widely used (see, e.g., Davidson and di Gregorio 2011; Kozinets et al. 2014; Marotzki et al. 2014). These forms of communication are used now as instruments for doing research as well together with other Web 2.0 developments. A recent study (RIN 2010) has focused on the use of Web 2.0 tools in particular for research purposes and on who is already using them and what developments this will lead to. Characteristics of Web 2.0 and their relevance for research purposes are outlined as follows:

> Web 2.0 encompasses a variety of different meanings that include an increased emphasis on user-generated content, data and content sharing and collaborative effort, together with the use of various kinds of social software, new ways of interacting with web-based applications, and the use of the web as a platform for generating, re-purposing and consuming content. (Anderson 2007, quoted in RIN 2010, p. 14)

The essential point is how communication and the production of knowledge are organized: "Web 2.0 services emphasize decentralized and collective generation, assessment and organization of information, often with new forms of technological intermediation" (RIN 2010, p. 14). In the context of qualitative research using this approach, the sharing of information is a central issue. This begins with retrieving information (publications, for example; see Chapter 6), communicating and making information accessible (sharing of data, public data sets, etc.), and reaches to new forms of publishing research (results, reports, etc.) online (see Chapter 30). Thus the main issue is how these new media are used to organize and facilitate scholarly communication. You can use these media for collaborative research (see Cornish, Gillespie, and Zittoun 2014) by sharing your data and experiences with other researchers. So you could work on the same data sets with other people, use blogs for this purpose, and make your results public in this context.

Examples of these forms of communication include public wikis (the best known may be Wikipedia, but there are other examples) or private wikis set up for a specific purpose. Other forms include writing (or contributing comments to) blogs, and posting presentations, slides, images, or videos publicly. These forms can be used for working in collaborative teams in one institution or across several institutions (see also www.oii.ox.ac.uk/microsites/oess/ for more information on this area in general). The use of social media (like Facebook) can play an important role here (see Kozinets et al. 2014). In the communication about research, the use of open access software and, even more, to use open access online journals for one's own publications, for seeking existing publications, and for commenting on other people's publications have become a major issue. There are also commercial services like SlideShare (www.slideshare.net), where slide presentations can be made public as a more informal way of communicating about research and findings. And finally, there is a strong trend towards open access repositories making the literature available online and for free (e.g., the Social Science Open Access Repository: www.ssoar.info/).

These developments underline how far online research has become established as an alternative design for doing qualitative research and how far elements of online research have become part of doing qualitative research in general and will continue to bring it forward (see also Chapter 28).

Basic Designs in Qualitative Research

Returning to our main focus—the general introduction to designing qualitative research—we can distinguish a number of basic designs in qualitative research (cf. also Creswell 2008), which you can take as a starting point, use in your research, or combine in parts with each other. In this you will define the central focus of your study in two respects regarding the perspectives of time and comparison taken in each alternative.

Case Studies

The aim of case studies is the precise description or reconstruction of cases (for more details see Ragin and Becker 1992). The term "case" is rather broadly understood here.

You can take persons, social communities (e.g., families), organizations, and institutions (e.g., a nursing home) as the subject of a case analysis. Your main problem then will be to identify a case that would be significant for your research question and to clarify what else belongs to the case and what methodological approaches its reconstruction requires. If your case study is concerned with the school problems of a child, you have to clarify, for instance, whether it is enough to observe the child in the school environment. Or do you need to interview the teachers and/or fellow pupils? To what extent should the family and their everyday life be observed as part of the analysis?

—CASE STUDY 9.1—

Mass Unemployment Studied Using the Case of a Village

In a study that is still regularly quoted in unemployment research, Jahoda, Lazarsfeld, and Zeisel (1933/1971) investigated the consequences of unemployment in a small Austrian industrial village at the time of the world economic crisis in the 1930s. For their study, they selected one case—the small village called "Marienthal." They used an imaginative combination of quantitative (e.g., measurement of walking speed, income statistics) and qualitative methods (e.g., interviews, housekeeping books, diary entries, young people's essays about their view of the future, document analysis, and so on). They also used some historical materials they developed, with the basic formula ("Leitformel") of a "tired society"—a concise characterization of the life-feelings and the everyday course of events in a community affected by unemployment. At the same time they were able to identify a variety of individual "behavioral types" in reaction to unemployment, such as "unbroken," "resigned," "desperate," and "apathetic"—a result that has proved to be of heuristic value in contemporary research.

What Are the Problems in Applying the Design?

However, the aim is not to make statements about only the concrete case. Rather you will study it because it is a typical or particularly instructive example of a more general problem. If you look at this the other way around, case studies raise the question of how to select the case under study in a way that permits more general conclusions to be drawn from analyzing it. Finally you should clarify how to delimit the case—what has to be included in analyzing it?

What Is the Contribution to the General Methodological Discussion?

Case studies can capture the process under study in a very detailed and exact way. They are not restricted due to an intended comparability and are able to fully use the potential of certain methods.

How Does the Design Fit into the Research Process?

In case studies, sampling is purposive (see Chapter 13). They will be most instructive when they are methodologically based on open case-sensitive approaches like the narrative interview (see Chapter 18) and ethnography (see Chapter 20) for collecting the data. Analytic methods like hermeneutics aimed at reconstructing a case (see Chapter 27) will be most fruitful, in particular if several methodological approaches are triangulated (see Chapter 14).

What Are the Limitations of the Design?

Concentration on one case often leads to problems of generalization—less so in a statistical than in a theoretical understanding. You can repair this by doing a series of case studies.

Comparative Studies

In a comparative study, you will not observe the case as a whole and in its complexity, but rather a multiplicity of cases with regard to particular excerpts. For example, you might compare the specific content of the expert knowledge of a number of people or biographies in respect of a concrete experience of illness and the subsequent life courses are compared to each other. Here the question arises about the selection of cases in the groups to be compared.

A further problem is what degree of standardization or constancy you need in the remaining conditions that are not the subject of the comparison (see Case Study 9.2 for this issue).

CASE STUDY 9.2

Health Concepts of Women in Portugal and Germany

In this project run by two students (Beate Hoose and Petra Sitta; see Flick, Hoose, and Sitta 1998) for their diploma thesis, we were interested in whether the representation of health and illness is a cultural phenomenon or not. To answer this question, we tried to show cultural differences in the views of health among Portuguese and German women. Therefore, we selected interview partners from both cultures. To be able to trace differences in the interviewees' health concepts, we kept as many other conditions in the case as constant as possible. Therefore, we had to ensure that the women we included in the study led similar lives in as many respects as possible (big-city life, professions, income, and education) under at least very similar conditions in order to be able to relate differences to the comparative dimension of "culture" (see Flick 2000b). The study was

(Continued)

---

planned as an exploratory study, so that we could limit the number of cases in each subgroup. The design of the study was a comparative design: two groups of women were compared for a specific feature, their health and illness concepts. In the planning of the interviews, we focused on the development of the current health and illness concept in the interviewees' biographies. Therefore, the study was a retrospective study, too.

We found different core concepts in the representations of health, which focus on culture-specific topics. The central phenomenon, which appeared in the interviews with Portuguese women again and again, is "lack of awareness" (in Portuguese, *falta de cuidado*). This term is difficult to translate into other languages but means "not to take care of oneself, not to be cautious for oneself." It seems to be a general problem in Portugal that people do not care for themselves and was named by different interviewees as the main source of illness. For the women we interviewed, Portuguese people "let things simply run." They know that there are things they should do for their health (eating, less stress, sport, prevention), but they see themselves as not having enough initiative. Many interviewees attribute this lack of awareness to themselves or to the people in Portugal in general.

However, they also mentioned many reasons for this lack of awareness arising from the Portuguese health system. One interviewee said, "Who depends on the public health system might die in the meantime." Waiting two or three months for an appointment with the doctor, waiting years for operations, and waiting five to six hours at the health center despite a fixed appointment are seen as quite normal.

In the German interviews, the central phenomenon was the feeling of being "forced to health." Interviewees linked it to their feeling that they have to be healthy. They see how society and the media make ill people outsiders rather than integrating them in society. The interviewees repeatedly stressed the importance of sport and healthy eating for their health. The knowledge mediated to them has become anchored in their social representations. The women linked not only negative impressions to "being forced to health," but also positive ones. The information offered by the media and health insurance was also evaluated positively. The women feel informed and have developed a critical awareness towards traditional medicine. Rules of when and how often certain forms of prevention should be used were experienced as a relief.

We can see from this brief case study how to create a comparative, retrospective design by keeping other dimensions constant in order to analyze differences on one dimension. This was only an exploratory study, but it does show this special aspect of how to plan such a study.

What Are the Problems in Applying the Design?

Here you will face the problem of how to select the "right" dimensions. Furthermore, you should reflect on which conditions should be kept constant in order to make the comparisons coherent on the selected dimensions. Finally, it can be asked: how do you take into account the complexity and the structure of the cases which are compared?

What Is the Contribution to the General Methodological Discussion?

Applied in a consequent way, this design offers a way to a focused and thus limitable comparative analysis of issues and experiences.

How Does the Design Fit into the Research Process?

Sampling should be purposive, with an eye on the dimensions that are relevant for the comparison (see Chapter 13). In collecting data, interviews, which allow more directed questions (see Chapter 16), are preferable. Coding and categories, perhaps with computers, are helpful in analyzing the data (see Chapters 26 and 28).

What Are the Limitations of the Design?

If the concentration on the dimensions of the comparison is too strict, your analysis may neglect other aspects. Then the analysis of the material does not pay enough attention to its context and inherent structures.

We can see the dimension of a single case–comparative study as one axis according to which we can classify the basic design of qualitative research. An interim stage consists of the interrelation of a number of case analyses, which can initially be carried out as such and then compared or contrasted to each other. A second axis for categorizing qualitative design follows the dimension of time, from retrospective analyses to snapshots and then to longitudinal studies.

Retrospective Studies

The principle of case reconstruction is characteristic of a great number of biographical investigations that operate with a series of case analyses in a comparative, typologizing, or contrastive manner. Biographical research is an example of retrospective studies. For example, Hermanns (1984), for his PhD thesis, did narrative interviews with engineers in order to find out how they decided to take this professional orientation, how they put it into concrete terms in their university training, and how they finally found access to a professional career by successfully establishing themselves in their professional field or how they failed on this path. For this study (we will come back to it in the context of Chapter 18 on narratives) Hermanns used the narrative interview and took the current situation of the participants and asked them to look back on their life history and to present their experiences in a narrative. Thus this research is an example of a retrospective study, in which, retrospectively from the point in time when the research is carried out, certain events and processes are analyzed in respect of their meaning for individual or collective life histories. Design questions in relation to retrospective research involve the selection of informants who will be meaningful for the process to be investigated. They also involve defining appropriate groups for comparison, justifying the boundaries of the time to be investigated, checking the research question, deciding which (historical) sources and documents (see Chapter 22) should be used in addition to interviews. Another issue is how to consider the influences of present views on the perception and evaluation of earlier experiences (see Bruner 1987).

What Are the Problems in Applying the Design?

One danger in any retrospective research is that the current situation (in which an event is recounted) influences and overlaps with an earlier situation (which is recounted) or influences any assessment of past events.

What Is the Contribution to the General Methodological Discussion?

This approach makes a consistent realization of a biographical perspective (see Chapters 7, 18, and 25) possible and allows a process perspective to be taken on orders of events that have already begun or are even terminated.

How Does the Design Fit into the Research Process?

Here, mostly a constructionist perspective is taken (see Chapters 7 and 8). Data are often (but not necessarily) collected with narrative methods (see Chapter 18). They are analyzed with narrative or hermeneutic approaches (see Chapter 27). The aim is often to develop theories from the material that is analyzed (see Chapters 10 and 25).

What Are the Limitations of the Design?

Unlike longitudinal studies (see below), it is more difficult here to include options of activities (how things could have developed). The perspective on the processes that are analyzed is distilled from the view of interviewees (see Chapter 16) or from studying documents which have been produced and filed (see Chapter 22).

Snapshots: Analysis of State and Process at the Time of the Investigation

A major part of qualitative research focuses on snapshots. For example, you might collect different manifestations of the expertise which exists in a particular field at the time of the research in interviews and compare them to one another. Even if certain examples from earlier periods of time affect the interviews, your research does not aim primarily at the retrospective reconstruction of a process. It is concerned rather with giving a description of circumstances at the time of the research.

Many process-oriented procedures are also strongly related to the present: they are, therefore, not interested in the reconstruction of past events. Rather, they are interested in the course of currents from a parallel temporal perspective. In ethnographic studies, researchers participate in the development of some event over an extended period in order to record and analyze this in parallel to its actual occurrence. In conversation analyses (see Chapter 27), a conversation is recorded and then analyzed in terms of its sequencing, while in objective hermeneutics (see Chapter 27) a protocol is interpreted in a strictly sequential manner "from beginning to end."

In these approaches, from the design point of view, there arises the question of how to limit the empirical material: How can your selection guarantee that the phenomenon that is relevant to the research question actually comes up in empirically documented extracts from conversations and processes? Where should the beginning and end (of a conversation or observation) be located? According to what criteria should you select and contrast material for comparison? For instance, what conversations or conversational extracts and what observational protocols should you compare exactly?

What Are the Problems in Applying the Design?

One problem here is the lack of a link to process or development, which can only be made by using retrospective questions, for example. Furthermore, there is the question of how to limit the material in an appropriate and reasonable way.

What Is the Contribution to the General Methodological Discussion?

This design allows one to run pragmatically focused studies, which are interested in describing the state of affairs in a field.

How Does the Design Fit into the Research Process?

Inventories of subjective views or descriptions of everyday routines (see Chapter 7) can be made by using this design. For this purpose, interviews (see Chapters 16 and 18), observations (see Chapter 20), and coding analyses (see Chapters 25 and 26) are used.

What Are the Limitations of the Design?

It is not possible to apply a process or developmental perspective to phenomena or experiences.

Longitudinal Studies

The final variant of a basic design in qualitative research consists of longitudinal studies, in which an interesting process or state is analyzed again at later times of data collection. This strategy has rarely been used, at least explicitly, in qualitative research. In most guides to qualitative methods, you will find little guidance on how they could be applied in longitudinal studies with several periods of data collection. In a longitudinal study, the same method of data collection is applied repeatedly in order to analyze how things have changed over time in the issue. Interviews for example have to be carefully adapted to this procedure, as it may produce an artificial situation if you just simply ask the same questions again. There should be enough time between the two points when data are collected. In ethnography a longitudinal perspective within a temporally limited framework is realized (see Chapter 20) by virtue of the researchers' extended participation in the field of study. Such a perspective—with a retrospective focus—is achieved too in biographical research, which considers an extended section of a life history.

The great strengths of a longitudinal study are that: (1) researchers are able to document changes of view or action through repeated data collection cycles; and (2) the initial state of a process of change can be recorded without looking at it from the situation at the end of the process. These two strengths can only be fully realized in a real longitudinal study, but not in a retrospective study. Case Study 9.3 presents an example of a longitudinal study.

CASE STUDY 9.3

Qualitative Longitudinal Study

Gerhardt (1986) carried out a study with families, in which the husband/father suffered from a chronic fatal disease (renal failure). In this study, married men between 20 and 50 years old were included, 68 cases in all. Not only were the male patients interviewed but also their wives. What makes this study an example of a longitudinal study is the second interview with all participants (who were still alive at the second dates) about one year after the first interview. The research team developed an "interview scheme" (1986, p. 75) of the areas and topics that should be addressed (e.g., the patients' medical and professional career). This scheme was applied again in the second interview for reactivating the state of affairs and developments at the moment of the first interview. It was complemented by asking the interviewees to recount what had happened since the first interview and for finding out how presentations and evaluations of events before the first interview might have changed since.

This study is an example of longitudinal qualitative research (see Chapter 13 where this example is discussed again for sampling issues), which shows the potential of repeated interviews. This approach allows research to be conducted in parallel to the development of the issue—the interviewees' patient careers. At the same time it demonstrates the problems and challenges of such an approach: that in the second interview things might be presented and evaluated differently by the interviewee (1986, p. 77) and that it could be an artificial situation to ask the same questions again about the interviewee's life history. One year is not a very long time between the two interviews, but in this case a longer period would have implied the risk of losing more participants (due to the development of their disease). Longer periods are often difficult to be realized in a funded project of, say, three to four years' running time in general.

What Are the Problems in Applying the Design?

If you want to make full use of the potential of a longitudinal study, you should identify the processes for a study before they begin. To apply qualitative methods, for example, the narrative interview, repeatedly at several points of data collection may produce very artificial situations. Longitudinal studies in general require considerable organizational expenditure and extended resources (time etc.).

What Is the Contribution to the General Methodological Discussion?

Longitudinal studies are the most consistent way of analyzing developments and process in their course.

How Does the Design Fit into the Research Process?

The starting point is the interesting changes. Sampling should be purposeful and then selection should be maintained in the process (see Chapter 13). Observation and ethnographic study (see Chapter 20) include an implicitly longitudinal approach, but can also be applied repeatedly. Interviews using interview schedules (see Chapter 16) can be applied repeatedly more easily than focus groups (see Chapter 17) or narrative interviews (see Chapter 18).

What Are the Limitations of the Design?

In research for a thesis or in very briefly funded projects, longitudinal designs can be applied only in parts, since such a design needs enough time between the moments of data collection to make development and change visible.

Starting Points for Selecting a Research Design

In Figure 9.2 the basic designs in qualitative research are arranged according to the two dimensions of time and comparison.

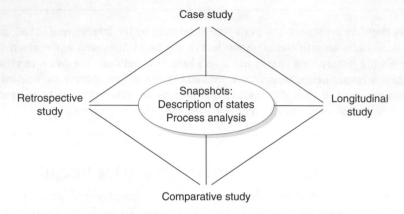

FIGURE 9.2   Basic Designs in Qualitative Research

These designs are discussed as the basic designs in qualitative research and I group them here along two dimensions. In research practice, you will often find combinations of these basic designs (e.g., a case study with a retrospective focus or a comparative, longitudinal study). In what follows, I will make some recommendations on how to decide between the research designs and between the essential alternatives in planning a study that were discussed above. This will include the conceptualization of the research process with the alternatives of linear and circular processes (see Chapter 10). Sampling is included with the basic alternatives of defining the sample in advance and of purposive sampling (see Chapter 13). The basic designs mentioned in this chapter are also juxtaposed. I will outline four points of reference for such a decision between different alternatives next.

1 Criteria-Based Comparison of the Approaches

A comparison of the various alternatives of constructing the research process, of sampling, and of the basic designs is the first point of reference for deciding among them. As criteria for such a decision, Table 9.1 shows the elements in each approach for guaranteeing sufficient openness for the issue or for interviewees' subjective views. Elements for producing a sufficient level of structure and depth in dealing with the thematic issue in the research are also listed. Further features shown are each approach's contribution to the development of the qualitative methodology in general and the fields of application that each was either created for or mainly used in. Finally, the problems of applying the approach and the limits that will be mentioned in the following chapters are noted for each approach. Thus, the field of methodological alternatives in the domain of constructing qualitative research designs is outlined so that the individual approach may be located within it.

TABLE 9.1 Comparison of Approaches for Constructing a Research Design

			Basic designs		
Criteria	Case study	Comparative study	Retrospective study	Snapshot	Longitudinal study
Openness to the issue by:	Focus on the case under study (individual, institution, field, etc.)	Integration of interviewing Understanding by participation	Process is often reconstructed from the views of the participants	Description of states without focus on process	Attendance of a process and the alternative options it includes
Structuring (e.g., deepening) the issue by:	Selection of one case	Definition of comparative dimensions Definition of what is kept constant	Looking back on (individual or institutional) developments Perspective on processes	Focus on the current state of affairs (e.g., in the knowledge under study)	Definition of the moments of data collection
Contribution to the general development of qualitative methods by:	Most consequent approach to the particular (case per se)	Focus on points of connection in the cases under study	Process perspective on developments that have begun or are already finished Biographical perspective	Approach for pragmatically focused studies	Perspective on process
Domain of application	Analysis of institutions Life histories	Focused research questions Bigger number of cases Comparative research questions	Life histories Institutional process of development Biographical experiences	Expert, lay, and institutional knowledge Practices and routines	Individual or institutional developments
Problems in applying the approach	Integration of the different perspectives on the case	Selection of the comparative dimensions Taking the structure or particularity of the case into account	Overlapping of the past by the present	How to delimit the material about the case	Identification of relevant issues in advance
Limitations of the approach	Generalization rather difficult	Perhaps neglecting other dimensions in favor of comparison on one specific dimension	Limited access to options of development which have not been realized	Dispensation of process and change as perspectives	Expenditure often beyond the resources of a project
References	Ragin and Becker (1992)	Glaser (1969)	Bude (2004)	Flick (2007c); Lüders (2004a)	Thomson, Plumridge, and Holland (2003)

2 The Selection of the Design and Checking its Application

If you select a design or its elements you should take several aspects into account and check your choice with reference to these aspects. First, you should find out whether the selected design is qualified for covering the essential elements of your research question. Is it appropriate to the conditions on the side of those who are involved in the study (participants, researchers)? Is there enough scope for them given in the design? Can the design be implemented under the given circumstances of the study in contact with the field and the participants? How far is it appropriate for how the data were collected data and the results will be used? Suggestions for making the decision about which design to use and for assessing the appropriateness of this decision are given in the checklist below.

Checklist for Selecting a Research Design

The following checklist is designed to give you some guidance on how to design your study and for checking back after your first field contacts on how well it works.

1 *Research question*

Can the design and its application address the essential aspects of the research question?

2 *Design*

The design must be applied according to the methodological elements and targets
  There should be no jumping between research designs, except when it is grounded in the research question or theoretically

3 *Researcher*

Are the researchers able to apply the design?
  What are the consequences of their own experiences and limits, resources, etc., in the realization?

4 *Participant*

Is the research design appropriate to the target group of the application?
  How can one take into account the fears, uncertainties, and expectations of (potential) participants?

5 *Scope allowed to the participant*

Can the participants present their views in the framework of the questions?
  Is there enough scope for the new, unexpected, and surprising?

6 *Interaction with the field*

Have the researchers applied the research design correctly?
  Have they left enough scope for the participants?

Have they fulfilled their role? (Why not?)

Were the participant's role, the researcher's role, and the situation clearly defined for the participant?

Could the participants fulfill their roles? (Why not?)

Analyze the breaks in order to validate the design between the first and second field contacts if possible

7 *Aim of the interpretation*

Are you interested in finding and analyzing limited and clear answers or complex, multifold patterns, contexts, etc.?

8 *Claim for generalization*

The level on which statements should be made:

- For the single case (the interviewed individual and his or her biography, an institution and its impact, etc.)?
- With reference to groups (about a profession, a type of institution, etc.)?
- As general statements?

3 Appropriateness of the Method to the Issue

For the construction of a research design we should keep in mind that there is no "ideal way" which fits every study. Research questions and issues under study should define how sampling is planned and what basic design should be selected. Theoretical sampling may be the most ambitious way to select cases in qualitative research. Nevertheless it is not the best choice in every study. Not all basic designs are appropriate and easy to apply in every study in the same way. The appropriateness for the issue under study and the concrete circumstances in which it is studied should be the main orientation in the decision for one or the other alternative discussed here.

4 Fitting the Approach into the Research Process

This point of reference concerns first selecting a sampling alternative or a research design and then fitting it into the research process. For planning a study, collecting data, and analyzing them, the soundness of the modules of the research should be checked. Is the flexibility in collecting the data or the case orientation in analyzing them compatible with the aims of a systematic comparison? Is the method for collecting data open and comprehensive enough for doing a complex case study with the data?

You will find the starting points for this assessment in the paragraphs on the fitting of the method into the research process given in the sections about each approach in this and the following chapters. You should compare the conceptualization of the research process and its components outlined in them, which characterize each approach, to your own research and how you plan it.

The above four points of reference should also be applied to procedures primarily aimed at verbal data (see Chapter 15), or at observation and data beyond talk (see Chapter 21), and alternatives for interpretation (see Chapter 25). As well as the appropriateness of the methods used for the object under study (see Chapter 2), the orientation to the process of research (see Chapter 29) is an essential criterion for evaluating methodological decisions.

KEY POINTS

- The design of a qualitative study is the result of a series of decisions.
- Both the knowledge interest of a study and the contextual conditions shape a study. These include resources, aims, and expectations of others.
- Qualitative online research is a growing area, in which some established qualitative approaches are transferred and adapted.
- Qualitative online research offers some advantages compared to real-world research (e.g., saving time for transcription) but presents many technical problems (such as accessibility and the identification of participants).
- A list of basic designs in qualitative research is available.
- Design in qualitative research has much to do with planning research. It has less to do with control than in quantitative research, though this too plays a part.

Exercise 9.1

1 Select a qualitative study from the literature, for example, Taylor (2012), and describe the design that the study is based on.
2 Reflect on the components of the design of your own study and plan your research with these aspects in mind.

Exercise 9.2

1 Select a qualitative study from the literature, for example, Thomson, Hadfield, Kehily, and Sharpe (2012), and assess how far the issues mentioned in Table 9.1 apply to it.

Exercise 9.3

1 Find an example on the Internet of online research (e.g., Paechter 2012) that reflects the example based on the background discussed in this chapter.
2 Take one of the methods discussed in Chapters 16 and 17 and specify (a) ways of transferring this method to online research and (b) the likely problems of doing so.

Designing Qualitative Research

These texts address the issue of research design in qualitative research in a systematic way:

Creswell, J.W. (2008) *Research Design: Qualitative, Quantitative, and Mixed Methods Approaches* (3rd edn.). Thousand Oaks, CA: Sage.

Flick, U. (2007c) *Designing Qualitative Research*. London: Sage.

Marshall, C. and Rossman, G.B. (2010) *Designing Qualitative Research* (5th edn). Thousand Oaks, CA: Sage.

Maxwell, J.A. (2012) *Qualitative Research Design: An Interactive Approach* (3rd edn). Thousand Oaks, CA: Sage.

Designing Qualitative Online Research

Fielding, N.G., Lee, R. and Blank, G. (eds.) (2008) *The SAGE Handbook of Online Research Methods*. London: Sage.

Kozinets, R.V., Dalbec, P.-Y. and Earley, A. (2014) "*Netnographic Analysis: Understanding Culture through Social Media Data*," *in* U. Flick (ed.), *The SAGE Handbook of Qualitative Data Analysis*. London: Sage. pp. 262–276.

Marotzki, W., Holze, J. and Verständig, D. (2014) "Analyzing Virtual Data," in U. Flick (ed.), *The SAGE Handbook of Qualitative Data Analysis*. London: Sage. pp. 450–463.

10
The Qualitative Research Process

┌─CHAPTER OBJECTIVES─┐

This chapter is designed to help you

- understand that there are alternatives to the traditional, linear, process of research;
- explain the different functions of theory in the qualitative research process;
- understand, by means of a case study, how (1) theory in qualitative research and (2) the research process work;
- see that the model of the research process in grounded theory research can give some inspiration for other forms of qualitative research as well.

Qualitative research cannot be characterized by the superiority of certain methods over and above others. Qualitative and quantitative research are not incompatible opposites: it is not the case that they should never be combined (see Chapter 3). Consequently, there is no need for us here to reopen old, often unfruitful, methodological debates concerning fundamental questions on the subject.

Qualitative research does, however, presuppose a different understanding of research in general—and this goes beyond, say, the decision to use a narrative interview or a questionnaire. Qualitative research entails a specific understanding of the relation between issue and method (see Becker 1996). Only in a very restricted way is it compatible with the logic of research familiar from experimental or quantitative research. Often in experimental research, the process of research may be conceived as neatly in a linear sequence of conceptual, methodological, and empirical steps. Each step can be taken and treated one after the other and separately. If you want to do qualitative research, there is in contrast a mutual interdependence between the single stages of the research process and you should take this into account much more. This conception of the research process has been developed by Glaser and Strauss (1967) in their grounded theory approach (see also Strauss 1987; Strauss and Corbin 1990; and Chapter 25).

Research as Linear Process?

But first, we should examine the traditional conception of the research process. The traditional version of quantitative social sciences ideally starts from building a model: before entering the field to be studied, and while still sitting at their desks, researchers construct a model of the assumed conditions and relations. The researchers' starting point is the theoretical knowledge taken from the literature or earlier empirical findings. From this, hypotheses are derived, which are then operationalized and tested against empirical conditions. The concrete or empirical "objects" of research, like a certain field or real people, have the status of the exemplary against which assumed general relations (in the form of hypotheses) are tested. The aim is to guarantee that a study is representative in its data and findings (e.g., because random samples of the people that are studied are drawn). A further aim is the breakdown of complex relations into distinct variables; this allows the researchers to isolate and test their effects. Theories and methods are prior to the object of research. Theories are tested and perhaps falsified along the way. If they are enlarged, it is through additional hypotheses, which are again tested empirically and so on.

Although much qualitative research is indeed oriented on such a step-by-step logic, I want here to outline a different understanding of the research process in qualitative research. This understanding comes from a specific approach (namely, grounded theory research), but provides an overall orientation for those forms of qualitative research that challenges the above step-by-step logic.

The Concept of Process in Grounded Theory Research

In contrast to the above theory-driven and linear model of the research process, the grounded theory approach prioritizes the data and the field under study over theoretical assumptions. According to this approach, theories should not be applied to the subject being studied but are "discovered" and formulated in working with the field and the empirical data to be found in it. People to be studied are selected according to their relevance to the research topic; they are not selected for constructing a (statistically) representative sample of a general population. The aim is not to reduce complexity by breaking it down into variables: rather it is to increase complexity by including context. Methods too have to be appropriate to the issue under study and have to be chosen accordingly.

The relation of theory to empirical work in this type of research is outlined as follows:

> The principle of openness implies that the theoretical structuring of the issue under study is postponed until the structuring of the issue under study by the persons being studied has "emerged." (Hoffmann-Riem 1980, p. 343)

Here it is postulated that researchers should at least suspend whatever a priori theoretical knowledge they bring into the field. However (in contrast to a widespread misunderstanding), this is postulated above all for the way to treat hypotheses and less for the decision concerning the research question (see the following Chapter 11):

> The delay in structuring implies the abandonment of the *ex ante* formulation of hypotheses. In fact, the research question is outlined under theoretical aspects. ... But the elaboration does not culminate in ... the set of hypotheses. (1980, p. 345)

This understanding of qualitative research suggests that the researcher should adopt an attitude of what, in a different context, has been termed "evenly suspended attention." According to Freud, this allows one to avoid the ensuing problems:

> For as soon as anyone deliberately concentrates his attention to a certain degree, he begins to select from the material before him; one point will be fixed in his mind with particular clearness and some other will be correspondingly disregarded, and in making this selection he will be following his expectations or inclinations. This, however, is precisely what must not be done. In making this selection, if he follows his expectations he is in danger of never finding anything but what he already knows; and if he follows his inclinations, he will certainly falsify what he may perceive. (1958, p. 112)

Applied to qualitative research, this means that researchers—partly because of their own theoretical assumptions and structures, which direct their attention to concrete aspects, but also because of their own fears—might remain blind to the structures in the field or person under study. As a result, their research fails to discover the actual "new."

The model of the process in grounded theory research includes the following aspects: theoretical sampling (see Chapter 13), grounded theory coding (see Chapter 25), and writing the theory (see Chapter 30). This approach focuses on the interpretation of data, no matter how they were collected. Here the question of which method to use for collecting data becomes minor. Decisions on data to be integrated and methods to be used for this are based on the state of the developing theory after analyzing the data already to hand at that moment.

Various aspects of Glaser and Strauss's model have become relevant in their own right in methodological discussions and qualitative research practice beyond grounded theory research. Theoretical sampling in particular, as a strategy of defining a sample step by step, is also applied in research in which methods of interpretation are used that are completely different from those Glaser and Strauss suggest or in which the claim for developing a theory is not made. Grounded theory coding as a method of analyzing texts has also gained its own relevance. The idea of developing theories by analyzing empirical material has become essential in its own right to the discussions of qualitative research, quite independently from using the methods of the approach at the same time.

Researchers often ignore the consistency with which the approach of Strauss connects its individual components. Theoretical sampling, for example, is feasible as a strategy only if the consequence is appreciated that not all interviews are completed in the first stage and the interpretation of the data starts only after interviewing is finished. It is rather the immediate interpretation of collected data that provides the basis for sampling decisions. These decisions are not limited to selecting cases, but also comprise the decisions about the type of data to integrate next and—in extreme cases—about changing the method.

Linearity and Circularity of the Process

This circularity of the parts of the research process in the model of grounded theory research is a central feature of the approach. It was the force behind a multitude of approaches starting from case analyses (e.g., Ragin and Becker 1992). However, this circularity causes problems where the general linear model of research (theory, hypotheses, operationalization, sampling, collecting data, interpreting data, validation) is used to evaluate research. In general, this is the case in two respects: in proposing a research project or in applying for a grant; and in the evaluation of this research and its results by the use of traditional quality indicators (see Chapter 29).

However, this circularity is also one of the strengths of the approach, because it forces the researcher to permanently reflect on the whole research process and on particular steps in the light of the other steps—at least when it is applied consistently. The close link between collecting and interpreting data and the selection of empirical material, unlike in the traditional linear method of proceeding, allows the researcher not only to ask the following question repeatedly, but also to answer it: How far do the methods, categories, and theories that are used do justice to the subject and the data?

Theories in the Research Process as Versions of the World

Now, what is the function of theories[1] in a research process in the style of Glaser and Strauss? There are two starting points for answering this question. The first is Goodman's (1978) concept that theories—similar to other forms of presenting empirical relations—are versions of the world. These versions undergo a continuous revision, evaluation, construction, and reconstruction. According to this view, theories are not (right or wrong) representations of given facts, but versions or perspectives through which the world is seen. By the formulation of a version and by the perspective on the world hidden in it, the perception of the world is determined in a way that feeds back into the social construction of this perspective, and thus the world around us (see Chapter 8). Thus theories as versions of the world become preliminary and relative. Further developing the version (e.g., by additional interpretations of new materials) leads to an increased empirical grounding in the object that is studied. But here the research process, too, does not start as a *tabula rasa*. The starting point is rather a pre-understanding of the subject or field under study.

Accordingly, the second point of reference for defining the role of theories in the model of grounded theory research is the first rule that Kleining formulates for qualitative research: "The initial understanding of the facts under study should be regarded as preliminary and should be exceeded with new, non-congruent information" (1982, p. 231).

Theoretical assumptions become relevant as preliminary versions of the understanding of and the perspective on the object being studied, which are reformulated and, above all, further elaborated in the course of the research process. These revisions of versions on the basis of the empirical material thrust the construction of the subject under study. The researcher's methodological decisions, as designed in the model of Glaser and Strauss, contribute to this construction.

CASE STUDY 10.1

Awareness of Dying

The following example represents one of the first and major studies using this form of research process and the goal of developing theories from qualitative research in the field. Barney Glaser and Anselm Strauss worked from the 1960s as pioneers of qualitative research and of grounded theory in the context of medical sociology. They did this study in several hospitals in the United States around San Francisco. Their research question was what influenced the various persons' interaction with dying people and how the knowledge—that the person will die soon—determines the interaction with that person. More concretely, they studied which forms of interaction between the dying person and the clinical staff in the hospital, between the staff and the relatives, and between the relatives and the dying person could be noted.

The starting point of the research was the observation when the researchers' own relatives were in the hospital that the staff in hospitals (at that time) seemed not to inform the patients with a terminal disease and their relatives about the state and the life expectancy of the patient. Rather the possibility that the patient might die or die soon was treated as taboo. This general observation and the questions it raised were taken as a starting point for more systematic observation and interviews in one hospital. These data were analyzed and used to develop categories. That was also the background for deciding to include another hospital and to continue the data collection and analysis there. Both hospitals, as cases, were immediately compared for similarities and differences.

The results of such comparison were used to decide which hospital to use next, until finally six hospitals were included in the study. These included a teaching hospital, a VA hospital, two county hospitals, a private Catholic hospital, and a state hospital. Wards included, among others, geriatrics, cancer, intensive care, pediatrics, and neurosurgery, in which the fieldworkers stayed two to four weeks each. The data from each of these units (different wards in one hospital, similar wards in different hospitals, various hospitals) were contrasted and compared to show similarities and differences.

At the end of the study, comparable situations and contexts outside hospitals and health care were included as another dimension of comparison. Analyzing and comparing the data allowed the development of a theoretical model, which then was transferred to other fields in order to develop it further. The result of this study was a theory of awareness contexts as ways of dealing with the information and with the patients' need to know more about their situation. Details of the results and ways of analyzing the data will be discussed further in Chapter 25.

This study provides a good example of using the research process outlined in this chapter to develop theoretically relevant insights from a series of case studies and their comparison (see Glaser and Strauss 1965a for details). Here theory was not a starting point: there was no theory available at that time to explain the initial experiences of the researchers with their own relatives in hospital. Theory was the end product of the research, and it was developed out of empirical material and the analysis of this material.

Qualitative research fits the traditional, linear logic of research only in a limited way. Rather, the circular interlinking of empirical steps, as the model of Glaser and Strauss suggests (see Figure 10.1), does justice to the character of discovery in qualitative research. The context of this model of the research process should be referred to when single parts, like theoretical sampling, are taken from it and used in isolation. This process-oriented understanding allows one to realize the epistemological

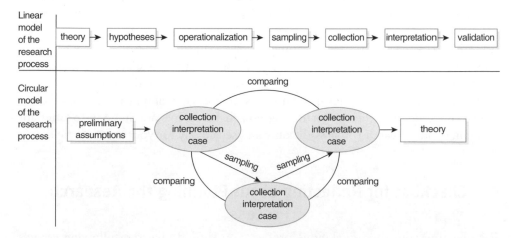

FIGURE 10.1   Models of Process and Theory

principle of *verstehen* with a greater degree of sensitivity than in linear designs. The relative relevance of theories as versions of the object to be reformulated takes the construction of reality in the research process into account more seriously. The central part reserved for the interpretation of data (compared to their collection or the a priori construction of elaborated designs) recognizes that text is the actual empirical material and the ultimate basis for developing the theory.

The Research Process in Qualitative Research in General

As discussed at the beginning of this chapter, a lot of qualitative research beyond the approach of grounded theory research is not completely oriented on the model outlined here. The endpoint of such research is not necessarily to develop a theory and there is theoretical knowledge about the issue at the outset of research. Most research is based on a specific method of data collection (e.g., a particular type of interview), which is not so much the case for grounded theory research. Also, sampling decisions in general (see Chapter 13) are taken in advance—you know that you are interested in a specific group of people's experiences (e.g., women with a specific chronic illness). Principles of theoretical and purposive sampling (see Chapter 13) are more relevant for the decision over which concrete cases you select for your interview, for example.

The circular model discussed above can highlight several important points for qualitative research beyond grounded theory. Qualitative research refrains from formulating hypotheses at the outset (and from testing them). Sampling decisions are taken or made more concrete in the research process. Data collection and analysis should be interlinked—it is often not very helpful to do all interviews first and then to think about what to do with them. It is more helpful to look at the first interviews, what could be a direction for analyzing them (which topics, categories, new areas in them are promising, relevant, or still missing), and what could be ways of improving the following interviews.

At the end of the research you should not merely have confirmed what you (or the literature) knew before, but you should have developed new insights (like a typology of women's experiences with chronic illness) that you found in analyzing your data. Your research will be more fruitful if the degree of standardization (see Chapter 9) you try to establish is not driven by the ideas of quantitative/standardized research, but if instead you leave room for adapting flexibly to your field and participants (as in the case study above). Thus qualitative research in general may not be based completely on grounded theory, yet that approach has some orientations to offer for designing your research (process) flexibly and sensitively for your concrete field.

Checklist for Reflecting about Planning the Research Process

For planning your own qualitative project, you should take the following aspects into account and find answers to the questions that arise:

1 Which steps in the research process are appropriate for the kind of study you plan?
2 Seek to clarify how developed the existing knowledge and research is about your issue of research.
3 Check what the gaps are in the empirical and theoretical knowledge about the issue of your study that you want to fill with your research.
4 Check which will be more adequate for your study: a more linear or a more circular process.
5 Check the procedures in your plan for their soundness: does the methodological plan of your study fit (a) the aims of your study, (b) its theoretical backgrounds, and (c) the state of research?
6 How compatible will this kind of research process be with (a) the issue you want to study and (b) the field in which you intend to do your research?

This checklist may help you plan your own study, but you can also use it for assessing the existing studies of other researchers.

KEY POINTS

- The research process in qualitative research is often difficult to divide into clearly separated phases.
- Qualitative research reveals its real potential when important parts of the research process are interlinked.
- An understanding of the interrelatedness of the various parts of the research process originates from grounded theory research. It is fruitful for other approaches too.
- Theories are versions of the world, which change and are further developed through the research.

Exercise 10.1

1 Select a qualitative study (e.g., Flick, Garms-Homolová, and Röhnsch 2012a) and identify the steps of the research process in it.
2 Decide whether the study you have selected was planned along the linear or circular model of the research process.

Exercise 10.2

Consider your own research project and plan it step by step. Then imagine how your research should be planned according to the circular model.

Note

1 Here "theories" mean assumptions about the subject under study, whereas the notion "theoretical positions" in Chapter 7 refers to differing assumptions about the methods and goals of research.

──Further Reading──

The epistemological positions of qualitative research are outlined in the first text, whereas the others provide both classical and more recent versions of the process model of grounded theory research:

Becker, H.S. (1996) "The Epistemology of Qualitative Research," in R. Jessor, A. Colby and R.A. Shweder (eds.), *Ethnography and Human Development*. Chicago, IL: University of Chicago Press. pp. 53–72.

Glaser, B.G. and Strauss, A.L. (1967) *The Discovery of Grounded Theory: Strategies for Qualitative Research*. Chicago, IL: Aldine.

Strauss, A.L. (1987) *Qualitative Analysis for Social Scientists*. Cambridge: Cambridge University Press.

11
Research Questions

CHAPTER OBJECTIVES

This chapter is designed to help you

- understand why research questions are so important for running a successful study;
- explain why it is important to carefully formulate and focus the research question;
- articulate the different types of research questions from which you can choose one for your project;
- distinguish good from bad research questions;
- understand the role of research questions in the research practice.

Research questions are like a door to the research field under study. Whether empirical activities produce answers or not depends on the formulation of such questions. Also dependent on this is the decision as to which methods are appropriate and who (i.e., which persons, groups, or institutions) or what (i.e., what processes, activities, or lifestyles) you should include in your study. The essential criteria for evaluating research questions include their soundness and clarity, but also whether they can be answered in the framework of given and limited resources (time, money, etc.; see

Chapter 9). You should take into account that formulating a research question means defining the overall guiding question for your entire project, rather than (for example) formulating the concrete questions you will ask in your interviews.

Origins of Research Questions

Research questions do not come from nowhere. How do research questions arise? First, an issue is discovered or defined, requiring empirical research. In many cases, the origin of such an issue lies in the researchers' personal biographies or their social contexts. Sometimes a personal experience leads researchers to decide to study a topic. One example is provided by the observations that Arlie Hochschild made of interactions in her childhood, when visitors with various cultural backgrounds came to her parents' house; this led Hochschild to later develop an interest in studying the management of emotions empirically (Hochschild 1983). Another example comes from the experiences with parents dying in hospitals and the lack of open communication observed in this situation that led to Glaser and Strauss (1965a) developing their interest in studying the awareness of dying empirically. In both cases, the development of research interests and later research questions was problem-driven.

In many other cases, research interests and questions are developed out of a more practical need—for example, when you need to do an empirical study to complete your masters thesis. Often, research questions start from earlier research and the issues and problems left open in a study recently finished. The decision about a specific question mostly depends on the researchers' practical interests and their involvement in certain social and historical contexts. Everyday and scientific contexts both play a part here. Recent research studying scientific processes has demonstrated how much traditions and styles of thinking influence the formulation of research questions in scientific laboratories and in work groups in social sciences.

If you want to start your qualitative study, a first and central step is how to formulate the research question(s). Though this step tends to be ignored in presentations of methods,[1] it essentially determines success in qualitative research. This challenge arises not just at the beginning of the research process, when you conceptualize your study or your project; you will need to formulate the research question at several stages of the process: when you conceptualize the research design, when you enter the field, when you select the cases, and when you collect the data. Reflecting on and reformulating the research question are central points of reference for assessing the appropriateness of the decisions you take at several points. The formulation of the research question becomes relevant when you decide on the method(s) of collecting data, when you conceptualize interview schedules, and also when you conceptualize the interpretation, which method you use, and which material you select.

You should formulate research questions in concrete terms with the aim of clarifying what the field contacts are supposed to reveal. The less clearly you formulate your research question, the greater is the danger that you will find yourself in the end confronted with mountains of data and helplessly trying to analyze them.

Although the quoted "principle of openness" questions the a priori formulation of hypotheses, it by no means implies that you should abandon attempts to define and formulate research questions. You need both to develop a clear idea of your research question and to remain open to new and perhaps surprising results. Clarity over research questions that are pursued is also necessary for checking the appropriateness of methodological decisions in the following respects: Which methods are necessary to answer the questions? Is it possible to study the research question with the chosen methods at all? Is qualitative research the appropriate strategy to answer these questions?[2] More generally, the elaboration of the research question in the research process may be characterized as in Figure 11.1.

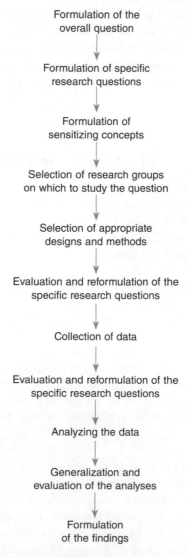

FIGURE 11.1   Research Questions in the Research Process

Cutting Questions to Size

The origin of research questions may lie (as noted above) in the researchers' personal biographies and their social contexts. The decision about a specific question typically depends on the researchers' practical interests and their involvement in certain social and historical contexts (Fleck, Trenn, and Merton 1979). In addition, research (e.g., Knorr-Cetina 1981; Knorr-Cetina and Mulkay 1983) studying scientific processes has demonstrated that traditions and styles of thinking influence the formulation of research questions in scientific laboratories and in work groups in social sciences.

If you decide upon a concrete research question certain aspects of your field will be brought to the fore, while others will be regarded as less important and (at least for the time being) left in the background or excluded. For instance, the decision on the research question will be crucial in the case of data collection through single interviews (see Chapters 15–18); if, however, you are collecting your data through a longer process—as for example in participant observation (see Chapter 20) or with repeated interviews—you can change the consequences of such a decision more easily.

Specifying an Area of Interest and Delimiting the Issue

The result of formulating research questions is that it helps you to circumscribe a specific area of a more or less complex field, which you regard as essential, although the field would allow various research definitions of this kind. For studying "counseling," for example, you could specify any of the following as areas of interest (with examples of possible research questions):

- Interactive processes between counselor and client—for example, how do they define and agree upon the client's problem as the issue of the consultation?
- Organization of the administration of clients as "cases"—for example, how may it be decided whether the counselor's institution is the right one for the client's problem?
- Organization and maintenance of a specific professional identity (e.g., to be a helper under unfavorable circumstances)—for example, how do counselors in the context of a prison maintain their identities as non-directive person-centered psychologists?
- Subjective or objective manifestations of the patient's "career"—for example, how do the counselors clarify the clients' earlier experiences with their problems or with other institutional forms of help?

All these areas are relevant aspects of the complexity of everyday life in an institution (counseling service, socio-psychiatric service). You can focus on each of these areas in a study and embody it in a research question. For example, you could approach a complex (e.g., institutional) field with the aim of focusing on gaining an understanding of the viewpoint of one person or of several persons acting in this field. You could also focus on describing a life world. Similarly, you could be dedicated to reconstructing subjective or objective reasons for activities and thus to explaining human behavior. Alternatively, you could concentrate on the relation between subjective interpretations and the structural features of activity environments that can be described objectively.

Only in very rare cases in qualitative research does it make sense to include such a multitude of aspects. It is crucial that you define the field and the research question in such a way that the question can be answered with the available resources and a sound research design can be derived. The research question must be formulated in such a way that it does not implicitly raise a lot of other questions at the same time.

Sensitizing Concepts and the Triangulation of Perspectives

At this stage, you will face the problem of which aspects (the essential, the manageable, the relevant perspective, and so on) to include and which to exclude (the secondary, the less relevant, and so on). How should you shape this decision in order to ensure the least "frictional loss" possible (i.e., ensure that the loss of authenticity remains limited and justifiable through an acceptable degree of neglect of certain aspects)?

Sensitizing concepts that provide access to a spectrum of processes relevant in a field may be the starting point of your research. Glaser and Strauss call these "analytical and sensitizing concepts" (1967, p. 38). For instance, when I studied the institutional everyday life of counseling, a concept like "trust" proved to be useful. This concept could be applied, for example, to aspects of interactions between counselor and client. I could also use it to study the counselor's task, the clients' impressions of the institution and their perceptions of the counselor's competence, the problematic of how to make a conversation a consultation, and so on.

Frictional loss in decisions between research perspectives can be reduced through systematic triangulation of perspectives (see Flick 2007b). This phrase refers to the combination of appropriate research perspectives and methods that are suitable for taking into account as many different aspects of a problem as possible. An example of this would be the combination of attempts at understanding people's points of view with attempts at describing the life world in which they act. According to Fielding and Fielding (1986, p. 34), structural aspects of a problem should be linked with reconstructing its meaning for the people involved (see Chapter 14 for triangulation). For example, in the case of my study of trust in counseling, I linked the reconstruction of counselors' subjective theories on trust with a description of the process of producing trust in a conversation in the special world of "counseling." If you use key concepts to gain access to the relevant processes and triangulation of perspectives to disclose as many different aspects as possible, you can increase the degree of proximity to the object of your research.

Generally speaking, the precise formulation of the research question is a central step when you conceptualize your research design. Research questions should be examined critically as to their origins (what has led to the actual research question?). They are points of reference for checking the soundness of your research design and the appropriateness of methods you intend to use for collecting and interpreting your data. This is relevant for evaluating any generalizations: the level of generalization that is appropriate and obtainable depends on the research questions pursued.

Types of Research Questions

There are various types of research questions (according to Lofland and Lofland 1984, p. 94), with which you can address an issue of research. For example:

1 What type is it?
2 What is its structure?
3 How frequent is it?
4 What are the causes?
5 What are its processes?
6 What are its consequences?
7 What are people's strategies?

If we take as an example our study on homelessness and health of adolescents, and focus on the aspect of chronic illness in the context of homelessness, we can formulate the following examples of research questions based on the above typology and suggest methodological approaches for answering them:

1 Type: What types of coping with a chronic illness can we identify among our participants?

  • This question would suggest interviews with the participants

2 Structure: What are the structural problems linked to specific forms of illness, which influence attempts at coping with them?

  • This would suggest doing expert interviews with service providers (see Chapter 16)

3 Frequency: How frequently do specific chronic diseases occur among homeless adolescents?

  • Again, expert interviews or, if available, statistics of treatments

4 Causes: What are the causes of homelessness in our sample? What causes of their situation do the participants see themselves? Which causes do they see for their illness?

  • Interviews with the adolescents

5 Processes: How do the adolescents seek help once their diseases become manifest?

  • Participant observation (see Chapter 20) and/or interviews with the adolescents

6 Consequences: What consequences can be identified for different forms of coping with the diseases?

  • Again, expert interviews with service providers

7 Strategies: How do the adolescents cope with their diseases (neglect, seek help, etc.)?

  • Participant observation and/or interviews with the adolescents

Lofland and Lofland recommend that researchers reflect on which "units" they want to choose for analyzing phenomena relevant for answering the research question. They suggest the following units (1984, p. 94), which could be complemented by others according to the specific research questions you have:

1 Meanings
2 Practices
3 Episodes
4 Encounters
5 Roles
6 Relationships
7 Groups
8 Organizations
9 Lifestyles

If we return to our example, we can nail down our examples of research questions based on the above typology as in the following examples:

1 Meanings: What is the meaning of the disease for our participants; how do they differ on this point?

- Interviews

2 Practices: How do they address or ignore their problem?

- Observations

3 Episodes: Which episodes show what determines whether the participants attend a doctor or not?

- Episodic interviews (see Chapter 18)

4 Encounters: What happens when they attend a doctor; what are the doctor's reactions to the adolescent?

- Observation or recording of doctor–patient situations

5 Roles: Does the role of the participant in the peer group change due to the disease?

- Observation and/or interviews

6 Relationships: Can we identify supportive relationships in the peer group?

- Observation

7 Groups: Can groups be identified which exclude the ill adolescents?

- Observation

8 Organizations: How do organizations like a hospital react when the adolescent seeks help?

- Interviews with staff and/or observation

9 Lifestyles: What are the effects of the lifestyle of "living on the street" on the development of the diseases?

- Interviews with adolescents and/or service providers

Generally speaking, we can differentiate between research questions oriented towards describing states and those describing processes. In the first case, you should describe how a certain given state (which type, how often) has come about (causes, strategies) and how this state is maintained (structure). In the second case, the aim is to describe how something develops or changes (causes, processes, consequences, strategies).

The description of states and the description of processes as the two main types of research question may be classified in terms of increasingly complex "units" (Lofland and Lofland 1984). This classification can be used for locating research questions in this space of possibilities and also for checking the selected research question for additional questions raised.

Finally, you can assess or classify research questions as to how far they are suitable for confirming existing assumptions (like hypotheses) or how far they aim at discovering new ones, or at least allow for this. Strauss calls the latter generative questions and defines them as follows: "Questions that stimulate the line of investigation in profitable directions; they lead to hypotheses, useful comparisons, the collection of certain classes of data, even to general lines of attack on potentially important problems" (1987, p. 22).

CASE STUDY 11.1

Adoption of a Public Health Orientation by Doctors and Nurses

In this project (Flick, Fischer, Walter, and Schwartz 2002), we were generally interested in whether and how far a public health orientation had reached some of the key institutions of home care services in the health field. This formulation is of course not yet a research question that could be used for starting an empirical study. We had first to zoom in from the general interest to a more focused perspective. Therefore, we focused on health concepts held by home care nurses and general practitioners. We then focused on the attitude towards prevention and health promotion as parts of their work, and more concretely with a specific part of their clientele—the elderly.

Against this background, we developed a set of questions that we wanted to pursue in a study using interviews. They were as follows:

- What are the concepts of health held by doctors and nurses?
- Which dimensions of health representations are relevant for professional work with the elderly?
- What is the attitude of professionals towards prevention and health promotion for the elderly?
- What are the concepts of ageing held by general practitioners and home care nurses? What is the relation of these concepts with those of health?
- What relevance do professionals ascribe to their own concepts of health and ageing for their own professional practice?
- Are there any relations between the concepts of health and ageing and professional training and experience?

We used these research questions to develop an instrument for episodic interviews (see Chapter 18) with doctors and nurses. Looking back on this project, we thought critically about the number of different research questions included in the above list. Particularly if you are a novice in qualitative research, I recommend that you concentrate on one or two such questions in planning a similar project to the one we did.

Good and Bad Research Questions

Let us consider further what tends to distinguish good research questions from bad ones in the next step.

Good Questions

What characterizes a good research question? First of all, it should be an actual question. For example, "The living situation of homeless adolescents in a West European country" is an interesting issue, but is not a (good) research question, because it is too broad and unspecific for orienting a research project. Implicitly, it addresses a variety of subgroups—and supposes that homeless adolescents in the United Kingdom and Germany for example are in the same situation. Also the term "living situation" is too broad; it would be better to focus on a specific aspect of the living situation, for example, their health problems and the use of professional services. Accordingly, it would be better to formulate a research question such as: "What characterizes the health problems and the use of professional services of adolescents in a West European country like Germany?" Here, we have a real question (What characterizes …?), a focus on two topics (health problems and use of services) and a clearer local focus (Germany). Thus, the issue has been turned into a research question.

There are three main types of research questions. (1) Exploratory questions focus on a given situation or a change: for example, "Has the health situation of homeless adolescents changed in the last 10 years?" (2) Descriptive questions aim at a description of a certain situation, state, or process: for example, "Do homeless adolescents come from broken homes?" or "How do adolescents find their way into the situation of being homeless?" (3) Explanatory questions focus on a relation. This means that more than just a state of affairs is investigated (so one goes further than asking a question such as "What characterizes …?): rather a factor or an influence is examined in relation to that situation. For example, "Is a lack of sufficient specialized health services a major cause of more serious medical problems among homeless adolescents?"

Bad Research Questions

Neuman (2000, p. 144) has characterized what he calls "bad research questions." He identifies five types of such questions, which I again illustrate with examples from my own fields of research: (1) questions that are non-scientific questions, for example, "Should adolescents live on the streets?"; (2) statements that include general topics but not a research question, for example, "Treatment of drug and alcohol abuse of homeless adolescents"; (3) statements that include a set of variables but no questions, for example, "Homelessness and health"; (4) questions that are too vague or ambitious, for example, "How to prevent homelessness among adolescents?"; and (5) questions that still need to be more specific, for example, "Has the health situation of homeless adolescents become worse?".

As these examples may show, it is important to have a research question that really is a question (not a statement) that can indeed be answered. It should be as focused and specific as possible instead of being vague and unspecific. All the elements of a research question should be clearly spelled out instead of remaining broad and full of implicit assumptions. To test your research question before you carry out your study, reflect on what possible answers to that question would look like.

Research Questions and Practice

Bryman (2007) carried out an interesting empirical study on the way researchers in their day-to-day practice deal with the issue of research questions—where questions come from, how they are treated and related to methods and the field. From the interviews he conducted, he identified two positions on the relation of the research question to the methodological approach applied in a study. The positions were (1) the particularistic and (2) the universalistic. The particularistic version emphasizes what is formulated in textbooks (and in this chapter): the research questions should be developed from a field of interest and then drive all the subsequent decisions—which methodological program is applied, which design and which methods are used for collecting and analyzing data. The universalistic position starts from a research program—like qualitative research, or for example discourse analysis or mixed-methods research—and sees it as universally appropriate to research issues in general. Research questions are then developed against the background of this research program. Methodological decisions—which design and which methods to use—are basically set by the orientation to the research program.

This universalistic view contradicts what textbooks say about the way research questions should drive all methodological decisions. But Bryman's interviews showed that it is at least as prominent in the research practice as the particularistic view and that researchers shift in their practices between both positions. However, if you start doing research and are not firmly entangled in a research context devoted to a specific research program, you should take the particularistic view as an orientation for planning your research, starting from a research question driving your subsequent methodological choices.

Checklist for Research Questions

The questions below list points that you should consider when formulating your research question(s):

1 Does your study have a clearly spelled out research question?
2 Where does your research question come from and what do you want to achieve in pursuing it?
3 Is your interest in the contents of the research question the main motivation? Or is answering the research question more a means to an end, like achieving an academic degree?
4 How many research questions does your study have? Are there too many? If you have more than one question, which is the main question?
5 Can your research question be answered?
6 What might an answer look like?
7 Can your research question be answered *empirically*?
8 Who can provide insights for that?
9 Can you reach these people?
10 Where can you find such people?
11 Which situations can give you insights for answering your research questions and are these situations accessible?
12 What are the methodological consequences of the research question?
13 What resources are needed? (For example, how much time?)

You can use these guideline questions both for planning your own study and for assessing existing studies by other researchers.

KEY POINTS

- It is essential to formulate a clear research question. You must ensure this is the case at all costs.
- Most issues of research can be addressed by more than one research question. It is important when you start your research to decide which one you will focus on.
- Typically, research questions get refined and reformulated as an empirical research project proceeds.

Exercise 11.1

1 Locate a qualitative study in the literature (e.g., Flick et al. 2010). Identify the study's guiding research question.
2 Assess this research question. Was it clear and well formulated?
3 Formulate a better research question for this study.

1 Decide on an issue you want to study and then formulate different research questions.
2 Decide which one you want to pursue.
3 Refine the research question so that it is one which you can answer with your research project.

Further Reading

The first three texts deal with linking perspectives in research questions in some detail. The fourth provides classical, more elaborate, information about how to deal with research questions in qualitative research:

Andrews, R. (2003) *Research Questions*. London: Continuum.
Bryman, A. (2007) "The Research Question in Social Research: What is its Role?" *International Journal of Social Research Methodology*, 10(1): 5–20.
Flick, U. (2007c) *Designing Qualitative Research*. London: Sage.
Lofland, J. and Lofland, L.H. (1984) *Analyzing Social Settings* (2nd edn). Belmont, CA: Wadsworth.

Notes

1 Almost no textbook dedicates a separate chapter to this topic. In most subject indexes, one looks for it in vain. Exceptions can be found in Andrews (2003), Silverman (1985, Ch.1; 1993), Strauss (1987, p. 17), and Strauss and Corbin (1990, pp. 37–40).
2 If the research question in a study implicitly or explicitly leads to the determination of the frequencies of a phenomenon, quantitative methods are both more appropriate and generally also simpler to apply.

12
Entering the Field

─CHAPTER OBJECTIVES─

This chapter is designed to help you to

- develop a sensitivity to this key step in the research process;
- understand that as a researcher you will have to actively locate yourself in the field;
- learn the strategies that institutions use to deal with researchers—and, sometimes, to keep them out;
- comprehend the dialectics of strangeness and familiarity in this context.

The Problem of Access

The question of how to gain access to the field under study is more crucial in qualitative research than in quantitative research. In qualitative research, the contact that researchers look for tends to be closer or more intense. For example, open interviews require that the interviewed person and the researcher get more closely involved than would be necessary for simply handing over a questionnaire. Or if you want to record everyday conversations, you would expect from participants a degree of disclosure of their own everyday lives, which they cannot easily control in advance. And as a participant observer, you normally come to the field for longer periods (see Chapter 20).

From a methodological point of view, research does more justice to its object through these procedures. From the perspective of everyday practicability, however, these procedures make a much more extensive demand on the people who are involved. This is why the question of how to gain access to a field deserves special attention.

The general term "field" here may refer to a certain institution, a subculture, a family, a specific group of people with a special biography, decision makers in administrations or enterprises, and so on. In each such case, you will face the same problems: How can you secure the collaboration of the potential participants in your study? How do you achieve not only that people express their willingness, but that this actually leads to concrete interviews or other data?

Role Definitions When Entering an Open Field

In qualitative research, you as the researcher and your respondent have a special importance. Your—and your respondent's—communicative competencies are the main "instruments" of collecting data and of recognition. Because of this, you cannot adopt a neutral role in the field and in your contacts with the people to be interviewed or observed. Rather you will have to assume certain roles and positions (sometimes vicariously or unwillingly). What information in your research you will gain access to (and which you will remain debarred from) will depend crucially on the successful adoption of an appropriate role or position. You should see the assumption of a role as a process of negotiation between researcher and participants, which runs through several stages. "Participants" here refers to those people to be interviewed or observed; for research in institutions, it also refers to those who have to authorize or facilitate access. The growing insight into the importance of the interactive process of negotiating and allocating roles to researchers in the field finds its expression in the metaphors that are used to describe this process and will be addressed in more detail later in this chapter.

Using the example of participant observation in ethnographic field research (see Chapter 20), Adler and Adler (1987) presented a system of membership roles in the field (see Figure 12.1). They show how, over the history of qualitative research, this problem has been variously treated. At one pole, they position the studies of the Chicago School (see Chapter 2) and their use of pure observation of the members in a field of open and well-directed interaction with them and of active participation in their everyday life. The problem of participation and observation becomes relevant in questions of necessary distancing (how much participation is needed for a good observation; how much participation is permissible in the context of scientific distancing?). For Douglas's (1976) "existential sociology," which they place in an intermediate position, Adler and Adler see the problem solved in participation aiming at revealing the secrets of the field. At the other pole, the concern of recent ethnomethodology (see Chapter 7) is with describing members' methods rather than their perspectives in order to describe the process under study from the inside. Here the problem of access is

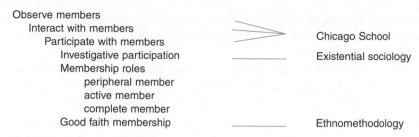

Observe members
  Interact with members
    Participate with members   Chicago School
      Investigative participation   _____ Existential sociology
      Membership roles
        peripheral member
        active member
        complete member
      Good faith membership   _____ Ethnomethodology

FIGURE 12.1   Membership Roles in the Field

Source: Adler and Adler (1987, p. 33)

managed by immersion in the work process observed and by membership of the researched field.

For Adler and Adler, the Chicago School's handling of this problem is over-committed to scientific distancing from the "object" of research. Yet they are rather critical too of the types of access obtained by ethnomethodology (positioned at different poles in their systematic). In both cases, access is obtained by completely fusing with the research object. Their concept of membership roles seems to be a more realistic solution, one located between these two poles. They work out the types of "membership roles: the peripheral, the active, and the complete member." For studying delicate fields (in their case, drug dealers), they suggest a combination of "overt and covert roles" (1987, p. 21). This means that, in order to gain insights that are as open as possible, they do not disclose their actual role (as researchers) to all the members of a field.

Access to Institutions

When you want to do your research in institutions (e.g., counseling services), this problem becomes more complicated. In general, different levels are involved in the regulation of access. First, there is the level of the people responsible for authorizing the research. In case of difficulties, they are held responsible for this authorization by external authorities. Second, there is the level of those to be interviewed or observed, who will be investing their time and willingness.

For research in administrations, Lau and Wolff (1983, p. 419) have outlined the process as follows. In an institution like social administration, researchers with their research interest are defined as clients. Like a client, the researcher has to make his or her request in formal terms. This request, its implications (research question, methods, time needed), and the researcher personally have to undergo an "official examination." The treatment of a researcher's request is "pre-structured" by the fact that the researcher has been sent by other authorities. This means that the authorization or support for the request by a higher authority in the first instance may produce distrust in the people to be interviewed (why is this higher authority in favor of this research?). Being endorsed by other people (e.g., colleagues from another institution), however, may facilitate access at the same time. In the end, the researcher's request can be fitted into administrative routines and treated using institutionally familiar procedures.

This process, termed "work of agreement," is a "joint product, in some cases an explicit working problem for both sides." For instance, the main task is the negotiation of common language regulations between researchers and practitioners. The analysis of this entry as a constructive process and, more importantly, the analysis of failures in this process allow the researcher to reveal central processes of negotiation and developing routines in the field in an exemplary manner (e.g., with "real" clients).

Wolff (2004a) summarizes the problems of entering institutions as a research field as follows:

1 Research is always an intervention into a social system.
2 Research is a disruptive factor for the system to be studied to which it reacts defensively.
3 A mutual opacity exists between the research project and the social system to be researched.
4 To exchange a whole mass of information on entering the research field does not reduce the opacity. Rather, it leads to increasing complexity in the process of agreement and may lead to increased "immune reactions." On both sides, myths are produced, which are fed by increased exchange of information.
5 Instead of mutual understanding at the moment of entry, one should strive for agreement as a process.
6 Data protection is necessary, but may contribute to increased complexity in the process of agreement.
7 The field discovers itself when the research project enters the scene (e.g., the limits of a social system are perceived).
8 The research project cannot offer anything to the social system. At most, it can be functional. The researcher should take care not to make promises about the usefulness of the research for the social system.
9 The social system has no real reasons for rejecting the research.

These nine points within themselves include various reasons for a possible failure in the agreement about the purpose and necessity of the research. A research project represents an intrusion into the life of the institution to be studied. Research is a disturbance, and it disrupts routines, with no perceptible immediate or long-term payoff for the institution and its members. Research unsettles the institution with three implications: that the limitations of its own activities are to be disclosed; that the ulterior motives of the "research" are and remain unclear for the institution; and, finally, that there are no sound reasons for refusing research requests. Thus, if the field and its members for some reason want to prevent researchers from doing their study, the members have to invent reasons and pretexts and to sustain them. Here the part played by irrationality in the ongoing process of agreement is situated.

Finally, providing more information on the background, intentions, procedure, and results of the planned research does not necessarily lead to more clarity. Rather it may lead to more confusion and produce the opposite of understanding. That is, negotiating entry to an institution is apt to be less a problem of providing information than of how to establish a relationship. In this relationship, enough trust must be developed in the researchers as people, and, in their request, that the institution—despite all reservations—accepts being involved in the research.

In principle the discrepancies of interests and perspectives between researchers and the institutions under study cannot be removed. However, you can minimize them if you manage to develop enough trust on the side of the participants and institutions to forge a working alliance in which research becomes possible.

Access to Individuals

Once you have gained access to the field or the institution in general, you will face the problem of how to reach those people within it who are the most interesting (see Chapter 13) participants. For example, how can you recruit experienced and practicing counselors for participation in the study and not simply trainees without practical experience who are not yet allowed to work with the relevant cases, but have—for that reason—more time to participate in the research? How can you access the central figures in a setting and not merely the minor ones? Here again, processes of negotiation, strategies of reference in the sense of snowballing, and, above all, competencies in establishing relationships play a major part. Often the reservations in the field caused by certain methods are different in each case.

CASE STUDY 12.1

Reservations against Research Methods

These reservations against various methods may be demonstrated by examining the methods that I used to study the question of trust in counseling. In this study I employed interviews and conversation analyses. I approached the individual counselors with two requests: permission to interview them for one to two hours; and permission to record one or more consultations with clients (who had also agreed beforehand). After the counselors had agreed in general to participate in the study, some of them had reservations about being interviewed (time, fear of "indiscreet" questions), whereas they saw the recording of a counseling session as routine. Other counselors had no problem with being interviewed, but had considerable reservations about allowing someone to delve into their concrete work with clients. Precautions guaranteeing anonymity may dispel such reservations only up to a point. This example shows that various methods may produce different problems, suspicions, and fears in different people.

With regard to access to people in institutions and specific situations, you will face above all the problem of willingness. However, with regard to access to individuals, the problem of how to find them proves just as difficult. In the framework of studying individuals who cannot be approached as employees or clients in an institution or as being present in a particular setting, the main problem is how to find them. We can take the biographical study of the course and subjective evaluation of professional careers as an example. In such a study, it would be necessary to interview men living alone after retirement. The question then becomes how and where you find this kind of person. Strategies could be to use the media (advertisements in newspapers, announcements in radio programs) or to post notices in institutions (education centers, meeting points) that these people might frequent. Another route to selecting interviewees is for the researcher to snowball from one case to the next. In using this strategy, often friends of friends are chosen and thus you would look for people from your own broader environment. Hildenbrand warns of the problems linked to this strategy:

> While it is often assumed that access to the field would be facilitated by studying persons well known to the researcher and accordingly finding cases from one's own circle of acquaintances, exactly the opposite is true: the stranger the field, the more easily may researchers appear as strangers, whom the people in the study have something to tell which is new for the researcher. (1995, p. 258)

Strangeness and Familiarity

Now we come back to the metaphors mentioned at the beginning of this chapter as useful for describing the process of field access. The question of how to get access (to people, institutions, or fields) raises a problem, which can be expressed by the metaphor of the researcher as professional stranger (Agar 1980) (Box 12.1). The need to orient oneself in the field and to find one's way around it gives the researcher a glimpse into routines and self-evidence. These have been familiar to the members for a long time and have become routines and unquestioned and taken for granted by them. The individuals no longer reflect on such routines, because they are often no longer accessible for them. A potential way of gaining further knowledge is to take and (at least temporarily) maintain the perspective of an outsider and to take an attitude of doubt towards any sort of social self-evidence.

BOX 12.1

Roles in the Field

- Stranger
- Visitor
- Initiant
- Refused

The status of a stranger can be differentiated—depending on the strategy of the research—into the roles of the "visitor" and the "initiate." As a visitor you appear in the field—in the extreme case—only once for a single interview, but you will be able to receive knowledge through questioning the routines mentioned above. In the case of the initiate, it is precisely the process of giving up the outsider's perspective step by step in the course of the participant observation that is fruitful.

Above all, the detailed description of this process from the subjective perspective of the researcher can become a fruitful source of knowledge. You should see entering the field as a process of learning.

Certain activities in the field, however, remain hidden from the view of the researcher as a stranger. In the context of social groups, Adler and Adler mention "two sets of realities about their activities: one presented to outsiders and the other reserved for insiders" (1987, p. 21). Qualitative research is normally not simply interested in the exterior presentation of social groups. Rather, you want to become involved in a different world or subculture and first to understand it as far as possible from inside and from its own logic. A source of knowledge here is that you gradually take an insider's perspective—to understand the individual's viewpoint or the organizational principles of social groups from a member's perspective.

The limitations of this strategy of dialectics become relevant in Adler and Adler's (1987) example mentioned above—dealing drugs. Here, aspects of reality remain hidden and are not disclosed to you as a researcher, even if you are integrated in the field and the group as a person. These areas will only be accessible if researchers conceal their role as researchers from certain members in the field. Fears of passing on information and of negative sanctions by third parties for the people researched are here trenchantly revealed, as well as ethical problems in the contact with the people under study. But they play a part in all research. Issues are raised here of how to protect the trust and interests of the people researched, of data protection, and of how the researchers deal with their own aims.

CASE STUDY 12.2

Street Corner Society

The following example comes from one of the classical studies of qualitative research using participant observation and ethnography (see Chapter 20) in a field. William F. Whyte was one of the most influential researchers in the sociology of the 1940s. He lived for three and half years with the community he studied. His classic ethnographic study of a street gang in a major city in the eastern United States in the 1940s offers, on the basis of individual observations, personal notes, and other sources, a comprehensive picture of a dynamic local culture.

Through the mediation of a key figure, Whyte (1955) had gained access to a group of young, second-generation Italian migrants. Whyte gives detailed descriptions of how he negotiated his access to the area he studied and how he used his key person to find access and to get accepted by the social group. He also describes the need to keep a distance from the field to avoid becoming a member of the group and going native in the group and the field.

(Continued)

(Continued)

As a result of a two-year period of participant observation, he was able to obtain information about the motives, values, and life awareness, and also about the social organization, friendships, and loyalties, of this local culture. These were condensed in theoretically important statements such as:

> Whyte's gangs can be seen simply as an example of a temporary non-adjustment of young people. They withdraw from the norms of the parental home and at the same time see themselves as excluded from the predominant norms of American society. Deviant behavior is to be noted both towards the norms of the parental home and towards the prevailing norms of the country of immigration. Deviant behavior, even as far as criminality, may be seen as a transient faulty adaptation that bears within itself both the option of adaptation and of permanent non-adaptation. (Atteslander 1996, p. XIII)

This study represents a paradigmatic example of how a researcher sought and gained access to a community and studied its rituals and routines making up a special form of daily life.

Strategies of Gaining Access—Examples

In Chapter 2, I mentioned studies with hard-to-reach people as a particular reason for doing qualitative research. In this case, access is a real challenge, even if the problems researchers are confronted with can be transferred to other contexts of qualitative research. In our study with homeless adolescents, we tried to gain access to potential interviewees by hanging out at the meeting spots of the adolescents to become familiar with them and give them a chance to become familiar with the person of the interviewer. This was a time-consuming way of obtaining access, although the time could be used for observations of the field, the participants, their activities and communication as well. A second form of approach was to approach the adolescents with the support of people working in the field, in particular social workers offering food and counseling to the adolescents. And finally the strategy of snowballing—asking our way from one adolescent or interviewee to the next.

In our research in nursing homes, we had to contact the various levels of directors (of the whole institution, of the single ward, etc.) to get permission to approach people in the field. Then we had to get in touch with the nurses both to ask them to take part in the study themselves and to support us in approaching the residents. For the latter, in many cases we had to ask their relatives to consent to the residents' participation in the study.

In summary, researchers face the problem of negotiating proximity and distance in relation to the person(s) studied. The problems of disclosure, transparency, and negotiation of mutual expectations, aims, and interest also pertain. Finally, you will have to make the decision between adopting the perspective of either an insider or an outsider with regard to the object of the research. Being an insider or outsider with regard to the field of research may be analyzed in terms of the strangeness and familiarity of the researcher. Where you locate yourself as researcher in this area of conflict between strangeness and familiarity will determine in continuation of the research which concrete methods are chosen and also which part of the field under study will be accessible and inaccessible for your research. A specific role is played by the partly unconscious fears that prevent the researcher from meddling in a certain field. For researchers, the form of access permitted by the field, and their personality, determine how instructive descriptions of the cases will be and how far the knowledge obtained remains limited to confirming what was known in advance.

Checklist for Entering the Field

For assessing the access you gained for your qualitative project, the questions in the checklist below might prove helpful:

1 Do the people you contacted know what you expect from them?
2 Have you obtained permissions from all the institutions that should be asked (e.g., the hospital in which you want to do your research)?
3 Have you involved the relevant levels in the hierarchy?
4 Have you asked all the persons who have to give you access (e.g., not only the children you want to interview, but also their parents)?
5 Have you taken care to avoid making any promises you cannot keep (e.g., about any immediate practical use of your research for the field)?

---KEY POINTS---

- Entering the field entails more than just being there: it involves a complex process of locating yourself and being located in the field.
- In particular, the process entails taking, and being allocated to, a role in the field.
- In institutions, there are often no good reasons to reject research in general. Therefore, representatives of institutions introduce reasons and use them as a pretext for rejecting a research project if they do not wish it to proceed. This makes negotiations more complex for the researcher.
- When researching individuals, you should try to include people you do not know personally in order to receive fruitful insights.

---Exercise 12.1---

1 Choose a study with qualitative methods from the literature (e.g., Reeves 2010). Try to identify from the text which problems of access the researcher mentions. In addition, try to imagine which problems arose when the researcher attempted to enter the field.
2 Think about your own study and plan how to access the field you want to study. From whom do you have to seek permission? What is the best way to approach those people you want to include in your study?

The following texts deal with concrete problems and examples of entering a field and taking a role and position in it. Schütz's paper is a good sociological description of the qualities of being a stranger, which allows insights into what is familiar to members of a field:

Adler, P.A. and Adler, P. (1987) *Membership Roles in Field Research*. Beverly Hills, CA: Sage.

Harrington, B. (2003) "The Social Psychology of Access in Ethnographic Research," *Journal of Contemporary Ethnography*, 32: 592–625.

Schütz, A. (1962) "The Stranger," in A. Schütz, *Collected Papers*, Vol. II. Den Haag: Nijhoff. pp. 91–105.

Wolff, S. (2004a) "Ways into the Field and their Variants," in U. Flick, E.v. Kardorff and I. Steinke (eds.), A *Companion to Qualitative Research*. London: Sage. pp. 195–202.

13
Sampling

CONTENTS

CHAPTER OBJECTIVES

This chapter is designed to help you

- understand the role and importance of sampling in qualitative research;
- identify the differences between theoretical and statistical sampling;
- distinguish various forms of sampling in qualitative research;
- comprehend how a case is constituted in qualitative research.

Frameworks of Sampling for Data Collection

The general issue of sampling is how to select cases or examples from a wider population (which might be too big to be studied completely) so that the research in the end can make statements that apply not just to the individual participant(s) of a study. For example, researchers may interview an individual or several individuals suffering from a specific chronic disease. The results in the end should not only elucidate the situation of the individual participant(s), but also refer more generally to the situations of patients with this disease. Thus the selection of the individuals included in the research should take that relation (sample to wider population) into account.

Sampling can be oriented on either formal or substantial criteria. Formal criteria (1) can be driven by the principle of representativeness of a sample for the population. This principle forms the background of a study based on random sampling (where every member of the population has the same chance to be a member of the sample, so that referring the findings from the sample to the population is no problem). This principle is applied in quantitative studies with statistical analyses of the data. In this kind of research, the single individuals and their features are not relevant for sampling decisions. Individuals become members of the sample because they were selected as a result of applying a random technique. This can be labeled as statistical sampling. Qualitative research normally does not apply such a formalized sampling routine. Instead, substantial criteria (2) are applied. In many of the sampling strategies discussed in this chapter (such as theoretical or purposive sampling), specific features of an individual (or a group) are relevant for deciding to include this individual in the sample.

This distinction between formal and substantive criteria should give an orientation in understanding the sampling strategies used in qualitative research (and how they differ from those in quantitative research). A second distinction refers to the point in the research process when sampling decisions about cases or material for data collection are taken. Here we find either sampling integrated in the process of collecting and analyzing data (see Chapter 10 and Figure 10.1 for this) and following a step-by-step logic, or strategies in which sampling is done according to criteria defined before data collection begins. Sampling beforehand is outlined in some detail below.

Defining the Sample Structure Beforehand
Using Defined Sampling Dimensions

In qualitative research as well, the sample structure can be organized around sampling dimensions that have been defined beforehand. Sampling criteria then start from an idea of the researched object's typicality and distribution. This should be represented in the sample of the material, which is studied (i.e., collected and analyzed) in a way that allows one to draw inferences from the relations in the object. This sampling strategy is similar to the logic of statistical sampling in which material is collected according to certain (e.g., demographic) criteria. In qualitative research with such samples defined beforehand, for example, a sample is drawn that is homogeneous in age or social situation (women with a certain profession at a specific biographical stage) or that represents a certain distribution of such criteria in the population. These criteria will have been developed independently of the concrete material analyzed and before its collection and analysis, as the following examples show.

Sampling with Social Groups Defined in Advance

In my study on the social representation of technological change in everyday life, I took three starting points. One was that the perceptions and evaluations of technological change in everyday life are dependent upon the profession of the interviewee. The second was that they depend on gender as well, and the third that they are influenced by cultural and political contexts.

In order to take these factors into account, I defined several dimensions of the sample. The professions of information engineers (as developers of technology), social scientists (as professional users of technology), and teachers in human disciplines (as everyday users of technology) should be represented in the sample by cases with a certain minimum of professional experience. Male and female persons should be integrated. I took the different cultural backgrounds into account by selecting cases from the contexts of West Germany, East Germany, and France. This led to a sample structure of nine fields (Table 13.1), which I filled as evenly as possible with cases representing each group. The number of cases per field depended on the resources (how many interviews could be conducted, transcribed, and interpreted in the time available?) and on the goals of my study (what do the individual cases or the totality of the cases stand for?).

This example shows how you can work with comparative groups in qualitative research that have been defined in advance, not during the research process or the sampling process.

Sampling cases for data collection is oriented towards filling the cells of the sample structure (found in Table 13.1) as evenly as possible or towards filling all cells sufficiently. Inside the groups or fields, theoretical sampling (see below) may be used in the decision on which case to integrate next.

TABLE 13.1 Example of a Sampling Structure with Dimensions Given in Advance

	Context and gender						
	West Germany		East Germany		France		
Profession	Female	Male	Female	Male	Female	Male	Total
Information engineers							
Social scientists							
Teachers							
Total							

Complete Collection

Gerhardt, in her study already mentioned in Chapter 9, applied an alternative method of sampling. She used the strategy of complete collection:

> In order to learn more about events and courses of patients' careers in chronic renal failure, we decided to do a complete collection of all patients (male, married, 30 to 50 years at the beginning of the treatment) of the five major hospitals (renal units) serving the south-east of Britain. (1986, p. 67)

The sampling is limited in advance by certain criteria: a specific disease, a specific age, a specific region, a limited period, and a particular marital status characterize the relevant cases. These criteria delimit the totality of possible cases in such a way that all the cases may be integrated in the study. But here, as well, sampling is carried out because virtual cases which do not meet one or more of these criteria are excluded in advance. It is possible to use such methods of sampling particularly in regional studies.

Limitations of the Method

In this strategy, the structure of the groups taken into account is defined before data collection. This restricts the range variation in the possible comparison. At least on this level, there will be no real new findings. If the aim of your study is the development of theory, this form of sampling restricts the developmental space of the theory in an essential dimension. Thus this procedure is suitable for further analyzing, differentiating, and perhaps testing assumptions about common features and differences between specific groups.

Defining the Sample Structure Step by Step

Strategies of sampling step by step are often based on the theoretical sampling developed by Glaser and Strauss (1967). Decisions about choosing and putting together empirical material (cases, groups, institutions, etc.) are made in the process of collecting and interpreting data. Glaser and Strauss describe this strategy as follows:

> Theoretical sampling is the process of data collection for generating theory whereby the analyst jointly collects, codes, and analyzes his data and decides what data to collect next and where to find them, in order to develop his theory as it emerges. This process of data collection is controlled by the emerging theory. (1967, p. 45)

Sampling decisions in theoretical sampling may start from either of two levels: they may be made on the level of the groups to be compared; or they may directly focus on specific persons. In both cases, the sampling of concrete individuals, groups, or fields is not based on the usual criteria and techniques of statistical sampling. You would employ neither random sampling nor stratification to make a sample representative. Rather, you would select individuals, groups, and so on according to their (expected) level of new insights for the developing theory in relation to the state of theory elaboration so far. Sampling decisions aim at the material that promises the greatest insights, viewed in the light of the material already used, and the knowledge drawn from it. The main questions for selecting data are: "*What* groups or subgroups does one turn to *next* in data collection? And for *what* theoretical purpose? … The possibilities of multiple comparisons are infinite, and so groups must be chosen according to theoretical criteria" (Glaser and Strauss 1967, p. 47).

Given the theoretically unlimited possibilities of integrating further persons, groups, cases, and so on, it is necessary to define the criteria for a well-founded limitation of the sampling. These criteria are defined here in relation to the theory. The theory developing from the empirical material is the point of reference. Examples of such criteria are how promising the next case is and how relevant it might be for developing the theory.

An example of applying this form of sampling is found in Glaser and Strauss's (1965a) study on awareness of dying in hospitals. In this study, the authors undertook participant observation in different hospitals in order to develop a theory about how dying in hospital is organized as a social process (see also Chapter 25 for more details). The memo in the following case study describes the decision and sampling process.

CASE STUDY 13.2

Example of Theoretical Sampling

The pioneers of grounded theory research, Glaser and Strauss, developed theoretical sampling during their research in medical sociology in the 1960s. They describe in the following passage how they proceeded in theoretical sampling:

> Visits to the various medical services were scheduled as follows. I wished first to look at services that minimized patient awareness (and so first looked at a premature baby service and then at a neurosurgical service where patients were frequently comatose). Next I wished to look at the dying in a situation where expectancy of staff and often of patients was great and dying was quick, so I observed on an Intensive Care Unit. Then I wished to observe on a service where staff expectations of terminality were great but where the patient's might or might not be, and where dying tended to be slow. So I looked next at a cancer service. I wished then to look at conditions where death was unexpected and rapid, and so looked at an emergency service. While we were looking at some different types of services, we also observed the above types of services at other types of hospitals. So our scheduling of types of service was directed by a general conceptual scheme—which included hypotheses about awareness, expectedness, and rate of dying—as well as

(Continued)

(Continued)

> by a developing conceptual structure including matters not at first envisioned. Sometimes we returned to services after the initial two or three or four weeks of continuous observation, in order to check upon items which needed checking or had been missed in the initial period. (Glaser and Strauss 1967, p. 59)

This example is instructive as it shows how, in constructing their sample, the researchers went step by step in the contact with the field while they collected their data.

A second question, as crucial as the first, is how to decide when to stop integrating further cases. Glaser and Strauss suggest the criterion of theoretical saturation (of a category etc.): "The criterion for judging when to stop sampling the different groups pertinent to a category is the category's theoretical saturation. Saturation means that no additional data are being found whereby the sociologist can develop properties of the category" (1967, p. 61; see also Chapter 25). Sampling and integrating further material is finished when the "theoretical saturation" of a category or group of cases has been reached (i.e., nothing new emerges any more).

For highlighting the specific features of theoretical sampling in distinction from statistical sampling (see the beginning of this chapter), Table 13.2 compares both approaches for some essential differences. As this comparison shows, in statistical sampling much more is defined in advance than in theoretical sampling, in which researchers will know what characterizes the population they study only after the sampling—and thus the research—has been completed. This sometimes makes it difficult to calculate in advance how many cases you need (see the expert discussion on this point in Baker and Edwards 2012).

TABLE 13.2   Theoretical versus Statistical Sampling

Theoretical sampling	Statistical sampling
Extension of the basic population is not known in advance	Extension of the basic population is known in advance
Features of the basic population are not known in advance	Distribution of features in the basic population can be estimated
Repeated drawing of sampling elements with criteria to be defined again in each step	One-shot drawing of a sample following a plan defined in advance
Sample size is not defined in advance	Sample size is defined in advance
Sampling is finished when theoretical saturation has been reached	Sampling is finished when the whole sample has been studied

Source: Wiedemann (1995, p. 441)

In Case Study 13.2, the procedure of theoretical sampling was described for a study in which participant observation (see Chapter 20) was applied in several institutions. In the example in Case Study 13.3, this step-by-step approach to sampling is used for selecting interview partners in several institutional contexts.

Step-by-Step Integration of Groups and Cases

In my study of the role of trust in therapy and counseling, I included cases coming from specific professional groups, institutions, and fields of work. I selected them step by step in order to fill in the blanks in the database that became clear according to the successive interpretation of the data incorporated at each stage. First, I collected and compared cases from two different fields of work (prison versus therapy in private practice). After that I integrated a third field of work (socio-psychiatric services) to increase the meaningfulness of the comparisons on this level.

When I interpreted the collected material, sampling on a further dimension promised additional insights. I extended the range of professions in the study up to that point (psychologists and social workers) by a third one (physicians) to further elaborate the differences of viewpoints in one field of work (socio-psychiatric services).

Finally, it became clear that the epistemological potential of this field was so big that it seemed less instructive for me to contrast this field with other fields than to systematically compare different institutions within this field. Therefore, I integrated further cases from other socio-psychiatric services (see Table 13.3, in which the sequence and order of the decisions in the selection are indicated by the letters A to C).

TABLE 13.3 Example of a Sample Structure Resulting from the Process

	Prison	Private practice	Socio-psychiatric services
Psychologists	A	A	B
Social workers	A	A	B
Physicians			C

This example illustrates how you can develop a sample and a sample structure step by step in the field while collecting your data.

In the end, you can see that the use of this method leads to a structured sample, as do the use of statistical sampling in quantitative research or sampling with sampling dimensions defined beforehand in qualitative research. However, you will not define the structure of the sample here before you collect and analyze your data. You will develop it step by step while you collect data and analyze them, and complete it by new dimensions or limited to certain dimensions and fields.

Sampling Step by Step as a General Principle

If we compare different conceptions of qualitative research in this respect, we can see that this principle of selecting cases and material has also been applied beyond Glaser and Strauss. The basic principle of theoretical sampling is to select cases or case groups according to concrete criteria concerning their substantial criteria instead of using formal methodological criteria. Sampling proceeds according to the *relevance* of cases, rather than their representativeness.

This principle is also characteristic of related strategies of collecting data in qualitative research.

On the one hand, parallels can be drawn with the concept of "data triangulation" in Denzin (1989b), which refers to the integration of various data sources, differentiated by time, place, and person (see Chapter 14). Denzin suggests studying "the same phenomenon" at different times and places and with different persons. He also claims to have applied the strategy of theoretical sampling in his own way as a purposive and systematic selection and integration of persons and groups of persons, and temporal and local settings. The extension of the sampling procedure to temporal and local settings is an advantage of the system of access in Denzin's method compared to that of Glaser and Strauss. In the example just mentioned, I took this idea into account by purposively integrating different institutions (as local settings) and professions and by using different sorts of data.

Analytic induction has been proposed by Znaniecki (1934) (see Chapter 29) as a way of making concrete and further developing theoretical sampling. But here attention is focused less on the question of which cases to integrate into the study in general. Rather, this concept starts from developing a theory (pattern, model, and so on) at a given moment and state and then specifically looking for and analyzing deviant cases (or even case groups). It is helpful here to contrast theoretical and analytic sampling. Theoretical sampling aims mainly to enrich the developing theory; analytic induction is concerned with securing it by analyzing or integrating deviant cases. Similarly, theoretical sampling wants to control the process of selecting data by the emerging theory; analytic induction uses the deviant case to control the developing theory. The deviant case here is a complement to the criterion of theoretical saturation. This criterion remains rather indeterminate but is used for continuing and assessing the collection of data. In the example mentioned above, cases were minimally and maximally contrasted in a purposeful way instead of applying such strategies starting from deviant cases (see Chapter 29).

This brief comparison of different conceptions of qualitative research demonstrates that theoretical sampling is the genuine and typical form of selecting material in qualitative research. This assumption may be supported by reference to Kleining's (1982) idea of a typology of social science methods. According to this idea, all research methods have the same source in everyday techniques: qualitative methods are the first and quantitative methods are the second level of abstraction from these everyday techniques. If this is applied analogously to strategies for selecting empirical material, theoretical sampling (and basically related strategies as mentioned before) is the more concrete strategy and is closer to everyday life. Criteria of sampling like being representative of a population and so on are the second level of abstraction.

This analogy of levels of abstraction may support the thesis that (1) theoretical sampling is the more appropriate sampling strategy in qualitative research, whereas (2) formal sampling procedures remain oriented to the logic of quantitative research. To what extent the latter should be imported into qualitative research has to be checked in every case. Here we can draw parallels with the discussion about the appropriateness of quality indicators (see Chapter 29).

Purposive Sampling

Step-by-step selection is not merely the original principle of sampling in various traditional approaches in qualitative research. More recent discussions, which describe strategies for how to proceed with purposive sampling by selecting cases and empirical material, continue to employ the principle. In the framework of evaluation research, Patton (2002) contrasts random sampling in general with purposive sampling and makes some concrete suggestions, which I illustrate with examples of sampling interviewees according to these suggestions:

1 One suggestion is to integrate purposively *extreme* or deviant cases. In order to study the functioning of a reform program, particularly successful examples of realizing it are chosen and analyzed. Or cases of failure in the program are selected and analyzed for the reasons for this failure. Here the field under study is disclosed from its extremities to arrive at an understanding of the field as a whole. In the case of interviews in a study on changes in a professional field, for example, you may sample interviewees with the longest experience in the field and those who have just recently arrived to work there.

2 Another suggestion is to select particularly *typical* cases (i.e., those cases in which success and failure are particularly typical for the average or the majority of the cases). Here the field is disclosed from inside and from its center. To return to our example, here you would try to find out how long people typically work in this field, and you would try to find interviewees meeting this criterion.

3 A further suggestion aims at the *maximal variation* in the sample—to integrate only a few cases, but those which are as different as possible, to disclose the range of variation and differentiation in the field. In our example, you would look for people with very different periods of being part of the field, try to vary the professional backgrounds, and gender if possible, or according to other criteria relevant for your study.

4 Additionally, cases may be selected according to the *intensity* with which the interesting features, processes, experiences, and so on are given or assumed in them. Either cases with the greatest intensity are chosen or cases with different intensities are systematically integrated and compared. In our example you could try to identify those people who identify themselves most intensely with their work and those who do this work just as a job (as interns, for example).

5 The selection of *critical cases* aims at those cases in which the relations to be studied become especially clear (e.g., in the opinion of experts in the field) or which are particularly important for the functioning of a program to be evaluated. Here in our example you would ask experts at which institutions you should do your interviews.

6 It may be appropriate to select a politically important or *sensitive case* in order to present positive findings in evaluation most effectively, which is an argument for integrating them. However, where these may endanger the program as a whole, due to their explosive force, they should rather be excluded. In our example you would try to find out which interviewee or institution represents such a sensitive case and then decide whether or not to do this interview.

7 Finally, Patton mentions the criterion of *convenience*, which refers to the selection of those cases that are the easiest to access under given conditions. This may simply be to reduce the effort. However, from time to time it may be the only way to do an evaluation with limited resources of time and people. That means that you give up specific criteria for

choosing interviewees in a field but do your interviews with those people ready to help you out. This is not the most valuable strategy of finding research participants but sometimes the only one that works. But you should turn to convenience sampling only after other more criterion-oriented strategies did not work.

In the end, it depends on these strategies of selection and how you can generalize your results. This may be greatest in random sampling, whereas in the strategy of least effort, mentioned last, it will be most restricted. However, it must be noted that generalization is not in every case the goal of a qualitative study, whereas the problem of access may be one of the crucial barriers.

Correspondingly, Morse (1998, p. 73) defines several general criteria for a "good informant." These may serve more generally as criteria for selecting meaningful cases (especially for interviewees). They should have the necessary knowledge and experience of the issue or object at their disposal for answering the questions in the interview or—in observational studies—for performing the actions of interest. They should also have the capability to reflect and articulate, should have time to be asked (or observed), and should be ready to participate in the study. If all these conditions are fulfilled, this case is most likely to be integrated into the study.

Integrating such cases is characterized by Morse as *primary selection*, which she contrasts with *secondary selection*. The latter refers to those cases that do not fulfill all the criteria previously mentioned (particularly of knowledge and experience), but are willing to give their time for an interview. Morse suggests that one should not invest too many resources in these cases (e.g., for transcription or interpretation). Rather, one should work with them further only if it is clear that there really are not enough cases of the primary selection to be found.

Box 13.1 summarizes the sampling strategies discussed.

BOX 13.1

Sampling Strategies in Qualitative Research

- Definition of sampling dimensions beforehand
- Complete collection
- Theoretical sampling
- Extreme case sampling
- Typical case sampling
- Maximal variation sampling
- Intensity sampling
- Critical case sampling
- Sensitive case sampling
- Convenience sampling
- Primary selection
- Secondary selection

RESEARCH DESIGN

Aims of Sampling: Width or Depth

What is decisive when you choose one of the sampling strategies just outlined, and for your success in putting together the sample as a whole, is whether it is rich in relevant information. Sampling decisions always fluctuate between the aims of covering as wide a field as possible and of doing analyses which are as deep as possible. The former strategy seeks to represent the field in its diversity by using as many different cases as possible in order to be able to present evidence on the distribution of ways of seeing or experiencing certain things. The latter strategy seeks to further permeate the field and its structure by concentrating on single examples or certain sectors of the field.

Given that resources (people, money, time, etc.) are limited, you should see these aims as alternatives rather than projects to combine. In the example mentioned above, the decision to deal more intensively with one type of institution (socio-psychiatric services), and (due to the limitation in resources) not to collect or analyze any further data in the other institutions, resulted from weighing width (to study trust in counseling in as many different forms of institutions) against depth (to proceed with the analyses in one type of institution as far as possible).

Case Constitution in the Sample

In this context, the question arises of what is the case that is considered in a sample and, more concretely, what this case represents. In my studies of trust in counseling (see Case Study 13.3 above and Case Study 12.1 in Chapter 12) and technological change in everyday life (see Case Study 13.1 above and Case Study 8.1 in Chapter 8), I treated the *case as a case*: sampling as well as collecting and interpreting data proceeded as a sequence of case studies. For the constitution of the sample in the end, each case was representative in five respects:

1 The case represents itself. According to Hildenbrand, the "single case dialectically can be understood as an individualized universal" (1987, p. 161). Thus, the single case is initially seen as the result of specific individual socialization against a general background (e.g., as physician or psychologist with a specific individual biography against the background of the changes in psychiatry and in the understanding of psychiatric disorders in the 1970s and 1980s). This also applies to the socialization of an information engineer against the background of the changes in information science and in the cultural context of each case. This socialization has led to different, subjective opinions, attitudes, and viewpoints, which can be found in the actual interview situation.

2 In order to find out what the "individualized universal" here meant in concrete terms, it proved to be necessary to also conceptualize the case as follows. The case represents a specific institutional context in which the individual acts and which he or she also has to represent to others. Thus the viewpoints in subjective theories on trust in counseling are influenced by the fact that the case (e.g., as doctor or social worker) orients his or her practices and perceptions to the goals of the institution of "socio-psychiatric services." Or he or she may even transform these viewpoints into activities with clients or statements in the interview, perhaps in critically dealing with these goals.

3 The case represents a specific type of professionalization (as doctor, psychologist, social worker, information engineer, etc.), which he or she has attained and which is represented in his or her concepts and ways of acting. Thus despite the existence of teamwork and co-operation in the institution, it was possible to identify differences in the ways professionals from the same socio-psychiatric services presented clients, disorders, and starting points for treating them.

4 The case represents a developed subjectivity as a result of acquiring certain stocks of knowledge and of evolving specific ways of acting and perceiving.

5 The case represents an interactively made and make-able context of activity (e.g., counseling, developing technology).

Sampling decisions cannot be made in isolation. There is no decision or strategy which is right per se. The appropriateness of the structure and contents of the sample, and thus the appropriateness of the strategy chosen for obtaining both, can be assessed only with respect to the research question of the study: which and how many cases are necessary to answer the questions of the study? The appropriateness of the selected sample can be assessed in terms of the degree of possible generalization that is striven for. It may be difficult to make generally valid statements based only on a single case study. However, it is also difficult to give deep descriptions and explanations of a case which was found by applying the principle of random sampling. Sampling strategies describe ways of disclosing a field. This can start from extreme, negative, critical, or deviant cases and thus from the extremities of the field. It may be disclosed from the inside, starting from particularly typical or developed cases. It can be tapped by starting from its supposed structure—by integrating cases as different as possible in their variation. The structure of the sample may be defined in advance and filled in through collecting data, or it may be developed and further differentiated step by step during selection, collection, and interpretation of material. Here, in addition, the research question and the degree of generalization one is seeking should determine the decision between defining in advance and developing the sample step by step.

Sampling Decisions in the Research Process

The issue of sampling will become relevant at different stages in the research process (Table 13.4). In an interview study, for example, sampling is connected to the decision about which persons you will interview (case sampling) and from which groups these should come (sampling groups of cases). Furthermore, it is related to the decision about which of the interviews should be treated further—that is, transcribed and analyzed (material sampling). During interpretation of the data, the question again arises when you decide which parts of a text you should select for interpretation in general or for particular detailed interpretations (sampling within the material). Finally, it arises when presenting the findings: which cases or parts of text best demonstrate your findings (presentational sampling)?

Table 13.4 illustrates these sampling decisions for interviews and for observations. The background for these illustrations is that sampling for interviews focuses on the persons you want to work with, whereas in observations it is rather situations you will look for as "material units".

TABLE 13.4 Sampling Decisions in the Research Process

Stage in research	Sampling decisions	Example for interviews	Example for observation
While collecting data	Case sampling Sampling groups of cases	Selecting an interviewee Selecting a professional group whose members are to be interviewed	Selecting a situation to observe Selecting types of situations to observe
While interpreting data	Material sampling Sampling within the material	Selecting an interview to begin the analysis with Selecting statements or excerpts from the interview(s) to analyze (in more detail)	Selecting an observation to begin the analysis with Selecting excerpts from protocols to analyze (in more detail)
While presenting the findings	Presentational sampling	Selecting statements and interpretations for illustrating or evidence	Selecting observations and interpretations for illustrating or evidence

In research designs using definitions of the sample structure beforehand, sampling decisions will be taken with a view to selecting cases or groups of cases. In complete collection, the exclusion of interviews already done will be less likely in that data collection and analysis are aimed at keeping and integrating all cases available in the sample. Thus, while the sampling *of* materials is less relevant, other questions arise, questions concerning: (1) sampling *in* the material (e.g., which parts of the interview are interpreted more intensely, which cases are contrasted?); and (2) sampling *in* presentation are as relevant here as in step-by-step definition of the sampling structure. When the sample structure is developed step by step in the research process, this approach applies mainly to sampling *of* materials, but also to sampling *in* the material which is collected and analyzed in this process. What is selected for a deeper interpretation and for presenting the findings will be decided in the progress of the research.

The characteristics of qualitative research mentioned in Chapter 7 also apply to sampling strategies. Implicit in the selection made in sampling decisions is a specific approach to understanding the field and the selected cases. In a different strategy of selection, the understanding would be different in its results. As sampling decisions start from integrating concrete cases, the origin of reconstructing cases is concretely realized. In sampling decisions, the reality under study is constructed in a specific way: certain parts and aspects are highlighted and others are phased out. Sampling decisions determine substantially what becomes empirical material in the form of text, and what is taken from available texts concretely and how it is used.

Sampling Checklist

For assessing your literature review for an empirical project in social research, the questions in the checklist below might be helpful:

1 Does your sampling follow one of the methods outlined in this chapter?
2 Is there a systematic approach on which it is based?
3 Have you included the relevant cases (e.g., people, groups, institutions) you need for research?
4 If you are applying convenience sampling, have you tried a more systematic way before?
5 Which dimensions are covered by your sample?
6 What was your reason for stopping sampling or limiting the sample to a concrete number of cases?

KEY POINTS

- In qualitative research, sampling is a very important step.
- Sampling decisions (who or which group next?) are often taken during *and* as a result of data collection and analysis.
- Sampling decisions in qualitative research are often taken on a substantive level rather than on a formal level: they may be based on purposeful decisions for a specific case rather than random sampling.
- In sampling, you will construct the cases you study in your research.

Exercise 13.1

1 Take a qualitative study from the literature (e.g., Coltart and Henwood 2012). First (a) describe how the authors did their sampling and then (b) define the rationale or plan visible in the presentation of the study.
2 Consider your own research. How would you plan your sampling? How would you proceed?
3 What are the limitations of the alternatives of sampling discussed in this chapter?
4 After you have read Box 13.1, review the discussion in the chapter, asking yourself: (a) what is the meaning of each concept; and (b) what relationships between these concepts have been identified?

Further Reading

The first text below is the classic reading on theoretical sampling. The other texts offer recent concepts for refining strategies of sampling in qualitative research. The last paper gives an overview about discussion concerning sample size in interviewing.

Glaser, B.G. and Strauss, A.L. (1967) *The Discovery of Grounded Theory: Strategies for Qualitative Research*. Chicago, IL: Aldine.
Merkens, H. (2004) "Selection Procedures, Sampling, Case Construction," in U. Flick, E.v. Kardorff and I. Steinke (eds.), *A Companion to Qualitative Research*. London: Sage. pp. 165–171.

Morse, J.M. (1998) "Designing Funded Qualitative Research," in N. Denzin and Y.S. Lincoln (eds.), *Strategies of Qualitative Research*. London: Sage. pp. 56–85.

Patton, M.Q. (2002) *Qualitative Research and Evaluation Methods* (3rd edn). London: Sage.

Gobo, G. (2004) "Sampling, Representativeness and Generalizability," in C. Seale, G. Gobo, J.F. Gubrium and D. Silverman (eds.), *Qualitative Research Practice*. London: Sage. pp. 435–456.

Rapley, T. (2014) "Sampling Strategies," in U. Flick (ed.), *The SAGE Handbook of Qualitative Data Analysis*. London: Sage. pp. 49–63.

Baker, S.E. and Edwards, R. (2012) "How Many Qualitative Interviews is Enough?", Discussion Paper, National Center of Research Methods: http://eprints.ncrm.ac.uk/2273/.

14
Triangulation

┌─ CHAPTER OBJECTIVES ───┐

This chapter is designed to help you

- develop an overview of the use of triangulation in qualitative research;
- see triangulation as an issue in designing qualitative research and not just an issue of quality;
- appreciate when triangulation is a useful strategy;
- know how to plan triangulation in qualitative research;
- develop an awareness of possible stumbling blocks in using triangulation.

In the preceding chapters, I introduced you to issues of how to design qualitative research and covered steps such as planning the research process, sampling, and access to the field. In this chapter I want to extend this discussion by considering a more complex way of designing qualitative research. The number of research issues that require more than one methodological approach is increasing. This does not necessarily mean combining qualitative and quantitative research (or mixed methods) as outlined in Chapter 3; it may instead refer to combining several qualitative methods. For some time now, such an approach has been discussed by using the concept of triangulation. Below I spell out this concept in more detail as a way of designing qualitative research.

Types and Definition of Triangulation

Triangulation refers to the combination of different methods, study groups, local and temporal settings, and different theoretical perspectives in dealing with a phenomenon. Its applications include (1) formalizing the relation between qualitative and quantitative research (see Chapter 3), (2) strengthening the quality of qualitative research (see Chapter 29), and (3) designing and conducting qualitative research in an appropriate way.

Types of Triangulation

The concept of triangulation was taken up by Denzin in the 1970s. He developed a more systematic approach of triangulation for social research. Denzin distinguished four types of triangulation (1989b, pp. 237–241). The first is *data triangulation*, which refers to the use of different data sources (as opposed to the use of different methods for producing data). As "subtypes of data triangulation," Denzin makes a distinction between (1) time, (2) space, and (3) persons; he recommends studying phenomena at different dates and places and from different persons. Thus he comes close to Glaser and Strauss's strategy of theoretical sampling. In both cases, the starting point is purposively and systematically to involve persons, study groups, and local and temporal settings in the study.

As the second type of triangulation, Denzin names *investigator triangulation*. Different observers or interviewers are employed to detect or minimize biases resulting from the researcher as a person. This does not mean a simple division of labor or delegation of routine activities to assistants, but rather a systematic comparison of different researchers' influences on the issue and the results of the research.

Theory triangulation is the third type in Denzin's systematology. The starting point is "approaching data with multiple perspectives and hypotheses in mind. … Various theoretical points of view could be placed side by side to assess their utility and power" (1989b, pp. 239–240). However, the purpose of the exercise is to extend the possibilities for producing knowledge.

As the fourth type, Denzin mentions *methodological triangulation*. Here again, two subtypes should be differentiated: within-method and between-method triangulation. A more traditional example of the first strategy outside qualitative research is to use different subscales for measuring an item in a questionnaire; an example of the second is to combine the questionnaire with a semi-structured interview.

Triangulation was first conceptualized as a strategy for validating results obtained with the individual methods. The focus, however, has shifted increasingly towards further enriching and completing knowledge and towards transgressing the (always limited) epistemological potential of the individual method. Thus Denzin has emphasized in the meantime that the "triangulation of method, investigator, theory, and data remains the soundest strategy of theory construction" (1989b, p. 236).

An extension of this approach is the systematic triangulation of several theoretical perspectives (Flick 1992) linked to the various qualitative methods. For example, in a study of, say, trust in counseling, a researcher might conduct interviews for reconstructing a subjective theory and then employ conversation analysis to study how the subjective theory is mobilized and trust is invoked during counseling conversations. Thus the orientation to the subject's point of view is linked to the perspective of producing social realities (see Chapter 7).

Triangulation may be used as an approach for further grounding the knowledge obtained with qualitative methods. Grounding here is not a matter of confirming results by using a second methodological approach. Triangulation is less a strategy for validating results and procedures than an alternative to validation (see Denzin and Lincoln 2000b; Flick 1992; 2004a; 2007b). Using triangulation allows systematically extending the possibilities of knowledge production by using a second methodological approach. This extension increases scope, depth, and consistency in methodological proceedings and thus puts findings on a more solid foundation.

Definition of Triangulation

If we want to use triangulation in a more comprehensive way in qualitative research, the definition (see also Flick 2007b, p. 41) in Box 14.1 provides a foundation.

BOX 14.1

Definition of Triangulation

Triangulation means that researchers take different perspectives on an issue under study or—more generally speaking—in answering research questions. These perspectives can be substantiated by using several methods and/or in several theoretical approaches. They are, or should be, linked. Furthermore, triangulation refers to combining different sorts of data on the background of the theoretical perspectives, which are applied to the data. As far as possible, these perspectives should be treated and applied on an equal footing and in an equally consequent way. At the same time, triangulation (of different methods or data sorts) should allow a principal surplus of knowledge. For example, triangulation should produce knowledge on different levels, which means insights that go beyond the knowledge made possible by one approach and thus contribute to promoting quality in research.

Triangulation Step by Step

Step 1: Deciding When and Why to Use Triangulation

Although triangulation can be very fruitful, there is no need to undertake triangulation in every qualitative study. One should certainly avoid any temptation to use the term "triangulation" tactically—that is, merely to make funding easier to obtain or to gain acceptance for publication in a journal. As in any other approach, you should first clarify why you want to use triangulation in your study and what the expected benefit will be. As in the decision for specific methods, you should reflect on the indication (see Chapter 29) of triangulation in your specific research. The points of reference for deciding to use triangulation should be the research question and the field or participants of your study.

The following questions can be used to guide your decisions on the use of triangulation, especially concerning the employment of more than one method of data collection:

1 Does my issue under study require several methodological approaches?
2 Does my research question focus on a number of aspects or levels of my issue?
3 Do I have several theoretical perspectives on my issue?
4 Are there different levels of information I need to collect for understanding my issue under study?
5 Does the time frame for my study and my resources in general allow triangulation to be used?
6 Can I expect my participants to be exposed to several methods (e.g., being observed and interviewed) or would this overly challenge them?

Before answering such questions in detail, consider the following case study. It will be referred to in our subsequent discussion.

---CASE STUDY 14.1---

Chronic Illness of Homeless Adolescents

This study is outlined in another chapter (see Case Study 20.4). It concerns the health concepts and practices of adolescents in a large city in Germany. In a first project, participant observation of adolescents was triangulated with episodic interviews of 24 adolescents concerning their situation, and health and illness in particular (Flick and Röhnsch 2007). In a second project, the focus was on how adolescents on the street live and cope with chronic illness. To answer this question, we continued participant observation and carried out episodic interviews with a different focus on 12 adolescents aged from 14 to 25 years and with a variety of chronic illnesses. This was complemented by interviews of 12 experts (physicians and social workers) from several institutions that the adolescents could address with their health problems—or (seen the other way round) institutions and services that are supposed to work with this clientele. In the process, we applied different theoretical perspectives for approaching: (1) the subjective experiences of lay people in dealing with health, illness, and health services; (2) a social interactionist analysis of a specific life world and how the members deal with these issues among each other; and (3) a professional perspective on a very specific clientele.

Step 2: Designing a Study Using Triangulation

Triangulation is not a research design per se, but can be incorporated in a variety of qualitative research designs. In most cases, triangulation is used in a cross-sectional study (snapshot, see Chapter 9). But triangulation can also be used in a longitudinal study. It can be very fruitful to use different methodological approaches in a case study, although usually the focus is comparative. Methods can be applied either one after the other or in parallel. Triangulation is used in the context of various research strategies. For example, it can be integrated in a grounded theory or in an ethnographic approach. Which of these design alternatives you choose when you carry out a triangulation study should depend on your research question and the field you do your research in.

Resources and Funding

When planning a triangulation study, you should bear in mind the extra resources needed for applying several methods. Several resources are worth mentioning. First of all, you will need (more) time for a triangulation study, because collecting data with different methods produces methodological problems and affects the time frames of each of the methods. Interviews need some time for arranging a date and traveling to meet the interviewee. Observation in most cases means coming back to the field several times over a longer period. In both approaches you need to establish a relation to the field and find access to its members (see Chapter 12).

It is also necessary to plan (extra) time and costs for documenting the data; for example, transcriptions of interviews (see Chapter 24) in triangulation studies working with several methods of data collection.

Other resources sometimes underestimated in this context include competencies for applying different qualitative methods in a skillful or professional way. A one-person project is sometimes difficult if several methods or research perspectives are to be applied. Sometimes time is needed for training the researchers in using the method(s).

If your study is based on external funding, you should calculate these costs and time in your budget.

Sampling in Triangulation

In a triangulation study, sampling may become more differentiated depending on the ways in which you collect data. Often it is not possible to rely strictly on one strategy like theoretical sampling for all approaches in data collection in one study. Sampling in studies using triangulation should be considered from three angles: (1) How can we guarantee that a sampling strategy fitting each single method can also be put into practice in the context of triangulation? (2) Which options of an interlaced sampling make sense? (3) How can we take into account or bring together the different logics of sampling of different methods or approaches?

In our example (Case Study 14.1) we were looking for adolescents with different chronic illnesses. We therefore applied a combination of initial sampling and theoretical sampling (see Chapters 25 and 13 for these concepts) in order to find a theoretically relevant variation of experiences with chronic illness. In the observations we sought to include situations from different contexts, in which health and (chronic) illness became relevant as a topic in practices or interactions. In the expert interviews we included professionals working in a variety of health and social services, who might be working with homeless adolescents in the case of illness. Thus we applied purposive sampling in this part of the study. In particular, in the sampling of interviewees among the adolescents, we used the sample of participants in the observations first and then went on to find other cases beyond that group. Here, we applied interlaced sampling, which means selecting cases for one approach from a sample set up for another approach.

As may already have become evident, different methods and types of data are linked to different logics of sampling. In our example, we have purposive sampling of persons in the expert interview part of the study. In the observation, sampling was directed to situations and issues becoming relevant in these situations. People were not so much the focus of sampling. For the interviews with the adolescents, we applied a sampling procedure which was increasingly oriented on principles of theoretical sampling.

Step 3: Triangulation in Collecting Data

If researchers apply methodological triangulation, in most cases they refer to different ways of collecting data. Here, it is important that triangulation does not just lead to "more of the same." For example, it does not make much sense to interview the same people twice with different methods of interviewing. Rather you should seek approaches on different levels. For example, combining interviews with observation focuses on subjective knowledge and experience and allows issues of the past to be introduced in the first approach. Observation rather focuses on practices and interactions at a specific moment and thus adds a new perspective. The data obtained from both approaches are located on different levels. If you combine a semi-structured interview based on an interview schedule of questions with a narrative interview focusing on the life history of the participant, you will not obtain data on different levels: rather, you will obtain similar data in different shapes. Both sets of data remain on the level of talking about experiences from a subjective point of view. In this case, a better idea might be to combine question–answer sequences with narratives stimulated by invitations to recount specific situations as in the episodic interview (see Chapter 18). In this case you use within-method triangulation, because you are taking different methodological perspectives in the framework of one method. If you want to apply between-method triangulation, you should try to combine methodological approaches which are rather clearly distinct in their focus and in the data they provide.

In the example in Case Study 14.1, we used participant observation (see Chapter 20) at open spaces, where homeless adolescents hang out and meet, in order to observe their health practices and what they do once a health problem comes up or intensifies. Not everything was accessible to observation in the strict sense of the word and many issues were only mentioned in interactions among the adolescents talking about their own problems or those of fellows from the scene. The second approach in this study was to run episodic interviews (see Chapter 18) with the adolescents, which allowed an issue to be addressed in a wider perspective of development and change. A third approach was to do expert interviews with health and social work professionals, in order to obtain an external perspective complementing the subjective experiences reported by the adolescents themselves. Here the focus was on the professionals' perception of this specific clientele and its way of using or avoiding professional help.

Thus the three ways of collecting data addressed different levels of the "same" problem, the levels being (1) subjective knowledge, (2) practices/interactions, (3) professional expert knowledge of health problems, and (4) help-seeking behavior of homeless adolescents with chronic illness. At the same time, these ways produced different sorts of data with different characteristics requiring different ways of analyzing them.

Step 4: Triangulation in Analyzing Data

There are various ways of using triangulation in this step. The first is to apply several methods of analyzing the (same) data—for example, content analysis (see Chapter 26) and a narrative–sequential approach (see Chapter 27) to interview data. The second is to bear in mind the different characteristics of the data collected with different methods and to apply a different approach to each of the data sets.

In our example we looked for interpretive patterns in the interviews with adolescents by comparing all of the interviews in the domains of the interviews and across these domains using thematic coding (see Chapter 26). The observational data were analyzed for situations of health-related behaviors and interactions, which then were compared to each other. The expert interviews were categorized with different forms of coding.

A third way is to think about how to link the different sets of data in the process of the analysis as a whole. In Chapter 3, I mentioned that there are two basic alternatives for the relation of qualitative and quantitative results. These two alternatives also apply for linking two (or more) sorts of data in the analysis in a project triangulating several qualitative methods in data collection. The first alternative is to look for links on the level of the single case.

In our example (Case Study 14.1), this would mean analyzing the interview with a participant for what he or she sees as health and how to act in a health-oriented way in a specific area—for example, healthy eating. Then we could examine the observational data for activities of that interviewee in this area: are there any situations in which he or she ate in a healthy way according to what was said in the interview or to the other adolescents about this issue? Finally, we could look at the expert interviews for statements referring to that adolescent and his or her way of eating healthily or not. We can then compare the three findings: are they convergent (revealing the same) or are they contradictory or complementary? Analyzing the three forms of data in this way allows them to be linked on the level of the single case (this specific interviewee) and using the potential of triangulation on this level.

An alternative is to look for links on the level of the data sets. This means analyzing the interview data first and looking for patterns in them. Then we analyze the observations for patterns in them and do the same with the expert interview data. In the next step, we compare the patterns we obtain in each analysis for similarities and differences: Do we find similar patterns of help-seeking behavior in the interviews with the adolescents and in the observations? Are there differences between the patterns in both sets of data? Are there similar patterns in the expert interviews? Or do we find different patterns in each of the data sets? Analyzing the three forms of data in this way allows them to be linked on the level of the data sets (the interviews and the observations) and using the potential of triangulation on this level (see Figure 14.1).

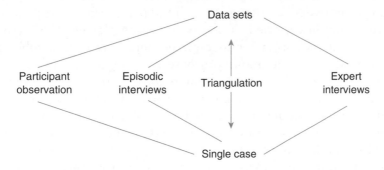

FIGURE 14.1 Levels of Triangulation with Three Forms of Qualitative Data

In many studies, only the second way seems possible. For example, in our study it was not possible to ask the experts directly about specific adolescents for anonymity reasons. So some of the experts might refer to a specific adolescent by chance only. In the observations in the field, one cannot always expect that every interviewee will be around or involved in interactions referring to a specific issue. In general, the observation is focused on situations rather than on single participants—from the sampling to the analysis. Expert interviews follow a logic which is different from interviews with lay people or patients. Therefore, we have good reason to establish and analyze links on the level of the data sets rather than expecting links on the level of the single case.

Issues Arising from Triangulation
Results of Using Triangulation

As mentioned in Chapter 3, the use of triangulation of several methods may lead to three types of results: converging results, complementary results, and contradictions. If a study using different methods ends up with completely convergent results, it might have been enough to concentrate on one method. A better justification for triangulation is results which are different in focus and level, which means that they complement each other or even contradict at first sight. In this case, you should not so much question the confirmability of your results: rather you should look for (theoretical) explanations of where these differences come from and what this diversity may tell you about your research and the issue you study. Then triangulation becomes most fruitful—as a strategy for a more comprehensive understanding and a challenge to look for more and better explanations.

Ethics of Triangulation

Using several methods in one study may raise additional ethical issues or increase their relevance compared to single method studies (see Chapter 5). For example, it is quite easy to arrange that all the participants give their informed consent for being interviewed. If you want to complement this by observing them in their interaction in a public place, there may be a number of other people involved in the situations you observe, who are not involved in your research in other ways. Here, it may be more difficult to organize informed consent. The multitude of information coming from several methods may intensify the problem of context and anonymity for the single participant in the study. The same is the case for confronting the participants with their problems or their life situation in general—the more you approach members with questions and interventions in the research, the more you confront them or the more the research may become a burden to them.

All this requires a well-reflected use of triangulation in your project. Only if there is a good reason for using several methods is it justified to expect participants to be ready to collaborate in several ways with the research.

Quality Issues in Using Triangulation

In triangulation studies, you can approach the quality question from two angles. The first is: How do you analyze the quality of data and procedures for each method you apply in an appropriate way? Can you use the same criteria for all of the methods? For example, we could use member checks for interviews but not for observations. So we may need different criteria for different methods or maybe different strategies (see Chapter 29).

The second angle is to assess the quality of using triangulation: How were the methods combined? What relevance did the single method have in the research? Did it address different levels, for example, subjective meaning and social structure, process and state, knowledge and activity, or knowledge and discourse? Have these methods been used systematically? How purposefully have they been chosen and used? Did the triangulation go beyond the simple combination of methods and include the integration and reflection of the theoretical backgrounds of the different methods? In general, was the use of different methods grounded in taking their background into account? Was the decision for the different methods and for triangulation grounded in the research question and in the issue(s) under study?

These questions raise issues which can be reflected on to check the quality of a study using triangulation on the level of the concrete way of application.

Stumbling Blocks in Using Triangulation

Some of the stumbling blocks you might come across in applying triangulation in your study have already been mentioned. One problem may be that you overly challenge your participants, or they may have reservations about one of your methods but are ready to respond to another (see Case Study 12.1). Another problem may be that you end up with data from different methods, which are difficult to link as they address overly heterogeneous aspects of your phenomenon under study. A third problem may arise from overly challenging your research team with the variety of methods and planning issues to be solved in your study. Again my suggestion is to decide carefully what you expect from using triangulation and then employ it at those stages where you most expect it to be worthwhile.

Triangulation as Systematization of Qualitative Methods

Using triangulation in a qualitative study is a way of making a more systematic use of the variety of qualitative research methods and approaches. On the one hand, we can find hybrid approaches that subordinate the explicit use of methods to a more general research strategy or attitude. This is the case for grounded theory research (see Chapter 25). It is also true in some ways for doing ethnography (see Chapter 20) and in those approaches which put a stronger focus on reflexivity and political change than on the production of knowledge (several of the contributions to Denzin and Lincoln's handbook (2005a) are examples of this). On the other hand, an explicit use of methods that seriously considers the appropriateness of methods to issues under study (see Chapter 2) will sooner or later end up needing more than one method and more than one methodological–theoretical approach for understanding complex phenomena. For such a way of doing qualitative research, triangulation can provide a more systematic option.

The use of the triangulation concept is often quite narrow and does not always fully acknowledge the potential of the approach. In the contexts of mixed-methods research, for example, triangulation is reduced to confirming qualitative results with quantitative methods (or vice versa, e.g., in Bryman 2004). In qualitative research, it is often reduced to an approach for assessing the quality of qualitative research (see Lincoln and Guba 1985). I hope this chapter has given you an idea of how to use triangulation as an approach for a more complex design in qualitative research.

Checklist for Designing and Assessing Triangulation

If you consider using triangulation in your own study, the questions below may be useful to guide your decisions:

1 What are the limitations of each method, which can be overcome by combining two or more approaches?
2 What is the gain in knowledge that you can expect from combining them?
3 Do the methods really address different levels or qualities in the data, so as to justify their combination?
4 How far can the extra efforts required for combining various methods be accommodated in your framework of research (within the constraints of resources, time, etc.)?
5 Are these efforts worthwhile, relative to the gain in knowledge they allow for?
6 Are the combined methods compatible with each other?
7 How should you sequence the methods you will use? How will sequencing affect the study?
8 How far are the methods applied according to their characteristics, so that their specific strengths are taken into account?

KEY POINTS

- Triangulation may extend your methodological and theoretical access to the issue and the field that you have chosen to study.
- Using triangulation requires effort and resources. Thus before one embarks on such a process, the prospective benefit should be evident.
- The approach will be most fruitful if it produces new and additional insights. Often this entails contradictory or complementary results arising from the use of a number of methods.
- All in all, triangulation allows the integration of a variety of qualitative approaches into a more general research design.

Exercise 14.1

1 Look for a study referring to triangulation (e.g., Sands and Roer-Strier 2006) and analyze what the purpose of integrating triangulation was, which of the principles discussed in this chapter was applied, and what the additional outcome due to triangulation was.
2 Consider your own research. Could triangulation be useful for your study? If so, how? If not, why not?

Further Reading

These texts discuss the strategy of triangulation in qualitative research:

Denzin, N.K. (1989b) *The Research Act* (3rd edn). Englewood Cliffs, NJ: Prentice Hall.
Flick, U. (2004a) "Triangulation in Qualitative Research," in U. Flick, E.v. Kardorff and I. Steinke (eds.), *A Companion to Qualitative Research.* London: Sage. pp. 178–183.
Flick, U. (2007b) *Managing Quality in Qualitative Research.* London: Sage.

PART 4
Verbal Data

Contents

Part 4 will introduce you to the variety of methods that are used to collect data focused mainly on the spoken word. Here three basic approaches to collecting verbal data will be presented. The first strategy is to use interviews based on questions and the answers that are elicited by them. This approach is explained in Chapter 16. Alternatively, people's stories can be used as collectable data for research. These may result from narrative interviews designed to elicit stories about people's lives or concerning specific situations. A similar strategy is to ask a group, say a family, to tell their joint story (joint narratives). These narrative methods are described in Chapter 18. A third option is not to interview a single person, but to collect data from groups by making them discuss the issue in the research study. Here we can use group discussions and the more trendy approach of focus groups. These group-oriented strategies are outlined in Chapter 17. Chapter 15 provides an overall introduction to this kind of research.

15
Collecting Verbal Data

┌─CHAPTER OBJECTIVES─┐

This chapter is designed to help you

- compare the different approaches to verbal data in order to make a decision about which to use for your own research;
- assess your decision critically in the light of your (initial) experiences when applying the method you chose;
- understand the method in the context of the research process and of the other stages of your research plan.

What Are Verbal Data?

The term "verbal data" is an umbrella term covering a variety of data that have in common that they primarily consist of words. They result from various methodological approaches which have in common that research participants speak about events, their experiences, their views or practices, and the like. These methodological approaches can consist of interviews with (a number of) single participants (or, more rarely, a group of participants), in which they have answered questions. The data can also come from storytelling, either spontaneous narratives recorded by the researcher or narratives elicited for the research. Or the data can stem from discussions in focus groups or group discussions. All these methods can be applied in real-world (face-to-face) interactions or online (e-mail interviews, online focus groups, etc.). In most cases data collection includes an audio (sometimes also audio-visual) recording allowing a more or less detailed transcription of the conversations in the interviews or focus groups.

In research focused on verbal data, other forms of expressions—such as facial expressions, gestures, movements, etc.—are treated as additional information, sometimes documented in interview protocols but seen as less central than the content of the talking. If, however, they are more in the focus, we would rather refer to such studies as visual or video research (see Chapter 21). If the data consist of written statement or other forms of written words, the research would fall into the category of documentary analysis (see Chapter 22).

Why Verbal Data? Aims and Target Groups

Sometimes the decision to collect verbal data is determined by pragmatic reasons—for example, there is only one contact per participant, there are a limited number of dates for focus groups, it is not possible to spend longer periods in the field. But there are also a number of positive reasons to use interviews or focus groups as the following example may demonstrate. In the field of health services research about a specific disease, there are many aims that can be pursued by using verbal data, as follows.

To Analyze Patients' Experiences

A first indication for interviews or focus groups in this context can be the analysis of patients' experiences—with their disease, of how their lives changes after diagnosis of the disease, or with the support they received (or missed). These experiences can form the subject of narratives concerning the development (of the disease, life, and treatment) or be addressed in open-ended interviews or focus groups of several patients exchanging their views.

To Analyze the Needs of Hard-to-Reach Groups

Sometimes the health system is confronted with the problem that some groups are more difficult to reach for services and support than others, although their needs may be even stronger than those of the "average" patients. Such hard-to-reach groups include migrants, homeless people, and patients with rare diseases. In most cases they are hard to reach both for the health services and for research, so they tend to be underrepresented in surveys, for example. In such cases interviews can offer a better solution for reaching these groups.

To Analyze Professional Experiences and Knowledge

The other side can also be studied by collecting verbal data. Practitioners often have an extensive implicit knowledge about their practices with specific issues or target groups, which can be made explicit—in interviews, for example.

To Analyze Expert Knowledge

To return to our example of hard-to-reach groups, it can be fruitful to approach experts for interviewing them about where members of this group seek help. Other issues include the following: What happens if they turn to a specific institution for seeking help? Which institutions are available for them (or in general for a problem like theirs)? Which institutions collaborate in such cases? How many cases might this group include and what are the deficiencies in the service system if this target group is concerned?

Evaluation of Services

Finally, interviews or focus groups can be a useful instrument for evaluating services— by asking clients, staff, or public utility providers for their criteria and estimates of success of the specific services.

There are various levels on which verbal data can be used in this context for understanding different perspectives on the issue of service utilization by hard-to-reach groups in the field of health.

Types of Verbal Data

As already mentioned, we can distinguish several types of verbal data depending on how they were produced.

Semi-structured Interviews

Semi-structured interviews are based on a set of prepared, mostly open-ended questions, which guide the interview and the interviewer. This interview guide should be applied flexibly and leave room for the interviewee's perspective and topics in addition to the questions. The format of the interviewees' contributions basically comprises statements and answers (see Chapter 16 for several forms of semi-structured interviews).

Narrative Interviews

Here, the interview is based on the interviewee's narration about his or her life, a specific process or development in this life, etc. The narration is stimulated by the interviewer's "generative narrative question," which defines the issue and the period the narration should address. Once the narration has started, the interviewer should refrain as much as possible from any interventions that might interrupt the narrator or the narration (see Chapter 18 for the narrative interview).

Combinations of Both

As it is not always necessary to have a full life history (although narratives can contribute much to the researchers' insights in the interviewees' perspectives on the issue under study), combinations of semi-structured and narrative interviews have been developed. In the episodic interview, narrations should refer to situations and episodes, and telling them is embedded in questions to be answered (see Chapter 18 for the episodic interview).

Interviews for Specific Target Groups

Most semi-structured and narration-oriented interviews focus on the interviewee comprehensively as a person and can be applied to all kinds of interviewees. We also find interviews that are used for specific target groups, for example, experts and elites. In that case, it is not the whole person who is in the focus of the interview, but rather a specific kind of knowledge that the interviewee is expected to have—that is, expert knowledge about a particular issue or experiences in an exposed position (as a member of an elite).

Focus Groups

Interviews are mostly done with individuals. Alternatively, groups may provide the medium for collecting verbal data. In most such cases, the expectation is that the groups discuss an issue, with the result that the data produced go beyond what a series of single interviews would provide (see Chapter 17 for focus groups and group discussions).

Online Interviews and Focus Groups

Interviews and focus groups have a long tradition in qualitative research. In most cases they are conducted face to face: the interviewer (or group moderator) and participants meet for specific sessions. For various reasons, these methods are now also applied online: communication is organized as computer-mediated communication (see Chapters 16 and 17 for more details about online interviews and focus groups).

In the next step, some clarification of what is linked to these concepts is offered.

What Are Interviews?

Rubin and Rubin (2012, p. 29) outline interviews as "in-depth qualitative interviewing" which is characterized by three features: (1) interviewers look for "rich and detailed information, not for yes-or-no, agree-or-disagree responses." Instead of giving answer categories, questions are open-ended. Questions and their order are not fixed: they can be adapted to the flow of the interview conversation. This adaptation is a task for the interviewers in the exchange with the interviewee. It raises the challenge of how to bring the flow of the interview and the original set of questions together.

What Characterizes Narratives?

Narratives are stories with a beginning, a development, and a state of affairs at the end about an event or process. Typically, they involve a complex structure that links facts and details to an overarching whole. They can cover a life history or smaller entities, such as situation narratives. Using narratives for collecting verbal data should take the structure of the narrative into account instead of isolating single statements from it.

What Are Focus Groups?

Focus groups are initiated by the researchers for their study and consist of five to twelve people who in most cases meet only once. They are prompted to discuss the issue of the study by some sort of stimulus material (a statement, a cartoon, a short film, etc.) introduced by the researcher, who acts as a moderator in the group. There are several ways to compose a group, for example, of people who know each other or not, who are rather similar in their features or rather heterogeneous, etc. (see Chapter 17). The context of the group and its interaction may be used for stimulating statements from the members (which they might not have made in a single interview) and should be taken into account in analyzing the data.

Starting Points for Selecting an Approach for Collecting Verbal Data

Collecting verbal data is one of the major methodological approaches in qualitative research. You can use various strategies to produce as much openness as possible towards the object under study and the views of the interviewee, narrator, or participant in discussions. At the same time, the methodological alternatives include specific elements for structuring the collection of data. Thus, you should make topics referring to the research question an issue in the interview or you should direct their treatment towards a greater depth or towards being more comprehensive. Additionally, you should introduce aspects of the research question not yet mentioned.

The methods alternate between these two goals: producing openness and producing structure. Each method orients to one or the other of these aims. In their central part, at least, narrative interviews are oriented towards openness and scope for the interviewee's presentation. The interviewer's directive interventions should be limited to the generative narrative question and to the stage of narrative inquiries at the end. In semi-structured interviews, the thematic direction is given much more preference and the interviews may be focused much more directly on certain topics. Therefore, depending on the goal of the research and on the chosen goal (openness or structure), specific methods are recommended to a greater or lesser extent for each concrete research question. In this chapter I will outline four points of reference for such a decision between the different methods for collecting verbal data.

1 Criteria-Based Comparison of the Approaches

A comparison of the various forms of semi-structured interviews, narratives, and group methods may be taken as a first point of reference for deciding between them. As criteria for such a decision, Table 15.1 shows the elements in each method for guaranteeing sufficient openness for interviewees' subjective views. Elements for producing a sufficient level of structure and depth in dealing with the thematic issue in the interview are also listed. Further features shown are each method's contribution to the development of the interview method in general and the fields of application which each was created for or is mainly used in. Finally, the problems of conducting the method and the limits mentioned in the following chapters are noted for each approach. Thus the field of methodological alternatives in the domain of verbal data is outlined so that the individual method may be located within it.

TABLE 15.1 Comparison of Methods for Collecting Verbal Data

Criteria	Interviews					Interviews for collecting narrative data		Group procedures	
	Focused interview	Semi-standardized interview	Problem-centered interview	Expert and elite interviews	Ethnographic interview	Narrative interview	Episodic interview	Group discussion	Focus groups
Openness to the interviewee's subjective view by:	Non-direction by unstructured questions	Open questions	Object and process orientation Room for narratives	Limited because only interested in the expert, not the person	Descriptive questions	Non-influencing of narratives once started	Narratives of meaningful experiences Selection by the interviewee	Non-directive moderation of the discussion Permissive climate in the discussion	Taking the context of the group into account
Structuring (e.g., deepening) the issue by:	Giving a stimulus Structured questions Focusing on feelings	Hypothesis-directed questions Confrontational questions	Interview guide as basis for turns and ending unproductive presentations	Interview guide as instrument for structuring	Structural questions Contrastive questions	Generative narrative questions Part of narrative questioning at the end Balancing part	Connection of narratives and argumentation Suggestion of concrete situations to be recounted	Dynamics developing in the group Steering with a guide	Using an interview guide to direct the discussion
Contribution to the general development of the interview as a method	Four criteria for designing interviews Analyzing the object as a second data sort	Structuring the contents with structure-laying technique Suggestions for explicating implicit knowledge	Short questionnaire Postscript	Highlighting of direction: limitation of the interview to the expert	Highlighting the problem of making interview situations	Localization of structuring the interview at the beginning and the end Exploring narratives as research instrument systematically	Systematic connection of narrative and argumentation as data sorts Purposive generative narrative question	Alternative to single interview due to group dynamics	Simulation of the way discourses and social representations are generated in their diversity
Domain of application	Analysis of subjective meanings	Reconstruction of subjective theories	Socially or biographically relevant problems	Expert knowledge in institutions	In the framework of field research in open fields	Biographical courses	Change, routines, and situations in everyday life	Opinion and attitude research	Marketing and media research

(Continued)

TABLE 15.1 (Continued)

Criteria	Interviews					Interviews for collecting narrative data		Group procedures	
	Focused interview	Semi-standardized interview	Problem-centered interview	Expert and elite interviews	Ethnographic interview	Narrative interview	Episodic interview	Group discussion	Focus groups
Problems in conducting the method	Dilemma of combining the criteria	Extensive methodological input Problems of interpretation	Unsystematic change from narrative to question–answer schema	Role diffusion of the interviewee Blocking by the expert	Mediation between friendly conversation and formal interview	Extremely unilateral interview situation Problems of the narrator Problematic *zugzwangs*	Explication of the principle Handling the interview guide	Mediation between silent and talkative people Course can hardly be planned	How to sample groups and members
Limitations of the method	Assumption of knowing objective features of the object is questionable Hardly any application in its pure form	Introducing a structure Need to adapt the method to the issue and the interviewee	Problem orientation Unsystematic combination of most diverse partial elements	Limitation of the interpretation on expert knowledge	Mainly sensible in combination with observation and field research	Supposed analogy of experience and narrative Reducing the object to what can be recounted	Limitation on everyday knowledge	High organizational effort Problems of comparability	Documentation of data Identification of single speakers and several speakers at the same time
References	Merton and Kendall (1946)	Groeben (1990)	Witzel (2000)	Bogner, Littig, and Menz (2009)	Heyl (2001) Spradley (1979)	Hermanns (1995) Riemann and Schütze (1987) Rosenthal (2004)	Flick (1994; 1995; 2000a; 2007b)	Blumer (1969) Bohnsack (2004)	Barbour (2007) Lunt and Livingstone (1996)

2 The Selection of the Method and Checking its Application

The various methodological alternatives aiming at the collection and analysis of verbal data suggest that it is necessary to make a well-founded decision according to your own study, its research question, its target group, and so on. Which method do you select for collecting data? My recommendation is that you assess such a decision on the basis of the character of the material that you want to collect. Not all methods are appropriate to every research question: biographical processes of events may be presented in narratives rather than in the question–answer schema of the semi-structured interview. For studying processes of developing opinions, the dynamic of group discussions is instructive, whereas this feature rather obstructs the analysis of individual experiences. The research question and the issue under study are the first anchoring points for deciding for or against a concrete method. Some people are able to narrate and others are not. For some target groups, attempting to reconstruct their subjective theory would prove a curious experience, whereas others can become involved in the situation without any problem. The (potential) interviewees are the second anchoring points for methodological decisions and for assessing their appropriateness.

But such differences in becoming involved in specific interview situations are not restricted to individual differences. If you take into account the research question and the level of statements your study is aiming at, then you can regard systematically the relation between method, subject(s), and issue. The criterion here is the appropriateness of the method you choose and of how you apply it. However, you should ask questions concerning this point—not only at the end of your data collection, when all the interviews or discussions have been conducted, but also earlier in the procedure after one or two trial interviews or discussions.

One aspect for checking the appropriateness of the methodological choice is to examine if and how far you have applied the method in its own terms. For example, has a narrative interview really been started with a generative narrative question? Have changes of topics and new questions been introduced only after the interviewees have had enough time and scope to deal with the preceding topic in sufficient detail in a semi-structured interview?

The analysis of the initial interviews may show that it is not only the interviewees who have more problems with certain methods than with others; interviewers may also have more problems in applying a certain method than in others. One reason for this is that it may overly challenge the interviewer's ability either to decide when and how to return to the interview guide if the interviewee deviates from the subject, or to deploy the necessary active listening skills in the narrative interview. Thus you should also check how far an interviewer and method match.

If problems emerge at this level, there are two possible solutions. Careful interview training may be given (for this, see the sections on the focused and semi-standardized interviews in Chapter 16 and on the narrative and episodic interviews in Chapter 18) in order to reduce these problems. If this is not sufficient, I would consider changing the method. A basis for such decisions may be provided by analyzing the interaction during data collection so as to establish the scope allowed to the interviewee by the interviewer and to see how clearly the roles of both have been defined.

A final factor you should consider in choosing and assessing a method relates to how the data are to be interpreted later and at which level of generalization the findings will be obtained.

Suggestions for making the decision about which method of data collection to use and for assessing the appropriateness of this decision are given in the checklist at the end of this chapter.[1]

3 Appropriateness of the Method to the Issue

Certain procedures are considered the "ideal way" to study an issue in a practical and legitimate way during a methodological discussion. In such discussions, one central feature of qualitative research is typically ignored: that is, methods should be selected and evaluated according to their appropriateness to the subject under study (see Chapter 2). An exception to this consists of studies that explore certain methods primarily in order to obtain findings about their conduct, conductibility, and problems. Then the object of research has only exemplary status for answering such methodological questions. In all other cases, the decision to use a certain method should be regarded as subordinate: the issue, research question, individuals studied, and statements striven for are the anchoring points for assessing the appropriateness of concrete methods in qualitative research.

4 Fitting the Method into the Research Process

Finally, you should assess how the method you selected fits into the research process. The aim is to find out whether the procedure for collecting data suits the procedure for interpreting them. It does not make sense to use the narrative interview during the data collection in order to allow the presentation a wide scope, if the data received then undergo a content analysis using only categories derived from the literature and paraphrases of the original text (for this see Chapter 26). It also does not make sense to want to interpret an interview that stresses the consistent treatment of the topics in the interview guide with a sequential procedure (see Chapter 27), which is used to uncover the development of the structure of the presentation. In a similar way, you should check the compatibility of the procedure for collecting data with your method of sampling cases (see Chapter 13). And you should assess its compatibility with (1) the theoretical background of your study (see Chapter 7) and (2) the understanding of the research process as a whole (e.g., developing theories versus testing hypotheses; see Chapter 10) that you took as starting points.

You will find the starting points for this assessment in the paragraphs about the fitting of the method into the research process given in the sections on each method. They outline the method's inherent understanding of the research process and its elements. The next step is to check how far the design of your study and the conceptualization of the single steps are compatible with the method's inherent conceptualization.

Checklist for Selecting a Method for Collecting Verbal Data

1 *Research question*

Can the interview type and its application address the essential aspects of the research question?

2 *Interview type*

Has the method been applied according to the methodological elements and target?

Has jumping between interview types been avoided, except when it is grounded in the research question or theoretically?

3 *Interviewer*

Are the interviewers able to apply the interview type?

What are the consequences of their own fears and uncertainties in the situation?

4 *Interviewee*

Is the interview type appropriate to the target group of the application?

How can one take into account the fears, uncertainties, and expectations of (potential) interviewees?

5 *Scope allowed to the interviewee*

Can the interviewees present their views within the framework of the questions?

Can they assert their views against the framework of the questions?

6 *Interaction*

Have the interviewers conducted the interview according to the correct procedure?

Have they left sufficient scope for the interviewee?

Did they fulfill their role? (Why not?)

Were the interviewee's role, the interviewer's role, and the situation clearly defined for the interviewee?

Could the interviewee fulfill his or her role? (Why not?)

Analyze the breaks in order to validate the interview between the first and second interview if possible.

7 *Aim of the interpretation*

Are you interested in finding and analyzing limited and clear answers or complex, multiple patterns, contexts, etc.?

8 *Claim for generalization*

On which level should statements be made:

- For the single case (the interviewed individual and his or her biography, an institution and its impact, etc.)?
- With reference to groups (about a profession, a type of institution, etc.)?
- General statements?

KEY POINTS

- All methods for collecting verbal data have their own particular strengths and weaknesses.
- They all provide ways to give the participants room for presenting their experiences and views.
- At the same time, each method structures the study in specific ways.
- Before and while applying a specific method, assess whether the method you selected is appropriate for answering your research question.

Exercise 15.1

1 Take a study from the literature which is based on interviewing people (e.g., Terrill and Gullifer 2010), and reflect on the extent to which the applied method was (or was not) appropriate for the issue under study and the people involved in the research.
2 Reflect on your own study: what were your main reasons for using this specific method?

Further Reading

The following texts give overviews of the different forms of collecting verbal data mentioned in the next chapters:

Flick, U. (2000a) "Episodic Interviewing," in M. Bauer and G. Gaskell (eds.), *Qualitative Researching with Text, Image and Sound: A Practical Handbook*. London: Sage. pp. 75–92.

Flick, U. (2007b) *Managing Quality in Qualitative Research*. London: Sage.

Hermanns, H. (2004) "Interviewing as an Activity," in U. Flick, E.v. Kardorff and I. Steinke (eds.), *A Companion to Qualitative Research*. London: Sage. pp. 209–213.

Mason, J. (2002) "Qualitative Interviewing: Asking, Listening and Interpreting," in T. May (ed.), *Qualitative Research in Action*. London: Sage. pp. 225–241.

Puchta, C. and Potter, J. (2004) *Focus Group Practice*. London: Sage.

Rubin, H.J. and Rubin, I.S. (2012) *Qualitative Interviewing: The Art of Hearing Data* (3rd edn). London: Sage.

Note

1 For more clarity, only the term "interview" is used. If you replace it with "group discussion" or "focus group," the same questions may be asked and answers found in the same way.

16
Interviews

CONTENTS

CHAPTER OBJECTIVES

This chapter is designed to help you

- understand the characteristics of various types of interviews;
- know the principles and recognize the pitfalls of interviewing;
- construct an interview guide;
- select the appropriate interview technique from the repertoire available.

Much methodological discussion (especially in the United States and in earlier periods of qualitative research) has revolved around observation as a central method for collecting data. Open interviews are more dominant in the German-speaking areas (e.g., Hopf 2004a) and now attract more attention in the Anglo-Saxon areas as well (see, e.g., Gubrium and Holstein 2001; Kvale 2007). Semi-structured interviews, in particular, have attracted interest and are widely used. This interest stems from the view that the interviewed subjects' viewpoints are more likely to be expressed in an openly designed interview situation than in a standardized interview or a questionnaire. Several types of interviews can be distinguished. The main types are discussed below, both in terms of their own logic and in terms of their contribution to further developing the interview as a method in general.

How to Conduct Interviews

It is characteristic of interviews that you will bring more or less open questions to the interview situation in the form of an interview guide. You will hope that the interviewee will answer these questions freely.

Style of Interviewing—The Responsive Interview

In their overview of qualitative interviewing, Rubin and Rubin (2012) use their term "responsive interview" for illustrating the interviewer's helpful attitude for successfully doing interviews in general:

> Responsive interviewing is a style of qualitative interviewing. It emphasises the importance of building a relationship of trust between the interviewer and interviewee that leads to more give-and-take in the conversation. The tone of questioning is basically friendly and gentle, with little confrontation. The pattern of questioning is flexible; questions evolve in response to what the interviewees have just said, and new questions are designed to tap the experience and knowledge of each interviewee. (2012, p. 37)

This description fits most interviews quite well, as the focus is typically on what the interviewee has experienced and sees as important in relation to the issue of the study. The aim is to develop a fuller picture from interviewees' points of view, rather than just simple, short, general, or abstract answers to the interviewer's questions. Rubin and Rubin accordingly state as "key elements" of a (responsive) interview: "In the responsive interviewing model, you are looking for material that has depth and detail and is nuanced and rich with vivid thematic material" (2012, p. 101). Accordingly, interviewers formulate first an interview *guide* consisting of questions designed to elicit the kinds of answers implied by this quotation.

The second instrument then consists of *probes* to the interviewees' answers, which lead them to more depth, detail, and illustration. This probing can consist of spontaneous interventions by the interviewer (e.g., "Could you please tell me more about what you just mentioned?"). But it can also be based on prepared questions for how to stimulate more details or depth at certain points in the interview. Thus Rubin and Rubin (2012, pp. 116–119) distinguish three question types: "main questions," "follow-up questions," and "probes." The tricky issue for the interviewer is when to ask follow-up questions and to probe. The authors suggest balancing these three types of questions in the actual interview, but the decision of when to follow up or not, when to probe or not, can only be taken in the concrete interview situation. This may lead to a number of problems, as follows.

Bureaucratic Use of the Interview Guide

The starting point of qualitative interviewing is the presumption that inputs, which are characteristic of standardized interviews or questionnaires and which restrict the sequence of topics dealt with, obscure rather than illuminate the subject's viewpoint. Problems also arise when trying to secure topically relevant subjective perspectives in an interview—problems of mediating between the input of the interview guide and the aims of the research question on the one hand, and the interviewee's style of presentation on the other. Thus the interviewer can and must decide during the interview when and in which sequence to ask the questions. Whether a question has already been answered *en passant* and may be left out can only be decided ad hoc. Interviewers will also face the question of whether and when to probe in greater detail and to support the interviewee if roving far afield, or when to return to the interview guide when the interviewee is digressing. The term "semi-standardized interview" is also used with respect to choice in the actual conduct of the interview. You will have to choose between trying to mention certain topics given in the interview guide and at the same time being open to the interviewee's individual way of talking about these topics and other topics relevant for the interviewee. These decisions, which can only be taken in the interview situation itself, require a high degree of sensitivity to the concrete course of the interview and the interviewee. Additionally, they require a great deal of overview of what has already been said and its relevance for the research question in the study. Here a continuous mediation between the course of the interview and the interview guide is necessary.

Hopf (1978) warns against applying the interview guide too bureaucratically. This might restrict the benefits of openness and contextual information because the interviewer is sticking too rigidly to the interview guide. This might encourage him or her to interrupt the interviewee's account at the wrong moment in order to turn to the next question instead of taking up the topic and trying to get deeper into it. According to Hopf (1978, p. 101), there may be several reasons for this. They include:

- the protective function of the interview guide for coping with the uncertainty due to the open and indeterminate conversational situation;
- the interviewer's fear of being disloyal to the targets of the research (e.g., because of skipping a question);
- finally, the dilemma between pressure of time (due to the interviewee's limited time) and the researcher's interest in information.

Therefore, detailed interview training has proved necessary, in which the application of the interview guide is taught in role-plays. These simulated interviews are recorded (if possible on videotape). Afterwards they are evaluated by all the interviewers taking part in the study—for interview mistakes, for how the interview guide was used, for procedures and problems in introducing and changing topics, the interviewers' non-verbal behavior, and their reactions to the interviewees. This evaluation is made in order to make different interviewers' interventions and steering in the interviews more comparable. This allows one to take up so-called "technical" problems (how to design and conduct interviews) and to discuss solutions to them in order to further back up the use of interviews.

Stage Directions for Interviewing

For preparing and conducting the interview itself, Hermanns (2004) has made some helpful suggestions. He sees the interview interaction as an evolving drama. The interviewer's task is to facilitate the evolution of this drama. He also warns interviewers not to be too anxious about using a recording device during the interview: he emphasizes that most interviewees have no problems with the recording of an interview and that it is often the interviewers who project their own uneasiness of being recorded onto the interviewee.

In his stage directions for interviewing (2004, pp. 212–213), you will find suggestions on such matters as: how to explain to the interviewees what you expect from them during the interview; how to create a good atmosphere in the interview; and how to give room to allow your interviewees to open up. Most crucial in his suggestions (in my experience) is that during the interview you should try to discover not theoretical concepts, but rather the life world of the interviewee. Of similar importance is that you should be aware that research questions are not the same as interview questions and you should try to use everyday language instead of scientific concepts in the questions. Discovering theoretical concepts and using scientific concepts is something for the data analysis process; using concrete everyday wordings is what, in contrast, should happen in your questions and the interview.

Evaluation of Questions in the Interview Guide

If you want to check your instruments before conducting your interviews, you can use a list of key points for checking the way you constructed your interview guide and how you formulated your questions, as Ulrich (1999) suggests (see Box 16.1).

BOX 16.1

Key Points for Evaluating Questions in Interviews

1 Why do you ask this specific question?

   - What is its theoretical relevance?
   - What is the link to the research question?

2 For what reason do you ask this question?

   - What is the substantial dimension of this question?

---

3 Why did you formulate the question in this way (and not differently)?

   - Is the question easy to understand?
   - Is the question unambiguous?
   - Is the question productive?

4 Why did you position this question (or block of questions) at this specific place in the interview guide?

   - How does it fit into the rough and detailed structure of the interview guide?
   - How is the distribution of types of question spread across the interview guide?
   - What is the relation between single questions?

The advantage of this method is that the consistent use of an interview guide increases the comparability of the data and means that they will be more structured as a result of the questions in the guide. If concrete statements about an issue are the aim of the data collection, a semi-structured interview is the more economic way. If the course of a single case and the context of experiences are the central aims of your research, you should consider narratives of the development of experiences as the preferable alternative.

In the remainder of this chapter a number of specific forms of interview are presented. This overview begins with a method that was suggested rather early and can still give some guidance for semi-structured interviews in general. Then a number of alternatives are presented, sometimes linked to specific fields or forms of research.

The Focused Interview

Robert Merton was one of the most influential sociologists in the United States. He worked over a long period in fields like media research. Patricia Kendall worked with him and later became a professor in medical sociology. In the 1940s Merton, Kendall, and their colleagues developed the focused interview (Merton and Kendall 1946). I will describe this method in some detail, because you can learn much from Merton and Kendall about how to plan and conduct interviews in qualitative research in general.

In the focused interview, you proceed as follows. After a uniform stimulus (a film, a radio broadcast, etc.) is presented, its impact on the interviewee is studied using an interview guide. The original aim of the interview was to provide a basis for interpreting statistically significant findings (from a parallel or later quantified study) on the impact of media in mass communication. The stimulus presented is content analyzed beforehand. This enables a distinction to be made between the "objective" facts of the situation and the interviewees' subjective definitions of the situation with a view to comparing them.

During the design of the interview guide and the conducting of the interview itself, use the following four criteria: (1) non-direction, (2) specificity, (3) range, and (4) the depth and personal context shown by the interviewee. The different elements of the method will serve to meet these criteria.

What Are the Elements of the Focused Interview?

Non-direction is achieved by using several forms of questions.[1] The first is unstructured questions (e.g., "What impressed you most in this film?"). In the second form, namely, semi-structured questions, either the concrete issue (e.g., a certain scene in a film) is defined and the response is left open (e.g., "How did you feel about the part describing Jo's discharge from the army as a psychoneurotic?"), or the reaction is defined and the concrete issue is left open (e.g., "What did you learn from this pamphlet which you hadn't known before?"). In the third form of questioning, structured questions, both are defined (e.g., "As you listened to Chamberlain's speech, did you feel it was propagandistic or informative?"). You should ask unstructured questions first and introduce increased structuring only later during the interview; this prevents the interviewer's frame of reference being imposed on the interviewee's viewpoints (Box 16.2).

—BOX 16.2—

Example Questions from the Focused Interview

- What impressed you most in this film?
- How did you feel about the part describing Jo's discharge from the army as a psychoneurotic?
- What did you learn from this pamphlet, which you hadn't known before?
- Judging from the film, do you think that the German fighting equipment was better, as good as, or poorer than the equipment used by the Americans?
- Now that you think back, what were your reactions to that part of the film?
- As you listened to Chamberlain's speech, did you feel it was propagandistic or informative?

Source: Merton and Kendall (1946)

In this respect, Merton and Kendall call for the flexible use of the interview schedule. The interviewer should refrain as far as possible from making early evaluations and should perform a non-directive style of conversation. Problems may arise if questions are asked at the wrong moment and interviewees are thus prevented from, rather than supported in, presenting their views, or if the wrong type of question is used at the wrong time.

The criterion of *specificity* requires that the interview should bring out the specific elements which determine the impact or meaning of an event for the interviewees so as to prevent the interview from remaining on the level of general statements. For this purpose, the most appropriate forms of questions are those that handicap the interviewee as little as possible. To increase specificity, you should encourage *retrospective inspection*. You can support the interviewees in recalling a specific situation by using materials (e.g., an excerpt of a text, a picture) and corresponding questions ("Now that you think back, what were your reactions to that part of the film?"). Alternatively, you may achieve this criterion by "explicit reference to the stimulus situation" (e.g., "Was there anything in the film that gave you that impression?"). As a general rule, Merton and Kendall suggest that "specifying questions should be explicit enough to aid the subject in relating his responses to determinate aspects of the stimulus situation and yet general enough to avoid having the interviewer structure it" (1946, p. 552).

The criterion of *range* aims at ensuring that all aspects and topics relevant to the research question are mentioned during the interview. The interviewees must be given the chance to introduce new topics of their own in the interview. The interviewer's double task is mentioned here at the same time: step by step to cover the topical range (contained in the interview guide) by introducing new topics or initiating changes in the topic. This means as well that interviewers should lead back to those topics that have already been mentioned yet not detailed deeply enough, especially if responses gave the impression that the interviewee led the conversation away from a topic in order to avoid it. Here interviewers should reintroduce the earlier topic again with "reversional transitions" (1946, p. 553).

However, in realizing this criterion, Merton and Kendall see the danger of "confusing range with superficiality" (1946, p. 554). To what extent this becomes a problem depends on the way the interviewers introduce the topical range of the interview guide and whether they become too dependent on the interview guide. Therefore, interviewers should only mention topics if they really want to ensure that they are treated in detail.

Depth and *personal context* shown by the interviewees mean that the interviewers should ensure that emotional responses in the interview go beyond simple assessments like "pleasant" or "unpleasant." The goal is rather "a maximum of self-revelatory comments concerning how the stimulus material was experienced" by the interviewee (1946, pp. 554–555). A concrete task for interviewers resulting from this goal is to continuously diagnose the current level of depth in order to "shift that level toward whichever end of the 'depth continuum' he finds appropriate to the given case." Strategies for raising the degree of depth are for example to "focus on feelings," "restatement of implied or expressed feelings," and "referring to comparative situations." Here reference to the non-directive style of conducting a conversation can also be seen.

The application of this method in other fields of research is mainly oriented to the general principles of the method. Focusing in the interview is understood as related to the topic of study, rather than to the use of stimuli such as films.

CASE STUDY 16.1

People's Concepts of Human Nature

Based on Merton and Kendall's method, cultural psychologist Rolf Oerter (Oerter 1995; see also Oerter, Oerter, Agostiani, Kim, and Wibowo 1996, pp. 43–47) developed the "adulthood interview" for studying concepts of human nature and adulthood in different cultures (United States, West Germany, Indonesia, Japan, and Korea) (Box 16.3).

The interview is divided into four main parts. In the first part, general questions about adulthood are asked: for example, what should an adult look like; what is appropriate for adulthood? The second part deals with the three main roles of adulthood: the family, occupational, and political. The third part draws attention to the past of the interviewee, asking for developmental changes during the previous two or three years. The last part of the interview deals with the near future of the interviewee, asking for his or her goals in life and his or her further development:

> The interviewee is then confronted with dilemma stories, which are followed again by a focused interview: The subject is asked to describe the situation [in the story] and to find a solution. The interviewer is asking questions and tries to reach the highest possible level the subject can achieve. Again, the interviewer must be trained in understanding and assessing the actual level of the individual in order to ask questions at the level proximal to the individual's point of view. (Oerter 1995, p. 213)

In order to focus the interview more on the subject's point of view, the interview guide includes "general suggestions" like "Please encourage the subject as often as necessary: Can you explain this in more detail? What do you mean by …?" (Oerter et al. 1996, pp. 43–47). This provides a good example of how the focused interview may be taken as a starting point for developing a form of interview, which is tailor-made for a specific issue of research.

BOX 16.3

Example Questions from the Adulthood Interview

1 General Questions about Adulthood:

 (a) How should an adult behave? Which abilities/capabilities should he or she have?

   What is your idea of an adult?

 (b) How would you define real adults? How do real adults differ from ideal adults?

   Why are they as they are?

 (c) Can the differences between the ideal and the real adult (between how an adult should behave and how an adult actually does behave) be narrowed down? How?

   (If the answer is "no," then why not?)

VERBAL DATA

(d) Many people consider responsibility to be an important criterion of adulthood. What does responsibility mean to you?

(e) Striving for happiness (being happy) is often viewed as the most important goal for human beings. Do you agree? What is happiness, and what is being happy in your opinion?

(f) What is the meaning of life in your opinion? Why are we alive?

2 Further Explanations about the Three Leading Roles of an Adult:

(a) Conceptions about one's professional role:

What do you think you need to get a job?

Are work and a job really necessary? Are they part of being an adult or not?

(b) Conceptions about one's future family:

Should an adult have a family of his or her own?

How should he or she behave in his or her family? How far should he or she be involved in it?

(c) Political role:

What about an adult's political role? Does he or she have political tasks? Would he or she engage in political activities?

Should he or she care about public affairs? Should he or she take on responsibilities for the community?

What Are the Problems in Conducting the Interview?

The criteria that Merton and Kendall (1946) suggest for conducting the interview incorporate some targets that cannot be matched in every situation. For example, the requirements of "specificity" and depth orient an interview towards matters of detail in what is said, whereas the requirement of "range" leads the interview in the direction of developing a broader overview of the whole issue. The interviewers have to decide in their probing, for example, which of the directions they want to follow in the concrete situation. Fulfilling these criteria cannot be realized in advance (e.g., through designing the interview guide). How far they are met in an actual interview depends to a great extent on the interview situation and how it goes in practice. These criteria highlight the decisions that the interviewers have to make and the necessary priorities they have to establish ad hoc in the interview situation. The authors also mention there is no "right" behavior for the interviewer in the focused (or any other semi-structured) interview.

The successful conduct of such interviews depends essentially on the interviewer's situational competence. This competence may be increased by practical experience of making decisions necessary in interview situations, in rehearsal interviews, and in interview training. In such training, interview situations are simulated and analyzed afterwards with a view to providing trainee interviewers with some experience. Some examples are given of typical needs for decisions between more depth (obtained by probing) and guaranteeing the range (by introducing new topics or the next question of the interview guide), with the different solutions at each point. This makes the difficulties of pursuing contradictory targets easier to handle, although they cannot be completely resolved.

What Is the Contribution to the General Methodological Discussion?

The four criteria identified above and the problems linked to them can be applied to other types of interviews without using an advance stimulus and pursuing other research questions. They have become general criteria for designing and conducting interviews and a starting point for describing dilemmas in this method (e.g., in Hopf 2004a). All together, the concrete suggestions that Merton and Kendall made for realizing the criteria and for formulating questions may be used as an orientation for conceptualizing and conducting interviews more generally. To focus as far as possible on a specific object and its meaning has become a general aim of interviews. The same is the case for the strategies that Merton and Kendall have suggested for realizing these aims—mainly to give the interviewees as much scope as possible to introduce their views.

How Does the Method Fit into the Research Process?

With this method, you can study subjective viewpoints in different social groups. The aim may be to generate hypotheses for later quantitative studies, but also the deeper interpretation of experimental findings. The groups investigated are normally defined in advance and the research process is linear in design (see Chapter 10). Research questions focus on the impact of concrete events or the subjective handling of the conditions of one's own activities. Interpretation is not fixed to a specific method. However, coding procedures (see Chapters 25 and 26) seem to be most appropriate.

What Are the Limitations of the Method?

The specific feature of the focused interview—the use of a stimulus like a film in the interview—is a variation of the standard situation of the semi-structured interview, which is rarely used but which nevertheless gives rise to some specific problems that need consideration. Merton and Kendall are concerned less with how interviewees perceive and assess the concrete material and more with general relations in the reception of filmed material. In this context, they are interested in subjective views on concrete material. It may be doubted that they obtain the "objective facts of the case" (1946, p. 541) by analyzing this material that can be distinguished from the "subjective definitions of the situation." However, they receive a second version of the object in this way. They can relate subjective views of the single interviewee as well as the range of perspectives of the different interviewees to this second version. Furthermore, they have a basis for answering questions like: Which elements of the interviewee's presentations have a counterpart in the result of the content analysis of the film? Which parts have been left out on his or her side, although they are in the film according to the content analysis? Which topics has the interviewee introduced or added?

A further problem with this method is that it is hardly ever used in its pure and complete form. Its current relevance is defined rather by its impetus for conceptualizing and conducting other forms of interviews, which have been developed from it and are often used. Furthermore, the suggestion to combine open interviews with other methodological approaches to the object under study may be noted. These approaches might provide a point of reference for interpreting subjective viewpoints in the interview. This idea is discussed more generally under the heading of "triangulation" (see Chapter 14).

The Semi-standardized Interview

In their method for reconstructing subjective theories, Scheele and Groeben (1988) suggest a specific elaboration of the semi-structured interview (see also Groeben 1990). Brigitte Scheele and Norbert Groeben are psychologists, who have developed the approach of studying subjective theories as a special model for studying everyday knowledge. They developed their approach in the 1980s and 1990s to study subjective theories in fields like schools and other areas of professional work.

I have chosen this method here both because it has contributed much to the development of the method of interviewing and because it might be interesting for designing other forms of interviews. The term "subjective theory" refers to the fact that the interviewees have a complex stock of knowledge about the topic under study. For example, people have a subjective theory of cancer: what cancer is; what the different types of cancer are; why they think people fall ill with cancer; what the possible consequences of cancer will be; how it might be treated; and so on. This knowledge includes assumptions that are explicit and immediate and which interviewees can express spontaneously in answering an open question. These are complemented by implicit assumptions. In order to articulate these, the interviewees must be supported by methodological aids, which is why different types of questions (see below) are applied here. They are used to reconstruct the interviewee's subjective theory about the issue under study (e.g., the subjective theories of trust used by counselors in activities with their clients). The actual interview is complemented by a graphic representation technique called the "structure laying technique" (described more fully below). By applying it together with the interviewees, their statements from the preceding interview are turned into a structure. Also, this allows their communicative validation (i.e., the interviewee's consent to these statements is obtained).

What Are the Elements of the Semi-standardized Interview?

During the interviews, the contents of the subjective theory are reconstructed. The interview guide mentions several topical areas. Each of these is introduced by an open question and ended by a confrontational question. The following examples (Box 16.4) come from my study about subjective theories of trust held by professionals in the health system. *Open questions* ("What do you think, and why are people in general ready to trust each other?") may be answered on the basis of the knowledge that the interviewee has immediately at hand.

BOX 16.4

Example Questions from the Semi-standardized Interview

- Briefly, could you please tell me what you relate to the term "trust" if you think of your professional practice?
- Could you tell me what are the essential and the decisive features of trust between client and counselor?
- There is a proverb: "Trust is good, control is better." If you think of your work and relations to clients, is this your attitude when you approach them?
- Can counselors and clients reach their goals without trusting each other?
- Will they be ready to trust each other without a minimum of control?
- How do people who are ready to trust differ from people who are not willing to trust?
- Are there people who are more easily trusted than others? How do those trustworthy people differ from the others?
- Are there activities in your work which you can practice without trust between you and your client?
- If you think of the institution you work in, what are the factors that facilitate the development of trust between you and your clients? What are the factors that make it more difficult?
- Does the way people come to your institution influence the development of trust?
- Do you feel more responsible for a client if you see that he or she trusts you?

Additionally, *theory-driven, hypotheses-directed questions* are asked. These are oriented to the scientific literature about the topic or are based on the researcher's theoretical presuppositions ("Is trust possible among strangers, or do the people involved have to know each other?"). In the interview, the relations formulated in these questions serve the purpose of making the interviewees' implicit knowledge more explicit. The assumptions in these questions are designed as an offer to the interviewees, which they might take up or refuse according to whether they correspond to their subjective theories or not.

The third type of questions, *confrontational questions*, respond to the theories and relations that the interviewee has presented up to that point in order to critically re-examine these notions in the light of competing alternatives. It is stressed that these alternatives have to stand in "real thematic opposition" to the interviewee's statements in order to avoid the possibility of their integration into the interviewee's subjective theory. Therefore, the interview guide includes several alternative versions of such confrontational questions. Which one is used concretely depends on the view of the issue developed in the interview up to that point.

Conducting the interview here is characterized by introducing topical areas and by the purposive formulation of questions based on scientific theories of the topic (in the hypotheses-directed questions) (Box 16.4).

The Structure Laying Technique

In a second meeting with the interviewee, no more than one or two weeks after the first interview, the structure laying technique (SLT) is applied. In the meantime, the interview just outlined has been transcribed and a first content analysis has been applied to it. In the second meeting, the interviewee's essential statements are presented to him or her as concepts on small cards for two purposes. The first is to assess the contents: the interviewees are asked to recall the interview and check if its contents are correctly represented on the cards. If this is not the case, they may reformulate, eliminate, or replace statements with other more appropriate statements. This assessment regarding the contents (i.e., the communicative validation of the statements by the interviewees) is finished for the moment.

The second purpose is to structure the remaining concepts in a form similar to scientific theories by applying the SLT rules. For this purpose, the interviewees are given a short paper introducing the SLT, in order to familiarize them with the rules for applying it and—as far as necessary and possible—with the way of thinking it is based on. Also given in the paper is a set of examples. Figure 16.1 shows an excerpt from an example of the application of the technique and some of the possible rules for representing causal relations among concepts, such as "A is a precondition for B" or "C is a promoting condition of D."

The result of such a structuring process using the SLT is a graphic representation of a subjective theory. At the end, the interviewee compares his or her structure to the version that the interviewer has prepared between the two meetings.

This comparison—similar to the confrontational questions—serves the purpose of making the interviewee reflect again on his or her views in the light of competing alternatives.

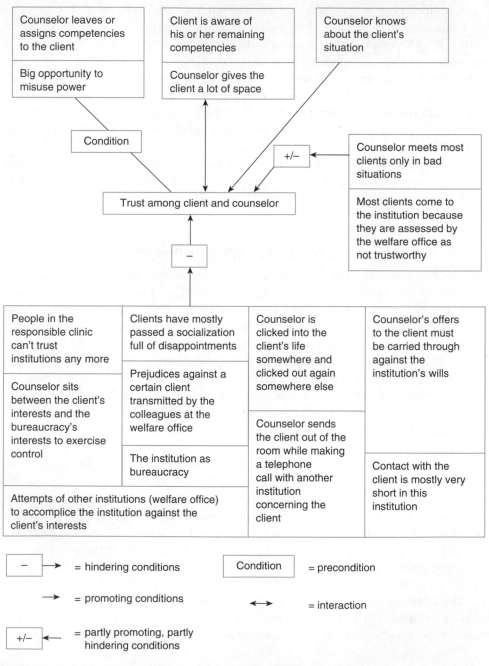

Figure 16.1   Excerpt from a Subjective Theory on Trust in Counseling

Subjective Theories on Trust in Counseling

In my study of trust in counseling, I used this method to interview 15 counselors from different professional backgrounds (e.g., psychologists, social workers, and physicians). The interview schedule included such topics as the definition of trust, the relation of risk and control, strategy, information and preceding knowledge, reasons for trust, its relevance for psychosocial work, and institutional framework conditions and trust (see Box 16.4). As a response to the question "Could you please tell me briefly what you relate to the term 'trust,' if you think of your professional practice?", an interviewee gave as her definition:

> If I think of my professional practice – well … very many people ask me at the beginning whether they can trust me in the relationship, and – because I am representing a public agency – whether I really keep confidential what they will be telling me. Trust for me is to say at this point quite honestly how I might handle this, that I can keep it all confidential up to a certain point, but if they tell me any jeopardizing facts that I have difficulties with then I will tell them at that point. Well, this is trust for me: to be frank about this and the point of the oath of secrecy, that actually is the main point.

The interviews revealed how subjective theories consisted of stocks of knowledge in store for identifying different types of opening a counseling situation, target representations of ideal types of counseling situations and their conditions, and ideas of how at least to approximately produce such conditions in the current situation. Analyzing counseling activities showed how counselors act according to these stocks of knowledge and use them for coping with current and new situations.

This study showed the content and the structure of the individual subjective theories and differences in the subjective theories of counselors working in the same field but coming from different professional backgrounds. The structuration of the questions as part of the interview guide and developed using the SLT later on allowed the context of single statements to be revealed.

What Are the Problems in Applying the Method?

The main problem in both parts of the method is how far the interviewers manage to make the procedure plausible to interviewees and deal with irritation, which may be caused by confrontational questions. If you carefully introduce alternative viewpoints (e.g., "One could perhaps see the problem you just mentioned in the following way: …") this could be a way of handling such annoyances. The rules of the SLT and the way of thinking they are based on can produce irritation, because it is not always standard procedure for people to put concepts into formalized relations in order to visualize their interconnections. Therefore, I suggest that you make clear to the interviewee that applying the SLT and its rules by no means should be understood as a performance test, but that they should rather be used playfully. After initial inhibitions have been overcome, in most cases it is possible to give the interviewee the necessary confidence in applying the method.

What Is the Contribution to the General Methodological Discussion?

The general relevance of this approach is that the different types of questions allow the researchers to deal more explicitly with the presuppositions they bring to the interview in relation to aspects of the interviewee. The "principle of openness" in qualitative research has often been misunderstood as encouraging a diffuse attitude. Here this principle is transformed into a dialogue between positions as a result of the various degrees of explicit confrontation with topics. In this dialogue, the interviewee's position is made more explicit and may also be further developed. The different types of questions, which represent different approaches to making implicit knowledge explicit, may point the way to the solution of a more general problem of qualitative research. A goal of interviews in general is to reveal existing knowledge in a way that can be expressed in the form of answers and so become accessible to interpretation.

The SLT also offers a model for structuring the contents of interviews in which different forms of questions have been used. That this structure is developed with the interviewee during data collection, and not merely by the researcher in the interpretation, makes this structure an element of the data. Whether the shape that Scheele and Groeben suggest for this structure, and the suggested relations, correspond with the research issue can only be decided in an individual case. In summary, a methodological concept has been proposed here, which explicitly takes into account the reconstruction of the object of research (here a subjective theory) in the interview situation instead of propagating a more or less unconditional approach to a given object.

How Does the Method Fit into the Research Process?

The theoretical background to this approach is the reconstruction of subjective viewpoints. Presuppositions about their structure and possible contents are made. But the scope of this method for shaping the contents of the subjective theory remains wide enough for the general target of formulating grounded theories to be realized, as well as the use of case-oriented sampling strategies. Research questions that are pursued with this method concentrate partly on the content of subjective theories (e.g., psychiatric patients' subjective theories of illness) and partly on how they are applied in (e.g., professional) activities.

What Are the Limitations of the Method?

The fastidious details of the method (types of questions, rules of the SLT) need to be adapted to the research question and the potential interviewees. One way is to reduce or modify the rules suggested by Scheele and Groeben. Another way is perhaps also to abandon confrontational questions (e.g., in interviews with patients on their subjective theories of illness). In the major part of the research on subjective theories, only a short version of the method is applied. Another problem is the interpretation of the data collected with it, because there are no explicit suggestions for how to proceed. Experience shows that coding procedures fit best (see Chapters 25 and 26). Due to the complex structure of the single case, attempts at generalization face the problem of how to summarize different subjective theories to groups. For research questions related to (e.g., biographical) processes or unconscious parts of actions, this method is not suitable.

The Problem-centered Interview

The problem-centered interview suggested by Andreas Witzel (Witzel 2000; see also Witzel and Reiter 2012) has attracted some interest and been applied mainly in German psychology. Witzel developed it in the context of biographical research interested in professional biographies of different groups of people. We will look at it in some detail here, as it includes some suggestions of how to formulate questions and of how to probe during the interview itself. In particular, by using an interview guide incorporating questions and narrative stimuli it is possible to collect biographical data with regard to a certain problem. This interview is characterized by three central criteria: *problem centering* (i.e., the researcher's orientation to a relevant social problem); *object orientation* (i.e., that methods are developed or modified with respect to an object of research); and finally *process orientation* in the research process and in the understanding of the object of research.

What Are the Elements of the Problem-centered Interview?

Witzel originally named four "partial elements" for the interview he has conceptualized: "qualitative interview," "biographical method," "case analysis," and "group discussion" (2000, p. 3). His conception of a qualitative interview comprises a preceding short questionnaire, the interview guide, the tape recording, and the postscript (an interview protocol). The interview guide is designed to support the narrative string developed by the interviewee. But above all, it is used as a basis for giving the interview a new turn "in the case of a stagnating conversation or an unproductive topic." The interviewer has to decide on the basis of the interview guide "when to bring in his or her problem-centered interest in the form of exmanent [i.e., directed] questions in order to further differentiate the topic" (Box 16.5).

─BOX 16.5─

Example Questions from the Problem-centered Interview

1 What comes spontaneously to your mind when you hear the keywords "health risks or dangers?"
2 Which health risks do you see for yourself?
3 Do you do anything to keep yourself healthy?
4 Many people say that poisons in air, water, and food impair our health.

   (a) How do you estimate that problem?
   (b) Do you feel environmental pollutants endanger your health? Which ones?
   (c) What made you concern yourself with the health consequences of environmental pollutants?

   ...

   (a) How do you inform yourself about the topic "environment and health?"
   (b) How do you perceive the information in the media?
   (c) How credible are scientific statements in this context? What about the credibility of politicians?

Source: Ruff (1990)

Four central communicative strategies in the problem-centered interview are mentioned: the conversational entry, general and specific prompting, and ad hoc questions. In a study on how adolescents found their occupation, Witzel used as a conversational entry: "You want to become [a car mechanic etc.]; how did you arrive at this decision? Please, just tell me that!" General probing provides further "material" and details of what has so far been presented. For this purpose, additional questions like "What happened there in detail?" or "Where do you know that from?" are used. Specific probing deepens the understanding on the part of the interviewer by mirroring (summarizing, feedback, interpretation by the interviewer) what has been said, by questions of comprehension, and by confronting the interviewee with contradictions and inconsistencies in his or her statements. Here, it important that the interviewer makes clear his or her substantial interest and is able to maintain a good atmosphere in the conversation.

─CASE STUDY 16.3─

Subjective Theories of Illness in Pseudo-croup

The example here shows how this method can be applied, if you concentrate on its core elements. The example comes from an area of health problems. The study is a typical example of using interviews in a qualitative study. The issue under study was a relatively new one, with little research available at that time. The research focused on lay knowledge and the perspective of the participants on the issue under study. Therefore, this example was selected to show what you can do with problem-centered or similar interviews.

In his study about the subjective theories of illness[2] of 32 children with pseudo-croup (a strong cough in children caused by environmental pollution), Ruff (1998) conducted problem-centered interviews with the subjects' parents. The interview guide included the following key questions (see also Box 16.5):

- How did the first illness episode occur, and how did the parents deal with it?
- What do the parents see as the cause of their children's illness?
- What are the consequences of the parents' view of the problem for their everyday lives and further planning of their lives?
- According to the parents' judgment, which environmental pollutants carry risks for their children's health? How do they deal with them? (Ruff 1998, p. 287)

As a main finding, it was stated that in their subjective theories of illness about two-thirds of the interviewed parents assumed a relation between their children's illness of the respiratory tract and air pollution. Although in the main they saw air pollution as only one reason among possible others and linked the causal assumptions with high uncertainty, the majority of these parents had adapted their everyday lives and also partly the planning of their further lives to that new view of the problem (1998, pp. 292–294).

This example shows how some of the basic ideas of the problem-centered interview were taken up by the author and adapted to his specific research question.

What Is the Contribution to the General Methodological Discussion?

For a general discussion beyond his own approach, Witzel's suggestion to use a short questionnaire together with the interview is fruitful. Using such a questionnaire will allow you to collect the data (e.g., demographic data), which are less relevant than the topics of the interview itself, before the actual interview. This permits you to reduce the number of questions and—what is particularly valuable in a tight time schedule—to use the short time of the interview for more essential topics. Contrary to Witzel's suggestion to use this questionnaire before the interview, I think it makes more sense to use it at the end: this will prevent its structure of questions and answers imposing itself on the dialogue in the interview.

As a second suggestion, the postscript may be carried over from Witzel's approach into other forms of interviews. Immediately after the end of the interview, the interviewer should note his or her impressions of the communication, of the interviewee as a person, of him- or herself and his or her behavior in the situation, external influences, the room in which the interview took place, and so on. Thus, context information that might be instructive is documented. This may be helpful for the later interpretation of the statements in the interview and allow the comparison of different interview situations.

With regard to the tape recording of interviews suggested by Witzel for being able to take the context of statements into account better, this practice has already been established for a long time in using interviews. The different strategies for probing the interviewee's answers that Witzel suggests (general and specific probing) are another suggestion that might be carried over to other interview forms.

How Does the Method Fit into the Research Process?

The theoretical background of the method is the interest in subjective viewpoints. The research is based on a process model with the aim of developing theories (see Chapter 10). Research questions are oriented to knowledge about facts or socialization processes. The selection of interviewees should proceed gradually (see Chapter 13) in order to make the process orientation of the method work. This approach is not committed to any special method of interpretation but mostly to coding procedures: qualitative content analysis (see Chapter 26) is mainly used (see also Witzel (2000) for suggestions on how to analyze this form of interviews).

What Are the Limitations of the Method?

The combination of narratives and questions suggested by Witzel is aimed at focusing the interviewee's view of the problem on which the interview is centered. At some points, Witzel's suggestions of how to use the interview guide give the impression of an over-pragmatic understanding of how to handle the interview situation. He therefore suggests introducing questions to shortcut narratives about an unproductive topic. Witzel includes group discussions and "biographical method" with the aim of integrating the different approaches. As the author discusses these parts under the heading of elements of the problem-centered interview, the role of the group discussion, for example, remains unclear here: it might be added as a second or additional step, but a group discussion cannot be part of an interview with one person.

There have been reservations about the criterion of problem centering. This criterion is not very useful in distinguishing this method from others as most interviews are focusing on special problems. However, the name and the concept of the method make the implicit promise that it is—perhaps more than other interviews—centered on a given problem. This makes the method often especially attractive for beginners in qualitative research.

Witzel's suggestions for the interview guide stress that it should comprise areas of interest but does not mention concrete types of questions to include. Although instructions about how to shape deeper inquiries to interviewee's answers are given to the interviewer with the "general and specific probing," applications of the method have shown that these instructions do not save the interviewers from facing the trade-off between depth and range outlined in the discussion of focused interviews above.

The interviews discussed up to now have been presented in greater detail with regard to methodological aspects. The focused interview has been described because it was the driving force behind such methods in general and because it offers some suggestions on how to realize interviews in general. The semi-standardized interview includes different types of questions and is complemented by ideas about how to structure its contents during data collection. The problem-centered interview offers additional suggestions about how to document the context and how to deal with secondary information. In what follows some other types of semi-structured interviews, which have been developed for specific fields of application in qualitative research, are briefly discussed.

Expert and Elite Interviews

The methods of interviewing discussed so far are not specified in terms of their target group. They have been designed for being applied with all kinds of interviewees, whatever the requirements of the research question are. In this section, two approaches will be presented, which are designed for specific and limited groups of potential interviewees: experts in institutions, who have specific insights and knowledge because of their professional position and expertise; and elite interviews addressing rather high-ranking representatives of organizations or in public life. In both cases a specific preparation of and for the interview is necessary. A second problem is how to identify the right experts or elites and that the number of potential interviewees is rather limited.

Expert Interviews

Meuser and Nagel (2009) discuss the expert interview as a specific form of applying semi-structured interviews. In contrast to biographical interviews, here the interviewees are of less interest as a (whole) person than their capacities as experts for a certain field of activity. They are integrated into the study not as a single case but as representing a group (of specific experts; see also Chapter 13). But who should be seen as an expert? We find different opinions about this:

> The answer to the question, who or what are experts, can be very different depending on the issue of the study and the theoretical and analytical approach used in it. … We can label those persons as experts who are particularly competent as authorities on a certain matter of facts. (Deeke 1995, pp. 7–8)

This definition also covers people as experts for their own biography or chronically ill persons as experts for their illness. If expert interviews are used, mostly staff members of an organization with a specific function and a specific (professional) experience and knowledge are the target groups. Bogner and Menz (2009, p. 19) give a more clearly formulated definition of expert and expert knowledge for this purpose:

> Experts have technical process oriented and interpretive knowledge referring to their specific professional sphere of activity. Thus, expert knowledge does not only consist of systematized and reflexively accessible specialist knowledge, but it has the character of practical knowledge in big parts. Different and even disparate precepts for activities and individual rules of decision, collective orientations and social interpretive patterns are part of it. The experts' knowledge and orientations for practices, relevancies etc. have also – and this is decisive – a chance to become hegemonic in a specific organizational or functional context. This means, experts have the opportunity to assert their orientations at least partly. By becoming practically relevant, the experts' knowledge structures the practical conditions of other actors in their professional field in a substantial way.

The experts' function in their field often leads to a certain time pressure if interviews are planned. Therefore, expert interviews are normally based on an interview schedule, even if the narrative interview (see Chapter 18) originally was created for interviewing experts (local politicians) for a specific political process—local decision making. The concentration on the status of the authority in a specific function restricts the scope of the potentially relevant information that the interviewee is expected to provide, and does so much more than in other forms of interviews.

Aims and Forms of Expert Interviews

Expert interviews can be used with different aims. Bogner and Menz (2009, pp. 46–49) suggest a threefold typology of expert interviews. Such interviews can be used (1) for exploration, for orientation in a new field in order to give the field of study a thematic structure and to generate hypotheses (2009, p. 46). This type of interview can also be used for preparing the main instrument in a study for other target groups (e.g., patients). The systematizing expert interview (2) can be used to collect context information complementing insights coming from applying other methods (e.g., interviews with patients). Theory-generating expert interviews (3) aim at developing a typology or a theory about an issue from reconstructing the knowledge of various experts—for example, about contents and gaps in the knowledge of people working in certain institutions concerning the needs of a specific target group.

In this context, the distinction made by Meuser and Nagel (2002, p. 76) becomes relevant: both process knowledge and context knowledge can be reconstructed in expert interviews. In the former, the aim is to have information about a specific process: how does the introduction of a quality management instrument in a hospital proceed; which problems occurred in concrete examples; how were they addressed? What happens if people in a specific situation (e.g., being homeless) become chronically ill; who do they address first; what barriers do they meet; how does the typical patient career develop? From such a process knowledge, we can distinguish context knowledge: how many of these cases can be noted; which institutions are responsible for helping them; what role is played by health insurance or by the lack of insurance etc.?

Bogner and Menz (2009, p. 52) further distinguish between technical knowledge (1), which "contains information about operations and events governed by rules, application routines that are specific for a field, bureaucratic competences and so on," and process knowledge (2). This knowledge:

> relates to inspection of and acquisition of information about sequences of actions and interaction routines, organizational constellations, and past or current events, and where the expert because of his or her practical activity is directly involved or about which he or she at least has more precise knowledge because these things are close to his or her field of action.

The third type is interpretive knowledge (3), that is, "the expert's subjective orientations, rules, points of view and interpretations," which can be accessed in expert interviews to be seen "as a heterogeneous conglomeration" (p. 52).

How to Conduct an Expert Interview

Due to time pressure and to the narrow focus in its application, the interview guide here has a much stronger directive function with regard to excluding unproductive topics. On this point, Meuser and Nagel discuss a series of problems and sources of failing in expert interviews. The main question is whether or not the interviewer manages to restrict and determine the interview and the interviewee to the expertise of interest. Meuser and Nagel (2009, pp. 71–72) identify a number of forms of failure, as follows:

- The expert blocks the interview in its course, because he or she proves not to be an expert for this topic as previously assumed.
- The expert tries to involve the interviewer in ongoing conflicts in the field and talks about internal matters and intrigues in his or her work instead of talking about the topic of the interview.
- He or she often changes between the roles of expert and private person, so that more information results about him or her as a person than about his or her expert knowledge.
- As an intermediate form between success and failure, the "rhetoric interview" is mentioned. In this, the expert gives a lecture on his or her knowledge instead of joining the question–answer game of the interview. If the lecture hits the topic of the interview, the latter may nevertheless be useful. If the expert misses the topic, this form of interaction makes it more difficult to return to the actual relevant topic.

Interview guides have a double function here:

> The work, which goes into developing an interview guide, ensures that researchers do not present themselves as incompetent interlocutors. ... The orientation to an interview guide also ensures that the interview does not get lost in topics that are of no relevance and permits the expert to extemporize his or her issue and view on matters. (Meuser and Nagel, 2002, p. 77)

Ways of Using Expert Interviews

Like other methods, you can use the expert interview as a stand-alone method, if your study aims at a comparison of contents and differences of expert knowledge in a field, which is held by representatives of different institutions. Then you select the relevant people, do enough interviews in a sufficient variety, and analyze them. But, at least at the same frequency, expert interviews are used to complement other methods—beforehand for developing the main instrument or for orientation in the field (see above) or parallel to rounding up information from other interviews. Finally they can also be used after the main data collection, for example, in an expert validation of findings resulting from interviews. Then the expert interview often is not used as a single, but rather as a complementary, method. Both can be seen as an example of triangulation (see Chapters 29 and 14) of different perspectives on an issue under study.

Elite Interviews

Littig (2009) compares the approach of interviewing experts, which she sees as more prominent in the German-speaking discussions, to the tradition of interviewing elites, which is more prominent in the Anglo-Saxon discussion. In the latter, elites are defined as:

> a group of individuals, who hold, or have held, a privileged position in society and, as such, as far as a political scientist is concerned, are likely to have had more influence on political outcomes than general members of the public. (Richards 1996, p. 199)

This definition shows that, here, more the top positions in the hierarchies of institutional or public life are in the focus, whereas the experts mentioned above are often located in middle-range positions and have more of an insight into institutional routines and processes than a top-down perspective. The potential target person for an elite interview is described as:

> an informant (usually male) who occupies a senior or middle management position; has functional responsibility in an area which enjoys high status in accordance with corporate values; has considerable industry experience and frequently also long tenure with the company; possesses a broad network of personal relationships; and has considerable international exposure. (Welch, Marschan-Piekkari, Penttinen, and Tahvanainen 2002, p. 613)

Harvey (2011) gives some advice about strategies for conducting elite interviews, whereas Mikecz (2012) addresses methodological and practical issues, such as how to gain access to and the trust of potential interviewees. He mentions the influence of doing the interview in the interviewee's office, of the problem of getting "the respondents' honest opinions, however subjective or emotional they are" (p. 484) and the major question of the researcher's positionality. Referring to Welch et al. (2002), he suggests that researchers should attempt to take the position of the "informed outsider," which again—as in the expert interview—underlines the importance of being informed and a competent dialogue partner as expectations to be fulfilled by the interviewer. As the first problem often is to define and identify the "right" people as the elites who are relevant for the study, and then the second is that the interviewer has to manage to be taken seriously as a competent exchange partner, Mikecz draws the conclusions:

> The key insight of this article is that the success of elite interviews hinges on the researcher's knowledgeability of the interviewees. … The researcher's positionality is central to successful elite interviewing. It is not determined on an "insider/outsider" dichotomy but is on an "insider/outsider" continuum that can be positively influenced by the researcher through preparation. (2012, pp. 491–492)

What Are the Problems in Conducting Expert and Elite Interviews?

First of all, it is often not easy to identify the "right" experts (or elites) when you are interested in processes in institutions, for example. In the next step it can be difficult to convince them to give an interview. Here and during the interview, the issue of time restrictions comes up—expert interviews often have to be calculated and run much tighter than other forms of interviews. Finally, they demand a high level of expertise from the interviewer—for understanding the relevant, often rather complex processes the interview is about and for asking the right questions and probing in an appropriate way. Furthermore, the problem of confidentiality comes up here—often delicate issues for an organization, also in competition with other players in the market, are mentioned. This may lead to answers being refused or to reservations about tape recording; it can also lead to complicated processes of approving the research by higher authorities.

What Is the Contribution to the General Methodological Discussion?

In this field of application, you will find the highlights of various interview problems. Problems of directing arise more intensely here, because the interviewee is less interesting as a person than in a certain capacity. The expert interview makes some of the methodological problems of a pragmatically oriented qualitative research visible or allows them to be demonstrated: how can we get methodologically controlled access to subjective experiences in a limited time, with a specific focus, without taking the whole person or life history into account? The need for interviewers to make clear in the interview that they are also familiar with its topic is in general a condition for successfully conducting such interviews.

How Does the Method Fit into the Research Process?

The theoretical background is to reconstruct subjective views in a specific aspect (see Chapter 7). The selection of interviewees will be based on purposive sampling. Theoretical sampling is only one option here. The alternatives suggested by Patton (2002) may be more appropriate (see Chapter 13). The interpretation of expert interviews mainly aims at analyzing and comparing the content of the expert knowledge by using specific forms of coding (see Chapters 25 and 26).

What Are the Limitations of the Method?

The focus in using the method can be a reason that is often only applied as a complementary instrument. Time pressure and other technical problems which may come up can mean that it reaches its limits as a single method. For many research questions, the exclusive focus on the knowledge of a specific target group may be too narrow.

The Ethnographic Interview

In the context of ethnographic field research, participant observation is mainly used. In applying it, however, interviews also play a part. A particular problem is how to shape conversations arising in the field into interviews in which the unfolding of the other's specific experiences is aligned with the issue of the research in a systematic way. The local and temporal frameworks are less clearly delimited than in other interview situations, where time and place are arranged exclusively for the interview. Here opportunities for an interview often arise spontaneously and surprisingly from regular field contacts. Explicit suggestions for conducting such an ethnographic interview are made by Spradley:

> It is best to think of ethnographic interviews as a series of friendly conversations into which the researcher slowly introduces new elements to assist informants to respond as informants. Exclusive use of these new ethnographic elements, or introducing them too quickly, will make interviews become like a formal interrogation. Rapport will evaporate, and informants may discontinue their co-operation. (1979, pp. 58–59)

According to Spradley (1979, pp. 59–60), ethnographic interviews include the following elements that distinguish them from such "friendly conversations":

- a specific request to hold the interview (resulting from the research question);
- ethnographic explanations in which the interviewer explains the project (why an interview at all) or the noting of certain statements (why he or she notes what); these are completed by everyday language explanations (with the aim that informants present relations in their language), interview explanations (making clear why this specific form of talking is chosen, with the aim that the informant gets involved), and explanations for certain (types of) questions, explicitly introducing the way of asking;
- ethnographic questions, that is, descriptive questions, structural questions (answering them should show how informants organize their knowledge about the issue), and contrast questions (they should provide information about the meaning dimensions used by informants to differentiate objects and events in their world).

With this method, the general problem of making and maintaining interview situations arises in an emphatic way because of the open framework. The characteristics that Spradley mentions for designing and explicitly defining interview situations apply also to other contexts in which interviews are used. In these, some of the clarifications may be made outside the actual interview situation. Nonetheless, the explicit clarifications outlined by Spradley are helpful for producing a reliable working agreement for the interview, which guarantees that the interviewee really joins in. The method is mainly used in combination with field research and observational strategies (see Chapter 20).

You can find a more recent overview of using ethnographic interviews in Heyl (2001). Following Kvale (1996), a stronger focus is on the interview as a co-construction by the interviewer and the interviewee. Heyl links the field of ethnographic interviewing with current works concerning how to shape interviews in general (e.g., Bourdieu 1996; Gubrium and Holstein 1995; Kvale 1996; Mishler 1986; and others), but does not develop a specific approach in ethnographic interviewing.

Online Interviewing

When qualitative research is based on interviews, it is often the face-to-face contact and the personal relationship, based on verbal and non-verbal communications, that are its strengths. In this situation, the researcher stimulates the dialogue in details and specifics, which then is a condition for the quality of data. Transcribing interviews as data collection is a cost to the researchers before they analyze the data. Also, you have to meet people to interview them. That means they may have to come to your office or you have to travel to see them. It is easier to work with a local sample. If you do your research while living in the countryside or if your interviewees are spread across the country or even several countries, this can be more difficult to organize and to finance. This may reduce your sample from relevant to accessible people. Finally, there may be some people who feel uneasy spontaneously answering a series of questions over an hour or two, which may lead them to reject participation in your research. All these practical issues are reasons on one level that might lead researchers to do interviews online if the target groups of their study are likely to be reached by e-mail or the Internet. But of course there are also good reasons on another level for doing online interviews: for example, if the research issue has much to do with Internet usage or if the target group is best to be found in online contexts. For these reasons online interviewing has developed as a specific way of doing interviews and complements the repertoire of interview methods. On a methodological level, guiding questions for integrating online interviewing in this repertoire might be: What are the differences and common features of traditional and online interviewing? How can the different forms of interviewing be transferred to online research? How do you proceed in collecting and analyzing the data?

Online interviewing can be organized in a synchronous form, which means that you get in touch with your participant in a chatroom where you can directly exchange questions and answers while you are both online at the same time. This comes closest to the verbal exchange in a face-to-face interview. But online interviews can also be organized in an asynchronous form, which means that you send your questions to the participants and they send their answers back after some time and you are not necessarily online at the same time. The latter version is mostly done in the form of e-mail exchanges, but researchers may also use messaging systems or websites for sharing questions and answers.

E-mail Interviewing

On the practical level, online interviewing will be organized differently from face-to-face interviewing. Semi-structured interviews are normally run in a single meeting with the interviewee. A set of questions is prepared in advance. In an online interview, you could try to do the same by sending a set of questions to participants and asking them to send back the answers. But this comes closer to the situation of sending out a questionnaire in a survey than to the situation of a semi-structured interview. Therefore, some authors suggest that you design the collection of data more interactively by sending one or two questions, which will be answered by the participants. After that you can spend the next (one or two) questions asking for answers and so on. Thus the online interview forms a series of e-mail exchanges.

Practicalities of E-mail Interviewing

Where do you find your participants for an e-mail interview? The easiest way is to address people whose e-mail address you already have or whose e-mail address you are able to retrieve (from their home pages or from the home pages of their institutions, such as universities). You can also use snowballing techniques, which means that you ask your first participants for the addresses of other potential participants for your study. You can also go into discussion groups or chatrooms and post information about your research, asking people to contact you if they are interested in participating.

However, you will face several problems in following these ways. First, using these ways, in some cases, will mean you have only abbreviated information, like people's e-mail address or the nickname they use in discussion groups or chatrooms. In some cases, you will know no more about them or have to rely on the information they give you about their gender, age, location, and so on. This may raise questions of reliability of such demographic information and lead to problems of contextualizing the statements in the later interview. As Markham (2004, p. 360) holds: "What does it mean to interview someone for almost two hours before realizing (s)he is not the gender the researcher thought (s)he was?" In contrast to face-to-face interviews, in online interviews the supposed interviewee may have delegated the task of answering to someone else or run the draft responses past someone else for approval before sending them to you. This may contradict one of the major aims of interviewing—to elicit spontaneous and subjective views of the interviewee—without giving the interviewer the chance to become aware of this.

For example, if you want to compare statements in the context of the age of the participants, you should have reliable information about the age of every participant. These ways of access—and degrees of retaining the anonymity of the participants you accessed—may also lead to problems in sampling in your research. It is not just that traditional parameters of representativeness are difficult to apply and check in such a sample; it can also be difficult to apply strategies of theoretical or purposive sampling (see Chapter 13) here.

Once you have found a solution for how to sample and address participants for your study, you should prepare instructions for them about what you expect from them when they participate in your study. In face-to-face research, you can explain your expectations in a direct oral exchange when recruiting people or before you start your questions in the interview situation and respond to your participants' questions. In online interviewing you have to prepare instructions in written form, and they have to be clear and detailed, so that the participant knows what to do. At the same time, the instructions should not be too long in order to avoid confusion and neglect on the side of the interviewee.

As in face-to-face interviewing, it is necessary in online interviewing to build up a temporal relationship (rapport) with the interviewees, even if the communication may be asynchronous and responses come with some delay (even days). Face-to-face communication (and interviewing) may be more spontaneous than online communication, but the latter allows the participants to reflect on their answers more than the former. Following Baym (1995), Mann and Stewart (2000, p. 129) see five factors as important to consider as influences on computer-mediated interaction in interviews:

1 What is the purpose of the interaction/interview? This will influence the interest of possible participants of whether or not to become involved in the study.
2 What is the temporal structure of the research? Are synchronous or asynchronous methods used and will there be a series of interactions in the research or not?
3 What are the possibilities and limitations coming from the software influencing the interaction?
4 What are the characteristics of the interviewer and the participants? What about the experience of and attitude to using technology? What about their knowledge of the topics,

writing skills, insights, etc.? Is one-to-one interaction or researcher–group interaction planned? Has there been any interaction between researcher and participant before? How is the structure of the group addressed by the research (hierarchies, gender, age, ethnicity, social status, etc.)?

5 What is the external context of the research—inter/national culture and/or communities of meaning that are involved? How do their communicative practices outside the research influence the latter?

When running the interview itself, you can send one question or a couple of questions, wait for the answers, and then probe (as in a face-to-face interview) or go on with sending the next questions. If there is a longer delay before answers come, you can send a reminder (after a few days, for example). Bampton and Cowton (2002) view a decline in length and quality of responses as well as answers that are coming more slowly as signs of fading interest on the side of the participant and for the interview to come to an end.

What Are the Problems in Conducting the Method?

Online interviewing is a way to transfer face-to-face interviewing to Internet research. There is a much greater amount of anonymity for the participants, which may protect them from any detection of their person during the research and from the results. For the researchers, this makes any form of (real-life) contextualization of the statements and the persons in their study much more difficult.

What Is the Contribution to the General Methodological Discussion?

Online interviewing is a way of making qualitative research in the context of Internet research work. It can be very helpful if you want to integrate participants in your study who are not easily accessible, because they live far away or because they do not want to talk to a stranger (about a possibly sensitive topic). Online research can also allow its participants to have anonymity, which can be an advantage. Online interviewing produces data which are already available in the form of texts, so that you can skip the time-consuming step of transcribing your interviews.

How Does the Method Fit into the Research Process?

Most forms of interviewing can be adapted and applied to Internet research. Sampling will have to be purposive sampling (see Chapter 13), which again has to be adapted and faces some problems if you do not get enough information about your participants. Online interviews can be analyzed quite easily by coding and categorization (see Chapters 25 and 26), whereas hermeneutic approaches have to be adapted to these sorts of data.

What Are the Limitations of the Method?

Online interviewing is a kind of simulation of real-world interviewing and spontaneity of verbal exchange is replaced by the reflexivity of written exchanges. Nonverbal or paralinguistic elements of communication are difficult to transport and integrate. Finally, the application of this approach is limited to people ready and willing to use computer-mediated communication or this kind of technology and communication in general.

How to Analyze Interviews

There are a variety of interviews (some have been discussed here, some will be topics of Chapter 18), which come with a number of common issues for the step of analyzing them. Basically the whole range of analytic methods discussed in Part 6 of this book can be applied to interviews in general, although some forms call for specific treatment.

Common steps in interviewing across the methodological range are that interviews should be recorded and transcribed (see Chapter 24) so that there is a solid database for the analysis. Roulston (2014, p. 301) holds: "In broad terms, analyzing interview data includes the phases of (1) data reduction; (2) data reorganization; and (3) data representation." In her article, she unfolds this general statement for a more differentiated perspective including narrative and hermeneutic approaches and grounded theory forms of coding. However, she sees the identification of relevant passages in the interview(s) as the first step, which then should be categorized and ordered again around the issue of the research. The next step (for her) is to make an interpretation of these relevant parts of the material. As challenges, she mentions the management of bigger data sets and how to avoid statements being forced to fit into existing categories or even hypotheses.

Another issue for the analysis of interviews is how much attention is paid to the single interview (and interviewee) from a case-oriented perspective: Are we interested in a collection of statements about one (or more) specific topic as part of the issue coming from all interviewees, or are we interested in a fuller picture concerning the single interviewee? Both can be applied in series—topic-related comparisons about a series of issues as well as a series of case-related analyses that are then compared—and in combinations. For expert interviews, Meuser and Nagel (2009, pp. 35–37) suggest a rather pragmatic approach: for example, to transcribe only the relevant passages, to work with paraphrases, coding, and thematic comparison of the main statements (and not of all the material). According to Meuser and Nagel, transcription should be limited to the parts that are relevant for the research question and to those which were not affected by the forms of failing discussed above. Transcription should be limited to contents more than formal aspects of how something was said. Categorization is also based on formulating headings for parts of the interviews, which then are used for a "thematic comparison" (p. 36), before sociological conceptualization and theoretical generalization follow.

Finally, for interviews (as for other forms of qualitative data), ways of storing and making them available in archives have been discussed for some time (see the special issues of the online journal *FQS* (2005, Vol. 5(2) and 2011, Vol. 12(3) www.qualitative-research.net/index.php/fqs/issue/archive) for overviews. Major issues in this discussion are about how to make qualitative (interview) data available for reanalysis by other researchers or for new research questions (see Wästersfors, Åkerström, and Jacobsson 2014), but also accessible for critical re-examination of the researcher's interpretations by other researchers. Once such archives are publicly accessible they require an infrastructure (see, e.g., Corti 2011) that is maintained and funded permanently.

Checklist for Doing Interviews

The following checklist is designed to help you to decide whether to use interviews and which form might be best for your research. You may also apply these questions to studies with interviews you read.

1 How far can the issue of your research be studied by asking people about it?
2 What is the main focus of your study; what should be the main focus of your interview?
3 Who will be your interview partners—lay people, professionals, experts, elites?
4 Where and how can you access your interview partners?
5 What good reasons are there, if any, for doing your interviews online?
6 How will you document your data—recording and transcription? If not, why not?
7 How will you manage ethical issues like informed consent in your interviews?
8 What is important to document about the context of your interviews as part of the data?

KEY POINTS

- The interview forms in this chapter proceed in different ways towards similar goals. Interviewees should be given as much scope as possible to reveal their views. At the same time, they should be given a structure for what to talk about.
- The interview forms can be applied in themselves, but more often they provide an orientation for designing an interview and a list of questions to cover the research issue.
- A very important step is planning for probing interviewees. Decide what you will ask if the interviewees' answers remain too general or if they miss the point that you intended.
- Interviews can be extended to a second meeting with two aims: first, to check the adequacy of the main statements with the interviewee (communicative validation); second, to develop with interviewees a representation of the structure of their statements.

1 Look in a journal for a qualitative study based on interviews (e.g., Flick et al. 2012a). Try to identify which of the methods presented in this chapter was used in it or could be seen as an orientation in relation to the study.
2 Consider the study's questions and then improve them by using one or more of the interviewing methods presented in this chapter.
3 Think of your own study and develop an interview guide for your research question according to one of the interview forms presented here.
4 Take one of the methods of interviewing discussed in this chapter and think about ways and problems of transferring this method to online research.

─Further Reading─

How to Conduct Interviews

The first text below is typical of a more attitudinal approach to interviewing, while the others treat more concrete and also technical problems:

Fontana, A. and Frey, J.H. (2000) "The Interview: From Structural Questions to Negotiated Texts," in N. Denzin and Y.S. Lincoln (eds.), *Handbook of Qualitative Research*. London: Sage. pp. 645–672.
Hermanns, H. (2004) "Interviewing as An Activity," in U. Flick, E.v. Kardorff and I. Steinke (eds.), *A Companion to Qualitative Research*. London: Sage. pp. 209–213.
Kvale, S. (1996) *Interviews: An Introduction to Qualitative Research Interviewing*. London: Sage.
Kvale, S. (2007) *Doing Interviews*. London: Sage.
Rubin, H. J. and Rubin, I. S. (2012) *Qualitative Interviewing: The Art of Hearing Data* (3rd edn). London: Sage.
Wengraf, T. (2001) *Qualitative Research Interviewing: Biographic Narrative and Semi-Structured Methods*. London: Sage.

The Focused Interview

The second text below is the classic text on the focused interview, whereas the other two offer more recent developments and applications of this strategy:

Merton, R.K. (1987) "The Focused Interview and Focus Groups: Continuities and Discontinuities," *Public Opinion Quarterly*, 51: 550–556.
Merton, R.K. and Kendall, P.L. (1946) "The Focused Interview," *American Journal of Sociology*, 51: 541–557.
Oerter, R., Oerter, R., Agostiani, H., Kim, H.O. and Wibowo, S. (1996) "The Concept of Human Nature in East Asia: Etic and Emic Characteristics," *Culture & Psychology*, 2: 9–51.

The Semi-standardized Interview

The first text outlines methodological strategies for realizing the aims of this kind of method, whereas the second gives an introduction to the theoretical background and assumptions they are based on:

Flick, U. (1992) "Triangulation Revisited: Strategy of or Alternative to Validation of Qualitative Data," *Journal for the Theory of Social Behavior*, 22: 175–197.

Groeben, N. (1990) "Subjective Theories and the Explanation of Human Action," in G.R. Semin and K.J. Gergen (eds.), *Everyday Understanding: Social and Scientific Implications*. London: Sage. pp. 19–44.

The Problem-centered Interview

These texts outline the method and the problems of applying it:

Witzel, A. (2000, January) "The Problem-Centered Interview [27 paragraphs]," *Forum Qualitative Sozialforschung/Forum: Qualitative Social Research* [Online Journal], 1(1), www. qualitative-research.net/fqs-texte/1-00/1-00witzel-e.htm (date of access: March 25, 2013).

Witzel, A. and Reiter, H. (2012) *The Problem-centred Interview*. London: Sage.

Expert and Elite Interviews

This text outlines the methods and the problems of applying it:

Bogner, A., Littig, B. and Menz, W. (eds.) (2009) *Interviewing Experts*. Basingstoke: Palgrave Macmillan.

The Ethnographic Interview

The first text is an outline of the method and the second puts it in the framework of participant observation:

Heyl, B.S. (2001) "Ethnographic Interviewing," in P. Atkinson, A. Coffey, S. Delamont, J. Lofland and L. Lofland (eds.), *Handbook of Ethnography*. London: Sage. pp. 369–383.

Spradley, J.P. (1979) *The Ethnographic Interview*. New York: Holt, Rinehart and Winston.

Online Interviewing

The first text describes e-mail interviewing in some detail, while the second refers to both areas and is a very good introduction to qualitative online research:

Bampton, R. and Cowton, C.J. (2002, May) "The E-Interview," *Forum Qualitative Sozialforschung/Forum: Qualitative Social Research*, 3(2), www.qualitative-research.net/fqs/fqs-eng.htm (date of access: February 22, 2005).

Gaiser, T.J. and Schreiner, A.E. (2009) *A Guide to Conducting Online Research*. London: Sage.

How to Analyze Interviews

This text describes ways of analyzing interviews in some detail:

Roulston, K. (2014) "Analyzing Interviews", in U. Flick (ed.), *The SAGE Handbook of Qualitative Data Analysis*. London: Sage. pp. 297–312.

1 The examples are taken from Merton and Kendall (1946).
2 Whereas the method described earlier was developed especially for reconstructing subjective theories, the problem-centered interview is used for this purpose as well. Thus it is rather coincidental that subjective theories are the object in both examples.

17
Focus Groups

┌─CHAPTER OBJECTIVES─

This chapter is designed to help you

- familiarize yourself with the different ways of collecting data in a group;
- understand the differences between group interviews, group discussion, and focus groups;
- understand the differences between focus groups and the single interviews;
- identify the problems related to using groups for collecting qualitative data.

The preceding chapter presented several forms of open-ended interviews as a way to collect qualitative data. Semi-structured and narrative interviews (see Chapters 16 and 18) were developed starting from a critique of standardized interview situations. The skepticism about the standardized interview situation was based in part on the argument of its artificiality, because the interviewee is separated from all everyday relations during the interview. Also, the interaction in the standardized interview is not comparable in any way to everyday interactions. Particularly when studying opinions and attitudes about taboo subjects, it was repeatedly suggested that the dynamics of a group discussing such topics should be used, because this is more appropriate than a clear and well-ordered single interview situation.

These methods have been discussed in terms of (1) group interviews, (2) group discussions, or (3) focus groups. By thus extending the scope of data collection, the aim is to collect the data in context and to create a situation of interaction that comes closer to everyday life than the (often one-off) encounter of interviewer and interviewee or narrator permits.

Group Interviews

One way to extend the interview situation is to interview a group of people. Beginning with Merton, Fiske, and Kendall (1956), group interviews have been conducted in a number of studies (Fontana and Frey 2000; Merton 1987). Patton, for example, defines the group interview as follows:

> A focus group interview is an interview with a small group of people on a specific topic. Groups are typically six to eight people who participate in the interview for one-half to two hours. (2002, p. 385)

Several procedures are differentiated, which are more or less structured and moderated by an interviewer. In general, the interviewer should be "flexible, objective, empathic, persuasive, a good listener" (Fontana and Frey 2000, p. 652). Objectivity here mainly means the mediation between the different participants. The interviewer's main task is to prevent single participants or partial groups from dominating the interview and thus the whole group with their contributions. Furthermore, the interviewer should encourage reserved members to become involved in the interview and to give their views and should try to obtain answers from the whole group in order to cover the topic as far as possible. Finally, interviewers must balance their behavior between (directively) steering the group and (non-directively) moderating it.

Patton sees the focus group interview as a highly efficient qualitative data collection technique, which provides some quality controls on data collection: "Participants tend to provide checks and balances on each other which weeds out false or extreme views. The extent to which there is a relatively consistent, shared view can be quickly assessed" (2002, p. 386). He also discusses some weaknesses of the method such as the limited number of questions one can address and the problems of taking notes during the interview. Therefore, he suggests the employment of pairs of interviewers, one of whom is free to document the responses while the other manages the interview and the group. In contrast to other authors, Patton underlines the fact that: "The focus group interview is, first and foremost, an interview. It is not a problem-solving session. It is not a decision-making group. It is not primarily a discussion, although direct interactions among participants often occur. It is an *interview*" (2002, pp. 385–386).

In summary, the main advantages of group interviews are that they are low cost and rich in data, that they stimulate the respondents and support them in remembering events, and that they can lead beyond the answers of the single interviewee.

Group Discussions

The elements of group dynamics and of discussion among the participants are high-lighted when a group discussion is conducted. Blumer, for example, holds that:

> A small number of individuals, brought together as a discussion or resource group, is more valuable many times over than any representative sample. Such a group, discussing collectively their sphere of life and probing into it as they meet one another's disagreements, will do more to lift the veils covering the sphere of life than any other device that I know of. (1969, p. 41)

The methods of open interviews and group discussions both arise from a critique of standardized interviews. However, although the two forms have that in common, group discussions have been used as an explicit *alternative* to open interviews, especially in the German-speaking areas. They have been proposed as a method of interrogation since the studies of the Frankfurt Institute for Social Research (Pollock 1955).

Unlike the group interview, the group discussion both stimulates a discussion and uses the dynamic of developing conversation in the discussion as the central source of knowledge. The method has attracted a lot of interest and is rarely omitted from any textbook. Marketing research and other fields use it often now (for a more general overview, see also Bohnsack 2004). People have different reasons for using this method. In methodological debates about group discussions, there is also the problem of contradictory understandings of what an appropriate group is like. However, it is up to the researcher actually using the method to decide on the "right" conception (i.e., the one which is best fitted to the research object). The alternatives to be found in the literature will be discussed here briefly.

Why Use Group Discussions?

Group discussions are used for various reasons. Pollock prefers them to single interviews because "studying the attitudes, opinions and practices of human beings in artificial isolation from the contexts in which they occur should be avoided" (1955, p. 34). The starting point here is that opinions, which are presented to the interviewer in interviews and surveys, are detached from everyday forms of communication and relations. Group discussions on the other hand correspond to the way in which opinions are produced, expressed, and exchanged in everyday life.

Another feature of group discussions is that corrections by the group concerning views that are not correct, not socially shared, or extreme are available as means for validating statements and views. The group becomes a tool for reconstructing individual opinions more appropriately. However, some researchers studied the group opinion (i.e., the participants' consensus negotiated in the discussion about a certain issue). Mangold (1973) takes the group opinion as an empirical issue, which is expressed in the discussion but exists independently of the situation and applies for the group outside the situation.

Another aim of group discussions is the analysis of common processes of problem solving in the group. Therefore, a concrete problem is introduced and the group's task is to discover, through a discussion of alternatives, the best strategy for solving it. Thus approaches that take group discussions as a medium for better analyzing individual opinions can be differentiated from those that understand group discussions as a medium for a shared group opinion which goes beyond individuals. However, studying processes of negotiating or of solving problems in groups should be separated from analyzing states such as a given group opinion that is only expressed in the discussion.

Forms of Groups

A brief look at the history of, and methodological discussion about, this procedure shows that there have been different ideas about what a group is. A common feature of the varieties of group discussions is to use as a data source the discussion on a specific topic in a natural group (i.e., existing in everyday life) or an artificial group (i.e., put together for the research purpose according to certain criteria). Sometimes it is even suggested that real groups are used, which means groups that are concerned by the issue of the group discussion also independently of the discussion and as a real group including the same members as in the research situation. One reason for this is that real groups start from a history of shared interactions in relation to the issue under discussion and thus have already developed forms of common activities and underlying patterns of meaning.

Furthermore, there is a distinction between homogeneous and heterogeneous groups. In homogeneous groups, members are comparable in the essential dimensions related to the research question and have a similar background. In heterogeneous groups, members should be different in the characteristics that are relevant for the research question. This is intended to increase the dynamics of the discussion so that many different perspectives will be expressed and also that the reserve of individual participants will be broken down by the confrontation between these perspectives.

CASE STUDY 17.1

Student Dropouts: How to Set Up a Group

In a study of the conditions and the subjective experience of students dropping out of teaching programs, a homogeneous group would consist of students of the same age, from the same discipline, and who dropped out of their studies after the same number of terms. If the concrete question focuses on gender differences in the experiences and the reasons for not completing their studies, a homogeneous group is put together comprising only female students, with male students being put into a second group. A heterogeneous

(Continued)

(Continued)

group should include students of various ages, of both genders, from different disciplines (e.g., psychology and information sciences), and from different terms (e.g., dropouts from the first term and from shortly before the end of their studies). The expectation linked to this is that the different backgrounds will lead to intensified dynamics in the discussion, which will reveal more aspects and perspectives of the phenomenon under study.

However, in a homogeneous group the members may differ in other dimensions which were not considered as relevant for the composition of the group. In our example, this was the dimension of the students' current living situation—alone or with their own family.

Another problem is that heterogeneous groups in which the members differ too much may find few starting points for a common discussion. If the conditions of studying the various disciplines are so different, there may be little that the student dropouts can discuss in a concrete way with each other and the discussion may end up in exchanging only general statements.

These considerations show that the distinction between "homogeneous" and "heterogeneous" is only relative. Groups normally comprise five to ten members. Opinions vary about the best size of a group.

This example shows how groups can be composed to meet the needs of a research question. It should also make clear that the definition of homogeneous or heterogeneous is always relative, depending on the research question and the dimension that is important.

What Is the Role of the Moderator?

Another aspect that is treated differently in the various approaches is the role and function of the moderator in the discussion. In some cases, the group's own dynamic is trusted so much that moderation by researchers is abandoned altogether in order to prevent any biasing influence on the discussion in process and content that may arise as a result of their interventions.

However, it is more often the case that moderation of the discussion by a researcher is found to be necessary for pragmatic reasons. Here three forms are distinguished. *Formal direction* is limited to control of the agenda of the speakers and to fixing the beginning, course, and end of the discussion. *Topical steering* additionally comprises the introduction of new questions and steering the discussion towards a deepening and extension of specific topics and parts. Beyond this, *steering the dynamics* of the interaction ranges from reflating the discussion to using provocative questions, polarizing a slow discussion, or accommodating relations of dominance by purposively addressing those members remaining rather reserved in the discussion.

Another possibility is the use of texts, images, and so on to further stimulate the discussion or topics dealt with during the discussion. However, these interventions should only support the dynamics and the functioning of the group. To a large extent the discussion should find its own dynamic level.

In general, the moderator's task is not to disturb the participants' own initiative, but rather to create an open space in which the discussion keeps going, first through the exchange of arguments.

If you decide to use group discussions, you should choose a combination from the alternatives available concerning the aims, the kind and composition of the group, and the function of the moderator chosen for the particular application.

─CASE STUDY 17.2─

Group Discussion with Bank Employees

Krüger (1983) has studied restrictive contexts of actions for a professional future. She conducted eight group discussions with bank employees on the lowest hierarchical level (i.e., officials in charge of specific departments in the credit business). These were real groups because the group members came from one department and knew each other. The groups were homogeneous, as she did not involve superiors in order to exclude any inhibitions. An average group included seven participants.

Krüger emphasizes a non-directive style of moderating in which the moderator should always try to stimulate narrative–descriptive statements. Pointing out phenomena of the situation that have not (yet) been mentioned is suggested as a way to achieve this. The researcher gave stimuli for the discussion. A protocol of the process was made in order to be able to identify speakers in the transcript later. Krüger also underlines that it is essential for the practical conduct of a group discussion that the research question is restricted to a delimited area of experience. In terms of defining cases, she sees the text of each group discussion. This text had to undergo successive stages of interpretation.

This example illustrates the practical issues of making a group discussion fruitful for a specific research question.

What Is the Process, and What Are the Elements, of Group Discussions?

A single scheme cannot show how you should proceed when running a group discussion. The dynamics and the composition of the group essentially influence the way a group discussion unfolds. In real or natural groups, the members already know each other and possibly have an interest in the topic of the discussion. In artificial groups, introducing members to one another and enabling members to make one another's acquaintance should be the first step.

The following steps provide a rough outline of procedure:

- At the beginning, an explanation of the (formal) procedure is given. Here the expectations for the participants are formulated. Expectations can be to be involved in the discussion, perhaps to argue certain topics, to manage a common task, or to solve a problem together. (For example, "We would like you to openly discuss with each other the experiences you have had with your studies, and what it was that made you decide not to continue any further with them.")

- Then follows a short introduction of the members to one another and a phase of warming up to prepare the discussion. Here the moderator should emphasize the common ground of the members in order to facilitate or to reinforce community (e.g., "As former students of psychology, you all should know the problems, the …").
- The actual discussion starts with a "discussion stimulus," which may consist of a provocative thesis, a short film, a lecture on a text, or the unfolding of a concrete problem for which a solution is to be found. Note here some of the parallels to the focused interview (see Chapter 16 and Merton 1987). In order to stimulate discussions about the change of work and living conditions with workers, Herkommer (1979, p. 263) used the discussion stimulus shown in Box 17.1.
- In groups with members that did not know each other in advance, phases of strangeness with, of orientation to, adaptation to, and familiarity with the group, as well as conformity and the discussion drying up, are gone through.

BOX 17.1

Example of a Discussion Stimulus in a Group Discussion

In the following example, a group discussion in the area of research into economic crisis and the resulting uncertainty—a still very relevant issue—is stimulated as follows:

The current economic situation in Germany has become more difficult; this is indicated for example by continuously high unemployment, by problems with pensions and social security, and by tougher wage bargaining. From this, a series of problems in occupations and in workplaces has resulted for workers. In general, a decline in the working climate of factories has occurred. But there are also other problems in everyday life and in the family, e.g., in children's school education. With respect to the problems just mentioned, we would like to hear your opinion on the position: "One day our children will have a better life!" (Herkommer 1979, p. 263)

What Are the Problems in Conducting the Method?

The proclaimed strength of the method compared to interviewing single persons is also the main source of problems in applying it. The dynamics, which are determined by the individual groups, make it more difficult to formulate distinct patterns of process in discussions and also to clearly define the tasks and multiple conducts for the moderators beyond the individual group. For this reason, it is hardly possible to design relatively common conditions for the collection of data in different groups involved in a study.

It is true that the opening of discussions may be shaped uniformly by a specific formulation, a concrete stimulus, and so on. But the twists and turns of the discussion during its further development can hardly be predicted. Therefore, methodological interventions for steering the group may only be planned approximately and many of the decisions on data collection can only be made during the situation.

Similar conditions apply to the decision about when a group has exhausted the discussion of a topic. Here no clear criteria are given, which means that the moderator has to make this decision on the spot.

Problems similar to those that occur in semi-structured interviewing emerge. The problem that the researchers face in mediating between the course of the discussion and their own topical inputs is relevant here too. Indeed, it becomes more serious. It is aggravated here because the researchers have to accommodate the developing dynamics of the group and, at the same time, to steer the discussion in order to integrate all the participants. Thus it remains difficult to handle the problem because of the dynamics of the situation and the group; individual members may dominate while others may refrain from entering into the discussion. In both cases, the result is that some individual members and their views are not available for later interpretation.

Finally, the apparent cost-effectiveness of interviewing several persons at the same time is clearly reduced by the high organizational effort needed to make an appointment which all members of a group can meet.

What Is the Contribution to the General Methodological Discussion?

Group discussions may reveal how opinions are created and above all changed, asserted, or suppressed in social exchange. In a group discussion, verbal data can be collected in their context. Statements and expressions of opinion are made in the context of a group, and these may be commented upon and become the subject of a more or less dynamic process of discussion. A result of the debates about the group discussion as a method is that dynamic and social negotiations of individual views have increasingly been taken into account in the methodological literature as an essential element for understanding social constructions of reality.

How Does the Method Fit into the Research Process?

The theoretical background to applying the method is often provided by structuralist models (see Chapter 7), starting from the dynamic and from the unconscious in the generation of meanings, as becomes evident in group discussions. In more recent applications, the development of theories has been to the fore. Earlier attempts to test hypotheses with this procedure have failed due to the lack of comparability of the data. The close link between the collection and the interpretation of data suggests a circular concept of the research process (see Chapter 10). Research questions focus on how opinions are produced and how they are distributed or shared in a group. In accessing cases and in sampling, researchers face the problem that the groups in which the individuals are assembled for data collection become units themselves. Theoretical sampling (see Chapter 13) may focus on the characteristics of the groups to be integrated (e.g., if groups of psychology students and medical students have been involved so far, would it be better now to integrate engineering students from technical universities or from colleges?), or it may focus on the features of the individual members.

In the interpretation of the data, the individual group again is the unit to start from. Sequential analyses (e.g., objective hermeneutics, see Chapter 27) are suggested, which start from the group and the course of discussion in it. In terms of generalizing the findings, the problem arises of how to summarize the different groups.

What Are the Limitations of the Method?

Group discussions are strongly oriented on conflict, argumentation, and diversity in the data analysis, with the aims of making the data more substantial and of revealing implicit or unconscious parts of participants' relation to the topic of research or the issue of the discussion. This strong impact of the method on the issue is not always adequate, for example, for very sensitive topics.

Focus Groups

Whereas the term "group discussion" was dominant in earlier studies, especially in the German-speaking areas (see Bohnsack 2004), the method has more recently had some kind of renaissance as "focus group" in Anglo-Saxon research (for overviews see Barbour 2007; 2014; Lunt and Livingstone 1996; Merton 1987; Puchta and Potter 2004). Focus groups may be defined broadly as follows: "Any group discussion may be called a focus group as long as the researcher is actively encouraging of, and attentive to, the group interaction" (Kitzinger and Barbour 1999, p. 20).

When to Use Focus Groups

Focus groups are used especially in marketing and media research. Again, the stress is laid on the interactive aspect of data collection. The hallmark of focus groups is the explicit use of group interaction to produce data and insights that would be less accessible without the interaction found in a group (Morgan 1988, p. 12). Focus groups are used as a method on their own or in combination with other methods—surveys, observations, single interviews, and so on. Morgan (1988, p. 11) sees focus groups as useful for:

- orienting oneself to a new field;
- generating hypotheses based on informants' insights;
- evaluating different research sites or study populations;
- developing interview schedules and questionnaires;
- getting participants' interpretations of results from earlier studies.

Barbour (2007) discusses a number of uses for focus groups on the level of research interests. Often one finds an exploratory use of focus groups for developing a questionnaire. The groups can be employed for studying sensitive topics. In particular, Barbour sees their value for accessing the reluctant, which means people who tend to refrain from other forms of social science data collection and in general for accessing hard-to-reach people. Finally they can be used for studying "Why not" questions—what participants think—for example, why their services are not used by a specific target group.

Barbour also identifies a number of ways in which focus groups are used, from a methodological point of view. They can be applied as a stand-alone instrument, which means the research is only based on this method. They can be used together with other methods for exploratory purposes—for gathering information that is necessary for designing a questionnaire or an interview schedule, for example. She also identifies a confirmatory use for other forms of research, for example, for feeding back results from interviews to participants (see below, Case Study 17.3). And they can be useful as one method in mixed-methods (see Chapter 3) or triangulation designs (see Chapter 14).

How to Conduct Focus Groups

A short overview of the literature provides some suggestions for conducting focus groups. The number of groups you should conduct depends on your research question and on the number of different population subgroups required (Morgan 1988, p. 42). It is generally suggested that it is more appropriate to work with strangers instead of groups of friends or people who know each other very well, because the level of things taken for granted, which remain implicit, tends to be higher in the latter (1988, p. 48). It is also suggested that you should begin with groups as heterogeneous as possible and then run a second set of groups that are more homogeneous (1988, p. 73). In each case, it is necessary to start the group with some kind of warming up, as in the examples in Box 17.2.

—BOX 17.2—

Examples for Beginning a Focus Group

These two openings of focus groups are very typical and helpful:

Before we begin our discussion, it will be helpful for us to get acquainted with one another. Let's begin with some introductory comments about ourselves. X, why don't you start and we'll go around the table and give our names and a little about what we do for a living?

(Continued)

(Continued)

Today we're going to discuss an issue that affects all of you. Before we get into our discussion, let me make a few requests of you. First, you should know that we are tape recording the session so that I can refer back to the discussion when I write my report. If anyone is uncomfortable with being recorded please say so and, of course, you are free to leave. Do speak up and let's try to have just one person speak at a time. I will play traffic cop and try to assure that everyone gets a turn. Finally, please say exactly what you think. Don't worry about what I think or what your neighbor thinks. We're here to exchange opinions and have fun while we do it. Why don't we begin by introducing ourselves?

Source: Stewart and Shamdasani (1990, pp. 92–93)

According to Puchta and Potter (2004), it is important when running focus groups to produce informality in the discussion. The moderators need to create a liberal climate, facilitating members to contribute openly both their experiences and opinions. At the same time, it is important that the participants do not drift into just chatting or presenting endless anecdotes with little reference to the issue of the focus group (and the study). Puchta and Potter suggest several strategies on how to balance formality and informality in the practice of focus groups.

It is suggested that you use the contents of the discussions or systematic coding or content analyses as an analytic technique for focus group data. Think about the point of reference in the comparisons. You could try to take the single participants' statements and compare them across all groups. This can be difficult because of the group dynamics and the different development of each group. Therefore, the second alternative might be more adequate. This means that you take the single group as a unit and compare it to the other groups you did. Comparison then focuses on the topics mentioned, the variety of attitudes towards these topics among the members in the group, the stages the discussion ran through, and the results of the discussion in each group.

─CASE STUDY 17.3─

Using Focus Groups for Feedback of Results and Member Check

In our study on health professionals' concepts of health and ageing (Flick, Fischer, Neuber, Walter, and Schwartz 2003; Flick, Walter, Fischer, Neuber, and Schwartz 2004b), we first used episodic interviews (see Chapter 16) to collect data on these concepts, including the interviewees' ideas and experiences with prevention and health promotion. After analyzing these data, we ran focus groups with general practitioners and nurses with three goals. We wanted to give the participants feedback about our study's results.

We also wanted to receive their comments on these results as a way of applying the concept of member check or communicative validation (see Chapter 29 for this). And we wanted to discuss with them practical consequences of the findings for improving day-to-day routines in home care nursing and medicine. This improvement should be directed towards a stronger focus on health, health promotion, and prevention.

To prevent the discussions in the groups from becoming too general and heterogeneous, we looked for a concrete sensitizing concept as an input, which opened up the overall issue. We used the results referring to the barriers against a stronger focus on prevention in their own practice that the interviewees had mentioned in the interviews. We presented the results concerning the patients' and the professionals' readiness and resistance. First, we presented an overview of the barriers that had been mentioned. Then we asked the participants for a ranking of their importance. Next, we asked them to discuss the results in the wider context of health in their own practice. When the discussion started to calm down, we asked them to make suggestions on how to overcome the barriers discussed before, and to discuss such suggestions. In the end, we had a list of comments and suggestions from each group, which we then compared and analyzed as part of our study.

In this example, focus groups were used for a specific purpose. They were not used as a stand-alone method for data collection, but for feedback and member check of the first results of a study. The participants in the focus groups were the same as in the single interviews. However, not all the interviewees accepted our invitation to come and contribute again to our study. Using a stimulus—in this case, the presentation of a selection of results—was helpful to start and structure the discussion. In the end, when we compared the results, we had to use each group as a case, but ended up with comparable views and results.

When Not to Use Focus Groups

In the literature (e.g., Barbour 2007; 2014) a number of research purposes are discussed for which focus groups should not be used, because other methods are more appropriate. Accessing narratives for example is not an aim best reached by focus groups, because the group dynamics will confound and disturb the narrative in its development. An exception might be situations where you are interested in joint narratives (coming from a family, for example; see Chapter 18). But then the design is different from a focus group discussion, which aims at discussions as the format of talk about an issue and not the narrative.

Another aim that cannot really be achieved by using focus groups is the collection and analysis of individual experiences. Here, you will be more successful by using individual interviews, which will allow you to probe much more in detail what is mentioned as an individual experience ("as I found out that I have a chronic disease ..." for example). The main point here is that we should keep in mind that a focus group discussion will lead to a format of exchange that is very different from that in a face-to-face interview: focus groups are not a way of "doing several interviews at the same time."

Another misunderstanding of the use of focus groups is the belief that you can do representative studies with this method. As we will discuss later on, doing a number of focus groups is not the same as doing interviews with the same (number of) people and issues of representativity are more difficult to solve in focus groups. If the aim of the study is to access attitudes of the participants, a questionnaire study will be much more adequate than a focus group study, as you will have difficulties in identifying every participants' attitude in the end from analyzing the discussions of the group.

Another limitation of focus groups becomes evident when you try to study topics with it that are too sensitive: it may be more difficult to talk about such topics in a group of strangers than to an interviewer in a face-to-face situation. The intention of using focus groups in order to save time and money compared to doing interviews is often more difficult to fulfill than expected. The organizational efforts that are often necessary for getting the groups finally to sit down together in the right composition, in the right place, at the right time, and to discuss are one reason. Technical challenges—such as the more demanding ways of recording and transcribing group discussions compared to individual interviews—are another.

What Is the Contribution to the General Methodological Discussion?

Focus groups can be used as simulations of everyday discourses and conversations or as a quasi-naturalistic method for studying the generation of social representations or social knowledge in general (Lunt and Livingstone 1996). The general strength of focus groups is twofold:

> First, focus groups generate discussion, and so reveal both the meanings that people read into the discussion topic and how they negotiate those meanings. Second, focus groups generate diversity and difference, either within or between groups, and so reveal what Billig (1987) has called the dilemmatic nature of everyday arguments. (Lunt and Livingstone 1996, p. 96)

What Are the Limitations of the Method?

This method faces problems similar to those already mentioned for group discussion. A specific problem is how to document the data in a way that allows the identification of individual speakers and the differentiation between statements of several parallel speakers.

How Does the Method Fit into the Research Process?

Focus groups start from an interactionist point of view (see Chapter 7) and want to show how an issue is constructed and changed in a group discussing this issue.

Sampling is often oriented towards diversity of the members of the various groups in a study (see Chapter 13). The analysis of data is often very pragmatic—statements rather than extensive interpretations are the focus of the analysis. A more recent development is the use of online focus groups.

Online Focus Groups

In a similar way to online interviews (see Chapter 16), the use of focus groups has been transferred to Internet research. Here, we find similar distinctions and discussions as in the context of online interviewing. Again, you can distinguish between synchronous (or real-time) and asynchronous (non-real-time) groups. The first type of online focus group requires that all participants are online at the same time and may take part in a chatroom or by using specific conferencing software. This latter version means that all participants need to have this software on their computers or that you should provide it to your participants who are supposed to load it onto their computers. Besides the technical problems this may cause, many people may hesitate to receive and install software for the purpose of taking part in a study.

Asynchronous focus groups do not require all participants to be online at the same time (and this prevents the problems of co-ordinating this precondition). As in an e-mail interview, people can take their time to respond to entries by the other participants (or to your questions or stimulus). The interventions by every participant will be addressed to a conference site and stored in a folder to which all participants have access. This type of focus group has its advantages when people from different time zones participate or when people vary in their speed of typing or responding, which might produce differences in the chance to articulate in the group.

In order to make online focus groups work, easy access for the participants must be set up. Mann and Stewart (2000, pp. 103–105) describe in some detail the software you can use for setting up synchronous focus groups ("conferencing software"). They also describe the alternatives of how to design websites, and whether these should facilitate access for those who are intended to participate and exclude others not intended to have access. The authors also discuss how the concepts of naturalness and neutrality for designing the venue of a focus group can be transferred to online settings. For example, it is important that the participants can take part in the discussions from their computers at home or at their workplace and not from a special research site. As a beginning, it is important to create a welcome message, which invites the participants, explains the procedures and what is expected from the participants, what the rules of communication among the participants should be like (e.g., "please be polite to everyone …"), and so on (for an example, see 2000, p. 108). The researcher should—as with any focus group—create a permissive environment.

For the recruitment of participants, you can basically use the same sources as for an online interview (see above), snowballing, or looking in existing chatrooms or discussion groups for possible participants. Here again you will face the problem that you cannot really be sure that the participants meet your criteria or that the representation they give of themselves is correct. This can become a problem if you want to set up a homogeneous group (see above) of girls of a certain age, for example: "Unless online focus group participation combines the textual dimensions of chat rooms or conferencing with the visual dimension of digital cameras and/or voice, the researcher will be unable to be sure that the focus group really is comprised of, for example, adolescent girls" (Mann and Stewart 2000, p. 112).

The number of participants in real-time focus groups should be limited because too many participants might make the discussion in the group too fast and superficial. You can manage this problem more easily in asynchronous groups. Therefore, the number of participants does not have to be restricted in the latter case but should be limited in the former.

Compared to face-to-face focus groups, you can manage the issue of participant or group dynamics more easily in (especially asynchronous) online groups, yet it can also become a problem. Shy participants may hesitate to intervene when they are unsure of the procedure or the issue, but the researcher has more options to intervene and work on this problem than in normal focus groups. The greater anonymity in online focus groups that is produced by the use of usernames, nicknames, and the like may facilitate topical disclosures of participants in the discussion more than in focus groups, in general.

Finally, it is important that you choose a topic for the discussion that is relevant for the group and participants in your study, so that it is attractive for them to join the group and the discussion. Or, the other way around, it is important that you find groups for whom your topic is relevant in order to have fruitful discussions and interesting data.

What Are the Problems in Conducting the Method?

Online focus groups can be a fruitful way to use the communication on the Internet for research purposes. Here as well, anonymity for the participants is much greater and so may protect them from any detection of their person during the research and from the results. Again, for the researchers, this makes any form of (real-life) contextualization of the statements and the persons in their study much more difficult and leads to sampling problems if they want to construct homogeneous groups, for example.

What Is the Contribution to the General Methodological Discussion?

In online focus groups, you can manage the problem of quiet participants more easily. You can also produce group interactions among people in anonymity and safety from being identified by the other participants or the researcher. This may lead to more disclosure than in real-world groups. The data are more easy to document and the loss of contributions due to hearing problems during transcription can be reduced.

How Does the Method Fit into the Research Process?

If you receive enough information about your participants, you can adapt and apply most forms of focus groups to Internet research. Sampling will be purposive sampling (see Chapter 13). Online focus groups can be analyzed quite easily by coding and categorization (see Chapters 25 and 26), whereas hermeneutic approaches have to be adapted to these sorts of data.

What Are the Limitations of the Method?

Online focus groups can be affected by external influences on the participants who take part in their everyday context. This may lead to dropouts or distractions and influences on the data and their quality. This is difficult to control for the researcher. Technical problems in the online connection of one or more participants may also disturb the discussion and influence the quality of the data. Finally, again, the application of this approach is limited to people ready and willing to use computer-mediated communication or this kind of technology and communication in general.

The group procedures briefly mentioned here stress different aspects of the task of going beyond interviewing individuals to data collection in a group. Sometimes it is the reduction in time spent interviewing—one group at a time instead of many individuals at different times—that is important. Group dynamics may be attributed as being a helpful or a disturbing feature in realizing the goal of receiving answers from all interviewees. In a group discussion, however, it is precisely this dynamic and the additional options of knowledge produced by the group which are given priority. In each case, the verbal data gathered are more complex than in the single interview.

The advantage of this complexity is that data are richer and more diverse in their content than in an individual interview. The problem with this complexity is that it is more difficult to locate the viewpoints of the individuals involved in this common process of meaning making than in an individual interview.

How to Analyze Focus Groups

After much has been discussed in the literature about how to prepare, set up, and run focus groups, the number of publications addressing the analysis of the data produced in this way is growing (see Barbour 2007; 2014; Halkier 2010; Puchta and Potter 2004). There is a range of approaches from just catching statements (in market research) coming from focus groups to paying much more or most attention to the interaction in focus groups (e.g., Puchta and Potter 2004), or a combination of the two (Barbour 2014; Halkier 2010; see for the following also Barbour 2007).

Integrating Interaction and Group Dynamics in Analyzing Focus Groups

This approach takes into account that statements in focus groups should not be seen as isolated individual statements: rather, they are embedded in the group interaction and dynamic. Thus the analysis should include an approach to analyze how the group (maybe different from other groups) interacts, and how the conversation in the group is organized, developing, and changing. This means combining (for example) a coding analysis (see Chapters 25 and 26) of the contents of a focus group discussion with a conversation or discourse analytic approach (see Chapter 27) focusing on turn taking and other linguistic aspects in the discussion. For example, if the group leads to developing a consensus about an issue, it could be interesting how this consensus was built up step by step, how the integration of statements and views was organized, how participation and exclusion were managed in this process, and the like.

Differences Within and Between Groups as Starting Points for Comparison

The analysis of focus group data will take on a comparative perspective in most cases. In contrast to analyzing interviews, for example, comparisons will go in two directions on the two levels mentioned above (content and process). First, in analyzing the single group, a within comparison will be possible and necessary: How do the statements of participants differ; what do they have in common? And how does the discussion develop and change over time? The second perspective will then focus comparisons between groups: How do they differ in the contents and in the process of discussing? What is the variety of speaking about an issue across all groups? (See Table 17.1.)

Identification of Patterns

The aim of analyzing focus groups is to identify patterns in dealing with an issue again on the two levels of content and process of discussion and again in the two directions (see Table 17.1). Patterns can be identified not only for the whole group or the issue of the research as a whole (e.g., talking about foreigners), but also for specific topics (e.g., problems of integration of foreigners).

TABLE 17.1 Analytic Dimensions for Analyzing Focus Groups

Analytic dimensions	Within the single group	Across the groups	Overall range
Contents: What is said?			
Process: How is the group interaction?			
Development over time			

Identification of Typologies

A specific approach to analyzing focus groups has been developed by Bohnsack (2004; 2014). Here the aim of inferring from the contents of the discussion to the structure of the group is also pursued in the analysis: "It is important to distinguish what is said, reported or discussed, that is, what becomes a topic, from what is documented about the group in what is said" (Bohnsack 2004, p. 220). The analysis is pursued on two levels, which can also be seen as two steps. The first focuses on the contents: "The basic structure of *formulating interpretation* is the thematic composition, that is, the thematization of themes, the decoding of the normally implicit thematic structure of texts" (p. 220). The second step of analysis is integrating the formal aspects of the discussion:

> *Reflecting interpretation* aims at the reconstruction of the orientation pattern or framework. Its basic tool is the reconstruction of the formal structure of texts (beyond that of their thematic structure). In the case of group discussion this means reconstructing the *discourse organization*, that is, the manner in which the participants relate to each other. (2004, p. 221)

This process of interpretation then is completed by developing typologies from the material and the analysis:

> In the formation of types, on the basis of common features of cases (e.g. experience common to all students from the education milieu of dealing with the everyday world of work), specific contrasts typical of a particular milieu for coping with these experiences are worked out (...). The contrast in common features is a basic principle of the generation of individual types and also of the structure that holds a whole typology together. The unambiguity of a type depends on the extent to which it can be distinguished from all other possible types. The formation of types is the more valid, the more clearly other types can also be demonstrated with reference to a particular case, and the more fully a type can be fixed within a typology. (2004, p. 221)

Starting Points for Explaining Differences Between Groups

In analyzing focus group data, the first step can be to identify differences between the various groups. The second step then can be to describe the differences in greater detail by comparing the groups. In most cases, researchers will look for explanations for the differences they have found in these comparisons. A starting point for such an explanation is to look at the composition of the group and how the members of each group differ in features like age, gender, background, relations to the issue, etc. A second approach is to look for specific features like professional backgrounds. In our example above (see Case Study 17.3) we had two different backgrounds (nurses and physicians) and composed the groups according to these differences. Thus a first step in explaining differences between the groups was to link statements, arguments, and consensus back to the respective backgrounds of the participants. In this context again, looking at the group dynamics in each group can be helpful for explaining why some (maybe rather radical) statements were made in one group but not in the other.

What Are the Analytic Challenges of the Method?

For the reasons mentioned above, a first challenge is to keep in mind that the smallest analytic unit for analyzing focus group data is always the group, and not the individual participant or the single statement without the context of the group. A second challenge relates to situations in which one or more participants have remained silent at relevant stages of the discussion or throughout the whole group session. How can we interpret their silence? Which effect can be assumed as resulting from this individual silence for the group interaction as a whole (e.g., have some issues no longer been mentioned after one or more participants fell silent?). A third, more technical, challenge is how to prevent parts of the data from not being suitable for analysis because a number of people have been talking at the same time and it is difficult to understand the contents or to allocate statements to a speaker.

What Are the Limitations of the Method?

During the interpretation of the data, problems often arise due to differences in the dynamics of the groups, the difficulties of comparing the groups, and of identifying the opinions and views of the individual group members within the dynamics. As the smallest analytical unit, only the whole discussion group or subgroups should be considered. In order to enable some comparability among the groups and among the members as cases in the whole sample, non-directed groups are now rarely used. Because of the major effort in conducting, recording, transcribing, and interpreting group discussions, their use makes sense mainly for research questions which focus particularly on the social dynamics of generating opinions in a group. Attempts to use group discussions to economize on individual interviewing of many people at the same time have proved less effective. Often this method is combined with other methods (e.g., additional single interviews or observations).

Checklist for Doing Focus Groups

The checklist below should give you an orientation about when and how to use focus groups:

1. What are your expectations for doing focus groups in your research?
2. Is your topic an issue that can be better addressed in a group than in an individual interview, for example?
3. Is it an issue that can be best addressed in a discussion (and not in a personal narrative, for example)?

4   What is the best form of group composition for your issue?
5   Which one will fit your research participants?
6   How can you take into account that events and experiences will become topical in groups only in the context of the group dynamics?
7   How can you take the interaction in the group into account in your analysis of the data?
8   What level of comparison will you aim for in your data analysis (within or between groups)?

KEY POINTS

- Compared to focus groups, group interviews are seldom used.
- Use focus groups instead of single interviews only when the research question provides a good reason. Saving time is not a likely benefit of working with groups, because of the more difficult organizational details and the work required to analyze group protocols.
- Focus groups can be very fruitful where the interaction of the members adds to the knowledge produced in data collection.
- The analysis of focus group discussions needs to take the interaction in the group into account.
- The methods selected for the analysis should allow the combination of conversation and thematic analyses if possible.

Exercise 17.1

1   Locate a study in the literature using focus groups as a research method (e.g., Halkier 2010). Identify what kind of group was given in this case.
2   Seek too to identify how the researcher conducted the group.
3   Suggest your own idea for a research issue that would be best studied by using focus groups or group discussions.

Further Reading

Group Interviews

Both these texts deal explicitly with group interviews as a method:

Fontana, A. and Frey, J.H. (2000) "The Interview: From Structured Questions to Negotiated Text," in N. Denzin and Y.S. Lincoln (eds.), *Handbook of Qualitative Research* (2nd edn). London: Sage. pp. 645–672.
Patton, M.Q. (2002) *Qualitative Evaluation and Research Methods* (3rd edn). London: Sage.

Group Discussions

The following text discusses methodological problems and applications of the method and links it to the discussion of focus groups:
Bohnsack, R. (2004) "Group Discussions and Focus Groups," in U. Flick, E.v. Kardorff and I. Steinke (eds.), *A Companion to Qualitative Research*. London: Sage. pp. 214–221.

Focus Groups

The second text discusses recent applications and methodological problems, while the others give general overviews of the method:

Barbour, R. (2007) *Doing Focus Groups*. London: Sage.

Lunt, P. and Livingstone, S. (1996) "Rethinking the Focus Group in Media and Communications Research," *Journal of Communication*, 46: 79–98.

Morgan, D.L. and Krueger, R.A. (eds.) (1998) *The Focus Group Kit* (6 vols.). Thousand Oaks, CA: Sage.

Puchta, C. and Potter, J. (2004) *Focus Group Practice*. London: Sage.

Stewart, D.M. and Shamdasani, P.N. (1990) *Focus Groups: Theory and Practice*. Newbury Park, CA: Sage.

Analysis of Focus Groups

The first three texts below discuss recent methodological problems of analyzing focus group data, whereas the last one outlines the combination of content and interaction-oriented analysis:

Barbour, R. (2014) "Analyzing Focus Groups", in U. Flick (ed.), *The SAGE Handbook of Qualitative Data Analysis*. London: Sage. pp. 313–326.

Bohnsack, R. (2004) "Group Discussions and Focus Groups," in U. Flick, E.v. Kardorff and I. Steinke (eds.), *A Companion to Qualitative Research*. London: Sage. pp. 214–221.

Bohnsack, R. (2014) "Documentary Method," in U. Flick (ed.), *The SAGE Handbook of Qualitative Data Analysis*. London: Sage. pp. 217–233.

Halkier, B. (2010) "Focus Groups as Social Enactments: Integrating Interaction and Content in the Analysis of Focus Group Data," *Qualitative Research*, 10(1): 71–89.

18
Using Narrative Data

CONTENTS

CHAPTER OBJECTIVES

This chapter is designed to help you

- use narratives in qualitative research;
- identify the difference between life histories and episodes as a basis for narratives;
- distinguish the advantages and disadvantages of various forms of narratives in interviews;
- identify how the narrative approach may be used for analyzing life histories and other forms of data;
- appreciate that it is not always the big stories which form the focus of narrative research;
- recognize that narratives can be used for studying both individual biographies and social issues.

Narratives: Why and How? Backgrounds and Approaches

Why Study Narratives?

Narrative analysis has become a major approach in qualitative research. This development has been supported by three theoretical developments. First, Barthes has argued that narratives play a central role in social life:

The narratives of the world are numberless. Narrative is first and foremost a prodigious variety of genres, themselves distributed amongst different substances – as though any material were fit to receive man's stories. Able to be carried by articulated language, spoken or written, fixed or moving images, gestures, and the ordered mixture of all these substances; narrative is present in myth, legend, fable, tale, novella, epic, history, tragedy, drama, comedy, mime, painting, …, stained glass windows, cinema, comics, news item, conversation. Moreover, under this almost infinite diversity of forms, narrative is present in every age, in every place, in every society; it begins with the very history of mankind and there nowhere is nor has been a people without narrative. All classes, all human groups, have their narratives. … Caring nothing for the division between good and bad literature, narrative is international, transhistorical, transcultural: it is simply there, like life itself. (1977, p. 79)

Second, narrative has become prominent as a mode of knowing and of presenting experiences and also increasingly analyzed in psychology (e.g., Bruner 1990; 1991; Flick 1996; Murray 2000; Sarbin 1986). Concepts such as episodic knowledge and memory are based on stories as a format for knowing about issues and for remembering events. In addition, links between narrative and identity have been studied (Brockmeier and Carbaugh 2001).

Third, narratives are seen as a way of communicating personal experiences, social events, and even political and historical developments. Not only in oral history, but also in social sciences, political changes like the fall of the Berlin wall have been studied by analyzing the stories linked to that event, to the times and ways of living in the political systems before and after it.

How to Make Use of Narratives in Qualitative Research?

Accordingly, we find several ways of making use of narratives as data in qualitative research:

- to analyze existing written or recorded narratives;
- to stimulate narratives in special forms of interview or focus group for research purposes;
- to analyze narratives which emerge in interviews;
- to integrate the stimulation of narratives into the design of interview approaches.

A useful distinction has been made by Bamberg (2012, p. 77) between "research *on* narratives" and "research *with* narratives." The former refers to occasions when the narratives are analyzed to understand how narratives work, are constructed, and used; the latter refers to the use of narratives for understanding something else, like experiences, biographies, the representation of social problems, and the like.

When working with narratives in your research, you can use narratives produced by interviewees as a form of data as an alternative to semi-structured interviews. Sometimes also in semi-structured interviews, narratives are integrated as an element (e.g., in the problem-centered interview, see below). In case of doubt, if they are unproductive, they are subordinated to the interview guide. More generally, Mishler (1986,

p. 235) has studied what happens when interviewees in the semi-structured interview start to narrate, how these narratives are treated, and how they are suppressed rather than taken up. One methodological starting point for using narratives systematically is skepticism over how far subjective experiences may be tapped in the question–answer scheme of traditional interviews (even when this method is handled in a flexible way). Narratives, in contrast, allow the researcher to approach the interviewee's experiential yet structured world in a comprehensive way. But we can also integrate the stimulation of narratives into interviews working with questions and answers.

What Is a Narrative?

A narrative is characterized as follows:

> First the initial situation is outlined ("how everything started"), then the events relevant to the narrative are selected from the whole host of experiences and presented as a coherent progression of events ("how things developed"), and finally the situation at the end of the development is presented ("what became"). (Hermanns 1995, p. 183)

In this chapter, I first present a method specifically designed to stimulate narratives for research purposes and to position narratives in the center of data collection (the narrative interview). I then outline an alternative to this approach that integrates narrative data into an interview using questions and answers parallel to narratives. Instead of always aiming at individuals' narratives, these can also be collected as joint narratives (of a family, for example). Specific approaches for analyzing the narratives form the subject of the chapter's final part.

The Narrative Interview

The narrative interview was introduced by Schütze (see Riemann and Schütze 1987; Rosenthal 2004) as a special method for collecting narrative data. The method mainly employs a biographical approach. It does so in two ways. Either it is used in the context of biographical research (for an overview see Bertaux 1981; Rosenthal 2004), or participants are asked to remember and recount their experiences with specific larger changes and developments (e.g., the collapse of East Germany). Originally, however, the method was developed in the context of a project on local power structures and political decision processes. Here the narratives stimulated by this method focused not on the narrators' biographies, but rather on their stories about this political decision process.

The narrative interview's basic principle of collecting data is described as follows:

> In the narrative interview, the informant is asked to present the history of an area of interest, in which the interviewee participated, in an extempore narrative. ... The interviewer's task is to make the informant tell the story of the area of interest in question as a consistent story of all relevant events from its beginning to its end. (Hermanns 1995, p. 183)

Elements of the Narrative Interview

A narrative interview is begun using a "generative narrative question" (Riemann and Schütze 1987, p. 353); this will refer to the topic of the study and is intended to stimulate the interviewee's main narrative. The latter is followed by the stage of narrative probing in which narrative fragments that were not exhaustively detailed before are completed. The final stage of the interview is the "balancing phase, in which the interviewee may also be asked questions that aim at theoretical accounts of what happened and at balancing the story, reducing the 'meaning' of the whole to its common denominator" (Hermanns 1995, p. 184). At this stage, the interviewees are taken as "experts" and "theoreticians of themselves" (Schütze 1983). This means they are asked questions about why they think something developed in the way it did in their lives, about relations between events, or their general or specific viewpoints about some relevant issues. The main difference to the earlier parts of the interview is that the format changes from narration to question–answer sequences. Now argumentations and explanations, not just narrations, are the aim.

If you wish to elicit a narrative that is relevant to your research question, you must formulate the generative narrative question broadly, yet at the same time sufficiently specifically for the interesting experiential domain to be taken up as a central theme. The interest may refer to the informant's life history in general. In this case, the generative narrative question is rather unspecified, for example: "I would like to ask you to begin with your life history." Or it may aim at a specific, temporal, and topical aspect of the informant's biography, for example, a phase of professional reorientation and its consequences. An example of such a generative question is shown in Box 18.1.

BOX 18.1

Example of a Generative Narrative Question in the Narrative Interview

This is a typical example of a good generative narrative question:

> I want to ask you to tell me how the story of your life occurred. The best way to do this would be for you to start from your birth, with the little child that you once were, and then tell all the things that happened one after the other until today. You can take your time in doing this, and also give details, because for me everything is of interest that is important for you.

Source: Hermanns (1995, p. 182)

It is important to check whether the "generative question" really is a narrative stimulus. In the example by Hermanns in Box 18.1, clear prompts on the course of events told are given. These refer to several stages and include the explicit request for a narration and for detailing it.

If the interviewee begins a narrative in response to this question, it is crucial for the quality of the data in this narrative that the interviewer does not interrupt or obstruct the narration. For example, you should not ask questions in this part (e.g., "Who is this about?") or interrupt with directive interventions (e.g., "Could this problem not have been managed in a different way?") or evaluations ("That was a good idea of yours!"). Instead, as an active listener, you should signal (e.g., by reinforcing "*hm's*") that you empathize with the narrated story and the perspective of the narrator. Thus, you will support and encourage the interviewees to continue their narratives until the end.

Typically, the end of the story is indicated by a "coda," for instance "I think I've taken you through my whole life" (Riemann and Schütze 1987, p. 353) or "That's pretty well it by and large. I hope that has meant something to you" (Hermanns 1995, p. 184). In the next stage—the questioning period—the story's fragments that have not been further carried out are readdressed or the interviewer takes up with another generative narrative question those passages that had been unclear. For example, "You told me before how it came about that you moved from X to Y. I did not quite understand how your disease went on after that. Could you please tell me that part of the story in a little more detail?"

In the balancing phase, more and more abstract questions are asked, which aim for description and argumentation. Here, it is suggested first to ask "how" questions, for example: "How would you describe the symptoms of your disease in some detail?" or "How often did your have to consult a doctor at that time?", and then only afterwards complement them with "why" questions aiming at explanations, for example: "Why could you not continue to work after your disease became known to your colleagues?"

A main criterion for the validity of the information in the main part of the narrative interview is whether the interviewee's account is primarily a narrative. Although to some extent descriptions of situations and routines or argumentation may be incorporated in order to explain reasons or goals, the dominant form of presentation should be a narrative of the course of events (if possible from the beginning to the end) and of developmental processes. This distinction is clarified by Hermanns (1995, p. 184) who uses the following example:

> My attitude towards nuclear plants cannot be narrated, but I could tell the story about how my present attitude came about. "Well, I walked, it must have been 1972, across the site at Whyl, all those huts there and I thought, well that is great, what these people have got going here, but with their concern about nuclear energy they are kind of mad. I was strongly M/L at that time."[1]

That this method works, and the main narrative provides a richer version of the events and experiences than the other forms of presentation that are argued as consequences, are the main reasons that the narrators become entangled in certain constraints ("threefold narrative zugzwangs"). This entangling will start as soon as they have got involved in the situation of the narrative interview and started the narrative.

The constraints are the *constraint of closing gestalt*, the *constraint of condensing*, and the *constraint of detailing*. The first makes narrators bring a narrative to an end once they have started it. The second requires that only what is necessary for understanding the process in the story becomes part of the presentation. The story is condensed not only because of limited time, but also so that the listener is able to understand and follow it. The constraint of detailing is the reason why the narrative provides background details and relationships necessary for understanding the story. This constraint makes the narrator tell as many details as seems necessary to give the listener the chance to fully understand the story. Thus details about personal motives, about features of other persons involved, and so on are provided.

Through these narrative constraints, the narrator's control, which dominates in other forms of oral presentation, is minimized to such an extent that awkward topics and areas are also mentioned:

> Narrators of unprepared extempore narratives of their own experiences are driven to talk also about events and action orientations, which they prefer to keep silent about in normal conversations and conventional interviews owing to their awareness of guilt or shame or their entanglements of interests. (Schütze 1976, p. 225)

With the narrative interview, a technique for eliciting narratives of topically relevant stories has been created that provides data that cannot be produced in other forms of interviewing for three reasons. First, the narrative takes on some independence during its recounting. Second, "people 'know' and are able to present a lot more of their lives than they have integrated in their theories of themselves and of their lives. This knowledge is available to informants at the level of narrative presentation but not at the level of theories" (Hermanns 1995, p. 185). Finally, an analogous relationship between the narrative presentation and the narrated experience is assumed: "In the retrospective narrative of experiences, events in the life history (whether actions or natural phenomena) are reported on principle in the way they were experienced by the narrator as actor" (Schütze 1976, p. 197).

─CASE STUDY 18.1─

Excerpt from a Narrative Interview

As an illustration, the following text is taken from the beginning of a biographical main narrative of a mental patient (E) given to the interviewer (I). Gerd Riemann is one of the protagonists of biographical research with narrative interviews. This example comes from his PhD project, which is a typical study of biographies using the narrative interview (Riemann 1987, pp. 66–68). While reading it, look for when the interviewee comes to the topic of the interview (mental illness). References to villages and areas are replaced by general words in double brackets ((...)). Words in italics are strongly emphasized; a slash indicates the interruption of a word by another; and the interviewer's reinforcing signals ("hmh," "Oh yes") are represented exactly at the position they occurred:

```
 1  E   Well, I was born in ((area in the former East Germany))
 2  I   hmh
 3  E   actually in ((...)) which is a purely Catholic, purely/mainly.
 4      Catholic district of ((area, western part))
 5  I   Oh yes
 6  E   ((town))
 7  I   hmh
 8  E   My Father uh ... was captain
 9  I   hmh
10  E   and ... uh was already county court judge ...
11      and then was killed in the war.
12  I   hmh
13  E   My mother got stuck alone with my elder brother/he is three years
14      older than me and uh – fled with us.
15  I   hmh
16  E   About the journey I don't know anything in detail, I only remember –
17      as a memory that I once uh sat in a train and felt terrible/uh
18      terrible thirst or anyhow hunger
19  I   hmh
20  E   and that then somebody came with a pitcher and a cup for us
21      uh poured coffee and that I felt that to be very refresh-
22  I   hmh
23  E   -ing.
24      But other memories are also related to that train which
25      maybe point uh to very much later, well, when
26  I   hmh
27  E   came into psychiatry, see.
28      Namely, uh – that comes up again as an image from time to time.
29      And we had laid down in that train to go to sleep
30      and I was somehow raised ... uh to be put to sleep
31  I   hmh
32  E   And I must have fallen down in the night without waking
33      up.
34  I   hmh
35  E   And there I rem/remember that a uh female, not my
36      mother, a female person took me in her arms and smiled
37      at me.
38  I   hmh
39  E   Those are my earliest memories.
40  I   hmh.
```

This narrative continues over another 17 pages of transcript. The interview is continued in a second meeting. A detailed case analysis is presented by Riemann (1987, pp. 66–200).

(Continued)

(Continued)

In this example, you can see how a narrative interview begins, how the interviewee's life history is unfolded in it, and how the interview slowly approaches issues directly relevant for the research question, but also provides a lot of information that might look less relevant at first glance. This information seems less relevant at first glance because it does not refer directly. However, as the research issue unfolds its relevance may become clear during the analysis of the interview.

In the narrative interview, on the one hand, the expectation is that factual processes will become evident in it, that "how it really was" will be revealed, and this is linked to the nature of narrative data. On the other hand, analyzing such narrated life histories should lead to a general theory of processes. Schütze (1983) calls this "process structures of the individual life course." In some areas, such typical courses have been demonstrated empirically, as in the following (see Case Study 18.2).

CASE STUDY 18.2

Professional Biographies of Engineers

Harry Hermanns is another of the main protagonists in developing and using the narrative interview, in his case in the context of professional biographies. Hermanns (1984) has applied this method in his PhD study to 25 engineers in order to elaborate the patterns of their life histories—patterns of successful professional courses and patterns of courses characterized by crises.

The case studies showed that at the beginning of his or her professional career, an engineer should go through a phase of seeking to acquire professional competencies. The central theme of the professional work of the following years should result from this phase. If one fails with this, the professional start turns into a dead-end.

From the analyses, a series of typical fields for the engineer's further specialization resulted. A decisive stage is to build up "substance" (i.e., experience and knowledge), for example, by becoming an expert in a technical domain. Other types of building up substance are presented by Hermanns.

The next stage of engineers' careers is to develop a line of continuity in career specialism (i.e., to link themselves to some professional topic for a sustained time and construct a foundation of expertise from which they can act). The development of continuity in specialisms can be accelerated by successes, but also may "die" (e.g., because the requisite competence may be missing or because the selected topic loses its value over time).

Professional careers fail when one does not succeed in constructing a basis, developing and securing a continuity in career specialism, building up competence and substance when one of the central professional tasks distilled from the analysis of professional biographies is not managed successfully.

This example shows how patterns of biographical courses can be elaborated from case studies of professional biographies. These patterns and the stages of the biographical processes contained in them can be taken as points of reference for explaining success and failure in managing the tasks of successful biographies.

What Are the Problems in Conducting the Interview?

One problem in conducting narrative interviews is the systematic violation of the role expectations of both participants. First, expectations relating to the situation of an "interview" may be violated, because (at least for the most part) questions in the usual sense of the word are not asked. Second, the expectations linked to the situation "everyday narration" are violated, because in everyday life narrators are rarely given so much space and time for telling their stories. These violations of situational expectations often produce irritation in both parties, which prevent them from settling down into the interview situation. Furthermore, although being able to narrate may be an everyday competence, it is mastered to varying degrees. Therefore, it is not always the most appropriate social science method: "We must assume that not all interviewees are capable of giving narrative presentations of their lives. We meet reticent, shy, uncommunicative, or excessively reserved people not only in everyday social life but also in biographical interviews" (Fuchs 1984, p. 249). Additionally, some authors see problems in applying this method in foreign cultures, because the validity of the narrative schema dominant in Western culture cannot simply be presumed for other, non-Western cultures.

Because of these problems, interview training that focuses on active listening (i.e., signaling interest without intervention and on how to maintain the relationship with the interviewee) is necessary. This training should be tailor-made for the concrete research question and the specific target group whose narratives are sought. For this, role-plays and rehearsal interviews are recommended here as well. The recordings of these should be systematically evaluated by a group of researchers for problems in conducting the interview and with the interviewer's role behavior.

A precondition for successfully conducting the interview is to explain the specific character of the interview situation to the interviewee. For this purpose, I suggest paying special attention to explaining, in detail, targets and procedures during the phase of recruiting interviewees.

What Is the Contribution to the General Methodological Discussion?

The narrative interview and its attached methodology highlight a qualitative interview's making of the responsive structure and experiences. A model that reconstructs the internal logic of processes stresses the narrative as a gestalt loaded with more than statements and reported "facts." This also provides a solution to the dilemma of the semi-structured interview: how to mediate between freedom to unfold subjective viewpoints and the thematic direction and limitation of what is mentioned. This solution includes three elements:

- The primary orientation is to provide the interviewees with the scope to tell their story (if necessary, for several hours) and to require them to do so.
- Concrete, structuring, or thematically deepening interventions in the interview are postponed until its final part in which the interviewer may take up topics broached before and ask more direct questions. The restriction of the structuring role of the interviewer to the end of the interview and to the beginning is linked to this.
- The generative narrative question serves not only to stimulate the production of a narrative, but also to focus the narrative on the topical area and the period of the biography with which the interview is concerned.

The methodological discussion so far has dealt mainly with questions of how interviewers should behave to keep a narrative going once it is stimulated and to enable it to be finished with the least disturbance possible. But the argument that a good generative narrative question highly structures the following narrative has not yet fully been taken into account. Imprecise and ambiguous generative narrative questions often lead to narratives which remain general, disjointed, and topically irrelevant. Therefore, this method is far from the completely open interview that it is often erroneously presented as being in some textbooks. However, the structuring interventions by the interviewer are more clearly localized than in other methods—in their limitation to the beginning and end of the interview. In the framework thus produced, the interviewees are allowed to unfold their views unobstructed by the interviewer as far as possible. Thus this method has become a way of employing the potential of narratives as a source of data for social research.

How Does the Method Fit into the Research Process?

Although dependent on the method used for interpretation, the theoretical background of studies using narrative interviews is mainly the analysis of subjective views and activities. Research questions pursued from within this perspective focus biographical processes against the background and in the context of concrete and general circumstances (e.g., life situations such as a phase of professional orientation and a certain social context and biographical period—the postwar period in Germany). The procedure is mainly suitable for developing grounded theories (see Chapter 10).

A gradual sampling strategy according to the concept of theoretical sampling (see Chapter 13) seems to be most useful. Special suggestions for interpreting narrative data gathered using this method have been made that take into account their formal characteristics as well as their structure (see below). The goal of analysis is often to develop typologies of biographical courses as an intermediate step on the way to theory building (see Chapter 25).

What Are the Limitations of the Method?

One problem linked to the narrative interview is that it rests on the following assumption: that it allows the researcher to gain access to factual experiences and events. This assumption finds its expression in Schütze's idea that narrative and experience are homologous: if the interviewee really narrates, it can be assumed that what is told has really happened as it is told. This assumption may not be valid, because what is presented in a narrative is constructed in a specific form during the process of narrating, and memories of earlier events may be influenced by the situation in which they are told. These are further problems which obstruct the realization of some of the claims to the validity of the data, which are linked to the narrative interview.

Furthermore, it is necessary to ask, critically, another question before applying the method: is it as appropriate for your own research question, and above all for the interviewees, to rely on the effectiveness of narrative constraints and entanglements in a narrative, as it was during the developmental context of the method? The local politicians whom Schütze originally interviewed with this method probably had different reasons for and better skills at concealing awkward relations than other potential interviewees. In the latter case, using this kind of strategy for eliciting biographical details also raises questions of research ethics.

A more practical problem is the sheer amount of textual material in the transcripts of narrative interviews. Additionally, these are less obviously structured (by topical areas, by the interviewer's questions) than semi-structured interviews. At the very least, it is more difficult to recognize their structure. The sheer mass of unstructured texts produces problems in interpreting them. The consequence is often that only a few, extremely voluminous, case studies result from applying this method. Therefore, before choosing this method you should decide beforehand whether it is really the course (of a life, a patient's career, a professional career) that is central to your research question. If it is not, the purposive topical steering allowed by a semi-structured interview may be the more effective way to achieve the desired data and findings.

Critical discussions provoked by this method have clarified the limits of narratives as a data source. These limits may be based on the issue of the interview in each case: "It is always only 'the story of' that can be narrated, not a state or an always recurring routine" (Hermanns 1995, p. 183). In the face of these limitations, the researcher should determine, before applying this method, whether narratives are appropriate as the only approach to the research question and the potential interviewees, and whether and with which other sorts of data they should be combined.

The Episodic Interview

The starting point for the episodic interview (Flick 2000a; 2007b, Ch. 5) is the assumption that subjects' experiences of a certain domain are stored and remembered in forms of narrative–episodic and semantic knowledge. Whereas episodic knowledge is organized closer to experiences and linked to concrete situations and circumstances, semantic knowledge is based on concepts, assumptions and relations which are abstracted from these and generalized. For the former, the course of the situation within its context is the main unit around which knowledge is organized. In the latter, concepts and their relation to each other are the central units (Figure 18.1).

To access both forms of knowledge about a domain, I have designed a method to collect and analyze narrative–episodic knowledge using narratives, while semantic knowledge is made accessible by concrete pointed questions. However, it is intended not as a time-saving, pragmatic jumping between the data types "narrative" and "answer", but rather as a systematic link between forms of knowledge that both types of data can make accessible.

The episodic interview yields context-related presentations in the form of a narrative, because these are closer to experiences and their generative context than other presentational forms. They make the processes of constructing realities more readily accessible than approaches that aim at abstract concepts and answers in a strict sense. But the episodic interview is not an attempt to artificially stylize experiences as a "narrate-able whole." Rather it starts from episodic–situational forms of experiential knowledge. Special attention is paid in the interview to situations or episodes in which the interviewee has had experiences that seem to be relevant to the question of the study. Both the form of the presentation (description or narrative) of the situation and the selection of other situations can be chosen by the interviewee according to aspects of subjective relevance.

In several domains, the episodic interview facilitates the presentation of experiences in a general, comparative form. At the same time it ensures that those

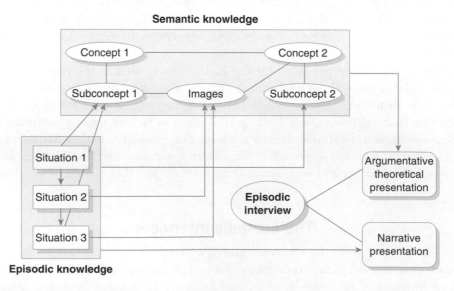

FIGURE 18.1   Forms of Knowledge in the Episodic Interview

situations and episodes are told in their specificity. Therefore, it includes a combination of narratives oriented to situational or episodic contexts and argumentation that peel off such contexts in favor of conceptual and rule-oriented knowledge. The interviewee's narrative competence is used without relying on narrative constraints ("zugzwangs") and without forcing the interviewee to finish a narrative against his or her intentions.

What Are the Elements of the Episodic Interview?

The central element of this form of interview is that you recurrently ask the interviewee to present narratives of situations (e.g., "If you look back, what was your first encounter with television? Could you please recount that situation for me?"). Also, you can mention chains of situations ("Please could you recount how your day went yesterday, and where and when technology played a part in it?").

You should prepare an interview guide in order to orient the interview to the topical domains for which such a narrative is required. In order to familiarize the interviewee with this form of interview its basic principle is first explained (e.g., "In this interview, I will ask you repeatedly to recount situations in which you have had certain experiences with technology in general or with specific technologies").

A further aspect is the interviewee's imaginations of expected or feared changes ("Which developments do you expect in the area of computers in the near future? Please imagine and tell me about a situation which would make this evolution clear for me!"). Such narrative incentives are complemented by questions in which you ask for the interviewee's subjective definitions ("What do you link to the word 'television' today?"). Also, you should ask for abstractive relations ("In your opinion, who should be responsible for change due to technology, who is able to or should take the responsibility?"). This is the second large complex of questions aimed at accessing semantic parts of everyday knowledge.

CASE STUDY 18.3

Technological Change in Everyday Life

In a comparative study, I conducted 27 episodic interviews on the perception and evaluation of technological change in everyday life. In order to analyze different perspectives on this issue, I interviewed information engineers, social scientists, and teachers as members of professions dealing with technology in different degrees (as developers of technology, as professional and everyday users of technology). The interview mentioned the following topical fields.

The interviewees' "technology biographies" (the first encounter with technology they remember, their most important experiences linked to technology) formed one point of

(Continued)

---

reference. The interviewees' technological everyday life (e.g., how yesterday went with regard to where and when technology played a part in it; domains of everyday life like work, leisure, household, and technology) was the second.

As a response to the narrative incentive "If you can recall, what was your first encounter with technology? Could you please recount that situation?", the following situation was recounted, for example:

I was a girl, I am a girl, let's say, but I was always interested in technology, I have to say, or and, well I was given puppets as usual. And then sometime, my big dream, a train set, and uh yeah that train. I wound it up and put it on the back of my sister's head, and then the little wheels turned. And the hair got caught up in the train wheels. And then it was over with the technology, because then my sister had to go to the hairdresser. The train had to be taken to pieces, it was most complicated, she had no more hair on her head, everybody said, "Oh how awful," I cried because my train was taken to pieces. That was already the end of the technology. Of course, I did not know at all what had happened, I did not realize at all what would happen. I don't know what drove me, why I had the devil in me. She was sitting around and I thought, "put the train on her head." How long I actually played with the train before, don't really know. Probably not very long, and it was a great train. Yeah, then it was over for a while. That was an experience, not a very positive experience.

Another example is the following situation, which is remembered as a first encounter with technology:

Yes, electric lights on the Christmas tree. I knew that already from that time, yeah and that has impressed me deeply. I saw those candles at other children's houses and actually, nowadays would say that this is much more romantic, much more beautiful. But at that time, of course, it was impressive, if I turned on a candle, all the lights went off, yes, and when I wanted. And that was just the case on the first Christmas holiday, it's a holiday, the parents sleep longer. And the children, of course, are finished with sleeping very early. They go out to the Christmas tree to continue playing with the gifts, which had had to be stopped on Christmas Eve. And I could then turn on the candles again and everything shone again, and with wax candles, this was not the case.

A large part of the interview focused on the use of various exemplary technologies which determine changes in everyday life in an extraordinary way (computer, television). For these examples, definitions and experiences were mentioned. As a response to the question "What do you link to the word 'computer' today?", a female information engineer gave the following definition:

Computer, of course I must have an absolutely exact conception of that. ... Computer, well, uh, must have a processor, must have a memory, can be reduced to a Turing machine. These are very technical details. That means a computer can't do anything except go left, go right and write on a tape, that is a model of the computer. And I don't link more to it at all at first. This means, for me, a computer is a completely dull machine.

Consequences of technological change in different areas (e.g., family life, children's lives, etc.) were focused across the different technologies. In each of these areas, narrative incentives were complemented by conceptual–argumentative questions (Box 18.2). A context protocol was written for every interview, which included information about the interviewee (profession, age, gender, etc.) and about details of the interview situation (disturbances, specific ways of interacting or non-verbal aspects, etc.; for more details see Box 24.2 in Chapter 24). The interviews showed the common aspects of the different views, so that in the end an everyday theory of technological change could be formulated across all cases. They also showed group-specific differences in the views, so that every group-specific accentuation of this everyday theory could be documented.

In this example, you can see how the episodic interview is applied to study a social psychological issue. Here, narratives of specific situations are given and concepts and definitions are mentioned.

BOX 18.2

Example Questions from the Episodic Interview

- What does "technology" mean for you? What do you associate with the word "technology"?
- When you look back, what was your first experience with technology? Could you please tell me about this situation?
- If you look at your household, what part does technology play in it, and what has changed in it? Please tell me about a situation typical of that.
- On which occasion did you first have contact with a computer? Could you please tell me about that situation?
- Have your relations with other people changed due to technologies? Please tell me about a typical situation.
- Please recount how your day went yesterday and when technologies played a part in it.
- Which parts of your life are free of technology? Please tell me about a typical situation.
- What would life without technology look like for you? Please tell me about a situation of this type, or a typical day.
- If you consider the life of (your) children today and compare it to your life as a child, what is the part played by technology in each case? Please tell me about a situation typical of that which makes this clear for you and me.
- What do you link to the word "television" today? Which device is relevant for that?

(Continued)

(Continued)

- What part does TV play in your life today? Please tell me about a typical situation.
- What determines if and when you watch TV? Please tell me about a situation typical of that.
- If you look back, what was your first encounter with TV? Please tell me about that situation.
- On which occasion did TV play its most important role in your life? Please tell me about that situation.
- Are there areas in your life in which you feel fear when technology enters? Please tell me about a situation typical of that.
- What gives you the impression that a certain technology or a device is outdated? Please tell me about a typical situation.

─CASE STUDY 18.4─

Patients' Self-determination in Nursing Homes

In a study for her PhD, Delia Struppek investigated several perspectives on the issue of how residents' self-determination in nursing homes is supported, maintained, or reduced by the institution and the staff working in it (Struppek 2010). She conducted episodic interviews with 13 nursing home residents about their perceptions, experiences, and evaluations of health care. These interviews were complemented by episodic interviews with 8 members of the nursing home where the interviewed residents lived, 14 doctors they had mentioned in the interviews, and 9 relatives. The interviews with all these groups focused on diseases, contact with nurses and doctors, medication, wishes, and ideas.

The data were analyzed according to grounded theory coding (see Chapter 25). Results showed the need for giving comprehensive information to the residents about their health status and problems and about treatments for giving them a chance to participate in any decisions taken on their treatment. It also became evident how maintaining self-determination is a process of communication between all the groups involved and a process of negotiation between them.

The episodic interview proved to be helpful in giving the residents space for presenting their experiences in detail. The professionals' interviews also provided a range of substantiated reflections about situations in which residents' self-determination is at stake—whether it is promoted or inhibited.

What Are the Problems in Conducting the Interview?

The general problem of interviews generating narratives—that some people have greater problems with narrating than others—is also the case here. But the difficulty is qualified here, because a single overall narrative is not requested—as in the narrative interview—but rather several delimited narratives are stimulated. The problem of how to mediate the principle of recounting certain situations to the interviewee has to be handled carefully in order to prevent situations (in which certain experiences have been encountered) from being merely mentioned without being recounted.

As in other forms of interviews, it is an essential precondition that you as the interviewer have really internalized the principle of the interview. Therefore, I suggest careful interview training using concrete examples here as well. This should focus on how to handle the interview guide and, above all, how to stimulate narratives and—where necessary—how to probe.

What Is the Contribution to the General Methodological Discussion?

In episodic interviews, you should try to employ the advantages of both the narrative interview and the semi-structured interview. These interviews use the interviewee's competence to present experiences in their course and context as narratives. Episodes as an object of such narratives and as an approach to the experiences relevant for the subject under study allow a more concrete approach than does a narrative of the life history. In contrast to the narrative interview, routines and normal everyday phenomena are analyzed with this procedure. For a topic like technological change, these routines may be as instructive as the particulars of the interviewee's history with technology.

In the episodic interview, the range of experiences is not confined to those parts that can be presented in a narrative. As the interviewer you have more options to intervene and direct it through a series of key questions concerning a subject recounting and defining situations. Thus the extremely one-sided and artificial situation given in the narrative interview here is replaced by a more open dialogue in which narratives are used as only one form of data. By linking narratives and question–answer sequences, this method realizes the triangulation of different approaches as the basis of data collection.

How Does the Method Fit into the Research Process?

The theoretical background of studies using the episodic interview is the social construction of reality during the presentation of experiences. The method was developed as an approach to social representations. Therefore, research questions have until now focused mainly on group-specific differences in experiences and everyday knowledge. The comparison between certain groups is the goal of sampling cases (see Chapter 13). The connection between a linear and a circular understanding of the research process underlies its application. The data from episodic interviews should be analyzed with the methods of thematic and theoretic coding (see Chapters 26 and 25).

Limitations of the Method

Apart from the problems already mentioned in conducting episodic interviews, their application is limited to the analysis of everyday knowledge of certain objects and topics and interviewees' own history with them. As with other interviews, episodic interviews give direct access neither to activities nor to interactions. You will only receive reports about what the interviewees did or how they interacted with other people. However, these can be reconstructed from the participants' viewpoints and group-specific differences in such experiences may be clarified.

Between Biography and Episode

Interviews primarily aiming at interviewees' narratives collect data in the form of a more or less comprehensive and structured whole—as a narrative of life histories or of concrete situations in which interviewees have had certain experiences. Thus these interviews are more sensitive and responsive to interviewees' viewpoints than other interviews in which concrete topics and the way these should be treated are pre-structured to a considerable extent by the questions that are asked. Procedures generating narratives, however, are also based on interviewers' inputs and ways of structuring the situation of collecting data. Which form of narrative you should prefer as a source of data—the comprehensive biographical narrative in the narrative interview or the narrative of details that are linked to situations in the episodic interview—should be decided with regard to the research question and the issue under study. Such decisions should not be made on the basis of the fundamentally postulated strength of one method compared to all other methods of collecting data, as the programmatic discussions around the narrative interview sometimes suggest. An alternative to creating a myth about narratives in such a programmatic way is to reintroduce a dialogue between the interviewer and the interviewee in the episodic interview. A second alternative is to stimulate this dialogue among the members of a family in joint narratives of family histories.

Joint Narratives

The narrative approach to data collection has been extended by Hildenbrand and Jahn (1988) to a method that can be applied to groups. Their starting point was the observation that families under study jointly narrate and thus restructure and reconstruct domains of their everyday reality. Starting from this observation, the authors stimulate such joint narratives more systematically and use them as data. All the persons belonging to a household are present in the situation of data collection, which should take place at the family's home: "At the beginning of the conversation, the family members are invited to recount details and events from their former and current family life. We abandoned the use of an explicit narrative stimulus, because it produces unnecessary restrictions on the variety of topics" (1988, p. 207). In order to allow the family members to shape the conversation, the authors refrained from methodologically directed interventions. This was intended to bring the research situation as close as possible to the everyday situation of narratives in the family. Finally, by using a checklist, those social data are completed, together with the family, which have not been mentioned during the narrative. At the end, extended observational protocols were made, which refer to the context of the conversation (generative history, living conditions of the family, description of the house and its furniture).

What Is the Contribution to the General Methodological Discussion?

With this approach, the situation of the monologue of a single narrator (in the narrative interview) is extended to a collective storytelling. Analyses of the interaction are made, which refer to the realization of the narrative and to the way in which the family construct reality for themselves and the listener.

This approach has been developed in the context of a specific field of research—family studies. The natural structure of this field or research object is given as a particular reason for the interest in this method. It should be possible to transfer this idea of joint narratives to other forms of communality beyond families. You could imagine using the method to analyze a specific institution (e.g., a counseling service, its history, activities, and conflicts, by asking the members of the teams working in it to jointly recount the history of their institution). This would make not only the narrated course of development an analytic issue, but also the dynamics of the different views and presentations of the members.

How Does the Method Fit into the Research Process?

The theoretical background of the method is the joint construction of reality. The aim is the development of theories grounded in these constructions (see Chapter 10). The starting point is the single case (a family in Hildenbrand and Jahn 1988), where later on other cases are included step by step (see Chapter 13). Interpretation of the material proceeds sequentially (see Chapter 27), with the aim of arriving at more general statements from the comparison of cases (see Chapter 29).

What Are the Limitations of the Method?

The method has been developed in the context of a study using several other methods. Its independent use remains to be tested. A further problem is that large textual materials result from a single case. This makes interpretations of single cases very voluminous. Therefore, analyses remain mostly limited to case studies. Finally, the rather far-reaching abstinence from methodological interventions makes it more difficult to purposively apply the method to specific research questions and to direct its application in collecting data. It is possible that not only the strengths, but also the problems, of the narrative interview are combined with those of group discussions.

How to Analyze Narratives

Narrative analyses of data resulting from using the narrative interview start from a specific sequential order. The individual statement that you wish to interpret is first considered in terms of whether it is part of a narrative and is then analyzed. Narratives are stimulated and collected in the narrative interview in order to reconstruct biographical processes. More generally, life is conceptualized as narrative in order to analyze the narrative construction of reality (Bruner 1987; 1991) without necessarily using a procedure of data collection explicitly aimed at eliciting narratives.

Analyzing Narrative Interviews for Reconstructing Events

In the literature you will find several suggestions for analyzing narrative interviews. The "first analytic step (i.e., formal text analysis) is to eliminate all non-narrative passages from the text and then to segment the 'purified' narrative text for its formal sections" (Schütze 1983, p. 286). A structural description of the contents follows, specifying the different parts of narratives ("temporally limited processual structures of the life course on the basis of formal narrative connectors" (Riemann and Schütze 1987, p. 348)), such as "and then" or pauses. The analytic abstraction—as a third step—moves away from the specific details of the life segments. Instead its intention is to elaborate "the biographical shaping *in toto*, i.e., the life historical sequence of experience-dominant processual structures in the individual life periods up to the presently dominant processual structure" (Schütze 1983, p. 286). Only after this reconstruction of patterns of process do you integrate the other, non-narrative, parts of the interview into the analysis. Finally, the case analyses produced in this way are compared and contrasted to each other. The aim is less to reconstruct the narrator's subjective interpretations of his or her life but more to reconstruct the "interrelation of factual processual courses" (1983, p. 284).[2]

An alternative procedure has been outlined by Haupert (1991). In preparation for the actual fine analysis, he first draws up the narrator's short biography. This includes a chronological display of the "events identified as meaningful" in the life history. This is followed by the segmentation of the interviews according to Schütze's method and by formulating headings for the single sequences. The identification of the "sequential thematic," and the attachment of quotations explaining it, is the next step. Finally, the core of the biography with the central statements of the interview is formulated. Paraphrases of statements from the text and the explication of the contexts and milieus of the interviews lead to further abstraction. After condensing the case stories to core stories, they are classified into types of processes. These types are related to life-world milieus. This procedure also reconstructs the course of the biography from the course of the narrative.

This reconstruction of factual courses from biographical narratives starts from the "assumption of homology." According to Bude, this includes the premise that "The autobiographical unprepared extempore narrative is seen ... as a truly reproductive recapitulation of past experience" (1985, pp. 331–332). This premise has been questioned, and not only by Bude (for similar arguments, see Bruner 1987). The constructions involved in narratives are now attracting more attention.

The Analysis of Narrative Data as Life Constructions

Accordingly, Bude (1984) outlines a different view on narratives, the data contained in them, and their analysis by suggesting the "reconstruction of life constructions." Here he takes into account that narratives, like other forms of presentation, include subjective and social constructions in what is presented—life constructions in narrative interviews, for example. In a similar way, authors in psychology, such as Bruner (1987), understand life histories as social constructions. In their concrete shaping, they draw on basic cultural narratives and life histories offered by the culture. The goal of analyzing narrative data is more to disclose these constructive processes than to reconstruct factual processes. Rosenthal and Fischer-Rosenthal (2004) see a difference between a life story told in the interview and the life history which was lived by the interviewee. They analyze narrative interviews in five steps: analysis of the biographical data; thematic field analysis (reconstruction of the *life story*); reconstruction of the life *history*; microanalysis of individual text segments; and contrastive comparison of life history and life story (see also Box 18.3).

BOX 18.3

The Sequence of Stages in the Practical Analysis

1 **Analysis of biographical data (dates of events)**

   Here the dates of the narrator's life history (e.g., birth, siblings, training, marriage, relocations, retirement) are analyzed in their temporal sequence.

2 **Text and thematic field analysis (sequential analysis of textual segments from the self-presentation in the interview)**

   Here the thematic gestalt of the text is analyzed. For example, it is asked why a topic is introduced at a specific location in the text or why it is introduced in a specific format, or why so extensively or briefly, and what bigger issues are linked to this topic.

3 **Reconstruction of the case history (life as lived)**

   In this step, the biographical dates (see step 1) are contrasted and compared to the interviewee's narratives and self-interpretations. This aims at the decoding of the gestalt of the biographical life narrative.

(Continued)

(Continued)

4 Detailed analysis of individual textual locations

Here, a detailed analysis links the interpretation of single passages of the narrative to the biographical overall view and to the biographical interpretation of single events and experiences.

5 Contrasting the life story as narrated with life as lived

Now the questions can be pursued about which functions a specific way of presenting one's own life history can have for the narrator and what relevance any differences between the sequence of events (see step 1) and the sequence in the presentation (see step 3) may have for understanding the interviewee's way of coping with events in his or her life.

6 Formation of types

Now the analysis goes beyond the single case and aims at developing a typology based on contrasting several cases in a comparative way. The result should be a typology of ways of living with a specific chronic disease, for example, which allows several cases to be allocated to one type and other cases to a second type.

Source: Rosenthal and Fischer-Rosenthal (2004)

Denzin outlines the procedure for such an interpretation as follows:

(1) Securing the interactional text; (2) displaying the text as a unit; (3) subdividing the text into key experiential units; (4) linguistic and interpretive analysis of each unit; (5) serial unfolding and interpretation of the meanings of the text to the participants; (6) development of working interpretations of the text; (7) checking these hypotheses against the subsequent portions of the text; (8) grasping the text as a totality; and (9) displaying the multiple interpretations that occur within the text. (1989a, p. 46)

CASE STUDY 18.5

Example of a Case Reconstruction

Gabriele Rosenthal and Wolfram Fischer-Rosenthal have developed a practical model (see Box 18.3) for analyzing narrative data from narrative interviews. They have applied it in many studies of biographical experiences in certain historical periods (e.g., during and after World War II).

Rosenthal and Fischer-Rosenthal (2004, pp. 261–264) present a detailed analysis of excerpts from a narrative interview referring to a period in a life history. Here the interviewee starts her story with the sequence: "*Nothing is as you imagined it. Everything turned out differently*" and then immediately embarks on the following report: "*The great love of my youth, met my husband at 15 and was engaged at 18 and married at 20 and at 21 had my son (laughing) that was already in '42, when there was already war then.*"

The authors analyze the self-presentation in this statement on different levels. They consider the biographical meaning of the events presented here for the interviewee and ask why the interviewee might have chosen to start her life story with this issue ("young love"). In order to understand this in greater detail, they formulate hypotheses at the level of the story of life as lived and at the level of the narrated life story. They also use further information about the life as it was lived and about the way such a life developed normally in that period. Differences from that normal life course can be analyzed as "life unlived."

In the thematic field analysis, the self-presentation is reconstructed by means of complexes of topics; that is to say, by expanding thematic fields in the order of their treatment. The analysis proceeds on the basis that self-presentation cannot—or can only occasionally—be intentionally controlled: the story of experience is manifest in the text that corresponds to the uninterrupted opening narrative.

In preparing this step, the interview passage is sequenced. That is, it is segmented according to the turn taking in the interview, the text type, and the change of topic (see p. 263). Questions are formulated, such as:

- Why are topics introduced at a specific point?
- Which topics are or are not mentioned?
- Why are some topics presented in greater detail and others not?
- What is the thematic field this topic fits into?

In answering these questions and testing the hypotheses, the authors develop an extensive interpretation of this case. The case study is then contrasted with other cases from the same study or field.

This example shows how the authors develop an approach to narrative data referring to life histories, which takes into account the difference between the story as it is developed and the life which is narrated in its course. The example also shows how extensive an analysis of this type normally is (see Rosenthal and Fischer-Rosenthal 2004, pp. 261–264, again only for an excerpt of such an analysis).

How to Analyze Joint Narratives

For analyzing joint narratives of families and the processes of constructing reality that take place in them (see Chapter 7), Hildenbrand and Jahn (1988, p. 208) suggest the following sequential analytic procedure. First, the "hard" social data of the family (birth, marriage, educational situation, stages in professional life, etc.) are reconstructed from the narrative. Then they are interpreted with respect to the room for decisions, compared to the decisions actually made. Then a hypothesis is generated. This is systematically tested during further interpretation of the case of the studied family. Two components, (1) the opening sequence of the narrative and (2) the "members' self-presentation" evident within it, provide the basis for the analytic procedure. Sampling of further cases follows. The case structures elaborated in the analyses can be contrasted, compared, and generalized. The inspiration behind this procedure was the objective hermeneutics (see Chapter 27).

Levels of Narrative Analysis

In the context of research in health psychology, Murray (2000) proposes four levels of analyzing narratives: the personal, interpersonal, positional, and ideological levels. Most research focuses on the personal level of narratives—what does a narrative reveal of an individual's biography and life history? The interpersonal level focuses on the process of co-constructing events and issues as a shared achievement of narrator and listener. On a positional level, we can analyze how people in their narratives position themselves towards the issues they talk about— for example, towards their chronic illness as successful managers or as failing victims in dealing with it. On an ideological level, narratives contribute to constituting and delimiting social groups and also to hold up boundaries. This level is related to social representations theory (see Chapter 7 and Flick 1998) and comes closer to what Hildenbrand and Jahn discuss as "joint narratives" of families, for example.

What Is the Contribution to the General Methodological Discussion?

Common to all the procedures for analyzing narrative data presented here is that in the interpretation of statements they start from the gestalt of the narrative. In so doing they view the statements in the context of the way the narrative proceeds. Furthermore, they include a formal analysis of the material, indicating which passages of the text are narrative passages, and which other sorts of text can be identified.

The procedures differ in how they view the role of the narrative in the analysis of the studied relations. Schütze sees the narrative presented in the interview as a true representation of the events recounted. The other authors see narratives as a special form of constructing events. This form can also be found in everyday life and knowledge and so this mode of construction is particularly suited to research purposes. A characteristic feature of narrative analysis is the combination of formal analysis and sequential procedure in the interpretation of constructions of experiences.

How Does the Method Fit into the Research Process?

The theoretical background is the orientation to the analysis of subjective meaning (see Chapter 7). For this purpose, narrative interviews are used for collecting data (see above). Research questions focus on the analysis of biographical processes (see Chapter 9). Cases are usually selected gradually (see Chapter 13), and generalizations made in order to develop theories (see Chapter 10). Therefore, case analyses are contrasted with one another (see Chapter 29).

What Are the Limitations of the Method?

In the main, those analyses based on Schütze's method exaggerate the quality of reality in narratives. The influence of the presentation on what is recounted is underestimated; the possible inference from narrative to factual events in life histories is overestimated. Only in very rare examples are narrative analyses combined with other methodological approaches in order to overcome their limitations.

A second problem is the degree to which analyses stick to individual cases. The time and effort spent analyzing individual cases restricts studies from going beyond the reconstruction and comparison of a few cases. The more general theory of biographical processes that was originally aimed at has yet to be realized, although there are instructive typologies in particular domains.

Small Narratives and Constructionist Analysis

Narrative research is an increasingly prominent approach that is in the process of still further development and proliferation. Here we may mention two recent examples. As Ochs and Capps (2001, p. 57) discuss, narrative analysis often focuses on ideal typical narratives which can be characterized by several qualities:

> A coherent temporal progression of events that may be reordered for rhetorical purposes and that is typically located on some past time and place. A plotline that encompasses a beginning, a middle, and an end, conveys a particular perspective and is designed for a particular audience who apprehend and shape its meaning.

This understanding forms the basis of research based on the narrative interview described. But narration often happens under circumstances and conditions in everyday life that limit its shape and full-fledged development. A consequence is to limit the stimulation of narratives to recounting situations as in the episodic interview also described above.

More generally, Bamberg (see Bamberg 2012; Bamberg and Georgakopoulou 2008) has developed a new approach for using narrative data in qualitative research. He distinguishes "small stories" from the big narratives (as being produced in the narrative interview or in mundane storytelling). Small stories comprise "tellings of ongoing events, future or hypothetical events and shared (known) events, but ... also ... allusions to (previous) tellings, deferrals of tellings and refusals to tell" (Bamberg and Georgakopoulou 2008, p. 381). The aim of analyzing such small stories is: "We are interested in how people use small stories in their interactive engagements *to construct* a sense of who they are, while big story research analyzes the stories as *representations* of world and identities" (p. 382).

Such developments show how the focus has shifted—away from the idea that narratives offer a better access to how things really occurred (as was the driving assumption behind the narrative interview for some time) and towards how narratives construct meaning and interpretation in a specific way. In a similar way, the constructionist approach to narrative analysis developed by Esin et al. (2014) is interested in issues like how audiences have a constructing effect on stories that are told and how this becomes relevant for analyzing narratives coming from interviews in other languages.

Checklist for Using Narratives in Qualitative Research

The checklist below should give you some orientation of when and how to use narratives in qualitative research:

1 What are your expectations for analyzing narratives in your research?
2 Are there any existing narratives you can use?
3 Which form of narrative data collection is the most appropriate for your issue?
4 Which one will best suit your research participants?
5 How do you take into account that narratives are a way of (re)constructing events and experiences?
6 How does the situation in which narratives are produced for your research affect what is narrated?
7 If you work with the narrative interview, how far does your method of analysis take into account the complexity of the data you receive?

KEY POINTS

- Narratives can be used in interviews to elicit a more comprehensive and contextualized account of events and experiences.
- This can be achieved either with overall life histories—biographical narratives—or with situation-oriented narratives.
- There are different ways of conceiving narratives in interviews—as the main form, standing alone, or embedded in different forms of questions.
- Not everything constitutes a suitable issue for a narrative presentation; sometimes other forms of accessing experiences are needed to complement, or even replace, narratives.
- Joint narratives can be very fruitful where the interaction of the members adds to the knowledge produced in data collection.
- Narrative approaches take into account the structure of the text.
- Narrative analysis follows the structure of the text (sequentially) and sees the statements in this context.
- Biographical texts are analyzed in the light of the sequence of the events that is reported so that (1) the internal structure of the life history and (2) the external structure of the life reported in it may be related to each other.
- It is not always the "big" narrative that is the best way of collecting narrative data. "Small" narratives also have a role to play.
- Narratives are constructions of events that are reported.

1 When would you use a narrative interview, when would you prefer the episodic interview, and when a different type of interview?
2 If you have a research question in your own research project for which the narrative interview is adequate, develop a narrative generative question.
3 Develop an interview guide for an episodic interview for a research question of your own.

Exercise 18.2

1 Take your own interview data and look for any biographical information. Identify the dates that are mentioned in them and reconstruct the case history (in the excerpts that are mentioned).
2 Analyze how the interviewee presents him- or herself in the interview at various stages of the text, especially at the beginning of the interview.

Further Reading

The Narrative Interview

The first two texts deal with the topic of biographical research, whereas the third introduces the method in English:

Bertaux, D. (ed.) (1981) *Biography and History: The Life History Approach to Social Sciences.* Beverly Hills, CA: Sage.
Denzin, N.K. (1988) *Interpretive Biography.* London: Sage.
Rosenthal, G. (2004) "Biographical Research," in C. Seale, G. Gobo, J. Gubrium and D. Silverman (eds.), *Qualitative Research Practice.* London: Sage. pp. 48–65.

The Episodic Interview

In these texts, some applications and the methodological background of the episodic interview can be found:

Flick, U. (1994) "Social Representations and the Social Construction of Everyday Knowledge: Theoretical and Methodological Queries," *Social Science Information*, 33: 179–197.
Flick, U. (1995) "Social Representations," in R. Harré, J. Smith and L.v. Langenhove (eds.), *Rethinking Psychology.* London: Sage. pp. 70–96.
Flick, U. (2000a) "Episodic Interviewing," in M. Bauer and G. Gaskell (eds.), *Qualitative Researching with Text, Image and Sound: A Practical Handbook.* London: Sage. pp. 75–92.
Flick, U. (2007b) *Managing Quality in Qualitative Research.* London: Sage. Ch. 5.

Joint Narratives

Each text here deals with a field of application of group narratives:

Bruner, J. and Feldman, C. (1996) "Group Narrative as a Cultural Context of Autobiography," in D. Rubin (ed.), *Remembering Our Past: Studies in Autobiographical Memory*. Cambridge: Cambridge University Press. pp. 291–317.

Hildenbrand, B. and Jahn, W. (1988) "Gemeinsames Erzählen und Prozesse der Wirklich keitskonstruktion in familiengeschichtlichen Gesprächen," *Zeitschrift für Soziologie*, 17: 203–217.

Narrative Analyses

These texts give an overview of different ways of analyzing narratives:

Bruner, J. (1987) "Life as Narrative," *Social Research*, 54: 11–32.

Denzin, N.K. (1988) *Interpretive Biography*. London: Sage.

Rosenthal, G. and Fischer-Rosenthal, W. (2004) "The Analysis of Biographical-Narrative Interviews," in U. Flick, E.v. Kardorff and I. Steinke (eds.), *A Companion to Qualitative Research*. London: Sage. pp. 259–265.

Czarniawska, B. (2004) *Narratives in Social Science Research*. London: Sage.

Esin, C., Fathi, M. and Squire, C. (2014) "Narrative Analysis: The Constructionist Approach," in U. Flick (ed.), *The SAGE Handbook of Qualitative Data Analysis*. London: Sage. pp. 203–216.

Narratives between Biography and Episode

To enter into a discussion of these questions more deeply, these two works of Bruner are very instructive:

Bruner, J. (1987) "Life as Narrative," *Social Research*, 54: 11–32.

Bruner, J. (1991) "The Narrative Construction of Reality," *Critical Inquiry*, 18: 1–21.

Small Stories

Bamberg, M., and Georgakopoulou, A. (2008) "Small Stories as a New Perspective in Narrative and Identity Analysis," *Text & Talk*, 28(3), 377–396.

Bamberg, M. (2012) "Narrative Analysis," in H. Cooper (Editor-in-chief), *APA Handbook of Research Methods in Psychology* (3 vols.). Washington, DC: APA Press.

Notes

1. Whyl is a place in Germany where a nuclear power plant was planned and built and where big anti-nuclear demonstrations took place in the 1970s, with lots of people camping on the site of the planned plant. M/L was a quite influential Marxist–Leninist political group at that time, which did not support this kind of demonstration.

2. The study of Hermanns (1984) has already been presented briefly above as an example of a convincing application of this procedure (see Case Study 18.2).

PART 5
Data Beyond Talk

The approaches presented in Part 4 have one point in common: for all of them, the spoken word is central. In these approaches, other information beyond what participants in a study say has only limited relevance. However, it has increasingly become recognized in research that this focus on verbal data can accommodate only a limited part of what is relevant for qualitative research about specific issues. Data beyond talk (Chapter 19) have attracted more and more attention. As a consequence, methods designed to overcome this limitation have grown in importance. Part 5 will make you familiar with such methods.

Observation and participant observation have a long tradition in qualitative research: they are currently sailing, under the flag of ethnography, to new relevance and influence. E-mail, the Internet, the Word Wide Web, chatrooms, and newsgroups have become familiar ways of communicating for many people. It is no surprise, then, that the Internet has been not only discovered as an object of research, but also used as a tool for reaching people and for doing research. A special interest has been developed in using this approach to study virtual worlds and communication on the Internet. Characteristic of such research is the use of a variety of methods and data. These include observation sometimes complemented by interviews, documents, and other traces of interaction and practices. This approach is outlined in Chapter 20.

Visual research—using photographs, films, or videos as data—has been attracting greater attention. Whereas over the previous few decades the field of verbal data saw a narrative turn, we now see other turns: they include the **iconic turn** or the **performative turn**, which make extended forms of data necessary to study the research questions linked to these turns. Films and photographs are ubiquitous and images dominate much of our lives. It is, therefore, no surprise that films, photographs, and videos have become formats to produce data as well as issues of research in qualitative studies. Chapter 21 is devoted to such forms of visual data. Qualitative research also employs other forms of documents as data, beyond the visual ones just mentioned. The use of documents for study has a long tradition in qualitative research; for example, diaries can be seen as traces of personal experiences or records as traces of institutional interactions (see Chapter 22).

19
Collecting Data Beyond Talk

CHAPTER OBJECTIVES

This chapter is designed to help you

- compare various approaches to observation and visual and documentary data;
- evaluate your decisions on data collection in the light of your (first) experiences when applying the method you choose;
- understand your method in the context of the research process and of the other stages of your research plan.

Strategies of using data beyond talk are becoming increasingly widespread in qualitative research. Visual data in particular are increasingly being discovered in qualitative research. The use of observation and ethnography is a major trend; the Internet is becoming both a resource and issue for qualitative research in the virtual sphere. Various sorts of documents are employed as data in qualitative research.

There are different reasons for using observational data or documents instead of, or in addition to, verbal data. First, there is the desire on the part of the researcher to go beyond the spoken word and what participants report about actions in favor of analyzing the actions themselves as they naturally occur. Second, there is the advantage to be gained from the fact that some forms of observations work without the need for the researcher to make any interventions in the field under study. Finally, there is the possibility of obtaining knowledge through observing by participating and by intervening in the field and then observing the consequences in the field.

Observation, in its various forms, tries to understand practices, interactions, and events that occur in a specific context in one of two ways: either from the inside, as a participant, or from the outside, as a mere observer. In observation, different starting points are taken to reconstruct the single case: for example, the events in a specific setting, the activities of a specific person, or the concrete interaction between several persons.

Furthermore, it is increasingly being recognized that the media of film and the camera have an influence on the events under study and their presentation for the observer. Thus observational procedures contribute to the construction of the very reality they seek to analyze, a reality which is already the result of processes of social construction before being observed. Observational methods provide a specific access to trace such construction processes as they occur in interaction. In the end, observational methods also lead to the production of text as empirical material. The texts range from observation protocols, through transcripts of recorded interactions, to verbal descriptions of the events in films, or the content of photographs.

Other forms of documents provide a fruitful way to approach everyday lives and institutional routines across the traces that these lives and routines produce and leave in records, for example.

Aims of Collecting Data beyond Talk

There are several aims linked to the decision to use other forms of data beyond asking members of a field for their version of an issue or their experience, as Lüders (2004a, p. 222) emphasizes:

> Anyone who wishes to make an empirical investigation of human beings, their everyday practice and lifeworlds has, in principle, two possibilities: one can hold conversations with participants about their actions and collect appropriate documents in the hope of obtaining, in this way, rich information *about* the practice in which one is interested. Or else one looks for ways or strategies for taking part, for as long as possible, in this everyday practice and becoming familiar with it, so as to be able to observe its everyday performance. The second strategy ... is that which has long been described ... as *participant observation* ... recently replaced by the term "ethnography."

The idea behind such a distinction is that there is "first-hand" information that can be obtained by observing a field and taking part in it or by using existing data (e.g., documents) and "second-hand" information coming from reports (narratives, descriptions, etc.) of individuals or groups.

Another aim is to take into account how far specific forms of visualization have intruded on our daily lives. Knoblauch, Tuma, and Schnettler (2014, p. 435), for example, speak of the "omnipresence of video in everyday life"; films are influencing viewers' and public images of their issues and documents are produced in all steps of our history and presence. It is necessary to develop appropriate methods for analyzing these parts of everyday (and institutional) life.

Types of Data beyond Talk

This umbrella term "data beyond talk" is used for approaches that do not restrict data collection to interviews, to collecting narratives, or to running focus groups in which participants report their experiences and views about a certain issue. One option is first to go into the field where the action happens—by observing what goes on and by becoming more or less part of the action for a shorter or longer period. An alternative is to use visual data that documents practices and interactions including mimics, gestures and other visual elements part of them. And finally, written documents may allow traces of everyday or institutional lives to be accessed beyond the single participants' views and reports. These three types of data will be discussed in some detail in this and the following chapters.

What Is Observation?

In their book on the history of observation, Daston and Lunbeck give a very broad definition of the term:

> Observation is the most pervasive and fundamental practice of all modern sciences, both natural and human. It is also among the most refined and variegated. Observation educates the senses, calibrates judgment, picks out objects of scientific inquiry, and forges "thought collectives." Its instruments include not only the naked senses, but also tools such as the telescope and the microscope, the questionnaire, the photographic plate, the glassed-in beehive, the Geiger counter, and a myriad of other ingenious inventions designed to make the invisible visible, the evanescent permanent, and the abstract concrete. Where is society? How blue is the sky? Which ways do X-rays scatter? Over the course of centuries, scientific observers have devised ways to answer these and many other riddles. (Daston and Lunbeck 2011, p. 1)

This definition refers to the basic scientific practice of observation, not necessarily to narrower conceptions such as doing a participant or non-participant observation. Under this broad definition, observation means to collect data and analyze them and to use the variety of existing methods to do so. In qualitative research, such an understanding of observation can be fruitful for taking into account that there are many ways of collecting data and that there are many types of data, which result from these ways of collecting. Thus, in distinction to the prominent approach of asking members of a field to talk about an issue or their view of it, in the remainder of this chapter, the term "observation" will be used in a broader sense, as the use of documents, photos, video, or of communications on the Internet are forms of observing interactions and other processes, too.

What Is Participant Observation?

In qualitative research, several forms of observation are used (see Chapter 20). From the beginning and for a long while, participant observation was the most prominent way of doing observation. This means the researchers go into the field and try to become part of the field and an active member of it. The researchers do not refrain from activities in the field; they participate in them.

Participation represents a step towards developing insights into the field and towards finding better access to relevant processes and practices that the researchers want to observe for their study. Participation also includes talking to members of the field—informally, in ethnographic interviews (see Chapter 16) as part of the observation process, or in other forms of interviews separated from the observation and in addition to it. The major challenge here is how to balance the two activities "participation" and "observation," which means how to become a member of the field as far as possible and at the same time keep the distance big enough to remain a researcher and observer. Schensul, Schensul, and LeCompte (1999) define participant observation as "the process of learning through exposure to or involvement in the day-to-day or routine activities of participants in the researcher setting" (p. 91). Data collection is mainly based on the field notes the researchers write during the observations; in some cases video recording is used in the field for documentation.

What Is Ethnography?

In more recent discussions, the term "ethnography" has become more common than participant observation. This has two reasons. First, this term underlines that observation is just one of the techniques used in the field, which is complemented by all sorts of other ways of collecting data (interviews, documents, images, graffiti, etc.). Second, this term more strongly highlights the part of writing about the field for the research as a whole. Writing starts from field notes (see Chapter 20) and memos (see Chapter 25) and extends to presenting the findings and describing the process of research in the final report or publication (see Chapter 30). Ethnography is a much more flexible strategy, also based on longer participation in the field. But it is more the "analytic inspiration" that Gubrium and Holstein (2014) mention, which is important for identifying the best sites for the study and the best ways to find out what is relevant for describing and understanding the phenomenon and the field on which the research focuses.

Gobo (2008, p. 12) gives the following definition of ethnography, showing both the centrality of (participant) observation in ethnography and how ethnography goes beyond observation:

A methodology which privileges (the cognitive mode of) observation as its primary source of information. This purpose is also served, in a secondary and ancillary manner, by other sources of information used by ethnographers in the field: informal conversations, individual or group interviews and documentary materials (diaries, letters, essays, organizational documents, newspapers, photographs and audiovisual aids). Ethnography comprises two research strategies: non-participant observation and participant observation.

What Is Virtual Ethnography?

Ethnography is based on the researchers' presence in the field under study. If this field falls within the realm of the Internet and a virtual field, virtual ethnography can be applied. This means, basically, that the techniques of ethnography are transferred to online research and the researchers participate in online communication to study it. Kozinets, for example, labels this approach as netnography and gives the following definition:

> virtual ethnography is ethnography conducted on the Internet; a qualitative, interpretive research methodology that adapts the traditional, in-person ethnographic research techniques of anthropology to the study of online cultures and communities formed through computer-mediated communications. (2006, p. 135)

Here again, we find participation as an element of the research and observation as a basic strategy.

What Is Visual Qualitative Research?

Visual research is based on the assumption that we need to understand the iconic qualities of an issue by integrating images, films, and video in the data collected for understanding the issue. Images are not only seen as representing an issue and the practices of dealing with it; they are also assumed to influence individual and public views of the issue. And they are embedded in forms of social use—interpretations and communications referring to them on the users' side. The visual material in this sense becomes a medium for understanding and communicating social meanings of an issue.

Visual material can be addressed on various levels: by looking at its content (1), by analyzing its formal composition etc. (2), by asking for the intentions behind producing it (3)—whether individual or institutional intentions—and analyzing its reception (4) and social use on the side of viewers.

This diversity of approaches to visual material is reflected in the difficulties of defining the term "visual methodology" coherently. Pink, for example, argues that:

> as a field of scholarship, visual methodology is complex and diverse. Its uniting themes tend to be the focus on the (audio)visual; the media and technologies engaged; and

attention to a specific range of ethical issues. There are sometimes vast differences in terms of the ways that the status of the image is understood, and the theoretical and discipline-specific foundations that distinguish some approaches to the visual in research methodology. (2012, p. 9)

Therefore, she "considers visual methodologies as a set of approaches to working with the visual in research and representation that are constantly in progress and development" (p. 4) and as a set of practices rather than a set of methods:

The question of defining visual methodology as a field of practice is further complicated by the fact that within it discipline and also task-specific uses and understandings of the visual exist alongside and in relation to visual work that is self-consciously interdisciplinary. (p. 8)

This series of quotations from Pink shows that visual qualitative research is not so much based on a common understanding or procedure but shares the interest and approach to use visual material in concrete research projects. Pink also highlights that the methodologies here cannot be seen or discussed independently from the findings produced with them (p. 4).

There are, however, some methodological issues at stake for any visual research project. After defining a research issue and questions, the next step will be to identify visual materials which can be used for studying the issue in the light of the research question. The materials can be existing images, recordings, or films or they can be produced for the research. Sampling questions (see Chapter 13) refer to the visual material—which photo (or film) to select for the study—or to parts in the material—which sequence in a film or video, which part of a photo to analyze? Then the main question is what the material represents on the four levels mentioned above—what are the researchers' expectations towards using this specific material in their study? Specific ethical issues arise here due to the much more comprehensive exposure of research participants in visual material compared to that in research limited to talk (see Chapter 5). This becomes relevant in particular when quotations from the material are used for illustration or as evidence in the presentation of findings or in publications.

The advantage of visual data over verbal data methods is that processes can be analyzed in the making and how they unfold, instead of having (only) reports about them. The advantage of visual data over observation is that they are less volatile—images or video recording can be watched again and again, while from observations only the condensed version in the researchers' field notes remain available. Nevertheless, images are not innocent: they are not "just there"; their meaning comes from those who produce them for a specific purpose and from those who consume them and read a certain meaning into them or use them for some purpose.

What Are Documents?

Although visual materials can be seen as documents as well, the following definition shows that the analysis of documents mostly means written documents:

> What can be included as a "document" in social research covers a potentially broad spectrum of materials, both textual and otherwise. There are of course "official" records of various kinds – organisational and "state" documents designed as records of action and activity such as large data sets and public records. There are also everyday documents of organisations and lives – notes, memoranda, case records, email threads and so forth; semi-public or routine documents that are at the heart of everyday social practice. There are also private papers of various kinds that we can treat as documentary data or evidence – for example diaries, testimony, letters and cards. (Coffey 2014, p. 367)

Here the guiding idea is that most parts of our daily life, and even more of institutional life, leave traces somewhere as they are documented. Again a driving force behind analyzing these traces, instead of talking to people in interviews (for example), is the assumption that the interesting events become available without the filters of individual memory and meaning making. But, again, documents are not "just there"—they were made by someone for some purpose and become relevant for the research only through the researchers' interpretations. In particular, the intentions and purposes for documenting something in a specific form have to be taken into account in analyzing the documents. For documents as well, central methodological issues are what to select as material, what to select in the material, and for what this selection is seen as relevant.

Starting Points for Selecting an Approach for Collecting Data beyond Talk

The types of data mentioned in this part can be seen as an alternative or as an addition to using verbal data. Observations are also made for the research so that in this approach, new data are produced for the study. In the other approaches mentioned here, the researchers can either use existing material (e.g., photos in a family's photo album) or produce new materials (e.g., by asking a family to document a certain part of their everyday lives in photos taken for the researchers). Which kind of approach should be taken in a concrete study is a major decision in this context. Four points of orientation are outlined below.

1 Criteria-based Comparison of the Approaches

A starting point can be to compare approaches to observation, visual data, and documents with the criteria used for comparing the approaches to verbal data (see Chapter 15). A central question here, again, is how (far) each procedure produces or guarantees openness in the research process. Because observations and visual material start mostly from interactions and actions, the participants' subjective perspectives are often ascertained in additional interviews. In addition to such efforts for openness, observational methods include how to structure data collection to garner in-depth content. The various approaches to visual data also contribute to

TABLE 19.1 Comparison of Methods for Collecting Data beyond Talk

Criteria	Observation and ethnography				Visual data			Documents
	Observation	Participant observation	Ethnography	Virtual ethnography	Use of photos	Film analysis	Video analysis	Using documents
Openness to the participants' subjective view by:	Integration of interviews	Integration of interviews Empathy through participation	Linking observation and interviewing	Participants can act without the researchers' physical presence	Subject as photographer	Subversive interpretations focus one protagonist's perspective	Asking the participant to do the video recording	Taking the context of the document into account (who produced it; for which purpose?)
Openness to the process of actions and interactions by:	Not influencing the observed field	Distance despite participation Most open observation	Participation in the life world which is observed	Participation in the online world that is observed	Documentation in photo series	Analysis of stories and processes in films	Comprehensive documentation of context	Using records of processes produced for everyday purposes
Structuring (e.g., deepening) the analysis by:	Increased focusing Selective observation	Integration of key persons Increased focusing	Plurality of the applied methods	Focusing on specific contents and ways of communicating virtually	Slice and angle Photograph at the decisive moment	Contrasting "realistic" and "subversive" interpretations	Focus of the camera on certain aspects	Selection of the documents and taking their structure into account
Contribution to the general development of methods for collecting data beyond talk	Refraining from interventions in the field Elucidating the gendered nature of fieldwork Self-observation for reflection	Elucidating the conflicts between participation and distance	Highlighting the appropriateness of methods Sensitizing for problems of description and presentation	Making distant participants available for the research Making use of an up-to-date form of communication for research	Enriching other methods (observation, interviews)	Fixing visual data Documentation and detailed analysis of non-verbal components	Extension of limits of other methods	Ways of using data not originally produced for research purposes

Criteria	Observation and ethnography				Visual data			Documents
	Observation	Participant observation	Ethnography	Virtual ethnography	Use of photos	Film analysis	Video analysis	Using documents
Area of application	Open fields Public places	Delimited fields Institutions	Everyday life worlds	Analyses of online communication in ethnography	Strange cultures Biographical experiences	Social problems Cultural values	Workplace studies Interactions in institutional context	Analyses of institutional or everyday processes
Problems in conducting the method	Agreement of (unknown) people observed in public places	Going native Problems of access Inundation of the observer	Unspecified research attitude instead of using specific methods	Uncertainty about the identity of participants Limited to users of the Internet	Selectivity of the medium and its application	Interpretation at the level of the image or at the level of the text	How to restrict the influence of the presence of technology	How to select and how to take contexts of documents into account
Limits of the method	Covert observation as a problem of ethics	Relation between statements and actions in the data	Limited interest in methodological questions	Allows only a very special part of everyday life to be approached (virtual communication)	Photo analysis as text analysis	No specific method for analyzing filmed data	Selectivity of the camera	Functions and purposes of the documents often can only be indirectly concluded
References	Adler and Adler (1998) Marvasti (2014)	Lüders (2004a) Spradley (1980)	Atkinson et al. (2001) Gubrium and Holstein (2014) Lüders (2004a)	Bergmann and Meier (2004) Marotzki et al. (2014) Kozinets et al. (2014)	Becker (1986a) Harper (2004) Banks (2014)	Denzin (2004b) Mikos (2014)	Heath and Hindmarsh (2002) Knoblauch, Schnettler, Raab, and Soeffner (2006b) Knoblauch et al. (2014)	Coffey (2014) Prior (2003) Wolff (2004b)

the development of observation and the analysis of documents and of visual data as methods in general. They can also be characterized by the fields of applications in which they are mainly used or for which they were developed.

The methods discussed here each raise specific problems in applying them and have their own limitations; these are shown in Table 19.1. The methods are grouped in three categories: observation and ethnography, visual data methods, and documents. The comparison in the table delimits the field of methodological alternatives in the area of using such data and facilitates their positioning in this range.

2 Selection of the Method and Checking its Application

Researchers should select the appropriate method for collecting observational, visual, or documentary data on the basis of their own investigation: its research question, the field that is to be observed, and the persons (or materials) that are most crucial. They should check the selected method against the material obtained with it. Not every method is appropriate to every research question. Events of the past may best be analyzed by using those visual materials that emerged at the time the events took place. Photos provide a path in this direction. One may study how a society defines cultural values and deals with social problems in general (i.e., across various situations) by analyzing films shown in cinemas and on television.

How such values and problems are concretely treated in situations of interaction may become clear in observing the fields and persons to whom they are relevant. But observation has access only to the actions realized in the situation, and the social and individual biographical background, knowledge, or attention can only be reconstructed in a mediated way from them. If the situation, the field, and the members can be sufficiently confined, the additional options of knowledge resulting from the researcher's participation in the field under study should be integrated. Non-participant observation makes sense mainly where the field cannot be delimited in a way that makes participation possible or where the actions to be observed prevent participation due to the dangers linked to them or their illegality. Traces left in documents and on the Internet can reveal a specific part of social processes and changes.

After the research question, the persons to be studied are a second consideration when deciding between methods of collecting observational visual or documentary data. Some people are more irritated and embarrassed by mere observation than by the researcher's temporary participation in their daily lives, whereas others have problems with the disturbance created by the presence of the participant observer in the domain of interest. Some researchers have bigger problems in finding their way in the studied field, whereas others have more problems with the withdrawal required in mere observation. With respect to the participants in the study, it may be helpful if you clarify the situation and the researchers' procedures and check the appropriateness of the method you selected for this concrete purpose.

For the observers and for solving their problems, observational training may be offered. Observed situations can be analyzed in order to find out if the relevant aspects have been taken into account or not. Field contacts should be analyzed additionally for problems in orienting and staying in the field. If this training does not solve the researcher's problems in the field, the choice of method or the choice of observer should be reconsidered.

The analysis of the first observation should also concentrate on the question of how far the selected method has been applied according to its rules and aims. For example, have observational sheets been applied as exactly and as flexibly as the method requires? Have the researchers maintained the necessary distance in their participation? Did the participation correspond in extension and intensity to the goals of the research? Here one should also take into account, in selecting and assessing a method, what kind of statements one will obtain at the end and at what level of generalization. Only by taking these factors into account is it possible to specify what a good observation is (see the Checklist below).

By using the questions in the Checklist at the end of this chapter, the appropriateness of the method and of its application can be assessed from different angles. This assessment should be done after the first field contacts and repeatedly in the further proceeding of the observation.

3 Appropriateness of the Method to the Issue

Generally, there is no valid ideal method for collecting observational and visual data. The research question and the issue under study should determine whether participant observation or a film analysis is applied. Non-participant observation can only provide insights that are limited to actions and interactions in concrete situations. The extension to participation in the events to be observed and to parallel conversations with the persons in the field is the more appropriate way of getting to grips with the subjective perspectives and the life world of the participants. The problem of appropriateness of methods is solved in the field of observation particularly by combining different methods in ethnographic studies.

4 Fitting the Method into the Research Process

Locating observational methods in the research process is the fourth point of reference. The form of data collection should be cross-checked with the intended method of interpretation to find out if the effort to realize openness and flexibility towards the issue under study is comparable in both cases. It does not make much sense to design the observation in the field so that it is free of methodological restrictions and is as flexible and comprehensive as possible, if afterwards the data are exclusively analyzed with categories derived from existing theories (see Chapter 26). It has proved extremely difficult to analyze data that are only documented in field notes with hermeneutic methods (see Chapter 27), like objective hermeneutics (for this problem see Lüders 2004a). Methods of interpretation located between these two poles (e.g., grounded theory coding, see Chapter 25) are more appropriate for these data. In a similar way, you should cross-check your form and design of observation with your method of sampling fields and situations and with the theoretical background of your study.

Starting points for this cross-checking can be found in the considerations about fitting the method into the research process given for each method in the preceding chapters. The understanding of the research process outlined in these considerations should be compared to the understanding of the research process on which the concrete study and its design are based.

Thus, the choice of the concrete method may be taken and assessed with respect to its appropriateness to the subject under study and to the process of research as a whole.

Checklist for Using Data beyond Talk

Suggestions for deciding on a method for collecting data beyond talk, and for checking the appropriateness of this decision, are given in the checklist below:

1 *Research* question

Can the method and its application address the essential aspects of the research question?

2 *Form of data collection*

Has the method been applied according to the methodological rules and goals? Has jumping between the forms of data collection been avoided except when it is grounded in the research question and/or theoretically?

3 *The researchers*

Are the researchers able to apply the method?
What parts do their own fears and uncertainties play in the situation?

4 *The participants*

Is the form of data collection appropriate to the target group?
How can the fears, uncertainties, and expectations of (potential) participants in the study be taken into account?

5 *Field*

Is the form of data collection appropriate to the field under study?
How are its accessibility and feasibility and ethical problems taken into account?

6 *Scope for the members*

How are the perspectives of the persons that are studied and their variability taken into account?

Do the members' perspectives have a chance of asserting themselves against the methodological framework of the study (e.g., are the observational sheets flexible enough for the unexpected)?

7 *Course of the data collection*

Have the researchers realized the form of data collection?

Have they left enough scope to the members?

Has the researcher managed his or her roles? (Why not?)

Were the participants' role, the researcher's role, and the situation sufficiently clearly defined for the participants?

Could they fulfill their roles? (Why not?)

Analyze the breaks in order to validate the data collection between the first and second field contact, if possible.

8 *Aim of the interpretation*

What are the clearly defined actions, multifold patterns, contexts, and so on?

9 *Claim for generalization*

What is the level on which statements should be made:

- For the single case (the participants and their actions, an institution and the relations in it, etc.)?
- Referring to groups (findings about a profession, a type of institution, etc.)?
- General statements?

┌─KEY POINTS─

- All methods for collecting observational, visual, and documentary data have their own particular strengths and weaknesses.
- All methods offer ways to give the participants room for presenting their experiences.
- At the same time, each method structures what is studied in a specific way.
- Before and while applying a specific method for answering your research question, assess whether the method selected is appropriate.

┌─Exercise 19.1─

1 Find a study from the literature which is based on using observational or visual data (e.g., Mondada 2012). How appropriate was the method for the issue under study and the people involved in the research?
2 For your own study reflect on what your main reasons were for using one of the methods to collect observational or visual data.

These texts deal with some of the methods for analyzing the data mentioned in this part of the book:

Banks, M. (2007) *Using Visual Data in Qualitative Research*. London: Sage.

Bergmann, J. and Meier, C. (2004) "Electronic Process Data and their Analysis," in U. Flick, E.v. Kardorff and I. Steinke (eds.), *A Companion to Qualitative Research*. London: Sage. pp. 243–247.

Coffey, A. (2014) "Analyzing Documents," in U. Flick (ed.), *The SAGE Handbook of Qualitative Data Analysis*. London: Sage. pp. 367–379.

Denzin, N.K. (2004a) "Reading Film: Using Photos and Video as Social Science Material," in U. Flick, E.v. Kardorff and I. Steinke (eds.), *A Companion to Qualitative Research*. London: Sage. pp. 234–247.

Hammersley, M. and Atkinson, P. (2007) *Ethnography: Principles in Practice* (3rd edn). London: Routledge.

Harper, D. (2004) "Photography as Social Science Data," in U. Flick, E.v. Kardorff and I. Steinke (eds.), *A Companion to Qualitative Research*. London: Sage. pp. 231–236.

Kozinets, R. Dolbec, P.Y., and Earley, A. (2014) "Netnographic Analysis: Understanding Culture through Social Media Data," in U. Flick (ed.), *The SAGE Handbook of Qualitative Data Analysis*. London: Sage. pp. 262–276.

Marotzki, W., Holze, J. and Verständig, D. (2014) "Analyzing Virtual Data," in U. Flick (ed.), *The SAGE Handbook of Qualitative Data Analysis*. London: Sage. pp. 450–463.

DATA BEYOND TALK

20
Observation and Ethnography

CHAPTER OBJECTIVES

This chapter is designed to help you

- appreciate the various types of observation you can use for your own study;
- understand the specific problems of participant observation;
- identify ethnography as a current trend in the context of these traditions;
- see how virtual ethnography can be used for studying interaction and communication.

If you look at the history of qualitative research, you will find that methodological discussions about the role of observation as a sociological research method have been central to it. This is particularly so in the United States. Various conceptions of observation and of the observer's role can be found in the literature. There are studies in which the observer does not become an active part of the observed field (e.g., in the tradition of Goffman 1961). These studies are complemented by approaches that try to accomplish the goal of gaining an insider's knowledge of the field through the researcher's increasing assimilation as a participant in the observed field. Ethnography has taken over in recent years what was previously participant observation.

In general, these approaches stress that practices are accessible only through observation; interviews and narratives merely make the accounts of practices accessible rather than the practices themselves. The claim is often made for observation that it enables the researcher to find out how something factually works or occurs. Compared to that claim, presentations in interviews are said to comprise a mixture of how something is and how something should be, which still needs to be untangled.

In this chapter, we first address observation as the method that is at the heart of the strategies presented here. We then turn to participation and observation and ethnography, in which this method is embedded in specific relations to the field that is observed. Finally, we will focus on virtual ethnography as a way of applying observation to communication on the Internet.

Observation

Besides the competencies of speaking and listening used in interviews, observation is another everyday skill, which is methodologically systematized and applied in qualitative research. Practically all the senses—seeing, hearing, feeling, and smelling—are integrated into observations.

Forms of Observation

According to different authors, observational methods are generally classified along five dimensions, which can be differentiated by asking the following questions:

1 Covert versus overt observation: how far is the observation revealed to those who are observed?
2 Non-participant versus participant observation: how far does the observer have to go to become an active part of the observed field?
3 Systematic versus unsystematic observation: is a more or less standardized observation scheme applied or does the observation remain flexible and responsive to the processes themselves?
4 Observation in natural versus artificial situations: are observations done in the field of interest or are interactions "moved" to a special place (e.g., a laboratory) to make them observable more systematically?
5 Self-observation versus observing others: mostly other people are observed, so how much attention is paid to the researcher's reflexive self-observation for further grounding the interpretation of the observed?

You can also apply this general classification to observation in qualitative research, except that here data are (in general) collected from natural situations. In this chapter, the method of non-participant observation is discussed first. This form refrains from interventions in the field, in contrast to interviews and participant observations. The expectations linked to this are outlined as follows: "Simple observers follow the flow of events. Behavior and interaction continue as they would without the presence of a researcher, uninterrupted by intrusion" (Adler and Adler 1998, p. 81).

Roles in the Field

Here you can take the typology of participant roles developed by Gold (1958) as a starting point to define the differences from participant observation. Gold distinguishes four types of participant roles:

- the complete participant;
- the participant-as-observer;
- the observer-as-participant;
- the complete observer.

The complete observer maintains distance from the observed events in order to avoid influencing them. You may accomplish this in part by replacing the actual observation in the situation by videotaping. Alternatively, attempts may be made to distract the attention of those under observation from the researcher so that they become oblivious to the process of observation. In this context, covert observation is applied, in which observed people are not informed that they are being observed. This procedure, however, is ethically contestable (see Chapter 5), especially if the field can be easily observed, and there are no practical problems in informing the observed people or obtaining their consent. Often, however, this kind of observation is practiced in open spaces (e.g., in train stations or public places, in cafés with frequently changing clientele) where this agreement cannot be obtained.

What Are the Phases of Observation?

Authors such as Adler and Adler (1998), Denzin (1989b), and Spradley (1980) identify the following phases of such an observation:

1 the selection of a setting (i.e., where and when the interesting processes and persons can be observed);
2 the definition of what is to be documented in the observation and in every case;
3 the training of the observers in order to standardize such focuses;
4 descriptive observations that provide an initial, general presentation of the field;
5 focused observations that concentrate on aspects that are relevant to the research question;
6 selective observations that are intended to purposively grasp central aspects;
7 the end of the observation, when theoretical saturation has been reached, which means that further observations do not provide any further knowledge.

Leisure Behavior of Adolescents

In the following example, you can see the attempt and the limitations of a study keeping strictly to non-participant observation. The researcher, Mechthild Niemann, carried out her study in the context of education. She observed adolescents "parallel at two times of measurement" in two discotheques, ice stadiums, shopping malls, summer baths, football clubs, concert halls, and so on. She selected situations randomly and documented "developmental tasks" which were specific to these situations (e.g., realizing the goal of integration in the peer group) on protocol sheets.

In order to better prepare the researcher, a period of training in observational techniques was given prior to the actual research in which different and independent observations of a situation were analyzed for their correspondence with the aim of increasing the latter. An observational manual was applied in order to make the notes more uniform:

> Observations of situations in principle were given a protocol only after they finished … mostly based on free notes on little pieces of scrap paper, beer mats or cigarette boxes. Here, however, there was a danger of bias and imprecise representations, which would interfere with the goal of minimizing the influence on the adolescents' behavior. (Niemann 1989, p. 79)

The attempt to avoid reactivity (i.e., feedback of the procedure of observation on the observed) determines the data collection, which in this case was complemented by interviews with single juveniles.

Merkens characterizes this strategy of "non-participant field observation" as follows:

> The observer here tries not to disturb the persons in the field by striving to make himself as invisible as possible. His interpretations of the observed occur from his horizon. … The observer constructs meanings for himself, which he supposes direct the actions of the actors in the way he perceives them. (1989, p. 15)

The example in Case Study 20.1 demonstrates the dilemmas of a non-participant observation in which the researcher tries to maintain methodological standards and thus allows the methods to strongly influence and determine the issue under study. The attempt to avoid influencing the participants' behavior in the field in the end decisively constricts the interpretation of the data, which has to be undertaken from an external perspective on the field under study.

What Are the Problems in Conducting the Method?

A main problem here is to define a role for the observers that they can take and that allows them to stay in the field or at its edge and observe it at the same time (see the discussion of participant roles in Chapter 12). The more public and unstructured the field is, the easier it will be to take a role that is not conspicuous and does not influence the field. The easier a field is to overlook, the more difficult it is to participate in it without becoming a member.

Niemann outlines how to position a researcher in the field for observing the leisure activities of adolescents at leisure sites: "The observations were covert in order to avoid influencing the behavior of the adolescents that was typical for a specific site" (1989, p. 73).

What Are the Contributions to the General Methodological Discussion?

Triangulation of observations with other sources of data and the employment of different observers increase the expressiveness of the data gathered. Gender differences are a crucial aspect also, particularly when planning to observe in public places, where the possibilities of access and moving around are much more restricted due to particular dangers for women than for men. Women's perceptions of such restrictions and dangers, however, are much more sensitive, which makes them observe differently and notice different things compared to male observers. This shows the "gendered nature of fieldwork" (Lofland, quoted in Adler and Adler 1998, p. 95), and this is the reason for the suggested use of mixed-gender teams in observational studies.

A further suggestion is painstaking *self*-observation of the researcher while entering the field, during the course of the observation, and when looking back on its process in order to integrate implicit impressions, apparent incidentals, and perceptions in the reflection of the process and results.

How Does the Method Fit into the Research Process?

The theoretical background here is the analysis of the production of social reality from an external perspective. The goal is (at least often) the testing of theoretical concepts for certain phenomena on the basis of their occurrence and distribution (see Chapter 10). Research questions aim at descriptions of the state of certain life worlds (e.g., adolescents in Berlin). The selection of situations and persons occurs systematically according to criteria of how to get a representative sample, and random sampling therefore is applied (see Chapter 13). Data analyses are based on counting the incidence of specific activities by using the procedures of categorizing (see Chapters 25 and 26).

What Are the Limitations of the Method?

All in all, this form of observation represents an approach to the observed field from an external perspective. Therefore, you should apply it mainly to the observation of public spaces in which the number of the members cannot be limited or defined. Furthermore, it is an attempt to observe events as they naturally occur. How far this aim can be fulfilled remains doubtful, because the act of observation influences the observed in any case. Sometimes the argument is made for the use of covert observation, which eliminates the influence of the researcher on the field; however, this is highly problematic with respect to research ethics. Furthermore, the researcher's abstinence from interacting with the field leads to problems in analyzing the data and in assessing the interpretations, because of the systematic restraint on disclosing the interior perspective of the field and of the observed persons. This strategy is associated more with an understanding of methods based on quantitative and standardized research.

Participant Observation

More commonly used in qualitative research is participant observation. Denzin gives a definition:

> Participant observation will be defined as a field strategy that simultaneously combines document analysis, interviewing of respondents and informants, direct participation and observation, and introspection. (1989b, pp. 157–158)

The main features of the method are that you as a researcher dive headlong into the field. You will observe from a member's perspective, but also influence what you observe due to your participation. The differences from non-participant observation and its aims, as just discussed, are elucidated in the seven features of participant observation listed by Jorgensen:

1 a special interest in human meaning and interaction as viewed from the perspective of people who are insiders or members of particular situations and settings;
2 location in the here and now of everyday life situations and settings as the foundation of inquiry and method;
3 a form of theory and theorizing stressing interpretation and understanding of human existence;
4 a logic and process of inquiry that is open-ended, flexible, opportunistic, and requires constant redefinition of what is problematic, based on facts gathered in concrete settings of human existence;
5 an in-depth, qualitative, case study approach and design;
6 the performance of a participant role or roles that involves establishing and maintaining relationships with natives in the field; and
7 the use of direct observation along with other methods of gathering information. (1989, pp. 13–14)

Openness is essential when collecting data based solely on communicating with the observed. This method is often used for studying subcultures.

What Are the Phases of Participant Observation?

Participant observation should be understood as a process in two respects. First, the researcher should increasingly become a participant and gain access to the field and to people (see below). Second, the observation should also move through a process of becoming increasingly concrete and concentrated on the aspects that are essential for the research questions. Thus, Spradley (1980, p. 34) distinguishes three phases of participant observation:

1 *descriptive observation*, at the beginning, serves to provide the researcher with an orientation to the field under study. It provides nonspecific descriptions and is used to grasp the complexity of the field as far as possible and to develop (at the same time) more concrete research questions and lines of vision;
2 *focused observation* narrows your perspective on those processes and problems, which are most essential for your research question;
3 *selective observation*, towards the end of the data collection, is focused on finding further evidence and examples for the types of practices and processes, found in the second step.

Sometimes observation schemes—defining which aspects should be in the focus of the observer's attention—and observation sheets—which consist of a grid of issues to note while observing—are used, with differing degrees of structure. More often, protocols of situations are produced (see below), which are as detailed as possible in order to allow "thick descriptions" (Geertz 1973) of the field. Whether you prefer the use of field notes to the use of structured protocol sheets, which concretely define those activities and situational features to be documented in every case, depends both on the research question and on the phase in the research process in which observations are made.

The more a protocol sheet differentiates between aspects, the greater the risk of failing to perceive or record those aspects not identified on the sheet; the greater, too, of not perceiving a situation in the round (of not "seeing the wood for the trees"). Therefore, descriptive observation should refrain from using heavily structured sheets in order to prevent the observer's attention from being restricted and from limiting his or her sensitivity to the new.

In selective observation, however, structured protocol sheets may be helpful for grasping fully the relevant aspects elaborated in the previous phase. However, participant observations are confronted with the problem of the observer's limited observational perspective, as not all aspects of a situation can be grasped (and noted) at the same time. Bergmann holds that: "We have only a very limited competence of remembering and reproducing amorphous incidents of an actual social event. The participant observers thus have no other choice than to note the social occurrences which they were witness to mainly in a typifying, resuming, fashion of reconstruction" (1985, p. 308). The question of whether to work with overt observation (where the observed know that they are observed) or with covert observation arises here as well, but less as a methodological than as an ethical question.

┌─ CASE STUDY 20.2 ─

Boys in White

The following example is one of the classic studies of qualitative research in the medical sociology of the 1960s. The research team included several of the pioneers of qualitative research at that time and for the following decades, among them Howard Becker, Blanche Geer, and Anselm Strauss.

Becker, Geer, Hughes, and Strauss (1961) studied a state medical school in order:

> to discover what a medical school did to students other than give them a technical education. We assumed that students left medical school with a set of ideas about medicine and medical practice that differed from the ideas they entered with. ... We did not know what perspectives a student acquired while in school. (Becker and Geer 1960, p. 269)

For this purpose, over a period of one or two months, participant observations in lectures, practical exercises, dormitories, and all departments of the medical school were carried out, which sometimes extended to the whole day. The orientations that were found were examined for the degree to which they were collectively held, which means how far they were valid for the studied groups as a whole as against only for single members.

This example remains an instructive example of using participant observation with the intention of going beyond the focus of the single member of a community and of knowledge and talk. It shows how you can study communication and the development of attitudes from observing interaction and practices.

Sampling in Participant Observation

In participant observation, several steps in the research process require specific attention. Selecting a field of research, a site, which is relevant for the issue under study, is a major step and decision. Access to the site then is a longer and sensitive process. Sampling in participant observation is—different from interviews—in most cases not focused on individuals but on situations, in which specific activities or interactions are expected to happen. An exception is "shadowing," which means following, like a shadow, the person under observation: this is a method to follow specific individuals through their everyday or institutional routines for research purposes. This technique is mainly applied in organizational research (see McDonald 2005).[1] Then sampling decisions refer to individuals. In all other cases, the sampling is situation-oriented.

Finding and Accessing a Site in Participant Observation

One problem is how to delimit or select observational situations in which the problem under study becomes really "visible." According to Spradley, social situations generally may be described along nine dimensions for observational purposes:

1 *space*: the physical place or places
2 *actor*: the people involved
3 *activity*: a set of related acts people do
4 *object*: the physical things that are present
5 *act*: single actions that people do
6 *event*: a set of related activities that people carry out
7 *time*: the sequencing that takes place over time
8 *goal*: the things people are trying to accomplish
9 *feeling*: the emotions felt and expressed. (1980, p. 78)

If you cannot observe for the whole day in an institution, for example, the problem of selection arises. How can you find those situations in which the relevant actors and interesting activities can be assumed to take place? At the same time, how can you select situations which are as different from one another as possible, from the range of an average day's events, in order to increase the variation and variety of what you actually observe?

Another problem is how to access the field or the studied subculture. In order to solve this, key persons are sometimes used who introduce the researchers and make contacts for them. It is sometimes difficult, however, to find the right person for this job. However, the researchers should not leave themselves too much at the mercy of key persons. They should take care as to how far they accept the key persons' perspectives uncritically and should be aware of the fact that they may only be providing the researchers with access to a specific part of the field. Finally, key persons may even make it more difficult to gain access to the field under study or to approach certain people within it, for example, if the key persons are outsiders in the field.

Going Native

In participant observation, even more than in other qualitative methods, it becomes crucial to gain as far as possible an internal perspective on the studied field and to systematize the status of the stranger at the same time. Only if you achieve the latter will your research enable you to view the particular in what is everyday and routine in the field. To lose this critical external perspective and to unquestioningly adopt the viewpoints shared in the field is known as "going native." The process of going native, however, is discussed not only as a researcher's fault, but also as an instrument for reflecting on one's own process of becoming familiar with and for gaining insights into the field under study, which would be inaccessible by maintaining distance.

However, the goal of the research is not limited to becoming familiar with the self-evidence of a field. This may be sufficient for a successful participation but not for a systematic observation. Researchers who seek to obtain knowledge about relations in the studied field, which transcends everyday understanding, also have to maintain the distance of the "professional stranger" (see Agar 1980). Thus, Koepping underlines the fact that, for participant observation, the researcher:

as social figure must have exactly those features that Simmel has elaborated for the stranger: he has to dialectically fuse the two functions in himself, that of commitment and that of distance. ... [The researcher therefore tries to realize] what is outlined by the notion of participation in observation, the task of which is to understand through the eyes of the other. In participating, the researcher methodologically authenticates his theoretical premise and furthermore he makes the research subject, the other, not an object but a dialogical partner. (1987, p. 28)

CASE STUDY 20.3

Participant Observation in Intensive Care Units

The following example is intended to show the role of preparation for a study using participant observation in a very special field and the problem of being absorbed by the field, by the members, and by the dynamics of activities in the field during observation.

Before carrying out participant observation in intensive care units, Sprenger (1989, pp. 35–36) first had to learn the basics of intensive care medicine in order to become familiar with the terminology (syndromes, treatment concepts, etc.) in the field. In collecting data, observational guides were used, which were geared to the different scenarios that were to be analyzed (e.g., the doctoral round, visits by family members). During data collection, several activities served to widen the perspective on the field under study. A weekly exchange with a professional consulting group (doctors, nurses) was the first of these. The systematic variation of the observational perspective, namely, observations centering on physicians, nurses, or patients and scene-oriented observations (doctoral rounds, washing, setting a catheter, etc.), was the second. Special problems (here as well) resulted from the selection of an appropriate location and the "right" moment for observing, as the following notes about the researcher's experience may clarify:

> In the room, there is a relative hurry, permanently something has to be done, and I am successfully overrun by nurse I.'s whisky business. (No minutes at the "nurses' desk".) After the end of the shift, I remark after leaving the ward that I was a quasi-trainee today. The reason is for me mainly related to the moment of my arrival in the ward. Afterwards I consider it ineffective to burst into the middle of a shift. To participate in the handing over, in the beginning of the shift, means for us as well as for the nurses the chance to adapt to each other. I did not find any time today to orient myself calmly. There was no phase of feeling or growing into the situation, which would have allowed me a certain sovereignty. So I unexpectedly slipped into the mechanisms of the little routines and constraints and before I could get rid of them, my time was gone. (1989, p. 46)

This account elucidates two aspects. The choice of the moment or of the actual beginning of an observational sequence determines essentially what can be observed and, above all, how. In addition, it becomes clear here that especially in very hectic settings, the observer's inundation by the events leads to his or her being (mis)used as "quasi-trainee" for managing the events. Such participation in activities can lead to observation obstacles, for which Sprenger offers a remedy:

This problem of being inundated by the field events is virulent during the whole course of the research, but may be controlled quite well. In addition to choosing the optimal beginning for the observation, as already mentioned in the presented protocol, defining the observational goals and leaving the field intentionally as soon as the researcher's observational capacity is exhausted have proved very effective control strategies. However, this requires the researchers to learn about their own capacity limits. (1989, p. 47)

This example shows that steering and planning the observation as well as reflecting on one's own resources may reduce the danger (just outlined) of the researcher being absorbed by the field as well as the danger of "going native," and therefore of adopting perspectives from the field without reflecting it.

What Are the Problems in Conducting the Method?

In terms of Gold's (1958) typology of observer roles, the role of the participant-as-observer best fits the method of participant observation. Linked to the approach of diving headlong into the field is often the experienced sense of culture shock on the part of the observer. This is particularly obvious in ethnographic field studies in foreign cultures. But this phenomenon also occurs in observations in subcultures or generally in strange groups or in extreme situations such as intensive medicine: familiar self-evidence, norms, and practices lose their normality, and the observer is confronted with strange values, self-evidence, and so on. These may seem hard to understand at first but he or she has to accept them to be able to understand them and their meaning. In particular in participant observation, the researcher's action in the field is understood not only as a disturbance, but also as an additional source of or as cornerstones for knowledge: "Fortunately, the so-called 'disturbances' created by the observer's existence and activities, when properly exploited, are the cornerstones of a scientific behavioural science, and not – as is currently believed – deplorable *contretemps*, best disposed of by hurriedly sweeping them under the rug" (Devereux 1967, p. 7).

What Is the Contribution to the General Methodological Discussion?

All in all, participant observation elucidates the tension between increasing participation in the field, from which understanding alone results, and the maintenance of a distance, from which understanding becomes merely scientific and verifiable. Furthermore, this method still comes closest to a conception of qualitative research as a process, because it assumes a longer period in the field and in contact with the persons and contexts to be studied, whereas interviews mostly remain one-off encounters.

Strategies like theoretical sampling (see Chapter 13) can be applied here more easily than in interview studies. If it becomes evident that a specific dimension, a particular group of persons, concrete activities, and so on are needed for completing the data and for developing the theory, the researchers are able to direct their attention to them in the next observational sequence. For interviews, this is rather unusual and needs detailed explanation if researchers want to make a second appointment.

Furthermore, in participant observation, the interaction with the field and the object of research may be realized most consistently. Also, by integrating other methods, the methodical procedures of this strategy may be especially well adapted to the research issue. Methodological flexibility and appropriateness to the object under study are two main advantages of this procedure.

How Does the Method Fit into the Research Process?

The use of participant observation is rooted in the theoretical backgrounds of more recent versions of symbolic interactionism (see Chapter 7). In terms of pursuing the goal of developing theories about the research object (see Chapter 10), questions of how to access the field become a decisive methodological issue (see Chapter 12). Research questions (see Chapter 11) focus on the description of the field under study and of the practices in it. In the main, step-by-step strategies of sampling (see Chapter 13) are applied. Coding strategies are used to carry interpretations (see Chapters 25 and 26).

What Are the Limitations of the Method?

One problem with this method is that not all phenomena can be observed in situations. Biographical processes are difficult to observe. This also applies to comprehensive knowledge processes. Events or practices that seldom occur—although they are crucial to the research question—can be captured only with luck or if at all by a very careful selection of situations of observation.

As a way of solving these problems, additional interviews of participants are integrated into the research program, which allow the reconstruction of biographical processes or stocks of knowledge that are the background of observable practices. Therefore, the researchers' knowledge in participant observation is based only in part on the observation of actions. A large part is grounded in participants' verbal statements about certain relations and facts.

TABLE 20.1 Dependability of Observations

		Volunteered	Directed by the observer	Total
Statements	To observer alone			
	To others in everyday conversations			
Activities	Individual			
	Group			
Altogether				

Source: Becker and Geer (1960, p. 287)

DATA BEYOND TALK

In order to be able to use the strengths of observation compared to interview studies and to assess how far this strength applies for the data received, Becker and Geer (1960, p. 287) suggest the scheme in Table 20.1 for locating the data.

The authors are interested in answering the question of how likely it is that an activity or an attitude that is found is valid for the group they studied in general or only for individual members or specific situations. They start from the notion that the group most likely shares attitudes deduced from activities in the group, because otherwise the activities would have been corrected or commented on by the other members. You can more likely see statements within the group as shared attitudes rather than as member's statements in face-to-face contact with the observer. Spontaneous activities and statements seem more reliable than those responding to an observer's intervention (e.g., a direct question). The most important thing again is to answer the question of how likely the observed activities and statements are to occur independently of the researcher's observation and participation.

Another problem arises out of the advantages of the methods that were discussed with key phrases like flexibility and appropriateness to the object of research. Participant observation can hardly be standardized and formalized beyond a general research strategy, and it does not make sense to see this as a goal for further methodological developments (Lüders 2004a). Correspondingly, methodological discussions have stagnated in recent years. Attempts to codify participant observation in textbooks are based on the discussions of the early 1970s or else are reported from the workshops on observation.

Ethnography

In recent discussions, interest in the method of participant observation has faded into the background, while the more general strategy of ethnography, in which observation and participation are interwoven with other procedures, has attracted more attention:

> In its most characteristic form it involves the ethnographer participating, overtly or covertly, in people's daily lives for an extended period of time, watching what happens, listening to what is said, asking questions – in fact, collecting whatever data are available to throw light on the issues that are the focus of the research. (Hammersley and Atkinson 1995, p. 1)

What Are the Features of Ethnographic Research?

The concrete definition and formulation of methodological principles and steps are subordinated to practicing a general research attitude in the field, which is observed or, more generally, studied. However, in a more recent overview, Atkinson and Hammersley (1998, pp. 110–111) note several substantial features of ethnographic research as shown in Box 20.1.

┌─ BOX 20.1 ─┐

Features of Ethnographic Research

- A strong emphasis on exploring the nature of a particular social phenomenon, rather than setting out to test hypotheses about them.
- A tendency to work primarily with "unstructured" data: that is, data that have not been coded at the point of data collection in terms of a closed set of analytic categories.
- Investigation of a small number of cases, perhaps just one case, in detail.
- Analysis of data that involves explicit interpretation of the meanings and functions of human actions, the product of which mainly takes the form of verbal descriptions and explanations, with quantification and statistical analysis playing a subordinate role at most.

Source: Atkinson and Hammersley (1998, pp. 110–111)

Gubrium and Holstein (2014) emphasize the role of analytic inspiration in ethnographic fieldwork. Here data collection is most consistently subordinated to the research question and the circumstances in the respective field. Methods are subordinated to practice (for the plurality of methods in this context, see also Atkinson et al. 2001). Lüders (1995, pp. 320–321; 2004a) sees the central defining features of ethnography as follows:

> first [there is] the risk and the moments of the research process which cannot be planned and are situational, coincidental and individual. ... Second, the researcher's skilful activity in each situation becomes more important. ... Third, ethnography ... transforms into a strategy of research which includes as many options of collecting data as can be imagined and are justifiable.

Methodological discussions focus less on methods of data collection and interpretation and more on questions of how to report findings in a field (see Chapter 30). However, methodological strategies applied in the fields under study are still very much based on observing what is going on in the field by participating in the field. Interviews and the analysis of documents are integrated into this kind of participatory research design where they hold out the promise of further knowledge.

In their overview of ethnography, Atkinson et al. stated:

> Contemporary ethnographic research is characterized by fragmentation and diversity. There is certainly a carnivalesque profusion of methods, perspectives, and theoretical justifications for ethnographic work. There are multiple methods of research, analysis, and representation. (2001, p. 2)

Ethnography as a research strategy (like participant observation at its outset) has been imported from anthropology into different substantial areas in other disciplines such as sociology or education. Whereas, at the beginning, ethnography studied remote cultures in their unfamiliarity, current ethnography starts its research around the corner and wants to show the particular aspects of what seem familiar to us all.

Small life worlds of do-it-yourselfers, members of parliaments, and body builders for example are studied and analyzed (see Honer 2004).

From a more methodological point of view, current ethnographic research is characterized by an extended participation in the field, which studies a flexible research strategy, employing all sorts of methods and focusing on writing and reporting experiences in that field (Lüders 2004a).

Smith (2002) outlines an approach called institutional ethnography in which the focus is not so much the daily practices, but how these are institutionalized in rules and general relations, in which individuals' everyday practices are embedded. In her approach, a strong link to feminist theories and topics is given, when she studies women's mothering work, for example.

CASE STUDY 20.4

Homeless Adolescents' Health Behavior

In our recent project studying the health behavior and practices of homeless adolescents (see Flick and Röhnsch 2007), we study adolescents aged 14 to 20 years and distinguish two groups among them according to the time, how long they hang out on the streets, and how far they are involved in the communities of street kids. The degree of perpetuation of their homelessness is relevant here. We observe them at different locations in a big city. If the adolescents are identified in participant observation as being members of the community over time, we ask them for an interview about their experiences with health problems and services in the health system, their health concepts, and how they recount their way into homelessness. In the study, we use different methodological approaches to develop a fuller picture of our participants' living situations.

This example shows how you can use an open approach such as ethnography for studying a concrete issue (health concepts and behavior) when you use several methods addressing different levels of the issue under study, here knowledge (via interviews) and practices (via observation).

What Are the Problems in Conducting the Method?

Methods define which aspects of the phenomenon are especially relevant and deserve particular attention. At the same time, they give an orientation for the researcher's practice. In ethnography, both are given up in favor of a general attitude towards the research, through the use of which the researchers find their own ways in the life world under study. In this study, a pragmatic use of all sorts of methods— and data—is central. As some researchers in the field have observed critically, the methodological flexibility that contemporary ethnography requires means that researchers have to be familiar with, or even experts in, quite a variety of methods to do ethnographic studies. This requirement may be overly challenging, especially to novices in research.

What Is the Contribution to the General Methodological Discussion?

Ethnography has attracted special attention in recent years due to two circumstances. First, in this context, an extensive debate about the presentation of observation has begun (Clifford and Marcus 1986), which has not been and will not be without consequences for other domains of qualitative research (see Chapter 30 for this). Second, the fairly recent methodological discussion about qualitative methods in general in the Anglo-Saxon area (e.g., in the contributions to Denzin and Lincoln 2000a) has been strongly influenced by strategies and discussions in ethnography. Ethnography has been the most powerful influence on the transformation of qualitative research into some kind of postmodern research attitude, which is opposed to the more or less codified application of specific methods. In addition, ethnography has been rediscovered in developmental and cultural psychology (cf. the volume by Jessor et al. 1996) and has stimulated a new interest in qualitative methods in this area.[2]

How Does the Method Fit into the Research Process?

Ethnography starts from the theoretical position of describing social realities and their making (see Chapter 7). It aims at developing theories (see Chapter 10). Research questions focus mainly on detailed descriptions of case studies (see Chapter 11). Entering the field has central importance for the empirical and theoretical disclosure of the field under study and is not simply a problem which has to be solved technically (see Chapter 12). Sampling strategies generally orient towards theoretical sampling or procedures based on this (see Chapter 13). Interpretations are mainly done using sequential and coding analyses (see Chapters 25 and 26). More recently, approaches like virtual ethnography have been developed (see below) to use ethnography as a method for analyzing interactions in cyberspace.

What Are the Limitations of the Method?

In the discussion about ethnography, data collection methods are treated as secondary. Strategies of participation in the field under study, the interpretation of data, and, above all, styles of writing and the question of authority and authorship in the presentation of results (see Chapter 30 for this in greater detail) receive more attention. This approach may be interpreted (in a positive way) as showing flexibility towards the subject under study, but it also holds the danger of methodological arbitrariness. The concretely applied methods make ethnography a strategy that uses the triangulation (see Chapters 14 and 29) of various methodological approaches in the framework of realizing a general research attitude.

Writing Field Notes

The classic medium for documentation in qualitative research with observation has been the researcher's notes. You will find good overviews, reflections, and introductions in Emerson, Fretz, and Shaw (1995), Lofland and Lofland (1984), and Sanjek (1990). The notes taken in interviews should contain the essentials of the interviewee's answers and information about the proceeding of the interview. The participant observers repeatedly interrupt their participation to note important observations, as the description in Box 20.2 of the classic documentation technique, its problems, and the chosen solution to them makes clear.

─BOX 20.2 ─

Field Notes in Practice

The following example comes from a study used previously as an example, which was run by Anselm Strauss and his colleague in the 1960s in a psychiatric hospital. The example shows the authors' practices in writing field notes:

> Our usual practice was to spend limited periods of time in the field, perhaps two or three hours. When we could appropriately leave the field, we headed immediately for a typewriter or Dictaphone. If leaving was impossible, we took brief memory-refreshing notes whenever lulls occurred and recorded them fully as soon thereafter as possible. The recording of field notes presented a number of problems involving discrimination among events seen and heard, as well as an interviewer's impressions or interpretations. As professionals, all of us were mindful of the pitfalls attending recall and the all-too-easy blurring of fact and fancy. We attempted therefore to make these discriminations clearly, either by stating them unmistakably or by developing a notational system for ensuring them. Verbal material recorded within quotations signified exact recall; verbal material within apostrophes indicated a lesser degree of certainty or paraphrasing; and verbal material with no markings meant reasonable recall but not quotation. Finally, the interviewer's impressions or inferences could be separated from actual observations by the use of single or double parentheses. Although this notational system was much used, none of us was constrained always to use it.

Source: Strauss, Schatzman, Bucher, Ehrlich, and Sabshin (1964, pp. 28–29)

Lofland and Lofland (1984) propose as a general rule that such notes should be made immediately—or at least as soon as possible. The withdrawal necessary for this may introduce some artificiality in the relation to interaction partners in the field. Especially in action research when the researchers take part in the events in the field and do not merely observe them, it is difficult to maintain this freedom for the researchers. An alternative is to note impressions after ending the individual field contact. Lofland and Lofland (1984, p. 64) recommend that researchers use a "cloistered rigor" in following the commandment to make notes immediately after the field contact, and furthermore that researchers estimate the same amount of time for carefully noting the observations as for spending on the observation itself. It should be ensured that later a distinction can still be made between what has been observed and what has been condensed by the observer in his or her interpretation or summary of events (see Chapter 29 on procedural reliability of protocols). Researchers may develop a personal style of writing notes after a while and with increasing experience.

The production of reality in texts starts with the taking of field notes. The researcher's selective perceptions and presentations have a strong influence on this production. This selectivity concerns not only the aspects that are left out, but also and above all those which find their way into the notes. It is only the notation that raises a transitory occurrence out of its everyday course and makes it into an event to which the researcher, interpreter, and reader can turn their attention repeatedly. One way to reduce or at least qualify this selectivity of the documentation is to complement the notes by diaries or day protocols written by the subjects under study in parallel with the researcher's note taking. Thus their subjective views may be included in the data and become accessible to analysis. Such documents from the subject's point of view can be analyzed and contrasted with the researcher's notes. Another way is to add photos, drawings, maps, and other visual material to the notes. A third possibility is to use an electronic notebook, a dictating machine, or similar devices for recording the notes.

Correspondingly, Spradley (1980, pp. 69–72) proposes four forms of field notes for documentation:

- the condensed accounts in single words, sentences, quotations from conversations, etc.;
- an expanded account of the impressions from interviews and field contacts;
- a fieldwork journal, which like a diary "will contain ... experiences, ideas, fears, mistakes, confusions, breakthroughs, and problems that arise during fieldwork" (1980, p. 71);
- some notes about analysis and interpretations, which start immediately after the field contacts and extend until finishing the study.

Virtual Ethnography

In Chapters 16 and 17, we have already discussed ways of transferring methods for collecting verbal data of interviewing individuals or stimulating groups into online research. There, the Internet becomes a *tool* to study people you could not otherwise reach, which is different from and goes beyond traditional interviewing or group discussions. But you can also see the Internet as a *place* or as a *way of being* (for these three perspectives, see Markham 2004). In these cases, you can study online contexts as a form of milieu or culture in which people develop specific forms of communication or, sometimes, specific identities. Both suggest a transfer of ethnographic methods to Internet research and to studying the ways of communication and self-presentation on the Internet: "Reaching understandings of participants' sense of self and of the meanings they give to their online participation requires spending time with participants to observe what they do online as well as what they say they do" (Kendall 1999, p. 62). For example, this led Kendall in her study of a multiple user group first to observe and note the communication going on in this group and after a while to become an active participant in the group to develop a better understanding of what was going on there. This is similar to how ethnographers become participants and observers in real-world communities and cultures.

The difference is that virtual ethnography is located in a technical environment instead of a natural environment. As many studies (see as an example Flick 1995; 1996) have shown, technology should not be seen as something just given and taken for granted, because its use and impact are strongly influenced by the representations and beliefs referring to it on the side of the users and non-users. A similar approach is suggested for virtual ethnography, which should start from research questions like the ones mentioned in Box 20.3.

┌ BOX 20.3 ┐

Research Questions for Virtual Ethnography

- How do the users of the Internet understand its capacities? What significance does its use have for them? How do they understand its capabilities as a medium of communication, and whom do they perceive their audience to be?
- How does the Internet affect the organization of social relationships in time and space? Is this different to the ways in which "real life" is organized, and if so, how do users reconcile the two?
- What are the implications of the Internet for authenticity and authority? How are identities performed and experienced, and how is authenticity judged?
- Is "the virtual" experienced as radically different from and separate from "the real"? Is there a boundary between online and offline? (Hine 2000, p. 8)

These research questions focus on representations of the virtual context on the side of the actors, on the building of virtual communities or social groups, on identity online, and on the links between the virtual and the real. In this context, the definition of what to understand by virtual communities may be helpful:

> Virtual communities are social aggregations that emerge from the Net when enough people carry on those public discussions long enough, with sufficient human feeling, to form webs of personal relationships in cyberspace. (Rheingold 1993, p. 5)

Thus ethnography undergoes a second transformation: the first was its transfer from studying foreign cultures to our own culture; the second is to transfer it from the "real" world to the virtual world as online ethnography (Marotzki 2003).

Practicalities of Virtual Ethnography

As in online interviews, the exchange of questions and answers has to be reconceptualized: some of the core elements of ethnography can be transported to virtual ethnography without problems, while others have to be reformulated. This becomes evident in the 10 principles of virtual ethnography suggested by Hine (2000, pp. 63–65). In these principles, the author claims that the sustained presence of an ethnographer in the field and the intensive engagement with the everyday life of its inhabitants are also in virtual ethnography a need for developing ethnographic knowledge. But in cyberspace, notions like the site of interaction or the field site are brought into question. What are the boundaries of the field? They cannot be defined in advance but become clear during the study. There are many links between cyberspace and "real life," which should be taken into account. In this way, the Internet is a culture and a cultural product at the same time. Mediated communication can be spatially and temporally dislocated. You do not have to be at the same time or space to observe what is going on among members of a virtual group. You can engage in a lot of other things and then come back to your computer where your e-mails or entries in a discussion group are waiting for you and you can access them from computers anywhere in the world.

Virtual ethnography is never holistic but always partial as you will not be in touch with the research partners face to face, but only with the image they present of themselves online. You should be skeptical towards any idea of studying "pre-existing, isolable and describable informants, locales and cultures" online—they will exist, but the access of virtual ethnography is not an immediate one to those entities; instead we find knowledge based on "ideals of strategic relevance rather than faithful representations of objective realities," as Hine (2000, p. 65) holds. Virtual ethnography is virtual in the sense of being disembodied and also carries a connotation of "not quite" or not strictly the real thing (2000, p. 65).

This kind of virtual ethnography is applied to studying the contents of communications on the Internet and the textual ways in which participants communicate. Hine's own study focuses on web pages around a trial and the way these reflected the trial, the case, and the conflicts linked to them.

Data in Virtual Ethnography

For virtual ethnographies a growing range of new forms of data are available and can be used. Marotzki et al. (2014, p. 452) distinguish "static data" (i.e., "the kind of data that 1) are not created by different users interacting with each other and 2) remain basically unchanged while they are continuously accessible") from *dynamic data* in situations of interaction, which means that they react to data generated by other users, as in a thread in a bulletin board discussion" (p. 452). The forms of communication that can be studied are not only verbal or written exchanges, but also digital games played interactively on the Web. A new dimension comes from the use of mobile data—for example, text messages on mobile/cell phones, Twitter, or Internet used on smartphones etc. (see Marotzki et al., 2014).

Virtual Ethnography

In her study, Hine (2000) took a widely discussed trial (the Louise Woodward case—a British au pair who was tried for the death of a child she was responsible for in Boston) as a starting point. She wanted to find out how this case was constructed on the Internet by analyzing web pages concerned with this issue. She also interviewed Web authors by e-mail about their intentions and experiences and analyzed the discussions in newsgroups in which ten or more interventions referring to the case had been posted.

She used the Dejanews website, www.dejanews.com, for finding newsgroups. At this site, all newsgroup postings are stored and can be searched by using keywords. Her search was limited to one month in 1998. She posted a message to several of the newsgroups, which had dealt with the issue more intensively. But, in contrast to the Web authors, the response was rather limited, an experience researchers had obviously had repeatedly (2000, p. 79). Hine also set up her own home page and mentioned it while contacting prospective participants or in posting messages about her research. She did that to make herself and her research transparent for possible participants.

In summarizing her results, she had to state:

The ethnography constituted by my experiences, my materials and the writings I produce on the topic is definitely incomplete. ... In particular, the ethnography is partial in relation to its choice of particular applications of the Internet to study. I set out to study "the Internet," without having made a specific decision as to which applications I intended to look at in detail. (2000, p. 80)

Nevertheless, Hine produced interesting results of how people dealt with the issue of the trial on the Internet and her thoughts and discussions of virtual ethnography are very instructive beyond her own study. However, they also show the limitations of transferring ethnography—or more generally, qualitative research—to online research, as Bryman's critical comment illustrates: "Studies like these are clearly inviting us to consider the nature of the Internet as a domain for investigation, but they also invite us to consider the nature and the adaptiveness of our research methods" (2004, p. 473).

According to Marotzki (2003), several structural features of virtual communities can be studied in online ethnography: the rules and socio-graphic structures of a community and its communicative, informational, presentational, and participative structures—for example, who communicates with whom in a chatroom and what the rules are in this communication.

Going one step further, Bergmann and Meier (2004) start from a conversation analytic, ethnomethodological background, when they suggest analyzing the formal parts of interaction on the Web. Conversation analysis is more interested in the linguistic and interactive tools (like taking turns, repairing, opening up closings; see Chapter 27) people use when they communicate about an issue. In a similar way, the authors suggest that to identify the traces online communication produces and leaves is to understand how communication is practically produced online. There-fore, they use electronic process data, which means "all data that are generated in the course of computer-assisted communication processes and work activities – either automatically or on the basis of adjustments by the user" (2004, p. 244).

These data are not just simply at hand: they must be reconstructed on the basis of a detailed and ongoing documentation of what is happening on the screen and—if possible—in front of it, when someone sends an e-mail, for example. This includes the comments of the sender while typing an e-mail, or paralinguistic aspects, like laughing and so on.

It is also important to document the temporal structure of using computer-mediated communication. Here one can use special software (like Lotus Screen-Cam) that allows filming of what is happening on the computer screen together with recording the interaction in front of the screen with video, for example.

A particular combination of Internet research and ethnography is proposed by Kozinets et al. in what they call "netnography":

> As netnography is a naturalistic method, its interpretations can be built from a com-bination of elicited and, more often, non-elicited data. These data emerge and are captured through the researcher's observation of and participation with people as they socialize online in regular environments and activities (Kozinets, 2010). Online cultural research is far less intrusive than traditional ethnography, as the online researchers can gather a vast amount of data without making their presence visible to culture members. (2014, p. 263)

This approach is basically applied to studying online communication in the so-called social media (e.g., Facebook) and the social context of their use. Three forms of data are collected "in netnography: archival data, elicited data, and field note data" (p. 266). The first form refers to any sort of traces of communication on the Internet including websites. The second group of data results from online interview-ing (see Chapter 16) and the researchers' participation in chatrooms and the like. The third group, field note data, is not produced with the participants but by the researchers, although they "may contain captures of data such as texts, screen shots, moving images, and so on" (p. 268). Data analysis then uses the approaches of cod-ing (see Chapters 25 and 26) mainly and mostly applied in CAQDAS software (see Chapter 28).

What Are the Problems in Conducting the Method?

Internet ethnography has to take into account how the users—individuals or communities—construct the Internet. As the example of Hine (2000, pp. 78–79) shows, it is sometimes quite difficult to receive a good response to newsgroup postings. This is seen by Bryman (2004, p. 474) as a general problem of skepticism against such cyber-areas to be used by researchers. Hine concentrated on analyz-ing web pages relevant for her issue more than on analyzing interactions.

What Is the Contribution to the General Methodological Discussion?

The approach challenges several essentials of ethnographic research—concepts such as being there, being part of the everyday life of a community or culture, and so on. These challenges lead to interesting ways of rethinking these concepts and to adapting them to the needs of studying the virtual instead of real-world communities. After the controversies about writing and representation, authorship, and authority (see Chapters 2 and 30), it is an interesting contribution to the highly reflexive discussion about ethnography.

How Does the Method Fit into the Research Process?

This approach has been developed against the background of the more general discussions of ethnography (see above) and of writing and text in qualitative research (see Chapters 8 and 30). Sampling is purposive and analysis of the collected material is, like other forms of ethnography, rather flexible.

What Are the Limitations of the Method?

As the argumentation of several authors in this context shows, researching online communication entails more than just communication online: to develop a comprehensive ethnography of the virtual, it would be necessary to include the links to real-world activities—in front of the screen or in the social life beyond computer use. To find a way from virtual communities to the real life of the participants is, as has been said before, rather difficult. Therefore, virtual ethnography remains much more partial and limited than other forms of ethnography and than ethnographers claim as necessary for their approach.

Analyzing Observations and Ethnographies

Analyzing Data from Participant Observation

The analysis of data coming from (participant) observation should be done in a more integrative process, as Coffey and Atkinson highlight:

> The process of analysis should not be seen as a distinct stage of research; rather, it is a reflexive activity that should inform data collection, writing, further data collection, and so forth. Analysis is not, then, the last phase of the research process. It should be seen as part of the research design and of the data collection. The research process, of which analysis is one aspect, is a cyclical one. (1996, p. 6)

As Marvasti (2014) holds, the analysis is often strongly inductive, with categories developed from the material. It is important to analyze the researchers' relations to the field ("rapport") as a part of the data. It is also necessary to reflect the process of getting into the field and of managing the relations with it in the analysis. Writing memos throughout the process and writing as a substantial part of the analysis have been highlighted in the move from participant observation to ethnography.

Analyzing Ethnographic Data

Much of what has been said above about the analysis of participant observation-based data applies to ethnographic data, too. In their textbook, Hammersley and Atkinson (2007, pp. 158ff.) describe data analysis in ethnography quite closely linked to grounded theory approaches (see Chapter 25) in emphasizing concept development from the data. They also discuss concepts like triangulation (see Chapter 14) and analytic induction as strategies for better grounding the analysis in the field and data, and see typologies (see Chapter 30) as an aim for their analysis. Gubrium and Holstein (2014) emphasize the role of analytic inspiration in ethnography-based data analysis. Together with the emphasis on writing (see Chapter 30 and Denzin 2014) in ethnography, the methodological approach to actual analysis is less emphasized here than in other kinds of research.

Checklist for Doing Observation and Ethnography

1 Is the issue of your research accessible to observation?
2 Where will it "happen," which sort of situation or interaction will make it "visible?"
3 Which other methods—like in/formal interviews, for example—will you need for studying your issue?
4 If your issue has to do with virtual communication, how and where would you find it for a virtual ethnography?
5 How will you design your relation to the field and its members—participation or just observation?
6 How will you manage ethical issues like informed consent in your observation?
7 What is important to document in field notes as the data in your research?

KEY POINTS

- In qualitative research, observation can be used with different degrees of the researcher's participation in the field under study.
- In each version, the relation of methodological rigor and flexibility is different. Non-participant observation is characterized by keeping a distance from the field and maintaining general methodological standards.
- At the other end of the spectrum, ethnography is characterized by extended participation and a methodological pragmatism oriented towards adapting methods to the field and using whatever methods lead to more insights.

- Ethnography replaced participant observation. However, participant observation is the central methodological basis for any ethnographic research. Questions of how to do ethnographic research in an ethically sound way, and of how to avoid any form of going native in the field, pertain to all research based on observation and participation.
- Virtual ethnography makes specific issues accessible for ethnography, such as virtual communities or distant members of a community or new forms of communication like social media, Twitter, etc.

Exercise 20.1

1 Look for an example of an ethnographic study in the literature (e.g., McGibbon, Peter, and Gallop 2010). Identify which methods were used in this study, how the authors organized their participation in the field, and how they managed issues of involvement and distance in their field contacts.
2 Go to open spaces in your university (like the library or cafeterias) and do some participant observation in order to find out mechanisms and practices of integration and segregation among the people in these spaces. Are there different groups? How do they get in touch, maintain boundaries, etc.? Write down your observations in field notes. After you have finished your observations, write an account of what you saw and of what puzzled you in the field.
3 Look on the Internet for an example of online research (e.g., Paechter 2012) and reflect on this example based on the background discussed in this chapter.

Further Reading

Observation

This text gives an overview of participant observation in qualitative research:

Adler, P.A. and Adler, P. (1998) "Observation Techniques," in N. Denzin and Y.S. Lincoln (eds.), *Collecting and Interpreting Qualitative Materials*. London: Sage. pp. 79–110.

Participant Observation

The first text is a classic example of the application of this method; the textbooks and handbook chapter discuss the method in greater depth:

Becker, H.S., Geer, B., Hughes, E.C. and Strauss, A.L. (1961) *Boys in White: Student Culture in Medical School*. Chicago, IL: University of Chicago Press.
Jorgensen, D.L. (1989) *Participant Observation: A Methodology for Human Studies*. London: Sage.
Spradley, J.P. (1980) *Participant Observation*. New York: Holt, Rinehart and Winston.
Marvasti, A. (2014) "Analyzing Observations," in U. Flick (ed.), *The SAGE Handbook of Qualitative Data Analysis*. London: Sage. pp. 354–366.

Ethnography

The different approaches to ethnography that are characteristic of recent discussions are outlined in the textbooks and the handbook chapter and also in the reader from cultural psychology:

Angrosino, M. (2007) *Doing Ethnographic and Observational Research*. London: Sage.

Atkinson, P., Coffey, A., Delamont, S., Lofland, J. and Lofland, L. (eds.) (2001) *Handbook of Ethnography*. London: Sage.

Atkinson, P. and Hammersley, M. (1998) "Ethnography and Participant Observation," in N. Denzin and Y.S. Lincoln (eds.), *Strategies of Qualitative Inquiry*. London: Sage. pp. 110–136.

Gubrium, J. and Holstein, J. (2014) "Analytic Inspiration in Ethnographic Fieldwork," in U. Flick (ed.), *The SAGE Handbook of Qualitative Data Analysis*. London: Sage. pp. 35–48.

Hammersley, M. and Atkinson, P. (2007) *Ethnography: Principles in Practice* (3rd edn). London: Routledge.

Jessor, R., Colby, A. and Shweder, R.A. (eds.) (1996) *Ethnography and Human Development*. Chicago, IL: University of Chicago Press.

Writing Field Notes

These three books are very informative about how to write and analyze field notes in the context of participant observation and ethnography:

Emerson, R., Fretz, R. and Shaw, L. (1995) *Writing Ethnographic Fieldnotes*. Chicago, IL: Chicago University Press.

Lofland, J. and Lofland, L.H. (1984) *Analyzing Social Settings* (2nd edn). Belmont, CA: Wadsworth.

Sanjek, R. (ed.) (1990) *Fieldnotes: The Making of Anthropology*. Albany, NY: State University of New York Press.

Virtual Ethnography

The first text discusses a more conversation analytic approach to Internet communication, the second discusses the use of ethnography in online research in detail. The other two texts describe more practical issues and approaches to online ethnographic research:

Bergmann, J. and Meier, C. (2004) "Electronic Process Data and their Analysis," in U. Flick, E.v. Kardorff, and I. Steinke (eds.), *A Companion to Qualitative Research*. London: Sage. pp. 243–247.

Hine, C. (2000) *Virtual Ethnography*. London: Sage.

Kozinets, R., Dolbec, P.Y. and Earley, A. (2014) "Netnographic Analysis: Understanding Culture through Social Media Data," in U. Flick (ed.), *The SAGE Handbook of Qualitative Data Analysis*. London: Sage. pp. 262–276.

Marotzki, W., Holze, J. and Verständig, D. (2014) "Analyzing Virtual Data," in U. Flick (ed.), *The SAGE Handbook of Qualitative Data Analysis*. London: Sage. pp. 450–463.

1 Researchers should reflect on why their key person is ready to take this role. In the literature, you will find a range of social positions from which people start to become key persons in participant observation. Most of these positions are characterized by social deficits concerning the social status of the key person in the group or in the field (e.g., the outsider, the novice, the frustrated, people needing loving care, the subordinate). That does not necessarily mean that social acceptance must be the only motive for supporting the researcher in this respect. But the consequences of the key person's motivation and role for the researcher's access and the observation should be taken into account. Thus not only observation by key persons, but also observation of key persons in the field should be integrated as a basis for such reflection.

2 However, you can find that there are positions different from the dominant postmodern ethnography. For example, Shweder (1996) in his concept of "true ethnography argues against the solipsism and superficiality" of postmodern ethnography and instead makes claims for "mind reading."

21
Visual Data: Photography, Film, and Video

┌─CHAPTER OBJECTIVES─

This chapter is designed to help you

- understand the opportunities and limitations concerning visual data methods;
- appreciate that using archival photographs and taking new photographs constitute forms of data collection;
- comprehend the relevance of movies as a reflection of and influence on the social construction of social realities;
- realize the potential of using video as a source of data production and analysis;
- see that visual methods in general are necessarily selective in what they make available as data;
- understand that every kind of camera *constructs* a specific image, rather than innocently documenting phenomena.

Photographs as an Instrument and Object of Research

Interest has been growing in the use, both as research topic and as method, of second-hand observation in the form of visual media. Photographs, films, and videos are increasingly recognized as genuine forms and sources of data (see Becker 1986a; Denzin 2004a; Harper 2004; for a discussion on the use of video cameras for recording conversations or interviews see Chapter 24). Photography, in particular, has a long tradition in anthropology and ethnography. Bateson and Mead's (1942) study of the "Balinese character" is repeatedly treated as classic.

─CASE STUDY 21.1 ─

Bateson and Mead's Study of the "Balinese Character"

Gregory Bateson and Margaret Mead were pioneers of cultural anthropology. They developed a comprehensive methodology for their study, which included the production and analysis of visual material like photos and film to document everyday life, routines, and rituals in Bali. In their investigation of a Balinese mountain village, Bateson and Mead (1942) collected 25,000 photos, 2000 meters of film, pictures, sculptures, and children's drawings.

Photos and films are especially important both as data and as an instrument of knowledge. The authors presented the developed film to the inhabitants of the village and documented their reactions again on film. Photographs and films were understood not as mere reproductions of reality but as presentations of reality, which are influenced by certain theoretical assumptions. Bateson and Mead were aware that photographs and films—not unlike sculptures and drawings—were not mirror images of reality but only presentational forms, which remain blind without analysis.

The photos and their analysis in so-called image plates are essential in the presentation of their results. Image plates are groups of photographs together with related (textual) analyses. The images were sorted according to cultural categories assumed to be typical for Bali (such as "spatial orientation and levels," "learning," "integration and disintegration of the body," and "stages of child development"): "The images were arranged in groups that allowed several perspectives on a single subject to be presented simultaneously or in sequences that showed how a social event evolved through time" (Harper 1998, p. 132).

In this study, visual material for the complementary documentation of the analyzed culture and practices is called into play and contrasted with the presentations and interpretations in textual form in order to develop integrated perspectives on the subject. It is already taken into account that visual material is both accomplished against a certain theoretical background and is perceived and interpreted from a specific point of view.

The Camera as an Instrument for Collecting Data

A visual sociology using photography and film has been developed. Becker (1986a) inaugurated the approach. Before that Mead (1963) summarized the central purpose of using cameras in social research: they allow detailed recordings of facts as well as providing a more comprehensive and holistic presentation of lifestyles and conditions. They allow the transportation of artifacts and the presentation of them as pictures. They also overcome constraints of time and space. They can capture facts and processes that are too fast or too complex for the human eye. Moreover, cameras also allow non-reactive recordings of observations, and, finally, they are less selective than observations. Photographs are available for reanalysis by others. Notwithstanding these advantages of using photographs, we should not ignore the dangers of an uncritical view of photographs: they can be edited, reworked, or digitally made up to involve a specific focus on the issue and the aspects of the issue captured on them. This means that cameras—as other instruments of data collection—are selective, focused, and limited in the way they reveal issues for research: that is, as media they play a role in constructing the issue of research.

Following Barthes (1996), four types of relation can be distinguished between the researcher and the researched. The researcher can show photos (as demonstrator) to people under study (as spectators) and ask them about the material (type I). The operator (who takes the photograph) can use the researched individual as a model (type II). The researchers (as spectators) may ask the subject to show them photos concerning a certain topic or period (as demonstrator) (type III). Finally, the researcher (as spectator) may observe the subjects (as operators) while they take a picture and conduct an analysis of the choice of subject matter being photographed (type IV; see Wuggenig 1990).

More generally, the question discussed is "how to get information on film and how to get information off film" (Hall 1986, quoted in Denzin 1989b, p. 210). One approach, for example, is to use the photographs in family albums to analyze the history of the family or subjects documented in the albums over time. Also, in family or institutional research, the integration of their members' self-presentation in photos and their images on the walls in rooms can reveal social structures in the social field.

In general, several methodological questions have been discussed, centered on the following topics (see Denzin 1989b, pp. 213–214):

- How do theoretical presumptions determine what is photographed and when and which feature is selected from the photograph for analysis? How do they leave their mark on the use of photographs as data or for the documentation of relations?
- Are cameras incorruptible in terms of their perception and documentation of the world? It is often assumed that they do not forget, do not get tired, and do not make mistakes. However, photographic material can fade, technical and mechanical errors can occur, films and files may get lost, and the like. Thus we should keep in mind that photographs do not merely document the world, they also transform it: they present the world in a specific shape.
- Do photos tell the truth (Becker 1986a)? How far are photos also marked by the interpretation and ascription of meaning by those who take or regard them?
- How far do photos (and films) reveal an approach to the symbolic world of the subjects and their views—for example, if participants are asked to provide the researcher with photos that represent a certain topic for them or are interviewed about the meaning of certain photos for them?
- Photos are only meaningful when they are taken at the right moment—when the interesting action occurs and the relevant people step into the camera's field of vision. This is not only a question of aesthetics, but a question of sampling—that is, selecting the most relevant moment for taking a picture which then will be useful for analyzing the research issue. What does this mean for using photographs as data for research?

- How to take into account that not only the participant, but also the photographing observer, have to find and take a role and an identity in the field?

Using Photos in the Context of Interviews

A different use of the medium of photography is outlined by Dabbs (1982). The people under study receive cameras and are asked "to take (or have someone else take) photographs that tell who they are" (1982, p. 55). This may be extended to a photographic diary in which people capture aspects and events of their daily lives as these unfold. In such cases, the subject decides the events or aspects worthy of photographing, not the researcher. What the subjects select and take as a picture allows the researcher to draw conclusions about the views of the subjects towards their own everyday lives. This is especially the case when comparing the perspectives of different subjects in the field expressed in their photographs and the features highlighted in them.

Wuggenig (1990, pp. 115–118) applies a similar procedure in order to study significance in the area of living. People were instructed to use a camera to document in 12 photos their ways of living and the interiors of their apartments typical of people like themselves. The instruction in Box 21.1 was given to them.

― BOX 21.1 ―

Instruction for the Photo Interview

When you want to use photographs as part of data collection in the context of interviews, you should give your participants an instruction like the following one:

What do you like most about your own room and in the flat (or house)? What do you like least about your room and in the flat (or house)? Please photograph first the three motifs you like the most in your room and then the three you like the least. Then please repeat this for the rest of the apartment. It does not matter which room you choose. All in all, you can use 12 pictures.

Source: Wuggenig (1990, p. 116)

In the "photo elicitation interview" (Harper 2000, p. 725), photos from people's own lives are taken to stimulate interview partners to produce narratives or answers—first about the photo and then starting from this about their daily lives. This procedure may also be seen as a way of using the focused interview (see Chapter 16) in more concrete version. Whereas here visual material is used as a support for conducting the interview, in the following example photos are used as data in their own right.

┌─CASE STUDY 21.2─┐

Analysis of Soldiers' Photos

In the following case, photos were not produced for research purposes, but existing photos were used as material for research. Haupert (1994) analyzed soldiers' photos using the method of objective hermeneutics (see Chapter 27) in order to reconstruct biographical processes. Here, photos are not produced for research purposes, but existing photos are analyzed for the general relations to the photographed period and the individual fate traced in this material. Photos here have their own special importance as genuine documents. Their analysis can be referred to other forms of data (biographical interviews). Photo analysis is explicitly understood and practiced as a form of textual analysis. This means that photos are studied here:

> whose textual quality in the sense of social research – although the grammar of the image for the moment remains unclear – ... can finally be singled out by a programmatic procedure of telling grammatically correct stories which are adequate in meaning and model the contextual framework of the image. (1994, p. 286)

This is an example of how to use existing photographic material from earlier times to support the elicitation of memories about that period so that interviews referring to it can be conducted.

In general, photos have a high iconic quality, which may help to activate people's memories or to stimulate or encourage them to make statements about complex processes and situations.

┌─CASE STUDY 21.3─┐

Photographs for Analyzing the Use of Public Space by Homeless People

In this study (see Hodgetts, Radley, Chamberlain, and Hodgetts 2007), photos are used to explore how homeless people make use of and represent public space in a major city in Europe. Participants were given cameras and asked to take pictures of their everyday lives and then interviewed about the pictures and their day-to-day experiences. For example, in the following extract, a participant, Jean, discusses the photograph in Figure 21.1 which depicts a back street in which she links stress and stigma to a loss of self, associated with being reduced to an abandoned physical object:

JEAN: I live and eat and work with it and I haven't had a break for years. ... And the street, can claim you. ... It has various ways of claiming you. That's why this ... photograph I feel epitomises completely my view. That street, just one back alley will claim you as a homeless person.

INTERVIEWER: How does the street keep you?

JEAN: Well, how does a car, end up being parked in one street for a very long time? I've often seen cars like this, has been abandoned, right. Now if a car could speak, the car would say I've got no choice. My driver's gone; I've run out of petrol. … I'm stuck in this street and there are lots of time when you think, I'm not human anymore.

FIGURE 21.1   Street Context Symbolizing Homelessness and Stigma for a Participant

Source: Hodgetts et al. (2007)

FIGURE 21.2   Science of Begging in the Context of Street Life

Source: Hodgetts et al. (2007)

(Continued)

(Continued)

In a different excerpt, another participant (Keith) explains his "science of begging" as an important knowledge base for survival on the street. He recounts how, depending on location and pedestrian flows, a person can select different tactics for begging:

KEITH: There's two different kinds of begging. You can sit down with a blanket and beg or you can walk about and beg. I used to beg like this [Figure 21.2]. Sit down with a sign when it's really busy at rush hour, but now I stand around and beg and walk about.

In this example, the researchers take photographs taken by the participants as a starting point for exploring the everyday life of a vulnerable group. The visual material is less analyzed for its pictorial qualities and features, but becomes a starting point for inviting participants to talk about their experiences and views.

Analyzing Images

John Berger introduced the concept of "ways of seeing" (Berger 1972) for illustrating that we do not just simply look at images: how we see a painting or a photograph depends on the perspective and (e.g., theoretical) framework we apply. Banks (2014) refers in the context of visual research to this concept for highlighting that there can be differing ways of looking at the "same" picture and that several viewers may see differing things in the same image. Regarding the analysis of images, Banks refers to Rose (2012), who "for example, … discusses five sociological modalities: 'compositional interpretation' (i.e., a detailed study of the various elements within the image frame), content analysis, semiotic analysis, psychoanalytical analysis, and discourse analysis" (Banks 2014, p. 398). Both Banks's references show that the there is neither one way of seeing this kind of data—which means images are subject of varying interpretations—nor a single method of doing the analysis. Both—seeing and analyzing—depend on the actual research interest and research question for which images are produced, or selected from existing ones and analyzed. As Lynn and Lea (2005, p. 219) highlight, "for the visual researcher, an exposition of text and context is integral to understanding the social phenomenon of interest." Again this emphasizes that visual data cannot be seen as existing data but are embedded in various contexts, in which they appear in the field and in which they are located in the research.

What Are the Problems in the Application of the Method?

Denzin (1989b, pp. 214–215) takes up Gold's typology of observer roles (see Chapter 20) in order to describe the problems associated with finding the most appropriate role for the photographing observer. One problem is the influence of the medium. Arranging the subjects in a photo results in losing the moment's expressiveness. The same is the case if the subjects pose for the photos (self-presentation photos). The insights that photos can provide about the everyday life under study will be greatest if the photographing researchers can manage to integrate their use of the camera in a way that attracts the least possible attention.

Another problem is the possibility of influencing or manipulating the photographic presentation. Denzin identifies montage and retouch or the attempt to take artistic photos in this respect. He argues that these techniques may lead to details being left out that are relevant to the research question. Denzin (1989b, p. 220) also mentions various forms of censorship (by official agencies, by the photographed persons, or by the photographer) that may restrict the realization and reliability of photos as social science data. Becker discusses this point under the heading of the photographer's control over the final image:

> The choice of film, development and paper, of lens and camera, of exposures and framing, of moment and relations with subjects—all of these, directly under the photographer's control, shape the end product. … A second influence on the image the photographer produces, is his theory about what he is looking at, his understanding of what he is investigating. (1986a, pp. 241–242)

Furthermore, Becker raises the question "Do photographs tell the truth?" and tries to specify ways of answering it by discussing sampling questions and the problem of reactivity produced by the very act of taking the photos. A special problem is the question of framing (what is in the picture, what is focused on, what is left out?) and how much the personal aesthetic style of the photographer determines the content of the photo.

Overall, these problems raise the question of how far the sample of the reality under study contained in the scope of the photo introduces bias into the presentation of reality, and what part the medium of photography plays in the construction of the reality under study.

How Does the Method Fit into the Research Process?

The theoretical background of using photos is structuralist models such as objective hermeneutics or symbolic interactionism (see Chapter 7) in Denzin's case. Research questions focus on descriptions of aspects of reality contained in the photographs (see Chapter 11). Material is selected in a step-by-step manner (see Chapter 13). Sequential procedures are used for interpretation (see Chapter 27). The analysis of visual material is mostly triangulated with other methods and data (see Chapters 14 and 29).

What Are the Limitations of the Method?

Attempts at hermeneutics of images aim at extending the range of what counts as possible data for empirical social research into the visual domain. However (at least up to now), procedures of interpretation familiar from analyses of verbal data have been applied to them. In this respect, such visual data are also regarded as texts. Photos tell a story; text descriptions, summaries, or transcription often accompany visual data before textual interpretation methods are carried out on visual material. Genuine analytical procedures that directly relate to images still remain to be developed.

Film Analysis as an Instrument of Research

Television and films influence everyday life. Qualitative research uses these media to tell us about the social construction of reality. "As media of communication, films are embedded in the circumstances by which society communicates and interacts. Movies are part of discursive and social practices. They reflect the conditions and structures of society and of individual life," as Mikos (2014, p. 409) highlights before referring to Teays:

> I will tell you something about movies. They aren't just entertainment; they are powerful ways to see into the workings of our minds and hearts. With movies, we can get a better sense of what we are doing here, why we are doing it, and what in the world we need to do to bring about the changes we seek. (Teays 2012: XI)

Denzin (1989b) analyzes Hollywood movies that contain social reflections on social experiences (such as alcoholism, corruption, and so on). Such films reflect also on key moments of history (e.g., the Vietnam War), on certain institutions (e.g., hospitals), on social values (such as marriage and family) and relations, on domains of everyday life, and on emotions.

These movies and the practices presented can be interpreted on different levels of meaning. Denzin distinguishes "realistic" and subversive reading (2004a, p. 240). Realistic readings understand a film as a truthful description of a phenomenon, whose meaning can be (completely) disclosed through a detailed analysis of the contents and the formal features of the images. The interpretation serves to validate the truth claims that the film makes about reality. Subversive readings take into account that the author's ideas of reality influence the film as well as that those of the interpreter will influence its interpretation. Different interpretations influence the analysis of film material. Various constructions of reality (see Chapter 7) should be used to analyze and compare the interpretations.

Steps in Conducting a Film Analysis

For film analyses, Denzin (2004a, pp. 241–242) suggests four phases as a general model:

1 "Looking and feeling": the films are regarded as a whole, and impressions, questions, and patterns of meaning which are conspicuous are noted.
2 What research question are you asking? Formulate the questions to pursue. Therefore, note key scenes.

3 Structured microanalysis is conducted of individual scenes and sequences, which should lead to detailed descriptions and patterns in the display (of conflicts and so on) in these excerpts.
4 When answering the research question, search for patterns in the entire film. Searching for patterns extends to the whole film in order to answer the research question. The film's realistic and subversive readings are contrasted and a final interpretation is written.

This procedure has been applied to several examples.

─CASE STUDY 21.4─

Alcoholism in Hollywood Movies

Using the example of the film *Tender Mercies*, Denzin studies the presentation and treatment of problems like "alcoholism" and "families of alcoholics" in order to find out "how cultural representations form lived experiences" (1989c, p. 37). Therefore, Denzin first studied the "realistic interpretations" of the film, which he derived from reviews and film guides for their "dominant ideological meanings" (1989c, p. 40).

The background assumption is that the interpretations of films and of social problems like alcoholism are often "patriarchally biased," because they are formulated from a male point of view (1989c, p. 38). Denzin contrasts this with his own "subversive reading" of the film and the problem, which he conducts from the standpoint of feminism. The focus is shifted from the main male character and his alcohol addiction to the women in his life and to the consequences that the main character's alcoholism has for the women and his family (1989c, p. 46). From this change of perspectives, an analysis of the cultural values and issues to do with the problem of alcoholism, such as family, gender relations, and the control of emotions in society, is derived (1989c, p. 49). Finally, the developed readings are assessed against the interpretations of different viewers of the film. The latter are related to the viewers' subjective experiences of the problems, which are mentioned (1989c, p. 40).

The following conclusions may be drawn from this study. Interpretation and analysis should be used to deconstruct films. Perspective determines the central focus of the interpretation and its results. The point that Denzin seeks to make is that this is the case not only for the analyses of film reviewers—for whom that will not be news—but also for the analyses of social scientists. How far the feminist perspective Denzin takes is the most appropriate one is a question that he does not want to decide with respect to the multiplicity of possible interpretations he highlights.

Analyzing Film

Mikos (2014, p. 420) discusses how the structural function of film texts is significant for their reception. For this purpose he suggests doing a film analysis on five levels:

- Content and representation
- Narration and dramaturgy
- Characters and actors
- Aesthetics and configuration
- Contexts

This list of levels to approach film material focuses in part on the images per se: what is their content, what do they represent? At they same time, the way the film texts are constructed should be analyzed: What are the aesthetic features of a movie? How are people and things configured in the images, in the scenes and sequences of scenes? What are the characteristics of the composition of films and images in the film? What is the relevance of these features for the meaning of the film and impact on the viewers? And, finally, the embedding of these features in internal structures of narration or dramaturgy and in external contexts should be taken into account. On most of these levels, language plays an important role for understanding the visual.

CASE STUDY 21.5

Nursing as a Profession in TV Serials

In their diploma theses, Brigitte Alzenauer and Gudrun Lang conducted a film analysis for studying the representation of nursing as a profession in the media starting from the following assumptions. At that time, nursing as an occupation had become increasingly professionalized for some decades. The range of duties and responsibilities had been widened, nursing had become more academic. These relevant developments are hardly reflected in the media's portrayal of nursing. Therefore the practice of nursing remains opaque for the public and the image of nursing stays low. Besides their function to inform and to entertain, TV films transfer social values. Serials about hospitals are presented weekly and with a rising tendency. Because it appears that these serials show a realistic workday routine, it has to be examined how far this routine was adjusted from the professional developments of nursing.

A qualitative film analysis focused on 18 episodes of the hospital serial *Für alle Fälle Stefanie* (*For all cases Stefenie*), which was broadcast by a private German TV program from 1997 to 1998. The research questions of the analysis were: How does the image of nursing as a profession drawn in the serial transport and reinforce traditional representations? How does the serial take the changes in the profession into account? Are single-sided role clichés presented in the representation of the relations between medicine and nursing in the serial?

The method of the analysis was based on Denzin's (2004a) approach of a realist and a subversive film analysis. This analytic concept was put into concrete terms in several steps. First, the selected episodes were watched repeatedly as a whole and impressions and more detail research questions were written down in memos. In a second step, this led then to three major questions: legal aspects of nursing practices, collaboration, and job profile of nursing as represented in the serial. Then three orienting guidelines for analyzing the material were formulated: "nursing as maternal labour of love," "nursing as assistance job," and "self-perception and public image of nursing." In the third step 15 key episodes were subjected to a microanalysis. The course of actions was analyzed by including facial expressions, gestures, intonation and paralinguistic features, the position of the actors towards each other, the composition of the images, and the position of the camera in the analytic focus. In the final step, the microanalyses were compared and summarized for commonalities and differences in identifying general patterns. For example, for "the maternal labor of love" as characterization of nurses' work in the episodes, the following indicators could be found. The nurses in the serials generally ignore their personal needs in favor of a permanent availability for patients and physicians. A separation between work and time off is not practiced. The nurses visit the ward in their days off work. They take care of private issues of the patients and their families after work or let former patients stay with them at their home when the patients have no home of their own.

The study showed that the representation of nursing in the TV serial corresponds to a very traditional view and is characterized by stereotypes and clichés. The picture of nursing conveyed does not help to improve the professional image of nursing. Thus the film analysis of this serial can contribute to an analysis of the image of nursing as a profession in the wider public as it is produced or reinforced by films and TV (see Alzenauer, Lang, and Flick 2000).

What Are the Problems in Conducting the Method?

Using films as data also leads to problems of selection (which films, which scenes are analyzed more closely?) and of interpretation (what should attention be paid to in the material?). Additionally, the question of working up the data for interpretation arises: should coding, categorization, and interpretation be done directly on the visual material or should transcriptions of dialogues and their contexts be made first, thus transforming visual material into text?

What Is the Contribution to the General Methodological Discussion?

Using media such as films and photographs as data in qualitative research crosses the boundaries between the various social science methods discussed in this book. Compared to interviews, they provide the non-verbal component of events and practices which could otherwise only be documented in context protocols. Observed situations are ephemeral, whereas events recorded with the media allow for repeat access. This may transgress the limitations of perception and documentation that are characteristic of observation. Finally, Petermann (1995) discusses the relation between reality and the presentation of reality in scientific documentary films.

How Does the Method Fit into the Research Process?

The theoretical background of using film materials is Denzin's interpretive interactionism (see Chapter 7). Research questions focus on descriptions of segments of reality contained in the film (see Chapter 11). Concrete examples of these are sampled step by step (see Chapter 13). Interpretation is often carried out using sequential procedures (see Chapter 27).

What Are the Limitations of the Method?

Film-makers construct versions of reality by their own choosing. But it is the viewers who interpret the material in different ways. Therefore, film analyses are rarely used as a genuine strategy but rather as an addition to or part of other methods aimed at analyzing verbal data. Up to now there has been no method of interpretation for such material which deals directly with the visual level. Films are understood as visual texts (Denzin 1989b, p. 228), transformed into text by transcription or by recounting the stories contained in them, and then analyzed as such.

Video Analysis in Qualitative Research

Another way of using visual data, which goes beyond the single photograph or a series of still photographs, is to videotape aspects of a specific life world. Videotaping has become a familiar everyday technique to document experiences—like holidays or festivities. It is also present in public places, underground stations, and the like, which are subject to video camera surveillance. You can use videotaping in different ways in qualitative research. One way is to use a video recorder instead of a tape recorder to document the interaction in an interview. This technical use of videotaping will be discussed in Chapter 24. But videotapes can be a source or data sorts themselves.

Knoblauch (2004b, p. 126) lists several data sorts which are used in video research:

- Scientific recording of natural social situations.
- Scientific recording of experimental social situations.
- Interviews.
- Natural social situations recorded by the actors (surveillance, audio recording).
- Posed situations recorded by actors (video diaries).
- Situations recorded and edited by actors (wedding videos).
- Situations recorded by actors and edited by professionals (wedding videos, documentations).

These forms of data are discussed in this context here, as video research is concerned not only with analyzing video material, but also with how a corpus of material is produced, which can then be analyzed: What is recorded, selected, or cut out of the tape? Which materials are selected for analyzing an issue? What sorts of material are produced for research purposes?

Knoblauch (2004b) develops a video interaction analysis as a method from using these sorts of video data, which he characterizes by three features: methodicity, order, and reflexivity. "Methodicity" refers not only to the *what*, but also to the *how* of the presentations of situations and actors in video material. "Order" focuses on sound ways of producing and interpreting the performed activities. "Reflexivity" or "performativity" means that the actors not only act, but also reflect what they do in their presentations.

Heath and Hindmarsh (2002) highlight that, in their research, video recordings in naturally occurring activities are the primary data, but that the researchers have also to undertake conventional fieldwork such as becoming familiar with the setting and so on when they produce these data. If they want to use video recordings of doctor–patient interactions, for example, it is crucial to do fieldwork, observation, etc., prior to recording material. This is necessary for deciding adequately where to place the camera, what to take as the best angle, or what to include of the context of the interaction, and so on.

Knoblauch, Schnettler, and Raab (2006a, pp. 14–16) identify four major problems confronting qualitative video analysis: (1) The complexity of the data produced in this context, which include information on several levels. This leads to a (necessary) selectivity in recording and analyzing the data and to the question of what becomes the analytic unit here. (2) The technological challenge (progress in the development of technical devices, influences on the events under study, complexity in using the devices, costs for purchasing new tools, etc.) in using video as a medium. (3) The relation of text and image has to be spelled out, which refers to questions of how to transcribe visual data (see Chapter 24). (4) Legal implications of video recording: who is permitted to record social interactions and carry out social interaction analysis for research purposes? For example, the use of surveillance (CCTV) of underground stations, street intersections, etc., is a matter of dispute. To use such recordings for research (see Heath and Luff 2006) leads to several ethical questions (how to organize an informed consent; see Chapter 5).

Qualitative video analysis can refer to producing and analyzing video data. But it can also study the use and analysis of video data in everyday life (Heath and Luff 2006): how is information on CCTV videos recognized in the observation room; how are they evaluated and taken as a reason for intervening?

CASE STUDY 21.6

Using Video for Studying Children in Their Everyday Context

In a study of the development of egocentrism in children and changes in their perspectives, Billman-Mahecha (1990) used videotaping as a method to collect data in an everyday context. After an initial period of participant observation in order to get acquainted with the family, she came back and videotaped a couple of hours of an afternoon with the family and of children's play. Then she sampled appropriate episodes from the video material, transcribed them, and made her own interpretation of them. The next step was to show these episodes to the parents and to interview both about them. These interviews were also transcribed and interpreted. Both perspectives (the researcher's interpretation of the video episodes and the interpretation of the parents' answers) were triangulated on the level of the single case. Then the episodes were analyzed on both levels in order to develop a typology of practices and statements of the children in the different episodes.

Analyzing Video Recordings

Knoblauch et al. (2014) distinguish standardized and interpretive video analysis:

> *interpretive* video analysis follows a different methodological premise: it assumes that the actions recorded are guided by meanings that must be understood by the actors themselves. It is only on the basis of the meanings of actions to the actors involved, that is "first order constructs", that researchers pursue their questions and create their "second order constructs". (p. 436)

Their own approach focuses on studying social interaction by employing video analysis and thus, of course, is not limited to the visual part of the recording but takes an audio-visual approach. In this it is similar to participant observation (see Chapter 20) but has the big advantage of having recorded data, which are available permanently and can be watched repeatedly. The analysis then follows the principle of sequentiality (see Chapter 27) and the interaction according to its temporal development. The second principle is reflexivity, assuming that the actors do not simply act, but "'indicate', 'frame' or 'contextualise' what they do while they are acting" (p. 14).

What Are the Problems in Conducting the Method?

One problem is how to limit the technical presence of the equipment. If you use this approach you should take care that the camera and recording equipment do not dominate the social situation. Another problem is the selectivity of the camera's focus—either you will have a very narrow focus in good quality and detail but without much of the context of the situation captured on the film, or you will have a good panoramic view of the social situation but without the details of facial expressions, for example. What you prefer should be determined by your research questions, but this already shows the limitations of the recording. Another issue is how to decide when to start and when to stop recording. Finally, you could—from a technical point of view—use recordings of surveillance cameras, which will give you an exhaustive overview of the activities in a place of interest. But, from an ethical point of view, you will have a lot of material which the actors never accepted for your research (or to be recorded at all). So, avoid using this kind of material.

What Is the Contribution to the General Methodological Discussion?

A video analysis extends the capacities of other approaches in several directions. Compared to an audio recording, video analyses include the non-verbal parts of interaction. Compared to interviewing, they allow the recording of actions in the making instead of accounts of actions from a retrospective point of view. In addition to observation, they allow the capturing of more aspects and details than participant observers in their field notes. Videotaping allows for repeat observation of fleeting situations. Thus video analysis reduces the selectivity of several methods. However, this method entails its own form of selectivity due to the limits of what can be documented and filmed at a specific moment. The method highlights again the selectivity and limitations of research methods in general.

How Does the Method Fit into the Research Process?

As the frequently used term of "videography" shows, video research is often part of an ethnographic approach to specific life worlds, such as workplace studies (Knoblauch, Heath, and Luff 2000). The theoretical interests linked to this research are to analyze interactions (in a form of interactionism, see Chapter 7) in such contexts and to understand the way social reality is constructed in these contexts and in or through videotapes. Concrete examples of these are sampled step by step (see Chapter 11). Often, video analyses are useful only in combination with other methods and other sorts of data (triangulation, see Chapters 14 and 29). The material is often analyzed against the background of ethnomethodology and conversation analysis (see Chapters 6 and 24).

What Are the Limitations of the Method?

As the above examples already show, video analysis is not a stand-alone method. It is best used in combination with other methods, fieldwork in the classical sense, additional interviewing, and observation beyond the camera. The technical development of the cameras is constantly progressing, but this will not make the camera disappear from the situation that is filmed, documented, and analyzed by using it.

Photos, film, and videos have become objects of research, which means existing examples become material that can be analyzed for answering a specific research question. At the same time, they have become media for producing data—videography of social situations or settings, for example. These materials as well as these media can be integrated in more comprehensive research strategies, notably in combination with interviews or in the context of ethnography. Seen this way, visual data methods complement verbal data methods and permit comprehensive research integrating mediated data of various forms.

Checklist for Using Visual Data

The questions in the following checklist should help you to reflect on the potentials and limits of using visual data:

1 Is the issue of your research accessible to visualization in photos or films?
2 Is your material original material for your research or was it produced for other purposes?

3 Which other methods—like in/formal interviews, for example—will you need for studying your issue?
4 Which forms or editing or reworking have influenced your visual material?
5 What are the ethical issues to consider when using this material?
6 How will you manage ethical issues like informed consent in your observation?
7 What are the technical influences on your material?

KEY POINTS

- Visual data methods provide new ways of analyzing the visual side of social settings and practices and of making these a part of research.
- Visual data can consist of existing materials or can be produced specifically for research purposes.
- Video analysis focuses on visual and acoustic parts of the recorded data.
- There is still a need for developing appropriate methods for analyzing the visual parts of the data made available by these methods.
- Visual data are—like other methods—selective in their focus and provide a specific perspective on the issues that are studied with them.

Exercise 21.1

1 Find a study in the literature in which videos, photos, or films were used as data (e.g., Mondada 2012). Reflect on (a) how the data were produced, (b) whether they were used as stand-alone data or in combination with other forms of data, and (c) how they were analyzed.
2 When you plan your own study, think about (a) how you could use visual material in it and (b) which parts of your research question it could or could not relate to.

Further Reading

Visual Data in General

The following text gives a good overview of approaches and methodological issues in using visual data:

Banks, M. (2007) *Using Visual Data in Qualitative Research*. London: Sage.

Photos

The problems of a visual sociology using photographs as data are discussed in these texts in greater detail:

Banks, M. (2014) "Analyzing Images," in U. Flick (ed.), *The SAGE Handbook of Qualitative Data Analysis*. London: Sage. pp. 394–408.
Becker, H.S. (1986a) *Doing Things Together: Selected Papers*. Evanston, IL: Northwestern University Press.

Denzin, N.K. (1989b) *The Research Act* (3rd edn). Englewood Cliffs, NJ: Prentice Hall.

Harper, D. (2004) "Photography as Social Science Data," in U. Flick, E.v. Kardorff and I. Steinke (eds.), *A Companion to Qualitative Research*. London: Sage. pp. 231–236.

Film Analysis

The approach of a visual sociology using films as data is discussed in these two texts in greater detail:

Denzin, N.K. (2004a) "Reading Film," in U. Flick, E.v. Kardorff and I. Steinke (eds.), *A Companion to Qualitative Research*. London: Sage. pp. 237–242.

Mikos, L. (2014) "Analysis of Film," in U. Flick (ed.), *The SAGE Handbook of Qualitative Data Analysis*. London: Sage. pp. 409–423.

Video Analysis in Qualitative Research

The use of video in the context of qualitative research is outlined here:

Heath, C. and Hindmarsh, J. (2002) "Analysing Interaction: Video, Ethnography and Situated Conduct," in T. May (ed.), *Qualitative Research in Action*. London: Sage. pp. 99–120.

Knoblauch, H., Schnettler, B., Raab, J. and Soeffner, H.-G. (eds.) (2006b) *Video Analysis: Methodology and Methods*. Frankfurt: Peter Lang.

Knoblauch, H., Tuma, R., and Schnettler, B. (2014) "Video Analysis and Videography," in U. Flick (ed.), *The SAGE Handbook of Qualitative Data Analysis*. London: Sage. pp. 435–449.

22
Using Documents as Data

┌─CHAPTER OBJECTIVES─

This chapter is designed to help you

- use documents for qualitative research;
- understand that documents need to be analyzed in the context of their production and use in the field;
- comprehend that documents are not just a simple representation of processes and experiences: they are communicative devices that construct a version of these processes;
- see the potential for analyzing Internet documents.

Our lives, as individuals as well as members of a society, and societal life as a whole have become subject to recording. Hardly any institutional activity occurs without producing a record. Birth and death certificates, like any other form of institutional record, produce data. These data are produced for institutional purposes on the more general level in the form of statistics (e.g., the number of people who got married this year) but also on a personal level (e.g., whether some person is already married; whether a marriage can be conducted without a divorce).

At the same time, most people produce many personal documents in their daily lives, from diaries to photographs to holiday letters. In between, there are biographies of people—autobiographies written by the persons themselves or biographies written about a specific person for a special occasion. Although these records and documents are not produced for research purposes, they and the information they contain can be used for research.

Here we are in the realm of analyzing documents. They can be analyzed in a quantitative way—statistics about marriages in a period or geographical area can be analyzed for the average age of marrying or the number of migrants' compared to non-migrants' marriages. And documents can also be analyzed in a qualitative way—how is the life history of a person constructed in the official records about this person in different institutional settings?

As with other approaches in qualitative research, you can use documents and their analysis as a complementary strategy to other methods, like interviews or ethnography. Or you can use the analysis of documents as a stand-alone method. Then your research will rely on how the reality under study is documented in these kinds of data. As we have already discussed the use of photographs in the preceding chapter, I want to focus on written (textual) documents here. Even if you apply the same methods for analyzing these texts as you do for, say, analyzing interviews, there is more to using documents than merely analyzing them.

What Characterizes Documents?

The following definition outlines what is generally understood as "documents":

> Documents are *standardized artifacts*, in so far as they typically occur in particular *formats*: as notes, case reports, contracts, drafts, death certificates, remarks, diaries, statistics, annual reports, certificates, judgements, letters or expert opinions. (Wolff 2004b, p. 284)

Prior gives a more dynamic, use-oriented definition:

> If we are to get to grips with the nature of documents then we have to move away from a consideration of them as stable, static and pre-defined artifacts. Instead we must consider them in terms of fields, frames and networks of action. In fact, the status of things as "documents" depends precisely on the ways which such objects are integrated into fields of action, and documents can only be defined in terms of such fields. (2003, p. 2)

Lincoln and Guba (1985, p. 277) make the distinction between documents and records with respect to both what they represent and how they become relevant for research accordingly. Documents are produced in personal activities and require a contextualized interpretation, whereas records are set up in administrative and political contexts (see also Hodder 2000, p. 703). When you decide to carry out an analysis of documents, you should take two distinctions into account: either you can use solicited documents for your research (e.g., ask people to write diaries for the next 12 months and then analyze and compare these documents), or you can use unsolicited documents (e.g., the diaries people have written as part of an everyday routine). In the tradition of research using unobtrusive methods, Webb, Campbell, Schwartz, and Sechrest (1966) and Lee (2000) distinguish running records, which are produced to document administrative processes, from episodic and private records, which are not produced continuously but occasionally. Documents may take the form of printed texts or digital files (a database, for example). Hodder (2000) sees them as part of a material culture, which "are produced so as to transform, materially, socially, and ideologically" (p. 706). For May, "documents, read as the sedimentations of social practices, have the potential to inform and structure the decisions which people make on a daily and longer-term basis: they also constitute particular readings of social events" (2001, p. 176).

Scott (1990, p. 14) distinguishes 12 types of documents, which are constituted by a combination of two dimensions: the authorship (who produced the document) and the access to the documents. The authorship can be divided into personal and official documents and the latter again into private and state documents. For example, I can have a personal document of my birth (e.g., a photograph taken immediately afterwards); there is a birth certificate, which I possess as a private but official document; and I can be registered as born in London, for example, and this registration is an official document produced, held, and used by the state.

All of these documents may be classified in terms of accessibility. Scott distinguishes four alternatives. The access can be closed (e.g., the medical records of a general practitioner are not accessible to third parties). The access can be restricted (e.g., juridical records are only accessible to specific professional groups like lawyers in a trial). The access can be open archival, which means that everyone can access the documents but (only) in a specific archive. And the access can be open published; then the documents are published and accessible to any interested party. Combining these two dimensions—authorship and access—gives the 12 types (see Scott 1990, pp. 14–18, for details).

CASE STUDY 22.1

The Polish Peasant in Europe and America

Thomas and Znaniecki's (1918–1920) study is one of the earliest uses of documents. Here the authors study experiences of migration—and migration as a sociological issue—by analyzing documents which Thomas called "undesigned records." These documents were produced not for research purposes, but in the everyday life of the Polish community in the United States.

The main data were family letters and letters to social institutions (newspapers, emigration offices, churches, welfare institutions, and courts). These documents were analyzed for attitudes and social values documented in them and especially for the change of such attitudes and values and for the decline of solidarity among the members of the Polish community the longer they were in the United States. Therefore, some central topics were identified in these letters, like social disorganization, patterns of family interaction, individualization, and so on.

The analysis of the documents focused on the frequencies with which the issues were raised and on the indicators of how the actors' definition of social situations in these communities changed over time. Beyond using letters and documents, the authors used only one other form of data when they asked an individual to write down his or her life history.

This study is seen as a pioneering study in qualitative research and instructive for the potential and the problems of using documents as data. It has also been a pioneering study for current biographical research.

Using Documents as Data: More than Textual Analysis

Scott's classification can be helpful for locating the documents you want to use in your research. It can also be helpful for assessing the quality of the documents. As the dimensions already make clear, documents are not just a simple representation of facts or reality. Someone (or an institution) produces them for some (practical) purpose and for some form of use (which also includes a definition of who is meant to have access to them). When you decide to use documents in your study, you should always see them as a means for communication. You also should ask yourself: Who has produced this document, for which purpose, and for whom? What were the personal or institutional intentions to produce and store this document or this kind of document? Therefore, documents are not just simple data that you can use as a resource for your research. Once you start using them for your research you should always focus on these documents as a topic of research at the same time: What are their features? What are the particular conditions of their production? And so on. According to Coffey (2014, p. 371), important analytic questions are: "What kind of reality is the document creating? How is the document accomplishing this task?"

Selecting Documents

For assessing the quality of documents, Scott proposes four criteria, which you can use for deciding whether or not to employ a specific document (or set of documents) for your research:

- Authenticity. Is the evidence genuine and of unquestionable origin?
- Credibility. Is the evidence free from error and distortion?
- Representativeness. Is the evidence typical of its kind, and, if not, is the extent of its untypicality known?
- Meaning. Is the evidence clear and comprehensible? (1990, p. 6)

The first criterion addresses the question of whether the document is a primary or secondary document: Is it the original report of an accident, for instance, or is it a summary of this original report by someone who did not witness the accident itself?

What was omitted or misinterpreted in writing this summary? Tertiary documents are sources to find other documents, like the library catalogue which lists primary source documents. Looking at internal inconsistencies or comparing to other documents, by looking at errors and by checking whether different versions of the same document exist, can assess *authenticity*.

Credibility refers to the accuracy of the documentation, the reliability of the producer of the document, the freedom from errors.

Representativeness is linked to typicality. It may be helpful to know if a specific record is a typical record (which contains the information an average record contains). However, it can also be a good starting point if you know a specific document is untypical and to ask yourself what that means for your research question.

In terms of meaning, we can distinguish between (1) the intended meaning for the author of the document, (2) the meaning for the reader of it (or for the different readers who are confronted with it), and (3) the social meaning for someone who is the object of that document. For example, the protocol of interrogation was written by the author in order to demonstrate that this was a formally correct interrogation. For a judge in court, the meaning of the content of the protocol is to have a basis for reaching a judgment. For an accused man, the meaning of the content of this protocol can be that he now has a conviction, which will have consequences for the rest of his life when he tries to find a job, and so on. And for the researcher, the meaning of this protocol might be that it demonstrates how guilt is constructed in a criminal trial.

Constructing a Corpus

If you have decided to use documents in your research and know the sort of documents you want to use, a major step will then be to construct a corpus of documents. This step entails issues of sampling: do you want to have a representative sample of all documents of a certain kind, or do you want to purposively select documents to reconstruct a case (see Chapter 13)?

One problem that arises here is the intertextuality of documents. Documents may be linked to each other explicitly (e.g., they may be about the same people referring to earlier events in their lives), but they may also be linked implicitly to other documents referring to other cases of a similar kind. For example, there are certain standards and routines on how to write a diagnostic report with a lot of general knowledge about a particular kind of disease, other cases, and so on in the background. So all documents refer to other documents in the way they document and construct social realities. For your research, it may be helpful to see these connections and to take them into account.

The Practicalities of Using Documents

How do you conduct an analysis using documents? Wolff (2004b) recommends that you should not start from a notion of factual reality in the documents compared to the subjective views in interviews, for example. Documents represent a specific version of realities constructed for specific purposes. It is difficult to use them for validating interview statements. They should be seen as a way of contextualizing information. Rather than using them as "information containers," they should be seen and analyzed as *methodologically created communicative turns* in constructing versions of events.

Another suggestion is to take no part of any document as arbitrary, but to start from the ethnomethodological assumption of order at all points. This should also include the way a document is constructed. Questions of layout or some standard or routine formulations used in a specific form of documents (e.g., juridical documents) are part of the communicative device "document" and should not be neglected. To see these parts of documents more clearly, it may be helpful to compare documents from different contexts—a record from juridical processes, say, to a record from the health system, referring to the same issue or even case.

What are the problems in accessing documents? As in other research, limitations of resources may force you to be selective instead of using all the available (or necessary) documents. Sometimes the necessary documents are not available, not accessible, or simply lost. Sometimes there are gatekeepers who will not let you through to use the documents you need. In other cases, some people may block access to documents referring directly or indirectly to their person. For example, the archives of the secret services of the former East Germany were opened after the reunification of the two parts of Germany. Persons of certain public interest (like former chancellors of West Germany) could prevent interested people (journalists, researchers, and the like) from having access to files referring to these persons of public interest. Publication of these materials might have damaged the memory of these persons or produced a public outcry.

Another practical problem may be that you have problems with understanding the content of the documents, because you cannot decipher the words, abbreviations, codes, or references that are used or because they are difficult to read (e.g., handwritten documents) or are damaged.

If you decide to use a certain type of document for your research, you should always ask yourself: who has produced this document and for what purpose? Documents in institutions are meant to record institutional routines and at the same time to record information necessary for legitimizing how things are done in such routines. This becomes relevant in particular when problems, failures, or mistakes have to be justified. So documents can be used, picked up, and reused in the practical context.

An example of this is an early study by Harold Garfinkel, in which he addressed the documentation of psychiatric treatments. Garfinkel (1967) studied files and folders on patients in psychiatric contexts and found out in how many cases substantial parts of the records were missing. He found and analyzed "good" organizational reasons for "bad clinical records" (hence the title of his study). Among these reasons, time was only one—to document what you do is often secondary to doing what you do when time is short. Therefore, essential data are forgotten or omitted.

Another reason is that a certain vagueness in documenting institutional practices prevents others from controlling these practices and, for example, cutting down the available time for certain routines. Thus, for researchers using such documents for their own research interest, it should also be asked: What has been left out in producing the record, by whom, and why? What are the social circumstances which may have influenced the production of the record?

The content of documents should be analyzed by asking: what are they referenced to, what are the patterns of referencing, and what are the patterns of producing and using these documents in their mundane context?

⌐CASE STUDY 22.2⌐

Analyzing Documents of Professional Training

In earlier chapters, our study on the health concepts of professionals (Flick et al. 2002; Flick et al. 2004b) was used as an example. We not only covered interviews and focus groups about the issue, but also analyzed documents about the professional training of the doctors and nurses. We analyzed the curricula that defined the medical training and the vocational education of nurses in the period when most of our interviewees received their training. We then compared them to more recent versions of the curricula and with the statements in the interviews. We analyzed the documents in which the aims and contents of training programs, exams, and practical parts of the training are outlined for several topics: the role of health, health promotion, prevention, and ageing. The intention in analyzing these materials was to contextualize our interviewees' general statements that these topics were not part of their training, but that they were confronted with them only during their later work as physicians and nurses. We were able to show that these issues have been given more space in more recent versions of the curricula. We also analyzed special programs of further education for doctors and nurses, which were on the market but not compulsory. They included more specialized programs referring to these issues.

What we found concerned the representation of these issues on the level of the planning of training and further education. There may be big differences between the planning and the actual training, so that one cannot refer directly from curricula (documents) to training (practice). Also, the fact that a curriculum includes a specific issue does not necessarily mean that this issue reaches the individual students during their training—they may simply have missed the lectures devoted to that issue.

This example shows different things: there may be a discrepancy between the planning of a program (in the document) and the practices in the teaching and in the reception of what is taught. Analyzing documents such as curricula can give you useful additional information, which you can relate to experiences mentioned in interviews, for example. As a stand-alone method, the analysis of documents has its limitations.

How to Analyze Documents

In this chapter, we have concentrated so far on documents in written form. However, as Prior (2003, pp. 5–9) shows, documentary analysis may be applied to a wider range of artifacts, understood as documents of practices or activities. Beyond analyzing *texts* as documents, Prior describes how, for instance, architectural plans of mental hospitals from various periods can be analyzed as representations of concepts of madness at a specific time: for example, stricter separation of closed-off areas for mentally ill patients indicates a less tolerant concept of mental illness, whereas open wards in a hospital plan document a more integrative and open attitude to mental illness in general. Another example is the analysis of paintings at cemeteries, which can be seen as representations of images of death in the periods they were painted. These examples show how widely the concept of "documents" can be defined for studying social issues with document analysis. In addition, photos or films can be seen and analyzed as documents (see Chapter 21), and the Internet or the Web can be added as a special sort of document (see below).

What Are the Problems in Conducting the Method?

If you want to analyze documents you should take into account who produced the documents, for what purpose, who uses them in their natural context, and how to select an appropriate sample of single documents. You should avoid focusing only on the contents of documents without taking their context, use, and function into account. Documents are the means for constructing a specific version of an event or process and often, in a broader perspective, for making a specific case out of a life history or a process. Again, this should go into analyzing the documents.

What Is the Contribution to the General Methodological Discussion?

Analyzing a document is often a way of using unobtrusive methods and data produced for practical purposes in the field under study. This can provide a new and unfiltered perspective on the field and its processes. Therefore, documents often permit going beyond the perspectives of members in the field.

How Does the Method Fit into the Research Process?

The background of much research focusing on documents is often ethnomethodology (see Chapter 7) and researchers analyze documents as communicative devices rather than as containers of contents. Depending on the specific research questions, all the methods of coding and categorizing (see Chapters 25 and 26) can be applied as well as conversation analytic approaches (see Chapter 27).

What Are the Limitations of the Method?

As a stand-alone method, analyzing documents gives you a very specific and sometimes limited approach to experiences and processes. However, documents can be a very instructive addition to interviews or observations. Major problems in analyzing documents include (1) how to conceptualize the relations between explicit content, implicit meaning, and the context of functions and use of the documents, and (b) how to take these relations into account in the interpretation of the documents.

Analyzing Internet Documents

In the context of online research, we also find the transfer of analyzing documents to the context of Internet research. The Web is full of material like personal and institutional home pages, documents, and files you can download from these pages, online journals, advertisements, and the like. If your research question asks for such documents to be analyzed, you will find an endless multitude of sites, often with links among them or to other specific sites.

Features of Internet Documents

An outstanding part of the Internet is the World Wide Web and its endless variety of web pages. These can be seen as a special form of document or text and analyzed as such. Special features characterize web pages, according to Mitra and Cohen (1999). One feature is the intertextuality of documents on the Web, organized and symbolized by (electronic) links from one text (or one page) to other texts. This kind of cross-referencing goes beyond the traditional definition and boundaries of a text and links a big number of single pages (or texts) to one big (sometimes endless) text.

This explicit linking of texts is more and more supplemented by the implicit linking of texts, which becomes visible when you use a search engine and see the number of links that are produced as a result of such a search. A related feature is that texts on the Web should rather be seen as hypertexts due to the connectedness to other texts, but also due to the impermanence and infiniteness of texts on the Web. Many web pages are permanently updated, changed, disappear, and reappear on the Web, which is why it is necessary to always mention the date you accessed a page when referring to it as a source.

Furthermore, Web texts are characterized by "non-linearity." Traditional texts have a linear structure—a beginning and an end, and often a temporal structure in the content (in a narrative, for example). Reading the text is normally oriented on this linearity. Web pages no longer conform to this linearity. They may have a drill-down structure, with its first page and subordinate pages.

But there is no need for the user to follow the structure in the way the author or the Web designer planned or created the pages. Mitra and Cohen see this as a redefinition of the relation of author and reader (as writer) where Web texts are concerned.

Other features of Web texts are that most of them go beyond the text as a medium and are multimedia products (including images, sounds, texts, popup pages, and so on) and that they are global. The latter is linked to the question of language; although most pages are in English, many pages are still constructed by using different languages.

Practicalities of Analyzing Internet Documents

Some problems result from the features just discussed when you want to analyze Internet documents. First, what kind of text needs analyzing: the single home page, an isolated web page, or the totality of a page with its links to other related pages? Where should you begin? If you start from a notion of sequentiality (see Chapter 27), you need the beginning of a text, a more or less linear structure, and an idea about the end of the text. But what is the beginning of a web page? Or, one step further, what are the criteria for selecting a page for your research, and what are the criteria for selecting a page for starting the analysis? A potential sequentiality could come from the main menu of a web page and then go on to subordinate menus. But, different from a written text, this is not a fixed order. The users can select which of the subordinated pages they go to next and so on.

Concerning the starting point and sampling of web pages, you could start by using theoretical sampling (see Chapter 13). This means you can start with any page that seems interesting for your research and then decide which one(s) to include next in your sample according to the insights or unsolved questions after analyzing the first one. A search engine like Google can be helpful for finding web pages for your topic. Here, it is important to have adequate keywords for the search, so it can be helpful to try out several if your search is not successful at the beginning. Also you should bear in mind that all search engines cover the Web only in parts, so it could be helpful to use more than one engine for your search.

As websites come and go it can be problematic to assume that a page once found will always be accessible in the same way again. You should store copies of the most important pages for your research on your computer. At the same time, it can be fruitful to come back to websites during your research to check if they have changed or were updated.

Depending on what you want to find out exactly, you can use methods for analyzing visual material (see Chapter 21) or textual material (see Chapters 23–27) and also the more sophisticated QDA software (see Chapter 28) for your study.

What Are the Problems in Conducting the Method?

Web pages are somehow beyond the routines of analyzing documents in qualitative research, because it is more difficult to define their boundaries and because they often change and disappear from the Web again. They have a different structure from texts and include different forms of data (images, sounds, text, links, and so on) at the same time.

What Is the Contribution to the General Methodological Discussion?

At the same time, web pages are a timely form of communication and self-presentation for individuals and organizations, and they are challenging the potential of qualitative research and methods.

How Does the Method Fit into the Research Process?

Analyzing Internet documents is a way of transferring document analysis to the realm of the virtual. Depending on the concrete research question, the analytic tools of qualitative research can be selected and applied, but may have to be adapted. Sampling should be oriented on theoretical or purposeful sampling (see Chapter 13). Web pages are good examples to study and show the social construction of reality and specific issues.

What Are the Limitations of the Method?

Web pages and other Internet documents represent a specific surface, a form of "presentation of self in everyday life" (Goffman 1959), which presents technical barriers to go back to what is presented here. To analyze a home page in order to make statements about the owner and creator (whether a person or institution) can be a tricky business. In such a case, I would strongly recommend triangulating your research (see Chapter 14), with other methods focusing on a real-world encounter with persons or institutions.

Checklist for Using Documents in Qualitative Research

The checklist below should give you some orientation of when and how to use narratives in qualitative research.

1 What are your expectations for analyzing documents in your research?
2 Are there existing documents you can use?

3   Which way of selecting the documents is the most appropriate for your issue?
4   Which one will best suit your research question?
5   How do you take into account that documents are a way of (re)constructing events and experiences?
6   How does the context in which documents are produced affect what is relevant for your research?
7   How do you take the communicative function of the documents in the institution or in the process into account in your research?

KEY POINTS

- Documents can be instructive for understanding social realities in institutional contexts.
- They should be seen as communicative devices produced, used, and reused for specific practical purposes, rather than as "unobtrusive" data in the sense of bias-free data.
- They can form a fruitful addition to other forms of data, provided the contexts of their production and use are taken into account.

Exercise 22.1

1   Take a newspaper and a lifestyle magazine and locate the "lonely hearts" section in the advertisements. Select several of these ads from both sources and try to analyze and compare them. Try to find out who wrote and posted them and for what kind of purpose. Are there any systematic differences that you can see between the ads in the newspaper and those in the lifestyle magazine?
2   What are the limitations of such documents for analyzing an issue like individualization or the way social relations are built? How could you overcome these limitations?
3   Take the study of Scourfield, Fincham, Langer, and Shiner (2012) and check (a) which sort of documents were used, (b) how they were selected, and (c) how they were analyzed.

Further Reading

Analyzing Documents

These five texts give a good overview of the principles and pitfalls of analyzing documents:

Coffey, A. (2014) "Analyzing Documents," in U. Flick (ed.), *The SAGE Handbook of Qualitative Data Analysis*. London: Sage. pp. 367–379.
Prior, L. (2003) *Using Documents in Social Research*. London: Sage.
Rapley, T. (2007) *Doing Conversation, Discourse and Document Analysis*. London: Sage.
Scott, J. (1990) *A Matter of Record: Documentary Sources in Social Research*. Cambridge: Polity Press.
Wolff, S. (2004b) "Analysis of Documents and Records," in U. Flick, E.v. Kardorff and I. Steinke (eds.), *A Companion to Qualitative Research*. London: Sage. pp. 284–290.

Analyzing Internet Documents

The first text listed below outlines a framework for analyzing Internet documents on a conceptual and practical level, the second gives an example of research, and the third covers the range of virtual data and the challenges they produce for using them in research:

Hine, C. (2000) *Virtual Ethnography*. London: Sage.

Mitra, A. and Cohen, E. (1999) "Analyzing the Web: Directions and Challenges," in S. Jones (ed.), *Doing Internet Research: Critical Issues and Methods for Examining the Net*. London: Sage. pp. 179–202.

Marotzki, W., Verständig, D., and Holze, J. (2014) "Analyzing Virtual Data," in U. Flick (ed.), *The SAGE Handbook of Qualitative Data Analysis*. London: Sage. pp. 450–463.

PART 6
Qualitative Data Analysis

So far we have looked at procedures for producing or selecting data. Now, we turn to the ways of analyzing data. In Chapter 23 (the first chapter of this part of the book) an introductory overview of qualitative data analysis issues provides a framework for a discussion of alternative ways of doing analysis: this is designed to prepare you for the subsequent detailed presentation of methods.

Before starting your data analysis, you will need to document your data—what you have observed or what you have been told—in order to have a basis for analyzing it. Chapter 24, on transcription and data management, introduces you to the use of field notes in observation and the transcription of interviews. It provides suggestions on how to reflect on these (not merely technical) steps in the research process.

Chapter 25 then introduces you to several techniques of grounded theory coding. This method can be inspiring for studies beyond theory development. Central features of this approach are that methodological decisions are subordinated to the field and phenomenon under study, on the one hand, and the overall goal of developing a theory out of the material, on the other. Mastering this process is more a matter of art and craft than by a strict orientation of methodological principles and rigor.

The methodological toolkit offered in the preceding chapters is used here in a pragmatic way to collect or produce the data in order to understand the field and phenomenon and to ground the theory empirically.

Chapter 26 presents alternative ways of coding and categorizing data. The common strategy underlying these techniques is prominent in qualitative research—that is, analyzing material by identifying relevant passages and parts and by naming and grouping these passages according to categories and types. Here you will find introductions to thematic analysis, thematic coding, and qualitative content analysis.

Chapter 27 focuses on a different strategy and presents methods to make it work. The main difference here from the preceding chapters is the use of naturally occurring data instead of data produced by methods such as interviews. A second principle is that content and form are considered—and sometimes form is more strongly considered than content in these methods. Third, the strategy here is to understand a text—and the material—by following its internal structure and then taking this strongly into account when analyzing the text and the material. Conversation and discourse analyses seek to demonstrate how issues are constructed in the way that people talk about them or how discourses are produced in more general forms of communication, such as media representations and the response on the part of the recipients. Hermeneutic procedures and narrative analysis need to understand a text according to the development and unfolding of the issue and its meaning.

Computer software for analyzing qualitative data has attracted much attention recently. The potential and the limitations of using such software are discussed in Chapter 28.

23
Qualitative Data Analysis

┌─CHAPTER OBJECTIVES───┐

This chapter is designed to help you

- develop an introductory understanding of qualitative data analysis;
- compare ways of analyzing your data;
- identify the strengths and weaknesses of methods of qualitative data analysis in context;
- understand your method of data analysis in the context of the research process and of the other stages of your research plan.

Aims of Qualitative Data Analysis

The analysis of qualitative data can be oriented to various aims. The first such aim may be to *describe* a phenomenon. The phenomenon could be, for example, the subjective experiences of a specific individual or group (e.g., the way people continue to live after a fatal diagnosis). Such a study could focus on the case (individual or group) and its special features and links between them. Or the analysis could focus on *comparing* several cases (individuals or groups) and on what they have in common, or on the differences between them. The second aim may be to identify conditions on which such differences are based—which means looking for *explanations* for such differences (e.g., circumstances which make it more likely that the coping with a specific illness situation is more successful than in other cases). The third aim may be to *develop a theory* of the phenomenon under study from the analysis of empirical material (e.g., a theory of illness trajectories).

The above are three general aims of qualitative data analysis. In addition we can distinguish the analysis of *content* (1) from that of *formal aspects* (2) and from approaches that *combine both* (3). For example, we can look at what participants report about their illness experiences and compare the contents of such reports to statements made by other participants (1). Or we can look at formal aspects of an interaction about these experiences (with a family member or a professional), when the language becomes unclear, pauses become longer, and the like (2). Or we can look for formal aspects and contents in a discourse about chronic illness in the public (3).

Not all of these aims can be pursued with every available method presented in the following chapters—each method has its own focus strengths and limits in reaching such aims. Before we go into more detail about the aims and approaches of qualitative data analysis, it is helpful to develop a short but general definition of the term.

What Is Qualitative Data Analysis?

By way of orientation, we can start from the following definition of qualitative data analysis (see Box 23.1).

BOX 23.1

What Is Qualitative Data Analysis?

Qualitative data analysis is the interpretation and classification of linguistic (or visual) material with the following aims: to make statements about implicit and explicit dimensions and structures of meaning making in the material and what is represented in it. Meaning making can refer to subjective or social meanings. Often qualitative data analysis combines rough analysis of the material (overviews, condensation, summaries) with detailed analysis (development of categories or hermeneutic interpretations). Often the final aim is to arrive at statements that can be generalized in one way or the other by comparing various materials or various texts or several cases.

This definition highlights that in qualitative data analysis, in most cases several levels of analysis are involved, for example, explicit and implicit levels of meaning. Thus we will need to read "between the lines" of what is said. Sometimes what is *not* said is also of interest. For example, in answering questions some fact may be mentioned by all interviewees bar one: we may then ask what that omission tells us about the issue or the interviewee. We would also want to find out what dimensions and structures can be identified which may influence what individuals say or experience.

Meaning can also be located beyond what the individual is aware of (which would refer to subjective meanings). For example, the actors have some ideas about their intention, why they do something. These intentions are part of the meaning their action has for them and they can talk about these meanings when asked to do so. Beyond individual awareness there are, for example, unconscious aspects of individual or social activities. For example, social meaning may come from professional routines or constraints on individual practices. It can also result from background conflicts in a family, which structure the members' interaction, although no member is really aware of that.

We can go deeply into some parts of the analysis by using categories and coding or in a hermeneutic analysis, but in some approaches we do a rough analysis beforehand—for example, setting up a list of topics in the material or writing a short description of a case. Finally, in most studies we do not stop when we have a description of what was said by the interviewee, for example, and how: instead, we then search for some kind of generalization, which means we ask ourselves how far this case or some statement is typical of other similar cases that were not part of the study.

A way of arriving at such generalizable statements is to compare statements within the case and even more findings coming from several cases or from using several empirical approaches. In grounded theory research (e.g., Strauss 1987, see here Chapter 25), the interpretation of data is the core of the empirical procedure, which, however, includes explicit methods of data collection. The interpretation of texts serves to develop the theory as well as the foundation for collecting additional data and for deciding which cases to select next. Therefore, the linear process of first collecting the data and later interpreting it is given up in favor of an interwoven procedure.

The analysis of texts may pursue two opposite goals. One is to reveal and uncover statements or to put them into their context in the text that normally leads to an augmentation of the textual material; for short passages in the original text, page-long interpretations are sometimes written. The other goal is to reduce the original text by paraphrasing, summarizing, or categorizing. These two strategies may be applied either alternatively or successively.

Data Management

Before you can start analyzing your data, you have to prepare and organize them. First you have to record what is said in an interview, for example, by tape recording, or what you see in observations (e.g., in field notes). Then you have to transcribe what was said or edit what you observed electronically. The next step is to organize the administration of your files with the data, so that you keep track of your interviews or notes. In this step you need to keep issues of anonymity and data protection in mind. Finally, larger data sets may be more easily analyzed when a preparatory global analysis is done first. Such techniques of data management are spelled out in more detail in the next chapter (see Chapter 24).

Using Naturally Occurring or Solicited Data

The interpretation of data is at the core of qualitative research, although its importance is seen differently in the various approaches. Sometimes, for example, in objective hermeneutics and conversation analysis and sometimes in discourse analysis (see Chapter 27), research refrains from using specific methods for data collection beyond making recordings of everyday situations. Instead of soliciting data with methods for research purposes, naturally occurring data (such as everyday conversations) are used and the researchers' methodological activity consists of recording these conversations. In these cases, the use of research methods consists of applying methods for the interpretation of text. In other approaches, it is a secondary step following more or less refined techniques of data collection. This is the case, for example, with qualitative content analysis or with some methods of handling narrative data.

Methods or Data as Points of Reference

When deciding on how to analyze qualitative data, you can take two points of reference (see also Flick 2014b). First, a number of methods of qualitative data analysis have been developed, which are widely applicable. For example, qualitative content analysis (see Chapter 26) can be applied to all sorts of data, as well as grounded theory coding (see Chapter 25). Second, we find approaches to qualitative data analysis which have been developed for specific forms of data, for example, the suggestions on how to analyze narrative data (see Chapter 18) or conversation analysis, which was designed for analyzing everyday and institutional talk (see Chapter 27). Then there are specific forms of data, such as documents (see Chapter 22), which require a specific analytic treatment, or visual data such as photos and films (see Chapter 21), which ask for extended analysis on several levels. Thus we can take methods of analysis as a starting point and apply them to our specific data set in our project. Or we can take the particular form of data we have as a starting point and use the approaches especially designed for these forms of data. The major question in both strategies is how far the analytic approach we want to apply fits the data we have collected. For example, it does not make sense to apply the rather limited approach of content analysis with predefined categories (see Chapter 26) to data coming from detailed life histories resulting from narrative interviews (see Chapter 18), because we will lose much of the potential of the data in using this approach for analyzing them.

What Is Coding?

There are various understandings of the term "coding," which have in common that they describe the relation of materials to categories used in the analysis. In grounded theory research (see Chapter 25), for example, coding has been defined as "naming segments of data with a label that simultaneously categorizes, summarizes, and accounts for each piece of data" (Charmaz 2006, p. 43). For qualitative content analysis (see Chapter 26) it is a central feature: "The method is also systematic in that it requires coding (i.e., assigning segments of the material to the categories of the coding frame) to be carried out twice (double-coding), at least for parts of the material" (Schreier 2014, p. 171). In qualitative content analysis, in contrast to other approaches, an emphasis is put on developing codes and categories mainly from the theory rather than from the material. Here, the focus is on developing a coding frame, which is a well-defined system of categories (see Chapter 26).

In general, coding is a process of labeling and categorizing data as a first step in the analysis. In several methods, there are several steps of coding—for example, initial and focused coding in recent grounded theory research or open and selective coding in earlier versions (see Chapter 25). Coding first is mainly oriented on developing concepts which can be used for labeling, sorting, and comparing excerpts of the data (e.g., several statements) and later for allocating further excerpts to the developing coding system.

It is helpful to distinguish between approaches to coding in ethnography and in grounded theory. In ethnography, coding is often oriented on generating "sensitizing concepts": Blumer (1970, p. 57) distinguishes between definitive and sensitizing concepts. Definitive concepts "refer precisely to what is common to a class of objects, by the aid of the clear definition of attributes or fixed bench marks." A sensitizing concept "gives the user a general sense of reference and guidelines in approaching empirical instances. Where definitive concepts provide prescriptions of what to see, sensitizing concepts merely suggest directions along which to look." Whereas the use of codes in qualitative content analysis is close to what Blumer defines as definitive concepts, the first steps in grounded theory research (open or initial coding) and the use of codes in ethnography are much closer to sensitizing concepts. Whereas coding in qualitative content analysis ideally is based on mutually exclusive categories, which allow one to code every excerpt of the data to only one category, in ethnography the process of coding is much more open:

> We code [the field notes] inclusively, that is to say, if we have any reasons to think that anything might go under the heading, we will put it in. We do not lose anything. We also code them in multiple categories, under anything that might be felt to be cogent. (Becker 1968, p. 245, quoted from Hammersley and Atkinson 2007, p. 153)

In general, coding is the work with materials for generating concepts and for allocating excerpts of the material to categories. This is then followed by interpretation: how we can understand and explain what the coding has revealed about the views in the field, their links among each other, their ties to context conditions, and the like.

What Is Sequential Analysis?

Coding procedures involve moving quite freely through and across the material—for example, for finding other or similar examples of a statement later in an interview or in a different interview. Sequential analysis, in contrast, requires the researcher to strictly follow the text to analyze its development from the beginning to the end. The aims of sequential analysis are to understand how meaning is built up in the development of the text or how the linguistic organization of a conversation proceeds and, also, how this contributes to the construction of the issues of the conversation. Most consistently, this principle is applied in objective hermeneutics and conversation analysis (see Chapter 27).

The principle of sequentiality means that the researchers refrain from using later parts of the text for understanding earlier parts. This means that, for example, you have to analyze the question before you can analyze and understand the answer in a dialogue. Let us suppose that the initial answer to this question is vague and that clarification is given some time later in the conversation: in sequential analysis you have to understand the answer in its vagueness, at the point in the conversation when it occurs, and not by using the clarification given for it in a later part of the dialogue. Because this vagueness is the problem, the other participant in the dialogue has to deal with this situation and has to refer to this vagueness in the next turn.

Coding, the use of concepts for the classification of statements, does not play a role here, except in the approach of social science hermeneutics (see also Chapter 27), into which concepts of open coding have been integrated. In general, the principle of sequentiality is linked to the question of how far we take the formal development of a text into account when we want to analyze its contents.

─ CASE STUDY 23.1 ─

Sequential Analysis

The following extract documents the beginning of a consultation, conducted by a social worker (B) with a client (K):

B: Hmm, well, your grandfather came to us (K_1: yes), huh, he seemed to be very worried about you?

K: Yeah, I was feeling quite bad

B: Yes, what was the matter at that time?

K: In May, (.) you know, I drank too much a couple of days in a series and then I was feeling soo bad, because of the circulation (B: hmm), well everything, what you-, break out of sweat (B: hmm) raving of the heart, uuuh, burning eyes and everything, anyhow, and I didn't feel like laughing at all

> B: And then your grandfather also said, uh, well (.) your family doctor had said, meanwhile you are in a very urgent danger of death. Do you have an urgent organic–
>
> K: Well, well, danger of death
>
> B: complaints?
>
> K: not really, ne? (B: hmm) There's just my fear, if I carry on that way, that still might come, (B: hmm) and that must not really happen, you know, I don't lay any stress on this (B: hmm) and therefore it's kind of a thing about drinking in my case.
>
> B: How did it begin?
>
> If we want to understand the specific aspects of this conversation, we have to work from the beginning to the end (of this excerpt). The social worker starts with a specific intervention, asking the client about something a third person (his grandfather: "he seemed to be very worried about you?") had said about him. The client tries to put this third-party information into perspective, but the social worker continues to clarify what third parties had said about the client ("your grandfather also said, uh, well (.) your family doctor had said, meanwhile you are in a very urgent danger of death"). Only then does the social worker turn to a usual start in consultation, exploring the client's view ("How did it begin?"). This deviation from the usual practice reveals some professional task or conflict for the social worker (Do I have to involve the physician in the team now?) and would not become evident if the analysis started right away by looking at the actual starter (How did it begin?). Sequential analysis means to strictly follow the sequence of contributions of the speakers in order to unfold how the meaning of issue is built up.

In summary, then, we can distinguish the following two basic strategies in working with texts. Coding the material has the aim of categorizing and/or theory development (see Chapter 25). The more or less strictly sequential analysis of the text aims at reconstructing the structure of the text and of the case. The latter strategy will be the topic of Chapter 27.

What Is Interpretation?

Interpretation is the core activity of qualitative data analysis for understanding or explaining what is in the data—whether explicitly mentioned or implicitly there to be elaborated. Coding is a preparatory step for accessing the data and making them ready for interpretation. Interpretation means to understand the internal logic of an excerpt of the data or to put it into context: for example, what has an interview statement about patients' needs to do with the fact that it comes from a male physician and not from a female nurse? As Willig holds:

> Interpretation is the challenge at the heart of qualitative research. Without interpretation, we cannot make sense of our data. As qualitative researchers, we aim to find out more

about people's experiences, their thoughts, feelings and social practices. To achieve this aim, we need to ask questions about their meaning and significance; we need to make connections between different components and aspects of the data in order to increase our understanding. In other words, we need to make the data meaningful through a process of interpretation. (2014b, p. 136)

The methods presented in the next chapters (and those methods of analysis presented in earlier chapters for specific forms of data, e.g., narratives) are alternative ways of accessing, understanding, dismantling, and reconstructing our data in a way that allows researchers to make sense of them and what their issue is.

Starting Points for Selecting an Approach for Qualitative Data Analysis

Sooner or later in qualitative research, texts become the basis of interpretative work and of inferences made from the empirical material as a whole. The starting point is the interpretative understanding of a text, namely, an interview, a narrative, an observation, as these may appear both in a transcribed form and in the form of other documents. In general, the aim is to understand and comprehend each case. However, different attention is paid to the reconstruction of the individual case. In content analysis, work is mainly in relation to categories rather than to cases. In a similar fashion, conversation analyses restrict their focus to the particular socio-linguistic phenomenon under study and dedicate their attention to collecting and analyzing instances of this phenomenon as opposed to attempting the analysis of complete cases.

In thematic coding (see Chapter 26), in the analysis of narrative interviews (see Chapter 18), and in objective hermeneutics (see Chapter 27), the focus is on conducting case studies. Only at a later stage does attention turn to comparing and contrasting cases. The understanding of the case in the different interpretative procedures can be located at various points in the range from a consequent idiographic approach to a quasi-nomothetic approach.

The first alternative takes the case *as* case and infers directly from the individual case (an excerpt of a conversation, a biography, or a subjective theory) to general structures or regularities. A particularly good example of this approach is objective hermeneutics and other related approaches of case reconstruction. In the second alternative, several examples are collected and—hence, "quasi-nomothetic"—the single statement is at least partly taken out of its context (the case or the process) and its specific structure in favor of the inherent general structure.

The procedures of text interpretation discussed in the preceding chapters may be appropriate to your own research question. As an orientation for a decision for or against a specific procedure, four points of reference can be identified. Each is outlined below.

Criteria-Based Comparison of Approaches

To gain an initial overview, the various alternatives for coding and sequential interpretation of texts may be compared using Table 23.1. You can then read about the approaches in greater detail for the purpose of deciding which one to use. The criteria I suggest for this comparison are as follows. The first is the degree to which precautions are taken in each method to guarantee sufficient openness to the specificity of the individual text with regard to both its formal aspects and its content. A second criterion is the degree to which precautions are taken to guarantee a sufficient level of structural and depth analysis in dealing with the text and the degree to which such structures are made explicit. Further criteria for a comparison are each method's contribution to developing the method of text interpretation in general and the main fields of application the methods were created for or are used in. The problems in applying each method and each method's limitations mentioned in the preceding chapters are again noted for each approach at the end. This display of the field of methodological alternatives of text interpretation allows the reader to locate the individual methods in it. The criteria used in Table 23.1 will be used again in the following chapters presenting the single methods in greater detail.

Appropriateness of the Method to the Issue

The interpretation of data is often the decisive factor in determining what statements you can make about the data and what conclusions you can draw from the empirical material. Here, as with other procedures in qualitative research, despite all the rhetoric surrounding certain approaches, no procedure is appropriate in every case. Procedures such as objective hermeneutics (see Chapter 27) were originally developed for the analysis of a specific domain of issues (interaction in families viewed from the perspective of socialization theory). Over time their field of application has been extended both in terms of materials used for analysis (interviews, images, art, TV programs, etc.) and in terms of issues and topics analyzed. Similarly, the approach of Strauss and Corbin (1998, see Chapter 25) is marked by a claim for more and more general applicability as made clear by the formulation of a very general "coding paradigm" (see Chapter 25).

Fitting the Method into the Research Process

Third, you should assess the method you choose for its compatibility with other aspects of the research process. Here you should clarify whether the procedure of interpreting data works well with the strategy of data collection you used. If, say, when conducting an interview, you paid great attention to the gestalt of the narrative in the interviewee's presentation, it would not make much sense to apply content analysis on the data in which only a few categories are used and which were defined in advance. Attempts to sequentially analyze field notes with objective hermeneutics have proved impractical and unfruitful. Similarly, it needs to be asked

TABLE 23.1 Comparison of Methods for the Interpretation of Data

Criteria	Grounded theory coding	Thematic coding	Qualitative content analysis	Conversation analysis	Discourse analysis	Objective hermeneutics	CAQDAS software
Openness to each text by:	Open coding	Principle of case analysis Short characterization of the case	Explicating content analysis	Sequential analysis of the "talk-in-interaction"	Reconstructing participants' versions	Sequential analysis of the case	Allowing open coding of material
Structuring (e.g., deepening) the issue by:	Axial coding Selective coding Basic questions Constant comparison	Elaboration of a thematic structure for case analysis Core and social distribution of perspectives	Summarizing content analysis Structuring content analysis	Comparative analysis of a collection of cases	Integration of other forms of texts	Group of interpreters Consulting context Falsification of hypotheses against the text	Supporting specific structures of categories (e.g., tree structures in NVivo)
Contribution to the general development of interpretation as a method	Combination of induction and deduction Combination of openness and structuring	Comparison of groups in relation to the issue after case analysis	Strongly rule-based procedure for reducing large amounts of data	Formal analysis of natural interaction shows how conversation and talk work	Reorientation of discourse analysis to contents and social science topics	Transgressing subjective perspectives Elaboration of a methodology of text interpretation	Making coding more explicit and documentation of coding
Domain of application	Theory building in all possible domains	Group comparisons	Large amounts of data from different domains	Formal analysis of everyday and institutional talk	Analysis of the contents of everyday and other discourses	All sorts of texts and images	All sorts of texts and images

Criteria	Grounded theory coding	Thematic coding	Qualitative content analysis	Conversation analysis	Discourse analysis	Objective hermeneutics	CAQDAS software
Problems in application	Fuzzy criteria for when to stop coding	Time-consuming due to case analysis as intermediate step	Applying the schematic rules often proves difficult	Limitation to formal order and to minimal sequences in conversations	Hardly developed genuine methodology	Transition from the single case to general statements	Compatibility with sequential methods
Limits of the method	Flexibility of methodological rules can be learned mainly through practical experience	Limited to studies to predefined comparative groups	Strongly oriented to quantitative methodology	Limited focus on social science-relevant contents	No concrete definition of the concept of discourse	Concept of structure Art instead of method	Not a method, only a tool Not enough for making an analysis explicit
References	Bryant and Charmaz (2007b) Strauss (1987) Thornberg and Charmaz (2014)	Flick (1994; 1995) Flick et al. (2003)	Mayring (2000; 2004) Schreier (2012; 2014)	Bergmann (2004b) Drew (1995) Toerien (2014)	Harré (1998) Potter and Wetherell (1998) Willig (2014a)	Reichertz (2004) Wernet (2014)	Gibbs (2007; 2014) www.surrey.ac.uk/ sociology/research/ researchcentres/ caqdas/

whether the method of interpreting data works well with the method of sampling the material (see Chapter 13). Also you should consider whether the theoretical framework of your study corresponds to the theoretical background of the interpretative method (see Chapters 7 and 8) and whether both understandings of the research process (see Chapter 10) correspond.

If the research process is conceptualized in the classical linear way, much is determined at the beginning of the interpretation—above all, which material was collected and how. In this case, you should answer the question of selecting and evaluating an interpretative procedure with regard to those parameters to which it should correspond. In a research process that is conceptualized in a more circular way, the method of interpretation may determine the decisions made about the procedure in the other steps. Here, the collection of data is oriented towards the sampling and the method towards the needs, which result from the type and the state of interpretation of data (see Chapter 10).

At this point, it is clear that you should make the evaluation of methodological alternatives and the decision between them with due consideration of the process of the research. Suggestions for answering these questions are provided by the paragraphs on fitting the individual method into the research process, and the research questions and the goals of the concrete empirical application.

CASE STUDY 23.2

Ways of Doing Qualitative Analysis

In their book, Wertz et al. (2011) take one interview and analyze it by five different methods (among them grounded theory (see Chapter 25), discourse analysis (see Chapter 26), and narrative research (see Chapter 18)). The book also provides some detailed comparisons of what pairs of methods produced as differences and similarities in analyzing the text. It also becomes evident that not only the procedure of how the text is analyzed, but also which aspects are put in the foreground vary across the five approaches. Thus we find "Constructing a grounded theory of loss and regaining a valued self" (Charmaz 2011) as the approach and result of the grounded theory approach. The discourse analysis of the same material focuses on "Enhancing oneself, diminishing others" (McMullen 2011). Thus this book provides an interesting insight into the differences and commonalities of various empirical approaches to the same transcript.

The Selection of the Method and Checking its Application

As with collecting data, not every method of interpretation is appropriate in each case. Your decision between the methodological alternatives discussed here should be grounded in your own study, its research question and aims, and in the data that you collected. You should review your decision against the material to be analyzed.

The evaluation of an interpretative method and the checking of its application should be done as early as possible in the process of interpretation—in the case of analyses, no later than after finishing the interpretation of the first case. A central feature of this evaluation is whether the procedure itself was applied correctly; for example, whether the principle of strict sequential interpretation was followed or whether the rules on content analysis were applied. The specific problems that the individual interpreter has with the attitude of interpretation demanded by the method should be taken into account. If any problems arise at this level, it makes sense that you, in a group of interpreters, reflect on them and the way you work with the text. If it is impossible to remedy the problems in this way, you should also consider changing the method.

Another point of reference for assessing the appropriateness of an interpretative procedure is the level at which you seek results. If you have to analyze large amounts of text with a view to ensuring that your results are representative on the basis of many interviews, approaches like objective hermeneutics may make the attainment of this goal more difficult or even obstruct it. Qualitative content analysis, which would be a more appropriate method for this type of analysis, is not recommended for deeper case analyses.

Checklist for Selecting a Method of Qualitative Data Analysis

Suggestions for deciding on a method of interpretation, and for checking the appropriateness of this decision are given in the checklist below:

1 *Research question*

Can the method of interpretation and its application address the essential aspects of the research question?

2 *Interpretative procedure*

Has the method been applied according to the methodological precautions and targets?
   Has jumping between forms of interpretation been avoided, except when this is based on the research question or theoretically?

3 *Interpreter*

Are the interpreters able to apply the type of interpretation?
   What is the effect of their personal fears and uncertainties in the situation?

4 *Text(s)*

Is the form of interpretation appropriate to the text or the texts?
   How is their structure, clarity, complexity, and so on taken into account?

5 *Form of data collection*

Does the form of interpretation fit the collected material and the method of data collection?

6 *Scope for the case*

Does the framework of the interpretation allow room for the case and its specificity?

How clearly can the distinctive features of the text emerge, using this framework of interpretation?

7 *Process of the interpretation*

Have the interpreters applied the form of interpretation correctly?

Have they left enough scope for the material?

Have they managed their roles successfully? (Why not?)

Was the way of handling the text clearly defined? (Why not?)

Analyze the breaks in order to validate the interpretation(s) between the first and second case if possible.

8 *Aim of the interpretation*

Are you looking for delimited and clear answers in their frequency and distribution, or for complex, multifold patterns or contexts?

Or do you want to develop a theory or distribution of viewpoints in social groups?

9 Claim for generalization

On what level do you wish to make statements:

- For the single cases (the interviewed individuals and their biographies, an institution, its impact, etc.)?
- Referring to groups (about a profession, a type of institution, etc.)?
- General statements?

If the applicability of approaches is extended like this, the criterion of appropriateness to the issue again needs to be taken into account. You should reflect on it in two respects: (1) to which issues is each method of interpretation appropriate; *and* (2) to which is it *not* appropriate? This reflection will help you to derive the concrete use of the method in a grounded way.

KEY POINTS

- None of the methods for analyzing data is the one and only method. Each of them has strengths and weaknesses in relation to your own study.
- You should carefully consider which method best fits your kind of data and your research question.
- Each method produces a specific structure through the way it enables you to work with the data.
- Before and while applying a specific method for answering your research question, assess whether the method you selected is appropriate.

---

1 Locate a study from the literature, based on analyzing textual material (e.g., Toerien and Kitzinger 2007). How appropriate was the method to (a) the issue under study and (b) the texts involved in the research?
2 For your own study, reflect on why you have chosen your specific method of data analysis.

—Further Reading—

Methods for Analyzing Texts in Qualitative Research

These resources will give you a comparative overview of analytic methods in qualitative research by presenting methods in more detail:

Flick, U. (2014b) "Mapping the Field", in U. Flick (ed.) *The SAGE Handbook of Qualitative Data Analysis*. London: Sage. pp. 3–18.

Flick, U., Kardorff, E.v. and Steinke, I. (eds.) (2004a) *A Companion to Qualitative Research*. London: SAGE (especially chapters 5.10–5.21).

Gibbs, G. (2007) *Analyzing Qualitative Data*. London: Sage.

Rapley, T. (2007) *Doing Conversation, Discourse and Document Analysis*. London: Sage.

Silverman, D. (1993/2001) *Interpreting Qualitative Data: Methods for Analyzing Talk, Text and Interaction* (2nd edn). London: Sage.

Strauss, A.L. (1987) *Qualitative Analysis for Social Scientists*. Cambridge: Cambridge University Press.

24
Transcription and Data Management

CHAPTER OBJECTIVES

This chapter is designed to help you

- understand the different ways of documenting observations;
- recognize the potential and pitfalls of transcription;
- distinguish the various ways in which the method of recording influences what is documented;
- see the necessity of data management—and the problems associated with it;
- understand the importance of this step in the research process.

The preceding chapters have detailed the main ways in which data are collected or produced. However, before you can analyze the data you may have generated in these ways, it needs to be documented and edited. In the case of interview data, an important part of this editing process is that you record the spoken words and then transcribe them. For observations, the most important task is that you document actions and interactions.

In both cases, a contextual enrichment of statements or activities should form a major part of the data collection. You can achieve this enrichment by documenting the process of data collection in context protocols, research diaries, or field notes (see Chapter 20). With these procedures, you transform the relations you study into texts, which are the basis for the actual analyses. And, finally, you need to develop a way of managing your data, so that you are able to find your interviews over time, but also to find excerpts in the data and, when you work with them, to retrace the context in which a statement or an observation was made.

This chapter discusses methodological alternatives for documenting collected data. The data you produce as a result of this process are substituted for the studied (psychological or social) relations so that you can proceed with the next stages of the research process (i.e., interpretation and generalization). The process of documenting the data comprises four steps: (1) recording the data; (2) editing the data (transcription); (3) constructing a "new" reality in and by the produced text; and (4) developing a systematic way of data management. All in all, this process plays an essential role in the construction of reality in the research process.

Technological Progress and Problems of Recording Data

The more sophisticated (acoustic and audio-visual) possibilities for recording events have had a telling influence on the renaissance of qualitative research over recent decades. One condition for this progress has been that the use of recording devices (tape, MP3, mini-disc, and video recorders) has become widespread in daily life itself as well. To some extent, their prevalence has made them lose their unfamiliarity for potential interviewees or for those people whose everyday lives are to be observed and recorded by their use. These technologies have made possible some forms of analyses such as conversation analysis and objective hermeneutics (see Chapter 27 for more details).

Acoustic and Visual Recordings of Natural Situations

The use of machines for recording renders the documentation of data independent of perspectives—those of the researcher as well as those of the subjects under study. It is argued that this achieves a naturalistic recording of events or a natural design: interviews, everyday talk, or counseling conversations are recorded on cassettes or videotape. After informing the participants about the purpose of the recording, the researcher hopes that they will simply forget about the tape recorder and that the conversation will take place "naturally"—even at awkward points.

Presence and Influence of the Recording

The hope of making a naturalistic recording is most likely to be fulfilled if you restrict the presence of the recording equipment. In order to get as close as possible to the naturalness of the situation, I recommend that you restrict the use of recording technology to the collection of data necessary to the research question and the theoretical framework. Where videotaping does not document anything essential beyond that obtained with an audio recording, you should prefer the less obtrusive machine. In any case, researchers should limit their recordings to what is absolutely necessary for their research question—in terms of both the amount of data that is recorded and the thoroughness of the recording.

In research about counseling, for example, you may ask counselors to record their conversations with clients using a voice recorder. In institutions where these kinds of recordings are continuously made for purposes of supervision, recording may have little influence on what is recorded. However, you should not ignore the fact that there may be some influence on the participants' statements. This influence is increased if the researchers are present in the research situation for technical reasons. The greater the effort in videotaping and the more comprehensive the insight it permits into the everyday life under study, the greater the possible skepticism and reservations on the part of participants in the study. This makes integration of the recording procedure in the daily life under study more complicated.

Skepticism about the Naturalness of Recordings

Correspondingly, you can find thoughtful reflections on the use of recording technology in qualitative research. These forms of recording have replaced the interviewers' or observers' notes, which were the dominant medium in earlier times. For Hopf, they provide "increased options for an inter-subjective assessment of interpretations … for taking into account interviewer and observer effects in the interpretation … and for theoretical flexibility" compared to "the necessarily more selective memory protocols" (1985, pp. 93–94). This flexibility leads "to a new type of 'qualitative data hoarding' owing to the delays in decisions about research questions and theoretical assumptions which are now possible."

Questions concerning research ethics, changes in the situations under study caused by the form of recording,[1] and a loss of anonymity for the interviewees arise here. With respect to research ethics, researchers should critically reflect on how much and how comprehensively they should audio and video record the situations they study. As participants are much more exposed and subject to identification and maybe misuse of their data by others, depending on how comprehensive and detailed the recording is, this also could develop into an issue for ethic committees. Thus, researchers should reflect on and give a detailed account of how they will record, document (and store) their data, and why they decided to do so.

Ambivalence over the technological options for recording qualitative data suggests that it is important to treat this point not as a problem of technical detail, but rather in the sense of a detailed "qualitative technology assessment." Also, you should include in your considerations about the appropriate method for documentation "out-of-date" alternatives such as field notes (see Chapter 20), which were displaced by the new technologies.

Research Diaries

There is a need for documentation of, and reflection on, the ongoing research process in order to increase the comparability of the empirical proceedings in the individual notes. This is especially the case if more than one researcher is involved.

One method of documentation is to use continually updated research diaries written by all participants. These should document the process of approaching a field, and the experiences and problems in the contact with the field or with interviewees and in applying the methods. Important facts and matters of minor importance or lost facts in the interpretation, generalization, assessment, or presentation of the results seen from the perspectives of the individual researcher should also be incorporated. Comparing such documentation and the different views expressed in them makes the research process more intersubjective and explicit.

Furthermore, diaries may be used as memos in the sense of Strauss (1987, in particular Ch. 5) for developing a grounded theory (see Chapter 25). Strauss recommends writing memos during the whole research process, which will contribute to the process of building a theory. Documentation of this kind not only is an end in itself or additional knowledge, but also serves in the reflection on the research process.

Several methods have been outlined for "catching" interesting events and processes, statements, and proceedings. In the noting of interventions in the everyday life under study, the researchers should be led in their decisions by the following *rule of economy*: record only as much as is definitely necessary for answering the research question. They should avoid any "technical presence" in the situation of the data collection that is not absolutely necessary for their theoretical interests. Reducing the presence of recording equipment and informing the research partners as much as possible about the sense and purpose of the chosen form of recording make it more likely that the researchers will truly "catch" everyday behavior in natural situations.

In the case of research questions where so-called "out-of-date" forms of documentation such as preparing a protocol of answers and observations are sufficient, I highly recommend using these forms. But you should produce these protocols as immediately and comprehensively as possible in order to mainly record impressions of the field and resulting questions.

Documentation Sheets

For interviews, I find it helpful to use sheets for documenting the context of data collection. What information they should include depends on the design of the study—for example, whether several interviewers are involved or interviews are conducted at changing locations (which might have influenced the interviews). In addition, the research questions determine what you should concretely note on these sheets. The example in Box 24.1 comes from my study of technological change in everyday life, in which several interviewers conducted interviews with professionals in different work situations on the influences of technology on childhood, children's education in one's own family or in general, and so on. The documentation sheet needed, therefore, to contain explicit additional contextual information.

BOX 24.1

Example of a Documentation Sheet

Information about the Interview and the Interviewee
Date of the interview:
Place of the interview:
Duration of the interview:
Interviewer:
Indicator for the interviewee:
Gender of the interviewee:
Age of the interviewee:
Occupation of the interviewee:
Working in this occupation since:
Professional field:
Where raised (countryside/city):
Number of children:
Age of the children:
Gender(s) of the children:
Special occurrences in the interview

....

....

....

....

....

Transcription

If data have been recorded using technical media, their transcription is a necessary step on the way to their interpretation. Several transcription systems are available which vary in their degree of exactness (for overviews see Kowall and O'Connell 2004; 2014).

How Exact and Comprehensive Has Transcription to Be?

A standard has not yet been established. In language analyses, interest often focuses on attaining the maximum exactness in classifying and presenting statements, breaks, and so on. Here you can also ask about the procedure's appropriateness. These standards of exactness contribute to the natural science ideals of precision in measurement and are imported into interpretive social science through the back door.

Also, the formulation of rules for transcription may tempt one into some kind of fetishism that no longer bears any reasonable relation to the question and the products of the research. Where linguistic and conversation analytic studies focus on the organization of language, this kind of exactness may be justified. For more psychological or sociological research questions, however, where linguistic exchange is a medium for studying certain contents, exaggerated standards of exactness in transcriptions are justified only in exceptional cases, when a strong linguistic focus is on the way things are said is essential for the research.

Transcription is often seen as a necessary and basic step in qualitative research. It is sometimes a tricky point, in particular if the research is pursued logically step by step and it is not exactly clear what to do with the transcripts later on, or how detailed the analysis will be on the level of how an interaction happened. If you do all your interviews first, then transcribe all the interviews and then start to analyze the material, it may be difficult to decide at which point the transcription is done, how exact and detailed it has to be. Here again it might be helpful to interlink the steps of the research in the beginning as suggested in Chapter 10 and also in Chapter 15: that is, to do the first interview, to do a first transcription of this interview, and to start with the analysis, and also to reflect on the kind of analysis you plan and apply that needs to be covered in the transcripts. The suggestion is to reflect on not only whether the interview worked as you expected, but also how appropriate the level of transcription is that you apply to your material. If you only collect the themes and who mentioned them from a focus group and are not interested in how the interaction (turn taking, interruptions, breaks and pauses) in the group went, the transcript could be limited to word protocols rather than very detailed transcripts.

It seems very reasonable to transcribe only as much as required by the research question, and exactly that (Strauss 1987). First, precise transcription of data absorbs time and energy, which could be invested more reasonably in interpreting the data instead. Second, the message and the meaning of what was transcribed are sometimes concealed rather than revealed in the differentiation of the transcription and the resulting obscurity of the protocols produced. Thus Bruce (1992, p. 145, quoted in O'Connell and Kowall 1995, p. 96) holds:

> The following very general criteria can be used as a starting point in the evaluation of a transcription system for spoken discourse: manageability (for the transcriber), readability, learnability, and interpretability (for the analyst and for the computer). It is reasonable to think that a transcription system should be easy to write, easy to read, easy to learn, and easy to search.

Beyond the clear rules of how to transcribe statements, namely, turn taking, breaks, ends of sentences, and so on, a second check of the transcript against the recording and the anonymization of data (names, local, and temporal references) are central features of the procedure of transcription. Transcription in conversation analysis (see Chapter 27) has often been the model for transcriptions in social science. Drew

(1995, p. 78) gives a "glossary of transcription conventions," which may be used after the criteria with regard to the research question mentioned above have been applied (Box 24.2).

─BOX 24.2─

Transcription Conventions

Overlapping speech: the precise point at which one person begins speaking while the other is still talking, or at which both begin speaking simultaneously, resulting in overlapping speech.

(0.2) Pauses: within and between speaker turns, in seconds.

"Aw:::": Extended sounds: sound stretches shown by colons, in proportion to the length of the stretch.

<u>Word</u>: Underlining shows stress or emphasis.

"<u>fishi</u>-": A hyphen indicates that a word/sound is broken off.

".hhhh": Audible intakes of breath are transcribed as ".hhhh" (the number of h's is proportional to the length of the breath).

WORD: Increase in amplitude is shown by capital letters.

(words...): Brackets bound uncertain transcription, including the transcriber's "best guess."

Source: Adapted from Drew (1995, p. 78)

A second version of transcribing interviews is shown in Box 24.3. I suggest using line numbers for the transcript and leaving enough space in the left and right margins for notes.

─BOX 24.3─

Rules for Transcription

Layout

Word processing	WORD
Font	Times New Roman 12
Margin	Left 2, right 5
Line numbers	5, 10, 15, etc., every page starts again
Lines	1,5

Page numbers	On top, right
Interviewer:	I: Interviewer
Interviewee:	IP: Interviewee

Transcription

Spelling	Conventional
Interpunctuation	Conventional
Breaks	Short break *; more than 1 sec *no of seconds*
Incomprehensible	((incomp))
Uncertain transcription	(abc)
Loud	With Commentary
Low	With Commentary
Emphasis	With Commentary
Break off word	Abc-
Break off sentence	Abc-
Simultaneous talk	#abc#
Paralinguistic utterance	With Commentary (e.g., sighs ...)
Commentary	With Commentary
Verbal quote	Conventional
Abbreviations	Conventional
Anonymization	Names with°

If you use these suggestions for transcribing your interviews, transcripts like the one in Box 24.4 should result.

BOX 24.4

Example from a Transcript

1 I: Yeah the first question is, what is this for you, health? ((telephone rings)) Do you want to pick it up first?
   N: No.
   I: No? Okay.

(Continued)

(Continued)

> 5 N: Health is relative, I think. Someone can be healthy, too, who is old and has a
> handicap and can feel healthy nevertheless. Well, in earlier times, before I came
> to work in the community, I always said, "someone is healthy if he lives in a very
> well ordered household, where everything is correct and super exact, and I would
> 10 like to say, absolutely clean". But I learnt better, when I started to work in the
> community (...). I was a nurse in the NAME OF THE HOSPITAL-1 before that, in
> intensive care and arrived here with ...
>
> I = Interviewer; N = Nurse

In qualitative online research with interviews and focus groups (see Chapters 16 and 17), the answers, statements, or narratives in interviews or focus groups come in written and electronic formats, so you can skip the step of transcription here.

Reality as Text: Text as New Reality

Recording the data, making additional notes, and transcribing the recordings transform the interesting realities into text. At the very least, the documentation of processes and the transcription of statements lead to a different version of events. Each form of documentation leads to a specific organization of what is documented. Every transcription of social realities is subject to technical conditions and limitations and produces a specific structure on the textual level, which makes accessible what was transcribed in a specific way. The documentation detaches the events from their transience. The researcher's personal style of noting things makes the field a presented field; the degree of the transcription's exactness dissolves the gestalt of the events into a multitude of specific details. The consequence of the following process of interpretation is that:

> Reality only presents itself to the scientist in substantiated form, as text – or in technical terms – as protocol. Beyond texts, science has lost its rights, because a scientific statement can only be formulated when and insofar as events have found a deposit or left a trace and these again have undergone an interpretation. (Garz and Kraimer 1994, p. 8)

This substantiation of reality in the form of texts is valid in two respects: as a process that allows access to a field; and, as a result of this process, as a reconstruction of the reality, which has been transformed into texts. The construction of a new reality in the text has already begun at the level of the field notes and at the level of the transcript and this is the only (version of) reality available to the researchers during their following interpretations. These constructions should be taken into account in the more or less meticulous handling of the text, which is suggested by each method of interpretation.

The more or less comprehensive recording of the case, the documentation of the context of origination, and the transcription all organize the material in a specific way. Coming back to the features of qualitative research as mentioned in Chapter 7, the epistemological principle of understanding may be more easily applied by being able to analyze as far as possible the presentations or the proceeding of situations according to their internal logic. How does the situation under study develop step by step? Therefore, the documentation has to be exact enough to reveal structures in those materials and it has to permit approaches from different perspectives. The organization of the data has the main aim of documenting the case in its specificity and structure. This allows the researcher to reconstruct it holistically and also to analyze it and reveal its structure—that is, the rules according to which it functions, the meaning underlying it, the parts that characterize it. Texts produced in this manner construct the studied reality in a specific way and make it accessible as empirical material for interpretative procedures.

Data Management

Data management comprises a number of practical issues, which have some ethical implications as well.

Indexing Data

First you will need a storage system for your transcripts. For example, when conducting a study with several interviewees, it would be wise to store each transcript with an indicator, for example, IP-1 for the first, IP-2 for the second, and so on. If you do repeated interviews with the same interviewees, I suggest using IP-1-1 for the first interview of interviewee number 1, IP-1-2 for the second interview with this person, IP-2-1 and IP-2-2 for the next interviewee, and so on. I would suggest using these indicators both for labeling the files in which you store the transcripts and in the header of the transcripts (indicated on every page). I also suggest producing transcripts with line numbers, indented as in Box 24.4 and with broad margins, so that you can note comments on the printed transcripts.

For ethical reasons, I recommend developing a system of nicknames for anonymization of the interviewee and other persons mentioned in the interviews and for names of institutions, enterprises, and so on. Sometimes it is even better to use an alphabetic list for labeling the interviewees. Anonymization is essential for confidentiality, but it is often not sufficient to guarantee confidentiality. It is also important that not too much information about the features and context of an anonymized person is kept together, which would allow (re)identification of the person. In video recordings as documentations (and in excerpts from them), it may be necessary to make faces unidentifiable (also of individuals in the background) or to avoid recognition of people due to uncovered context information (in the room, for example). Confidentiality also requires managing data in such a way that the risk of any, possibly unintended, identification of a participant is treated in a very reflective way by all involved in the research.

If you have someone do the transcription for you, you must find a way to guarantee that the transcribers do not use the information from the interviews (about the people or institutions involved) for any other purpose. It would be best to set up a data protection contract with them. You should store interview transcripts and recordings (and also field notes) in a safe place (password-protected files on computers, locked cabinets for printed transcripts). If you keep a list which allows you to re-identify anonymized persons, you should keep it separate from the transcripts, recordings, and interpretations of the materials. If you copy excerpts from a transcript into a category file or into a text you write during or about your interpretation, always copy information for relocating the excerpt with it (indicator of the interview, line numbers, page number if necessary).

In larger data sets with many interviews, for example, it can be very helpful to use CAQDAS programs for data management (see Chapter 28), even if you do your analysis later without this software. What has been said so far about interview data management should be applied in a similar way to field notes and observations (see Chapter 20), to audio and audio-visual recordings of group discussions or of conversations, and also to documents used for research (see Chapter 22).

Finally, data management includes ways of developing an overview and keeping tack of bigger data sets (e.g., a number of interviews and interviewees). One way here is global analysis (discussed below): other ways are described in the context of thematic coding (see Chapter 26).

Global Analysis

A pragmatically oriented supplement to other analytic procedures (mainly theoretical coding or qualitative content analysis) is provided by the global analysis suggested by Legewie (1994). Here, the aim is to obtain an overview of the thematic range of the text which is to be analyzed.

Clarification of one's own background knowledge and of the research question, which is applied to the text, is recommended as a preparatory step. When reading through the text, keywords are noted alongside the transcript and a structuring of the large passages of the text is produced. The next step refines this structure by marking central concepts or statements, and information about the communicative situation in the generation of each text is identified. Ideas are noted while reading the text.

This is followed by the production of the text's table of contents, which includes the structuring keywords noted previously with the numbers of the lines to which they refer. Themes (again with the line numbers) are ordered alphabetically and finally the ideas noted in the different steps are collected in a list.

The next step of the global analysis is to summarize the text and to evaluate whether to include it in the actual interpretation or not. The basis for this decision is the viewpoints of the participants. You should look for indicators that the reported facts are true, complete, and that the way of reporting them is appropriate to the communicative situation of the interview. Next, look for indicators for things left out, biased, or distorted in the interview.

The final step is to note keywords for the entire text and formulate the consequences for working with the material or for selecting or integrating further texts, cases, and information according to theoretical sampling.

This form of editing texts before their actual interpretation may be helpful for your initial orientation to the text. It is also useful for deciding whether it is worth choosing a certain interview over another one for a detailed interpretation, if the resources (e.g., of time) are limited. Combined with similar pragmatically oriented analytic procedures of qualitative content analysis, it may give you an overview of the material. In theoretical coding, this method may facilitate the finding and assignment of further passages, especially for later steps of axial and selective coding.

This method can supplement categorizing methods, but cannot replace them. Procedures like objective hermeneutics or conversation analysis, which aim at a sequential disclosure of the text (see Chapter 27), will not be compatible with this form of editing the material.

Checklist for Transcription and Data Management

This checklist gives you an orientation about how to plan transcription and data management for your study:

1 What aspects or features are important to document in transcripts as the data in your research?
2 How detailed does your transcription need to be in order to achieve your research purposes?
3 When does your transcription become over-detailed and too time-consuming?
4 Have you developed a system of managing and retrieving your data (excepts) that is adequate for your research questions?
5 Have you taken issues of anonymization into account in your ways of data management?
6 Have you developed a system indexing your data so that you can easily navigate through them?

KEY POINTS

- The documentation of data is not merely a technical step in the research process: it also influences the quality of the data that can be used for interpretations.
- Recording technologies have changed the possibilities of documentation and also the characteristics of qualitative data.
- Though transcription is an important step in the analysis of data, the concern (sometimes excessive) with exactness should not predominate.
- Field notes and research diaries can provide precious information about the experiences in research.
- In management of data, scale is a practical issue.
- Ethical issues pertain to all forms of data management.

─Exercise 24.1───

1 Record some interactions with a voice recorder and transcribe one or two pages from this recording. Then compare the recording to the written text to see how adequately the transcription represents what was said and how.

─Further Reading───

The second and third texts listed below give overviews and some critical reflections of transcription, while the first text links it more generally to data analysis.

Gibbs, G. (2007) *Analyzing Qualitative Data*. London: Sage.

Kowall, S. and O'Connell, D.C. (2004) "Transcribing Conversations," in U. Flick, E.v. Kardorff and I. Steinke (eds.), *A Companion to Qualitative Research*. London: Sage. pp. 248–252.

Kowall, S. and O'Connell, D.C. (2014) "Transcription as a Crucial Step of Data Analysis," in U. Flick (ed.), *The SAGE Handbook of Qualitative Data Analysis*. London: Sage. pp. 64–78.

More information about transcribing verbal or audio data can be found at: http://www.audiotranskription.de/english

More information about transcribing video data can be found at: http://www.feldpartitur.de/en/

─ Note ──

1 According to Bergmann, "an audiovisual recording of a social event is by no means the purely descriptive representation which it may seem to be at first. Owing to its time-manipulative structure it has rather a constructive moment in it" (1985, p. 317). Thus, after its recording, a conversation can be cut off from its unique, self-contained temporal course and monitored over and over again. Then it may be dissected into specific components (e.g., participants' non-verbal signals) in a way that goes beyond the everyday perceptions of the participants. This not only allows new forms of knowledge, but also constructs a new version of the events. From a certain moment, the perception of these events is no longer determined by their original or natural occurrence, but rather by their artificially detailed display.

25
Grounded Theory Coding

┌─ CHAPTER OBJECTIVES ───┐

This chapter is designed to help you

- develop an overview of one major approach of coding in qualitative data analysis;
- understand the various ways of doing grounded theory coding;
- appreciate the importance of integrating the key elements of the approach in your research;
- see how you may profit from applying grounded theory coding to other forms of qualitative data analysis.
└──┘

Grounded Theory Methodology

Grounded theory *methodology* is relevant for qualitative data analysis in several ways. It has provided several tools for doing qualitative analysis, which can be used also in other contexts—like the specific conceptualization of coding data and materials, which will be the focus of this chapter. However, these concepts of data analysis have been developed as part of an integrated conception of how to do qualitative research, which includes a specific conceptualization for the research process (see Chapter 10) and for the sampling of materials (see Chapter 13). Although grounded theory coding can be applied in other contexts, it will reveal its potential most fully when used in an integrated manner. Thus we will briefly outline the methodological context of the coding procedures presented in detail later on.

The key components of the original version of grounded theory outlined by Glaser and Strauss (1967) are summarized by Hood (2007; see Box 25.1).

BOX 25.1

Key Components of Grounded Theory

1 A spiral of cycles of data collection, coding, analysis, writing, design, theoretical categorization, and data collection.
2 The constant comparative analysis of cases with each other and to *theoretical categories* throughout each cycle.
3 *A theoretical sampling process based upon categories developed from ongoing data analysis.*
4 The size of sample is determined by the "*theoretical saturation*" of categories rather than by the need for demographic "representativeness", or simply lack of "additional information" from new cases.
5 The resulting theory is developed inductively from data rather than tested by data, although the developing theory is continuously refined and checked by data.
6 Codes "*emerge*" from data and are not imposed *a priori* upon it.
7 The substantive and/or formal theory outlined in the final report takes into account all the variations in the data and conditions associated with these variations. The report is an *analytical product rather than a purely descriptive account. Theory development is the goal.* (Hood 2007, p. 154, original italics)

Over the years, grounded theory methodology has proliferated in a number of textbooks (e.g., Charmaz 2006; Glaser 1978; Glaser and Strauss 1967; Strauss 1987; Strauss and Corbin 1990). Each of these books takes different starting points and takes different approaches to grounded theory or elements in this methodology. New protagonists have entered the field—like Juliet Corbin or Kathy Charmaz. Glaser (1992) has taken different stances and criticized the writings of Strauss and Corbin (1990). Charmaz and others have taken a more constructionist approach to grounded theory research. This includes reservations about the idea of discovering a theory in the field and the data and about aiming at constructing theories that are grounded in the field and the data. The role of "data" in the process has been discussed as well. Despite the further development, proliferation, and debates in the field over 40 years, Bryant and Charmaz (2007b, p. 12) and Wiener (2007) define the following aspects as integral for using grounded theory *methodology*:

- data gathering, analysis and construction proceed concurrently;
- coding starts with the first interview and/or field notes;
- memo writing also begins with the first interview and/or field notes;
- theoretical sampling is the disciplined search for patterns and variations;
- theoretical sorting of memos sets up the outline for writing the paper;
- theoretical saturation is the judgment that there is no need to collect further data;
- identify a basic social process that accounts for most of the observed behavior.

In this chapter, I seek to give a brief summary of doing grounded theory in a step-by-step perspective and to spell out these integral aspects in some more detail.

Key Steps Towards Grounded Theory Analysis

Finding a Relevant Problem: Discovering or Constructing it

There can be several starting points for a grounded theory study, as in other types of research. Charmaz (2006) gives examples in which the researchers' curiosity led them into taking something as a research problem for developing a grounded theory—for example, how the process of recovering from addiction works without treatment. A second motivation can be a personal experience or concern, as in the example of Glaser and Strauss (1965a) when the researchers' experience with how their parents' dying was "managed" in hospitals made them study this process (see Chapter 10, Case Study 10.1). A third point of departure can be based on gaps in the state of a scientific field—research questions resulting from earlier research, the lack of theoretical models, theories, or explanations for a certain problem. A fourth reason for a grounded theory study can be the emergence of a new phenomenon or the discovery of a new problem—for instance, a new kind of chronic illness may suggest a study of the experience of people concerned with it. Or the relevance of a certain context (e.g., homelessness) for living with traditional forms of chronic illness is identified as a research problem. In all these cases, researchers take a decision on what they want to study.

This process of identification gives the issue a specific shape—certain aspects are more interesting, others are less prominent. Identifying an issue as a topic for a grounded theory study entails a decision on a research perspective, aiming at developing a new theory, where so far a lack of theoretical knowledge exists. It also includes designing the problem in such a way that it is worth studying from a theory development perspective and then constructing a phenomenon as a specific research issue. It finally includes developing a research question (which aspects will be studied first or mainly etc.). Although the initial research question can be revised and although the researcher might find out along the way what the most important aspects of an issue under study are, any grounded theory study should start with making a research question explicit.

If we take these aspects of identifying an issue for research and of giving it a specific shape, it becomes clear that issues are not something just discovered but are constructed in a specific way.

Getting Started: Using Sensitizing Concepts and Finding Relevant Situations, People, or Events

A good starting point is to use sensitizing concepts. These are concepts that give the researcher a "general sense of references and guidance in approaching empirical instances ... suggest directions along which to look ... and rest on a general sense of what is relevant" (Blumer 1970, p. 58). They can be helpful as heuristic devices for giving researchers an orientation. Concepts such as "trust," "identity," and the like can be starting points for identifying relevant problems and first conceptualizations in a field. Once you have identified a specific problem, for which a lack of empirical analysis and theoretical explanation can be noted, the next step will be to find contexts in which you can begin to study it.

An example used elsewhere in this book (see Case Study 20.4) may illustrate this. Chronic illness for homeless adolescents is an issue which is not very well analyzed empirically or theoretically. In our study concerning the health practices of adolescents living on the streets in Germany (see Flick and Röhnsch 2007), we came across several cases of adolescents reporting a more or less severe chronic illness, which led to our starting a project on this issue. The next question is where to find people in this situation more systematically: where would you meet potential participants for such a story, what kind of chronic illness would be most instructive as a starting point for developing a first understanding of this phenomenon, etc.? In this phase of the research, the identification of participants and contexts to begin with is not a question of sampling, but rather a question of discovery, exploration, creativity, and imagination. Sometimes it is necessary to ask experts, professionals, or colleagues for their suggestions about where to take up your research. Once you have found this first case or first material, you should immediately begin to analyze it to advance your understanding of your issue.

Collecting or Producing Relevant Data

Grounded theory methodology (the literature) places a strong focus on two "steps": sampling and analyzing data. There is less emphasis on how to turn phenomena into data in the process, which means that there is less extensive advice on how to arrive at data to analyze once the fields or cases have been selected according to theoretical sampling. First of all, we find general statements like "All is data" (Glaser 2002). Looking at textbooks of grounded theory gives the impression that explicit methods of data collection are less covered than how to analyze them. Then we find a sometimes harsh debate about the status of data (collection) in the process of developing a grounded theory. This debate oscillates between the notion that data emerge in the field (Glaser), that data are collected by using specific methods (Strauss 1987), and the idea that data are constructed or produced by the researcher in the field (see Charmaz 2006). Beyond the epistemological differences in these notions, it seems obvious that researchers use methods for arriving at data. Grounded theory methodology is not linked to a preferable method for collecting or producing data.

However, the whole concept of the research process (see Chapter 10) has been developed in projects based on participant observation (see Chapter 20), including more or less formalized conversations or interviews with members of the field (see Case Study 10.1). This research strategy is based on repeated field contacts and allows returning to the field to collect more data and to adapt data collection to the needs and questions resulting from the analysis of the data so far. Interview studies are in most cases based on meeting the interviewee once and often rely on an interview schedule for all interviewees.

If you want to make the most out of using grounded theory methodology, you should consider a strategy that can accommodate several forms of data (as in observation or in ethnography) rather than expecting to do only a limited number of interviews. Furthermore, the epistemological debates mentioned above should not confuse you in your access to data: data do not emerge from a field and not everything *is* data. But you can use almost everything as data—whatever is helpful for understanding the process and the field you are interested in and to answer your research questions. Then you can use different sorts of phenomena and materials and turn them into data. And you can use different methods to collect and document such materials as data. Whatever method you use in this step will influence what you see as data and how phenomena and materials appear as data. Thus, as in other kinds of research, the use of certain methods will produce data, which you can use for constructing a theory that is grounded in these data.

Grounded Theory Analysis

Memoing: Producing Evidence through Writing

"Memo writing is essential to Grounded Theory methodological practices and principles" (Lempert 2007, p. 245). This statement highlights the central role of writing in the process of theory development. However, most theorists of grounded theory methodology locate memo writing basically in the step of analyzing the data, as Lempert holds: "Memos are not intended to describe the social worlds of the researcher's data, instead they *conceptualize* the data in narrative form" (p. 245). Memo writing can include references to the literature and diagrams for linking, structuring, and contextualizing concepts. They may also incorporate quotes from respondents in interviews or field conversations as further evidence in the analysis.

Memoing is not a standardized procedure but depends on the personal style of the researcher. However, it can be seen as a learned skill. Lempert sees four fundamental principles in memo writing. The intention is the discovery (1) and development of theory rather than application and confirmation. A major step in analyzing any sort of raw data is memo writing and diagramming of concepts (2), both of which help to shape the further collection and analysis of data (3). Memos are written, reread, and rewritten (4) in order to advance to more abstract levels of theorizing (2007, p. 262).

Memo writing helps to make the analysis more explicit and transparent for the researcher, other people in the team, and if used as part of a publication, for readers of the research and its results. However, a consistent use of memoing should go beyond this restriction to analyzing data. Your research will benefit a lot if you start memo writing right away by writing a research diary throughout the process. Writing field notes should complement this once you get in touch with your empirical area and the members of your field. If you do interviews, you should write an extended context protocol including your impressions, descriptions of the setting in which you did an interview, circumstances and intriguing events in relation to the field and the interviewee. This protocol complements the recording and transcription of what has been said in the interview. In general, try to make notes throughout the process of your research. Richardson (1994, p. 527) distinguishes four categories of notes helpful for documenting and reflecting on the process of research:

- Observation notes to cover perceptions in the field.
- Methodological notes about how methods are applied and how to frame that situation.
- Theoretical notes in the sense of what grounded theory researchers describe as memos.
- Personal notes in the sense of a research diary or journal.

This extension of memoing will make evident how your research advanced and how you produced evidence that allowed construction of your theory in the process.

Analysis through Coding

The central process in grounded theory research is coding the data. Different from other concepts of coding (which see the allocation of material to existing categories as coding), here the process of developing codes, categories, and concepts is seen as coding. As coding is so central to the process of grounded theory, it is not surprising that the controversies about the right way of doing grounded theory research focused on the way of coding and what that means for openness to material, data, and phenomena. Glaser (1992) criticizes Strauss and Corbin (1990) for forcing their categories upon the material and for obstructing the process of emergence rather than supporting it by their way of coding. Charmaz (2006) questions this understanding of categories as emerging. She sees the whole process, including the step of coding, as a way of constructing grounded theories rather than discovering them. This again produced harsh reactions from Glaser.

Thus researchers sometimes find that using grounded theory as a tool for studying their issue and field can result in confusion. This can be dealt with in various ways: either you adopt one of the perspectives and apply a Glaserian, Straussian, or Charmazian version of grounded theory methodology in your research and ignore the other versions; or you follow the eclectic way and pick those concepts and procedures from each of the approaches, which look most instructive for your research. Finally, you could try to see the common core of methodological approach in the different versions of grounded theory methodology and see the differences in the detail more as alternative ways of how to proceed depending on your research question.

If we want to outline the common core of this methodological approach in the various versions of grounded theory methodology, the following account provides common ground for analyzing data in grounded theory research. Coding means developing categories, properties, and relations between them. Coding is a process which includes at least three steps (or ways of coding) with different aims. The starting point is always open coding, sometimes called initial coding (e.g., by Charmaz). Later, some form of more structured coding is included. The ways of how to structure this coding can vary between the approaches. This step is discussed as "theoretical coding" (by Glaser), as "axial coding" (by Strauss and Corbin), or as "focused coding" (by Charmaz). Selective coding is the final step (although Glaser (1978) has presented it as a step prior to theoretical coding), which means that data are scanned for more evidence for core categories. Coding aims at identifying structures in the material. These structures are described as "core categories" (by Strauss), as "basic social processes" (by Glaser), or as "story lines" (by Strauss and Corbin). The different ways of coding should not be seen in a strictly sequential (one-after-the-other) logic. Rather the researcher will return to open coding if the other forms of coding raise questions that can only be answered by developing new categories. The endpoint of coding is reached when continuing coding does not lead to new theoretical insights. This situation is referred to as "theoretical saturation."

Grounded Theory Coding: Ways and Versions

Grounded theory coding (Charmaz (2006) uses this generic term for covering the different approaches) is the procedure for analyzing data that have been collected in order to develop a grounded theory. This procedure was introduced by Glaser and Strauss (1967) and further elaborated by Glaser (1978), Strauss (1987), and Strauss and Corbin (1990) or Charmaz (2006). As already mentioned, in this approach the interpretation of data cannot be regarded independently of their collection or the sampling of the material. Interpretation is the anchoring point for making decisions about which data or cases to integrate next in the analysis and how or with which methods they should be collected. In the years since the publication of the first introductory text by Glaser and Strauss (1967), proliferation of the approaches in the field has led to debates and distinctions about the right way to do grounded theory coding. Therefore it makes sense to briefly outline some of the different versions that exist in how coding proceeds.

Strauss and Corbin's Approach to Coding

In the process of interpretation, as Strauss (1987) and Strauss and Corbin (1990) characterize it, a number of "procedures" for working with text can be differentiated. They are termed "open coding," "axial coding," and "selective coding." You should see these procedures neither as clearly distinguishable procedures nor as temporally separated phases in the process. Rather, they are different ways of handling textual material between which the researchers move back and forth if necessary and which they combine. But the process of interpretation begins with open coding, whereas towards the end of the whole analytical process, selective coding comes more to the fore. Coding here is understood as representing the operations by which data are broken down, conceptualized, and put back together in new ways. It is the central process by which theories are built from data (Strauss and Corbin 1990, p. 3).

According to this understanding, coding includes the constant comparison of phenomena, cases, concepts, and so on, and the formulation of questions that are addressed to the text. Starting from the data, the process of coding leads to the development of theories through a process of abstraction. Concepts or codes are attached to the empirical material. They are formulated first as closely as possible to the text, and later more and more abstractly. Categorizing in this procedure refers to the summary of such concepts into *generic concepts* and to the elaboration of the relations between concepts and generic concepts or categories and superior concepts. The development of theory involves the formulation of *networks* of categories or concepts and the relations between them. Relations may be elaborated between superior and inferior categories (hierarchically) but also between concepts at the same level. During the whole process, impressions, associations, questions, ideas, and so on are noted in *memos*, which complement and explain the codes that were found.

Open Coding

This first step aims at expressing data and phenomena in the form of concepts. For this purpose, data are first disentangled ("segmented"). Units of meaning classify expressions (single words, short sequences of words) in order to attach annotations and "concepts" (codes) to them. In Box 25.2, you will find an example in which a subjective definition of health and the first codes attached to this piece of text are presented. This example should clarify this procedure. A slash separates two sections in the interview passage from each other and each superscript number indicates a section. The notes for each section are then presented: in some cases these led to the formulation of codes and in other cases they were abandoned in the further proceedings as being less suitable.

BOX 25.2

Example of Segmentation and Open Coding

This example comes from one of my projects about the health concepts of lay people. It demonstrates how one of the analysts applied the segmentation of a passage in one of the interviews in the context of open coding in order to develop codes. In this process, the analyst explored a number of associations more or less helpful or close to the original passage:

Well-1[1]/link[2]/personally[3]/to health[4]/: the complete functionality[5]/of the human organism[6]/all[7]/the biochemical processes[8] of the organism[9]/included in this[10]/all cycles[11]/but also[12]/the mental state[13]/of my person[14]/and of Man in general[15]/.

First associations on the way to codes

01 Starting shot, introduction.

02 Making connections.

03 Interviewee emphasizes the reference to himself, delimiting from others, local commonplace. He does not need to search first.

04 See 2, taking up the question.

05 Technical, learned, textbook expression, model of the machine, norm orientation, thinking in norms, normative claim (someone who does not fully function is ill).

Codes: functionality, normative claim

06 Distancing, general, contradiction to the introduction (announcement of a personal idea), textbook, reference to Man, but as a machine.

Code: mechanistic image of Man

07 Associations to "all": referring to a complete, comprehensive, maximal understanding of health; …; however, "all" does not include much differentiation.

08 Prison, closed system, there is something outside, passive, other directed, possibly an own dynamic of the included.

09 See 06.

10 Textbook category.

11 Comprehensive; model of the machine, circle of rules, procedure according to rules, opposite to chaos.

Code: mechanistic–somatic idea of health

12 Complement, new aspect opposite to what was said before, two (or more) different things belonging to the concept of health.

Code: multidimensionality

13 Static ("what is his state?"); mechanistic concept of human being ("state"), ….

14 Mentions something personal, produces a distance again immediately, talks very neutrally about what concerns him, defense against too much proximity to the female interviewer and to himself.

Code: wavering between personal and general level

15 General, abstract image of Man, norm orientedness, singularity easier to overlook.

Code: distance

This procedure cannot be applied to the whole text of an interview or an observation protocol. Rather, it is used for particularly instructive or perhaps extremely unclear passages. Often the beginning of a text is the starting point. This procedure serves to elaborate a deeper understanding of the text. Sometimes dozens of codes result from open coding (Strauss and Corbin 1990, p. 113). The next step in the procedure is to categorize these codes by grouping them around phenomena discovered in the data, which are particularly relevant to the research question. The resulting categories are again linked to codes, which are now more abstract than those used in the first step. Codes now should represent the content of a category in a striking way and above all should offer an aid to remembering the reference of the category. Possible sources for labeling codes are concepts borrowed from the social science literature (*constructed* codes) or taken from interviewees' expressions (*in vivo* codes). Of the two types of codes, the latter are preferred because they are closer to the studied material. The categories found in this way are then further developed. To this end the properties belonging to a category are labeled and dimensionalized (i.e., located along a continuum in order to define the category more precisely regarding its content):

> To explain more precisely what we mean by properties and dimensions, we provided another example using the concept of "color". Its properties include shade, intensity, hue, and so on. Each of these properties can be dimensionalized. Thus, color can vary in shade from dark to light, in intensity from high to low, and in hue from bright to dull. Shade, intensity, and hue are what might be called general properties. (1990, pp. 117–118)

Open coding may be applied in various degrees of detail. A text can be coded line by line, sentence by sentence, or paragraph by paragraph, or a code can be linked to whole texts (a protocol, a case, etc.). Which of these alternatives you should apply will depend on your research question, on your material, on your personal style as analyst, and on the stage that your research has reached. It is important not to lose touch with the aims of coding. The main goal is to break down and understand a text and to attach and develop categories and put them into an order in the course of time. Open coding aims at developing substantial codes describing, naming, or classifying the phenomenon under study or a certain aspect of it. Strauss and Corbin summarize open coding as follows:

> Concepts are the basic building blocks of theory. Open coding in grounded theory method is the analytic process by which concepts are identified and developed in terms of their properties and dimensions. The basic analytic procedures by which this is accomplished are: the asking of questions about the data; and the making of comparisons for similarities and differences between each incident, event and other instances of phenomena. Similar events and incidents are labelled and grouped to form categories. (1990, p. 74)

The result of open coding should be a list of the codes and categories attached to the text. This should be complemented by the code notes that were produced for explaining and defining the content of codes and categories, and a multitude of memos, which contain striking observations on the material and thoughts that are relevant to the development of the theory.

For both open coding and the other coding strategies it is suggested that the researchers regularly address the text with the following list of so-called basic questions:

1 *What?* What is the issue here? Which phenomenon is mentioned?
2 *Who?* Which persons/actors are involved? What roles do they play? How do they interact?
3 *How?* Which aspects of the phenomenon are mentioned (or not mentioned)?
4 *When?* How long? Where? Time, course, and location.
5 *How much?* How strong? Aspects of intensity.
6 *Why?* Which reasons are given or can be reconstructed?
7 *What for?* With what intention, to which purpose?
8 *By which?* Means, tactics, and strategies for reaching the goal.

By asking these questions, the text will be opened up. You may address them to single passages, but also to whole cases. In addition to these questions, comparisons between the extremes of a dimension ("flip-flop technique") or to phenomena from completely different contexts and a consequent questioning of self-evidence ("waving-the-red-flag technique") are possible ways for further untangling the dimensions and contents of a category.

Axial Coding

After identifying a number of substantive categories, the next step is to refine and differentiate the categories resulting from open coding. As a second step, Strauss and Corbin suggest doing a more formal coding for identifying and classifying links between substantive categories. In axial coding, the relations between categories are elaborated. In order to formulate such relations, Strauss and Corbin (1998, p. 127) suggest a coding paradigm model, which is symbolized in Figure 25.1.

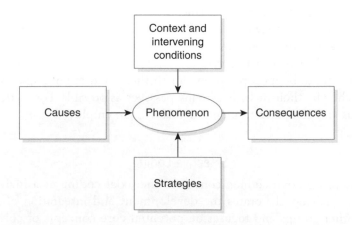

FIGURE 25.1 The Paradigm Model

This very simple and, at the same time, very general model serves to clarify the relations among a phenomenon, its causes and consequences, its context, and the strategies of those who are involved. This model is based on two axes: one goes from causes to phenomena and to consequences, the other one links context, intervening conditions, and action and interactional strategies of participants to the phenomenon.

Concepts may be classified in three ways: (1) as a *phenomenon* for this category; (2) as the *context* or *conditions* for other categories; or (3) as a *consequence*. It is important to note that the coding paradigm only names possible relations between phenomena and concepts: the purpose of coding is to facilitate the discovery or establishment of structures of relations between phenomena, between concepts, and between categories. Here as well, the questions addressed to the text and the comparative strategies mentioned above are employed once again in a complementary way.

The developed relations and the categories that are treated as essential are repeatedly verified against the text and the data. The researcher moves continuously back and forth between inductive thinking (developing concepts, categories, and relations from the text) and deductive thinking (testing the concepts, categories, and relations against the text, especially against passages or cases that are different from those from which they were developed). Axial coding is summarized as follows:

> Axial coding is the process of relating subcategories to a category. It is a complex process of inductive and deductive thinking involving several steps. These are accomplished, as with open coding, by making comparisons and asking questions. However, in axial coding the use *of* these procedures is more focused, and geared toward discovering and relating categories in terms of the paradigm model. (Strauss and Corbin, 1990, p. 114)

In axial coding, the categories that are most relevant to the research question are selected from the developed codes and the related code notes. Many different passages in the text are then sought as evidence of these relevant codes in order to elaborate the axial category on the basis of the questions mentioned above. In order to structure the intermediate results (means–end, cause–effect, temporal, or local) relations are elaborated between the different axial categories by using the parts of the coding paradigm mentioned above.

From the multitude of categories that were originated, the ones selected are those which seem to be most promising for further elaboration. These axial categories are enriched by their fit with as many passages as possible. For further refining, the questions and comparisons mentioned above are employed.

Selective Coding

The third step, selective coding, continues the axial coding at a higher level of abstraction. This step elaborates the development and integration of it in comparison to other groups and focuses on potential core concepts or core variables. In this step you look for further examples and evidence for relevant categories.

This then leads to an elaboration or formulation of the *story of the case*. At this point, Strauss and Corbin conceive the issue or the central phenomenon of the study as a case and not a person or a single interview. One should bear in mind here that the aim of this formulation is to give a short descriptive overview of the story and the case and should therefore comprise only a few sentences. The analysis goes beyond this descriptive level when the *story line* is elaborated—a concept is attached to the central phenomenon of the story and related to the other categories. In any case, the result should be *one* central category and *one* central phenomenon. The analyst must decide between equally salient phenomena and weigh them, so that one central category results together with the sub-categories which are related to it. The core category again is developed in its features and dimensions and linked to (all, if possible) other categories by using the parts and relations of the coding paradigm. The analysis and the development of the theory aim at discovering patterns in the data as well as the conditions under which these apply. Grouping the data according to the coding paradigm allocates specificity to the theory and enables the researcher to say, "Under these conditions (listing them) this happens; whereas under these conditions, this is what occurs" (1990, p. 131).

Finally, the theory is formulated in greater detail and again checked against the data. The procedure for interpreting data, like the integration of additional material, ends at the point where theoretical saturation has been reached (i.e., further coding, enrichment of categories, and so on no longer provide or promise new knowledge). At the same time, the procedure is flexible enough that the researcher can re-enter the same source texts and the same codes from open coding with a different research question and aim at developing and formulating a grounded theory of a different issue.

CASE STUDY 25.1

Unending Work and Care

Juliet Corbin and Anselm Strauss have further developed the approach of grounded theory coding and applied it in many studies in the context of nursing and medical sociology in the 1980s and since. In one of their more recent studies, Corbin and Strauss (1988) applied their methodology to the study of how people experiencing a chronic illness and their relatives manage to deal with this serious illness and manage to conduct their personal lives.

The empirical basis of this study is a number of intensive interviews with such couples at home and at work. These were undertaken to identify the problems these couples face in their personal lives in order to answer the question: "How can the chronically ill be helped to manage their illnesses more effectively?" (1988, p. xi).

Different from early conceptualizations of grounded theory research in which it was suggested *not* to develop a theoretical framework and understanding of the issue under study (e.g., in Glaser and Strauss 1967), the authors here start with an extensive presentation of

(Continued)

(Continued)

the theoretical tools used in their study, which builds on previous empirical work by the same researchers.

The main concept in the research is trajectory. This refers to the course of the illness as well as to the work of the people who attempt to control and shape this course. Corbin and Strauss identify several stages—trajectory phases—that are labeled as acute, come-back, stable, unstable, deteriorating, and dying stages of illness. In the theoretical framework, the authors analyze how a chronically ill member of a family changes the life plans of families and focus on biographical processes with which the victims try to manage and come to terms with the illness. In the second part of their book, the authors use this theoretical framework to analyze the various trajectory phases in greater detail.

This is not only one of the most important studies in the field of everyday management of chronic illness. It is also very fruitful in developing and differentiating a theoretical framework for this issue, which goes beyond existing concepts of coping, adjustment, and stress. Rather, the authors develop from their empirical work a much more elaborate concept (trajectory) for analyzing the experience of their research partners. They achieve this by analyzing the different stages of trajectory by asking a set of questions: "What are the different types of work? How do they get done? How do the central work processes and interactional developments enter into getting the work done? What are the biographical processes that accompany and affect those matters?" (1988, p. 168). All in all, this study is a very good example of how the research strategy developed by Glaser, Strauss, and Corbin in several steps can be used for analyzing a theoretically and practically relevant issue.

Glaser's Approach: Theoretical Coding

In many parts, Glaser and Strauss proceed in the same way when analyzing the material. Glaser (1992) more recently has criticized the way Strauss and Corbin have elaborated their approach and in particular the coding paradigm and the idea of axial coding. In the main he sees this as forcing a structure on the data instead of discovering what emerges as structure from the data and the analysis. In his version, open coding is the first step, too. But then he progresses in a different way. As an instrument for coding material more formally and in a theoretically relevant way, Glaser (1978) has suggested a list of basic codes, which he grouped as coding families. These families are sources for defining codes and at the same time an orientation for searching new codes for a set of data (see Table 25.1).

The third step is again selective coding – although in his earlier textbook (Glaser 1978), selective coding comes before theoretical coding based on the coding families. As Kelle (2007) holds, the list of coding families can be an heuristic tool for advancing an understanding of the material. However, he criticizes the lack of internal logic in the set of coding families and states that there is a lot of background knowledge implicit to the families.

Awareness of Dying and Awareness Contexts

Glaser and Strauss developed this method in the following study on the handling of death and dying in hospitals (Glaser and Strauss 1965a). Their research question was on what interacting with dying people depends upon and how the knowledge of a person's imminent death determines the interaction with him or her. More concretely, what they studied were the forms of interaction between the dying person and the clinical staff of the hospital, between the staff and the relatives, and between the relatives and the dying person: Which tactics are applied in the contact with dying people, and what part does the hospital play as a social organization here?

The central concept at the end of the analysis was "awareness contexts." This concept expresses what each of the interactants knows about a certain state of the patient and what he or she assumes about the other interactants' awareness of his or her own knowledge. This awareness context may change due to the patient's situation or to new information for one or all of the participants.

Four types of awareness were found. *Closed awareness* means the patients do not suspect their approaching death. *Suspicion awareness* means they have a suspicion concerning this issue. *Awareness of mutual pretence* is the case when everybody knows, but nobody says it openly. *Open awareness* is when the patients know about their situation and speak frankly about it with all others.

More generally, the analysis of awareness contexts included their description and the precondition of the social structure in each context (social relations etc.). It also comprised resulting interactions, which included the tactics and countertactics of the participants in order to bring about changes in the awareness context and also the consequences of each form of interaction for those who are involved, for the hospital, and for further interactions. The analysis was elaborated to a theory of awareness contexts through comparisons with other situations of mutual pretence and differing awareness of those who are involved, into which this typology fits. As examples, the authors mention buying and selling cars or "clowning at the circuses" (1965a, p. 277), and so on. Integrating such other fields and the grounded theories developed for them formulates a formal theory of awareness.

All in all, this very early research example allows us to follow the steps of grounded theory development based on one central concept. The study is not only instructive from a methodological point of view but was very influential in the sociology of illness and dying and in areas such as nursing, for example.

Charmaz's Approach to Coding in Grounded Theory Research

Kathy Charmaz is currently one of the leading researchers in the field of grounded theory. She develops (Charmaz 2003) an alternative view of the procedure in the development of grounded theory. Charmaz suggests doing open coding line by line, because it "also helps you to refrain from imputing your motives, fears, or unresolved personal issues to your respondents and to your collected data" (2003, p. 94). She also gives a concrete example of this procedure as in Box 25.3. You will find the codes that Charmaz developed in the left column and the excerpt of the interview in the right column of the box.

BOX 25.3

Example of Line-by-Line Coding

Shifting symptoms, having inconsistent days	If you have lupus, I mean one day it's my liver; one day it's my joints; one day it's
Interpreting images of self given by others	my head, and it's like people really think you're a hypochondriac if you keep com-
Avoiding disclosure	plaining about different ailments …. It's
Predicting rejection	like you don't want to say anything be-
Keeping others unaware	cause people are going to start thinking,
Seeing symptoms as connected	you know, 'God, don't go near her, all she is – is complaining about this.' And I
Having others unaware	think that's why I never say anything be-
Anticipating disbelief	cause I feel like everything I have is relat-
Controlling others' views	ed one way or another to the lupus but
Avoiding stigma	most of the people don't know I have lu-
Assessing potential losses and risks of disclosing	pus, and even those that do are not going to believe that ten different ailments are the same thing. And I don't want anybody saying, you know, [that] they don't want to come around me because I complain.

Source: Charmaz (2003, p. 96)

After line-by-line coding at the beginning (see Box 25.3), she continues by exploring some of the resulting codes more deeply. Charmaz's second step is called focused coding. In the example given in Box 25.3, these were the two codes "avoiding disclosure" and "assessing potential losses and risks of disclosing."

All three versions discussed here treat open coding as an important step. All see theoretical saturation as the goal and endpoint of coding. They all base their coding and analysis on constant comparison between materials (cases, interviews, statements, etc.). Glaser retains the idea of emerging categories and discovery as epistemological principle. In contrast, Charmaz (2006) sees the whole process more as "constructing grounded theory" (hence the title of her book). All see a need for developing also formal categories and links.

Identifying Structure, Reducing Complexity, and Developing a Theoretical Model

The aims of coding in this process are always twofold: first, to develop and unfold an understanding of the issue or field under study first, which demands an open access to what should be coded and how; and, secondly, to identify an underlying structure, an organizing principle, a basic social process, or core category. This asks for reduction and structuration. According to these aims, Glaser (1978) for example distinguishes between substantive and theoretical coding. For the first form of coding he suggests using either words and concepts from the language of the field ("in vivo codes"), or words and concepts drawn from the scientific (e.g., sociological) terminology ("sociological constructs"). Theoretical coding then aims at identifying relations among such substantive codes as the next step towards formulating a theory. Here we find suggestions to look for relations among codes like causes, contexts, consequences, and conditions (1978, p. 72).

Another tool that Glaser suggests is the coding 'families' (see Table 25.1). As Kelle (2007, p. 200) holds, this set of coding families comes with a lot of background assumptions that are not made explicit, which limits their usefulness for structuring substantive codes, in particular for beginners looking for an orientation of how to code. It can be used as an inspiration for which directions to look in if you are searching for possible links among your substantive codes.

In Strauss's concept of coding, the coding paradigm (or paradigmatic model) replaces the coding families in Glaser's approach. Here again an orientation is given for how to link substantive concepts with each other. Again this is an abstract and general model for how to link and contextualize substantive codes among each other. This model is constructed around two axes: one goes from causes to phenomena and to consequences, the other goes from context to intervening conditions and to action and interactional strategies of participants. Accordingly you may take a phenomenon which was labeled with a substantive code, and ask yourself along the first axis: what are the causes of this phenomenon and what are its consequences? On the second axis you may ask: what were the context and intervening conditions influencing this phenomenon, which strategies by participants were linked to this phenomenon, and what were the consequences? Of course these questions are not hypothetical but should be addressed to the empirical material and answered by coding and comparison.

In both approaches, substantive codes are linked by codes that are more about formal relations (something is a *cause* of something). Strauss's model around two axes led to his step of axial coding, which takes this model as a heuristic device for the further development of a grounded theory. In both approaches, the idea of selective coding is included, which focuses on potential core concepts or core variables (Holton 2007, p. 280). Also, constant comparison of materials during the coding process is beyond question for both approaches. Integration of materials and developing the structure of the theory is advanced by the theoretical sorting of codes and even more of memos written about them. Several authors suggest

TABLE 25.1   Coding Families Applied to Examples of Coding Pain Experiences

Coding families	Concepts	Examples
The six Cs	Causes, contexts, contingencies, consequences, covariances, conditions	Causes of pain Conditions of suffering from pain
Process	Stages, phases, phasings, transitions, passages, careers, chains, sequences	Career of a patient with chronic pain
The degree family	Extent, level, intensity, range, amount, continuum, statistical average, standard deviation	Extent of pain suffering
Type family	Types, classes, genres, prototypes, styles, kinds	Types of pain, e.g., burning, piercing, throbbing, shooting, sting, gnawing, sharp
The strategy family	Strategies, tactics, techniques, mechanisms, management	Strategies of coping with pain Techniques for reducing pain
Interactive family	Interaction, mutual effects, interdependence, reciprocity, asymmetries, rituals	Interaction of pain experience and coping Rituals of communicating about pain
Identity self-family	Identity, self-image, self-concept, self-evaluation, social worth, transformations of self	Self-concepts of pain patients Shifts in identity after continuous pain experience
Cutting point family	Boundary, critical juncture, cutting point, turning point, tolerance levels, point of no return	Turning point: when did the pain become chronic? New level in the medical career of pain patient
Cultural family	Social norms, social values, social beliefs	Social norms about tolerating pain, "feeling rules"
Consensus family	Contracts, agreements, definitions of the situation, uniformity, conformity, conflict	Compliance of the patient: taking pills according to the prescription

Source: Adapted from Glaser (1978, pp. 75–82)

doing this sorting by hand. The theoretical codes produced in one of the ways discussed above can be used as an orientation for theoretical sorting (see Charmaz 2006, pp. 115–118).

Which Approach to Choose?

In general, the outlined alternatives in applying grounded theory coding are different ways to the same aim. Strauss and Corbin have focused their approach to material more on a basic model (paradigm model) with a limited number of elements and links between them. Glaser has developed a broader set of basic ways of coding (coding families) from his experiences. Charmaz has developed that into a more constructivist approach to materials and to theories. This affects epistemological issues as well ("Finding or constructing theories?") whereas the distinction between Strauss's and Glaser's approaches is based more on how strict and how open the researcher's own approach to data is. Glaser may be more flexible here and less oriented on traditional models of science (the use of "paradigm" and the criteria suggested by Strauss and Corbin—see Chapter 29—may support this notion) but tends at some points to overemphasize his notion of flexibility in his approach to material (formulations like "All is data" and "Just do it" characterize some of his later writings, e.g., Glaser 2002). For your own research, you should look at the tools that each approach suggests for analyzing material and see which fits best for your own material and attitude towards it. Beyond the disputes between Glaser and Strauss/Corbin, the more current suggestions of Charmaz (e.g., Thornberg and Charmaz 2014; Case Study 25.3) may point the way for the future development of grounded theory coding.

—CASE STUDY 25.3—

Identity Dilemmas of Chronically Ill Men

Charmaz (1997) conducted a grounded theory study interested in gender and identity in the context of chronic illness. Research questions were for example:

What is it like to be an active productive man one moment and a patient who faces death the next? What is it like to change one's view of oneself accordingly? Which identity dilemma does living with continued uncertainty pose for men? How do they handle them? When do they make identity changes? When do they try to preserve a former self? (p. 38)

Her research was based on 40 interviews of 20 men with chronic illness; 80 interviews with chronically ill women were used for comparative purposes. Her sampling focused on (1) adult status (more than 21 years of age), (2) a diagnosis of a serious, but not terminal chronic illness, (3) a disease with an uncertain course, and (4) effects of illness upon daily life (p. 39).

The steps in her research included: (1) analysis of the interviews for gender differences; (2) a thematic analysis of the men's interviews; (3) building analytic categories from men's definitions of their situations; (4) further interviews for refining these categories; (5) rereading the data with a gender perspective; (6) studying a new set of personal accounts; and (7) making comparisons with women on selected key points.

She answered her research questions by looking at four major processes in men's experience of chronic illness: (1) awakening to death after a life-threatening crisis; (2) accommodating uncertainty once the lasting consequences of the illness were recognized by the men; (3) defining illness and disability; and (4) preserving a self to maintain a sense of coherence while experiencing loss and change (see p. 38). This again is discussed from the comparative focus on how participants were "preserving a public identity" and "changing a private identity" and finally of "strategies for preserving self." A core element of her grounded theory was how men maintain an identity and/or sink into

(Continued)

(Continued)

depression when facing their permanent illness and disability: "Life becomes struggling to live while waiting to die" (p. 57).

This study constitutes an example of research done by one of the major protagonists of grounded theory methodology. It uses core elements of the methodology, although it is neither entirely clear how far the sampling is based on theoretical sampling, nor clear about which of the coding strategies were used exactly to analyze the data. The study provides interesting and important insights about living with chronic illness and fills relevant blanks in the theoretical knowledge about this issue. However, what becomes visible as a grounded theory is less clearly shaped than what Glaser and Strauss (1965a) for example presented as their theory of "awareness of dying." This research therefore is an example of how differently grounded theory research can be pursued, without leaving the framework of the approach.

What Is the Contribution to the General Methodological Discussion?

This method aims at a consequent analysis of texts. The combination of open coding with increasingly focused procedures can contribute to the development of a deeper understanding of the content and meaning of the text beyond paraphrasing and summarizing it (which would be the central approaches in the qualitative content analysis which will be discussed later). The interpretation of texts here is methodologically realized and manageable. This approach allows room for maneuvering through the different techniques and flexibility in formulating rules. It differs from other methods of interpreting texts because it leaves the level of the pure texts during the interpretation in order to develop categories and relations, and thus theories. Finally, the method combines an inductive approach with an increasingly deductive handling of text and categories.

How Does the Method Fit into the Research Process?

The procedure outlined here is the main part of the research process that aims at developing theories (see Chapter 10). In terms of theoretical background, symbolic interactionism has very strongly influenced this approach (see Chapter 7). The material is selected according to theoretical sampling (see Chapter 13). Research questions and the development state of the emerging theory orient the selection of data collection methods. Which methods should be used for collecting data is not determined beyond that. First, generalization aims at grounded theories, which should be related directly to the data and finally at formal theories that are valid beyond the original contexts. Integrating grounded theories developed in other contexts in the study allows the testing of formal theories.

What Are the Limitations of the Method?

One problem with this approach is that the distinction between method and art becomes hazy. This makes it difficult to teach as a method in some places. Often, the extent of the advantages and strengths of the method only become clear in applying it.

A further problem is the potential endlessness of options for coding and comparisons. You could apply open coding to all passages of a text, and you could further elaborate all the categories which you found, and which in most cases are very numerous. Passages and cases could be endlessly compared to each other. Theoretical sampling could endlessly integrate further cases. The method gives you few hints about what the selection of passages and cases should be oriented to and what criteria the end of coding (and sampling) should be based on. The criterion of theoretical saturation leaves it to the theory developed up to that moment, and thus to the researcher, to make such decisions of selection and ending.

One consequence is that often a great many codes and potential comparisons result. One pragmatic solution for this potential infinity is to make a break, to balance what was found, and to build a list of priorities. Which codes should you definitely elaborate further, which codes seem to be less instructive, and which can you leave out with respect to your research question? The further procedure may be designed according to this list of priorities. It has proved helpful—for the specific purpose of further grounding such decisions and also more generally—to analyze texts with this procedure in a group of interpreters. Then you can discuss the results among the members and mutually check them.

Grounded Theory Coding: Integrated Approach or Starting Point?

The various ways of doing grounded theory coding have been spelt out here in some detail as they may inform qualitative analysis in several respects:

1 They have been developed without being linked to a specific form of data. Basically any sorts of data can be analyzed with them.
2 They have been developed as integrating part of a complex methodology of qualitative research.
3 As coding procedures, they may be used to provide an orientation for analysis of materials in other contexts of qualitative research with categories developed from the material.
4 They have provided the starting point for other approaches developed from them—such as thematic coding (see Chapter 26).
5 Finally, they have provided a foundation for implementing qualitative data analysis in QDA software like ATLAS.ti or MAXQDA (see Chapter 28).

Checklist for Using Grounded Theory Coding

1 What are your expectations for grounded theory coding in your research?
2 Are you aiming at developing a theory or just using the coding procedures?

3 Which approach of grounded theory is the most appropriate for your issue?
4 Have you integrated memo writing in your analysis?
5 How have you taken into account the fact that coding is a way of (re)constructing events and experiences?
6 Have you arrived at some general principle, basic social process, or central concept in your analysis?

---KEY POINTS---

- Grounded theory coding remains a major approach in qualitative data analysis.
- There are a number of common elements in this approach, but also different versions of how to do the analysis.
- The approach is most fruitful when the core elements of method, as defined in this chapter, are kept in mind.
- There are a number of versions of grounded theory coding procedure.

---Exercise 25.1---

1 Find a journal in which qualitative research is published and locate a research study (e.g., Neill 2010) applying grounded theory methodology. Analyze (a) which elements of the methodology are explicitly mentioned in the article as part of the study and (b) which version of grounded theory was applied.
2 Reflect on your own research and plan it according to the key elements of grounded theory research mentioned in this chapter.

---Exercise 25.2---

1 Look for part of an interview (perhaps the one from Exercise 24.1 in Chapter 24) and apply open coding to it. You could start from the beginning of the interview or select a part which looks particularly interesting to you and develop a label for this part (name a code).
2 Apply the basic questions suggested by Strauss and Corbin (mentioned in this chapter) to the selected piece of text.
3 Finally, apply the segmentation technique (see Box 25.2) to your piece of text.

---Further Reading---

Textbooks and Handbooks of Grounded Theory

These works go further into the details of how to do grounded theory research in different ways. The fourth text is a good example of not only the results that this strategy is able to produce, but also the study for which it was developed. The other texts discuss the method in its various degrees of elaboration:

Böhm, A. (2004) "Theoretical Coding," in U. Flick, E.v. Kardorff and I. Steinke (eds.), *A Companion to Qualitative Research*. London: Sage. pp. 270–275.

Bryant, A. and Charmaz, K. (eds.) (2007a) *The SAGE Handbook of Grounded Theory*. London: Sage.

Charmaz, K. (2006) *Constructing Grounded Theory: A Practical Guide Through Qualitative Analysis*. London: Sage.

Glaser, B.G. and Strauss, A.L. (1965a) *Awareness of Dying*. Chicago, IL: Aldine.

Glaser, B.G. (1978) *Theoretical Sensitivity*. Mill Valley, CA: University of California Press.

Strauss, A.L. and Corbin, J. (2008) *Basics of Qualitative Research* (3rd edn). London: Sage.

Thornberg, R. and Charmaz, K. (2014) "Grounded Theory and Theoretical Coding," in U. Flick (ed.), *The SAGE Handbook of Qualitative Data Analysis*. London: Sage. pp. 153–169.

26
Thematic Coding and Content Analysis

─CHAPTER OBJECTIVES─

This chapter is designed to help you

- know the different approaches to coding empirical material;
- apply the procedures of thematic coding;
- understand the techniques of qualitative content analysis;
- identify the potentials and limitations of coding and of categorizing approaches in general.

In the discussion of data analysis in the previous chapter, the emphasis lay on the development of grounded theory. However, qualitative research has many aims besides that. For example, many studies are interested in exploring a thematic range and company social groups' knowledge of it, rather than finding a core category and theory development. Moreover, researchers may have a stronger focus on individual participants' views than on an issue: they will, therefore, pay more attention to analyzing the case (i.e., the individual interview) as a whole than grounded theory analysts would do. Finally, qualitative analysis of interviews often focuses on some kind of (non-numerical) distribution of the views on an issue over several groups (e.g., how similar and different are psychologists' and physicians' views of a specific patient's situation in a study based on expert interviews?). This kind of study is again very different from grounded theory studies. Nevertheless, in all the alternatives mentioned so far, coding is a central approach to the data. In this chapter several ways of thematic analysis, thematic coding, and content analysis are presented.

Thematic Analysis

In the context of psychological research, Braun and Clarke (2006) propose a method that they call thematic analysis. The authors compare this method to approaches such as narrative analysis (see Chapter 18), discourse analysis (see Chapter 27), and grounded theory analysis (see Chapter 25). They present it, not as an extra or alternative approach, but rather as a strategy for *combining* other approaches. They define thematic analysis as:

> a method for identifying, analysing and reporting patterns (themes) within data. It minimally organizes and describes your data set in (rich) detail. However, frequently it goes further than this, and interprets various aspects of the research topic. (2006, p. 79)

To make their method as practical as possible, the authors provide step-by-step advice. First (Braun and Clarke 2006, pp. 81–83), they list several essential decisions or distinctions:

1 What counts as a theme? For them, a theme is something relevant for the research question which can be seen on "some level of patterned response or meaning within the data set" (2006, p. 82).
2 Is the aim of the analysis (a) a rich description of a data set or (b) a detailed analysis of a particular aspect (see 2006, p. 83)?
3 They distinguish between (a) "inductive thematic analysis," which develops codes and themes from the data, and (b) "theoretical thematic analysis," which is driven more by the researchers' theoretical or analytical interest (p. 84).
4 Next, a distinction between "semantic" and "latent" themes is made. The first type focuses on the "explicit or surface meanings of the data," whereas the second aims to "identify or examine the underlying ideas, assumptions, and conceptualizations – and ideologies" (p. 84) that lie behind what is mentioned explicitly in the text.
5 Epistemological clarity is then provided by deciding whether (a) a realist or (b) a constructionist approach of data analysis will be taken (p. 85).
6 Finally Braun and Clarke highlight the importance of distinguishing between two types of question: (a) the research questions of a study and (b) the actual questions asked in an interview.

From the above, Braun and Clarke develop a concept of thematic analysis that "involves the searching across a data set … to find repeated patterns of meaning" (2006, p. 86). Such analysis may be developed by taking the following six steps:

1 Familiarizing yourself with your data.
2 Generating initial codes.
3 Searching for themes.

4 Reviewing themes.
5 Defining and naming themes.
6 Producing the report. (pp. 87–93)

The first step focuses on doing the transcription (yourself) and reading the transcripts several times. In the second step, codes are developed from the material. Here the authors distinguish between semantic codes (meanings expressed verbally) and latent codes (underlying meanings). They suggest working systematically through the whole text, to keep the context of an extract in focus and to keep in mind that statements can be coded in different themes simultaneously. The third step entails sorting the codes into various themes and collation of the relevant data extracts in the themes. Step 4 aims at a refinement of the developing codes system by breaking down themes into subthemes, leaving out less relevant themes. In reviewing themes, the researcher can focus either on data extracts or on the entire data set. This should lead, in the fifth step, to thematic maps (visual representations of themes and subthemes and links between them). Then labels are given to the themes and reflect what they are actually representing. In the sixth (and final) step the results of this procedure are presented.

What Is the Contribution to the General Methodological Discussion?

This method pins down activities in qualitative data analysis on a practical level. The authors see their method as independent of any more developed theoretical and methodological program (like hermeneutics, conversation or discourse analysis—see Chapter 27). They suggest a procedure for use when the research aims beyond developing a theory from the material (see Chapter 25 for this). Such aims include, for example, producing descriptions or detailed accounts for one aspect by coding qualitative material.

The guidance that Braun and Clarke provide may helpfully be applied to approaches beyond their own. The phases the authors present as steps in using their method give some good advice on how to do this sort of analysis. These phases can also be instructive for further elaborating other forms of analyzing qualitative materials with coding. The reflections on what makes good (thematic) analysis of data that Braun and Clarke (2006, pp. 95–96) present in their article can also be instructive for using and reflecting on other approaches to coding.

How Does the Method Fit into the Research Process?

The authors emphasize that their method does not assume any defined or confined theoretical or methodological program: rather, they provide a description of what may be done with empirical material in a range of methodological contexts. Epistemological issues have to be clarified by the individual researchers. The method is compatible with various epistemological and theoretical conceptualizations. It is founded on analyzing subjective viewpoints (see Chapter 7) and, methodologically, on data coming from interviews (see Chapter 16) and focus groups (see Chapter 17). It is strongly rooted in psychological research.

What Are the Limitations of the Method?

Braun and Clarke's methodological suggestions seek to provide clear(er) advice on how to do an analysis that is based on coding and is not oriented to over-complex or over-challenging aims (such as developing a theory). However, on closer inspection, we can see that the concrete steps identified above are relatively close to what is suggested by grounded theory methodologies.

With the stripping away of data analysis from methodological and theoretical contexts comes the risk of reducing the analysis to a sort of hands-on procedure. Thematic analysis is presented here as a general and basic method in qualitative data analysis (or in psychology, as the title of Braun and Clarke's paper suggests). However, the method in the practical steps and in the examples presented by these authors is limited to the analysis of interviews.

The contradiction that arises here—between discussing a general method and basically outlining one that is limited to one sort of data (interviews)—is intensified by the authors' extensive discussion of other approaches (from grounded theory to content and discourse analysis), which are less limited in their indication for data sorts. What exactly should happen in steps 3 and 4 of the analysis remains relatively open: Braun and Clarke characterize these steps by providing illustrative examples, rather than an explicit description of what to do.

Thematic Coding

Although developed earlier than thematic analysis, the following method in effect combines ideas of that approach with those of grounded theory coding. I developed this procedure in the context of a study on technological change in everyday life in various contexts (Flick 1996). This was set against the background of limitations in grounded theory coding (e.g., Strauss 1987; Chapter 25 here), which became evident in analyzing the data in this project. The aim was to use coding for comparative studies in which the groups under study were derived from the research question and thus defined a priori. The research issue was the social distribution of perspectives on a phenomenon or a process. The underlying assumption was that in different social worlds or groups, differing views can be found. To assess this assumption and to identify patterns in such groups' specific ways of seeing and experiencing, it proved necessary to modify some details of the grounded theory procedures in order to increase the comparability of the empirical material. Sampling was oriented to the groups whose perspectives on the issue seemed to be most instructive for analysis, and which, therefore, were defined in advance (see Chapter 13) and not derived from the state of interpretation (in contrast to grounded theory procedures). Theoretical sampling was applied in each group in order to select the concrete cases to be studied. Correspondingly, the collection of data was conducted with a method designed to guarantee comparability by defining topics while at the same time remaining open to the views related to them. This may be achieved through, for example, episodic interviewing in which the topical domains defined, concerning the situations to be recounted, are linked either to the issue of the study (see Chapter 18) or to other forms of interviews (see Chapter 16).

The Procedure for Thematic Coding

In the interpretation of the material, thematic coding is applied as a multi-stage procedure—again, with respect to the comparability of the analyses. The first step addresses the cases involved, which will be interpreted in a series of case studies.

Short Description of Each Case

One begins by producing a short description of each case. This is then continuously checked—and modified if necessary—during further interpretation of the case.

Case descriptions include several elements. The first is a statement which is typical of the interview—the motto of the case. A short description should provide information about the person with regard to the research question (e.g., age, profession, number of children, if these are relevant for the issue under study). Finally, the central topics mentioned by the interviewee concerning the research issue are summarized. On finishing the case analysis, this case description comes to form part of the results.

The example in Box 26.1 comes from my comparative study on everyday knowledge about technological change in different professional groups.

BOX 26.1

Example of a Short Description of a Case

"For me, technology has a reassuring side"

The interviewee is a female French information technology engineer, 43 years old and with a son of 15. She has been working for about 20 years in various research institutes. At present, she works in a large institute of social science research in the computer center and is responsible for developing software, teaching, and consulting employees. Technology has a lot to do with security and clarity for her. To mistrust technology would produce problems for her professional self-awareness. To master technology is important for her self-concept. She narrates a good deal, using juxtapositions of leisure, nature, feeling, and family to technology and work, and she repeatedly mentions the cultural benefit from technologies, especially from television.

Developing a Thematic Structure

In contrast to grounded theory procedures, you first carry out a deepening analysis of a single case (i.e., the first interview). This case analysis pursues several aims: one is to preserve and elucidate the relations between meanings that the respective person presents concerning the topic of the study. This is why a case study is done for each and every case.

A second aim is to develop a system of categories for the analysis of the single case. To elaborate this system of categories (similar to grounded theory), it is necessary to apply, first, open coding and then selective coding. Here, selective coding aims less at developing a grounded core category across all cases than at generating thematic domains and categories for the single case first.

After analyzing the first cases, you then cross-check the categories and thematic domains identified for each case. From this cross-checking a thematic structure results; this will then underlie the analysis of further cases in order to increase their comparability.

The excerpts, which are given in Box 26.2 as an example (of such a thematic structure), come from the study on technological change in everyday life previously mentioned.

─BOX 26.2─

Example of the Thematic Structure of Case Analyses in Thematic Coding

1 First encounter with technology
2 Definition of technology
3 Computer

   3.1 Definition
   3.2 First encounter(s) with computers
   3.3 Professional handling of computers
   3.4 Changes in communication due to computers

4 Television

   4.1 Definition
   4.2 First encounter(s) with television
   4.3 Present meaning

5 Alterations due to technological change

   5.1 Everyday life
   5.2 Household equipment

The structure in Box 26.2 was developed from the first cases and then continually assessed for all further cases. It will need to be modified if new or contradictory aspects emerge. It is used to analyze all cases that are part of the interpretation.

Fine Interpretation of Thematic Domains: Key Questions

For a fine interpretation of the thematic domains, single passages of the text (e.g., narratives of situations) are analyzed in greater detail. The coding paradigm suggested by Strauss (1987, pp. 27–28) is taken as the starting point for deriving the following key questions for:

1 *Conditions*: Why? What has led to the situation? Background? Course?
2 *Interaction among the actors*: Who acted? What happened?
3 *Strategies and tactics*: Which ways of handling situations, for example, avoidance, adaptation?
4 *Consequences*: What changed? Consequences? Results?

The result of this process is a case-oriented display of the way the case specifically deals with the issue of the study. This result includes constantly recurring topics (e.g., strangeness of technology) that can be found in the viewpoints across different domains (e.g., work, leisure, household).

  The thematic structure thus developed may also serve for comparing cases and groups (i.e., for elaborating correspondences and differences between the various groups in the study). Thus you analyze and assess the social distribution of perspectives on the issue under study. For example, after the case analyses have shown that the subjective definition of technology is an essential thematic domain for understanding technological change, it is then possible to compare the definitions of technology and the related coding from all cases.

CASE STUDY 26.1

Subjective Definitions of Technology and Their Coding

Two examples of subjective definitions of technology will serve to demonstrate the results of this procedure in one thematic domain. A female information technology engineer from West Germany gave the following answer to a question regarding her definition of technology:

> Technology is for me a machine, somewhere, existing in everyday life, devices for helping people in order to somehow design life either more pleasantly or less pleasantly. What do I link to it? Yes, sometimes something positive, sometimes something negative, depending on what I have experienced with the machine, in contrast perhaps to nature, so nature and technology are in opposition.

Here, on the one hand, it becomes clear that technology equals machines and that an omnipresence of technology is seen. On the other hand, a functional understanding of technology, also a functional evaluation of technology, and finally an explicit juxtaposition of technology and nature are expressed. This definition is coded as "technology as device."

> **A female teacher from France answered the same question as follows:**
>
> For me, technology is something that does not really exist in my life, because if one speaks of technology, I understand it as something scientific. Well, if I further reflect, then I say to myself, maybe it is the use of machines whose functioning needs or would need several steps.
>
> This is coded as "technology as unfamiliar science." This aspect of unfamiliarity could be identified for the other French teachers in this study in general.
> These examples show how codes are allocated to excerpts from interviews.

The coding of technology definitions includes two forms of statements: (1) definitions in a descriptive sense (e.g., "technology as …") and (2) the specification of the dimensions used for classifying different technologies and machines (e.g., "professional technology versus everyday technology"). After coding the subjective definition of technology, the distribution in Table 26.1 results.

Similar codes in the individual groups are summarized and the specific topics of each (professional) group are elaborated. Following a thorough comparison of the cases on the basis of the developed structure, the topical range in the way the interviewees' deal with each theme can be outlined.

TABLE 26.1 Thematic Coding of Subjective Definitions of Technology

	Information engineers	Social scientists	Teachers
West Germany	Technology as device Professional technology versus everyday technology	Technology as necessary means to an end Dimension "size" for classification	Technology as facility Technology as strange cold world
East Germany	Technology as device and its vulnerability Dimension "functional principle" for classification	Technology as unfamiliar device Dimension "complexity" for classification	Descriptive definitions of technology Dimension "everyday life versus profession" for classification
France	Technology as the opposite and application of science	Technology as application of science Dimension "everyday life" versus professional for classification	Technology as unfamiliar science Technology as means to an end Dimension "everyday life versus profession" for classification
Specific themes of the professions	Technology as professional device Opposition of technology and science "Functional principle" for classification	Application Technology as means to an end Classification: complexity and size	Unfamiliarity with technology "Everyday life versus profession" for classification

What Is the Contribution to the General Methodological Discussion?

This procedure specifies Strauss's (1987) approach to studies, which aims at developing a theory starting from the distribution of perspectives on a certain theme, issue, or process. Group-specific correspondences and differences are identified and analyzed.

In contrast to Strauss's procedure, however, the first step consists of a single case analysis: only in the second step will you undertake group comparisons beyond the single case (e.g., an interview).

By developing a thematic structure, which is grounded in the empirical material for the analysis and comparison of cases, you will increase the comparability of interpretations. At the same time, the procedure remains sensitive and open to the specific contents of each individual case and the social group with regard to the issue under study.

How Does the Method Fit into the Research Process?

The theoretical background is the diversity of social worlds as assumed in the concept of social representations (see Chapter 7) or more generally by constructivist approaches (see Chapter 8). Research questions focus on the analysis of the variety and distribution of perspectives on issues and processes in social groups (see Chapter 11). Cases are involved for specific groups (see Chapter 13). In addition, elements of theoretical sampling are used for the selection in the groups. Data are collected with methods that combine structuring inputs and openness with regard to contents (e.g., episodic interviews; see Chapter 18). Generalization is based on comparisons of cases and groups and aims at the development of theories (see Chapter 29).

What Are the Limitations of the Method?

The procedure is above all suitable for studies in which theoretically based group comparisons are to be conducted in relation to a specific issue. Therefore, the scope for a theory to be developed is more restricted than in Strauss's (1987) procedure. The analysis of texts consists of coding statements and narratives in categories, which are developed from the material. It is oriented to elaborating correspondences and differences between the groups defined in advance. These correspondences and differences are demonstrated on the basis of the distribution of codes and categories across the groups that are studied. The analysis plunges deep into text and case studies in the first step. If the case analyses are to be conducted consequently, the procedure may become somewhat time-consuming.

Qualitative Content Analysis

Content analysis is one of the classical procedures for analyzing textual material, no matter where this material comes from—it may range from media products to interview data (Bauer 2000). An essential feature is the use of categories that are often derived from theoretical models: that is, categories are brought to the empirical material and not necessarily developed from it (although they may be repeatedly assessed against it and modified if necessary). Above all, and contrary to other approaches, the goal here is to reduce the material.

Schreier (2012; 2014) has elaborated the approach of qualitative content analysis, while Mayring (2000; 2004) has developed a procedure for a qualitative content analysis, which offers a model of text analysis and different techniques for applying it. According to Schreier (2014, pp. 170), "qualitative content analysis is a method for systematically describing the meaning of qualitative data. ... This is done by assigning successive parts of the material to the categories of a coding frame."

The Process of Qualitative Content Analysis

Schreier (2014, p. 174) outlined the process of qualitative content analysis in a series of steps as follows (see Box 26.3).

— BOX 26.3—

The Process of Qualitative Content Analysis

1   Deciding on a research question
2   Selecting material
3   Building a coding frame
4   Segmentation
5   Trial coding
6   Evaluating and modifying the coding frame
7   Main analysis
8   Presenting and interpreting the findings. (Schreier 2014, p. 174)

In this approach, building a coding frame is central. First, material is selected. The coding frame is the result of structuring (which means developing its main categories) and generating (which means creating the subcategories for each main category). Both can be applied in a concept or data-driven way: categories result either from the existing literature or from the research interest behind the study. Developing categories from the material that is analyzed—as in grounded theory or thematic coding—should be used only in exceptional cases, as Schreier holds (in common with other theorists of qualitative content analysis). The coding frame and the use of theory-based categories are features that are supposed to make qualitative content analysis more systematic than other methods of qualitative data analysis. With the possibility of adding categories developed from the material, this method has some degree of flexibility.

However, the major aim of qualitative content analysis according to Schreier (2012) or Mayring (2004) is to work with rather large data sets, which have to be reduced in the analysis. Before the coding frame is applied, the categories are defined by giving them a name, describing what this name means, and giving positive examples and decision rules for applying it. If necessary the coding frame is adapted by revising and expanding it.

With this emphasis on the use of a coding frame, the three features that characterize the method according to Schreier can be put into practice: qualitative content analysis reduces data; it is systematic; and it is flexible (2014, p. 170 see above). Mayring (e.g., 2004; 2010) has suggested some concrete procedures for how to analyze qualitative material with qualitative content analysis, which will be outlined next.

The Procedure of Qualitative Content Analysis

According to Mayring, the first step is to define the material, to select the interviews or those parts that are relevant for answering the research question. The second step is to analyze the situation of data collection: how was the material generated, who was involved, who was present in the interview situation, where do the documents to be analyzed come from? In the third step, the material is formally characterized: was the material documented with a recording or a protocol, was there an influence on the transcription of the text when it was edited? In the fourth step Mayring defines the direction of the analysis for the selected texts and "what one actually wants to interpret out of them" (1983, p. 45). This means that the research question for analyzing the material is defined (again) and the researchers define what they intend to do with material in the analysis—for example, compare the specific experiences the participants had in their first period of working as a teacher. The research question is further differentiated on the basis of theories in the next step. Mayring emphasizes the role of defining the research question before starting to analyze materials in a qualitative content analysis and also that the categories should be defined in advance. He holds in this context that the "research question of the analysis must be clearly defined in advance, must be linked theoretically to earlier research on the issue and generally has to be differentiated in sub-questions" (1983, p. 47; see also Figure 26.1).

Finally, analytic units are defined. Here, Mayring differentiates the units as follows: the "coding unit" defines what is "the smallest element of material which may be analyzed, the minimal part of the text which may fall under a category"; the "contextual unit" defines what is the largest element in the text which may fall under a category; the "analytic unit" defines which passages "are analyzed one after the other." In the last but one step, the actual analyses are conducted before, in the final step, their results are interpreted with respect to the research question and questions of validity are asked and answered.

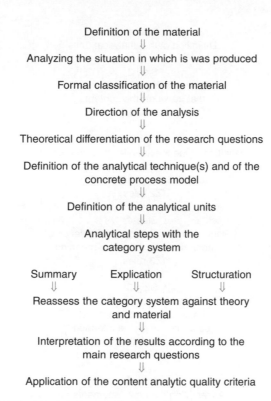

Definition of the material
⇓
Analyzing the situation in which is was produced
⇓
Formal classification of the material
⇓
Direction of the analysis
⇓
Theoretical differentiation of the research questions
⇓
Definition of the analytical technique(s) and of the
concrete process model
⇓
Definition of the analytical units
⇓
Analytical steps with the
category system

Summary   Explication   Structuration
⇓   ⇓   ⇓
Reassess the category system against theory
and material
⇓
Interpretation of the results according to the
main research questions
⇓
Application of the content analytic quality criteria

FIGURE 26.1   General Content Analytic Process Model

Source: Adapted from Mayring (1983)

Techniques of Qualitative Content Analysis

The concrete methodical procedure essentially includes three techniques: summarizing content analysis; explicative content analysis; and structuring content analysis.

Summarizing Qualitative Content Analysis

In *summarizing content analysis*, the material is paraphrased (see Figure 26.2). Less relevant passages and paraphrases with the same meanings are skipped; this is the first way in which material is reduced. Similar paraphrases are then bundled and summarized (the second reduction). This process allows the material to be reduced by turning several concrete statements in the original text into paraphrases, which abstract more and more from the concrete formulations. If for example 10 statements are represented by the same paraphrase, this one paraphrase is used in the further analysis; thus the original text of 10 statements is cut down to 1 statement. In order to make this reduction more effective, the paraphrases are then reformulated on a more abstract, general level. This again allows a reduction of the material. For this process of summarizing statements, a number of rules are formulated (see Box 26.4; similar rules are formulated for the other steps).

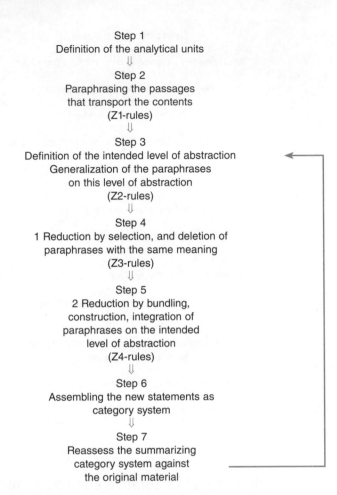

Step 1
Definition of the analytical units
⇓
Step 2
Paraphrasing the passages
that transport the contents
(Z1-rules)
⇓
Step 3
Definition of the intended level of abstraction
Generalization of the paraphrases
on this level of abstraction
(Z2-rules)
⇓
Step 4
1 Reduction by selection, and deletion of
paraphrases with the same meaning
(Z3-rules)
⇓
Step 5
2 Reduction by bundling,
construction, integration of
paraphrases on the intended
level of abstraction
(Z4-rules)
⇓
Step 6
Assembling the new statements as
category system
⇓
Step 7
Reassess the summarizing
category system against
the original material

FIGURE 26.2   Summarizing Content Analysis

Source: Adapted from Mayring (1983)

—BOX 26.4—

Rules of Summarizing Content Analysis

Z1   *Paraphrase*
Z1.1   Delete all passages that transport no or only little content (like ornamenting, repeating, explicating formulations!)
Z1.2   Translate the passages transporting content onto a coherent level of language
Z1.3   Transform them to a grammatical short version!

Z2   *Generalization to the level of abstraction*
Z2.1   Generalize die issues of the paraphrases to the defined level of abstraction, so that the old issues are included in the new ones!

Z2.2	Generalize die predicates in the same way!
Z2.3	Keep the paraphrases, which are above the intended level of abstraction!
Z2.4	Employ theoretical assumptions in cases of doubt!
Z3	*First Reduction*
Z3.1	Delete paraphrases of the same meaning within the analytic unit
Z3.2	Delete paraphrases which are not seen as substantial on the new level of abstraction
Z3.3	Keep the paraphrases that are still seen as transporting central contents (selection)!
Z3.4	Employ theoretical assumptions in cases of doubt!
Z4	*Second Reduction*
Z4.1	Summarize paraphrases with identical (similar) issues and similar statements to one paraphrase (bundling)!
Z4.2	Summarize paraphrases with several statements about one issue (construction/integration)!
Z4.3	Summarize paraphrases with identical (similar) issues and different statements to one paraphrase (construction/integration)!
Z4.4	Employ theoretical assumptions in cases of doubt!

Source: Mayring (1983, p. 57)

An example of summarizing content analysis is given in Box 26.5 (see also Figure 26.2).

BOX 26.5

Example: Summarizing Content Analysis

Psychologist Philipp Mayring developed this method in a study about psychological coping with unemployment. It involved a large number of interviews with unemployed teachers.

In an interview with an unemployed teacher, the statement "and actually, quite the reverse, I was well very very keen on finally teaching for the first time" (Mayring 1983) emerges. This is *paraphrased* as "quite the reverse, very keen on practice" and *generalized* as "rather looking forward to practice." Similarly, the statement "therefore, I have already waited for it, to go to a seminar school, until I finally could teach there for the first time" is paraphrased as "waited to teach finally" and generalized as "looking forward to practice."

Due to the similarity between the two generalizations, the second one is then skipped and reduced with other statements to "practice not experienced as shock but as big fun" (1983, p. 59).

As the example in Box 26.5 illustrates, you can reduce the source text by skipping those statements that overlap at the level of the generalization.

Explicative Content Analysis

Explicative content analysis works in the opposite way. It clarifies diffuse, ambiguous, or contradictory passages by involving context material in the analysis. Definitions taken from dictionaries or derived from the grammar are used. A distinction is made between *narrow content analysis* and *wide content analysis*. Narrow context analysis picks up additional statements from the text in order to explicate the passages to be analyzed, whereas wide context analysis seeks information outside the text (about the author, the generative situations, from theories). On this basis an *explicating paraphrase* is formulated and tested.

An example of explicative content analysis is given in Box 26.6.

BOX 26.6

Example: Explicative Content Analysis

In an interview, a teacher expresses her difficulties in teaching, stating that she—unlike successful colleagues—was no "entertainer type" (Mayring 1983, p. 109). In order to find out what she wishes to express by using this concept, definitions of "entertainer" are assembled from two dictionaries. Then the characteristics of a teacher who fits this description are identified from statements made by the teacher in the interview. Further passages are consulted.

Based on the descriptions of such colleagues included in these passages, an "explicating paraphrase can be formulated: an entertainer type is somebody who plays the part of an extroverted, spirited, sparkling, and self-assured human being" (1983, p. 74). This explication is assessed again by applying it to the direct context in which the concept was used.

Structuring Content Analysis

Structuring content analysis looks for types or formal structures in the material. Structuring is done on the formal, typifying, scaling level or as regards content:

> According to formal aspects, an internal structure can be filtered out (formal structuring); material can be extracted and condensed to certain domains of content (structuring as regards content). One can look for single salient features in the material and describe them more exactly (typifying structuring); finally, the material may be rated according to dimensions in the form of scales (scaling structuring). (Mayring 1983, pp. 53–54)

Box 26.7 presents an example of structuring content analysis.

─BOX 26.7─

Example: Structuring Content Analysis

One of the main questions in the project was: "Did the 'shock of the practice' influence the individual's self-confidence?" (Mayring 1983, p. 88). Therefore, the concept "self-confidence" (SC) was the subject of a simple scaling, which produced four categories: "C1, high SC; C2, medium SC; C3, low SC; C4, not inferable" (1983, p. 90). For each degree, a definition is formulated (e.g., for C2: "I maneuvered through this somehow, but often it was a tightrope walk" (1983, p. 91)). The next step is to formulate rules of coding. These are used to search the text for passages where statements about self-confidence can be found. These classifications finally pass a rating, which for example may aim at an analysis of frequencies of the different degrees in a category. But the fact is that for this form of content analysis: "for editing the results, no general rule can be defined. It depends on the respective research question" (1983, p. 87).

What Is the Contribution to the General Methodological Discussion?

Due to the schematic elaboration of the proceedings, this procedure seems more clear, less ambiguous, and easier to handle than other methods of data analysis. This is also due to the possible reduction of the material outlined above. The many rules that are formulated underline this impression of greater clarity and unambiguity. The approach mainly suits a reductive analysis of large masses of text, which is oriented to the surface of these texts. The formalization of the procedure produces a uniform schema of categories, which facilitates the comparison of the different cases to which it is applied throughout. This is an advantage over more inductive or case-oriented analytic procedures.

How Does the Method Fit into the Research Process?

The method is not limited to a particular theoretical background. It is used mainly to analyze subjective viewpoints (see Chapters 7 and 9), collected with interviews (see Chapter 16). The selection of materials mainly follows criteria that are defined in advance, but may also proceed step by step (see Chapter 13).

What Are the Limitations of the Method?

Often, however, the application of the rules given by Mayring proves at least as costly as in other procedures. Due particularly to the schematization of the proceedings and to the way the single steps are tidied up, the approach is strongly marked by the ideal of a quantitative methodology. Categorization of text based on theories may obscure the view of the contents, rather than facilitate analyzing the text in its depth and underlying meanings. Interpretation of the text as in other methods is done rather schematically with this method, especially when the technique of explicative content analysis is used, but without really reaching the depths of the text. Another problem is the use of paraphrases, which are used not only to explain the basic text, but also to replace it—mainly in summarizing content analysis.

The methods discussed in this chapter have a unifying feature, namely, the analysis of textual material through coding. Categories are mostly developed from the text but are also received from the literature. The internal (formal or meaning) structure of the analyzed text is not the (main) point of reference for the interpretation. Sooner or later, all these approaches turn to finding evidence for certain categories in the text and to assigning these to the categories.

The treatment of the individual case becomes important in different ways. In thematic coding, first a case analysis is produced before the material is analyzed across cases. The other procedures take the textual material altogether as a point of reference and develop or apply a system of categories, which transcends the single case.

Checklist for Using Thematic Coding and Qualitative Content Analysis

The following checklist may give you an orientation when deciding which form of coding to apply or for using coding at all for analyzing your material:

- What are your expectations for coding material in your study?
- Are you aiming (a) at describing the material or (b) to develop a typology for certain themes in the coding procedures?
- Which approach of coding is the most appropriate for your issue?
- Do you bring your categories or a coding frame to your material or develop categories from it?
- Do you want to reduce your material first of all?
- Is your analysis systematic in a way suggested by qualitative content analysis?
- How do you take into account the fact that coding is a way of (re)constructing events and experiences?

KEY POINTS

- Coding can either start from the text, in order to develop a set of categories (thematic coding), or take a set of categories as a starting point (content analysis).
- Often a combination of the two strategies will be encountered. In qualitative content analysis, for example, development of categories can be a strategy in addition to using theory-based categories.
- Most important is the researcher's sensitivity in coding the material in line with what is happening within the text.
- Coding often involves a combination of a very fine analysis of some parts of the text and a rough classification and summary of other parts.

Exercise 26.1

1 Take a passage of text (perhaps the one from Exercise 24.5) and apply thematic coding to it. Formulate a slogan for the text. Write a short description of what is going on in the text.
2 Apply the coding paradigm mentioned above to the text.

Exercise 26.2

1 Take a piece of text and apply qualitative content analysis to it. Try to identify similar statements and paraphrase them in order to skip identical paraphrases (summarizing content analysis).
2 Now look for unclear words or statements in the text and apply explicative content analysis to them.

Further Reading

Thematic Analysis

In this article, the concept of thematic analysis is spelled out in relation to other methods of data analysis:

Braun, V. and Clarke, V. (2006) "Using Thematic Analysis in Psychology," *Qualitative Research in Psychology*, 3(2): 77–101.

Thematic Coding

In these texts, some applications and the methodological background of thematic coding can be found:

Flick, U. (1994) "Social Representations and the Social Construction of Everyday Knowledge: Theoretical and Methodological Queries," *Social Science Information*, 2: 179–197.
Flick, U. (1995) "Social Representations," in R. Harré, J. Smith and L.v. Langenhove (eds.), *Rethinking Psychology*. London: Sage. pp. 70–96.
Flick, U., Fischer, C., Neuber, A., Walter, U. and Schwartz, F.W. (2003) "Health in the Context of Being Old: Representations Held by Health Professionals," *Journal of Health Psychology*, 8: 539–556.

Qualitative Content Analysis

These texts discuss the method in greater detail:

Mayring, P. (2000) "Qualitative Content Analysis" [28 paragraphs]. *Forum Qualitative Sozialforschung / Forum: Qualitative Social Research*, 1(2), Art. 20, http://nbn-resolving.de/urn:nbn:de:0114-fqs0002204. (last access: August 13, 2013)

Mayring, P. (2004) "Qualitative Content Analysis," in U. Flick, E.v. Kardorff and I. Steinke (eds.), *A Companion to Qualitative Research*. London: Sage. pp. 266–269.

Schreier, M. (2012) *Qualitative Content Analysis in Practice*. London: Sage.

Schreier, M. (2014) "Qualitative content analysis," in U. Flick (ed.), *The SAGE Handbook of Qualitative Data Analysis*. London: Sage. pp. 170–183.

Coding and Categorizing

This text gives a good overview:

Gibbs, G. (2007) *Analyzing Qualitative Data*. London: Sage.

27

Naturally Occurring Data: Conversation, Discourse, and Hermeneutic Analysis

CHAPTER OBJECTIVES

This chapter is designed to help you

- understand the principles of conversation analysis;
- identify the developments coming from this approach;
- distinguish the various versions of discourse analysis;
- complete a discourse analysis;
- understand genre analysis;
- understand the principle of sequential analysis as the guiding principle of hermeneutic analysis;
- explain what objective hermeneutics means.

In the preceding chapters (Chapters 25 and 26), the main focus was on the content of statements solicited in, for example, an interview or a focus group. The focus was mainly on *what* the speaker said. This chapter, in contrast, considers approaches that focus on *how* something is said, in addition to the content of what is said.

Sometimes, in conversation analysis, for example, it is more the formal organization of a dialogue rather than its context, which is the focus of the analysis. The approaches introduced in this chapter have in common that they give more attention to how texts develop over time—they look at how an argument or discussion develops and is built up step by step, rather than looking for specific contents across the (whole) data set.

These approaches also have in common that they originally refrained from using data produced by such methods as interviews or focus groups: instead they used naturally occurring data, for example, everyday conversations that are recorded for research purposes. Subsequently, however, some of these approaches—notably discourse analysis—have been applied to interview or focus group data as well.

To understand and analyze statements, it is necessary to take into account the contexts in which they occur. "Context" here refers to both the discursive context and the local context in the interaction. This notion is more or less unarguable in qualitative research. For this reason, in qualitative interviews open-ended questions are asked, which encourage the respondents to say more rather than less, and in doing so produce enough textual material for the researcher to analyze in terms of contextual considerations. In analyzing data, coding is open for this reason, at least in the beginning.

The interpretative procedures discussed in the preceding chapters increasingly ignore the shape and structure of the text as a whole in the course of the rearrangement of statements into categories. As an alternative to this approach, one finds approaches that pay more attention to the text as a whole. Therefore, these approaches "let themselves be guided by the principle of sequential analysis. … The sequential analysis puts the idea of social order, which reproduces itself in the performance of the interaction, into methodological terms" (Bergmann 1985, p. 313).

Such approaches are guided by the assumptions that (a) order is produced turn by turn (conversation analysis), or that meaning accumulates in the performance of activity (objective hermeneutics), and (b) contents of interviews are presented in a reliable way only if they are presented in the form of a narrative (narrative analyses, see Chapter 18 for more details). In each case, a specific form of context sensitivity is the methodological principle.

Conversation Analysis

Conversation analysis is less interested in interpreting the content of texts that have been explicitly produced for research purposes, for instance interview responses. Rather it is more interested in the formal analysis of everyday situations. Bergmann outlines this approach, which may be considered to be the mainstream of ethnomethodological research, as follows:

Conversation Analysis (or CA) denotes a research approach dedicated to the investigation, along strictly empirical lines, of social interaction as a continuing process of producing and securing meaningful social order. CA proceeds on the basis that in all forms of linguistic and non-linguistic, direct and indirect communication, actors are occupied with the business of analyzing the situation and the context of their actions, interpreting the utterances of their interlocutors, producing situational appropriateness, intelligibility and effectiveness in their own utterances and co-coordinating their own dealings with the dealings of others. The goal of this approach is to determine the constitutive principles and mechanisms by means of which actors, in the situational completion of their actions and in reciprocal reaction to their interlocutors, create the meaningful structures and order of a sequence of events and of the activities that constitute these events. In terms of method CA begins with the richest possible documentation – with audio-visual recording and subsequent transcription – of real and authentic social events, and breaks these down, by a comparative-systematic process of analysis, into individual structural principles of social interaction as well as the practices used to manage them by participants in an interaction. (2004b, p. 296)

In this way, emphasis is placed less on the analysis of the contents of a conversation and more on the formal procedures through which the contents are communicated and certain situations are produced. As Toerien (2014, p. 329) puts it: "our starting point is to ask: *what* is being *done* in the talk, and *how?*" One historical starting point of conversation analysis as a research program was the work of Sacks, Schegloff, and Jefferson (1974) on the organization of turn taking in conversations. Another point of departure was the work of Schegloff and Sacks (1974) in explaining closings in conversations. First, conversation analysis assumes that interaction proceeds in an orderly way and nothing in it should be regarded as random. Second, the context of interaction not only influences this interaction, but also is produced and reproduced in it. And, third, the decision about what is relevant in social interaction and thus for the interpretation can only be made through the interpretation and not by *ex ante* settings.

Drew (1995, pp. 70–72) has outlined a series of methodological precepts for conversation analysis (CA), shown in Box 27.1.

BOX 27.1

Methodological Precepts for Conversation Analysis

1 Turns at talk are treated as the product of the sequential organization of talk, of the requirement to fit a current turn, appropriately and coherently, to its prior turn.

2 In referring … to the observable relevance of error on the part of one of the participants … we mean to focus analysis on participants' analyses of one another's verbal conduct.

3 By the "design" of a turn at talk, we mean to address two distinct phenomena: (1) the selection of an activity that a turn is designed to perform; and (2) the details of the verbal construction through which the turn's activity is accomplished.

(Continued)

(Continued)

4 A principal objective of CA research is to identify those sequential organizations or patterns ... which structure verbal conduct in interaction.

5 The recurrences and systematic basis of sequential patterns or organizations can only be demonstrated ... through collections of cases of the phenomena under investigation.

6 Data extracts are presented in such a way as to enable the reader to assess or challenge the analysis offered.

Source: Drew (1995, pp. 70–72)

Research in conversation analysis was at first limited to everyday conversation in a strict sense (e.g., telephone calls, gossip, or family conversations in which there is no formal distribution of roles). However, it is now becoming increasingly occupied with dialogue involving specific role distributions and asymmetries like counseling conversation, doctor–patient interactions, and trials (i.e., conversations occurring in specific institutional contexts). The approach has also been extended to include analysis of written texts, mass media, or reports—text in a broader sense (Bergmann 2004a).

The Procedure of Conversation Analysis

Ten Have (1999, p. 48) suggests the following steps for research projects using CA as a method:

1 getting or making recordings of natural interaction;
2 transcribing the tapes, in whole or in part;
3 analyzing selected episodes;
4 reporting the research.

The procedure of conversation analysis of the material itself includes the following steps. First, you identify a certain statement or series of statements in transcripts as a potential element of order in the respective type of conversation. In the second step you assemble a collection of cases in which this element of order can be found. You then specify how this element is used as a means for producing order in interactions and for which problem in the organization of interactions it is the answer. This is followed by an analysis of the methods with which those organizational problems are dealt with more generally. Thus a frequent starting point for conversation analyses is to inquire into how certain conversations are opened and which linguistic practices are applied for ending these conversations in an ordered way.

Toerien (2014, p. 330) lists four key stages of conversation analysis:

1 Collection building;
2 Individual case analysis;
3 Pattern identification;
4 Accounting for or evaluating your patterns.

A central distinction should be kept in mind between "ordinary" talk (occurring in everyday life) and "institutional" talk (as occurs in the professional practice of physicians, for example): conversation analysis was originally conceived for analyzing the former. Subsequently, it has been extended to the latter. In both cases, the principle is that the talk to be analyzed must have been a "naturally occurring" interaction, which was only recorded by the researcher. Thus conversation analysis does not work with data that have been stimulated for research purposes—like interviews that are produced for research purposes. Rather the research limits its activities of data collection to recording occurring interaction with the aim of coming as close as possible to the processes that actually happened, as opposed to reconstructions of those processes from the view of participant (e.g., reconstructions created through the interview process). This recorded interaction then is transcribed systematically and in great detail and thus transformed in the actual data that are analyzed.

Collection building means collecting all available (or accessible) cases of the format of interaction that should be analyzed—for example, all examples of a specific situation of counseling interaction that you can get hold of and record.

The individual case analysis (e.g., the single interaction session of counseling) then focuses on two fundamental principles: How are turns designed (what happens when the talking turns from one speaker to the other, how is that organized and working in the single case?) and how is the sequence organized (what is the sequential relationship between such turns, how is the structure of the interaction organized in this sequence (in more detail see Toerien 2014).

The third step (pattern identification) is based on comparing several examples of similar situations for the actions occurring in them, the organization of turn taking and of sequence that occurs in these situations. In the example in Case Study 27.1, a number of opening situations of counseling interactions are analyzed and compared in order to ascertain what the problem is that the participants have to deal with in each case, how the participants organize the turn taking in these situations, and how the sequence is organized. Thus such an analysis will seek to understand how the interaction works specifically as an example of counseling addressing a specific topic for the session.

The fourth step mentioned above by Toerien looks for the actual problem for which a pattern that was identified offers a solution or which it turns into a manageable problem in the conversation.

CASE STUDY 27.1

Socio-psychiatric Counseling

In my (PhD) study in the field of community psychiatry, I was able to show for counseling conversations how entrance into a conversation is organized via authorized starters (Wolff 1986, p. 71), regardless of the various conditions under which the individual conversation came about. Their:

> task is to mark that point for all who are involved in a comprehensible way, at which organizational principles of everyday conversation (for example to be able to talk about any possible topic) only apply in a limited way which is characteristic for that specific type of activity.

In the conversations analyzed, such starters may be designed rather than open-ended (e.g., "What made you come to us?" or "And, what is it about?" or "What is your desire?"). In other cases, they name the (given) topic for the counseling, or specific characteristics in the way the counseling conversation came into being. These openings, which begin the actual counseling relationship and delimit it from other forms of talk, are sometimes linked to explanations about the way the conversation came about. These explanations are specific to the situation (e.g., "So, your brother gave me a call").

My analysis showed two points concerning the ending of the first contacts in the counseling processes. First, a timely ending of the conversation has to be ensured. At the same time, the counselor has to guarantee continuation of the relation (e.g., "We have … two communities in T-street, which have just been opened. Well, Mr S, we have to wind the whole thing up for today, we must finish it"). In the last example, the ending of the consultation is introduced with a reference to other caring services. This produces continuity in the contact with the client as well as doing the work, which finishes the conversation "for today".

This analysis indicated which formal steps counseling conversations ran through more or less regularly. It also showed how these steps not only built up the conversation in itself, but also were influential in processing the clients and their cases—regardless of the specific contents of their problems. So, the analysis was more formal than content-oriented, but shows the construction of cases in the conversations.

An essential feature of conversation analytic interpretation is the strictly sequential procedure (i.e., ensuring that no later statements or interactions are consulted for explaining a certain sequence). Rather, the order of the occurrence must show itself in understanding it sequentially. The turn-by-turn production of order in the conversation is clarified by an analysis, which is oriented to this sequence of turns. Another feature is the emphasis on context. This means that the efforts in producing meaning or order in the conversation can only be analyzed as local practices—that is, only related to the concrete contexts in which they are embedded in the interaction and in which the interaction again is embedded (e.g., institutionally).

Analysis always start from the concrete case, its embedding, and its course to arrive at general statements.

Ten Have (1999, p. 104) suggests in conjunction with Schegloff's work three steps for analysis of repair in conversation, for example. "Repair" means the way people start a repair organization in cases of comprehension problems in a conversation. According to ten Have, you should proceed as follows:

1 Check the episode carefully in terms of *turn taking*: the construction of turns, pauses, overlaps, etc.; make notes of any remarkable phenomenon, especially on any "disturbances" in the fluent working of the turn-taking system.
2 Then look for *sequences* in the episode under review, especially adjacency pairs and their sequels.
3 And finally, note any phenomena of *repair*, such as repair initiators, actual repairs, etc.

What Is the Contribution to the General Methodological Discussion?

Conversation analysis and the empirical results it produces help to explain the social production of everyday conversations and specific forms of discourse. The results document the linguistic methods that are used in these discourses. Furthermore, they show the explanatory strength of the analysis of natural situations and how a strictly sequential analysis can provide findings, which accord with and take into account the compositional logic of social interaction.

How Does the Method Fit into the Research Process?

The theoretical background of conversation analysis is ethnomethodology (see Chapter 7) and its interest in understanding the methods used for organizing everyday life and practices. Research questions focus on members' formal procedures for constructing social reality (see Chapter 11). Empirical material is selected as a collection of examples of a process to be studied (see Chapter 13). Research avoids using explicit methods for collecting data in favor of recording everyday interaction processes as precisely as possible (see Chapter 24).

What Are the Limitations of the Method?

Formal practices of organizing interaction remain the point of reference for analyses here. Subjective meaning or the participants' intentions are not relevant to the analysis. This lack of interest in the contents of conversations in favor of analyzing how the "conversation machine" functions, which is at the forefront of many conversation analytic studies, has been repeatedly criticized (e.g., by Coulter 1983; Harré 1998).

Another point of critique is that conversation analytic studies often get lost in the formal detail—they isolate smaller and smaller particles and sequences from the context of the interaction as a whole (for this, see Heritage 1985, p. 8). This is enforced by the extreme exactness in producing transcripts.

Discourse Analysis

Discourse analysis has developed from various backgrounds, including conversation analysis. Both share the interest in how something is said as a relevant approach. This link also can be found in the following short definition of discourse analysis:

> Discourse analysis is concerned with the ways in which language constructs and mediates social and psychological realities. Discourse analysts foreground the constructive and performative properties of language, paying particular attention to the effects of our choice of words to express or describe something. (Willig 2014a, p. 341)

A major difference from conversation analysis is that discourse analysis is not limited to naturally occurring interaction: it is also applied to texts, such as interviews or group discussions, produced specifically for research and thus influenced by the researcher. However, discourse analysis of interviews pays the same attention to what the interviewer says as to what the interviewees says, so that the interview dialogue is in focus and not just the answers. A second difference to conversation analysis is that in discourse analysis coding is a step of the analysis (Willig 2003), which documents the turn from the (only) formal analysis in conversation analysis to contents and form in discourse analysis. There are several versions of discourse analysis available now.

Discursive psychology was developed by Edwards and Potter (1992), Harré (1998), and Potter and Wetherell (1998) in a critique of the theoretical and methodological program of social representations (see Chapter 7 and the contributions from both camps to Flick 1998). It is interested in showing how, in conversations, "participants' conversational versions of events (memories, descriptions, formulations) are constructed to do communicative interactive work" (Edwards and Potter 1992, p. 16). Although conversation analysis is named as a starting point, the empirical focus is more on the "content of talk, its subject matter and with its social rather than linguistic organisation" (1992, p. 28). This allows the analysis of psychological phenomena like memory and cognition as social and, above all, discursive phenomena. Special emphasis is placed on the construction of versions of the events in reports and presentations. The "interpretative repertoires," which are used in such constructions, are analyzed.

Discourse analytic procedures refer not only to everyday conversations, but also to other sorts of data such as interviews (e.g., in Potter and Wetherell (1998) on the topic of racism) or media reports (in Potter and Wetherell (1998) about the construction of versions in coverage of the Gulf War).

Willig (2014a, p. 344) mentions a number of questions that a discourse analysis should address (see Box 27.2).

Questions to Address in a Discourse Analysis

- What sorts of assumptions (about the world, about people) appear to underpin what is being said and how it is being said?
- Could what is being said have been said differently without fundamentally changing the meaning of what is being said? If so, how?
- What kind of discursive resources are being used to construct meaning here?
- What may be the potential consequences of the discourses that are used for those who are positioned by them, in terms of both their subjective experience and their ability to act in the world?
- How do speakers use the discursive resources that are available to them?
- What may be gained and what may be lost as a result of such deployments?

Willig's (2003, pp. 92–93) research process in discursive psychology first describes the steps of using naturally occurring text and talk. The first step is the audio recording of interactions. The second step is to produce texts in the form of transcripts of conversations, for example. Then, careful reading of the transcripts is the third step. This is followed by coding the material, then analyzing it. According to Potter and Wetherell (1987, p. 167), guiding questions are: Why am I reading this passage in this way? What features of the text produce this reading? The analysis focuses on context, variability, and constructions in the text and finally on the interpretative repertoires used in the texts. The last step, according to Willig, is writing up the discourse analytic research. Writing should be part of the analysis and return the researcher back to the empirical material.

Racism in New Zealand

Jonathan Potter and Margret Wetherell are leading protagonists of discourse analysis in social psychology in the United Kingdom. In one of their studies, they analyze the social construction of racism in New Zealand using the example of the white majority's treatment of the Maori culture, an indigenous minority. Interviews were conducted with over 80 representatives of the white majority population (professionals from middle-income classes like doctors, farmers, managers, teachers, and so on). Reports on parliamentary debates and informational material from the mass media were included as well.

The results of this type of cultural study pointed to the existence of different interpretative repertoires such as "Culture as Heritage." In this repertoire the core idea is of Maori culture as a set of traditions, rituals, and values passed down from earlier generations. Culture becomes defined in this repertoire as an archaic heritage, something to be preserved

(Continued)

(Continued)

and treasured, something to be protected from the rigors of the "modern world," like great works of art or endangered species. Here is a typical example:

> I'm quite, I'm certainly in favour of a bit of Maoritanga it is something uniquely New Zealand, and I guess I'm very conservation minded (yes) and in the same way as I don't like seeing a species go out of existence I don't like seeing (yes) a culture and a language (yes) and everything else fade out. (Potter and Wetherell 1998, p. 148)

This is opposed, for example, to the repertoire of "Culture as Therapy," in which "culture is constructed as a psychological need for Maoris, particularly young Maoris who have become estranged and need to rediscover their cultural 'roots' to become 'whole' again" (1998, p. 148).

This study shows that discourse analysts often use interview material (in contrast to conversation analysts, for example) and it also can exemplify the concept of interpretative repertoires.

Over the years a proliferation in discourse analysis has arisen. Parker (2004b), for example, has developed a model of critical discourse analysis, built on the background developed by Michel Foucault (e.g., Foucault 1980), which is why this is also referred to as *Foucauldian Discourse Analysis* (e.g., in Willig 2003). Here issues of critique, of ideology, and of power are more in focus than in other versions of discourse analysis. Parker (2004a, p. 310) proposes a number of steps in the research process:

1 The researcher should turn the text to be analyzed into written form, if it is not already.
2 The next step includes free association to varieties of meaning as a way of accessing cultural networks, and these should be noted down.
3 The researchers should systematically itemize the objects, usually marked by nouns, in the text or selected portion of text.
4 They should maintain a distance from the text by treating the text itself as the object of the study rather than what it seems to "refer" to.
5 Then they should systematically itemize the "subjects"—characters, persona, role positions—specified in the text.
6 They should reconstruct presupposed rights and responsibilities of "subjects" specified in the text.
7 Finally, they should map the networks of relationships into patterns. These patterns in language are "discourses" and can then be located in relations of ideology, power, and institutions.

Willig (2003, pp. 109–113) has summarized Foucauldian discourse analysis in six steps. After selecting texts for analysis, the first step is to look for "discursive constructions" of the issue of the research (identify where it is mentioned in the material and how it is constructed). The second step ("discourses") focuses on the differences between the identified constructions of the discursive object in the text(s). The third step examines the "action orientation" revealed in these constructions and asks for their function in this respect (does the speaker construct him- or herself as actor in a process or as a victim of this process?). In the next step, the analysis focuses on the "positionings" of the actors in the text, again in relation to agency concepts that become visible. The fifth step looks for the relation between the discourses and "practices" (how do the discourse and orientation manifest in (reported) practices?). The final step looks for the relation of the discourses and "subjectivity" (what can be "felt, thought and experienced from within various subject positions?" (p. 111)).

Key differences between discursive psychology and Foucauldian discourse analysis are, according to Willig (2003, pp. 121–122), located on thee levels. First, research questions differ: discursive psychology asks, "How do participants use language to manage stake in social interactions?" Foucauldian discourse analysis asks, "What characterizes the discursive worlds people inhabit and what are their implications for possible ways-of-being?" (p. 121). Second, this leads to differing models of agency—the active agent versus the power of discourse to construct objects including the human subject (p. 122). Finally, "experience" is questioned by discursive psychology, whereas it is theorized in the other approach as being the result and impact of discourses.

Parker (2013), finally, has presented a panorama of discourse analytic approaches in psychology. The common feature is that they take a critical stance towards psychology in their research. In his overview, he stresses the fact of being critical as more important in discourse analysis than a specific methodological approach in research. In the eight approaches he sees as important for mapping the field, he sees some principles as important:

> The first principle for innovative discursive research is that in place of fixed method abstracted from context, we are concerned from the beginning of our work with the phenomena we study as *historically* constituted. … The second principle is that, in place of simple steps that should be followed, we know that we must bring to bear upon the phenomenon a theoretical understanding. … The third principle is to embed some kind of account of *subjectivity* into the research process, and even if that account is not immediately developed as a theory of the subjectivity of those inhabiting the discourse we describe, it should at least include the subjectivity of the researcher in forms of reflexivity. (2013, p. 3–4)

These three principles clearly demonstrate that discourse analysis, according to this understanding at least, is more a critical and theoretical program than a methodological approach providing guidance on how to conduct a study using the approach. The view has developed that the approach is somewhat fuzzy. In particular, it seems to subsume a number of distinct approaches. Parker identifies the following eight: (1) conversation analysis, (2) ethnomethodology, (3) narrative analysis, (4) thematic analysis (see here Chapter 26), (5) critical discourse analysis (see the contributions to Wodak and Meyer 2009), (6) Foucauldian discourse analysis, (7) semiotic analysis, and (8) political discourse analysis (based on the works of philosophers like Butler and Žižek). As, for example, Augoustinos (2013) has criticized, this subsuming approach obscures some of the distinctive features between conversation analysis and discourse analysis. It also turns the more or less clearly defined research program of discourse analysis into a vast and somewhat vague program of critique and theory. This has led to a fragmentation and marginalization of the approach in psychology. In particular, Augoustinos criticizes Parker for omitting from his bundle of discourse approaches the discursive psychology of Potter, Wetherell, Edwards, and others (which indeed was, for a long time, the most influential approach).

What Is the Contribution to the General Methodological Discussion?

Discourse analytic studies analyze issues that are closer to the topics of social sciences than those of conversation analysis (on this see Silverman 1993). They combine language analytic proceedings with analyses of processes of knowledge and constructions without restricting themselves to the formal aspects of linguistic presentations and processes.

How Does the Method Fit into the Research Process?

The theoretical background of discourse analysis is social constructionism (see Chapters 7 and 8). Research questions focus on how the making of social reality can be studied in discourses about certain objects or processes (see Chapter 11). Empirical material ranges from media articles to interviews (see Chapter 13). Interpretations are based on transcripts of those interviews or the texts to be found (see Chapter 24).

What Are the Limitations of the Method?

Methodological suggestions on how to carry out discourse analyses remain rather imprecise and implicit in most of the literature. Theoretical claims and empirical results are dominant in the works published. In some contexts, the fuzziness of the methodology behind discourse analysis is growing because more and more approaches in qualitative research are subsumed under this label by some major protagonists in the field.

Genre Analysis

A second development coming from conversation analysis is called genre analysis (see Knoblauch and Luckmann 2004). Communicative genres are socially rooted phenomena. Communicative patterns and genres are viewed as institutions of communication, which interactants communicate with others. The methodological steps include the recording of communicative events in natural situations and their transcription. The next step is that these data are hermeneutically interpreted and subjected to a sequential analysis (see also later in this chapter) before a conversation analysis is done with the material in order to show the language's level of organization. From these two steps of analysis, structural models are set up that are then tested for their appropriateness with further cases. In the final step, structural variants are considered that come about as a result of modalization. Examples of such communicative genres are irony, gossip, and the like.

The analysis of the data focuses first on the internal structure of communicative genres including:

- Prosody: intonation, volume, speech tempo, pauses, rhythm, accentuation, voice quality.
- Language variety: standard language, jargon, dialect, sociolect.
- Linguistic register: formal, informal, or intimate.
- Stylistic and rhetorical figures: alliteration, metaphor, rhythm, and so on.
- "Small" and "minimal forms": verbal stereotypes, idiomatic expressions, platitudes, proverbs, categorical formulations, traditional historical formulae, inscriptions, and puzzles.
- Motifs, topoi, and structural markers. (Knoblauch and Luckmann 2004, p. 305)

Finally, the external structure of communicative genres and the communicative economy of their use are analyzed.

What Is the Contribution to the General Methodological Discussion?

Genre analytic studies analyze larger communicative patterns than does conversation analysis, but use similar principles. Contrary to discourse analysis, they keep the focus on formal patterns of communication and on contents. So, they combine the methodological rigor of conversation analysis with a more content-oriented approach.

How Does the Method Fit into the Research Process?

The theoretical background of genre analysis is again social constructionism (see Chapters 7 and 8). Research questions focus on how the making of social reality can be studied in the patterns that are used to communicate about certain objects or processes and their function (see Chapter 11). Empirical materials are recordings of communication. Interpretations are based on transcripts of those recordings (see Chapter 24).

What Are the Limitations of the Method?

The definition of a communicative genre is less clear than other units of qualitative analysis. The methodology is more comprehensive and more rigorous than other analytic approaches in qualitative research. However, because it comprises several methodological approaches (hermeneutic and conversation analytic methods), it is rather complicated and time-consuming.

Objective Hermeneutics

Objective hermeneutics was originally formulated for analyzing natural interactions (e.g., family conversations). It includes similar approaches to conversation analysis in one step of its procedure (see below). Subsequently the approach has been used to analyze all sorts of other documents, including even works of art and photographs. Schneider (1988) has modified this approach for analyzing interviews. The general extension of the domain of objects of inquiry based on objective hermeneutics is expressed by the fact that authors characteristically understand the "world as text." This is indicated by the title of a volume of theoretical and methodological works in this field (Garz 1994).

This approach draws a basic distinction between the subjective meaning that a statement or activity has for one or more participants and its objective meaning. The latter is understood by using the concept of a "latent structure of meaning." This structure can be examined only by using the framework of a multi-step scientific procedure of interpretation. Due to its orientation to such structures, the label "structural hermeneutics" has also been used.

The Procedure for Objective Hermeneutics

In the beginning, the aim was focused on the "reconstruction of *objective* meaning structures" of texts. Analysis in objective hermeneutics was not interested in what the text producers thought, wished, hoped, or believed when they produced their text. Subjective intentions linked to text are held to be irrelevant in this context. The only relevant thing is the objective meaning of the text in a particular linguistic and interactive community. Later, the label "objective" was extended beyond the issue of study: not only were the findings claimed to have (greater) validity, but also the procedure was seen as a guarantor of objective research.

Analysis in objective hermeneutics must be "strictly sequential": one must follow the temporal course of the events or the text in conducting the interpretation. Analysis should be conducted by a group of analysts working on the same text. First, the members define what case is to be analyzed and on which level it is to be located. It could be defined as a statement or activity of a specific person, or of someone who performs a certain role in an institutional context, or of a member of the human race.

This definition is followed by a sequential *rough analysis* aimed at analyzing the external contexts in which a statement is embedded in order to take into account the influence of such contexts. The focus of this rough analysis is mainly on considerations about the nature of the concrete action problem for which the studied action or interaction offers a solution. First, case structure hypotheses, which are falsified in later steps and the rough structure of the text and of the case, are developed. The specification of the external context or the interactional embedding of the case serves to answer questions about how the data came about:

> Under the heading of interactional embedding, the different layers of the external context of a protocolled action sequence must be specified with regard to possible consequences and restrictions for the concrete practice of interaction itself, including the conditions of producing the protocol as an interactional procedure. (Schneider 1985, p. 81)

The central step is sequential *fine analysis*. This entails the interpretation of interactions on nine levels as in Box 27.3 (Oevermann et al. 1979, pp. 394–402). At levels 1 and 3 of the interpretation, an attempt is made to reconstruct the objective context of a statement by constructing several possible contexts in thought experiments and by excluding them successively. Here the analysis of the subjective meanings of statements and actions plays a minor role. Interest focuses on the structures of interactions. The procedure at level 4 is oriented to interpretations using the framework of conversation analysis, whereas at level 5 the focus is on the formal linguistic (syntactic, semantic, or pragmatic) features of the text. Levels 6 to 8 strive for an increasing generalization of the structures that have been found (e.g., an examination is made of whether the forms of communication found in the text can be repeatedly found as general forms—that is, communicative figures—and also in other situations). These figures and structures are treated as hypotheses and are tested step by step against further material.

─BOX 27.3─

The Sequence of Stages in Objective Hermeneutics

0 Explication of the context which immediately precedes an interaction.
1 Paraphrasing the meaning of an interaction according to the verbatim text of the accompanying verbalization.
2 Explication of the interacting subject's intention.
3 Explication of the objective motives of the interaction and of its objective consequences.
4 Explication of the function of the interaction for the distribution of interactional roles.
5 Characterization of the linguistic features of the interaction.
6 Exploration of the interpreted interaction for constant communicative figures.
7 Explication of general relations.
8 Independent test of the general hypotheses that were formulated at the preceding level on the basis of interaction sequences from further cases.

Source: Oevermann et al. (1979, pp. 394–402)

According to Schneider (1985), the elaboration of general structures from interaction protocols can be shown in the following steps in the procedure of sequential fine analysis. First, the objective meaning of the first interaction is reconstructed (i.e., without taking the contextual conditions into account). Therefore, the research group constructs stories about as many contrasting situations as consistently fit a statement. At the next step, the group compares general structural features to the contextual conditions in which the analyzed statement occurred. The meaning of an action can be reconstructed through the interplay of possible contexts in which it might have occurred and the context in which it actually occurred.

In thought experiments, the interpreters reflect on the consequences that the statement they have just analyzed might have for the next turn in the interaction. They ask: what could the protagonist say or do next? This produces a variety of possible alternatives of how the interaction *might* proceed. Then the next *actual* statement is analyzed. It is compared to those possible alternatives which might have occurred (but which did not in fact do so). By increasingly excluding such alternatives and by reflecting on why they were not chosen by the protagonists, the analysts elaborate the structure of the case. This structure is finally generalized to the case as a whole. For this purpose, it is tested against further material from the case—which means subsequent actions and interactions in the text.

According to Wernet (2014, p. 239–243), interpretive practices are based on four principles:

1 Exclude the context: According to this, a statement is analyzed independently of the specific context in which it was made. Therefore, thought experimental contexts that are compatible with the text are formulated. This clarifies which meanings the statement could have, after which an interpretation referring to the concrete context follows.
2 Take the literal meaning of a text seriously: According to this, the statement has to be interpreted in the way it was actually made and not how the speaker possibly meant it—in particular when a mistake is made. The principle of literality makes a direct interpretative approach to the difference between manifest meanings and latent meaning structures of a text.
3 Sequentiality: Here one does not search for contents in the text, but interprets its process step by step. For the sequential analysis, it is absolutely important *not* to consider the text that follows a sequence that is currently being interpreted.
4 Extensivity: This means to include a multitude of interpretations (meanings the text might have).

─CASE STUDY 27.3─

Counselor–Client Interactions

Sahle (1987) has used this procedure in her PhD research to study the interactions of social workers with their clients. Additionally, she interviewed the social workers. She presents four case studies. In each case, she has extensively interpreted the opening sequence of the interactions in order to elaborate the structure formula for the interaction, which is then tested against a passage randomly sampled from the further text.

From the analyses Sahle derives hypotheses about the professional self-concept of the social workers and then tests them in the interviews. In a very short comparison, she relates the case studies to each other and finally discusses her results with the social workers that were involved.

More generally, Reichertz (2004, pp. 291–292) outlines three variants of text explanation in research using objective hermeneutics:

1 The *detailed analysis* of a text at eight different levels in which the knowledge and the external context, and also the pragmatics of a type of interaction, are explained in advance and are borne in mind during the analysis.
2 The *sequential analysis* of each individual contribution to an interaction, step by step. This is done without clarifying in advance the internal or external context of the utterance. This is the most demanding variant of objective hermeneutics, since it is very strongly based on the methodological premises of the overall concept.
3 The full *interpretation of the objective social data* from all those who participate in an interaction before any approach is made to the text to be interpreted. This variant handles the fundamentals of a theory of hermeneutics interpretation very flexibly and uses them in a rather metaphorical way.

Further Developments

This procedure was developed for analyzing everyday language interactions, which are available in recorded and transcribed form as material for interpretation. The sequential analysis seeks to reconstruct the layering of social meanings from the process of the actions. When the empirical material is available as a tape or video recording and as a transcript, you can analyze the material step by step from beginning to end. Therefore, always begin the analysis with the opening sequence of the interaction.

When analyzing interviews with this approach, the problem arises that interviewees do not always report events and processes in chronological order. For example, interviewees may recount a certain phase in their lives and then go on to refer during their narrative to events that happened much earlier. In the narrative interview too (particularly in the semi-structured interview), events and experiences are not recounted in chronological order. When using a sequence analytic method for analyzing interviews, you first have to reconstruct the sequential order of the story (or of the action system under study) from the interviewee's statements. Therefore, it is necessary to rearrange the events reported in the interview in the temporal order in which they occurred. The sequential analysis should then be based on this order of occurrence, rather than the temporal course of the interview: "The beginning of a sequential analysis is not the analysis of the opening of the conversation in the first interview but the analysis of those actions and events reported by the interviewee which are the earliest 'documents' of the case history" (Schneider 1988, p. 234).

Other recent developments aim at deriving a hermeneutics of images from this approach. Starting from a critique of the increasingly narrow concept of structure in Oevermann et al.'s approach, Lüders (1991) attempts to transfer the distinction between subjective and social meaning to the development of an analysis of interpretative patterns.

What Is the Contribution to the General Methodological Discussion?

A consequence of this approach is that the sequential analytical procedure has developed into a program with clearly demarcated methodological steps. A further consequence of this is that it is made clear that subjective views provide only *one* form of access to social phenomena: meaning is also produced at the level of the social (on this in a different context, see Silverman 1993/2001). Finally, the idea of social sciences as textual sciences is preserved most consistently here. Another aspect is the call for conducting interpretations in a group in order to increase the variation of the versions and perspectives brought to the text and to use the group to validate interpretations that have been made.

How Does the Method Fit into the Research Process?

The theoretical backgrounds of this approach are structuralist models (see Chapter 7). Research questions focus on the explanation of social meanings of actions or objects (see Chapter 11). Sampling decisions are mostly taken successively (step by step) (see Chapter 13). Often, the researcher refrains from using explicit methods for collecting data. Instead, everyday interactions are recorded and transcribed, although interviews and, occasionally, field notes from observational studies are also interpreted using objective hermeneutics. Generalization in this procedure starts from case studies and is sometimes developed using contrasting cases (see Chapter 29).

What Are the Limitations of the Method?

A problem with this approach is that, because of the great effort involved in the method, it is often limited to single case studies. The leap to general statements is often made without any intermediate steps. Furthermore, the understanding of the method as art, which can hardly be transformed into didactic elaboration and mediation, makes it more difficult to apply generally (for general skepticism, see Denzin 1988). However, a relatively extensive research practice using this approach can be seen in German-speaking countries.

The common feature of the sequential methods discussed above is that they are based on the temporal–logical structure of the text, which they take as a starting point for their interpretation. Thus they follow the text more closely than do categorizing methods as discussed in Chapters 25 and 26. The relation of formal aspects and contents is shaped differently. Conversation analysis (see above) is mainly interested in formal features of the interaction. Narrative analyses (see Chapter 18) start from the formal distinction between narrative and argumentative passages in interviews. This distinction is used: (1) for deciding which passages receive (more extended) interpretative attention, which will generally be the narrative passages; and (2) for assessing the credibility of what has been said—as narratives are usually regarded as more credible than argumentative passages.

In contrast to conversation analysis, in interpretations using objective hermeneutics the formal analysis of the text is a rather secondary level of interpretation. It is more the *content* of what is said that is in the focus. Sometimes, these methods employ hypotheses derived from passages of the text in order to test them against others.

Social Science Hermeneutics and Hermeneutic Sociology of Knowledge

Recent approaches have taken up the basic ideas of objective hermeneutics, but have developed a different understanding of hermeneutics and of the issues of research. They no longer use the term "objective," focusing instead on the social construction of knowledge. Again, non-standardized data—protocols of interaction—are preferred to interview data. Researchers should approach the field under study as naively as possible and collect unstructured data.

Interpretations follow a three-step procedure. First, open coding according to Strauss (1987; see Chapter 25) is applied with a focus on the sequential structure of the document (line by line, sometimes word by word). Then, researchers look for highly aggregated meaning units and concepts that bind together the parts and units. In the third step, new data are sought with which the interpretation is falsified, modified, and extended by means of the later data collection (for more details, see Reichertz 2004; Soeffner 2004).

Checklist for Using Naturally Occurring Data

The following checklist may give you an orientation for using naturally occurring data in qualitative research and how to analyze them:

1 What is your focus in analyzing the data in your research?
2 To what extent are you aiming at understanding how language and verbal interaction (i.e., conversation) works in organizing a social situation?
3 To what extent is your focus the discourse about a specific issue and how it is organized in specific interactions?
4 What role do you see for subjectivity in your research?
5 (How far) do you want to address meaning beyond what is represented on the level of subjectivity?

6 How do you take into account in your analysis the sequentiality of a conversation or in the data in general?

7 How do you link formal aspects (e.g., of a conversation) with the contents which the conversation is about in your analysis?

-KEY POINTS-

- Conversation analysis was originally designed for studying everyday interaction with a formal focus. Subsequently, it has been used as a starting point for analyzing other materials.
- Discourse analysis has a broader focus concerning the material that can be analyzed, but also aims to show how communication about a specific issue is organized (as a discourse).
- Genre analysis extends this analytic attitude to broader conversational tools, which are applied by the participants. Genre analysts aim to study the use of such tools.
- Hermeneutic approaches take into account the structure of the text. The analysis follows the structure of the text (sequentially) and sees the statements in this context.
- Social science hermeneutics links such a sequential analysis with open coding according to grounded theory research.

-Exercise 27.1-

1 Take your own data or find a transcript of an interaction in the literature (e.g., in Toerien and Kitzinger 2007). Analyze how this interaction opens—how it begins, who says what, and what kind of argumentation is used.

2 Then look at the way taking turns is organized: how does the second speaker take over from the first one, how does the first one stop talking, etc.?

3 Finally, identify sequences in the transcript such as question–answer, greeting–greeting back, etc.

-Exercise 27.2-

1 Apply the guiding questions of discourse analysis given in Box 27.2 to a piece of text from your own data or from the literature.

2 Look for interpretive repertoires in that text.

-Exercise 27.3-

1 Analyze how the interviewee presents him- or herself in the interview in individual text locations, especially at the beginning of the interview.

2 Apply the levels of interpretation from objective hermeneutics (see Box 27.3) to the beginning of the interview.

Conversation Analysis

The first three texts give an overview of the theoretical and methodological background (ethnomethodology) of the research program, while the other two discuss the more recent state of the art:

Bergmann, J. (2004a) "Conversation Analysis," in U. Flick, E.v. Kardorff and I. Steinke (eds.), *A Companion to Qualitative Research.* London: Sage. pp. 296–302.

Garfinkel, H. (1967) *Studies in Ethnomethodology.* Englewood Cliffs, NJ: Prentice Hall.

Sacks, H. (1992) *Lectures on Conversation,* Vols. 1, 2 (ed. G. Jefferson). Oxford: Blackwell.

Ten Have, P. (1999) *Doing Conversation Analysis: A Practical Guide.* London: Sage.

Toerien, M. (2014) "Conversations and Conversation Analysis," in U. Flick (ed.), *The SAGE Handbook of Qualitative Data Analysis.* London: Sage. pp. 327–340.

Discourse Analysis

These four texts give an overview of the research program:

Edwards, D. and Potter, J. (1992) *Discursive Psychology.* London: Sage.

Parker, I. (2004a) "Discourse Analysis," in U. Flick, E.v. Kardorff and I. Steinke (eds.), *A Companion to Qualitative Research.* London: Sage. pp. 308–312.

Potter, J. and Wetherell, M. (1998) "Social Representations, Discourse Analysis and Racism," in U. Flick (ed.), *Psychology of the Social.* Cambridge: Cambridge University Press. pp. 138–155.

Willig, C. (2014a) "Discourses and Discourse Analysis," in U. Flick (ed.), *The SAGE Handbook of Qualitative Data Analysis.* London: Sage. pp. 341–353.

Genre Analysis

The second text gives some explanation of the theoretical backgrounds of this approach, while the first gives more information about how to do a genre analysis:

Knoblauch, H. and Luckmann, Th. (2004) "Genre Analysis," in U. Flick, E.v. Kardorff and I. Steinke (eds.), *A Companion to Qualitative Research.* London: Sage. pp. 303–307.

Luckmann, Th. (1995) "Interaction Planning and Intersubjective Adjustment of Perspectives by Communicative Genres," in E.N. Goody (ed.), *Social Intelligence and Interaction: Expressions and Implications of the Social Bias in Human Intelligence.* Cambridge: Cambridge University Press. pp. 175–189.

Objective Hermeneutics

There are only limited traces of this method in the Anglophone literature. The first two texts are examples; the third and fourth give introductions and overviews:

Denzin, N.K. (1988) *Interpretive Biography.* London: Sage.

Gerhardt, U. (1988) "Qualitative Sociology in the Federal Republic of Germany," *Qualitative Sociology,* 11: 29–43.

Reichertz, J. (2004) "Objective Hermeneutics and Hermeneutic Sociology of Knowledge," in U. Flick, E.v. Kardorff and I. Steinke (eds.), *A Companion to Qualitative Research.* London: Sage. pp. 290–295.

Wernet, A. (2014) "Hermeneutics and Objective Hermeneutics," in U. Flick (ed.), *The SAGE Handbook of Qualitative Data Analysis.* London: Sage. pp. 234–246.

Social Science Hermeneutics and Hermeneutic Sociology of Knowledge

These two chapters describe this approach:

Reichertz, J. (2004) "Objective Hermeneutics and Hermeneutic Sociology of Knowledge," in U. Flick, E.v. Kardorff and I. Steinke (eds.), *A Companion to Qualitative Research*. London: Sage. pp. 290–295.

Soeffner, H.G. (2004) "Social Science Hermeneutics," in U. Flick, E.v. Kardorff and I. Steinke (eds.), *A Companion to Qualitative Research*. London: Sage. pp. 95–100.

General Overview

Rapley, T. (2007) *Doing Conversation, Discourse and Document Analysis*. London: Sage.

28

Using Software in Qualitative Data Analysis

CHAPTER OBJECTIVES

This chapter is designed to help you

- identify how computers can make qualitative research easier;
- understand the role of software in supporting the qualitative analysis of material;
- appreciate that software neither does the analysis on its own, nor replaces the use of a method for analyzing material: it merely offers some tools for making analysis more convenient;
- select the appropriate program for your study.

New Technologies: Hopes, Fears, and Fantasies

Qualitative research is undergoing technological change and this is influencing the essential character of qualitative research. For example, see Chapter 24 for the discussion about new technologies of recording and the new forms of data they have made possible for the first time. Since the mid 1980s there has been far-reaching technological change in the analysis of data, which is linked to the use of computers in qualitative research. Here, note the general changes in working patterns in the social sciences brought about by the personal computer, word processing, cloud computing, and mobile devices. However, it is also important to see the specific developments in and for qualitative research. A wide range of software programs is available, mostly focused on the area of qualitative data analysis. The programs are sometimes referred to as QDA (Qualitative Data Analysis) software or as CAQDAS (Computer-Aided Qualitative Data Analysis Software). This chapter is designed to help readers decide whether to use one of the most prominent programs—ATLAS. ti, MAXQDA, or NVivo/N7—for coding, to use their Office program (e.g. Microsoft Office) for the same purpose, or do it in the traditional way, that is, with pencil and paper.

The introduction of software programs in the field of qualitative data analysis has produced mixed feelings: some researchers have high hopes about the advantages of using them, while others have concerns and fears about how the use of software will change or even distort qualitative research practice. Accordingly, as Friese (2011, p. 2) shows, "Welsh (2002) has described two camps of researchers: those who see software as central to their way of analyzing data and those who feel that it is peripheral and fear that using it leads to a 'wrong' way of analyzing data." Some of these hopes may be right, some of these fears may have a kernel of truth, but some parts of both are more fantasy than anything else. For both parts it should be emphasized that there is a crucial difference between this kind of software and programs for statistical analysis (like SPSS). QDA software does not *do* qualitative analysis itself or in an *automatic* way like SPSS can do a statistical operation or a factor analysis: "ATLAS.ti – like any other CAQDAS program – does not actually analyze data; it is simply a tool for supporting the process of qualitative data analysis" (Friese 2011, p. 1).

QDA software is more like a word processor, which does not write your text but makes it somewhat easier for you to write a text; in a similar way, QDA supports qualitative research but neither automates it nor actually performs it. Just as it is still the author who writes by using the word processor, it is still the researcher who does the coding and so on by using QDA.

In the meantime, several overviews of the perpetually developing market have been published. Some of them have been written from the program developer's and teacher's point of view (e.g., for NVivo, see Bazeley and Jackson 2013; for ATLAS.ti, Friese 2011) and some from that of the user (for MAXQDA, see Corbin and Strauss 2008; for comparative perspectives on several of the major programs, see Gibbs 2007; 2014; Schönfelder 2011) or based on users' experiences (see the KWALON experiment bringing together developers' and users' perspectives on using QDA software: Evers, Silver, Mruck, and Peeters 2011). As progress in software development continually leads to the improvement of existing programs and updated versions and the appearance of new programs, all of these overviews are of course to some extent outdated almost as soon as they are available.

Ways of Using Software and Computers in Qualitative Research

Although most software and computing in qualitative research are used for analyzing data, there are some other steps in the qualitative research process for which computers can be employed. In general, the following ways of using computers and software in the context of qualitative research are mentioned:

1. Data collection and fieldwork: making notes in the field; writing or transcribing field notes (see Chapter 20) and editing them (correcting, extending, or revising field notes); transcription of interviews; writing of a research diary collecting virtual data in online interviews (see Chapter 16) and focus groups (Chapter 17); virtual ethnographies (Chapter 20) and documents (see Chapter 22).

2. Processing of collected data: coding (attaching keywords or tags to segments of text to permit later retrieval); storage (keeping text in an organized database); archiving, storing, search and retrieval (locating relevant segments of text and making them available for inspection); data "linking" (connecting relevant data segments to each other, forming categories, clusters, or networks of information); memo writing (writing reflective commentaries on some aspect of the data, as a basis for deeper analysis); and content analysis (counting frequencies, sequence, or locations of words and phrases).

3. Finalizing and presentation of the analysis: data display (placing selected or reduced data in a condensed, organized format, such as a matrix or network, for inspection); the drawing of conclusions and their verification—aiding the analyst to interpret displayed data and to test or confirm findings; theory building (developing systematic, conceptually coherent explanations of findings and testing hypotheses); graphic mapping (creating diagrams that depict findings or theories); report writing (interim and final reports, see also Miles and Huberman 1994, p. 44; Weitzman 2000, p. 806).

4. Project management: collaboration and communication with other researchers by e-mail or social networks or using cloud applications ("apps"); dissemination of finding; publishing and peer reviews.

5. Studying online phenomena (like online discussions, websites, and other forms of communicating).

Why Use Software for Analyzing Qualitative Data?

In the literature, several claims may be found concerning the potential advantages—or "real hopes" (Weitzman 2000, p. 806)—of the use of QDA software. The first one is *speed* in handling, managing, searching, and displaying data and related items like codes, or memos, in links to the data. But you should take into account the time necessary for deciding on a program, installing it, and learning to use it (or even the computer). Thus the real gain of time will be worth the effort in the long run and with bigger projects and bigger data sets, rather than in the short run and with smaller amounts of data.

The second claim is that the use of QDA software will *increase the quality* of qualitative research or at least make quality easier to demonstrate. Here, the gain of consistency in analytic procedures is mentioned or the extra rigor in analysis. Authors like Kelle and Laurie (1995) or Welsh (2002) underline that the use of

QDA software increases the validity of analyses in qualitative research. Finally, the transparency of the research process can be increased and the use of QDA software can facilitate communication in a research team and by analyzing the way links between texts and codes were developed, for example. Weitzman (2000) and Friese (2011) also mention consolidation of the research as the computer allows the researcher to have all research documents (from initial field notes to final displays, tables, and writings about the findings) in one place—the computer's hard disk. Seale (2000) discusses *a facilitation of sampling* decisions based on the state of data analysis so far (according to theoretical sampling, see Chapter 13) due to using a computer program.

A major expectation has been that QDA software will facilitate *data management*. Kelle (2004, p. 278), for example, lists a series of data management techniques supported by QDA computer programs:

- the definition of pointers containing index words together with the "addresses" of text passages, which can be used to retrieve indexed text segments;
- the construction of electronic cross-references with the help of so-called "hyperlinks," which can be used to "jump" between linked text passages;
- facilities for storing the researchers' comments ("memos"), which can be linked to index words or text segments;
- features for defining linkages between index words;
- the use of variables and filters so that the search for text segments can be restricted by certain limitations;
- facilities for the retrieval of text segments with specified formal relations to each other (e.g., text segments that appear within a certain specified maximum distance of each other);
- facilities for the retrieval of quantitative attributes of the database.

QDA software (though not office programs or standard database systems) offers the first two, whereas the other five are offered only by more elaborate software packages for qualitative research. Better QDA programs facilitate the *representation* of data, of structures in the data, and of findings in graphic maps and other forms of displays that can be immediately imported into word processors for writing about research and findings. Finally, no technological development is safe from being "misused" for purposes other than it was created for. Some people use programs like N7 as a reference manager in their personal library or ATLAS.ti (see below) to do the project planning in their jobs.

The above list of claims and expectations is quite varied. As in the earlier days of word processing, the decision to use one of the software alternatives makes it more complicated to switch from one to another. There are problems of compatibility and data export. There is still no standard that allows the transfer of data and codes from one package to another, for example (see Corti and Gregory (2011) about this as a challenge for future development). Thus, the decision for one or another software package should be well considered and taken carefully. And finally, the potential user should bear in mind that there is "no one best program" (Weitzman 2000, p. 803).

History and State of Development of QDA Software

If you want to do your analysis with the support of software, you can turn to existing programs for specific ends or even write your own program. Many of the programs available today have been created in this way—starting from specific needs and necessities in a concrete research project. Some programs have had their range of options extended in a way that allows them to be used for other research questions and data sorts than originally intended.

As a result, more than 25 programs have become available at some point, which have been developed especially for analyzing qualitative data. As Davidson and di Gregorio (2011, p. 629ff.) in their overview of the history of QDA software show, this variety included many programs that were written for PCs based on DOS and some that were written for MAC computers. Once Windows replaced DOS as the operating system and after strong commercialization and marketing of software programs, the variety of programs reduced to three widely used software packages (ATLAS.ti, MAXQDA, NUD*IST/NVivo; see also below), although other programs continue to be used and further developed (e.g., the ETHNOGRAPH).

The dominant programs include many of the functions that were once typical of single programs:

- Text retrieval, which allows researchers to search, summarize, list, etc., certain word sequences.
- Text-based managing for administering, searching, sorting, and ordering text passages.
- Code and retrieval for splitting the text into segments, to which codes are assigned, and for retrieving or listing all segments of the text, marked with each code; marking, ordering, sorting, and linking texts and codes are supported and both (text and code) are presented and administered together.
- Code-based theory building by supporting steps and operations at the level of the text (attachment of one or more passages to a code), but also at the conceptual level (relations between codes, super- and subcategories, networks of categories), always going back to the attached text passages. In some programs, more or less sophisticated graphic editors are included and it is possible to integrate video data.
- Conceptual networking, which offers extensive options for developing and presenting conceptual networks, networks of categories, and various ways to visualize relations among the various parts of the network.

Software for Analyzing Qualitative Data: How to Choose?

The advantages and disadvantages of single programs compared to other programs can be assessed in three ways: first, general questions may be formulated and applied to single programs; second, researchers should ask themselves some key questions when selecting special software; and, finally, more empirical research focusing on users' experiences with QDA software might be helpful (one of the few studies in this field is by Fielding and Lee 1998).

Guiding Questions for Analyzing and Comparing Programs

I have found that the guiding questions in Box 28.1 have proved helpful for assessing computer programs for qualitative research. They were formulated against the background of ATLAS.ti being developed by taking the coding procedures of grounded theory (of Strauss and Corbin 1990; see Chapter 25) as a starting point. The ETHNOGRAPH, for example, was developed in the context of ethnographic research and took this type of research as its orientation.

BOX 28.1

Guiding Questions for Comparing QDA Software

- Data-related questions: For which kind of data was the program conceived? For which data can it be used beyond these original data? For which data should it not be used?
- Activity-related questions: Which activities can be carried out with this program? Which should not be carried out with it?
- Process-related questions: How does the program influence the handling of data and the part played by the researcher or interpreter according to experiences up to now? What new options does it offer? What is made more difficult or laborious in the process of interpretation due to the program?
- Technical questions: What are the necessary conditions for the hardware (type of computer, RAM, hard disk, graphic card, screen, etc.) or the software (systems software, other programs needed) and networking options to other programs (SPSS, word processors, databases, etc.)?
- Competence-related questions: Which specific technical skills does the program require from the user (programming skills, maybe in specific programming languages etc.)?

Key Questions before Deciding on Specific Software

Quite early in the development, authors like Weitzman (2000, pp. 811–815) or Weitzman and Miles (1995, pp. 7–9) suggested that potential users should ask themselves a series of key questions before selecting software for data analysis or deciding to use the computer in this step. Pertinent questions include:

1 What kind of computer user are you? Here, four levels of computer use may be distinguished:

   (a) The beginner (level 1) is new to the computer and engaged with learning the computer's functions and how to use software. These users are likely to be challenged by more elaborate CAQDAS software and should reserve some extra time for learning the software before analyzing their texts.
   (b) A user at level 2 has some experience with software and hardware and is comfortable learning and exploring new programs.
   (c) The user at level 3 has a real interest in exploring the features and capacities of computer programs.

(d) Level 4 (the hacker) is something between an expert and an addict.

(e) Additionally, the question arises: which kind of computer and operating system should be used or are already being used (Windows, UNIX, or Apple)?

(f) Finally, the question of your own experience with qualitative research should be considered. Beginners in qualitative research as well as beginners in using computers are usually overly challenged by the more demanding programs, the options they make, and by the decision about which program to use.

2 Are you looking primarily for a program for a specific project or, more generally, for use in research over the coming years? Three questions arise here:

(a) First, what is the balance of the costs of training with the program (i.e., compare the data preparation against time savings when using the computer), especially if only a very limited amount of data is to be analyzed with the computer?

(b) Second, how far is the program selected according to the current needs (the kind of data, the research question, etc.) and how far, with respect to later, possibly more complex studies?

(c) Third, what is the stage of the current project? If you are close to the end of funding and the motivation to choose a computer is to speed up the last steps of analyzing the data, it is more likely that the extra time needed to get the computer, software, and computer-aided analysis going will actually hamper the research project rather than help due to the equipment and program learning curves.

3 What kinds of data and project are involved (one or more data sources, case, or comparative study; structured or open data; uniform or various inputs of data; size of the databases)?

(a) Is it only text or are you using video or photos, acoustic data or moving images, or e-mail and Internet traces (Bergmann and Meier 2004)? Not all software is ready to work with these forms of data.

(b) Are there several data sources for each case or only one data sort, are you running a case study, or do you work with several cases?

(c) Are the records you want to use fixed in their format (e.g., the exactness of transcription) from beginning to end or might the format be changed (e.g., refined) during progress of the project?

(d) Are the data structured (e.g., by an interview guide applied in every case) or free format (e.g., a narrative of the individual life course without any external structuring)?

(e) Finally, consider the database's size and limits when making a selection.

4 What kind of analysis do you plan?

(a) Exploratory or confirming?

(b) Predefined coding scheme or one to be developed?

(c) Multiple or simple coding?

(d) One round through the data or multi-step analysis?

(e) How delicate is the analysis?

(f) Interest in the context of the data?

(g) How the data are to be presented?

(h) Only qualitative or also numeric analyses?

(i) Is a fixed coding system or an evolving set of categories used?

(j) How important is it to leave the data in their context or to have the context of a statement available?

(k) Is it necessary to be able to attach several codes to one element of text?

(l) Are several researchers working and coding the same text at the same time or in a sequence?

5 How important is the proximity of the data in the process of analyzing them? Should the text which is interpreted always be accessible (on the screen) or only the categories etc?

6 Limits of costs: Can you afford to buy the program and the computers needed for using it?

7 How fine is the analysis? For example, conversation analysts work very intensely with very small parts of their data (e.g., a turn in a conversation). Ten Have (1999) discusses ways of using computers for this kind of analysis.

Examples: ATLAS.ti, NUD*IST/NVivo, and MAXQDA

ATLAS.ti

ATLAS.ti was developed in a research project at the Technical University of Berlin. The software is based on the approach of grounded theory and coding according to Strauss (1987; see Chapter 25). The program can work with different sorts of text documents: plain text with soft line breaks, rich text with embedded objects (Excel tables, PowerPoint, etc.), or direct access to Word documents. Its more recent versions are able to process not only texts but also images, graphics, and sound. It supports operations on the textual and conceptual levels. A "hermeneutic unit" is formed on the screen that unifies the primary text (e.g., the interview to interpret) and the interpretations or coding related to it. The program shows the primary text with all codes attached to it and comments in different windows on the screen. It offers some functions, which are present on the screen in the form of symbols (retrieval, copy, cut, coding, networking, etc.).

Apart from the retrieval of sequences of words in the text and the attachment of codes, the presentation of codes and categories in conceptual networks is helpful. The relation to the passage to which the categories and supercategories are linked is maintained and can be presented immediately on the screen. Codes can be listed on the screen or printed. Interfaces to SPSS and other programs are integrated. Furthermore, it is possible for different authors to work on the same text on different computers. There is quite good support from the author and a very active electronic list of users. For more information about the program and contact with other users, see www.atlasti.com. A textbook providing an introduction to working with this program is available (see Friese 2011).

NUD*IST/NVivo

This software was originally developed as a Mac program with the acronym NUD*IST. Later it was transferred to Windows, though Mac versions are still produced. The latest version includes a full command language for automating coding and searching and allows the merging of analytic files from two or more research projects initially run separately. It also allows integration of Internet and social media data (like Facebook etc.).

This program was distributed commercially very early on and was promoted very actively by the authors. Typical features of the program include "system closure" (i.e., memo or search results can be added to the original data) and the display of codes on the screen ("indexing") in a hierarchical tree structure. Information and support can be found at www.qsrinternational.com. A textbook providing an introduction to working with this program is available (see Bazeley and Jackson 2013).

MAXQDA

MAXQDA is the successor to winMAX, a program developed from 1989 onwards. Objects, like photos, Excel tables, PowerPoint slides, etc., may be imported as embedded objects of an rtf file. The program has a hierarchical code system with up to 10 levels. Codings are visualized in 11 different-colored strips. Memos are visualized by little "Post-it" icons; they can be attached at any line right beside the text or at the codes (to give for instance code definitions). Eleven different icons can freely be assigned to a memo to indicate different types. A Code-Matrix Browser and a Code-Relations Browser visualize the distribution of codes over all texts and the intersections of codes respectively. The values can be exported to SPSS or Excel. Also you can automatically code search results and import attributes from SPSS, or any other quantitative package, as well as export them to MAXQDA. A project in MAXQDA is just one file. Special strengths are the teamwork functions and the features to merge qualitative and quantitative analyses. More information and manuals are available at www.maxqda.com.

This and the other two programs above are just examples of the continually developing range of available programs and versions. More information about the field and other programs (links to producers, references to newer literature, etc.) can be found from the CAQDAS project at Surrey University at http://www.surrey.ac.uk/sociology/research/researchcentres/caqdas/.

How to Use Software in Qualitative Research

In an overview of using computers in qualitative research, Kelle (2000, pp. 295–296) outlines two possible strategies for using software in qualitative research. The first one is rather typical for using computers in grounded theory-oriented research (see Chapter 25), starting with developing codes from the empirical material (the texts):

Step 1: formatting textual data
Step 2: coding data with ad hoc codes (open coding)
Step 3: writing memos and attaching them to text segments
Step 4: comparing text segments to which the same codes have been attached
Step 5: integrating codes and attaching memos to codes
Step 6: developing a core category. (Kelle 2000, p. 295)

The second strategy is much more formalized, developing a code scheme at the beginning and a numerical data matrix. Here the use of computers is planned with a strong interest in linking the qualitative analysis to a more quantitative analysis in a later step:

Step 1: formatting textual data
Step 2: defining a code scheme
Step 3: coding data with the predefined code scheme
Step 4: linking memos to the codes (not to text segments) while coding
Step 5: comparing text segments to which the same codes have been attached
Step 6: developing subcategories from this comparison
Step 7: recoding the data with these subcategories
Step 8: producing a numerical data matrix, whereby the rows represent the text documents, the columns the categories (codes), and the values of the categories the subcategories
Step 9: analyzing this data matrix with SPSS. (Kelle 2000, p. 296)

These two strategies should be seen as no more than suggestions about how to proceed. As a user of CAQDAS programs, you should develop your own strategy on the basis of the aims and research questions as well as the sorts of data and resources in the project.

CASE STUDY 28.1

Social Representation of AIDS among Zambian Adolescents

In their study, Joffe and Bettega (2003) used ATLAS.ti for analyzing interviews with adolescents in Zambia about AIDS. The authors did 60 semi-structured, in-depth interviews with Zambian adolescents aged 15 to 20. The interviews and results focused on representations of (1) the origin of HIV/AIDS; (2) the spread of HIV/AIDS; and (3) the personal risk of HIV/AIDS. With ATLAS.ti, the authors created thematic networks like the one in Figure 28.1, which represents the ideas about the origin of HIV/AIDS mentioned by the participants of the study.

This example shows how you can use software like ATLAS.ti to structure your categories and your results. The interesting thing about using such software is the link between the category and the original texts (statements, stories) it is linked to.

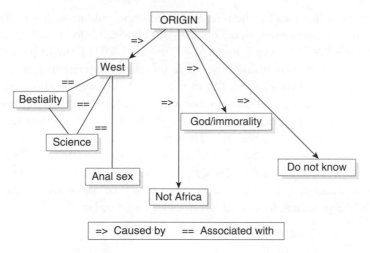

FIGURE 28.1   Origin of AIDS Represented in a Thematic Network Produced with ATLAS.ti

Source: Reproduced from Joffe and Bettega (2003)

Software's Impact on Qualitative Research: Examples

The discussion about the impact of software on qualitative research began with development of the very first programs. In this discussion one finds various concerns. First of all, some of the leading programs were developed on the back of a specific approach—coding according to grounded theory—and are more difficult to apply to other approaches. If the software does not fit a more sequential interpretation of data, is it just ignored by those researchers using this approach? Or does it change the way of analyzing data? And does it lead to some kind of common approach, a gold standard of qualitative research (Coffey, Holbrook, and Atkinson 1996)? Fielding and Lee (1998) already found in their empirical study on software use that in two-thirds of the projects the researchers they interviewed did not use grounded theory but used CAQDAS programs. This shows that the link between software and grounded theory is not as close as some authors suspect. Ten Have (1999) shows how this software can be applied to conversation analysis.

Another concern is that software implicitly forces its logical and display structure upon the data and the researcher's analysis. For example, NUD*IST/NVivo supports the development of a hierarchical tree structure of coding. Among its users, a certain inflation of tree-structured coding systems can be found. Seale (2000) gives a nice illustration of this problem when he applies NUD*IST and ATLAS.ti to a grounded theory developed by Glaser and Strauss and shows how different the display and the structure of this theory look in both programs.

Finally, there is a fear that the attention attracted by the computer and the software will distract the researcher from the real analytic work—reading, understanding, and contemplating the texts, and so on. Similarly, Richards and Richards, developers of one of the leading programs (NUD*IST), stated quite early: "The computer method can have dramatic implications for the research process and outcomes, from unacceptable restrictions on analysis to unexpected opening out of possibilities" (1998, p. 211). More recently, in the KWALON experiment (see Evers et al. 2011), the impact of software on qualitative analysis was studied by giving the same material to researchers using different software in their analyses. But in the end, it depends on the users and their ways of making the computer and the software useful for the ongoing research and how they reflect on what they are doing. Thus computers and software are pragmatic tools that support qualitative research. Their users should reflect on the technology's impact on the research itself. They should not be overloaded with hopes and expectancies, neither should they be demonized. Further developments in this field should be watched with interest, but a technological revolution of qualitative research due to using CAQDAS programs in general has not happened so far.

Future Developments: CAQDAS 2.0

In their account of the history and future of technology in qualitative research, Davidson and di Gregorio (2011) see us "in the midst of a revolution" (the phrase appears in the subtitle of their article). The authors show how the development of qualitative software use has paralleled the development of qualitative research in general (at least according to the stages in the model of Denzin and Lincoln 2011). They presented six stages in the field of QDA software development and use. Then they linked the developments in the field of QDA software to the developments in the field of Web 2.0 applications (like YouTube, Twitter, Facebook, etc.).

Their basic idea for the future of using technologies in qualitative analysis is that the software so far discussed in this chapter will be challenged or replaced by apps developed by interested users. At the same time, the authors report on research programs supporting the development of such kinds of devices and apps in the United Kingdom and other countries. The tools developed in such contexts focus on collaborative analysis (of video data, for example), collaborative analysis and developments (in wikis or cloud computing, for example), on blogging with hyperlinks as ways of collaborating, and the like. For CAQDAS tools and CAQDAS 2.0 tools, they list a number of basic requirements. For both sorts of tools the authors see as essential 'that these new tools

'Possess an intuitive and visually attractive interface;

Are easily accessible;

Have powerful, intuitive, and contextualized search tools;

Are easily combined to create new user-specialized tools;

Provide opportunities for visualization and spatialization;

Offer ease of integration with quantification tools; and

Offer strong functionality for collaborative work.' (Davidson and di Gregorio 2011, p. 638)

It can be expected that the existing CAQDAS programs will be further updated to integrate these requirements, where they do not yet meet them, but also that there will be set of tools beyond them in the near future, which will challenge and change the established software. In some ways the development of apps by users closes the circle to the beginning of QDA software, when programs were written by researchers for their own needs and data.

What Is the Contribution to the General Methodological Discussion?

The use of software has made the use of analytic techniques such as theoretical coding more explicit and transparent. Using software leads to more transparency about how the researcher has developed categories from the analyzed text and applied them to it. This can be documented and communicated among the researchers in the team as well as to readers of the research report, for example. Some authors see in such a form of transparency an increase of validity. Furthermore, such software allows new forms of administrating codes and texts and the links between both, and supports new forms of display. It also supports linking textual/verbal and non-textual/visual data in an analysis.

How Does the Method Fit into the Research Process?

Software originally best suited grounded theory research in which coding is applied to develop categories from the material, but subsequent developments have been more open to all sorts of analysis. The restrictions on the forms of data that can be used with this software have been reduced. Although other forms of data analysis are compatible with using QDA software, their link to coding and categorizing is still the closest.

What Are the Limitations of the Tools?

One problem with using QDA software is that it is only a tool for facilitating analysis and interpretation, which needs to be guided by a method. Often you will find in articles or other reports about qualitative research a statement from the authors that they used, for example, ATLAS.ti. When this is the only explanation of how the data were analyzed, I sometimes have the impression that the role of the software has been misunderstood. In such a case, the program is confused with a method instead of seeing it as a tool.

Checklist for Using Software in Qualitative Data Analysis

The checklist below may give you some orientation for using software in your study and which program to select:

1 What are your expectations for using software in analyzing the material in your study?
2 Which method of analysis do you want to apply?
3 Are you sufficiently familiar with this method of analysis?
4 Does QDA software fit the method and your aims in analyzing your data?
5 Do you have the skills necessary for learning and using the software?
6 How much support is available for you in case of problems?
7 Can you learn using the software by yourself or is there any tutoring available for you?
8 At what stage is your project—is it early enough for including software in your analysis?

KEY POINTS

- To maximize the benefits of using QDA software, it is important to decide early enough in the research process how to use it and have the time to prepare its use.
- The software available continues to develop quickly, though programs tend to converge towards similar features and capacities. In the end, selecting a program has more to do with availability and personal preferences.
- QDA software does not do the analysis for you. Its impact on the way the users do their research is more limited than some critics see. It is crucial to reflect on the way you use the software and to ensure that you subordinate it to your style of analysis (rather than the other way around).

Exercise 28.1

1 Follow one of the Internet links mentioned in this chapter and download a demonstration version of one (or more) of the programs (e.g., ATLAS.ti or MAXQDA). Explore the programs to understand their capabilities.
2 Consider how you could use the program in your study to make your analysis more transparent.
3 How could you use the program to save time or make your work easier?
4 Look for a study (e.g., Flick, Garms-Homolová and Röhnsch 2010) that was done without such software. How could software have improved the study you found? What would have been the impact of the software on the analysis?

Further Reading

These texts give concrete suggestions for using computers in qualitative research and also address problems associated with their use:

Bazeley, P. and Jackson, K. (2013) *Qualitative Data Analysis with NVivo* (2nd edn). London: Sage.
Davidson, J. and di Gregorio, S. (2011) "Qualitative Research and Technology: In the Midst of a Revolution," in N. Denzin and Y.S. Lincoln (eds.), *Handbook of Qualitative Research* (4th edn). London: Sage. pp. 627–643.

Friese, S. (2011) *Qualitative Data Analysis with ATLAS.ti*. London: Sage.

Gibbs, G. (2007) *Analyzing Qualitative Data*. London: Sage.

Gibbs, G. (2014) "Using Software in Qualitative Analysis," in U. Flick (ed.), *The SAGE Handbook of Qualitative Data Analysis*. London: Sage. pp. 277–294.

To remain updated with the rapid developments in this area, I suggest that you visit http://www.surrey.ac.uk/sociology/research/researchcentres/caqdas/

PART 7
Grounding, Writing, and Outlook

Contents

In this part, we address two major questions: how do you evaluate qualitative research, and how do you present results and the ways that you produced these results to your audience?

The first question becomes increasingly relevant the more that qualitative research becomes established, wants to be taken seriously, and competes with quantitative research in the social sciences or with research in the natural sciences for reputation, funding, and legitimacy.

In answering this question, you can go two ways. Either you can focus on the discussions about quality criteria and about which ones to employ. You will find quite a variety of suggestions for criteria in qualitative research, and you will also find plenty of argumentation criticizing these attempts. The first part of Chapter 29 provides an overview of the various criteria and the discussions linked to them. Or you can try to assess the quality of qualitative research beyond criteria, in which case you will use strategies of quality management as an alternative. In general, it is more the research process as a whole which becomes relevant for checking the quality of research, rather than a criterion-based assessment of some single step. The second part of Chapter 29 describes such process-oriented strategies of quality management in research.

After that, it is necessary to answer the question of indication and to think about why you use qualitative research in general and specific methods in particular for your own study.

Chapter 30 addresses the issue of how to present your research. Either you can see this as a technical problem—what are the best ways to write about your research? Or you can see it as a fundamental problem—how do the researchers' act of writing and their style cover the act of research, the realities in the field, and the perspectives of the people that were studied? Then the problem of writing becomes an issue of legitimacy and the problems linked to this issue may drive qualitative research back towards the tension between art and method.

In the final chapter, Chapter 31, an integrating overview of the state of the art of qualitative research is given as a kind of round-up, which leads to considerations of how to teach and learn qualitative research and about its future in the space between art and method.

29

Quality of Qualitative Research: Criteria and Beyond

CHAPTER OBJECTIVES

This chapter is designed to help you

- explore the relationships between qualitative research, criteria of quality, quality management, and quality assurance;
- understand the problems that arise when applying standard criteria from quantitative research to qualitative studies;
- identify ways of reformulating traditional criteria;
- learn about alternative criteria originating from qualitative researchers;
- recognize the general problems relating to the use of criteria in qualitative research;
- understand ways of assessing quality in qualitative research, beyond the use of criteria;
- distinguish problems, and the means, of generalization in qualitative research;
- recognize strategies of process evaluation and quality management in research and their contribution to answering the question of quality;
- identify the potential benefits and problems involved in the question of indication of methods.

The problem of how to assess qualitative research has not yet been solved. It is repeatedly taken up as an issue in order to raise general questions about the legitimacy of this kind of research. Should qualitative research be assessed with the same criteria and concepts as quantitative research or are there any specific ways to assess qualitative research? Are there any generally accepted criteria or strategies for assessing qualitative research and its results? Can research be "valid" and "reliable" without being subject to the traditional means of assessing validity and reliability? Such questions have dominated the discussions about the value of qualitative research as a specific approach or as part of a wider concept of empirical research.

Selective Plausibilization

One criticism of quality research stems from the observation that often interpretations and results are made transparent and comprehensible for the reader only by the interweaving of "illustrative" quotations from interviews or observation protocols. Especially where the researchers use this as "the only instrument for documenting their statements," Bühler-Niederberger (1985, p. 475) critically argues that "the credibility passed on by this is not sufficient." Why this is the case is clarified by Girtler, although involuntarily, in a very illustrative way:

> If I now prepare the publication about my research ... I finally present what is characteristic. In order to make vivid and provable these characteristics or the characteristic rules from which I "understand" the social practice to be studied or which I use to explain it, I quote the corresponding passages from my observational protocols or interviews. Of course, I quote only those passages which I believe illustrate the characteristics of the everyday world under study. (1984, p. 146)

This procedure, which may also be labeled "selective plausibilization," cannot solve the problem of comprehensibility in an adequate way. Above all, it remains unclear how the researchers handle cases and passages that they "believe" are not so illustrative of the characteristics, or cases and passages that may even be deviant or contradictory.

The different facets of the problem mentioned here could be summarized as "grounding qualitative research." Essentially, four topics fall under this heading:

1 Which criteria should be used to assess the procedure and results of qualitative research in an appropriate way?
2 What degree of generalization of the results can be obtained each time, and how can one guarantee generalization?
3 Are there other ways to address the question of quality in qualitative research more adequately?
4 How do you present procedures and results of qualitative research (see Chapter 30)?

Concerning the criteria for assessing the procedures and results of qualitative research, the following alternatives have been discussed in the literature. The first is to apply classical criteria like validity and reliability to qualitative research or to reformulate them in an adequate way for this purpose. The second is to develop new, "method-appropriate criteria," which do justice to the specificity of qualitative research because they have been developed from one of its specific theoretical backgrounds and so are designed to take the peculiarity of the qualitative research process into account. A third version engages with the discussion about how it is still possible to ask about validity, given the crises of representation and legitimation mentioned by Denzin and Lincoln (2000b, p. 17). This last version surely will neither contribute to further establishing the credibility of qualitative research, nor contribute to its results being considered as relevant in any way to the community. Therefore, attention will be given here to the first two ways. In terms of the use of classical criteria, the discussion concentrates on reliability and validity.

Using Classical Criteria

Here we examine three criteria, namely reliability, validity, and objectivity.

Reliability

In order to specify reliability as a criterion for assessing qualitative research, Kirk and Miller (1986) discuss three forms. They see *quixotic reliability* as the attempt to specify how far a particular method can consistently lead to the same measurements or results. The authors reject this specific form of reliability as trivial and misleading. Kirk and Miller discuss *diachronic reliability* in terms of the stability of measurements or observations in their temporal course. What becomes problematic here is the precondition that the phenomenon under study in itself may not undergo any changes, in order for this criterion to be effective: qualitative studies are seldom engaged in such unchanging objects.

Synchronic reliability is the constancy or consistency of results obtained at the same moment but using different instruments. Kirk and Miller emphasize that this criterion is most instructive when it is *not* fulfilled. The question then follows as to why this is the case and also raises questions concerning the different perspectives on the issue resulting from different methods applied by several researchers.

Procedural Reliability

Reliability gains its importance as a criterion for assessing qualitative research only against the background of a specific theory regarding the issue under study and the use of methods. But researchers can follow different ways in order to increase the reliability of data and interpretations. In ethnographic research, in terms of which Kirk and Miller discuss these criteria, the quality of recording and documenting data becomes a central basis for assessing their reliability and that of succeeding interpretations. One starting point for examining this is the field notes in which researchers document their observations. Standardization of notes increases the reliability of such data if several observers collect the data. The four forms of field notes that have already been discussed in Chapter 20 on observation (see also Spradley 1979) are one approach to this structuring.

For increasing their reliability, Kirk and Miller (1986, p. 57) suggest conventions for note taking, which are further developed by Silverman (1993, p. 147). These are shown in Box 29.1.

BOX 29.1

Conventions for Field Notes

Sign	Convention	Use
" "	Double quotation marks	Verbatim quotes
' '	Single quotation marks	Paraphrases
( )	Parentheses	Contextual data or fieldworker's interpretations
< >	Angled brackets	Emic concepts (of the member)
/ /	Slash	Etic concepts (of the researcher)
_____	Solid line	Beginning or end of a segment

Sources: Adapted from Kirk and Miller (1986) and Silverman (1993)

The underlying idea is that the use of conventions for how to write notes increases the comparability of the perspectives which have led to the corresponding data. In particular, the separation of concepts of the observed from those of the observers in the notes makes reinterpretation and assessment by different analysts possible. Transcription rules that clarify procedures for transcribing conversations have a similar function to conventions for writing notes in such a way.

For interview data, reliability can be increased by interview training for the interviewers and by checking the interview guides or generative questions in test interviews or following the first interview (see Chapter 15). For observations, the requirement to train the observers before they enter the field and to regularly evaluate the observing can be added. In the interpretation of data, training and reflexive exchange about the interpretative procedures and about the methods of coding can increase the reliability. From analyzing the opening sequence of a narrative, a hypothesis about the case structure can be derived and tested against the following sequences. This is another way to arrive at reliable interpretations. Assessing categories developed in open coding with other passages has a similar function in grounded theory research. In each of these examples, an attempt is made to check the reliability of an interpretation by testing it concretely against other passages in the same text or against other texts.

In general, the discussion about reliability in qualitative research comes down to the need for explication in two respects. First, the genesis of the data needs to be explicated in a way that makes it possible to check what is a statement of the subject and where the researcher's interpretation begins. Second, procedures in the field or interview and with the text need to be made explicit in training and rechecking in order to improve the comparability of different interviewers or observers' conduct. Finally, the reliability of the whole process will be greater, the more detailed the research process is documented as a whole.

Thus the criterion of reliability is reformulated in the direction of checking the dependability of data and procedures, which can be grounded in the specificity of the various qualitative methods. The implication is that one should reject other understandings of reliability, such as frequently repeated data collection leading to the same data and results. If this form of reliability is used, it may be more convenient to mistrust rather than to trust the dependability of the data. In interview studies, such a repetition is rather an indicator of a prepared statement, in which some relevant aspects may have been left out, rather than a confirmation of the correctness of what has been said.

Validity

In the discussions about grounding qualitative research, validity typically receives more attention than reliability (e.g., as in Hammersley 1990; 1992; Kvale 1989; Wolcott 1990a). The question of validity boils down to a question of whether the researchers in fact see what they think they see. Basically, three errors may occur: to see relationships where there are none or to identify relationships inaccurately (type 1 error); to reject them when they are indeed correct (type 2 error); and finally to ask the wrong questions (type 3 error) (Kirk and Miller 1986, pp. 29–30).

A basic problem in assessing the validity of qualitative research is how to specify the link between the relations that are studied and the version of them provided by the researcher. In other words, what would these relations look like if they were not issues of empirical research at that moment? And is the researcher's version grounded in the versions in the field, in the interviewee's biography, etc., and hence in the issue?

This implies less that there is an assumption that a reality exists independently of social constructions (i.e., perceptions, interpretations, and presentations) than that the question should be asked as to how far the researcher's specific constructions are empirically grounded in those of the members. In this context, Hammersley (1992, pp. 50–52) outlines the position of a "subtle realism." This position starts from three premises. (1) The validity of knowledge cannot be assessed with certainty: assumptions should be assessed on the basis of their plausibility and credibility. (2) Phenomena also exist independently of our claims concerning them: our assumptions about them can only approximate to these phenomena. (3) Reality becomes accessible across the (different) perspectives on phenomena. Research aims at presenting reality, not reproducing it.

If one starts from this position, the question of validity turns into a different question. How far the researchers' constructions are grounded in the constructions of those whom they studied (see Schütz 1962) and how far this grounding is transparent for others (see Chapter 8 on this) become the issues. Thus the production of the data becomes one starting point for judging their validity; the presentation of phenomena and of the inferences drawn from them, becomes another one.

Communicative Validation

Another version of specifying validity aims at involving the actors (subjects or groups) in the research process a little further. One way is to introduce communicative validation (sometimes called respondent validation or member check) at a second meeting after the interview and its transcription (for concrete suggestions see Chapter 16). The promise of further authenticity made here is twofold: (1) the interviewees' agreement with the contents of their statements is obtained after the interview; and (2) the interviewees develop a structure of their own statements in terms of the complex relations that the researcher is looking for (e.g., a subjective theory of trust as a form of everyday knowledge that is relevant for counseling; see Chapter 16 for an example).

For a more general application of such strategies, however, two questions remain to be satisfactorily answered. First, how can you design the methodological procedure of communicative validation in such a way that it really does justice to the issues under study and to the interviewees' views? Second, how can the question of grounding data and its results provide answers beyond the subjects' agreement? One way of proceeding here is to attempt a general validation of the reconstruction in a more traditional way.

Reformulating the Concept of Validity

Mishler (1990) goes one step further in reformulating the concept of validity. He starts from the *process* of validating (instead of from the state of validity) and defines "validation as the social construction of knowledge" (1990, p. 417) by which we "evaluate the 'trustworthiness' of reported observations, interpretations, and generalizations" (1990, p. 419). Finally, "reformulating validation as the social discourse through which trustworthiness is established elides such familiar shibboleths as reliability, falsifiability, and objectivity" (1990, p. 420). As an empirical basis for this discourse and the construction of credibility, Mishler discusses the use of examples from narrative studies.

Maxwell (1992) has developed a typology which comprises five types of validity and which is based on the discussions just mentioned:

1 *Descriptive* validity refers to the "factual accuracy" (p. 285) of researchers' accounts of what they saw or heard in the field they studied, so that they did not mis-hear or mis-transcribe the interviewees' statements, for example (see also the concept of procedural reliability above).
2 *Interpretive* validity builds on the first type, but focuses more on how far the meaning of statement (or observation) is developed, used, and presented adequately to the participants' view. This also includes the use of concepts taken from the participants' language for interpretation rather than theoretical abstractions right away (p. 289).
3 *Theoretical* validity goes one step further. It "refers to an account's validity as a *theory* of some phenomenon" (p. 291). Here two sorts of validity are at stake: the validity of concepts (developed from a field or used for analyzing it) and the validity of relations between the concepts (used for explaining the phenomenon).

These first three forms of validity mentioned by Maxwell refer to the analysis and presentation (account) provided by the researchers and thus mainly to the situation (or material) that was analyzed and how it was analyzed. The remaining two forms go beyond this close link to the material:

4 *Generalizability* refers to the accounts made on the grounds of analyzing the material to other fields or parts of the material (see below for this issue).
5 *Evaluative* validity is the last form Maxwell discusses. It refers to the adequacy of the evaluative framework used for analyzing or categorizing a statement (or activity) in a specific category (or as "typical" or "a-typical" for a group, for example).

Maxwell's suggestions are based on different forms of understanding when analyzing data. He emphasizes that the first form is the most crucial form of validity on which the other forms are based. He also mentions that the fourth form is similar to what is discussed as external validity in other contexts and that the last two forms of his typology are less important for most qualitative research than the first three. In general, this is an interesting attempt to maintain the concept of validity and make it fruitful and fit in the context of qualitative research (on this see also Maxwell 2012; Maxwell and Chmiel 2014b).

Procedural Validity

For the research process in ethnography, Wolcott suggests nine points which need to be realized in order to guarantee validity:

(1) The researcher should refrain from talking in the field but rather should listen as much as possible. He or she should (2) produce notes that are as exact as possible, (3) begin to write early, and in a way (4) which allows readers of his or her notes and

reports to see for themselves. This means providing enough data for readers to make their own inferences and follow those of the researcher. The report should be as complete (5) and candid (6) as possible. The researcher should seek feedback on his or her findings and presentations in the field or from his or her colleagues (7). Presentations should be characterized by a balance (8) between the various aspects and (9) by accuracy in writing. (1990a, pp. 127–128)

These steps for guaranteeing validity in the research process can be summarized as an attempt to act sensitively in the field, and, above all, as the transferral of the problem of validity in the research to the domain of *writing* about research (for this see the next chapter).

Finally, Altheide and Johnson formulate the concept of "validity as reflexive accounting," which creates a relation between researcher, issues, and the process of making sense. It locates validity in the process of research and the different relationships at work in it:

1 the relationship between what is observed (behaviors, rituals, meanings) and the larger cultural, historical, and organizational contexts within which the observations are made (the substance);
2 the relationship between the observer, the observed, and the setting (the observer);
3 the issue of perspective or point of view (whether the observer's or the members') used to render an interpretation of the ethnographic data (the interpretation);
4 the role of the reader in the final product (the audience);
5 the issue of representational, rhetorical, or authorial style used by the author(s) to render the description and/or interpretation (the style). (1998, pp. 291–292)

In the above suggestions, validation is discussed within the framework of the total research process. These suggestions, however, remain at the programmatic level rather than at the level at which concrete criteria or starting points are formulated, in terms of which individual studies or parts of them may be assessed.

All in all, attempts at using or reformulating validity and validation face several problems. Formal analyses of the way the data were produced, for example, in the interview situation, do not tell us anything about the contents of these interviews or whether they have been appropriately treated in the further proceeding of the research. The concepts of communicative validation or member check face a special problem: the subjects' consent becomes problematic as a criterion where the research systematically goes beyond the subject's viewpoint, for example, in interpretations, which want to permeate into social or psychological unconsciousness or which derive from the distinctiveness of various subjective viewpoints. The attempts to reformulate the concept of validity that were discussed here are marked by a certain fuzziness, which does not necessarily offer a solution for the problem of grounding qualitative research but rather provides questioning and programmatic statements. As a general tendency, there has been a shift from validity to validation and also from assessing the individual step or part of the research towards increasing the transparency of the research process as a whole.

Objectivity

The third classical criterion in empirical research, objectivity, seldom features in discussion about how to evaluate qualitative research. One of the few exceptions is a paper by Maddill, Jordan, and Shirley (2000). They discuss issues of objectivity and reliability in qualitative research for three epistemological backgrounds (realist, contextualist, and radical constructionist epistemologies). The authors show that objectivity, as a criterion, is appropriate only to a realist framework. In such a case, objectivity is interpreted as consistency of meaning, when two or more independent researchers analyze the same data or material. Where they arrive at the same conclusions, this indicates that the research is objective and reliable. The basic strategy employed here is to triangulate results from different researchers working independently.

The authors stress the need for researchers to make their epistemological position clear in order to make an appropriate evaluation of the research and its results possible. This paper is an attempt to discuss objectivity as a criterion for qualitative research, rather than a satisfying suggestion of how to apply it.

Classical Criteria in Qualitative Research?

Whether it makes sense to apply classical criteria to qualitative research is questioned, because "the 'notion of reality' in both streams of research is too heterogeneous" (Lüders and Reichertz 1986, p. 97). A similar reservation can be found in Glaser and Strauss, who:

> raise doubts as to the applicability of the canons of quantitative research as criteria for judging the credibility of substantive theory based on qualitative research. They suggest rather that criteria of judgment be based on generic elements of qualitative methods for collecting, analyzing and presenting data and for the way in which people read qualitative analyses. (1965b, p. 5)

From this skepticism, a series of attempts have been made to develop "method-appropriate criteria" in order to replace criteria like validity and reliability.

Alternative Criteria

Since the middle of the 1980s, various attempts have been made to develop alternative criteria for assessing qualitative research.

Credibility

Lincoln and Guba (1985) suggest trustworthiness, credibility, dependability, transferability, and confirmability as criteria for qualitative research. The first of these criteria is considered to be the main one, which will be discussed briefly as an example here. The authors outline five strategies for increasing the credibility of qualitative research:

1 activities for increasing the likelihood that credible results will be produced by a "prolonged engagement" and "persistent observation" in the field and the triangulation of different methods, researchers, and data;
2 "peer debriefing": regular meetings with other people who are not involved in the research in order to disclose one's own blind spots and to discuss working hypotheses and results with them;
3 the analysis of negative cases in the sense of analytic induction;
4 appropriateness of the terms of reference of interpretations and their assessment;
5 "member checks" in the sense of communicative validation of data and interpretations with members of the fields under study.

Procedural Dependability: Auditing

Dependability is checked through a process of auditing, modeled on the procedure of audits in the domain of financing. Thus an auditing trail is outlined in order to check procedural dependability in the following areas (see also Schwandt and Halpern 1988):

* the raw data, their collection and recording;
* data reduction and results of syntheses by summarizing, theoretical notes, memos, and so on, summaries, short descriptions of cases, etc.;
* reconstruction of data and results of syntheses according to the structure of developed and used categories (themes, definitions, relationships), findings (interpretations and inferences), and the reports produced with their integration of concepts and links to the existing literature;
* process notes (i.e., methodological notes and decisions concerning the production of trustworthiness and credibility of findings);
* materials concerning intentions and dispositions like the concepts of research, personal notes, and expectations of the participants;
* information about the development of the instruments including the pilot version and preliminary plan (see Lincoln and Guba 1985, pp. 320–327, 382–384).

This concept of auditing is discussed more generally in the framework of quality management (see below). Thus a series of starting points for producing and assessing the procedural rationality in the qualitative research process are outlined. In this way, proceedings and developments in the process of research can be revealed and assessed. In terms of the findings that have already been produced in a particular piece of research, the questions answered through the use of such an assessment procedure can be summarized as follows, according to Huberman and Miles:

* Are findings grounded in the data? (Is sampling appropriate? Are data weighed correctly?)
* Are inferences logical? (Are analytic strategies applied correctly? Are alternative explanations accounted for?)

- Is the category structure appropriate?
- Can inquiry decisions and methodological shifts be justified? (Were sampling decisions linked to working hypotheses?)
- What is the degree of researcher bias (premature closure, unexplored data in the field notes, lack of search for negative cases, feelings of empathy)?
- What strategies were used for increasing credibility (second readers, feedback to informants, peer review, adequate time in the field)? (1998, p. 202)

Although the findings are the starting point for evaluating the research, an attempt is made to do this by combining a result-oriented view with a process-oriented procedure.

Criteria for Evaluating the Building of Theories

The connection of outcome and process-oriented considerations about qualitative research becomes relevant when the development of a grounded theory (see Chapter 25) is the general aim of qualitative research. Corbin and Strauss (1990, p. 16) mention four points of departure for judging empirically grounded theories and the procedures that led to them. According to their suggestion, you should critically assess:

1 the validity, reliability, and credibility of the data;
2 the plausibility, and the value of the theory itself;
3 the adequacy of the research process which has generated, elaborated, or tested the theory;
4 the empirical grounding of the research findings.

For evaluating the research process itself, they suggest seven criteria:

Criterion 1	How was the original sampling selected? On what grounds (selective sampling)?
Criterion 2	What major categories emerged?
Criterion 3	What were some of the events, incidents, actions, and so on that indicated some of these major categories?
Criterion 4	On the basis of what categories did theoretical sampling proceed? That is, how did theoretical formulations guide some of the data collection? After the theoretical sampling was carried out, how representative did these categories prove to be?
Criterion 5	What were some of the hypotheses pertaining to relations among categories? On what grounds were they formulated and tested?
Criterion 6	Were there instances when hypotheses did not hold up against what was actually seen? How were the discrepancies accounted for? How did they affect the hypotheses?
Criterion 7	How and why was the core category selected? Was the selection sudden or gradual, difficult or easy? On what grounds were the final analytic decisions made? How did extensive "explanatory power" in relation to the phenomenon under study and "relevance" ... figure in decisions? (1990, p. 17)

The evaluation of theory development ends up by answering the question of how far the concepts—such as theoretical sampling and the different forms of coding—in

Strauss's approach were applied and whether this application corresponds with the methodological ideas of the authors. Thus efforts for evaluating proceedings and findings remain within the framework of their own system. A central role is given to the question of whether the findings and the theory are grounded in the empirical relations and data—whether it is a grounded theory (building) or not. For an evaluation of the realization of this aim, Corbin and Strauss suggest seven criteria for answering the question of the empirical grounding of findings and theories:

Criterion 1   Are concepts generated?
Criterion 2   Are the concepts systematically related?
Criterion 3   Are there many conceptual linkages and are the categories well developed? Do the categories have conceptual density?
Criterion 4   Is there much variation built into the theory?
Criterion 5   Are broader conditions that affect the phenomenon under study built into its explanation?
Criterion 6   Has "process" been taken into account?
Criterion 7   Do the theoretical findings seem significant and to what extent? (1990, pp. 17–18)

The point of reference, here again, is the procedure formulated by the authors and whether it has been applied or not. Thus the methodology of Strauss becomes more formalized. Its evaluation becomes more a formal one: were the concepts applied correctly? The authors see this danger and therefore they included the seventh criterion of relevance in their list. They emphasize that a formal application of the procedures of grounded theory building does not necessarily make for "good research." Points of reference like the originality of the results from the viewpoint of a potential reader, the relevance of the question, and the relevance of the findings for the fields under study, or even for different fields, play no role here.

In the meantime, Charmaz (2006, pp. 182–183) has considered this aspect in her specific suggestions of criteria for evaluating grounded theory studies. She proposes four criteria, namely, credibility, originality, resonance, and usefulness. Each criterion brings with it several questions:

Credibility

- Has your research achieved intimate familiarity with the setting or topic?
- Are data sufficient to merit your claims? Consider the range, number, and depth of observations contained in the data.
- Have you made systematic comparisons between observations and between categories?
- Do the categories cover a wide range of empirical observations?
- Are there strong logical links between the gathered data and your argument and analysis?
- Has your research provided enough evidence for your claims to allow the reader to form an independent assessment – and *agree* with your claims?

Originality

- Are your categories fresh? Do they offer new insights?
- Does your analysis provide a new conceptual rendering of the data?

- What is the social and theoretical significance of this work?
- How does your grounded theory challenge, extend, or refine current ideas, concepts, and practices?

Resonance

- Do the categories portray the fullness of the studied experience?
- Have your revealed both liminal and unstable taken-for-granted meanings?
- Have you drawn links between larger collectivities or institutions and individual lives, when the data so indicate?
- Does your grounded theory make sense to your participants or people who share their circumstances?
- Does your analysis offer them deeper insights about their lives and world?

Usefulness

- Does your analysis offer interpretations that people can use in their everyday worlds?
- Do your analytic categories suggest any generic processes?
- If so, have you examined these generic processes for tacit implications?
- Can the analysis spark further research in other substantive areas?
- How does your work contribute to knowledge? How does it contribute to making a better world? (Charmaz 2006, pp. 182–183)

Such aspects are also included in the criteria suggested by Hammersley (1992, p. 64) in a synopsis of various approaches for evaluating theories developed from empirical field studies (Box 29.2). These criteria are specific to the evaluation of qualitative research and its procedures, methods, and results, and they start from theory building as one feature of qualitative research. The procedures that led to the theory—the degree of development of the theory which is the result of this process, and finally the transferability of the theory to other fields and back into the studied context—become central aspects of evaluating all research.

— BOX 29.2 —

Criteria for Theory Development in Qualitative Research

1 The degree to which generic/formal theory is produced.
2 The degree of development of the theory.
3 The novelty of the claims made.
4 The consistency of the claims with empirical observations and the inclusion of representative examples of the latter in the report.
5 The credibility of the account to readers and/or those studied.
6 The extent to which findings are transferable to other settings.
7 The reflexivity of the account: the degree to which the effects on the findings of the researcher and of the research settings employed are assessed and/or the amount of information about the research process that is provided to readers.

Source: Hammersley (1992, p. 64)

In the context of qualitative research in psychology, Parker (2004b) has discussed the role of criteria. He suggests replacing the classical criteria by questions. For example, he wants to replace the question of objectivity by: "Have you described what theoretical resources you draw upon to make your subjectivity into a useful device and how those resources impact on the research?" (p. 102). Instead of checking the validity he suggests asking: "Have you made clear the ways in which the account you give is distinctive and paradigmatically different from other things that might be categorized along with it?" Reliability checks (which Parker sees based on an assumption of stability in what is studied) should be replaced by asking: "Have you traced a process of change in your understanding and other people's understanding of the topic and explored how views of it may continue to change?" (p. 102).

A second suggestion by Parker is that qualitative research (in psychology) should be based on three principles, which distinguish good from bad research examples. The principles concern apprenticeship, scholarship, and innovation. "Apprenticeship" (p. 103) means that the research is based in terminology, knowledge, and argumentation on the existing state of the discipline rather than starting from scratch in every case. "Scholarship" means that researchers dispose of a rhetorical skill to make an argument based on their research. Here we could add that scholarship should also refer to methodological skills in doing the research as well as possible. Finally, "innovation" refers to the question of how far methodological skills were applied in the project, but the research questions have been kept in mind so that in the end new insights about the issue are the outcome of the research. This suggestion goes beyond methodological issues in assessing the quality of research but includes issues of relevance to the study. Similar suggestions have been made by Charmaz (2006) for evaluating grounded theory research.

Traditional or Alternative Criteria: New Answers to Old Questions?

The approaches to grounding qualitative research discussed here provide a methodical approach to analyzing understanding as an epistemological principle. Criteria are defined which serve to judge the appropriateness of the procedures which were applied. The central questions concern how appropriately each case (whether a subject or a field) has been reconstructed, with how much openness it was approached, and what controls have been installed in the research process in order to assess this openness.

One starting point is to reflect upon the construction of social realities in the field under study and in the research process. The decisive question, however, is whose constructions were addressed and were successful in the process of knowledge production and in the formulation of the results—those of the researcher, or those met in the studied field? Then the problem of grounding qualitative research is made concrete with three questions: How far are the researchers' findings based

GROUNDING, WRITING, AND OUTLOOK

on the constructions in the field? How are the translation and documentation of these constructions in the field into the texts, which are the empirical material, made? How did the researcher proceed from the case study to the developed theory or to the general patterns found? Grounding qualitative research becomes a question of analyzing the research as process. After discussing the alternatives mentioned, the impression remains that both strategies—the application of traditional criteria and the development of alternative, specific criteria—have featured in recent discussions and that neither has yet given a wholly satisfactory answer to the problem of grounding qualitative research.

The equation or connection of alternative and traditional criteria by Miles and Huberman (1994, p. 278) outlines an interesting perspective for structuring this field. They have structured the major traditional criteria together with the most prominent alternative criteria in the following five groups:

- objectivity/confirmability;
- reliability/dependability/auditability;
- internal validity/credibility/authenticity;
- external validity/transferability/fittingness;
- utilization/application/action orientation.

But at the same time, this equation makes clear that attempts to reformulate criteria for qualitative research did not really lead to new solutions. Rather, the problems with traditional criteria derived from different backgrounds have to be discussed in the case of alternative criteria too.

Quality Assessment as a Challenge for Qualitative Research

The question of how to assess the quality of qualitative research currently arises in three respects. First, by the researchers who want to check and secure their proceeding and their results. Second, by the consumers of qualitative research, the readers of publications or the funding agencies, who want to assess what has been presented to them. And finally in the evaluation of research in reviewing research proposals and in peer reviews of manuscripts submitted to journals. In the last context, you will find a growing number of guidelines for evaluating research papers (articles, proposals, etc.). Seale (1999, pp. 189–192) presents a criteria catalogue of the British Sociological Association's Medical Sociology Group, which includes a set of questions referring to 20 areas from research questions on sampling, collection and analysis of data, or presentations and ethics. The guiding questions are helpful, but when you answer them, you will find that you are drawn back to your own—maybe implicit—criteria: for example, when you want an answer in area 19 ("Are the results credible and appropriate?"), the question "Do they address the research question(s)?" (1999, p. 192) is suggested.

Another catalogue has been presented by the National Institutes of Health, Office of Behavioral and Social Sciences (NIH 2001) for the field of public health.

Here especially, questions of design have been emphasized. Analysis and interpretations are summarized under design as well as the combination of qualitative and quantitative research. A checklist complements the catalogue with items like "Data collection procedures are fully explained" (p. 16).

Elliot, Fischer, and Rennie (1999) have developed a catalogue of guidelines for publishing qualitative research, with two parts. One can be applied to both quantitative and qualitative research; the second part is focused on the special character of qualitative research and includes concepts like member checks, peer debriefing, triangulation, etc. But as the strong reaction of Reicher (2000) shows, despite the rather general formulation of these guidelines, they are not consensual for different forms of qualitative research.

Quality Criteria or Strategies of Quality Assurance?

These catalogues show basically one thing: qualitative research will be confronted with issues of quality from the outside, even where it does not answer such questions internally. If criteria are set up, should they be applied to any form of qualitative research or do we need specific criteria for each approach? Can we set up criteria that include a benchmark for deciding the question of good and bad research? How much authenticity is necessary, and what is non-sufficient authenticity? In quantitative research, criteria like reliability come with benchmarks of enough and not enough reliability, which makes the decision between good and bad research simple. Therefore, another distinction may become relevant for qualitative research. Do we look for criteria or do we need strategies of quality assessment? Maybe it is very difficult to frame the "real" qualities of qualitative research in criteria. How can you evaluate in an exploratory study what this study really produced as new knowledge? How can you evaluate whether or not methods were appropriate to the field and the research question? How can you judge the originality in approaching the field and in creating or using methods? How can you evaluate creativity in collecting and analyzing empirical material? Yardley (2000) discusses "dilemmas in qualitative research" in this context. So in the end, perhaps thinking about *strategies*, which will be discussed in what follows, will be the more promising way than formulating criteria.

In the remainder of this chapter some issues of enhancing and ensuring the quality of qualitative research will be discussed that go beyond the idea of quality criteria. The idea behind this chapter is that quality in qualitative research cannot be reduced to formulating criteria and benchmarks for deciding about good and bad use of methods. Instead, the issue of quality in qualitative research is located on the level of research planning—from accessing the generalizability of findings, to quality management—on the level of process evaluation, research training, and the relation of attitude and technology—or art and method—in research (see also Chapter 31), and to checking the indication of research designs and methods. Thus the focus of this current chapter will be on when to use qualitative research and when to use which kind of qualitative research and on how to manage quality in the research as approaches to describe (good) qualitative research.

Strategies of Generalization in Qualitative Research

The generalization of concepts and relations found from analysis is another strategy of grounding qualitative research. At the same time, if the question is asked as to which considerations and steps have been applied in order to specify these domains, this forms a starting point for the evaluation of such concepts. This is discussed in terms of generalization. The central points to consider in such an evaluation are first the analyses and, second, the steps taken to arrive at more or less general statements.

The problem of generalization in qualitative research is that its statements are often made for a certain context or specific cases and based on analyses of relations, conditions, processes, etc., in them. This rootedness in contexts often allows qualitative research a specific expressiveness. However, when attempts are made at generalizing the findings, this context link has to be given up in order to find out whether the findings are valid independently of and outside specific contexts. In highlighting this dilemma, Lincoln and Guba (1985) discuss this problem under the heading of "the only generalization is: there is no generalization." But in terms of the "transferability of findings from one context to another" and "fittingness as to the degree of comparability of different contexts," they outline criteria and ways for judging the generalization of findings beyond a given context.

In a similar way Maxwell (2012, pp. 137–138; see also Maxwell and Chmiel 2014b) distinguishes between internal and external generalization: "Internal generalizability refers to the generalizability of a conclusion *within* the case, setting, or group studied, to persons, events, times, and settings that were not directly observed, interviewed, or otherwise represented in the data collected" (p. 137). In other terms, this could be discussed in terms of how far the findings are describing the case under study in a consistent way, which applies also to those aspects that were not part of the empirical material that was analyzed: "External generalizability, in contrast, refers to its generalizability *beyond* that case, setting, or group, to other persons, times, and settings" (2012, p. 137). Maxwell mentions in this context that the boundaries between the case and what is beyond the case depend on the researcher's definition of the case. Nevertheless, this distinction may offer an appropriate way of discussing issues of generalization for qualitative research in an appropriate way.

Various possibilities are discussed for mapping out the path from the case to the theory in a way that will allow you to reach at least a certain level of generalization. A first step is to clarify which degree of generalization you are aiming at and is feasible with the concrete study in order to derive appropriate claims for generalization. A second step is the cautious integration of different cases and contexts in which the relations under study are empirically analyzed. The generalizability of the results is often closely linked to the way the sampling is done. Theoretical sampling, for example, offers a way of designing the variation of the conditions under which a phenomenon is studied as broadly as possible. The third step is the systematic comparison of the collected material. Here again, the procedures for developing grounded theories can be drawn on. Finally, addressing the generalizability of results has much to do with checking the boundaries of the research and its findings, for example, by checking negative cases, that is, those which do not fit into a pattern or typology that was developed.

The Constant Comparative Method

In the process of developing theories, and additional to the method of "theoretical sampling" (see Chapter 13), Glaser (1969) suggested the constant comparative method as a procedure for interpreting texts. It basically consists of four stages: "(1) comparing incidents applicable to each category, (2) integrating categories and their properties, (3) delimiting the theory, and (4) writing the theory" (1969, p. 220). For Glaser, the systematic circularity of this process is an essential feature:

> Although this method is a continuous growth process—each stage after a time transforms itself into the next—previous stages remain in operation throughout the analysis and provide continuous development to the following stage until the analysis is terminated. (1969, p. 220)

This procedure becomes a method of *constant* comparison when interpreters take care to compare coding over and over again to codes and classifications that have already been made. Material which has already been coded is not finished with after its classification: rather it is continually integrated into the further process of comparison.

Contrasting Cases and Ideal Type Analysis

The constant comparison is further developed and systematized in strategies of contrasting cases. Gerhardt (1988) has made the most consistent suggestions based on the construction of ideal types, going back to Weber (1949). This strategy includes several steps. After reconstructing and contrasting the cases with one another, types are constructed. Then "pure" cases are tracked down. Compared to these ideal types of processes, the understanding of the individual case can be made more systematic. After constructing further types, this process comes to an end by structure understanding (i.e., the understanding of relationships pointing beyond the individual case). The main instruments are the *minimal* comparison of cases that are as similar as possible, and the *maximal* comparison of cases that are as different as possible. They are compared for differences and correspondences. The comparisons become more and more concrete with respect to the range of issues included in the empirical material. The endpoints of this range receive special attention in the maximal comparison, whereas its center is focused on the minimal comparison.

In a similar way, Rosenthal (1993) suggests the minimal and maximal contrasting of individual cases for a comparative interpretation of narrative interviews. Haupert (1991) structures the cases according to "reconstructive criteria" in order to develop a typology from such interviews. Biographies with maximal similarities are classified in groups, which are labeled as empirical types in the further proceedings. For each type, specific everyday situations are distilled from the material and analyzed across the individual cases.

Generalization in qualitative research entails the gradual transfer of findings from case studies and their context to more general and abstract relations, for example, a typology. The expressiveness of such patterns can then be specified for how far different theoretical and methodological perspectives on the issue—if possible by different researchers—have been triangulated and how negative cases were handled. The degree of generalization striven for in individual studies should also be taken into consideration. Then, the question of whether the intended level of generalization has been reached becomes a further criterion for evaluating the results of qualitative research and of the process which led to them.

Analytic Induction

Finally, these case-oriented strategies of generalizing in qualitative research should be complemented by assessing (and showing) how the researchers treated "negative cases" (Lincoln and Guba 1985) in the process of analyzing the data and of presenting the findings. Znaniecki (1934) introduced analytic induction. This strategy explicitly starts from a specific case. According to Bühler-Niederberger, it can be characterized as follows:

> Analytic induction is a method of systematic interpretation of events, which includes the process of generating hypotheses as well as testing them. Its decisive instrument is to analyze the exception, the case, which is deviant to the hypothesis. (1985, p. 476)

This procedure of looking for and analyzing deviant cases is applied after a preliminary theory (hypothesis pattern or model etc.) has been developed. Analytic induction is oriented to examining theories and knowledge by analyzing or integrating negative cases. The procedure of analytic induction includes the steps in Box 29.3.

BOX 29.3

Steps of Analytic Induction

1 A rough definition of the phenomenon to be explained is formulated.
2 A hypothetical explanation of the phenomenon is formulated.

(Continued)

(Continued)

3 A case is studied in the light of this hypothesis to find out whether the hypothesis corresponds to the facts in this case.
4 If the hypothesis is not correct, either the hypothesis is reformulated or the phenomenon to be explained is redefined in a way that excludes this case.
5 Practical certainty can be obtained after a small number of cases have been studied, but the discovery of each individual negative case by the researcher or another researcher refutes the explanation and calls for its reformulation.
6 Further cases are studied, the phenomenon is redefined, and the hypotheses are reformulated until a universal relation is established; each negative case calls for redefinition or reformulation.

Source: Adapted from Bühler-Niederberger (1985, p. 478)

Process Evaluation and Quality Management

The question of grounding qualitative research has not yet been answered in a definite way. There is a need to try new ways of evaluation and of specifying quality in qualitative research. One starting point comes from the process character of qualitative research (see Chapter 10) as well as from procedural specifications of reliability and of the evaluation of theory building (see above): the aim is to specify and, even more, to produce the grounding of qualitative research in relation to the research process.

Process Evaluation

Qualitative research is embedded in a process in a special way. It does not make sense to ask and answer questions of sampling or concerning special methods in an isolated way. Whether a sampling is appropriate can only be answered with regard to the research question, to the results, and to the generalizations that are aimed at and the methods used. Abstract measures like the representativeness of a sample, which can be judged generally, do not have any benefit here.

A central starting point for answering such questions is the sounding of the research process, which means examining whether the sampling that was applied harmonizes with the concrete research question and with the concrete process. Activities for optimizing qualitative research in the concrete case have to start from the stages of the qualitative research process. Correspondingly, there is a shift in the accent of evaluating qualitative methods and their use from mere evaluation of the application to process evaluation.

This kind of process evaluation was first realized in the "Berlin Research Association's Public Health," in which 23 research projects worked with qualitative or quantitative methods on various health-related questions. For example, questions of networking among social services and programs, ways of designing everyday life outside hospital, citizens' participation in health-relevant urban planning and administration, and the organization of preventative interventions were studied. The different projects used narrative and semi-structured interviews, participant observations, conversation analysis, or theoretical coding among other methods. I directed a cross-sectional project called "Qualitative Methods in Health Sciences" in that context, which served as methodological support and process evaluation. Starting from a process-oriented understanding of qualitative research, a continuous program of project consultations, colloquia, and workshops was established.

In this program, the different projects in the association were consulted and evaluated according to the stages of the qualitative research process (formulation and circumscription of the research question, sampling, collection and interpretation of data, grounding, and generalization of results). The program serves to define a framework for a discussion of methodological questions of operationalization of the research question and the application of methods across projects. This represents a shift in emphasis from an evaluation that views methods and their application in isolation to a process evaluation, which takes the specific character of research process and issue into account. The leitmotif of this shift is that the application of qualitative methods should be judged for its soundness with regard to its embedding in the process of research and to the issue of the study and less for its own sake.

Thus, the aspect of grounding is shifted to the level of the research process. The aim of this shift is also to underscore a different understanding of quality in qualitative research and to relate it to a concrete project.

Quality Management

Impulses for further developments can be provided by the general discussion about quality management (Kamiske and Brauer 1995), which lies mainly in the areas of industrial production but also of public services (Murphy 1994). This discussion surely cannot be transferred to qualitative research without restrictions. But some of the concepts and strategies used in this discussion may be adopted to promote a discussion about quality in research, which is appropriate to the issues and research concepts. The concept of auditing is discussed in both areas (see above; Lincoln and Guba 1985). It provides first intersections: "An audit is understood as a systematic, independent examination of an activity and its results, by which the existence and appropriate application of specified demands are evaluated and documented" (Kamiske and Brauer 1995, p. 5).

In particular, the "procedural audit" is interesting for qualitative research. It should guarantee that "the pre-defined demands are fulfilled and are useful for the respective application. ... Priority is always given to an enduring remedy of causes of mistakes, not only a simple detection of mistakes" (Kamiske and Brauer 1995, p. 8). Such specifications of quality are not conducted abstractly—for certain methods per se, but with regard to the client orientation (1995, pp. 95–96) and the co-workers' orientation (1995, pp. 110–111).

On the first point, the question is: who are the clients of qualitative research? Quality management differentiates between internal and external clients. Whereas the latter are the consumers of the product, the former are those who are involved in its production in a broader sense (e.g., employees in other departments). For qualitative research, this distinction may be translated as follows. External clients are those outside the project for whom its results are produced (supervisors, reviewers, and so on). Then, internal clients are those for and with whom one attempts to obtain the result (interviewees, institutions under study, etc.). Concepts like "member checks" or communicative validation (see above) explicitly take this orientation into account. Designing the research process and proceeding in a way which gives enough room to those who are studied realizes this orientation implicitly. For an evaluation, both aspects may be analyzed explicitly: how far did the study proceed in such a way that it answered its research question (orientation on external clients) and did it give enough room to the perspectives of those who were involved as interviewees (orientation on internal clients)?

BOX 29.4

Principles of Quality Management in the Qualitative Research Process

- Ensure that the definition of the goals and standards of the project are as clear as possible, and that all researchers and co-workers integrate themselves in this definition.
- Define how these goals and standards and, more generally, the quality are obtained; finally, a consensus about the way to apply certain methods (perhaps through joint interview training) and its analysis is a precondition for quality in the research process.
- Provide a clear definition of the responsibilities for obtaining quality in the research process.
- Allow transparency of the judgment and the assessment and quality in the process.

The co-worker orientation needs to take into account that "quality arises from applying suitable techniques but on the basis of a corresponding mentality" (Kamiske and Brauer 1995, p. 110). Transferred to qualitative research, this underlines that the application of methods essentially determines not only the quality of research, but also the attitude with which the research is conducted.

Another point of departure here is "to give responsibility (for quality) to the co-workers by introducing self-assessments instead of outside control" (1995, p. 111). Quality in the qualitative research process can be realized, as elsewhere, if it is produced and assessed together with the researchers involved. First, they define together what should be and what is understood as quality in this context. Quality management then includes "activities ... defining the quality policy, the goals and the responsibilities and realizing these by means of quality planning, quality steering, quality assessment/quality management, and quality improvement" (ISO 9004, quoted in Kamiske and Brauer 1995, p. 149).

These guiding principles of quality management are summarized in Box 29.4. They can be realized by defining the goals, documenting the process and problems, and regularly reflecting jointly on these processes and problems. Joint process evaluation in connection with consultation, training, and retraining, as outlined above, can be an instrument for realizing quality management in qualitative research. Other strategies will follow and advance the discussion about the appropriate realization and evaluation of qualitative research. A definition of quality in research, and how to guarantee it in the process which is appropriate to the issue, and the experience that quality can only be produced through a combination of methods and a corresponding attitude, are links to the discussion about quality management. A major issue in this process and in presenting it is how decisions for specific methods or for using qualitative research in general had been taken and on what these decisions were based. This can be discussed by using the concept of indication.

Indication of Qualitative Research

From a methodological point of view, one of the interesting questions in qualitative research is: what makes us decide to use some specific method in our research? Is it habit? Is it a tradition of research? Is it the researcher's experience with this method? Or is it the issue under study that drives the decision for or against certain methods?

Transferring the Idea of Indication from Therapy to Research

Not only in the field of qualitative research, but also in empirical research in general, textbooks of methodology hardly provide any help on deciding how to select a specific method for a study. Most books treat the single method or research design separately and describe their features and problems. In most cases, they do not arrive at a comparative presentation of the different methodological alternatives or at given starting points for how to select a specific method (and not a different one) for a research issue. Thus one need for qualitative research is to further clarify the question of indication. In medicine or psychotherapy, the appropriateness of a certain treatment for specific problems and groups of people is checked. This is named "indication." The answer to this question is whether or not a specific treatment is appropriate (indicated) for a specific problem in a specific case. If transferred to qualitative research, the relevant questions are: When are certain qualitative methods appropriate and also appropriate for which issue? Which research question? Which group of people (population) or fields are to be studied? When are quantitative methods or a combination of both indicated? And so on. (See Table 29.1.)

TABLE 29.1   Indication of Qualitative Research Methods

Psychotherapy and medicine			Qualitative research		
Which disease, symptoms, diagnosis, and population	**indicate**	which treatment or therapy?	Which issue, population, research question, knowledge of issue, and population	**indicate**	which method or methods?

1 When is a particular method appropriate and indicated?

2 How do you make a rational decision for or against certain methods?

Research Steps and Methods: Rules of Thumb and Key Questions

There is no one right method in qualitative research. This form of commitment is not appropriate to qualitative research. But there are some other forms of commitment necessary in qualitative research. Research should be methodologically planned and based on principles and reflection. Notions like fixed and well-defined paradigms obstruct the way to the issue under study rather than open new and appropriate ways to it. Take and reflect upon decisions for theory and method in qualitative research in a knowledge-based way. Box 29.5 below gives some rules of thumb about how to make decisions during the research process and contains some key questions to reflect on what has been decided and applied in the ongoing research process.

Taking these rules of thumb seriously and asking these questions should help qualitative researchers evaluate their decisions on a background of consideration and reflection. The rules will prevent qualitative researchers from sticking to methods not appropriate to the concrete case of their research and from being trapped in fundamentalist trench fights of qualitative versus quantitative research, as well as those fights among research paradigms in qualitative research (see also Chapter 3).

BOX 29.5

Research Steps and Methods: Rules of Thumb and Key Questions

1   Decide and reflect on whether to select qualitative or quantitative research.

Why qualitative research?
What reasons do you have for one or the other?
What are your expectations for the (qualitative) research that you plan?

2   Reflect on the theoretical background of your knowledge interest.

What is the impact of your setting on the research?
How open and how closed is your access to what you want to study?

---

3 Carefully plan your study, but allow for reconsidering the steps and modifying them according to the state of the study.

What are the resources available for the study?
How realistic are the aims of your research in relation to the available resources?
What are necessary and appropriate shortcuts?

4 Carefully plan your sampling.

What are your cases?
What do they stand for?

5 Think about who in the field you should contact and inform about your research. Reflect on the relation to establish with field subjects.

What can you learn about your research field and issues from the way you get into the field or are rejected?

6 Think about why you chose the special method of collecting data.

Was it a decision for a pet method (the one you or your colleagues have always used) due to habitual reasons?
What could or would alternative methods provide?
What are the impacts of the methods you use on your data and your knowledge?

7 Plan how to document your data and research experiences.

How exactly should you write your notes?
What do you need as information to document systematically?
What are the influences of the documentation on your research and on your field subjects?
What are the impacts of the documentation on your methods of collection and analysis?

8 Think about the aims of your data analysis.

Was it a decision for a pet method (the one you or your colleagues have always used) due to habitual reasons?
What could or would alternative methods provide?
What are the impacts of the methods you use on your data and your knowledge?

9 Think about the way you want to present what you have experienced in the field and found in your research.

Who are the target audiences of your writing?
What is it you want to convince them of with your research?
What is the impact of the format of your writing on your research and its findings?

10 Plan how to establish the quality of your research.

What are the quality criteria your research should meet?
How should these criteria be realized?
What is their impact on your research and your field subjects or relationships?

(Continued)

(Continued)

11 Think carefully about whether or not you want to use computers and software in the research.

Which computers or software do you want to use?
What are your expectancies and aims in using them?
Why do you use them?
What is their impact on your research and your field subjects or relationships?

To think about the question of indication of qualitative research methods and approaches is a way of arriving at methodological decisions. These decisions will then be driven by the idea of appropriateness of methods and approaches to the issue under study, to the research question you want to answer, and to the fields and people addressed by your research. It is the first step in ensuring the quality of qualitative research, which should be followed by strategies to enhance the quality of research. New ways of research evaluation are necessary.

Checklist for Selecting a Qualitative Research Method

The checklist below includes orienting questions that should be helpful for deciding which research design or method to select for a concrete study. Questions 1 and 2 in this checklist should be answered by checking the literature about the issue of the study. If there is little knowledge and a need for or an explicit interest in exploring the field and issue, the researcher should select methods that approach the issue, participants' views, or social processes in a very open way (e.g., ethnography or narrative rather than semi-structured interviews).

For selecting methods with more openness the information in the categories is as follows: "openness to the issue by" (see Chapter 9, Table 9.1), "openness to the interviewee's subjective view by" (see Chapter 15, Table 15.1), "openness to the participant's subjective view by" or "openness to the process of actions and interactions by" (see Chapter 19, Table 19.1), and "openness to each text" (see Chapter 23, Table 23.1) can be used. Questions 2, 5, and 7 in the checklist below refer to the way theory and method match in the study. You can also refer to Table 31.1 in Chapter 31 for an overview of the research perspectives and theoretical positions discussed in Chapters 7 and 8; it also allocates the methods of data collection and interpretation to them, which are discussed in Chapters 15–27.

Question 6 in the checklist below refers to the information given in the categories "structuring the issue by" (Tables 15.1 and 19.1) and "structuring the analysis by" (Table 23.1). Here, information is given as to what kind of structure the single method provides or supports. Questions 7 and 8 in the checklist refer to the decision for methods that are case-sensitive (e.g., narrative interviews or objective hermeneutics) or for those that are more oriented to immediately comparing cases (e.g., semi-structured interviews or coding and categorizing methods). This alternative is also alluded to in question 9 as case-sensitive methods are rather demanding in the resources (time and personnel in particular) needed.

The preceding chapters of this book have dealt with the major steps of the qualitative research process and with the different methods available and used in qualitative research. They, and especially the introductory overview chapters (9, 15, 19, and 23), give starting points for allocating methods to the answers to the questions in the following checklist. Not only should the decision be prepared by using this information, but also the decisions taken in this process should be considered for their consequences and impact on the data and the knowledge to be obtained.

1   What do I know about the issue of my study, or how detailed is my knowledge already?
2   How developed is the theoretical or empirical knowledge in the literature about the issue?
3   Am I more interested in exploring the field and the issue of my study?
4   What is the theoretical background of my study, and which methods fit this background?
5   What is it that I want to get close to in my study—personal experiences of (a group) of certain people or social processes in the making? Or am I more interested in reconstructing the underlying structures of my issue?
6   Do I start with a very focused research question right away, or do I start from a rather unfocused approach in order to develop the more focused questions during the process of my project?
7   What is the aggregate I want to study—personal experiences, interactions, or situations, or bigger entities like organizations or discourse?
8   Is it more the single case (e.g., of a personal illness experience or of a certain institution) I am interested in or the comparison of various cases?
9   What resources (time, money, personnel, skills, etc.) are available to run my study?
10 What are the characteristics of the field I want to study and of the people in it? What can I request of them and what not?
11 What is the claim of generalization of my study?

KEY POINTS

- Traditional criteria often miss the specific features of qualitative research and data.
- There are many suggestions for alternative criteria, but none of them solves the problem of adequate quality assessment.
- One issue is whether to develop criteria for (1) qualitative research as a whole or (2) specific approaches in qualitative research.
- Criteria can focus on formal aspects (was the method applied correctly?) or on the quality of the insights produced by the research (what's new?).

(Continued)

(Continued)

- Qualitative research is confronted by external entities (funding agencies, customers of qualitative research, and results) with the challenge of quality assessment.
- The quality of qualitative research often lies beyond what one can assess by applying criteria.
- A crucial and often neglected question is that of indication: why this method, why qualitative research, etc., in this specific research?
- Strategies such as triangulation and analytic induction can sometimes provide more insights about the quality of qualitative research than can criteria.
- Generalization in qualitative research entails asking two questions: To which social entities can I generalize or transfer my findings? And what are the limitations of my findings?
- Process evaluation and quality management extend the issue of quality to assessment of the whole research process.

Exercise 29.1

1 Consider several articles reporting qualitative research. Identify how the authors assess the quality of their research and which criteria they use.
2 Consider your own research and ask the question: why did I take these cases, and why did I take these examples, excerpts, and so on, for presenting my results?
3 Why are my results valid? And for what?

Exercise 29.2

1 Consider your own research and decide how to generalize your results.
2 Think about the forms of triangulation that could have extended your findings and what extra insights they offer.
3 Are there any negative cases (which your results do not fit to) in your study? How did you deal with them?
4 Apply the principles of quality management (Box 29.4) to your own research.

Further Reading

General Overview

Flick, U. (2007b) *Managing Quality in Qualitative Research*. London: Sage.

Reliability

The following texts give good overviews of the problematic of reliability in qualitative research:

Kirk, J.L. and Miller, M. (1986) *Reliability and Validity in Qualitative Research*. Beverly Hills, CA: Sage.
Silverman, D. (1993) *Interpreting Qualitative Data: Methods for Analyzing Talk, Text and Interaction* (2nd edn 2001). London: Sage.

Validity

The following texts provide good overviews of the problematics of validity in qualitative research:

Hammersley, M. (1990) *Reading Ethnographic Research: A Critical Guide.* London: Longman.
Hammersley, M. (1992) *What's Wrong with Ethnography?* London: Routledge.
Kvale, S. (ed.) (1989) *Issues of Validity in Qualitative Research.* Lund: Studentlitteratur.
Maxwell, J.A. (1992) "Understanding and Validity in Qualitative Research," *Harvard Educational Review*, 62: 279–300.

Alternative Criteria

In the following texts, the authors seek to develop alternative criteria for qualitative research:

Lincoln, Y.S. and Guba, E.G. (1985) *Naturalistic Inquiry.* London: Sage.
Seale, C. (1999) *The Quality of Qualitative Research.* London: Sage.

Theory Evaluation

The following give a good overview of how to evaluate theories grounded in and resulting from qualitative research:

Corbin, J. and Strauss, A. (1990) "Grounded Theory Research: Procedures, Canons and Evaluative Criteria," *Qualitative Sociology*, 13: 3–21.
Hammersley, M. (1992) *What's Wrong with Ethnography?* London: Routledge.

Generalization

The first text remains one of the classic texts on generalization in qualitative research, the second text covers the issue in a more general and up-to-date perspective:

Glaser, B.G. (1969) "The Constant Comparative Method of Qualitative Analysis," in G.J. McCall and J.L. Simmons (eds.), *Issues in Participant Observation.* Reading, MA: Addison-Wesley. pp. 217–227.
Maxwell, J.A. and Chmiel, M. (2014b) "Generalizing in and from Qualitative Analysis," in U. Flick (ed.), *The SAGE Handbook of Qualitative Data Analysis.* London: Sage. pp. 540–553.

30
Writing Qualitative Research

CHAPTER OBJECTIVES

This chapter is designed to help you

- understand different ways of presenting your research;
- understand the challenge of making qualitative findings accessible and relevant and see ways of doing so;
- comprehend problems involved in writing about others' and about one's own research experience;
- identify the basic problems raised by these discussions;
- appreciate what all this might imply for the further development of qualitative research as a whole.

The question of how to display research findings and proceedings has come to the fore in qualitative research—especially in ethnography—since the middle of the 1980s. In the social sciences, text is not only an instrument for documenting data and a basis for interpretation and thus an epistemological instrument, but also an instrument for mediating and communicating findings and knowledge. Sometimes writing is even seen as the core of social science:

> To do social science means mainly to produce texts. ... Research experiences have to be transformed into texts and to be understood on the basis of texts. A research process has

findings only when and as far as these can be found in a report, no matter whether and which experiences were made by those who were involved in the research. The observability and practical objectivity of social science phenomena is constituted in texts and nowhere else. (Wolff 1987, p. 333)

In this context, writing plays a role in qualitative research in four ways:

- for presenting the findings of a project;
- for making findings relevant in contexts of implementation;
- as a starting point for evaluating the proceedings which led to them and thus the results themselves;
- as a point of departure for reflexive considerations about the overall status of research altogether.

Pragmatic Function of Writing: Presentation of Results

You can locate the various alternatives for how to present the findings of your research between two poles. At one end, you may locate the aim of developing a theory from the data and interpretations according to the model of Strauss (1987). At the other end, you will find the "tales from the field" (van Maanen 1988), which are intended to illustrate the relations the researcher met.

Theories as a Form of Presentation

In Chapter 29, criteria for judging theories in the sense of Strauss (1987) were discussed. The presentation of such a theory requires, according to Strauss and Corbin:

(1) A clear analytic story. (2) Writing on a conceptual level, with description kept secondary. (3) The clear specification of relationships among categories, with levels of conceptualization also kept clear. (4) The specification of variations and their relevant conditions, consequences, and so forth, including the broader ones. (1990, p. 229)

In order to attain these goals, the authors suggest as a first step that the researcher outlines a logical draft of the theory. In this draft, you should develop the analytic logic of the story and note the contours of the theory. A clear summary of the central outline of the theory should be the second step.

As a third step, the authors suggest that you make a visual presentation of the "architecture" of the central draft (1990, pp. 230–231). Thus they lay the main stress in the presentation on clarifying the central concepts and lines of the developed theory. A visualization in the form of concept networks, trajectories, and so on is a way of presenting the theory in a concise form.

In order to avoid falling into the trap of wanting to write the perfect manuscript (which may never be finished), Strauss and Corbin suggest letting things go at the right moment and accepting a certain degree of imperfection in the theory and presentation (1990, pp. 235–236). Finally, they suggest taking the potential readership of the manuscript into account and formulating the text for the target readership. The suggestions of Lofland (1974) for presenting findings in the form of theories head in a similar direction. He identifies as criteria for writing the same criteria for evaluating such reports, that is, ensuring that:

(1) The report was organized by means of a *generic* conceptual framework; (2) the generic framework employed was *novel*; (3) the framework was *elaborated* or developed in and through the report; (4) the framework was *eventful* in the sense of being abundantly documented with qualitative data; (5) the framework was interpenetrated with the empirical materials. (1974, p. 102)

Tales from the Field

Van Maanen (1988) distinguishes three basic forms of presenting research findings and processes in ethnographic studies, which can be transferred to other forms of qualitative research. *Realist tales* are characterized by four conventions. First, the author is absent from the text: observations are reported as facts or documented by using quotations from statements or interviews. Interpretations are not formulated as subjective formulations. Second, emphasis in the presentation is laid on the typical forms of what is studied. Therefore, many details are analyzed and presented. Third, the viewpoints of the members of a field or of interviewees are emphasized in the presentation: How did they experience their own life in its course? What is health for the interviewees? Further, presentations may seek to give the impression of "interpretive omnipotence" (1988, p. 51). The interpretation does not stop at subjective viewpoints, but goes beyond them with various and far-reaching interpretations. The author demonstrates that he or she is able to provide a grounded interpretation and to transfer the subject's statements to a general level using experience-distant concepts (Geertz) taken from the social science literature for expressing relations. One example of this form of interpretive omnipotence is the presentation of findings after applying objective hermeneutics (see Chapter 27), in which the real causes for activities are sought in the elaborated structures far beyond the acting subject.

Van Maanen characterizes *confessional tales* by a personalized authorship and authority. Here, the authors express the role that they played in what was observed, in their interpretations, and also in the formulations that are used. The authors' viewpoints are treated as an issue in the presentation as well as problems, breakdowns, mistakes, etc. (van Maanen 1988, p. 79), in the field. Nevertheless, one's own findings may be presented as grounded in the issue that was studied. Naturalness in the presentation is one means of creating the impression of "a fieldworker and a culture finding each other and, despite some initial spats and misunderstandings, in the end making a match" (1988, p. 79). The result is a mixture of descriptions of the studied object and the experiences made in studying it. An example of this form of presentation is the description of entering the field as a learning process or descriptions of failing to successfully enter the field (see Wolff 2004a).

Impressionist tales are written in the form of dramatic recall:

> Events are recounted roughly in the order in which they are said to have occurred and carry with them all the odds and ends that are associated with the remembered events. The idea is to draw an audience into an unfamiliar story world and to allow it, as far as possible, to see, hear, and feel as the fieldworker saw, heard, and felt. Such tales seek to imaginatively place the audience in the fieldwork situation. (Van Maanen 1988, p. 103)

The knowledge in the report is presented step by step in a fragmentary way. Narratives are often chosen as a form of presentation. The aim is to maintain the tension for the readers and to convey consistency and credibility. But impressionist reports are never completely finished. Their meaning is further elaborated in the contact with the reader (1988, p. 120). A good example is the presentation of the Balinese cockfight by Geertz (1973).

Other forms are the *critical stories*, which seek to bring social issues to the reader's attention, and *formal stories*, which aim rather at the presentation of theoretical relationships. In these forms of reports, different emphases are placed on findings and processes. Sometimes, these forms of reports complement each other (e.g., initially a realistic tale is given and only in a second publication is a version of the field contact provided that is designed more as a confession). Conventions of writing ethnographic reports have changed, as van Maanen documents for his own styles of writing: today fewer realist and more impressionist or confessional tales are published. This change has occurred in two respects: more works are not only written in these styles, but also accepted for publication. There is a shift from realist tales to confessions and also an increasing awareness that there exists neither the perfect theory nor the perfect report about it. Thus the dimension of partial failure and the limits of one's own knowledge should be taken into account as elements of the findings which are worthy of presentation.

The Ability to Write and How to Develop It

When it comes to presenting findings—whether in the form of theory or of narrative—one needs to consider questions of writing. That is, it is not sufficient merely to have worthwhile findings: to present them effectively, one needs to develop competence in research *writing*. This is especially so when results cannot be reduced to statistics or tables.

Here the considerations of Howard Becker are useful. A pioneer of qualitative research in the United States, Becker has long experience of conducting research and writing about it. His considerations are based on his experience of leading seminars on writing in social science.

Becker (1986b) notes a certain fear among social scientists over taking up positions in their texts. He suggests that this tends to limit the persuasiveness of social science writing: "We write that way because we fear that others will catch us in obvious error if we do anything else, and laugh at us. Better to say something innocuous but safe than something bold you might not be able to defend against criticism" (1986b, pp. 8–9).

Considerations about grounding social science findings by systematically integrating negative cases and by contrasting extremely different cases (as discussed in Chapter 29) are particularly pertinent here. Such grounding of research can inspire in authors a more confident handling of findings and results, encouraging in turn a firmer, more concrete, treatment:

> Bullshit qualifications, making your statements fuzzy, ignore the philosophical and methodological tradition, which holds that making generalizations in a strong universal form identifies negative evidence which can be used to improve them. (1986b, p. 10)

According to Becker, attending to the manner of presentation requires a consideration of the prospective reader: the reader should become a central focus in the design of the text. Findings and results do not somehow exist in pure form: they are always influenced to some degree by the readership they are written for. Focusing on the reader should, Becker, suggests, help social scientists to decide how to shape their texts:

> Making your work clearer involves considerations of audience, who is it supposed to be clearer to? Who will read what you write? What do they have to know so that they will not misread or find what you say obscure or unintelligible? You will write one way for the people you work with closely on a joint project, another way for professional colleagues in other specialities and disciplines, and differently yet again for the "intelligent layman." (1986b, p. 18)

If the current trend in qualitative research towards textual science continues, questions of how to present research will loom larger in methodological discussions. Through their texts, writers construct a certain version of the world and seek to persuade their readers of this view. Persuasiveness here is a function of both the "what" and the "how" of the research communication. Becker notes that, in his seminars, "we talked about scientific writing as a form of rhetoric, meant to persuade, and which forms of persuasion the scientific community considered okay and which illegitimate" (1986b, p. 15). Correspondingly, recent debate has focused not just on the technique of writing: it has focused too on the constructive and interpretative processes involved in the production of texts—and also on questions of how the text, its construction, the version and interpretation of the world it offers, and the findings and results are grounded.

New Outlets for Writing about Qualitative Research

During the development of qualitative research, the medium of written—and printed—text has always been the main format for publishing and retrieving these results. Sometimes the amount of material produced in a qualitative study and necessary to make the concrete procedures transparent goes beyond what can be published in a journal article (and sometimes even exceeds the format of a book). The new media can provide an alternative here. Publishing on the Internet not only makes publications faster, but also is a way to go beyond such limitations in space and costs. Publications on the Internet may come with more material like interview excerpts, but also with photos and videos that were used as empirical material and would have lost a lot of their significance when printed as excerpts in black and white in a book. In particular, if you use data beyond talk as discussed in Part 5 of this book, you will face new challenges in presenting your results. Bergmann (2006, p. 496) outlines several alternatives of how to make mediated documents (images, photos, films, Internet documents) undergo a "data transformation":

- Descriptions in the form of text (which involve a high degree of interpretation by the researcher and of data reduction from image to text) may help to represent visual information in publications.
- Transcription and notation: Images—similar to spoken texts—are transcribed according to certain rules (see Chapter 24 for this) and excerpts are integrated in publications.
- Photo inserts: Images or drawings are exemplarily integrated in a published text.
- Photo series: As in the study by Bateson and Mead (1942), which was mentioned in Chapter 21, a series of images are integrated in the text or complement it in order to document processes.
- Ethnographic films are an alternative to a textual representation for presenting processes and results drawn from them.

If the text alone is not sufficient for a publication but if you do not want to choose a completely different format (e.g., a film), the new media can offer an alternative to book and print journal publications. Using CDs or DVDs as formats to publish the proceeding and results of qualitative research as a stand-alone medium or as a supplement to more conventional media like books can be a way of transferring richer material and analyses. These forms of publishing represent new options for transporting the insights from the research to its audience. However, they come with new questions of how to protect the privacy of the participants—whether it is more text (and context) from the empirical material that is provided with a publication or whether it is the rich and contextual image or series of images (see also Chapter 5). As with all technological progress in this area, we should see the positive and negative sides of such developments.

Legitimizing Function of Writing

That the communication of social science knowledge is essentially dependent on the forms in which it is presented has been neglected for a long time. Recently, however, this issue has been brought to the fore in methodological discussions within different areas of the social sciences, as Bude makes clear:

> One is made aware that scientific knowledge is always presented scientific knowledge. And the consequence is that a "logic of presentation" has to be considered as well as a

"logic of research." How researchers' constitution of experiences is linked to the way those experiences are saved in presentations has only begun to become an issue for reflection and research. (1989, p. 527)

As mentioned above, the background to these considerations is methodological discussion in different areas of the social sciences, notably considerations in historical sciences and the thoughts of Geertz (1988) about the role of the "anthropologist as author." Clifford Geertz himself is one of the most influential researchers in cultural anthropology; his considerations about the anthropologist as author come from his own experience of researching, writing, and analyzing the writings of his colleagues. The anthropologist as author provides less an image of the studied culture per se than a specific presentation of this culture, which is clearly marked by his or her style of writing. Thus Geertz deals with four classic researchers in anthropology (Malinowski, Evans-Pritchard, Levi-Strauss, Benedict) as four classic authors of anthropological texts and regards their texts from a literary viewpoint. In his considerations, the discussion that takes place in modern anthropology about the "crisis of ethnographic representation" plays a central role. In this discussion, the problems with traditional understandings of representation, which were mentioned in Chapter 8, are taken up and focused on the problem of the representation of the other (i.e., here, the other culture):

The turn towards the text discloses a dimension in the scientific process of knowledge, which remained underexposed up to now. Where knowledge is thematized as the production of text, as the transcription of discourse and practice, the conditions of possibility for discussing ethnographic practices of representation are created. (Fuchs and Berg 1993, p. 64)

In the ethnography of foreign and faraway cultures and the attempt to make them understandable to readers who do not have direct experience of them, the problem of presentation may be evident. However, in researchers' attempts to make a certain everyday life, a biography, an institutional milieu from their own cultural context comprehensible to readers, the problem of presentation, though less obvious, is equally relevant: "Ethnography always has to struggle with the mis-relation of limited personal experience, on which the process of knowledge is based, and the claim for an authoritative knowledge about a whole culture, which it makes with its product, i.e., the texts" (1993, p. 73).

As soon as social science adopts this critical re-examination of the conditions of the production of scientific texts and of their significance for what is described, explained, or narrated in these texts, the discussion about the appropriate form of displaying its findings arises. Writing then is not only a part of the research process, but also a method of research (Richardson 2000; Wolcott 1990b) that like other methods is subject to changes in historical and scientific contexts.

Postmodernity has influenced scientific writing especially in a lasting way and has questioned the foundations of scientific writing. Special importance is attributed to writing in the research process, because the "new criteria" for assessing qualitative research as a whole (discussed previously in Chapter 29) start from the ways in which processes and results are displayed. Where trustworthiness and credibility replace reliability and validity of data and findings as the central criteria (e.g., in Lincoln and Guba 1985), the problem of grounding is transferred to the level of the writing and reporting:

> The research report with its presentation of and reflection on the methodological proceedings, with all its narratives about access to and the activities in the field, with its documentation of various materials, with its transcribed observations and conversations, interpretations and theoretical inferences is the only basis for answering the question of the quality of the investigation. (Lüders 1995, p. 325)

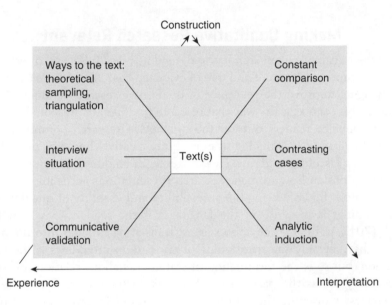

FIGURE 30.1   Grounding the Text

Thus, if the findings and procedures of scientific research are judged mainly according to their presentation and to the stylistic and other qualities of the report or article, the border between science and (fine) literature becomes blurred. In each case, the text is brought to the fore in the discussion about the grounding of qualitative research. In addition to the discussions in Chapter 8 (see Figure 8.2), the text becomes the central element for judging the translation of experiences into constructions and interpretations. The credibility of the presentation can be specified in the suggestions for realizing the criteria for grounding qualitative research, which were treated previously in Chapter 29. The following approaches ground the interpretation (see Figure 30.1): communicative validation, the analysis of the interview (or data collection) situation, a consequent application of theoretical (or purposive) sampling and of triangulation of methods, and perspectives on the methodological starting points for the generalization of findings by the constant comparison and contrasting of cases and the analysis of negative cases.

Reichertz goes one step beyond a text-centered treatment of credibility. He makes it clear that this form of persuasion concerning credibility is produced not only in the text, but also in the interaction of author, text, and reader:

> The decisive point, however, is the attitude, which is expressed in the text, with which the ethnographer turns toward his own interpretations and those of his colleagues in order to relate them to each other according to the needs of the individual case. It is not the way of accounting claimed for in the writing, which is relevant for the reader, but the attitude of accounting, which is shown in the text, which of course always has to use semiotic means, and these are means which are sensitive to cheating. (1992, p. 346)

Making Qualitative Research Relevant

In times when qualitative research has to defend its place in several directions—like the approach of mixed methods and that of evidence-based research as competitors—it is challenging to prove the relevance of qualitative research findings. An important issue in this context is the way that research findings are presented, so that they reach and convince readers outside the qualitative research community. Sandelowski and Leeman (2012) made this point quite clearly when they published their article "Writing Usable Qualitative Health Research Findings." They present a number of suggestions on how to make research presentations accessible, for example: "The key strategy for enhancing the accessibility and usability of qualitative health research findings is to write in the language of the readers to whom they are directed" (2012, p. 1407). They also suggest translating findings into thematic sentences, so that not only the mentioning of an issue in interviews is the basis of a presentation, but so is the formulation of statements about relations of issues and how they vary across the participants. For making findings relevant, the authors further suggest translating them into the languages of intervention and of implementation, so that the practical consequences of findings become more evident. These are suggestions coming from the context of qualitative health research, but they are helpful for other areas as well, where qualitative results are intended to be used for changing existing practices or for designing new ones.

Reflexive Function of Writing

Research includes not only the interaction between the researcher and the issue, but also the interaction between the researchers and their potential readers, for whom they finally write their presentations. This relationship—as well as the text produced for this purpose and the writing linked to it—is determined in multiple ways: "contextually ... rhetorically ... institutionally ... generically ... politically ... historically" (Clifford 1986, p. 6).

More generally, such considerations push the relationship between author, text, and readers and the conditions of producing scientific texts to the front of the relationship between researcher and issue, which is documented in the text in only summary form. A similar reflection can be noted for the production of research in (natural) science (see Knorr-Cetina 1981). In this case, social science (as it always did) is dealing with the "other" (i.e., concretely the (natural) scientists and their laboratories and the practices involved in the manufacturing of knowledge). The discussion about writing in ethnography and more generally in qualitative research, however, has led to self-reflection in social science research. Here, the role and the self-awareness of the qualitative researcher are increasingly questioned: "The qualitative researcher is not an objective, authoritative, politically neutral observer standing outside and above the text" (Bruner 1993, quoted in Lincoln and Denzin 2000, p. 1049).

This leads to the question of the validity that can be claimed for what is presented, given that the form of presentation used by the author essentially determines what is presented and how. This question is discussed under the heading of the authority of the text:

> By the *authority of the text*, we reference the claim any text makes to being accurate, true, and complete. ... Is a text, that is, faithful to the context and the individuals it is supposed to represent? Does the text have the right to assert that it is a report to the larger world that addresses not only the researcher's interests, but also the interests of those studied? (Lincoln and Denzin 2000, p. 1052)

Here questions about the claims of qualitative research arise—claims for an appropriate analysis and presentation of the contexts and persons that were studied and their legitimacy. The questioning of the authority of the text leads altogether to a questioning of the authority and legitimacy of the research. But, in such discussions, the original motive for the research—to produce knowledge about contexts of living and subjective points of view and their contexts—is in danger of getting lost in an endless discourse of self-referentiality. Lincoln and Denzin see a similar danger: "Endless self-referential criticisms by poststructuralists can produce mountains of texts with few referents to concrete human experience" (2000, p. 1050).

New Forms of Presenting Qualitative Research

In several contexts, discussion has started of how to present qualitative research beyond writing in the "classical" formats like articles and books about data referring to other people and situations and about how they were analyzed, with which results. First, we find trends to do autoethnography: "Autoethnography is an approach to research and writing that seeks to describe and systematically analyze (*graphy*) personal experience (*auto*) in order to understand cultural experience (*ethno*)" (Ellis et al. 2011, para 1). This trend is reframing both the formats of presentation and the ways of doing research. At the same time, functions of writing are seen as therapeutic for readers and participants (2011, para 26). Second, we find trends to move on from writing about research to forms of performative social science (see the special issue in the journal *FQS* (2009/2) and Guiney Yallop, Lopez de Vallejo, and Wright 2008). Here again, it is less the form of presentation of findings which has been reframed but rather the understanding of qualitative research in general (e.g., the role of methods and data in the process).

Dissolution of Social Science into Styles of Writing?

It is ironic that just as qualitative research has (with difficulties but successfully) achieved its place among the sciences, it now faces the danger of getting lost in endless debates about the role and problems of writing. Perhaps it does make sense to consider the writing styles of established ethnographers as authors (Geertz 1988 on Levi-Strauss and others; Wolff 1992 again on Geertz) in order to differentiate the style of writing in ethnography from that in other genres. Nevertheless, the claim made by qualitative research—for doing science, for specifying the borders with other genres of presentation, but also for marking the borders of a good, successful study from another, less successful, or even failed study—should not be given up. In favoring the discussion about writing in the research, one must neither give up the discussion about quality in research (and not only that of a good and credible text), nor reduce the emphasis on research practice.

But, in the end, writing not only has a reflexive function for the researchers, but is also a tool for communicating procedures and findings to the interested public and other researchers.

Checklist for Writing about Your Qualitative Research

The following checklist should give you some orientation in how to present your study and findings:

1 Have you made clear the aims of your project?
2 Have you explicitly formulated your research question and presented it?
3 Is it evident how you have selected which persons or situations to involve in your study and what your approach of sampling was?
4 How far can readers understand how you collected your data? For instance, did you present examples of questions you asked?
5 Is it transparent how data collection proceeded, which special occurrences played a role—perhaps for the quality of the data?
6 How clear will your analysis of your data be to readers?
7 Have you addressed questions (criteria and strategies) of quality assurances in the research?
8 Have you condensed your findings, so that the readers you intend to reach see their essentials?
9 Have you drawn (e.g., practical) consequences from your study and its findings and did you discuss them?
10 How easy is it to read and understand your report—and have you complemented the text with illustrations?
11 Have you provided enough evidence (e.g., quotations) to enable your readers to evaluate your results?

┌─KEY POINTS─┐

- Discussion about writing qualitative research goes beyond the question of which formal mode you wish to use to present your findings.
- Fundamental issues such as representation, legitimacy, and authority have made this discussion central.
- The danger with such a fundamental discussion is that it might prevent people from doing research and from finding interesting insights (and presenting them). It might lead them instead into endless reflexive loops.
- Nevertheless, the ways in which we write about what we have experienced in the field shape what we convey to our audiences.

Exercise 30.1

1 Take an example from the qualitative research literature (e.g., Flick et al. 2010). After reading it, ask yourself whether or not it was transparent for you, how the researchers found their access to the field and the people in it, how they collected their data and analyzed them (according to the checklist at the end of this chapter).
2 Look at it again and think about how much you heard the voices from the field in the version the authors presented, and whether this would have been necessary or helpful.
3 Look at any of your own papers about your research. What kind of presentation did you select? How far do the discussions about writing qualitative research meet your paper?

Further Reading

These texts go further into the details of the problems mentioned here concerning the different functions of writing in qualitative research:

Becker, H.S. (1986b) *Writing for Social Scientists*. Chicago, IL: University of Chicago Press.
Clifford, J. and Marcus, G.E. (eds.) (1986) *Writing Culture: The Poetics and Politics of Ethnography*. Berkeley, CA: University of California Press.
Geertz, C. (1988) *The Anthropologist as Author*. Stanford, CA: Stanford University Press.
Sandelowski, M. and Leeman, J. (2012) "Writing Usable Qualitative Health Research Findings," *Qualitative Health Research*, 10: 1404–1413.
Van Maanen, J. (1988) *Tales of the Field: On Writing Ethnography*. Chicago, IL: University of Chicago Press.

Suggestions for how to write about your research can be found at:
http://writeyourresearch.wordpress.com.

31

State of the Art and the Future

┌─CHAPTER OBJECTIVES─

This chapter is designed to help you

- develop an overview of the state of the art, and of the variety, of qualitative research;
- consider where further developments of qualitative research may lead;
- develop ideas on how to learn and teach qualitative research (and see those ideas in relation to one's conception of the subject as a whole);
- see that, despite all the methodological progress achieved, qualitative research still oscillates between art and method.

In the preceding chapters, I introduced you to the various steps in the research process in qualitative research. The history and common features of qualitative research were outlined in Chapter 2, and then the main part of the book focused on presenting, in a problem-oriented way, the various methodological approaches now available. As a result of the growth and diversification of the field of qualitative research, it is easy to lose track of the range of methods and approaches, of what they retain in common, and of where the developments can, will, or should lead.

This diversification has allowed many protagonists of qualitative research to feel comfortable with their own (or favorite) approach and no longer recognize what happens beyond this approach. To mitigate such tendencies, this chapter will give an overview of the main lines of development and trends in qualitative research, and end with some suggestions for teaching and learning qualitative research.

Qualitative Research Today

Recent developments in qualitative research have proceeded in different areas, each of them characterized by specific theoretical backgrounds, specific concepts of reality, and their own methodological programs. One example is ethnomethodology as a theoretical program, which first led to the development of conversation analysis and is differentiated in new approaches like genre analysis and discourse analysis (see Chapter 27). A number of such fields and approaches in qualitative research have developed, which unfold in their own ways and with little connection to the discussions and research in other fields of qualitative research. Other examples are objective hermeneutics (see Chapter 27), narrative-based biographical research (see Chapter 18), or ethnography (see Chapter 20). The diversification in qualitative research is intensified by the fact that German and Anglo-American discussions, for example, are engaged in very different topics and methods and there is only a limited exchange between both.

Research Perspectives in Qualitative Research

Although the various approaches in qualitative research differ in their theoretical assumptions, in their understanding of issues, and in their methodological focus, three major perspectives summarize them. Theoretical points of reference are drawn, first, from traditions of symbolic interactionism and phenomenology. The second main line is anchored theoretically in ethnomethodology and constructionism, in interested daily routines, and in the making of social reality. The third point of reference comprises structuralist or psychoanalytic positions that assume unconscious psychological structures and mechanisms and latent social configurations.

These three major perspectives differ in the objectives of research and in the methods they employ. Authors like Lüders and Reichertz (1986) distinguish between, first, approaches highlighting the "viewpoint of the subject" and, second, a group aiming at describing the processes in the production of existing (mundane, institutional, or more generally social) situations, milieus, and social order (e.g., in ethnomethodological analyses of language, see Chapter 27). The third approach is characterized by a (mostly hermeneutic) reconstruction of "deep structures generating action and meaning" in the sense of psychoanalytic or objective–hermeneutic conceptions (see Chapter 27).

The available range of methods for collecting and analyzing data can be allocated to these research perspectives as follows. The first perspective is dominated by semi-structured or narrative interviews and procedures of coding and content analyzing. In the second research perspective, data are collected from focus groups, ethnography or (participant) observation, and audio-visual recordings. Then, these data are

TABLE 31.1   Research Perspectives in Qualitative Research

	Approaches to subjective viewpoints	Description of the making of social situations	Hermeneutic analysis of underlying structures
Theoretical positions	Symbolic interactionism Phenomenology	Ethnomethodology Constructivism	Psychoanalysis Structuralism
Methods of data collection	Semi-structured interviews Narrative interviews	Focus groups Ethnography Participant observation Recording interactions Collecting documents	Recording interactions Photography Film
Methods of interpretation	Grounded theory coding Content analysis Narrative analysis Hermeneutic methods	Conversation analysis Discourse analysis Analysis of documents	Objective hermeneutics
Fields of application	Biographical research Analysis of everyday knowledge	Analysis of life worlds and organizations	Biographical research Visual research

analyzed by using discourse or conversation analyses. Lastly, the third perspective collects data by recording interactions and using visual material (photos or films) that undergo one of the different versions of hermeneutic analysis (Eberle 2014; Hitzler and Eberle 2004).

Table 31.1 summarizes these allocations and complements them with some exemplary fields of research characterizing each of the three perspectives.

Schools of Research

All in all, qualitative research in its theoretical and methodological developments and its research practice is characterized by an explicit building of schools of thought, which differ in their influence on the general debates.

Grounded Theory

Research in the tradition of Glaser and Strauss (1967) and their approach of building empirically grounded theories continues to prove very attractive for qualitative researchers (see Chapter 25). The idea of theory development is taken up as a general goal for qualitative research. Some concepts like theoretical sampling (to select cases and material on the background of the state of the empirical analyses in the project, see Chapter 13) or the different methods of coding (open, axial, and selective, see Chapter 25) are employed. A bigger part of qualitative research refers to one or another part of the program of Strauss and his colleagues (e.g., Chamberlain

1999). The approach has also left traces in the development of biographical research or is linked to other research programs.

Ethnomethodology; Conversation, Discourse, and Genre Analysis

Garfinkel's (1967) ethnomethodology is the starting point of the second school. It focuses on the empirical study of mundane practices, through which interactive order is produced in and outside of institutions. For a long time, conversation analysis (Sacks 1992) was the dominant way of making the theoretical project of ethnomethodology work empirically. Conversation analysis studies talk as a process and a form of interaction: which methods are employed to practically organize talk as processes which unfold in a regular way and, beyond this, to reveal how specific forms of interaction, such as conversations at the dinner table, gossip, counseling, and assessments, are organized (see Chapter 27).

In the meantime, conversation analysis has developed as an independent area of ethnomethodology. Studies of work designed by ethnomethodologists like Garfinkel as a second field of research (Bergmann 2004b) have remained less influential. Work extending conversation analytic research questions and analytical principles to bigger entities in genre analysis (Knoblauch and Luckmann 2004) have attracted more attention. Finally, ethnomethodology and conversation analysis have been patrons for formulating at least major parts of the heterogeneous research field of discourse analysis (see Harré 1998; Parker 2004a; Potter and Wetherell 1998; Rapley 2007). Data collection in all these fields is characterized by the attempt to collect natural data (like recording everyday conversations) without using explicit, reconstructing methods like interviews.

Ethnography

Ethnographic research has increased since the early 1980s. Ethnography has replaced studies using participant observation (see Chapter 20). It aims less at understanding social events or processes from reports about these events (e.g., in an interview) and more at understanding social processes of making these events from the inside by participating in the developments of the processes. Extended participation (instead of one-spot interviews or observations) and flexible use of different methods (including more or less formalized interviews or analyses of documents) characterize this research. Of central interest since the middle of the 1980s has been the place of writing about the observed events. More generally, this interest highlights the relation of the event and its presentation (see Chapter 30). Especially in the United States, "ethnography" (e.g., Denzin 1997) has replaced the label "qualitative research" (in all its facets).

Narrative Analysis and Biographical Research

Biographical research in German-language areas is essentially determined by a specific method used for collecting data and by the diffusion of this method. Here, mainly the narrative interview (see Chapter 18) stands to the fore. The narrative interview focuses on biographical experiences. This is applied in several areas of sociology and, in recent years, increasingly in education. Through analyzing narratives, bigger topics and contexts are studied (e.g., how people cope with unemployment, experiences of migration, and processes of illness or experiences in families linked to the Holocaust). Data are interpreted in narrative analyses (Rosenthal and Fischer-Rosenthal 2004). In recent years, group narratives (see Chapter 18), including multi-generational familial stories (Bude 2004), have become an extension of the narrative situation.

Box 31.1 summarizes the schools of qualitative research briefly mentioned here.

─BOX 31.1─

Schools of Qualitative Research

1 **Grounded theory**
2 **Ethnomethodology; conversation, discourse, and genre analysis**
3 **Ethnography**
4 **Narrative analysis and biographical research**

Methodological Developments and Trends

What Are the Current Methodological Trends in Qualitative Research?

Visual and Electronic Data

Visual data are important in the collection of qualitative research beyond the traditional forms of interviews, focus groups, or participant observations. Sociology analyzes videos and films just as in media studies (see Denzin 2004a; Harper 2004; Knoblauch et al. 2014; see also Chapter 21). Using them raises questions such as how to edit the data appropriately and whether methods originally created to analyze texts can be applied to these sorts of data. More books are being published with chapters on visual data, a sign of acceptability. Also, which new forms of data are available for studying the Internet and electronic communication (like e-mail) and which data have to be collected in order to analyze the processes of construction and communication that are involved? (See Chapters 16 and 17 and also Banks 2007; Bergmann and Meier 2004; Kozinets et al. 2014; Marotzki et al., 2014).

Qualitative Online Research

Several of the existing qualitative methods have been transferred and adapted to research using the Internet as a tool, resource, and issue of research. Such new areas as e-mail interviews, online focus groups, and virtual ethnography raise research questions on ethics and practical problems (see Chapters 16, 17, and 20).

Using Software

Field practitioners vary in their support for using software for qualitative research (e.g., Knoblauch 2004a). Analyzing texts is the main application of computers. Several computer programs are commercially available (e.g., ATLAS.ti, NUD*IST, and MAXQDA; see Chapter 28 and Gibbs 2014). In the end, are these programs just different ways to achieve a quite similar use and usability? Will they have a sustainable impact on the ways qualitative data are used and analyzed? What are the long-term relations of technical investments and efforts to the resulting facilitation of routines? These issues still have to be assessed (see Chapter 28). These devices support the handling and administration of data (e.g., matching codes and sources in the text, jointly displaying them, and tracing back categorizations to the single passage in the text they refer to). It still has to be determined if voice recognition software will lead to computer-supported transcription of interviews and whether this will be useful progress or not.

Hybridization

Hybridization is evident in many of the research perspectives and schools discussed above, such as ethnography, narrative studies, and grounded theory research. Researchers in the field select methodological and pragmatic approaches. Hybridization is labeled as the pragmatic use of methodological principles and the avoidance of a restricting subscription to a specific methodological discourse.

Triangulation

The idea of triangulation has been widely discussed. Linking different qualitative or qualitative and quantitative methods (Kelle and Erzberger 2004; see Chapter 3) becomes essential. Triangulation goes beyond the limitations of a single method by combining several methods and giving them equal relevance. It is becoming more fruitful if different theoretical approaches are combined or taken into account in combining methods (see for more details Chapter 14 and Flick 2007b).

Linking Qualitative and Quantitative Research

The literature identifies several positions linking qualitative and quantitative research. Especially in hermeneutic or phenomenological research, hardly any need is seen for linking with quantitative research and its approaches. This argument is based on the incompatibilities of the two research traditions, epistemologies, and their procedures. At the same time, models and strategies have been developed to link qualitative and quantitative research (see Chapter 3). Finally, in the everyday life of research practice beyond methodological discussions, a linking of both approaches is often necessary and useful for pragmatic reasons. Therefore, how do you conceptualize triangulation in a way that takes both approaches—their theoretical and methodological peculiarities—into serious account without any premature subordination of one approach to the other?

Writing Qualitative Research

In the 1980s and 1990s, the discussion about the appropriate ways of presenting qualitative procedures and results had a strong impact, especially in the United States (e.g., Clifford and Marcus 1986). Beyond comparing different strategies of reporting qualitative research, the main topics in this discussion included: How can qualitative researchers' writing do justice to the life worlds they studied and to the subjective perspectives they met there? How does the presentation and conceptualization affect the research itself? How does writing influence the assessment and the accessibility of qualitative research? The stress is laid in different ways. Ethnography sees the act of writing about what was studied as at least as important as collecting and analyzing data. In other fields, writing is seen in a rather instrumental way—how do I make my procedures and results in the field transparent and plausible to recipients (i.e., other scientists, readers, the general public, and so on)? All in all, the interest in the discussion about writing has decreased because of insights like this one: "Apart from a growth in self-reflection these debates yielded little in the way of tangible or useful results for research practice" (Lüders 2004a, p. 228; see Chapter 30).

Quality of Qualitative Research

Assessing the quality of qualitative research still attracts a lot of attention. Several books approach this topic from different angles (e.g., Seale 1999). The basic alternatives, however, are still determining the discussion: Should traditional criteria of validity, reliability, and objectivity be applied to qualitative research, and how? Or should new, method-appropriate criteria be developed for qualitative research? What are these, and how exactly can they be "operationalized" for assessing the quality of qualitative research? Discussions in the United States exhibit skepticism about using criteria in general. Distinguishing between good and bad research in qualitative research is an internal problem. At the same time, it is a need with regard to the attractiveness and the feasibility of qualitative research on the markets and arenas of teaching, to receive research grants, and impact policies in the social sciences (see Chapter 29 and Flick 2007b).

Between Establishing Schools of Research and Research Pragmatics

Methodological purism and research pragmatics cause tension in qualitative research. For example, as hermeneutic methods may over the years be continually elaborated, this may indeed result in a purer methodology—yet that methodology may then, when actually implemented, be more demanding in terms of time and personnel or other resources. This raises the question of how to use such approaches in research carried out for a ministry or company, or aiming at consulting politicians, in a pragmatic way so that the number of analyzed cases can be large enough to make results accountable (see Gaskell and Bauer 2000). This in turn leads to the question of what pragmatic, but nevertheless methodologically acceptable, shortcut strategies are available for collecting, transcribing, and analyzing qualitative data (Lüders 2004b) and for designing qualitative research (see Chapter 9 and Flick 2007c).

Internationalization

So far, there have been limited attempts to publish information about the methodological procedures that determine the German-speaking discussion, literature, and research practice, and also in English-language publications. Accordingly, the resonance of German-language qualitative research in the English-language discussion is rather modest. An internationalization of qualitative research is needed in several directions. Not only should German-language qualitative research pay more attention to what is currently discussed in the English—or French—literature, but it should also take it up in its own discourse. Also, it should invest in publishing "home-grown" approaches in international, English-language journals and at international conferences. And finally, the English-language discussion needs to open up more to what is going on in other countries' qualitative research (see also Knoblauch et al. 2005).

Indication

A final demand in qualitative research is to further clarify the question of indication. This is similar to how in medicine or psychotherapy the appropriateness of a certain treatment for specific problems and groups of people is checked (see Chapter 29). If this is transferred to qualitative research, the relevant questions include: When are certain qualitative methods appropriate—for which issue, which research question, which group of people or fields to be studied, and so on? When are quantitative methods or a combination of both indicated? This leads to the search for criteria to answer such questions. Finding these criteria can be a contribution to a realist assessment of single qualitative methods and of qualitative research in general. This will finally put an end to the fundamentalist trench fights of qualitative versus quantitative research (see Chapter 3).

Box 31.2 summarizes the trends and developments briefly mentioned here.

┌─ BOX 31.2 ─┐

Methodological Trends and Developments

1 Visual and electronic data
2 Qualitative online research
3 Using computers
4 Hybridization
5 Triangulation
6 Linking qualitative and quantitative research
7 Writing qualitative research
8 Quality of qualitative research
9 Qualitative research between establishing schools of research and research pragmatics
10 Internationalization
11 Indication

How to Learn and How to Teach Qualitative Research

Introductions to qualitative research face two basic problems. First, the alternatives summarized under the label of qualitative research are still very heterogeneous. Therefore, such introductions run the risk of giving a unified presentation to an issue which is and will remain rather diverse. At some points, an image of qualitative research as a whole is presented, which neglects the difference between various approaches and traditions in qualitative research. The risk is that a unified image of a qualitative "paradigm" is created, where there are various alternatives, schools, and research traditions. It is instructive to clarify the different theoretical, methodological, and general aims of the various alternatives.

Second, introductions to methods might obscure, rather than highlight, the idea that qualitative research does not merely involve the application of methods in a technological way. To understand qualitative research in its special potentials, we have to produce a sensitiveness for the relation of technique and art in the various methods. And we should convey in our teaching that qualitative research includes a specific research attitude. This attitude is linked to the primacy of the issue over the methods, to the orientation of the process of research, and to the attitude with which the researchers should meet their "objectives." In addition to curiosity, openness, and flexibility in handling the methods, this attitude entails a special degree of reflection on the issue, the appropriateness of the research question and methods, and indeed on the researcher's own perceptions and blind spots.

Two consequences result from this. First, there is a need in qualitative methods to find a way between teaching certain techniques (e.g., how to formulate a good question, or what is a good code) and teaching the necessary attitude. Curiosity and flexibility cannot simply be taught in lectures about the history and methods of qualitative research, but has be developed in practical experiences in the teaching. Learning how to use qualitative methods appropriately is often a function of gaining experience, encountering problems, experiencing failure, and continuing in the field. The pure methodological level should be separated from the level of application, as in all research. The concrete field, with its obstructions and necessities, often makes it difficult to apply, for example, certain interview techniques in an optimal way. Problems in qualitative methods intensify due to the scope of application and the need for flexibility, which influence decisions on a per situation basis. In the successful case, this flexibility in the interview situation allows the questions and their sequence to be adapted to the interviewee's way of talking about an issue and thus opens a way to the subjective viewpoint of the interviewee. In the case of failure, if the conversation in the interviews does not develop, or if time runs out, or if the interviewer is over-challenged by relating the interviewee's statements to the questions, this flexibility makes an orientation in the application of the interview more difficult, and a bureaucratic use of the interview guide (see Chapter 15) may be the result. Successfully used, procedures like theoretical coding or objective hermeneutics allow one to find a way into the structure of the text or of the case; when they fail, they leave the researcher in the situation of drowning in texts or data.

Second, an understanding of qualitative research can hardly be produced on only a theoretical level. Beyond that, learning and teaching should include practical experience in applying methods and in the contact with concrete research subjects. Qualitative researching is best introduced by combining teaching and research, allowing students to work continuously for a longer period of time on a research question using one method (or several methods). Learning by doing may provide a framework for practical experiences that are necessary to obtain an understanding of the options and limits of qualitative methods (see for example Flick and Bauer 2004). Ideally, the procedures of interviewing and interpreting data should be taught and understood from an applications perspective.

Failure of qualitative research is rarely discussed. As a result, the impression is sometimes given that validated knowledge and correct application are the bases of qualitative methods. Analyzing failures in qualitative research strategies (see the examples in Borman, LeCompte, and Goetz 1986; for focusing on entering the research field and failures in this process, see Chapter 12 and Wolff 2004a) can provide insights into how these strategies work in contact with concrete fields, institutions, or human beings. As the available literature about this issue is very limited, one way of making this an issue in teaching is to do interview training (as mentioned in Chapter 16, for example) with students. This means role-playing interviews in which one participant plays the interviewer, another the person who is interviewed, and the rest of the group observes the interaction. This can also include video recording the situation. Then the whole group discusses the interviewers' interventions—where probing was applied, where it was missing, which aspects should have been mentioned, what went wrong in the interaction, etc. The idea behind this is to take the discussion mistakes and failures in these (simulated) research situations as a starting point for learning how to conduct and how to do better in later (real) research situations. Similar forms of training and working on mistakes can be applied to observation and to data analysis.

The Future of Qualitative Research: Art or Method?

The other side of the coin is overemphasis on the part played by art in qualitative research. There is a debate over whether qualitative research may be best conceived as a matter of art or method. Those who emphasize the approach that qualitative research is a method with rules include for example Mayring, who set up a large number of rules on how to apply qualitative content analysis (see Chapter 26). But also conversation analysts have a strong focus on methods and data and see transcription exactness as an equivalent to measurement exactness in standardized research. Those who emphasize seeing qualitative research as art include for example researchers applying objective hermeneutics (see Chapter 27), which is not so much seen as a method but as an art, and which has been generally linked to hermeneutic approaches. They tend to stress that:

> Objective Hermeneutics does not provide methodical rules that instruct inexperienced colleagues how to organize fieldwork and to collect data. This lack of rules and techniques of research organization is due to the concept of an open, not-standardized process of research, which has to be newly adjusted for every research question. (Wernet 2014, p. 244).

Reichertz (2004, p. 290) supports this vision: "Objective hermeneutics, which looks upon itself as a *Kunstlehre [art]*, claims to be the fundamental method of investigation for *every* kind of sociological research."

For several methods it is explicitly claimed that they are indeed art and should be taught as such (e.g., for objective hermeneutics). For other methods, sometimes the impression is given that their application by those who have developed them are the best measure for assessing their potential. Furthermore, Denzin and Lincoln's handbook (2000a) gives the impression of qualitative research as art in many passages. A whole section is entitled "The art and practices of interpretation, evaluation, and representation" and then provides relatively little concrete advice on how to do an interpretation or evaluation. It is more the *art* than the practices or even the methods that are outlined. This last point turns also to the tension between art and method in grounded theory research. We find statements like "The process of memo writing in Grounded Theory is a learned skill, a practiced art" (Lempert 2007, p. 250). Other steps in the research process are difficult to nail down as methodological rules which can be applied unambiguously. This is the case for theoretical saturation, for developing categories in open coding, for the use of sensitizing concepts, and the like. A good grounded theory study is a good combination of art (creativity, flexibility, and curiosity towards what is studied) and of methods applied skillfully for reaching the goals of the study in a systematic way. This combination can best be learned by working with experienced researchers and scholars of the approach.

The description of the state of the art of qualitative research that Denzin and Lincoln (2000b) provide as an introduction underlines this impression. They give the impression that questions of methods and how to apply them are, as it were, strongly pushed to the back of queue: it is as if such questions are just outdated, belonging (so the claim goes) to a "modernist phase" of earlier times as opposed to the crises of representation and legitimation that they discuss as more recent developments. This may be linked to the two authors' strong orientation on ethnography, which characterizes the presentation of qualitative research in this handbook. According to Hammersley and Atkinson (1983) or Lüders (2004a), it is characteristic of ethnography that single methods are integrated in a pragmatic–pluralistic way or vanish behind such an attitude.

The debate about writing qualitative research (see Chapter 30) has attracted much attention. It has stimulated the discourse about the crises in qualitative research just mentioned. How far this debate and discourses have contributed to the further development of methods or to the more adequate application of the existing methods and has led to more and better research remains questionable.

Perhaps qualitative research should be understood as art *and* method. Progress should rather be expected from the combination of methodological developments and their successful and reflected application in as many fields and research questions as possible. Geertz underlined in his considerations about the "world in pieces" that the need for this kind of research is increasing:

> The same dissolution of settled groupings and familiar divisions, that has rendered the political world so angular and hard to fathom, has made the analysis *of* culture, of how it is people see things, respond to them, imagine them, judge them, deal with them, a far more awkward enterprise than it was when we knew, or rather thought that we knew what went with what and what did not. … What we need are ways of thinking that are responsible to particularities, to individualities, oddities, discontinuities, contrasts, and singularities, responsive to what Charles Taylor has called "deep diversity" – a plurality of ways of belonging and being, and that yet can draw from them – from it – a sense of connectedness, a connectedness that is neither comprehensive nor uniform, primal nor changeless, but nonetheless real. … But if what we are in fact faced with is a world of pressed-together dissimilarities variously arranged … there is nothing for it but to get down to cases, whatever the cost to generality, certainty or intellectual equilibrium. (2000, pp. 223–226)

Checklist for Locating Your Research Project

For locating a project you might plan to do in the current landscape of qualitative research, the questions in the checklist below might be helpful:

1 To what extent does your study fit into one (or more) of the schools mentioned in this chapter?
2 Which of the research perspectives mentioned above provides the context of your own research?
3 Which of the trends mentioned here are relevant for your study or for your issue of research?

These questions can be applied to the planning of your own study and in a similar way to locating other researchers' existing studies.

┌─ KEY POINTS ───┐

- Qualitative research exhibits a variety of approaches and continuously proliferates, leading to yet more methods and approaches. Also, its research perspectives are characterized by a variety of schools and trends.
- We can identify some trends that might change the field of qualitative research in the long run.
- There is debate over the extent to which qualitative research is best conceived in terms of (a) art or (b) method.

└──┘

Exercise 31.1

1 Locate an American and a European journal of qualitative research (e.g., *Qualitative Inquiry* or *Qualitative Research*). Examine the latest two volumes of each one: compare them for (a) common and (b) contrasting trends.
2 What trends and developments do you expect in qualitative research beyond those identified in this chapter?

Further Reading

Overviews of Qualitative Research

These texts go further into the details of the trends and developments mentioned here for qualitative research:

Denzin, N. and Lincoln, Y.S. (eds.) (2011a) *The SAGE Handbook of Qualitative Research* (4th edn). London: Sage.

Flick, U. (ed.) (2007a) *The SAGE Qualitative Research Kit* (8 vols.). London: Sage.

Flick, U. (ed.) (2014a) *The SAGE Handbook of Qualitative Data Analysis*. London: Sage.

Flick, U., Kardorff, E.v. and Steinke, I. (eds.) (2004a) *A Companion to Qualitative Research*. London: Sage.

Knoblauch, H., Flick, U., and Maeder, Ch. (eds.) (2005) "The State of the Art of Qualitative Research in Europe," *Forum Qualitative Sozialforschung/Forum: Qualitative Social Research*, 6(3), September, www.qualitative-research.net/fqs/fqs-e/inhalt3-05-e.htm.

The Future of Qualitative Research: Art or Method?

In their outlook, these authors make the tension of art and method evident in a specific way:

Lincoln, Y.S. and Denzin, N.K. (2005) "Epilogue: The Eighth and Ninth Moment," in N. Denzin and Y.S. Lincoln (eds.), *The SAGE Handbook of Qualitative Research* (3rd edn). London: Sage. pp. 1047–1065.

Learning and Teaching Qualitative Methods

Examples of teaching qualitative research by doing concrete research can be found in this source:

Flick, U. and Bauer, M. (2004) "Teaching Qualitative Research," in U. Flick, E.v. Kardorff and I. Steinke (eds.), *A Companion to Qualitative Research*. London: Sage. pp. 340–348.

Glossary

Adjacency pairs   Sequences of interaction like question–answer.

Analytic induction   Strategy to use negative or deviant cases for assessing and elaborating findings, models, or theories developed.

A priori   Latin expression for "beforehand." For example, working with categories defined before entering the field or before beginning to analyze material.

Auditing   Strategy to assess a process (in accounting or in research) in all its steps and components.

Authorized starters   Ways of beginning a formalized interaction, such as counseling.

Autoethnography   A form of research and writing aimed at describing and systematically analyzing the researchers' personal experiences in order to understand social or cultural experiences.

Background theories   Theories that inform qualitative research approaches with a specific concept of reality and research.

Canonization   A clear definition of methods by formulating standards of how to apply them leading to a consensus about it and general acceptance of it. For example, by defining rules of how to formulate questions in a specific form of interview.

Chicago School   A very influential group of researchers and approaches in the history of qualitative research at the University of Chicago who provided the methodological backgrounds of currently influential approaches like grounded theory. For example, research focused on how the community of (e.g., Polish) immigrants in Chicago was socially organized, how members maintained their cultural identity or adapted to a new one (of being American).

Closing gestalt   A specific format is completed. "Gestalt" refers to the fact that the whole is more than the sum of its parts. For example, to tell a story until its end, once the narrator started storytelling.

Codes of ethics   Sets of rules of good practice in research (or interventions) set up by professional associations or by institutions as an orientation for their members.

Coding   Development of concepts in the context of grounded theory. For example, to label pieces of data and allocate other pieces of data to them (and the label).

Coding families   An instrument in grounded theory research for developing relations between codes and for inspiring the researcher in which direction to look for categories.

Coding paradigm   A set of basic relations for linking categories and phenomena among each other in grounded theory research.

Communicative validation   Assessment of results (or of data) by asking the participants for their consensus.

Constant comparative method   Part of grounded theory methodology focusing on comparing all elements in the data to each other. For example, statements from an interview about a specific issue are compared to all the statements about this issue in other interviews and also to what was said about other issues in the same and other interviews.

Constructionism/constructivism   Epistemologies in which the social reality is seen as the result of constructive processes (activities of the members of processes in their minds). For example, living with an illness can be influenced by the way the individuals see their illness, which meaning they ascribe to it, and how this illness is seen by other members of their social world. On each of these levels, illness and living with are socially constructed.

Conversation analysis   Study of language (use) for formal aspects (how a conversation is started or ended, how turns from one to another speaker are organized).

Corpus   A set of materials or data for analyzing it (e.g., a corpus of newspaper texts for a discourse analysis).

Covert observation   A form of observation in which the observers do not inform the field or its members about the fact they are doing observations for research purposes. This can be criticized from an ethical point of view.

Cultural studies   A field of research particularly concerned with institutions such as the mass media and popular culture that represent convergences of history, ideology, and subjective experience.

Dialectics   Relation between two concepts, which includes contradiction and complementarity. For example, in entering the field, researchers have to build up enough familiarity with the field to understand it from within. At the same time, they have to maintain enough distance to be able to do a scientific analysis from an outsider's perspective.

Discourse analysis Studies of how language is used in certain contexts; for example, how specific identities, practices, knowledge, or meanings are produced by describing something in just that way compared to other ways. For instance, the way that the media write and people talk about a phenomenon like AIDS has changed over the years, which again has influenced the social relations to people having AIDS. This discourse and its consequences can be analyzed to better understand the phenomenon.

Disenchantment (of the world) Disentanglement of the mysteries of the world by rational, empirical analysis. The term was coined by sociologist Max Weber to describe the goal of social research—that is, to develop an analysis, a description, or an explanation for a phenomenon, which was unclear before.

Elite interviews A way of using interviews to study representatives of the top of any hierarchical system, for example, in enterprises, political parties, administrations, sports, sciences, or the like.

Episodic interview A specific form of interview, which combines question–answer sequences with narratives (of episodes).

Episodic knowledge Knowledge based on memories of situations and their concrete circumstances.

Epistemology Theories of knowledge and perception in science.

Ethics committees Committees in universities and sometimes also in professional associations, which assess research proposals (for dissertations or funding) for their ethical soundness. If necessary, these committees pursue violations of ethical standards.

Ethnography A research strategy combining different methods, but based on participation, observation, and writing about a field under study. For example, for studying how homeless adolescents deal with health issues, a participant observation in their community is combined with interviewing the adolescents. The overall image of details from this participation, observation, and interviewing is unfolded in a written text about the field. The way of writing gives the representation of the field a specific form.

Ethnomethodology Theoretical approach interested in analyzing the methods people use in their everyday lives to make communication and routines work.

Evidence-based practice Intervention (in medicine, social work, nursing, etc.) that is based on the results of research.

Experience-distant concept   A concept that is taken from (social) science and not from the life world of participants of a study for labeling social phenomena or subjective experiences. For example, the conceptual term "trajectory" used to describe the biographical processes (e.g., to lose a job) linked to the progress of a chronic illness.

Expert interview   A form of interview that is defined by the specific target group—people in certain professional positions, which enables them to inform about professional processes or a specific group of patients, for example.

Field notes   Notes taken by researchers about their thoughts and observations when they are in the field or "environment" they are researching.

First-degree constructions   Lay explanations of a phenomenon, which can be used to develop a scientific explanation (second-degree construction). For example, people's lay theories of their specific diseases can become a first step for developing a more general concept of everyday knowledge of the disease.

Focus groups   Research method used in market and other forms of research, in which a group is invited to discuss the issue of a study for research purposes.

Focused interview   A specific interview form, which was developed systematically for analyzing the effects of propaganda by asking a number of different types of questions. Its concept can still be very informative for developing semi-standardized interviews.

Folk psychology   Lay people's psychological explanations of phenomena.

Formal theory   A more general theory (in grounded theory research) referring to more than one area.

Generalization   Transfer of research results to situations and populations that were not part of the research situation.

Generative questions   Questions stimulating the investigation, leading to hypotheses, useful comparisons, the collection of certain classes of data.

Genre analysis   An extension of the concept of conversation analysis to bigger formats of interaction like gossip. For example, if people talk about a specific experience with an institution, they can use the format of gossiping about certain people instead of reporting facts and figures. The use of this interaction format can be analyzed for its effects.

Going native   A metaphor for describing the situation when researchers lose their professional distance to the field they study and become participants at the expense of their ability to observe.

Grounded theory   A theory developed from analyzing empirical material or from studying a field or process.

Group discussion   A research method in which data are collected by stimulating a discussion about an issue in a group of people who know each other already or who are strangers.

Hermeneutics   The study of interpretations of texts in the humanities. Hermeneutic interpretation seeks to arrive at valid interpretations of the meaning of a text. There is an emphasis on the multiplicity of meanings in a text, and on the interpreter's foreknowledge of the subject matter of a text.

Heuristic tool   Tools for dealing with a complex issue leading to first solutions and stimulating further analysis. For example, to ask questions about a text to be analyzed may be a first and fruitful step on the way to developing a category for classifying this text.

Hybridization   The pragmatic use of methodological principles and avoidance of a restricting subscription to a specific methodological discourse. For example, the use of observation and interviewing in ethnography in a pragmatic way.

Iconic turn   The shift from using text as empirical material to using images (in addition or instead). For example, the use of video material instead of doing interviews.

Indication   Decision about when exactly (under which conditions) a specific method (or combination of methods) should be used.

Informed consent   Participants' agreement, willingly provided, to co-operate with research that has been explained to them and that they are able to understand. This is a requirement for ethically sound research.

Interpretive repertoires   Ways of talking or writing about a specific phenomenon. For example, the culture of an ethnic group in society can be seen and talked about as a heritage and thus as something basically referring to the past, or as a therapy and thus something which is important in the present for building a social identity and for struggling against another group's dominance.

In vivo code   A form of coding based on concepts that are taken from an interviewee's statements.

Latent structures of meaning   Underlying and implicit levels of meaning production in actions and interactions, which can be identified in scientific hermeneutic analysis.

Leitmotif   Guiding idea or general principle in pursuing a goal. For example, to orient the decision between methodological alternatives on the characteristics of the issue under study can be a leitmotif.

Longitudinal studies   A design in which the researchers come back repeatedly to the field and the participants after some time to do interviews several times again in order to analyze development and changes.

Mediation   Finding a balance between two points of reference. For example, between pursuing the questions in the interview schedule and the spontaneous talk and contributions of the interviewee.

Member check   Assessment of results (or of data) by asking the participants for their consensus.

Membership roles   Ways of positioning for researchers in the field they study.

Memo   A document written in the research process to note ideas, questions, relations, results, etc. In grounded theory research, memos are building blocks for developing a theory.

Metaphysics of structures   Strong emphasis on structures assumed to underlie activities or interactions. For example, one person's unconscious motives in replying to another person's comments, which can be extrapolated from analyzing their interaction.

Mimesis   A form of representation of a process in a textual format by using this format for understanding this process at the same time. For example, people can unfold their own biography in the format of a narrative. They can also use this format or a specific type of narrative for better understanding their own lives and the processes in it—for instance, use a narrative of success for setting themselves in relation to technological change ("I master it") or a narrative of challenge and failure ("I always couldn't cope with new things").

Mixed methodologies   An approach combining qualitative and quantitative methods on a rather pragmatic level.

Modalization   A general format for transporting the content of a contribution to conversation. For example, to use irony for communicating one's dissatisfaction with something.

Monographic conception of science   Extensive study of a case, suitable for producing a book giving a comprehensive analysis of this case. For example, to write a book describing the variety of changes a community undergoes after unemployment results for many of its members when an industry breaks down, instead of analyzing a limited number of statistical variables and their relations referring to this problem.

Multiple realities   A concept describing the state in which there is more than one interpretation of a phenomenon, which makes it fruitful to analyze members' points of view in researching that phenomenon.

Narrative   A story told by a sequence of words, actions, or images, and more generally the organization of the information within that story.

Narrative interview   A specific form of interview based on one extensive narrative. Instead of asking questions, the interviewer asks participants to tell the story of their lives (or their illness, for example) as a whole, without interrupting them with questions.

Natural design   Data that have not been produced by using methods (such as an interview) but have rather been recorded from interactions in the daily life of the participants. For instance, instead of asking participants for their version of a conflict (and thus shaping the data with the questions), examples of such conflicts occurring among them are recorded without any other intervention by the researchers.

Naturalistic sociology   A form of field research trying to understand the field under study from within and with its own categories by using methods like participant observation and ethnography. Categories for analyzing data are developed from the material and not derived from existing theories.

Naturally occurring data   Data that are not produced by special methods (like interviews) but are only recorded in the way they can be found in the everyday life under study.

Objective hermeneutics   A way of doing research by analyzing texts for identifying latent structures of meaning underlying these texts and explaining the phenomena that are the issues of the text and the research. For example, analyzing the transcript of a family interaction can lead to identifying and elaborating an implicit conflict underlying the communication of the members in this interaction and on other occasions. This conflict as a latent structure of meaning shapes the members' interaction without their being aware of it.

Objectivity   The degree in which a research situation (the application of methods and their outcome) is independent of the single researcher.

OPAC   Online Public Access Catalogue, an electronic catalogue of a library, sometimes giving access to the catalogues of several libraries at the same time.

Paradigms   Fundamental conceptions of how to do research in a specific field with consequences on the levels of methodology and theory.

Paralinguistic elements of communication   Non-verbal part of communication, such as laughter, smiling, or certain looks. For example, the same wording can be accompanied by smiling or by looking angrily, both of which will influence how the message is received.

Paraphrase   A formulation of the core of information in a specific sentence or statement without taking the specific formulations into account.

Participant observation A specific form of observation based on the researcher becoming a member of the field under study in order to do the observation.

Performative turn The shift from analyzing texts as representations of data to using performative qualities in two respects: to see actions and interactions as performances in order to express specific meanings and to analyze the way they are performed (which means are used); and to use performative formats (dance, poems, acting) as ways of publishing the results of research.

Phenomenology Careful description and analyses of the subjects' life world and the meaning making and understanding in that life world. For example, how are small life worlds in communities like do-it-yourself people organized, and what are the rules and meanings they are built on?

Pluralization of life worlds The diversification of the ways of living in one society. For example, traditional class models (working, middle, and upper class) are no longer adequate to describe modern societies, as many local, subcultural, ethnic, etc., differences have become important as well.

Positivism A philosophy of science which bases the latter on the observation of data. The observation of data should be separated from the interpretation of their meanings. Truth is to be found by following general rules of method, largely independent of the content and context of the investigation.

Postmodernism A social theory which criticizes modernism and its concept of facts and science and takes the way science and facts are produced more into account.

Poststructuralism The result of a shift in social theory coming from literary theory, which questions the clear categories and general validity claims in several theories. Poststructuralism focuses on details rather than on generalization, on human agency rather than on social structure, and on change more than on continuity.

Pragmatism A movement in American philosophy. It focuses on ideas that the meaning of concepts can be found in their practical use, that thought guides action, and that the test for truth is the practical consequences of beliefs.

Principle of openness A principle in qualitative research, according to which researchers will mostly refrain from formulating hypotheses and formulate (interview) questions as open as possible in order to come as close as possible to the views of the participants.

Protocol Detailed documentation of an observation or of a group discussion. In the first case, it is based on the researchers' field notes; in the second case, interactions in the group are recorded and transcribed, often complemented by researchers' notes about the features of communication in the group.

Qualitative research Research interested in analyzing the subjective meaning or the social production of issues, events, or practices by collecting non-standardized data and analyzing texts and images rather than numbers and statistics.

Quality management Approach for promoting the quality of a process with a stress on a common development and clarification of the standards to be met in the process involving all members of the team.

Quantitative research Research interested in frequencies and distributions of issues, events or practices by collecting standardized data and using numbers and statistics for analyzing them.

Reflexivity A concept of research which refers to acknowledging the input of the researchers in actively co-constructing the situation which they want to study. It also alludes to the use to which such insights can be put in making sense of or interpreting data. For example, presenting oneself as an interviewer in an open-minded and empathic way can have a positive and intensifying impact on the interviewees' way of dealing with their experiences. Researchers' irritations after reading a transcript can be a starting point for asking specific questions about the text.

Reliability One of the standard criteria in standardized/quantitative research, measured for example by repeating a test and assessing whether the results are the same in both cases.

Repair organization A mechanism for correcting mistakes or deviations in interactions.

Representativeness A concept referring to the generalization of research and results. Either it is understood in a statistical way—is the population represented in the sample in the distribution of features (age, gender, employment, etc.)? Or it is understood in a theoretical way—are the study and its results covering the theoretically relevant aspects of the issue?

Research design A systematic plan for a research project including who to integrate in the research (sampling), who or what to compare for which dimensions, etc.

Research diaries A means for documenting researchers' experiences in the field. The researchers continually note their impressions and what happens during field contacts or in preparing the study, or during the analysis of the data.

Research perspectives Major approaches in (qualitative) research, under which the variety of methods can be summarized.

Research program A set of studies which are conducted according to the same theoretical or methodological principles and characterized by similar aims.

Resources Time, money, competencies, etc., available for the concrete study or research project.

Retrospective studies Research that analyzes a process by looking back at its development—for example, a biographical process seen from today.

Sampling Selection of cases or materials for the study from a larger population or variety of possibilities.

Second-degree constructions Scientific explanations or conceptualizations based on lay concepts in the life world, which are held by the members. For example, lay theories concerning a specific illness can be taken as a starting point for analyzing the social representations of this illness.

Segmentation Decomposition of a text into the smallest meaningful elements.

Semantic knowledge Knowledge organized around concepts, their meaning, and relation to each other.

Sensitizing concepts Concepts that suggest directions along which to look and rest on a general sense of what is relevant.

Sequential analysis Analysis of a text from beginning to end along the line of development in the text instead of categorizing it.

Shortcut strategies Pragmatic ways of using specific methods in situations of applied research, where it may be difficult to use these methods in their full versions (e.g., in the context of qualitative evaluation).

Social interaction analysis Research interested in analyzing the interactions among the members of a group from a social perspective. For example, how do other members respond to one member's account of seeing a doctor after detecting symptoms of a specific disease?

Social representation The way that social groups perceive or model scientific findings or other issues.

Standardization The degree of controlling a research situation by defining and delimiting as many features of it as necessary or possible.

Structure formula An underlying pattern of communication in a specific setting. For example, a social worker acts on the background of a specific interpretation of the client's situation, which leads repeatedly to misinterpreting the client's concrete problem accounts.

Structured microanalysis A detailed scene-by-scene interpretation of a film looking for patterns in the actions and discourses in the scenes. This analysis can help to identify major moments in the film in which conflicts over values occur and reveal how the film as a whole takes a position on these values.

Subjective theory   Lay people's knowledge about certain issues. This knowledge can be organized similar to scientific theories (e.g., subjective theories of health or illness).

Substantive theory   A more specific theory (in grounded theory research) referring to one area.

Subversive reading   A way of critically analyzing a film for its subtexts.

Symbolic interactionism   A background theory in qualitative research based on the assumption that people act and interact on the basis of the meaning of objects and their interpretation. For example, the use of a computer is influenced by the meaning ascribed to the machine by its users or in the communication about it—as something dangerous, mysterious, practical, or simply a tool for writing more easily and comfortably.

Tabula rasa   Latin for "empty table." This is used to describe an approach of starting research without reading the literature about the field or the issue and is also used for criticizing this approach. This notion was coined in the beginning of grounded theory research but is no longer held by most researchers in the area.

Thematic coding   An approach involving the analysis of data in a comparative way for certain topics after case studies (of interviews, for example) have been done.

Theoretical sampling   The sampling procedure in grounded theory research, where cases, groups, or materials are sampled according to their relevance for the theory that is developed and on the background of what is already the state of knowledge after collecting and analyzing a certain number of cases.

Theoretical saturation   The point in grounded theory research at which more data about a theoretical category do not produce any further theoretical insights.

Thomas's theorem   The theorem says that when a person defines a situation as real, this situation is real in its consequences. This is a basic concept from symbolic interactionism.

Transcription   Transformation of recorded materials (conversations, interviews, visual materials, etc.) into text for analyzing it.

Triangulation   The combination of different methods, theories, data, and/or researchers in the study of one issue.

Turn taking   Organizing principle of talk in interaction for when a participant begins to speak after another participant spoke.

Utilization research   A form of research interested in analyzing the way that results from earlier research projects and scientific knowledge in general are used in a practical context.

Validity   One of the standard criteria in standardized/quantitative research, analyzed for example by looking for confounding influences (internal validity) or for the transferability to situations beyond the current research situation (external validity).

Verbal data   Data produced by speaking (in an interview or a group discussion) about a topic.

Verstehen   German word for "to understand." It describes an approach to understanding a phenomenon more comprehensively than reducing it to one explanation (e.g., a cause–effect relation). For instance, to understand how people live with their chronic illness, a detailed description of their everyday lives may be necessary, rather than identifying a specific variable (e.g., social support) for explaining the degree of success in their coping behavior.

Virtual ethnography   Ethnography of online behavior (e.g., participation in a blog or discussion group).

Visual data   Data coming from images (photo, film, video).

Vulnerable population   People in a specific situation (social discrimination, risks, illness) requiring special sensitivity when studying them.

Zugzwangs (in narratives)   A term taken from the context of playing chess. It means that sometimes you are forced to take a second move once you have made a certain first move. For example, once you have started a narrative, a certain implicit force may drive you to continue this narrative to its end or to provide enough details so that your listeners may understand the situation, process, and point in your story.

References

Adler, P.A. and Adler, P. (1987) *Membership Roles in Field Research*. Beverly Hills, CA: Sage.

Adler, P.A. and Adler, P. (1998) "Observational Techniques," in N. Denzin and Y.S. Lincoln (eds.), *Collecting and Interpreting Qualitative Materials*. London: Sage. pp. 79–110.

Agar, M.H. (1980) *The Professional Stranger*. New York: Academic Press.

Alasuutari, P. (2004) "The Globalization of Qualitative Research," in C. Seale, G. Gobo, J.F. Gubrium and D. Silverman (eds.), *Qualitative Research Practice*. London: Sage. pp. 595–608.

Allmark, P. (2002) "The Ethics of Research with Children," *Nurse Researcher*, 10: 7–19.

Altheide, D.L. and Johnson, J.M. (1998) "Criteria for Assessing Interpretive Validity in Qualitative Research," in N. Denzin and Y.S. Lincoln (eds.), *Collecting and Interpreting Qualitative Materials*. London: Sage. pp. 293–312.

Alzenauer, B., Lang, G. and Flick, U. (2000) "Das Bild der Pflege im Fernsehen – Ergebnisse einer qualitativen Filmanalyse der Krankenhausserie 'Für alle Fälle Stefanie'," *psychomed*, 12: 184–189.

Andrews, R. (2003) *Research Questions*. London: Continuum.

Angrosino, M. (2007) *Doing Ethnographic and Observational Research*. London: Sage.

Atkinson, P., Coffey, A., Delamont, S., Lofland, J. and Lofland, L. (eds.) (2001) *Handbook of Ethnography*. London: Sage.

Atkinson, P. and Hammersley, M. (1998) "Ethnography and Participant Observation," in N. Denzin and Y.S. Lincoln (eds.), *Strategies of Qualitative Inquiry*. London: Sage. pp. 110–136.

Atteslander, P. (1996) "Auf dem Wege zur lokalen Kultur. Einführende Gedanken," in W.F. Whyte, *Die Street Corner Society. Die Sozialstruktur eines Italienerviertels*. Berlin: de Gruyter. pp. IX–XIV.

Augoustinos, M. (2013) "Discourse Analysis in Psychology: What's in a Name?," *Qualitative Research in Psychology, 10 (3): 244–248*

Baker, S.E. and Edwards, R. (2012) "How Many Qualitative Interviews is Enough?", Discussion Paper, National Center of Research Methods: http://eprints.ncrm.ac.uk/2273/.

Bamberg, M. (2012) "Narrative Analysis," in H. Cooper (Editor-in-chief), *APA Handbook of Research Methods in Psychology*. Washington, DC: APA Press. pp. 77–94.

Bamberg, M. and Georgakopoulou, A. (2008) "Small Stories as a New Perspective in Narrative and Identity Analysis," *Text & Talk*, 28(3): 377–396.

Bampton, R. and Cowton, C.J. (2002, May) "The E-Interview," *Forum Qualitative Sozialforschung/Forum: Qualitative Social Research*, 3(2), www.qualitative-research.net/fqs/fqs-eng.htm (date of access: February 22, 2005).

Banister, P., Burman, E., Parker, I., Taylor, M. and Tindall, C. (1994) *Qualitative Methods in Psychology: A Research Guide*. Buckingham: Open University Press.

Banks, M. (2007) *Using Visual Data in Qualitative Research*. London: Sage.

Banks, M. (2014) "Analyzing Images," in U. Flick (ed.), *The SAGE Handbook of Qualitative Data Analysis*. London: Sage. pp. 394–408.

Barbour, R. (2007) *Doing Focus Groups*. London: Sage.

Barbour, R. (2014) "Analyzing Focus Groups," in U. Flick (ed.), *The SAGE Handbook of Qualitative Data Analysis*. London: Sage. pp. 313–326.

Barthes, R. (1977) "Introduction to the Structural Analysis of Narratives," in *Image-Music-Text*. London: Fontana. pp. 79–124.

Barthes, R. (1996) *Camera Lucida: Reflections on Photography*. New York: Hill and Wang.

Barton, A.H. and Lazarsfeld, P.F. (1955) "Some Functions of Qualitative Analysis in Social Research," *Frankfurter Beiträge zur Soziologie*. I. Frankfurt a. M.: Europäische Verlagsanstalt. pp. 321–361.

Bateson, G. and Mead, M. (1942) *Balinese Character: A Photographic Analysis*, Vol. 2. New York: New York Academy of Sciences.

Bauer, M. (2000) "Classical Content Analysis: A Review," in M. Bauer and G. Gaskell (eds.), *Qualitative Researching with Text, Image and Sound – A Handbook*. London: Sage. pp. 131–150.

Bauer, M. and Gaskell, G. (eds.) (2000) *Qualitative Researching with Text, Image, and Sound – A Handbook*. London: Sage.

Baum, F. (1995) "Researching Public Health: Behind the Qualitative–Quantitative Methodological Debate," *Social Science and Medicine*, 40: 459–468.

Baym, N.K. (1995) "The Emergence of Community in Computer-Mediated Communication," in S. Jones (ed.), *Cybersociety: Computer-Mediated Communication and Community*. London: Sage. pp. 138–163.

Bazeley, P. and Jackson, K. (2013) *Qualitative Data Analysis with NVivo* (2nd edn). London: Sage.

Beck, U. (1992) *Risk-Society*. London: Sage.

Beck, U. and Bonß, W. (eds.) (1989) *Weder Sozialtechnologie noch Aufklärung? Analysen zur Verwendung sozialwissenschaftlichen Wissens*. Frankfurt: Suhrkamp.

Becker, H.S. (1986a) *Doing Things Together: Selected Papers*. Evanston, IL: Northwestern University Press.

Becker, H.S. (1986b) *Writing for Social Scientists*. Chicago, IL: University of Chicago Press.

Becker, H.S. (1996) "The Epistemology of Qualitative Research," in R. Jessor, A. Colby and R.A. Shweder (eds.), *Ethnography and Human Development*. Chicago, IL: University of Chicago Press. pp. 53–72.

Becker, H.S. and Geer, B. (1960) "Participant Observation: Analysis of Qualitative Data," in R.N. Adams and J.J. Preiss (eds.), *Human Organization Research*. Homewood, IL: Dorsey Press. pp. 267–289.

Becker, H.S., Geer, B., Hughes, E.C., and Strauss, A.L. (1961) *Boys in White: Student Culture in Medical School*. Chicago, IL: University of Chicago Press.

Berger, John (1972) *Ways of Seeing*. London: British Broadcasting Corporation.

Berger, P.L. and Luckmann, T. (1966) *The Social Construction of Reality*. Garden City, NY: Doubleday.

Bergmann, J.R. (1980) "Interaktion and Exploration: Eine konversationsanalytische Studie zur sozialen Organisation der Eröffnungsphase von psychiatrischen Aufnahmegesprächen," Dissertation, Konstanz.

Bergmann, J.R. (1985) "Flüchtigkeit und methodische Fixierung sozialer Wirklichkeit. Aufzeichnungen als Daten der interpretativen Soziologie," in W. Bonß and H. Hartmann (eds.), *Entzauberte Wissenschaft – Zur Realität und Geltung soziologischer Forschung.* Göttingen: Schwartz. pp. 299–320.

Bergmann, J.R. (2004a) "Conversation Analysis," in U. Flick, E.v. Kardorff and I. Steinke (eds.), *A Companion to Qualitative Research.* London: Sage. pp. 296–302.

Bergmann, J.R. (2004b) "Ethnomethodology," in U. Flick, E.v. Kardorff and I. Steinke (eds.), *A Companion to Qualitative Research.* London: Sage. pp. 72–80.

Bergmann, J.R. (2006) "Mediale Repräsentation in der qualitativen Sozialforschung," in R. Ayaß and J. Bergmann (eds.), *Qualitative Methoden in der Medienforschung.* Reinbek: Rowohlt. pp. 489–506.

Bergmann, J.R. and Meier, C. (2004) "Electronic Process Data and Their Analysis," in U. Flick, E.v. Kardorff and I. Steinke (ed.), *A Companion to Qualitative Research.* London: Sage. pp. 243–247.

Bertaux, D. (ed.) (1981) *Biography and History: The Life History Approach in Social Sciences.* Beverly Hills, CA: Sage.

Billig, M. (1987) *Arguing and Thinking: A Rhetorical Approach to Social Psychology.* Cambridge: Cambridge University Press.

Billman-Mahecha, E. (1990) *Egozentrismus und Perspektivenwechsel.* Göttingen: Hogrefe.

Blumer, H. (1938) "Social Psychology," in E. Schmidt (ed.), *Man and Society.* New York: Prentice Hall. pp. 144–198.

Blumer, H. (1969) *Symbolic Interactionism: Perspective and Method.* Berkeley and Los Angeles, CA: University of California Press.

Blumer, H. (1970) "What's Wrong with Social Theory?", in W.J. Filstead (ed.), *Qualitative Methodology: Firsthand Involvement with the Social World.* Chicago, IL: Markham. pp. 52–62.

Bogner, A., Littig, B. and Menz, W. (eds.) (2009) *Interviewing Experts.* Basingstoke: Palgrave Macmillan.

Bogner, A. and Menz, W. (2009) "The Theory-Generating Expert Interview," in A. Bogner, B. Littig and W. Menz (eds.), *Interviewing Experts.* Basingstoke: Palgrave Macmillan. pp. 43–80.

Böhm, A. (2004) "Theoretical Coding," in U. Flick, E.v. Kardorff and I. Steinke (eds.), *A Companion to Qualitative Research.* London: Sage. pp. 270–275.

Bohnsack, R. (2004) "Group Discussions and Focus Groups," in U. Flick, E.v. Kardorff and I. Steinke (eds.), *A Companion to Qualitative Research.* London: Sage. pp. 214–220.

Bohnsack, R. (2014) "Documentary Method," in U. Flick (ed.), *The SAGE Handbook of Qualitative Data Analysis.* London: Sage. pp. 217–233.

Bonß, W. (1982) *Die Einübung des Tatsachenblicks. Zur Struktur und Veränderung empirischer Sozialforschung.* Frankfurt: Suhrkamp.

Bonß, W. (1995) "Soziologie," in U. Flick, E.v. Kardorff, H. Keupp, L.v. Rosenstiel and S. Wolff (eds.), *Handbuch Qualitative Sozialforschung* (2nd edn). Munich: Psychologie Verlags Union. pp. 36–39.

Bonß, W. and Hartmann, H. (1985) "Konstruierte Gesellschaft, rationale Deutung – Zum Wirklichkeitscharakter soziologischer Diskurse," in W. Bonß and H. Hartmann (eds.), *Entzauberte Wissenschaft: Zur Realität und Geltung soziologischer Forschung.* Göttingen: Schwartz. pp. 9–48.

Borman, K.M., LeCompte, M. and Goetz, J.P. (1986) "Ethnographic Research and Qualitative Research Design and Why it Doesn't Work," *American Behavioral Scientist*, 30: 42–57.

Borneman, J. and Hammoudi, A. (eds.) (2009) *Being There – The Fieldwork Encounter and the Making of Truth.* Berkeley, CA: University of California Press.

Bourdieu, P. (1996) "Understanding," *Theory, Culture and Society*, 13(2): 17–37.

Braun, V. and Clarke, V. (2006) "Using Thematic Analysis in Psychology," *Qualitative Research in Psychology*, 3(2): 77–101.

Brockmeier, J. and Carbaugh, D. (eds.) (2001) *Narrative and Identity: Studies in Autobiography, Self and Culture*. Amsterdam: John Benjamins.

Bruce, G. (1992) "Comments," in J. Svartvik (ed.), *Directions in Corpus Linguistics: Proceedings of the Nobel Symposium 82, Stockholm, August 4–8, 1991*. Berlin: de Gruyter. pp. 145–147.

Bruner, E.M. (1993) "Introduction: The Ethnographic Self and the Personal Self," in P. Benson (ed.), *Anthropology and Literature*. Urbana, IL: University of Illinois Press. pp. 1–26.

Bruner, J. (1987) "Life as Narrative," *Social Research*, 54: 11–32.

Bruner, J. (1990) *Acts of Meaning*. Cambridge, MA: Harvard University Press.

Bruner, J. (1991) "The Narrative Construction of Reality," *Critical Inquiry*, 18: 1–21.

Bruner, J. and Feldman, C. (1996) "Group Narrative as a Cultural Context of Autobiography," in D. Rubin (ed.), *Remembering our Past: Studies in Autobiographical Memory*. Cambridge: Cambridge University Press. pp. 291–317.

Bryant, A. and Charmaz, K. (eds.) (2007a) *The SAGE Handbook of Grounded Theory*. London: Sage.

Bryant, A. and Charmaz, K. (2007b) "Introduction – Grounded Theory Research: Methods and Practices," in A. Bryant and K. Charmaz (eds.), *The SAGE Handbook of Grounded Theory*. London: Sage. pp. 1–28.

Bryman, A. (1992) "Quantitative and Qualitative Research: Further Reflections on their Integration," in J. Brannen (ed.), *Mixing Methods: Quantitative and Qualitative Research*. Aldershot: Avebury. pp. 57–80.

Bryman, A. (2004) *Social Research Methods* (2nd edn). Oxford: Oxford University Press.

Bryman, A. (2007) "The Research Question in Social Research: What Is its Role?", *International Journal of Social Research Methodology*, 10(1): 5–20.

Bude, H. (1984) "Rekonstruktion von Lebenskonstruktionen: eine Antwort auf die Frage, was die Biograpnieforschung bringt," in M. Kohli and G. Robert (eds.), *Biographie und soziale Wirklichkeit. Neuere Beiträge und Forschungsperspektiven*. Stuttgart: Metzler. pp. 7–28.

Bude, H. (1985) "Der Sozialforscher als Narrationsanimateur. Kritische Anmerkungen zu einer erzähltheoretischen Fundierung der interpretativen Sozialforschung," *Kölner Zeitschrift für Soziologie und Sozialpsychologie*, 37: 327–336.

Bude, H. (1989) "Der Essay als Form der Darstellung sozialwissenschaftlicher Erkenntnisse," *Kölner Zeitschrift für Soziologie und Sozialpsychologie*, 41: 526–539.

Bude, H. (2004) "Qualitative Generation Research," in U. Flick, E.v. Kardorff and I. Steinke (eds.), *A Companion to Qualitative Research*. London: Sage. pp. 108–112.

Bühler-Niederberger, D. (1985) "Analytische Induktion als Verfahren qualitativer Methodologie," *Zeitschrift für Soziologie*, 14: 475–485.

Chamberlain, K. (1999) "Using Grounded Theory in Health Psychology," in M. Murray and K. Chamberlain (eds.), *Qualitative Health Psychology: Theories and Methods*. London. Sage. pp. 183–201.

Charmaz, K. (1997) "Identity Dilemmas of Chronically Ill Men," in A. Strauss and J. Corbin (eds.), *Grounded Theory in Practice*. London. Sage. pp. 35–62.

Charmaz, K. (2003) "Grounded Theory," in J.A. Smith (ed.), *Qualitative Psychology: A Practical Guide to Research Methods*. London. Sage. pp. 81–110.

Charmaz, K. (2006) *Constructing Grounded Theory: A Practical Guide Through Qualitative Analysis*. London: Sage.

Charmaz, K. (2011) "A Constructivist Grounded Theory Analysis of Losing and Regaining a Valued Self," in F.J. Wertz, K. Charmaz, L.M. McMullen, R. Josselson, Ruthellen, R. Anderson and E. McSpadden, *Five Ways of Doing Qualitative Analysis*. New York: Guilford. pp. 165–204.

Charmaz, K. and Mitchell, R.G. (2001) "Grounded Theory in Ethnography," in P. Atkinson, A. Coffey, S. Delamont, J. Lofland and L. Lofland (eds.), *Handbook of Ethnography*. London: Sage. pp. 160–174.

Cicourel, A.V. (1964) *Method and Measurement in Sociology*. New York: Free Press.

Cicourel, A.V. (1981) "Notes on the Integration of Micro- and Macrolevels of Analysis," in K. Knorr-Cetina and A.V. Cicourel (eds.), *Advances in Social Theory and Methodology: Towards an Integration of Micro- and Macro-Sociologies*. London. Routledge & Kegan Paul. pp. 51–80.

Clifford, J. (1986) "Introduction: Partial Truths," in J. Clifford and G.E. Marcus (eds.), *Writing Culture: The Poetics and Politics of Ethnography*. Berkeley, CA: University of California Press. pp. 1–26.

Clifford, J. and Marcus, G.E. (eds.) (1986) *Writing Culture: The Poetics and Politics of Ethnography*. Berkeley, CA: University of California Press.

Coffey, A. (2014) "Analyzing Documents," in U. Flick (ed.), *The SAGE Handbook of Qualitative Data Analysis*. London: Sage. pp. 367–379.

Coffey, A. and Atkinson, P. (1996) *Making Sense of Qualitative Data: Complementary Research Strategies*. London: Sage.

Coffey, A., Holbrook, B. and Atkinson, P. (1996) "Qualitative Data Analysis: Technologies and Representations," *Sociological Research Online*, 1, http://www.socresonline.org.uk/1/1/4.html (Date of Access 13th. Aug. 2013

Coltart, C. and Henwood, K. (2012) "On Paternal Subjectivity: A Qualitative Longitudinal and Psychosocial Case Analysis of Men's Classed Positions and Transitions to First-Time Fatherhood," *Qualitative Research*, 12: 35–52.

Corbin, J. and Strauss, A. (1988) *Unending Work and Care: Managing Chronic Illness at Home*. San Francisco, CA: Jossey Bass.

Corbin, J. and Strauss, A. (1990) "Grounded Theory Research: Procedures, Canons and Evaluative Criteria," *Qualitative Sociology*, 13: 3–21.

Corbin, J. and Strauss, A.L. (2008) *Basics of Qualitative Research*. London: Sage.

Cornish, F., Gillespie, A. and Zittoun, T. (2014) "Collaborative Data Analysis," in U. Flick (ed.), *The SAGE Handbook of Qualitative Data Analysis*. London: Sage. pp. 79–93

Corti, L. (2011) "The European Landscape of Qualitative Social Research Archives: Methodological and Practical Issues" [77 paragraphs]. *Forum Qualitative Sozialforschung/Forum: Qualitative Social Research*, 12(3), Art. 11, http://nbn-resolving.de/urn:nbn:de:0114-fqs1103117.

Corti, L. and Gregory, A. (2011) "CAQDAS Comparability. What about CAQDAS Data Exchange?" [42 paragraphs]. *Forum Qualitative Sozialforschung/Forum: Qualitative Social Research*, 12(1), Art. 35, http://nbn-resolving.de/urn:nbn:de:0114-fqs1101352.

Coulter, J. (1983) *Rethinking Cognitive Theory*. London: Macmillan.

Creswell, J.W. (2008) *Research Design: Qualitative, Quantitative, and Mixed Methods Approaches* (3rd edn). Thousand Oaks, CA: Sage.

Czarniawska, B. (2004) *Narratives in Social Science Research*. London: Sage.

Dabbs, J.M. (1982) "Making Things Visible," in J. Van Maanen, J.M. Dabbs and R. Faulkner (eds.), *Varieties of Qualitative Research*. London: Sage. pp. 31–64.

D'Andrade, R.G. (1987) "A Folk Model of the Mind," in D. Holland and N. Quinn (eds.), *Cultural Models in Language and Thought*. Cambridge: Cambridge University Press. pp. 112–149.

Daston, L. and Lunbeck, E. (2011) "Introduction: Observation Observed," in L. Daston and E. Lunbeck (eds.), *Histories of Scientific Observation*. Chicago, IL: University of Chicago Press. pp. 1–9.

Davidson, J. and di Gregorio, S. (2011) "Qualitative Research and Technology: In the Midst of a Revolution," in N. Denzin and Y.S. Lincoln (eds.), *Handbook of Qualitative Research* (4th edn). London: Sage. pp. 627–643.

Deeke, A. (1995) "Experteninterviews – ein methodologisches und forschungspraktisches Problem. Einleitende Bemerkungen und Fragen zum Workshop," in C. Brinkmann, A. Deeke and B. Völkel (eds.), Experteninterviews in der Arbeitsmarktforschung. Diskussionsbeiträge zu methodischen Fragen und praktischen Erfahrungen. *Beiträge zur Arbeitsmarkt- und Berufsforschung* 191. Nürnberg: Bundesanstalt für Arbeit, pp. 7–22.

De Montfort University (September 2008) "How to Undertake a Literature Search and Review: For Dissertations and Final Year Projects," Department of Library Services (www.library.dmu.ac.uk/Images/Howto/LiteratureSearch.pdf).

Denzin, N.K. (1988) *Interpretive Biography.* London: Sage.

Denzin, N.K. (1989a) *Interpretive Interactionism.* London: Sage.

Denzin, N.K. (1989b) *The Research Act* (3rd edn). Englewood Cliffs, NJ: Prentice Hall.

Denzin, N.K. (1989c) "Reading *Tender Mercies:* Two Interpretations," *Sociological Quarterly*, 30: 1–19.

Denzin, N.K. (ed.) (1993) *Studies in Symbolic Interactionism*, Vol. 15. Greenwich, CT: JAI Press.

Denzin, N.K. (1997) *Interpretive Ethnography: Ethnographic Practices for the 21st Century.* Thousand Oaks, CA: Sage.

Denzin, N.K. (2000) "The Practices and Politics of Interpretation," in N. Denzin and Y.S. Lincoln (eds.), *Handbook of Qualitative Research* (2nd edn). London: Sage. pp. 897–922.

Denzin, N.K. (2004a) "Reading Film: Using Photos and Video as Social Science Material," in U. Flick, E.v. Kardorff and I. Steinke (eds.), *A Companion to Qualitative Research*. London: Sage. pp. 234–247.

Denzin, N.K. (2004b) "Symbolic Interactionism," in U. Flick, E.v. Kardorff and I. Steinke (eds.), *A Companion to Qualitative Research*. London: Sage. pp. 81–87.

Denzin, N.K. (2014) "Writing and/as Analysis or Performing the World," in U. Flick (ed.), *The SAGE Handbook of Qualitative Data Analysis*. London: Sage. pp. 569–584.

Denzin, N. and Giardina, M. (eds.) (2006) *Qualitative Inquiry and the Conservative Challenges*. Walnut Creek, CA: Left Coast Press.

Denzin, N. and Lincoln, Y.S. (eds.) (2000a) *Handbook of Qualitative Research* (2nd edn). London: Sage.

Denzin, N. and Lincoln, Y.S. (2000b) "Introduction: The Discipline and Practice of Qualitative Research," in N. Denzin and Y.S. Lincoln (eds.), *Handbook of Qualitative Research* (2nd edn). London: Sage. pp. 1–29.

Denzin, N. and Lincoln, Y.S. (eds.) (2005a) *The SAGE Handbook of Qualitative Research* (3rd edn). London: Sage.

Denzin, N. and Lincoln, Y.S. (2005b) "Introduction: The Discipline and Practice of Qualitative Research," in N. Denzin and Y.S. Lincoln (eds.), *The SAGE Handbook of Qualitative Research* (3rd edn). London: Sage. pp. 1–32.

Denzin, N. and Lincoln, Y.S. (eds.) (2011) *The SAGE Handbook of Qualitative Research* (3rd edn). London: Sage.

Department of Health (2001) *Research Governance Framework for Health and Social Care.* London: Department of Health.

Derrida, J. (1990) *Writing and Difference.* London: Routledge (original: *L'ecriture et la difference.* Paris: Editions du Seuil, 1967).

Devereux, G. (1967) *From Anxiety to Methods in the Behavioral Sciences.* The Hague: Mouton.

Douglas, J.D. (1976) *Investigative Social Research.* Beverly Hills, CA: Sage.

Drew, P. (1995) "Conversation Analysis," in J.A. Smith, R. Harré and L.v. Langenhove (eds.), *Rethinking Methods in Psychology.* London: Sage. pp. 64–79.

Eberle, T. (2014) "Phenomenology as a Research Method," in U. Flick (ed.), *The SAGE Handbook of Qualitative Data Analysis.* London: Sage. pp. 184–202.

Edwards, D. and Potter, J. (1992) *Discursive Psychology.* London: Sage.

Elliot, R., Fischer, C.T. and Rennie, D.L. (1999) "Evolving Guidelines for Publication of Qualitative Research Studies in Psychology and Related Fields," *British Journal of Clinical Psychology,* 38: 215–229.

Ellis, C., Adams, T.E. and Bochner, A.P. (2011) "Autoethnography: An Overview" [40 paragraphs]. *Forum Qualitative Sozialforschung/Forum: Qualitative Social Research,* 12(1), Art. 10, http://nbn-resolving.de/urn:nbn:de:0114-fqs1101108.

Emerson, R. Fretz, R. and Shaw, L. (1995) *Writing Ethnographic Fieldnotes.* Chicago, IL: Chicago University Press.

Erdheim, M. (1984) *Die gesellschaftliche Produktion von Unbewußtheit.* Frankfurt: Suhrkamp.

Esin, C., Fathi, M. and Squire, C. (2014) "Narrative Analysis: The Constructionist Approach," in U. Flick (ed.), *The SAGE Handbook of Qualitative Data Analysis.* London: Sage. pp. 203–216.

Ethik-Kodex (1993) "Ethik-Kodex der Deutschen Gesellschaft für Soziologie und des Berufsverbandes Deutscher Soziologen," *DGS-Informationen,* 1/93: 13–19.

Evers, J.C., Silver, C., Mruck, K. and Peeters, B. (2011) "Introduction to the KWALON Experiment: Discussions on Qualitative Data Analysis Software by Developers and Users" [28 paragraphs]. *Forum Qualitative Sozialforschung/Forum: Qualitative Social Research,* 12(1), Art. 40, http://nbn-resolving.de/urn:nbn:de:0114-fqs1101405.

Fielding, N.G. and Fielding, J.L. (1986) *Linking Data.* Beverly Hills, CA: Sage.

Fielding, N.G. and Lee, R.M. (eds.) (1991) *Using Computers in Qualitative Research.* London: Sage.

Fielding, N.G., Lee, R. and Blank, G. (eds.) (2008) *The SAGE Handbook of Online Research Methods.* London: Sage.

Fielding, N. and Lee, R.M. (1998) *Computer Analysis and Qualitative Research.* London: Sage.

Fink, A. (2009) *Conducting Research Literature Reviews: From the Internet to Paper* (3rd edn.). London: Sage.

Fleck, L., Trenn, T.J. and Merton, R.K. (1979) *Genesis and Development of a Scientific Fact.* Chicago, IL: Chicago University Press.

Flick, U. (1989) *Vertrauen, Verwalten, Einweisen – Subjektive Vertrauenstheorien in sozialpsychiatrischer Beratung.* Wiesbaden: Deutscher Universitätsverlag

Flick, U. (1992) "Triangulation Revisited: Strategy of or Alternative to Validation of Qualitative Data," *Journal for the Theory of Social Behavior,* 22: 175–197.

Flick, U. (1994) "Social Representations and the Social Construction of Everyday Knowledge: Theoretical and Methodological Queries," *Social Science Information,* 2: 179–197.

Flick, U. (1995) "Social Representations," in R. Harré, J. Smith and L.v. Langenhove (eds.), *Rethinking Psychology.* London: Sage. pp. 70–96.

Flick, U. (1996) *Psychologie des technisierten Alltags.* Opladen: Westdeutscher Verlag.

Flick, U. (ed.) (1998) *Psychology of the Social: Representations in Knowledge and Language.* Cambridge: Cambridge University Press.

Flick, U. (2000a) "Episodic Interviewing," in M. Bauer and G. Gaskell (eds.), *Qualitative Researching with Text, Image and Sound: A Practical Handbook.* London: Sage. pp. 75–92.

Flick, U. (2000b) "Qualitative Inquiries into Social Representations of Health," *Journal of Health Psychology*, 5: 309–318.

Flick, U. (ed.) (2003) "Health Concepts in Different Contexts" (Special Issue), *Journal of Health Psychology*, 8(5).

Flick, U. (2004a) "Triangulation in Qualitative Research," in U. Flick, E.v. Kardorff and I. Steinke (eds.), *A Companion to Qualitative Research.* London: Sage. pp. 178–183.

Flick, U. (2004b) "Constructivism," in U. Flick, E.v. Kardorff and I. Steinke (eds.), *A Companion to Qualitative Research.* London: Sage. pp. 88–94.

Flick, U. (2005) "Qualitative Research in Sociology in Germany and the US-State of the Art, Differences and Developments" [47 paragraphs]. *Forum Qualitative Sozialforschunq/Forum: Qualitative Social Research*, 6(3), Art, 23, http://nbn-resolving.de/urn:nbn:de:0114-fqs0503230.

Flick, U. (ed.) (2007a) *The SAGE Qualitative Research Kit* (8 vols.). London: Sage.

Flick, U. (2007b) *Managing Quality in Qualitative Research.* London: Sage.

Flick, U. (2007c) *Designing Qualitative Research.* London: Sage.

Flick, U. (2011) "Mixing Methods, Triangulation and Integrated Research: Challenges for Qualitative Research in a World of Crisis," in N.K. Denzin and M. Giardina (eds.), *Qualitative Inquiry and Global Crises.* Walnut Creek, CA: Left Coast Press. pp. 132–152.

Flick, U. (ed.) (2014a) *The SAGE Handbook of Qualitative Data Analysis.* London: Sage.

Flick, U. (2014b) "Mapping the Field", in U. Flick (ed.) *The SAGE Handbook of Qualitative Data Analysis.* London: Sage. pp. 3-18.

Flick, U. and Bauer, M. (2004) "Teaching Qualitative Research," in U. Flick, E.v. Kardorff and I. Steinke (eds.), *A Companion to Qualitative Research.* London: Sage. pp. 340–348.

Flick, U., Fischer, C., Neuber, A., Walter, U. and Schwartz, F.W. (2003) "Health in the Context of Being Old: Representations Held by Health Professionals," *Journal of Health Psychology*, 8(5): 539–556.

Flick, U., Fischer, C., Walter, U., and Schwartz, F.W. (2002) "Social Representations of Health Held by Health Professionals: The Case of General Practitioners and Home Care Nurses," *Social Science Information*, 41(4): 581–602.

Flick, U., Garms-Homolová, V. and Röhnsch, G. (2010) "'When They Sleep, They Sleep' – Daytime Activities and Sleep Disorders in Nursing Homes," *Journal of Health Psychology*, 15(5): 755–764.

Flick, U., Garms-Homolová, V. and Röhnsch, G. (2012a) "'And Mostly They Have a Need for Sleeping Pills': Physicians' Views on Treatment of Sleep Disorders with Drugs in Nursing Homes," *Journal of Aging Studies*, 26(4): 484–494.

Flick, U., Garms-Homolová, V., Herrmann, W.J., Kuck, J. and Röhnsch, G. (2012b) "'I Can't Prescribe Something Just Because Someone Asks for It …': Using Mixed Methods in the Framework of Triangulation," *Journal of Mixed Methods Research*, 6(2): 97–110.

Flick, U., Hoose, B. and Sitta, P. (1998) "Gesundheit und Krankheit gleich Saúde & Doenca? – Gesundheitsvorstellungen bei Frauen in Deutschland und Portugal," in Flick, U. (ed.), *Wann fühlen wir uns gesund? - Subjektive Vorstellungen von Gesundheit und Krankheit.* Weinheim: Juventa. pp. 141–159.

Flick, U., Kardorff, E.v. and Steinke, I. (eds.) (2004a) *A Companion to Qualitative Research*. London: Sage.

Flick, U. and Röhnsch, G. (2007) "Idealization and Neglect – Health Concepts of Homeless Adolescents," *Journal of Health Psychology*, 12: 737–750.

Flick, U., Walter, U., Fischer, C., Neuber, A. and Schwartz, F.W. (2004b) *Gesundheit als Leitidee? Gesundheitsvorstellungen von Ärzten und Pflegekräften*. Bern: Huber.

Flynn, L.R. and Goldsmith, R.E. (2013) *Case Studies for Ethics in Academic Research in the Social Sciences*. London: Sage.

Fontana, A. and Frey, J.H. (2000) "The Interview: From Structured Questions to Negotiated Text," in N. Denzin and Y.S. Lincoln (eds.), *Handbook of Qualitative Research* (2nd edn). London: Sage. pp. 645–672.

Foucault, M. (1980) *Power/Knowledge: Selected Interviews and Other Writings 1972–1977*. Hassocks: Harvester.

Freud, S. (1958) "Recommendations to Physicians Practising Psychoanalysis," in *The Standard Edition of the Complete Psychological Work of Sigmund Freud*, Vol. XII (trans. J. Strachey). London: Hogarth Press. pp. 109–120.

Friese, S. (2011) *Qualitative Data Analysis with ATLAS.ti*. London: Sage.

Fuchs, M. and Berg, E. (1993) "Phänomenologie der Differenz. Reflexionsstufen ethnographischer Repräsentation," in E. Berg and M. Fuchs (eds.), *Kultur, soziale Praxis, Text: Die Krise der ethnographischen Repräsentation*. Frankfurt: Suhrkamp. pp. 11–108.

Fuchs, W. (1984) *Biographische Forschung: Eine Einführung in Praxis und Methoden*. Opladen: Westdeutscher Verlag.

Gaiser, T.J. and Schreiner, A.E. (2009) *A Guide to Conducting Online Research*. London: Sage.

Garfinkel, H. (1967) *Studies in Ethnomethodology*. Englewood Cliffs, NJ: Prentice Hall.

Garfinkel, H. (1986) *Ethnomethodological Studies of Work*. London. Routledge & Kegan Paul.

Garfinkel, H. and Sacks, H. (1970) "On Formal Structures of Practical Actions," in J. McKinney and E. Tiryyakian (eds.), *Theoretical Sociology*. New York: Appleton.

Garz, D. (ed.) (1994) *Die Welt als Text*. Frankfurt: Suhrkamp.

Garz, D. and Kraimer, K. (1994) "Die Welt als Text. Zum Projekt einer hermeneutisch-rekonstruktiven Sozialwissenschaft," in D. Garz (ed.), *Die Welt als Text*. Frankfurt: Suhrkamp. pp. 7–21.

Gaskell, G. and Bauer, M. (2000) "Towards Public Accountability: Beyond Sampling, Reliability and Validity," in M. Bauer and G. Gaskell (eds.), *Qualitative Researching with Text, Image, and Sound – A Handbook*. London: Sage. pp. 336–350.

Gebauer, G. and Wulf, C. (1995) *Mimesis: Culture, Art, Society*. Berkeley, CA: University of California Press.

Geertz, C. (1973) *The Interpretation of Cultures: Selected Essays*. New York: Basic Books.

Geertz, C. (1983) *Local Knowledge: Further Essays in Interpretative Anthropology*. New York: Basic Books.

Geertz, C. (1988) *The Anthropologist as Author*. Stanford, CA: Stanford University Press.

Geertz, C. (2000) *Available Light: Anthropological Reflections on Philosophical Topics*. Princeton, NJ: Princeton University Press.

Gergen, K.J. (1985) "The Social Constructionist Movement in Modern Psychology," *American Psychologist*, 40: 266–275.

Gergen, K.J. (1994) *Realities and Relationship: Soundings in Social Construction*. Cambridge, MA: Harvard University Press.

Gergen, K.J. (1999) *An Invitation to Social Construction*. London: Sage.

Gergen, M. (2008) "Qualitative Methods in Feminist Psychology," in C. Willig and W. Stainton-Rogers (eds.), *The SAGE Handbook of Qualitative Research in Psychology*. London: Sage. pp. 280–295.

Gerhardt, U. (1986) *Patientenkarrieren. Eine medizinsoziologische Studie*. Frankfurt: Suhrkamp.

Gerhardt, U. (1988) "Qualitative Sociology in the Federal Republic of Germany," *Qualitative Sociology*, 11: 29–43.

Gibbs, G. (2007) *Analyzing Qualitative Data*. London: Sage.

Gibbs, G. (2014) "Using Software in Qualitative Analysis," in U. Flick (ed.), *The SAGE Handbook of Qualitative Data Analysis*. London: Sage. pp. 277–294

Gildemeister, R. (2004) "Gender Studies," in U. Flick, E.v. Kardorff and I. Steinke (eds.), *A Companion to Qualitative Research*. London: Sage. pp. 123–128.

Gilligan, C. (1982) *In a Different Voice: Psychological Theory and Women's Development*. Cambridge, MA: Harvard University Press.

Girtler, R. (1984) *Methoden der qualitativen Sozialforschung*. Vienna: Böhlau.

Glaser, B.G. (1969) "The Constant Comparative Method of Qualitative Analysis," in G.J. McCall and J.L. Simmons (eds.), *Issues in Participant Observation*. Reading, MA: Addison-Wesley. pp. 217–227.

Glaser, B.G. (1978) *Theoretical Sensitivity*. Mill Valley, CA: University of California Press.

Glaser, B.G. (1992) *Basics of Grounded Theory Analysis: Emergence vs. Forcing*. Mill Valley, CA: Sociology Press.

Glaser, B.G. (2002, September) "Constructivist Grounded Theory" [47 paragraphs]. *Forum Qualitative Sozialforschung/Forum: Qualitative Social Research* [Online Journal], 3 (3), http://www.qualitative-research.net/fqs-texte/3-02/3-02glaser-e.htm (date of access: May 9, 2008).

Glaser, B.G. and Strauss, A.L. (1965a) *Awareness of Dying*. Chicago, IL: Aldine.

Glaser, B.G. and Strauss, A.L. (1965b) "Discovery of Substantive Theory: A Basic Strategy Underlying Qualitative Research," *The American Behavioral Scientist*, 8: 5–12.

Glaser, B.G. and Strauss, A.L. (1967) *The Discovery of Grounded Theory: Strategies for Qualitative Research*. Chicago, IL: Aldine.

Glasersfeld, E.v. (1992) "Aspekte des Konstruktivsimus: Vico, Berkeley, Piaget," in G. Rusch and S.J. Schmidt (eds.), *Konstruktivismus: Geschichte und Anwendung*. Frankfurt: Suhrkamp. pp. 20–33.

Glasersfeld, E.v. (1995) *Radical Constructivism: A Way of Knowing and Learning*. London: Falmer Press.

Gobo, G. (2004) "Sampling, Representativeness and Generalizability," in C. Seale, G. Gobo, J.F. Gubrium and D. Silverman (eds.), *Qualitative Research Practice*. London: Sage. pp. 435–456.

Gobo, G. (2008) *Doing Ethnography*. London: Sage.

Goffman, E. (1959) *The Presentation of Self in Everyday Life*. New York: Doubleday.

Goffman, E. (1961) *Asylums: Essays on the Social Situation of Mental Patients and Other Inmates*. New York: Anchor Doubleday.

Gold, R.L. (1958) "Roles in Sociological Field Observations," *Social Forces*, 36: 217–223.

Goodman, N. (1978) *Ways of Worldmaking*. Indianapolis, IN: Hackett.

Grathoff, R. (1978) "Alltag und Lebenswelt als Gegenstand der phänomenologischen Sozialtheorie," in K. Hammerich and M. Klein (eds.), *Kölner Zeitschrift für Soziologie und Sozialpsychologie* Sonderheft 20: *Materialien zur Soziologie des Alltags*. pp. 67–85.

Groeben, N. (1990) "Subjective Theories and the Explanation of Human Action," in G.R. Semin and K.J. Gergen (eds.), *Everyday Understanding: Social and Scientific Implications*. London: Sage. pp. 19–44.

Guba, E.G. (ed.) (1990) *The Paradigm Dialog.* Newbury Park, CA: Sage.

Guba, E.G. and Lincoln, Y.S. (1998) "Competing Paradigms in Qualitative Research," in N. Denzin and Y.S. Lincoln (eds.), *The Landscape of Qualitative Research: Theories and Issues.* London: Sage. pp. 195–220.

Gubrium, J.F. and Holstein, J.A. (1995) *The Active Interview,* Qualitative Research Methods Series, 37. Thousand Oaks, CA: Sage.

Gubrium, J.F. and Holstein, J.A. (eds.) (2001) *Handbook of Interviewing Research.* Thousand Oaks, CA: Sage.

Gubrium, J.F. and Holstein, J.A. (2014) "Analytic Inspiration in Ethnographic Fieldwork," in U. Flick (ed.), *The SAGE Handbook of Qualitative Data Analysis.* London: Sage. pp. 35–48.

Guiney Yallop, J.J., Lopez de Vallejo, I. and Wright, P.R. (2008) "Editorial: Overview of the Performative Social Science Special Issue" [20 paragraphs]. *Forum Qualitative Sozialforschung/Forum: Qualitative Social Research,* 9(2), Art. 64, http://nbn-resolving.de/urn:nbn:de:0114-fqs0802649.

Habermas, J. (1967) *Zur Logik der Sozialwissenschaften.* Tübingen: Mohr.

Habermas, J. (1996) *The Habermas Reader.* Cambridge: Polity Press.

Halkier, B. (2010) "Focus Groups as Social Enactments: Integrating Interaction and Content in the Analysis of Focus Group Data," *Qualitative Research,* 10(1): 71–89.

Hall, E.T. (1986) "Foreword," in J. Collier Jr. and M. Collier (eds.), *Visual Anthropology: Photography as a Research Method.* Albuquerque: University of New Mexico Press. pp. xii–xvii.

Halperin, D.M. (1995) *Saint Foucault: Towards a Gay Hagiography.* Oxford: Oxford University Press.

Hammersley, M. (1990) *Reading Ethnographic Research: A Critical Guide.* London: Longman.

Hammersley, M. (1992) *What's Wrong with Ethnography?* London: Routledge.

Hammersley, M. (1995) *The Politics of Social Research.* London: Sage.

Hammersley, M. and Atkinson, P. (1983) *Ethnography: Principles in Practice.* London: Tavistock.

Hammersley, M. and Atkinson, P. (1995) *Ethnography: Principles in Practice* (2nd edn). London: Routledge.

Hammersley, M. and Atkinson, P. (2007) *Ethnography: Principles in Practice* (3rd edn). London: Routledge.

Harper, D. (1998) "On the Authority of the Image: Visual Methods at the Crossroads," in N. Denzin and Y.S. Lincoln (eds.), *Collecting and Interpreting Qualitative Materials.* London: Sage. pp. 130–149.

Harper, D. (2000) "Reimagining Visual Methods: Galileo to Neuromancer," in N. Denzin and Y.S. Lincoln (eds.), *Handbook of Qualitative Research* (2nd edn). London: Sage. pp. 717–732.

Harper, D. (2004) "Photography as Social Science Data," in U. Flick, E.v. Kardorff and I. Steinke (eds.), *A Companion to Qualitative Research.* London: Sage. pp. 231–236.

Harré, R. (1998) "The Epistemology of Social Representations," in U. Flick (ed.), *Psychology of the Social: Representations in Knowledge and Language.* Cambridge: Cambridge University Press. pp. 129–137.

Harrington, B. (2003) "The Social Psychology of Access in Ethnographic Research," *Journal of Contemporary Ethnography,* 32: 592–625.

Hart, C. (1998) *Doing a Literature Review.* London: Sage.

Hart, C. (2001) *Doing a Literature Search.* London: Sage.

Harvard, L. (2007) "How to Conduct an Effective and Valid Literature Search," Extended version of the article published in *Nursing Times,* 103: 45, 32–33 (www.nursingtimes.net/nursing-practice/217252.article).

Harvey, W.S. (2011) "Strategies for Conducting Elite Interviews," *Qualitative Research*, 11(4): 431–441.

Haupert, B. (1991) "Vom narrativen Interview zur biographischen Typenbildung," in D. Garz and K. Kraimer (eds.), *Qualitativ-empirische Sozialforschung*. Opladen: Westdeutscher Verlag. pp. 213–254.

Haupert, B. (1994) "Objektiv-hermeneutische Fotoanalyse am Beispiel von Soldatenfotos aus dem zweiten Weltkrieg," in D. Garz (ed.), *Die Welt als Text*. Frankfurt: Suhrkamp. pp. 281–314.

Have, P. ten (1999) *Doing Conversation Analysis: A Practical Guide*. London: Sage.

Heath, C. and Hindmarsh, J. (2002) "Analysing Interaction: Video, Ethnography, and Situated Conduct," in T. May (ed.), *Qualitative Research in Action*. London: Sage. pp. 99–120.

Heath, C. and Luff, P. (2006) "Video Analysis and Organisational Practice," in H. Knoblauch, B. Schnettler, J. Raab and H.-G. Soeffner (eds.), *Video Analysis: Methodology and Methods*. Frankfurt: Peter Lang. pp. 35–50.

Heritage, J. (1985) "Recent Developments in Conversation Analysis," *Sociolinguistics*, 15: 1–17.

Herkommer, S. (1979) *Gesellschaftsbewußtsein und Gewerkschaften*. Hamburg: VSA.

Hermanns, H. (1984) "Ingenieurleben – Der Berufsverlauf von Ingenieuren in biographischer Perspektive," in M. Kohli and G. Roberts (eds.), *Biographie und soziale Wirklichkeit. Neuere Beiträge und Forschungsperspektiven*. Stuttgart: Metzler. pp. 164–191.

Hermanns, H. (1995) "Narratives Interview," in U. Flick, E.v. Kardorff, H. Keupp, L.v. Rosenstiel and S. Wolff (eds.), *Handbuch Qualitative Sozialforschung* (2nd edn). Munich: Psychologie Verlags Union. pp. 182–185.

Hermanns, H. (2004) "Interviewing as an Activity," in U. Flick, E.v. Kardorff, and I. Steinke (eds.), *A Companion to Qualitative Research*. London: Sage. pp. 203–208.

Herrmann, W.J. and Flick, U. (2012) "Nursing Home Residents' Psychological Barriers to Sleeping Well: A Qualitative Study," *Family Practice* doi: 10.1093/fampra/cmr125.

Heyl, B.S. (2001) "Ethnographic Interviewing," in P. Atkinson, A. Coffey, S. Delamont, J. Lofland and L. Lofland (eds.), *Handbook of Ethnography*. London: Sage. pp. 369–383.

Hildenbrand, B. (1987) "Wer soll bemerken, daß Bernhard krank wird? Familiale Wirklichkeitskonstruktionsprozesse bei der Erstmanifestation einer schizophrenen Psychose," in J.B. Bergold and U. Flick (eds.), *Ein-Sichten: Zugänge zur Sicht des Subjekts mittels qualitativer Forschung*. Tübingen: DGVT Verlag. pp. 151–162.

Hildenbrand, B. (1995) "Fallrekonstruktive Forschung," in U. Flick, E.v. Kardorff, H. Keupp, L.v. Rosenstiel and S. Wolff (eds.), *Handbuch Qualitative Sozialforschung* (2nd edn). Munich: Psychologie Verlags Union. pp. 256–260.

Hildenbrand, B. and Jahn, W. (1988) "Gemeinsames Erzählen und Prozesse der Wirklichkeitskonstruktion in familiengeschichtlichen Gesprächen," *Zeitschrift für Soziologie*, 17: 203–217.

Hine, C. (2000) *Virtual Ethnography*. London: Sage.

Hitzler, R. and Eberle, T.S. (2004) "Phenomenological Analysis of Lifeworlds," in U. Flick, E.v. Kardorff and I. Steinke (eds.), *A Companion to Qualitative Research*. London: Sage. pp. 67–71.

Hochschild, A.R. (1983) *The Managed Heart*. Berkeley, CA: University of California Press.

Hodder, I. (2000) "The Interpretation of Documents and Material Culture," in N.K. Denzin and Y.S. Lincoln (eds) *Handbook of Qualitative Research*, 2nd edn, Thousand Oaks, CA: Sage. pp. 703–716.

Hodgetts, D., Radley, A., Chamberlain, C. and Hodgetts, A. (2007) "Health Inequalities and Homelessness: Considering Material, Spatial and Relational Dimensions," *Journal of Health Psychology*, 12: 709–725.

Hoffmann-Riem, C. (1980) "Die Sozialforschung einer interpretativen Soziologie: Der Datengewinn," *Kölner Zeitschrift für Soziologie und Sozialpsychologie*, 32: 339–372.

Hollingshead, A.B. and Redlich, F. (1958) *Social Class and Mental Illness*. New York: Wiley.

Holstein, J.A. and Miller, G. (eds.) (1993) *Reconsidering Social Constructionism: Debates in Social Problems Theory*. Hawthorne, NY: Aldine de Gruyter.

Holton, J.A. (2007) "The Coding Process and Its Challenges," in A. Bryant and K. Charmaz (eds.), *The SAGE Handbook of Grounded Theory*. London: Sage. pp. 265–290.

Honer, A. (2004) "Life-World Analysis in Ethnography," in U. Flick, E.v. Kardorff, and I. Steinke (eds.), *A Companion to Qualitative Research*. London: Sage. pp. 113–117.

Hood, J.C. (2007) "Orthodoxy versus Power: The Defining Traits of Grounded Theory," in A. Bryant and K. Charmaz (eds.), *The SAGE Handbook of Grounded Theory*. London: Sage. pp. 151–162.

Hopf, C. (1978) "Die Pseudo-Exploration: Überlegungen zur Technik qualitativer Interviews in der Sozialforschung," *Zeitschrift für Soziologie*, 7: 97–115.

Hopf, C. (1982) "Norm und Interpretation," *Zeitschrift für Soziologie*, 11: 309–327.

Hopf, C. (1985) "Nichtstandardisierte Erhebungsverfahren in der Sozialforschung. Überlegungen zum Forschungsstand," in M. Kaase and M. Küchler (eds.), *Herausforderungen der empirischen Sozialforschung*. Mannheim: ZUMA. pp. 86–108.

Hopf, C. (2004a) "Qualitative Interviews: An Overview," in U. Flick, E.v. Kardorff and I. Steinke (eds.), *A Companion to Qualitative Research*. London: Sage. pp. 203–208.

Hopf, C. (2004b) "Research Ethics and Qualitative Research: An Overview," in U. Flick, E.v. Kardorff and I. Steinke (eds.), *A Companion to Qualitative Research*. London: Sage. pp. 334–339.

Huberman, A.M. and Miles, M.B. (1998) "Data Management and Analysis Methods," in N. Denzin and Y.S. Lincoln (eds.), *Collecting and Interpreting Qualitative Materials*. London: Sage. pp. 179–211.

Humphreys, L. (1973) "Toilettengeschäfte," in J. Friedrichs (ed.), *Teilnehmende Beobachtung abweichenden Verhaltens*. Stuttgart: Enke. pp. 254–287.

Humphreys, L. (1975) *Tearoom Trade: Impersonal Sex in Public Places* (enlarged edn). New York: Aldine Transaction.

Hurrelmann, K., Klocke, A., Melzer, W. and Ravens-Sieberer, U. (2003*) Konzept und ausgewählte Ergebnisse der Studie*, www.hbsc-germany.de/pdf/artikel_hurrelmann_klocke_melzer_urs.pdf (date of access: 30 June 2008).

Iser, W. (1993) *The Fictive and the Imaginary: Charting Literary Anthropology*. Baltimore, MD: Johns Hopkins University Press.

Jacob, E. (1987) "Qualitative Research Traditions: A Review," *Review of Educational Research*, 57: 1–50.

Jahoda, M., Lazarsfeld, P.F. and Zeisel, H. (1933/1971) *Marienthal: The Sociology of An Unemployed Community*. Chicago, IL: Aldine-Atherton.

Jessor, R., Colby, A. and Shweder, R.A. (eds.) (1996) *Ethnography and Human Development*. Chicago, IL: Chicago University Press.

Jick, T. (1983) "Mixing Qualitative and Quantitative Methods: Triangulation in Action," in J.v. Maanen (ed.), *Qualitative Methodology*. London: Sage. pp. 135–148.

Joas, H. (1987) "Symbolic Interactionism," in A. Giddens and J.H. Turner (eds.), *Social Theory Today*. Cambridge: Polity Press. pp. 82–115.

Joffe, H. and Bettega, N. (2003) "Social Representations of AIDS among Zambian Adolescents," *Journal of Health Psychology*, 8: 616–631.

Johnson, R.B., Onwuegbuzie, A.J. and Turner, L.A. (2007) "Toward a Definition of Mixed Methods Research," *Journal of Mixed Methods Research*, 1: 112.

Jorgensen, D.L. (1989) *Participant Observation: A Methodology for Human Studies*. London: Sage.

Kamiske, G.F. and Brauer, J.P. (1995) *Qualitätsmanagement von A bis Z: Erläuterungen moderner Begriffe des Qualitätsmanagements* (2nd edn). Munich: Carl Hanser Verlag.

Kelle, U. (ed.) (1995) *Computer-aided Qualitative Data Analysis: Theory, Methods, and Practice*. London: Sage.

Kelle, U. (2000) "Computer Assisted Analysis: Coding and Indexing," in M. Bauer and G. Gaskell (eds.), *Qualitative Researching with Text, Image, and Sound*. London: Sage. pp. 282–298.

Kelle, U. (2004) "Computer Assisted Analysis of Qualitative Data," in U. Flick, E.v. Kardorff and I. Steinke (eds.), *A Companion to Qualitative Research*. London: Sage. pp. 276–283.

Kelle, U. (2007) "Development of Categories: Different Approaches in Grounded Theory," in A. Bryant and K. Charmaz (eds.), *The SAGE Handbook of Grounded Theory*. London: Sage. pp. 191–213.

Kelle, U. and Erzberger, C. (2004) "Quantitative and Qualitative Methods: No Confrontation," in U. Flick, E.v. Kardorff and I. Steinke (eds.), *A Companion to Qualitative Research*. London: Sage. pp. 172–177.

Kelle, U. and Laurie, H. (1995) "Computer Use in Qualitative Research and Issues of Validity," in U. Kelle (ed.), *Computer-aided Qualitative Data Analysis: Theory, Methods, and Practice*. London: Sage. pp. 19–28.

Kendall, L. (1999) "Recontextualising Cyberspace: Methodological Considerations for On-Line Research," in S. Jones (ed.), *Doing Internet Research: Critical Issues and Methods for Examining the Net*. London: Sage. pp. 57–74.

Kirk, J.L. and Miller, M. (1986) *Reliability and Validity in Qualitative Research*. Beverly Hills, CA: Sage.

Kitzinger, C. (2004) "The Internet as Research Context Research," in C. Seale, G. Gobo, J. Gubrium and D. Silverman (eds.), *Qualitative Research Practice*. London: Sage. pp. 125–140.

Kitzinger, J. and Barbour, R.S. (1999) "Introduction: The Challenge and Promise of Focus Groups," in R.S. Barbour and J. Kitzinger (eds), *Developing Focus Group Research: Politics, Theory and Practice*. London: Sage. pp. 1–20.

Kleining, G. (1982) "Umriss zu einer Methodologie qualitativer Sozialforschung," *Kölner Zeitschrift für Soziologie und Sozialpsychologie*, 34: 224–253.

Knoblauch, H. (2004a) "The Future Prospects of Qualitative Research," in U. Flick, E.v. Kardorff and I. Steinke (eds.), *A Companion to Qualitative Research*. London: Sage. pp. 354–358.

Knoblauch, H. (2004b) "Video-Interaktionsanalyse," *Sozialer Sinn*, 1: 123–139.

Knoblauch, H., Flick, U. and Maeder, Ch. (eds.) (2005) "The State of the Art of Qualitative Research in Europe," *Forum Qualitative Sozialforschung/Forum: Qualitative Social Research*, 6(3), www.qualitative-research.net/fqs/fqs-e/inhalt3-05-e.htm.

Knoblauch, H., Heath, C. and Luff, P. (2000) "Technology and Social Interaction: The Emergence of Workplace Studies," *British Journal of Sociology*, 51(2): 299–320.

Knoblauch, H. and Luckmann, Th. (2004) "Genre Analysis," in U. Flick, E.v. Kardorff and I. Steinke (eds.), *A Companion to Qualitative Research*. London: Sage. pp. 303–307.

Knoblauch, H., Schnettler, B. and Raab, J. (2006a) "Video Analysis: Methodological Aspects of Interpretive Audiovisual Analysis in Social Research," in H. Knoblauch, B. Schnettler, J. Raab and H.-G. Soeffner (eds.), *Video Analysis: Methodology and Methods*. Frankfurt: Peter Lang. pp. 9–27.

Knoblauch, H., Schnettler, B., Raab, J. and Soeffner, H.-G. (eds.) (2006b) *Video Analysis: Methodology and Methods*. Frankfurt: Peter Lang.

Knoblauch, H., Tuma, R. and Schnettler, B. (2014) "Video Analysis and Videography," in U. Flick (ed.), *The SAGE Handbook of Qualitative Data Analysis*. London: Sage. pp. 435–449.

Knorr-Cetina, K. (1981) *The Manufacture of Knowledge: An Essay on the Constructivist and Contextual Nature of Science*. Oxford: Pergamon.

Knorr-Cetina, K. and Mulkay, M. (eds.) (1983) *Science Observed: Perspectives on the Social Studies of Science*. London: Sage.

Koepping, K.P. (1987) "Authentizitat als Selbstfindung durch den Anderen: Ethnologie zwischen Engagement und Reflexion, zwischen Leben und Wissenschaft," in H.P. Duerr (ed.), *Authentizität und Betrug in der Ethnologie*. Frankfurt. Suhrkamp. pp. 7–37.

König, H.D. (2004) "Deep Structure Hermeneutics," in U. Flick, E.v. Kardorff and I. Steinke (eds.), *A Companion to Qualitative Research*. London: Sage. pp. 313–320.

Kowall, S. and O'Connell, D.C. (2004) "Transcribing Conversations," in U. Flick, E.v. Kardorff and I. Steinke (eds.), *A Companion to Qualitative Research*. London: Sage. pp. 248–252.

Kowall, S. and O'Connell, D.C. (2014) "Transcription as a Crucial Step of Data Analysis," in U. Flick (ed.), *The SAGE Handbook of Qualitative Data Analysis*. London: Sage. pp. 64–78.

Kozinets, R.V. (2006) "Netnography," in V. Jupp (ed.), *The SAGE Dictionary of Social Research Methods*. London: Sage. p. 135.

Kozinets, R. V. (2010) *Netnography*. Thousand Oaks, CA: Sage.

Kozinets, R.V., Dalbec, P.-Y. and Earley, A. (2014) "Netnographic Analysis: Understanding Culture through Social Media Data," in U. Flick (ed.), *The SAGE Handbook of Qualitative Data Analysis*. London: Sage. pp. 262–276.

Krüger, H. (1983) "Gruppendiskussionen: Überlegungen zur Rekonstruktion sozialer Wirklichkeit aus der Sicht der Betroffenen," *Soziale Welt*, 34: 90–109.

Kuckartz, U. (1995) "Case-oriented Quantification," in U. Kelle (ed.), *Computer-aided Qualitative Data Analysis*. London: Sage. pp. 158–166.

Kvale, S. (ed.) (1989) *Issues of Validity in Qualitative Research*. Lund: Studentlitteratur.

Kvale, S. (1996) *Interviews: An Introduction to Qualitative Research Interviewing*. London: Sage.

Kvale, S. (2007) *Doing Interviews*. London: Sage.

Lau, T. and Wolff, S. (1983) "Der Einstieg in das Untersuchungsfeld als soziologischer Lernprozeß," *Kölner Zeitschrift für Soziologie und Sozialpsychologie*, 35: 417–437.

Lee, R.M. (2000) *Unobtrusive Methods in Social Research*. Buckingham: Open University Press.

Legewie, H. (1994) "Globalauswertung," in A. Böhm, T. Muhr and A. Mengel (eds.), *Texte verstehen: Konzepte, Methoden, Werkzeuge*. Konstanz: Universitätsverlag. pp. 100–114.

Lempert, L.B. (2007) "Asking Questions of the Data: Memo Writing in the Grounded Theory Tradition," in A. Bryant and K. Charmaz (eds.), *The SAGE Handbook of Grounded Theory*. London: Sage. pp. 245–265.

Lincoln, Y.S. and Denzin, N.K. (2000) "The Seventh Moment," in N. Denzin and Y.S. Lincoln (eds.), *Handbook of Qualitative Research* (2nd edn). London: Sage. pp. 1047–1065.

Lincoln, Y.S. and Denzin, N.K. (2005) "Epilogue: The Eighth and Ninth Moment," in N. Denzin and Y.S. Lincoln (eds.), *The SAGE Handbook of Qualitative Research* (3rd edn). London: Sage. pp. 1047–1065.

REFERENCES

Lincoln, Y.S. and Guba, E.G. (1985) *Naturalistic Inquiry*. London: Sage.

Littig, B. (2009) "Interviewing Experts or Interviewing Elites: What Makes the Difference?", in A. Bogner, B. Littig and W. Menz (eds.), *Interviewing Experts*. Basingstoke: Palgrave Macmillan. pp. 98–113.

Livingston, E. (1986) *The Ethnomethodological Foundations of Mathematics*. London: Routledge & Kegan Paul.

Lofland, J.H. (1974) "Styles of Reporting Qualitative Field Research," *American Sociologist*, 9: 101–111.

Lofland, J. and Lofland, L.H. (1984) *Analyzing Social Settings* (2nd edn). Belmont, CA: Wadsworth.

Luckmann, Th. (1995) "Interaction Planning and Intersubjective Adjustment of Perspectives by Communicative Genres," in E.N. Goody (ed.), *Social Intelligence and Interaction: Expressions and Implications of the Social Bias in Human Intelligence*. Cambridge: Cambridge University Press. pp. 175–189.

Lüders, C. (1991) "Deutungsmusteranalyse: Annäherungen an ein risikoreiches Konzept," in D. Garz and K. Kraimer (eds.), *Qualitativ-empirische Sozialforschung*. Opladen: Westdeutscher Verlag. pp. 377–408.

Lüders, C. (1995) "Von der Teilnehmenden Beobachtung zur ethnographischen Beschreibung – Ein Literaturbericht," in E. König and P. Zedler (eds.), *Bilanz qualitativer Forschung*, Vol. 1. Weinheim: Deutscher Studien Verlag. pp. 311–342.

Lüders, C. (2004a) "Field Observation and Ethnography," in U. Flick, E.v. Kardorff and I. Steinke (eds.), *A Companion to Qualitative Research*. London: Sage. pp. 222–230.

Lüders, C. (2004b) "The Challenges of Qualitative Research," in U. Flick, E.v. Kardorff and I. Steinke (eds.), *A Companion to Qualitative Research*. London: Sage. pp. 359–364.

Lüders, C. and Reichertz, J. (1986) "Wissenschaftliche Praxis ist, wenn alles funktioniert und keiner weiß warum: Bemerkungen zur Entwicklung qualitativer Sozialforschung," *Sozialwissenschaftliche Literaturrundschau*, 12: 90–102.

Lunt, P. and Livingstone, S. (1996) "Rethinking the Focus Group in Media and Communications Research," *Journal of Communication*, 46: 79–98.

Lynn, N. and Lea, S. J. (2005) "Through the Looking Glass: Considering the Challenges Visual Methodologies Raise for Qualitative Research", *Qualitative Research in Psychology*, 2: 213–225

Machi, L.A. and McEvoy, B.T. (2012) *The Literature Review: Six Steps to Success*. Thousand Oaks, CA: Corwin Press.

Madill, A., Jordan, A. and Shirley, C. (2000) "Objectivity and Reliability in Qualitative Analysis: Realist, Contextualist, and Radical Constructionist Epistemologies," *British Journal of Psychology*, 91: 1–20.

Maijalla, H., Astedt-Kurki, P., and Paavilainen, E. (2002) "Interaction as an Ethically Sensitive Subject of Research," *Nurse Researcher*, 10: 20–37.

Malinowski, B. (1916) *Magic, Science, and Religion and Other Essays*. New York: Natural History Press, 1948.

Mangold, W. (1973) "Gruppendiskussionen," in R. König (ed.), *Handbuch der empirischen Sozialforschung*. Stuttgart: Enke. pp. 228–259.

Mann, C. and Stewart, F. (2000) *Internet Communication and Qualitative Research: A Handbook for Researching Online*. London: Sage.

Markham, A.M. (2004) "The Internet as Research Context Research," in C. Seale, G. Gobo, J. Gubrium and D. Silverman (eds.), *Qualitative Research Practice*. London: Sage. pp. 358–374.

Marotzki, W. (2003) "Online-Ethnographie – Wege und Ergebnisse zur Forschung im Kulturraum Internet," in B. Bachmair, P. Diepold and C. de Witt (eds.), *Jahrbuch Medienpädagogik 3*. Opladen: Leske & Budrich. pp. 149–166.

Marotzki, W., Holze, J., and Verständig, D. (2014) "Analyzing Virtual Data," in U. Flick (ed.), *The SAGE Handbook of Qualitative Data Analysis*. London: Sage. pp. 450–464.

Marshall, C. and Rossman, G.B. (2006) *Designing Qualitative Research* (4th edn). Thousand Oaks, CA: Sage.

Marshall, C. and Rossman, G.B. (2010) *Designing Qualitative Research* (5th edn). Thousand Oaks, CA: Sage.

Marvasti, A. (2014) "Analyzing Observations," in U. Flick (ed.), *The SAGE Handbook of Qualitative Data Analysis*. London: Sage. pp. 354–366.

Mason, J. (2002) "Qualitative Interviewing: Asking, Listening, and Interpreting," in T. May (ed.), *Qualitative Research in Action*. London: Sage. pp. 225–241.

Mauthner, M., Birch, M., Jessop, J. and Miller, T. (eds.) (2002) *Ethics in Qualitative Research*. London: Sage.

Maxwell, J.A. (1992) "Understanding and Validity in Qualitative Research," *Harvard Educational Review*, 62: 279–300.

Maxwell, J.A. (2005) *Qualitative Research Design: An Interactive Approach* (2nd edn). Thousand Oaks, CA: Sage.

Maxwell, J.A. (2012) *Qualitative Research Design: An Interactive Approach* (3rd edn). Thousand Oaks, CA: Sage.

Maxwell, J. and Chmiel, M. (2014a) "Notes Toward a Theory of Qualitative Data Analysis," in U. Flick (ed.), *The SAGE Handbook of Qualitative Data Analysis*. London: Sage. pp. 21–34.

Maxwell, J.A. and Chmiel, M. (2014b) "Generalizing in and from qualitative analysis," in U. Flick (ed.), *The SAGE Handbook of Qualitative Data Analysis*. London: Sage. pp. 540–553.

May, T. (2001) *Social Research: Issues, Methods and Process*. Buckingham: Open University Press.

Maynard, M. (1998) "Feminists' Knowledge and the Knowledge of Feminisms: Epistemology, Theory Methodology, and Method," in T. May and M. Williams (eds.), *Knowing the Social World*. Buckingham: Open University Press. pp. 129–137.

Mayring, P. (1983) *Qualitative Inhaltsanalyse. Grundlagen und Techniken* (7th edn 1997). Weinheim: Deutscher Studien Verlag.

Mayring, P. (2000) "Qualitative Content Analysis" [28 paragraphs]. *Forum Qualitative Sozialforschung / Forum: Qualitative Social Research*, *1*(2), Art. 20, http://nbn- resolving.de/urn:nbn:de:0114-fqs0002204. (last access: August 13th, 2013)

Mayring, P. (2004) "Qualitative Content Analysis," in U. Flick, E.v. Kardorff and I. Steinke (eds.), *A Companion to Qualitative Research*. London: Sage. pp. 266–269.

McDonald, S. (2005) "Studying Actions in Context: A Qualitative Shadowing Method for Organizational Research," *Qualitative Research*, 5: 455–473.

McGibbon, E., Peter, E. and Gallop, R. (2010) "An Institutional Ethnography of Nurses' Stress," *Qualitative Health Research*, 20(10): 1353–1378.

McKinlay, J.B. (1993) "The Promotion of Health through Planned Sociopolitical Change: Challenges for Research and Policy," *Social Science and Medicine*, 38: 109–117.

McKinlay, J.B. (1995) "Towards Appropriate Levels: Research Methods and Healthy Public Policies," in I. Guggenmoos-Holzmann, K. Bloomfield, H. Brenner and U. Flick (eds.), *Quality of Life and Health: Concepts, Methods, and Applications*. Berlin: Basil Blackwell. pp. 161–182.

McMullen, L. (2011) "A Discursive Analysis of Teresa's Protocol: Enhancing Oneself, Diminishing Others," in F.J. Wertz, K. Charmaz, L.M. McMullen, R. Josselson, R. Anderson and E. McSpadden, *Five Ways of Doing Qualitative Analysis*. New York: Guilford. pp. 205–223.

Mead, M. (1963) "Anthropology and the Camera," in W.D. Morgan (ed.), *The Encyclopedia of Photography*, Vol. I. New York: Greystone. pp. 163–184.

Merkens, H. (1989) "Einleitung," in R. Aster, H. Merkens and M. Repp (eds.), *Teilnehmende Beobachtung: Werkstattberichte und methodologische Reflexionen*. Frankfurt: Campus. pp. 9–18.

Merkens, H. (2004) "Selection Procedures, Sampling, Case Construction," in U. Flick, E.v. Kardorff and I. Steinke (eds.), *A Companion to Qualitative Research*. London: Sage. pp. 165–171.

Mertens, D.M. (2014) "Ethical Use of Qualitative Data and Findings," in U. Flick (ed.), *The SAGE Handbook of Qualitative Data Analysis*. London: Sage. pp. 510–523.

Mertens, D.M. and Ginsberg, P.E. (eds.) (2009) *Handbook of Social Research Ethics*. Thousand Oaks, CA: Sage.

Merton, R.K. (1987) "The Focused Interview and Focus Groups: Continuities and Discontinuities," *Public Opinion Quarterly*, 51: 550–556.

Merton, R.K., Fiske, M. and Kendall, P.L. (1956) *The Focused Interview*. Glencoe, IL: Free Press.

Merton, R.K. and Kendall, P.L. (1946) "The Focused Interview," *American Journal of Sociology*, 51: 541–557.

Meuser, M. and Nagel, U. (2002) "ExpertInneninterviews – vielfach erprobt, wenig bedacht. Ein Beitrag zur qualitativen Methodendiskussion," in A. Bogner, B. Littig and W. Menz (eds.), *Das Experteninterview*. Opladen: Leske & Budrich. pp. 71–95.

Meuser, M. and Nagel, U. (2009) "The Expert Interview and Changes in Knowledge Production," in A. Bogner, B. Littig and W. Menz (eds.), *Interviewing Experts*. Basingstoke: Palgrave Macmillan. pp. 17–42.

Mies, M. (1983) "Towards a Methodology for Feminist Research," in G. Bowles and R. Duelli Klein (eds.), *Theories of Women's Studies*. London: Routledge. pp. 120–130.

Mikecz, R. (2012) "Interviewing Elites: Addressing Methodological Issues," *Qualitative Inquiry*, 18(6): 482–493.

Mikos, L. (2014) "Analysis of Film," in U. Flick (ed.), *The SAGE Handbook of Qualitative Data Analysis*. London: Sage. pp. 409–423.

Miles, M.B. and Huberman, A.M. (1994) *Qualitative Data Analysis: A Sourcebook of New Methods* (2nd edn). Newbury Park, CA: Sage.

Mishler, E.G. (1986) "The Analysis of Interview-Narratives," in T.R. Sarbin (ed.), *Narrative Psychology*. New York: Praeger. pp. 233–255.

Mishler, E.G. (1990) "Validation in Inquiry-Guided Research: The Role of Exemplars in Narrative Studies," *Harvard Educational Review*, 60: 415–442.

Mitra, A. and Cohen, E. (1999) "Analyzing the Web: Directions and Challenges," in S. Jones (ed.), *Doing Internet Research: Critical Issues and Methods for Examining the Net*. London: Sage. pp. 179–202.

Mondada, L. (2012) "Video Analysis and the Temporality of Inscriptions within Social Interaction: The Case of Architects at Work," *Qualitative Research*, 12(3): 304–333.

Morgan, D.L. (1988) *Focus Groups as Qualitative Research*. Newbury Park, CA: Sage.

Morgan, D.L. and Krueger, R.A. (eds.) (1998) *The Focus Group Kit* (6 vols.). Thousand Oaks, CA: Sage.

Morse, J.M. (1998) "Designing Funded Qualitative Research," in N. Denzin and Y.S. Lincoln (eds.), *Strategies of Qualitative Research*. London: Sage. pp. 56–85.

Moscovici, S. (1973) "Foreword," in C. Herzlich, *Health and Illness: A Social Psychological Analysis*. London: Academic Press. pp. ix–xiv.

Murphy, E. and Dingwall, R. (2001) "The Ethics of Ethnography," in P. Atkinson, A. Coffey, S. Delamont, J. Lofland and L. Lofland (eds.), *Handbook of Ethnography*. London: Sage. pp. 339–351.

Murphy, J.A. (1994) *Dienstleistungsqualität in der Praxis*. Munich: Carl Hanser Verlag.

Murray, M. (2000) "Levels of Narrative Analysis in Health Psychology," *Journal of Health Psychology*, 5: 337–349.

Neill, S.H. (2010) "Containing Acute Childhood Illness within Family Life: A Substantive Grounded Theory," *Journal of Child Health Care*, 14(4): 327–344.

Neuman, W.L. (2000) *Social Research Methods – Qualitative and Quantitative Approaches* (4th edn). Boston, MA: Allyn & Bacon.

Nicca, D., Fierz, K., Happ, M.B., Moody, K. and Spirig, R. (2012) "Symptom Management in HIV/AIDS: A Mixed Methods Approach to Describe Collaboration and Concordance Between Persons Living with HIV and Their Close Support Persons," *Journal of Mixed Methods Research*, 6: 217–235.

Niemann, M. (1989) "Felduntersuchungen an Freizeitorten Berliner Jugendlicher," in R. Aster, H. Merkens and M. Repp (eds.), *Teilnehmende Beobachtung: Werkstattberichte und methodologische Reflexionen*. Frankfurt: Campus. pp. 71–83.

NIH (Office of Behavioral and Social Sciences Research) (ed.) (2001) *Qualitative Methods in Health Research: Opportunities and Considerations in Application and Review*, No. 02-5046, December. Washington, DC.

Northway, R. (2002) "Commentary," *Nurse Researcher*, 10: 4–7.

Oakley, A. (1999) "People's Ways of Knowing: Gender and Methodology," in S. Hood, B. Mayall and S. Olivier (eds.), *Critical Issues in Social Research: Power and Prejudice*. Buckingham: Open University Press. pp. 154–170.

Ochs, E. and Capps, L. (2001) *Living Narrative*. Cambridge, MA: Harvard University Press.

O'Connell, D. and Kowall, S. (1995) "Basic Principles of Transcription," in J.A. Smith, R. Harré and L.v. Langenhove (eds.), *Rethinking Methods in Psychology*. London: Sage. pp. 93–104.

Oerter, R. (1995) "Persons Conception of Human Nature: A Cross-Cultural Comparison," in J. Valsiner (ed.), *Comparative Cultural and Constructivist Perspectives*. Vol. III, *Child Development within Culturally Structured Environments*. Norwood, NJ: Ablex. pp. 210–242.

Oerter, R., Oerter, R., Agostiani, H., Kim, H.O. and Wibowo, S. (1996) "The Concept of Human Nature in East Asia: Etic and Emic Characteristics," *Culture & Psychology*, 2: 9–51.

Oevermann, U., Allert, T., Konau, E. and Krambeck, J. (1979) "Die Methodologie einer 'objektiven Hermeneutik' und ihre allgemeine forschungslogische Bedeutung in den Sozialwissenschaften," in H.G. Soeffner (ed.), *Interpretative Verfahren in den Sozial- und Textwissenschaften*. Stuttgart: Metzler. pp. 352–433.

Olesen, V. (2011) "Feminist Qualitative Research in the Millenium's First Decade," in N. Denzin and Y. Lincoln (eds.), *The SAGE Handbook of Qualitative Research* (4th edn). Thousand Oaks, CA: Sage. pp. 129–146.

Paechter, C. (2012) "Researching Sensitive Issues Online: Implications of a Hybrid Insider/Outsider Position in a Retrospective Ethnographic Study," *Qualitative Research*, 13(1): 71–86.

Parker, I. (2004a) "Discourse Analysis," in U. Flick, E.v. Kardorff and I. Steinke (eds.), *A Companion to Qualitative Research*. London: Sage. pp. 308–312.

Parker, I. (2004b) "Criteria for Qualitative Research in Psychology," *Qualitative Research in Psychology*, 1(2): 95–106.

Parker, I. (2013) "Discourse Analysis: Dimensions of Critique in Psychology," *Qualitative Research in Psychology*, 10(3): 223–239.

Parsons, T. and Shils, E.A. (1951) *Towards a General Theory of Action*. Cambridge, MA: Harvard University Press.

Patton, M.Q. (2002) *Qualitative Evaluation and Research Methods* (3rd edn). London: Sage.

Paulson, S. and Willig, C. (2008) "Older Women and Everyday Talk about the Ageing Body," *Journal of Health Psychology*, 13(1): 106–120.

Petermann, W. (1995) "Fotografie- und Filmanalyse," in U. Flick, E.v. Kardorff, H. Keupp, L.v. Rosenstiel and S. Wolff (eds.), *Handbuch Qualitative Sozialforschung* (2nd edn). Munich: Psychologie Verlags Union. pp. 228–231.

Pink, S. (2012) *Advances in Visual Methodology*. London: Sage.

Plummer, K. (2011) "Critical Humanism and Queer Theory: Postscript 2011: Living with the Tensions," in N. Denzin and Y. Lincoln (eds.) *The SAGE Handbook of Qualitative Research* (4th edn). Thousand Oaks, CA: Sage. pp. 195–212.

Pollock, F. (1955) *Gruppenexperiment: Ein Studienbericht*. Frankfurt: Europäische Verlagsanstalt.

Potter, J. and Wetherell, M. (1987) *Discourse and Social Psychology: Beyond Attitudes and Behaviour*. London: Sage.

Potter, J. and Wetherell, M. (1998) "Social Representations, Discourse Analysis, and Racism," in U. Flick (ed.), *Psychology of the Social: Representations in Knowledge and Language*. Cambridge: Cambridge University Press. pp. 177–200.

Prior, L. (2003) *Using Documents in Social Research*. London: Sage.

Puchta, C. and Potter, J. (2004) *Focus Group Practice*. London: Sage.

Ragin, C.C. (1994) *Constructing Social Research*. Thousand Oaks, CA: Pine Forge Press.

Ragin, C.C. and Becker, H.S. (eds.) (1992) *What Is a Case? Exploring the Foundations of Social Inquiry*. Cambridge: Cambridge University Press.

Rapley, T. (2007) *Doing Conversation, Discourse and Document Analysis*. London: Sage.

Rapley, T. (2014) "Sampling Strategies," in U. Flick (ed.), *The SAGE Handbook of Qualitative Data Analysis*. London: Sage. pp. 49–63.

Reeves, C. (2010) "A Difficult Negotiation: Fieldwork Relations with Gatekeepers," *Qualitative Research*, 10(3): 315–331.

Reicher, S. (2000) "Against Methodolatry: Some Comments on Elliot, Fischer, and Rennie," *British Journal of Clinical Psychology*, 39: 11–26.

Reichertz, J. (1992) "Beschreiben oder Zeigen: über das Verfassen ethnographischer Berichte," *Soziale Welt*, 43: 331–350.

Reichertz, J. (2004) "Objective Hermeneutics and Hermeneutic Sociology of Knowledge," in U. Flick, E.v. Kardorff and I. Steinke (eds.), *A Companion to Qualitative Research*. London: Sage. pp. 290–295.

Rheingold, H. (1993) *The Virtual Community: Homesteading on the Electronic Frontier*. Reading, MA: Addison-Wesley.

Richards, D. (1996) "Elite Interviewing: Approaches and Pitfalls," *Politics*, 16(3): 199–204.

Richards, T.J. and Richards, L. (1998) "Using Computers in Qualitative Research," in N. Denzin and Y.S. Lincoln (eds.), *Collecting and Interpreting Qualitative Materials*. London: Sage. pp. 211–245.

Richardson, L. (1994) "Writing: A Method of Inquiry," in N. Denzin and Y.S. Lincoln (eds.), *Handbook of Qualitative Research*. London: Sage. pp. 516–529.

Richardson, L. (2000) "Writing: A Method of Inquiry," in N. Denzin and Y.S. Lincoln (eds.), *Handbook of Qualitative Research* (2nd edn). London: Sage. pp. 923–948.

Richter, M., Hurrelmann, K., Klocke, A., Melzer, W. and Ravens-Sieberer, U. (eds.) (2008) *Gesundheit, Ungleichheit und jugendliche Lebenswelten: Ergebnisse der zweiten internationalen Vergleichsstudie im Auftrag der Weltgesundheitsorganisation WHO*. Weinheim: Juventa.

Ricoeur, P. (1981) "Mimesis and Representation," *Annals of Scholarship*, 2: 15–32.

Ricoeur, P. (1984) *Time and Narrative*, Vol. 1. Chicago, IL: University of Chicago Press.

Riemann, G. (1987) *Das Fremdwerden der eigenen Biographie: Narrative Interviews mit psychiatrischen Patienten*. Munich: Fink.

Riemann, G. and Schütze, F. (1987) "Trajectory as a Basic Theoretical Concept for Analyzing Suffering and Disorderly Social Processes," in D. Maines (ed.), *Social Organization and Social Process: Essays in Honor of Anselm Strauss*. New York: Aldine de Gruyter. pp. 333–357.

RIN (2010) *If you build it, will they come? How researchers perceive and use web 2.0*, www.rin.ac.uk/our-work/communicating-and-disseminating-research/use-and-relevance-web-20-researchers.

Roller, E., Mathes, R. and Eckert, T. (1995) "Hermeneutic-Classificatory Content Analysis," in U. Kelle (ed.), *Computer-aided Qualitative Data Analysis*. London: Sage. pp. 167–176.

Rose, Gillian (2012) *Visual Methodologies: An Introduction to Researching with Visual Materials*, 3rd edition. London: Sage.

Rosenthal, G. (1993) "Reconstruction of Life Stories: Principles of Selection in Generating Stories for Narrative Biographical Interviews," *The Narrative Study of Lives*, 1(1): 59–81.

Rosenthal, G. (2004) "Biographical Research," in C. Seale, G. Gobo, J. Gubrium and D. Silverman (eds.), *Qualitative Research Practice*. London: Sage. pp. 48–65.

Rosenthal, G. and Fischer-Rosenthal, W. (2004) "The Analysis of Biographical-Narrative Interviews," in U. Flick, E.v. Kardorff and I. Steinke (eds.), *A Companion to Qualitative Research*. London: Sage. pp. 259–265.

Roulston, K. (2014) "Analyzing Interviews," in U. Flick (ed.), *The SAGE Handbook of Qualitative Data Analysis*. London: Sage. pp. 297–312.

Rubin, H.J. and Rubin, I.S. (2012) *Qualitative Interviewing: The Art of Hearing Data*. (3rd edn). London: Sage.

Ruff, F.M. (1990) *Ökologische Krise und Umweltbewußtsein: zur psychischen Verarbeitung von Umweltbelastungen*. Wiesbaden: Deutscher Universitätsverlag.

Ruff, F.M. (1998) "Gesundheitsgefährdungen durch Umweltbelastungen: Ein neues Deutungsmuster," in U. Flick (ed.), *Wann fühlen wir uns gesund?* Weinheim: Juventa. pp. 285–300.

Sacks, H. (1992) *Lectures on Conversation*, Vols. 1, 2 (ed. by G. Jefferson). Oxford: Blackwell.

Sacks, H., Schegloff, E. and Jefferson, G. (1974) "A Simplest Systematics for the Organization of Turntaking for Conversation," *Language*, 4: 696–735.

Sahle, R. (1987) *Gabe, Almosen, Hilfe*. Opladen: Westdeutscher Verlag.

Salmons, J. (2010) *Online Interviews in Real Time*. London: Sage.

Sandelowski, M. and Leeman, J. (2012) "Writing Usable Qualitative Health Research Findings," *Qualitative Health Research*, 22(10): 1404–1413.

Sands, R.G. and Roer-Strier, D. (2006) "Using Data Triangulation of Mother and Daughter Interviews to Enhance Research about Families," *Qualitative Social Work*, 5: 237–260.

Sanjek, R. (ed.) (1990) *Fieldnotes: The Making of Anthropology*. Albany: State University of New York Press.

Sarbin, T.R. (ed.) (1986) *Narrative Psychology: The Storied Nature of Human Conduct*. New York: Praeger.

Schatzmann, L. and Strauss, A.L. (1973) *Field Research*. Englewood Cliffs, NJ: Prentice Hall.

Scheele, B. and Groeben, N. (1988) *Dialog-Konsens-Methoden zur Rekonstruktion Subjektiver Theorien*. Tübingen: Francke.

Schegloff, E. and Sacks, H. (1974) "Opening up Closings," in R. Turner (ed.), *Ethnomethodology*. Harmondsworth: Penguin. pp. 233–264.

Schensul, S.L., Schensul, J.J. and LeCompte, M.D. (1999) *Essential Ethnographic Methods: Observations, Interviews, and Questionnaires* (Book 2 in Ethnographer's Toolkit). Walnut Creek, CA: AltaMira Press.

Schneider, G. (1985) "Strukturkonzept und Interpretationspraxis der objektiven Hermeneutik," in G. Jüttemann (ed.), *Qualitative Forschung in der Psychologie*. Weinheim: Beltz. pp. 71–91.

Schneider, G. (1988) "Hermeneutische Strukturanalyse von qualitativen Interviews," *Kölner Zeitschrift für Soziologie und Sozialpsychologie*, 40: 223–244.

Schnell, M.W. and Heinritz, C. (2006) *Forschungsethik: Ein Grundlagen- und Arbeitsbuch mit Beispielen aus der Gesundheits- und Pflegewissenschaft*. Bern: Huber.

Schönberger, Ch. and Kardorff, E.v. (2004) *Mit dem kranken Partner leben*. Opladen: Leske & Budrich.

Schönfelder, W. (2011) "CAQDAS and Qualitative Syllogism Logic—NVivo 8 and MAXQDA 10 Compared" [91 paragraphs], *Forum Qualitative Sozialforschung/Forum: Qualitative Social Research*, 12(1), Art. 21, http://nbn-resolving.de/urn:nbn:de:0114-fqs1101218.

Schreier, M. (2012) *Qualitative Content Analysis in Practice*. London: Sage.

Schreier, M. (2014) "Qualitative Content Analysis," in U. Flick (ed.), *The SAGE Handbook of Qualitative Data Analysis*. London: Sage. pp. 170–183.

Schütz, A. (1962) *Collected Papers*, Vols. I, II. The Hague: Nijhoff.

Schütze, F. (1976) "Zur Hervorlockung und Analyse von Erzählungen thematisch relevanter Geschichten im Rahmen soziologischer Feldforschung," in Arbeitsgruppe Bielefelder Soziologen (eds.), *Kommunikative Sozialforschung*. Munich: Fink. pp. 159–260.

Schütze, F. (1977) "Die Technik des narrativen Interviews in Interaktionsfeldstudien, dargestellt an einem Projekt zur Erforschung von kommunalen Machtstrukturen," Manuskript der Universität Bielefeld, Fakultät für Soziologie.

Schütze, F. (1983) "Biographieforschung und Narratives Interview," *Neue Praxis*, 3: 283–93.

Schwandt, T.A. and Halpern, E.S. (1988) *Linking Auditing and Metaevaluation: Enhancing Quality in Applied Research*. Thousand Oaks, CA: Sage.

Scott, J. (1990) *A Matter of Record: Documentary Sources in Social Research*. Cambridge: Polity Press.

Scourfield, J., Fincham, B., Langer, S. and Shiner, M. (2012) "Sociological Autopsy: An Integrated Approach to the Study of Suicide in Men," *Social Science & Medicine* 74: 466–473.

Seale, C. (1999) *The Quality of Qualitative Research*. London: Sage.

Seale, C. (2000) "Using Computers to Analyse Qualitative Data," in D. Silverman (ed.), *Doing Qualitative Research: A Practical Handbook*. London: Sage. pp. 154–174.

Shweder, R.A. (1996) "True Ethnography: The Lore, the Law, and the Lure," in R. Jessor, A. Colby and R.A. Shweder (eds.), *Ethnography and Human Development*. Chicago, IL: University of Chicago Press. pp. 15–32.

Silverman, D. (1985) *Qualitative Methodology and Sociology*. Aldershot: Gower.

Silverman, D. (1993) *Interpreting Qualitative Data: Methods for Analyzing Talk, Text and Interaction* (2nd edn 2001). London: Sage.

Skeggs, B. (2001) "Feminist Ethnography," in P. Atkinson, A. Coffey, S. Delamont, J. Lofland and L. Lofland (eds.), *Handbook of Ethnography*. London: Sage. pp. 426–442.

Smith, D.E. (1978) "'K is Mentally Ill': The Anatomy of a Factual Account," *Sociology*, 12(1): 23–53.

Smith, D.E. (2002) "Institutional Ethnography," in T. May (ed.), *Qualitative Research in Action*. London: Sage. pp. 17–52.

Soeffner, H.G. (2004) "Social Science Hermeneutics," in U. Flick, E.v. Kardorff and I. Steinke (eds.), *A Companion to Qualitative Research*. London: Sage. pp. 95–100.

Spradley, J.P. (1979) *The Ethnographic Interview*. New York: Holt, Rinehart and Winston.

Spradley, J.P. (1980) *Participant Observation*. New York: Holt, Rinehart and Winston.

Sprenger, A. (1989) "Teilnehmende Beobachtung in prekären Handlungssituationen: Das Beispiel Intensivstation," in R. Aster, H. Merkens and M. Repp (eds.), *Teilnehmende Beobachtung: Werkstattberichte und methodologische Reflexionen*. Frankfurt: Campus. pp. 35–56.

Stewart, D.M. and Shamdasani, P.N. (1990) *Focus Groups: Theory and Practice*. Newbury Park, CA: Sage.

Strauss, A.L. (1987) *Qualitative Analysis for Social Scientists*. Cambridge: Cambridge University Press.

Strauss, A.L. and Corbin, J. (1990) *Basics of Qualitative Research* (2nd edn 1998; 3rd edn 2008). London: Sage.

Strauss, A.L. and Corbin, J. (eds.) (1997) *Grounded Theory in Practice*. London: Sage.

Strauss, A.L., Schatzmann, L., Bucher, R., Ehrlich, D. and Sabshin, M. (1964) *Psychiatric Ideologies and Institutions*. New York: Free Press.

Strauss, A.L. and Corbin, J. (2008) *Basics of Qualitative Research* (3rd edn). London: Sage.

Struppek, D. (2010) *Patientensouveränität im Pflegeheim. Sichtweisen hochaltriger mehrfach erkrankter Pflegeheimbewohner, ihrer Pflegekräfte, Ärzte und privaten Bezugspersonen*. Bern: Huber.

Stryker, S. (1976) "Die Theorie des Symbolischen Interaktionismus," in M. Auwärter, E. Kirsch and K. Schröter (eds.), *Seminar. Kommunikation, Interaktion, Identität*. Frankfurt: Suhrkamp. pp. 257–274.

Tashakkori, A. and Teddlie, Ch. (eds.) (2003a) *Handbook of Mixed Methods in Social & Behavioral Research*. Thousand Oaks, CA: Sage.

Tashakkori, A. and Teddlie, Ch. (2003b) "Major Issues and Controversies in the Use of Mixed Methods in Social and Behavioral Research," in A. Tashakkori and Ch. Teddlie (eds.), *Handbook of Mixed Methods in Social & Behavioral Research*. Thousand Oaks, CA: Sage. pp. 3–50.

Tashakkori, A. and Teddlie, Ch. (eds.) (2010) *Handbook of Mixed Methods in Social & Behavioral Research* (2nd edn). Thousand Oaks, CA: Sage.

Taylor, S. (2012) "'One Participant Said …': The Implications of Quotations from Biographical Talk," *Qualitative Research*, 12: 388–401.

Teays, W. (2012) *Seeing the Light: Exploring Ethics through Movies*. Malden, MA: Wiley-Blackwell.

Terrill, L. and Gullifer, J. (2010) "Growing Older: A Qualitative Inquiry into the Textured Narratives of Older, Rural Women," *Journal of Health Psychology*, 15(5): 707–715.

Thomas, W.I. and Znaniecki, F. (1918–1920) *The Polish Peasant in Europe and America*, Vols. 1–2. New York: Knopf.

Thomson, R., Hadfield, L., Kehily, M.J. and Sharpe, S. (2012) "Acting Up and Acting Out: Encountering Children in a Longitudinal Study of Mothering," *Qualitative Research*, 12(2): 186–201.

Thomson, R., Plumridge, L. and Holland, J. (eds.) (2003) "Longitudinal Qualitative Research" (Special issue), *International Journal of Social Research Methodology – Theory & Practice*, 6(3).

Thornberg, R. and Charmaz, K. (2014) "Grounded Theory and Theoretical Coding," in U. Flick (ed.), *The SAGE Handbook of Qualitative Data Analysis*. London: Sage. pp. 153–169.

Toerien, M. (2014) "Conversations and Conversation Analysis," in U. Flick (ed.), *The SAGE Handbook of Qualitative Data Analysis*. London: Sage. pp. 327–340.

Toerien, M. and Kitzinger, C. (2007) "Emotional Labour in Action: Navigating Multiple Involvements in the Beauty Salon," *Sociology*, 41(4): 645–662.

Toulmin, S. (1990) *Cosmopolis: The Hidden Agenda of Modernity*. New York: Free Press.

Ulrich, C.G. (1999) "Deutungsmusteranalyse und diskursives Interview," *Zeitschrift für Soziologie*, 28: 429–447.

Ussher, J. (1999) "Feminist Approaches to Qualitative Health Research," in M. Murray and K. Chamberlain (eds.), *Qualitative Health Psychology: Theories and Methods*. London. Sage. pp. 98–110.

Van Maanen, J. (1988) *Tales of the Field: On Writing Ethnography*. Chicago: University of Chicago Press.

Wästersfors, D., Åkerström, M. and Jacobsson, K. (2014) "Reanalysis of Qualitative Data," in U. Flick (ed.), *The SAGE Handbook of Qualitative Data Analysis*. London: Sage. pp. 467–480.

Webb, E.J., Campbell, D.T., Schwartz, R.D. and Sechrest, L. (1966) *Unobtrusive Measures: Nonreactive Research in the Social Sciences*. Chicago: Rand McNally.

Weber, M. (1919) "Wissenschaft als Beruf," in J. Winkelmann (ed.) (1988), *Max Weber: Gesammelte Aufsätze zur Wissenschaftslehre*. Tübingen: Mohr. pp. 582–613.

Weber, M. (1949) *The Methodology of the Social Sciences* (trans. and ed. E.A. Shils and H.A. Finch). New York: Free Press.

Weitzman, E.A. (2000) "Software and Qualitative Research," in N. Denzin and Y.S. Lincoln (eds.), *Handbook of Qualitative Research* (2nd edn). London: Sage. pp. 803–820.

Weitzman, E.A. and Miles, M.B. (1995) *Computer Programs for Qualitative Data Analysis: A Software Sourcebook*. London: Sage.

Welch, C., Marschan-Piekkari, R., Penttinen, H. and Tahvanainen, M. (2002) "Corporate Elites as Informants in Qualitative International Business Research," *International Business Research Review*, 11: 611–628.

Welsh, E. (2002) "Dealing with Data: Using NVivo in the Qualitative Data Analysis Process" [12 paragraphs]. *Forum Qualitative Sozialforschung/Forum: Qualitative Social Research*, 3(2), Art. 26, http://nbn-resolving.de/urn:nbn:de:0114-fqs0202260.

Wengraf, T. (2001) *Qualitative Research Interviewing: Biographic Narrative and Semi-Structured Methods*. London: Sage.

Wernet, A. (2014) "Hermeneutics and Objective Hermeneutics," in U. Flick (ed.), *The SAGE Handbook of Qualitative Data Analysis*. London: Sage. pp. 234–246.

Wertz, F.J., Charmaz, K., McMullen, L.M., Josselson, R., Anderson, R. and McSpadden, E. (2011) *Five Ways of Doing Qualitative Analysis*. New York: Guilford.

West, C. and Zimmerman, D.H. (1991) "Doing Gender," in J. Lorber and S.A. Farrell (eds.), *The Social Construction of Gender*. Newbury Park, CA: Sage. pp. 13–37.

Whyte, W.F. (1955) *Street Corner Society* (enlarged edn). Chicago, IL: University of Chicago Press.

Wiedemann, P.M. (1995) "Gegenstandsnahe Theoriebildung," in U. Flick, E.v. Kardorff, H. Keupp, L.v. Rosenstiel and S. Wolff (eds.), *Handbuch Qualitative Sozialforschung* (2nd edn). Munich: Psychologie Verlags Union. pp. 440–445.

Wiener, C. (2007) "Making Teams Work in Conducting Grounded Theory," in A. Bryant and K. Charmaz (eds.), *The SAGE Handbook of Grounded Theory*. London: Sage. pp. 293–310.

Wilkinson, S. (1999) "Focus Groups: A Feminist Method," *Psychology of Women Quarterly*, 23: 221–244.

Williamson, G. and Prosser, S. (2002) "Illustrating the Ethical Dimensions of Action Research," *Nurse Researcher*, 10: 38–49.

Willig, C. (2003) *Introducing Qualitative Research in Psychology: Adventures in Theory and Method*. Buckingham: Open University Press.

Willig, C. (2014a) "Discourses and Discourse Analysis," in U. Flick (ed.), *The SAGE Handbook of Qualitative Data Analysis*. London: Sage. pp. 341–353.

Willig, C. (2014b) "Interpretation and Analysis," in U. Flick (ed.) *The SAGE Handbook of Qualitative Data Analysis*. London: Sage. pp. 136–149.

Willig, C. and Stainton-Rogers, W. (eds.) (2007) *The SAGE Handbook of Qualitative Research in Psychology*. London: Sage.

Wilson, T.P. (1982) "Quantitative 'oder' qualitative Methoden in der Sozialforschung," *Kölner Zeitschrift für Soziologie und Sozialpsychologie*, 34: 487–508.

Winograd, T. and Flores, F. (1986) *Understanding Computers and Cognition*. Reading, MA: Addison-Wesley.

Witzel, A. (2000, January) "The Problem-Centered Interview" [27 paragraphs], *Forum Qualitative Sozialforschung/Forum: Qualitative Social Research* [Online Journal], 1(1), www. qualitative-research.net/fqs-texte/1-00/1-00witzel-e.htm (date of access: March 25, 2013).

Witzel, A. and Reiter, H. (2012) *The Problem-centred Interview*. London: Sage.

Wodak, R. and Meyer, M. (eds.) (2009) *Methods for Critical Discourse Analysis* (2nd revised edition). London: Sage.

Wolcott, H.F. (1990a) "On Seeking and Rejecting: Validity in Qualitative Research," in W. Eisner and A. Peshkin (eds.), *Qualitative Inquiry in Education: The Continuing Debate*. New York: Teachers College Press. pp. 121–152.

Wolcott, H.F. (1990b) *Writing up Qualitative Research*. London: Sage.

Wolff, S. (1986) "Das Gespräch als Handlungsinstrument: Konversationsanalytische Aspekte sozialer Arbeit," *Kölner Zeitschrift für Soziologie und Sozialpsychologie*, 38: 55–84.

Wolff, S. (1987) "Rapport und Report. Über einige Probleme bei der Erstellung plausibler ethnographischer Texte," in W.v.d. Ohe (ed.), *Kulturanthropologie: Beiträge zum Neubeginn einer Disziplin*. Berlin: Reimer. pp. 333–364.

Wolff, S. (1992) "Die Anatomie der Dichten Beschreibung: Clifford Geertz als Autor," in J. Matthes (ed.), *Zwischen den Kulturen? Sozialwissenschaften vor dem Problem des Kulturvergleichs*. Soziale Welt Sonderband 8. Göttingen: Schwartz. pp. 339–361.

Wolff, S. (2004a) "Ways into the Field and Their Variants," in U. Flick, E.v. Kardorff and I. Steinke (eds.), *A Companion to Qualitative Research*. London: Sage. pp. 195–202.

Wolff, S. (2004b) "Analysis of Documents and Records," in U. Flick, E.v. Kardorff and I. Steinke (eds.), *A Companion to Qualitative Research*. London: Sage. pp. 284–290.

Wolff, S., Knauth, B. and Leichtl, G. (1988) "Kontaktbereich Beratung. Eine konversations-analytische Untersuchung zur Verwendungsforschung," Manuskript. Projektbericht, Hildesheim.

Wuggenig, U. (1990) "Die Photobefragung als projektives Verfahren," *Angewandte Sozialforschung*, 16: 109–131.

Wundt, W. (1928) *Elements of Folk Psychology*. London: Allen & Unwin.

Yardley, L. (2000) "Dilemmas in Qualitative Health Research," *Psychology and Health*, 15: 215–228.

Znaniecki, F. (1934) *The Method of Sociology*. New York: Farrar and Rinehart.

Author Index

Coltart, C. 180
Corbin, J. 18, 40, 69, 70, 137, 156, 377, 398,
    402, 403–4, 406, 407, 408, 409, 410,
    414, 415, 418, 419, 462, 466, 489–90,
    507, 509–10
Cornish, F. 121
Corti, L. 238, 464
Coulter, J. 445
Cowton, C.J. 236, 240
Creswell, J.W. 29, 112, 121, 135
Czarniawska, B. 41, 290

Dabbs, J.M. 337
Dalbec, P.-Y. 118, 119, 120, 121, 135, 301, 306,
    328, 332, 524
D'Andrade, R.G. 87
Daston, L. 295
Davidson, J. 120, 465, 472, 474
Deeke, A. 227
Delamont, S. 42, 62, 240, 301, 320, 332
Denzin, N.K. 18, 19, 19–20, 21, 24, 47, 81,
    83, 84, 88, 93, 97, 174, 181, 183, 184,
    191, 192, 239, 261, 284, 289, 290, 301,
    306, 309, 312, 322, 330, 331, 332, 334,
    336, 340, 341, 342–3, 344, 345, 346,
    351, 456, 459, 472, 474, 481, 517, 523,
    524, 530, 532
Derrida, J. 88
Devereux, G. 317
di Gregorio, S. 120, 465, 472, 474
Dingwall, R. 50, 51, 54, 62
Douglas, J.D. 158
Drew, P. 379, 389–90, 441–2

Earley, A. 118, 119, 120, 121, 135, 301, 306,
    328, 332, 524
Eberle, T. 522
Eckert, T. 33
Edwards, D. 446, 450, 451, 459
Edwards, R. 172, 181
Ehrlich, D. 323
Elliot, R. 494
Ellis, C. 19, 42, 517
Emerson, R. 323, 332
Erdheim, M. 87
Erzberger, C. 34, 35, 38, 525
Esin, C. 41, 288, 290
Evers, J.C. 462, 472

Fathi, M. 41, 288, 290
Feldman, C. 290
Fielding, J.L. 149
Fielding, N.G. 21, 135, 149, 465, 471
Fierz, K. 38
Fincham, B. 363
Fink, A. 71, 73
Fischer, C.T. 152, 252, 494

Fischer-Rosenthal, W. 20, 283–4, 284–5, 290, 524
Fiske, M. 243
Fleck, L. 76, 148
Flick, U. 20, 24, 27, 30, 34, 35, 38, 45, 46, 51,
    62, 72, 82, 83, 84, 88, 90, 92, 97, 103,
    106, 112, 123, 131, 134, 143, 149, 152,
    155, 156, 184, 185, 192, 202, 206, 239,
    252, 264, 273, 286, 289, 290, 321, 324,
    345, 358, 372, 379, 400, 423, 437, 446,
    459, 474, 506, 519, 525, 526, 528, 529,
    532, 47, 57, 527, 532, 533
Flores, F. 18, 97
Flynn, L.R. 54, 57
Fontana, A. 239, 243, 261
Foucault, M. 83, 448
Fretz, R. 323, 332
Freud, S. 42, 138
Frey, J.H. 239, 243, 261
Friese, S. 462, 464, 468, 475
Fuchs, M. 514
Fuchs, W. 271

Gaiser, T.J. 58, 240
Gallop, R. 331
Garfinkel, H. 20, 40, 84, 85, 86, 93, 357,
    459, 523
Garms-Homolová, V. 38, 46, 72, 143, 155, 474
Garz, D. 392, 452
Gaskell, G. 36, 206, 289, 527
Gebauer, G. 99, 101, 102, 106
Geer, B. 18, 314, 318, 319, 331
Geertz, C. 12, 18, 83, 313, 510, 511, 514, 518,
    519, 531
Georgakopoulou, A. 287, 290
Gergen, K.J. 76, 77
Gergen, M. 78, 79
Gerhardt, U. 128, 170, 459, 496
Giardina, M. 19
Gibbs, G. 21, 379, 383, 396, 438, 462, 475, 525
Gildemeister, R. 79, 80, 93
Gillespie, A. 121
Gilligan, C. 78
Ginsberg, P.E. 62
Girtler, R. 480
Glaser, B. 18, 20, 40, 43, 66, 67, 70, 81, 112,
    113, 115, 131, 137, 138, 139, 140–1, 144,
    146, 149, 170, 171–2, 173, 174, 180, 183,
    398, 399, 400, 402, 403, 409, 410, 411–12,
    413, 414–15, 415, 416, 419, 471, 487, 496,
    507, 522
Glaserfeld, E. v. 76, 77
Gobo, G. 181, 289, 296
Goetz, J.P. 529
Goffman, E. 20, 307, 362
Gold, R.L. 309
Goldsmith, R.E. 54, 57
Goodman, N. 98, 103, 106

Grathoff, R. 20
Gregory, A. 464
Groeben, N. 202, 207, 217, 222, 223, 240
Guba, E.G. 18, 26, 90, 191, 353, 487, 488, 495, 497, 499, 507, 515
Gubrium, J.F. 42, 207, 233, 289, 296, 301, 320, 330, 332
Guiney Yallop, J.J. 517–18
Gullifer, J. 206

Habermas, J. 12, 20
Hadfield, L. 134
Halkier, B. 257, 261, 262
Hall, E.T. 336
Halperin, D.M. 80
Halpern, E.S. 488
Hammersley, M. 76, 306, 319, 320, 330, 332, 373, 483, 491, 507, 531
Hammoudi, A. 42
Happ, M.B. 38
Harper, D. 301, 306, 334, 335, 337, 351, 524
Harré, R. 86, 106, 289, 397, 437, 445, 446, 523
Harrington, B. 166
Hart, C. 70, 73
Hartmann, H. 14
Harvard, L. 71, 73
Harvey, W.S. 231
Haupert, B. 282, 338, 497
Have, P. ten 41, 442, 445, 459, 468, 471
Heath, C. 301, 347, 349, 351
Heinritz, C. 49, 50
Henwood, K. 180
Heritage, J. 85, 446, 447
Herkommmer, S. 248
Hermanns, H. 43, 125, 202, 206, 210, 239, 265, 266, 267, 268, 270, 273, 290
Herrmann, W.J. 38, 56, 57, 72
Heyl, B.S. 202, 233, 240
Hildenbrand, B. 162, 177, 280, 281, 285, 286, 290
Hindmarsh, J. 301, 347, 351
Hine, C. 325, 326, 327, 328, 332, 364
Hitzler, R. and Eberle, T.S. 522
Hochschild, A.R. 146
Hodder, I. 353, 354
Hodgetts, A. 338, 339
Hodgetts, D. 338, 339
Hoffmann-Riem, C. 20, 138
Holbrook, B. 471
Holland, J. 131
Hollingshead, A.B. 16
Holstein, J.A. 42, 82, 207, 233, 296, 301, 320, 330, 332
Holton, J.A. 413
Holze, J. 118, 120, 135, 301, 306, 326, 332, 364, 524
Honer, A. 321

Hood, J.C. 398
Hoose, B. 123
Hopf, C. 32, 54, 62, 207, 209, 216, 386
Huberman, A.M. 18, 29, 114, 115, 463, 488, 493
Hughes, E.C. 18, 314, 331
Humphreys, L. 52
Hurrelmann, K. 27

Iser, W. 99

Jackson, K. 462, 469, 474
Jacob, E. 18
Jacobsson, K. 238
Jahn, W. 280, 281, 285, 286, 290
Jahoda, M. 122
Jefferson, G. 441
Jessop, J. 52
Jessor, R. 144, 301, 322, 332
Jick, T. 30
Joas, H. 81
Joffe, H. 23, 470, 471
Johnson, J.M. 486
Johnson, R.B. 36
Jordan, A. 487
Jorgensen, D.L. 312, 331
Josselson, R. 59, 380

Kamiske, G.F. 499, 500, 501
Kardorff, E.v. 20, 24, 31, 62, 290
Kehily, M.J. 134
Kelle, U. 21, 34, 35, 38, 410, 413, 463, 464, 469, 470, 525
Kendall, P.L. 202, 211, 212, 213, 214, 215, 216, 239, 241, 243, 325
Kim, H.O. 214, 239
Kirk, J.L. 481–2, 483, 506
Kitzinger, C. 79, 383, 458
Kitzinger, J. 250
Kleining, G. 20, 28, 140, 174
Klocke, A. 27
Knauth, B. 85
Knoblauch, H. 47, 294, 301, 346, 347, 349, 351, 450, 451, 459, 523, 524, 525, 527, 532
Knorr-Cetina, K. 76, 86, 148, 517
Koepping, K.P. 315
Konau, E. 20, 28, 87, 88, 453, 456
König, H.D. 87
Kowall, S. 388, 389, 396
Kozinets, R.V. 118, 119, 120, 121, 135, 297, 301, 306, 328, 332, 524
Kraimer, K. 392
Krambeck, J. 20, 28, 87, 88, 453, 456
Krueger, R.A. 262
Krüger, H. 247
Kuck, J. 38, 72

Kuckartz, U. 33
Kvale, S. 207, 233, 239, 483, 507

Lang, G. 345
Langenhove, L.v. 437
Langer, S. 363
Lau, T. 159
Laurie, H. 463
Lazarsfeld, P.F. 29, 122
Lea, S.J. 340
LeCompte, M.D. 296, 529
Lee, R.M. 21, 135, 354, 465, 471
Leeman, J. 516, 519
Legewie, H. 394
Leichtl, G. 85
Lempert, L.B. 401, 530
Lincoln, Y.S. 18, 19–20, 24, 26, 47, 88, 90, 93,
     97, 181, 191, 239, 261, 331, 332, 353,
     472, 474, 481, 487, 488, 495, 497, 499,
     507, 515, 517, 530, 532
Littig, B. 202, 230, 240
Livingstone, S. 202, 250, 254, 262
Lofland, J.H. 42, 62, 150, 151, 152, 156, 240,
     301, 320, 323, 324, 332, 510
Lofland, L.H. 42, 62, 150, 151, 152, 156, 240,
     301, 320, 323, 324, 332
Lopez de Vallejo, I. 517–18
Luckmann, Th. 76, 450, 451, 459, 523
Lüders, C. 59, 88, 131, 294, 301, 303, 319, 320,
     321, 456, 487, 515, 521, 526, 527, 531
Luff, P. 347, 349
Lunbeck, E. 295
Lunt, P. 202, 250, 254, 262
Lynn, N. 340

McDonald, S. 314
McEvoy, B.T. 71
McGibbon, E. 331
Machi, L.A. 71
McKinlay, J.B. 28, 36
McMullen, L.M. 59, 380
McSpadden, E. 59, 380
Maddill, A. 487
Maeder, Ch. 47, 527, 532
Maijalla, H. 59
Malinowski, B. 18, 514
Mangold, W. 244
Mann, C. 52, 118, 120, 235, 255, 256
Marcus, G.E. 97, 322, 519, 526
Markham, A.M. 235, 324
Marotzki, W. 118, 119, 120, 135, 301, 306,
     325, 326, 327, 332, 364, 524
Marschan-Piekkari, R. 230, 231
Marshall, C. 116, 135
Marvasti, A. 301, 329, 331
Mason, J. 206
Mathes, R. 33

Mauthner, M. 52
Maxwell, J.A. 93, 112, 113, 135, 485, 495, 507
May, T. 206, 351, 354, 374
Maynard, M. 79
Mayring, P. 379, 429, 430, 431, 432, 433, 434,
     435, 437, 438, 530
Mead, G.H. 81
Mead, M. 335, 513
Meier, C. 119, 301, 306, 327, 332, 467, 524
Melzer, W. 27
Menz, W. 202, 228, 229, 240
Merkens, H. 180, 310
Mertens, D.M. 59, 62
Merton, R.K. 76, 148, 211, 212, 213, 214, 215,
     216, 239, 241, 243
Meuser, M. 227, 228, 229, 230, 237
Meyer, M. 449
Mies, M. 78
Mikecz, R. 231
Mikos, L. 301, 342, 343, 351
Miles, M.B. 18, 21, 29, 114, 115, 463,
     466, 488, 493
Miller, G. 82
Miller, M. 481–2, 483, 506
Miller, T. 52
Mishler, E.G. 233, 264, 484, 485
Mitchell, R.G. 43
Mitra, A. 118, 360, 361, 364
Mondada, L. 305, 350
Moody, K. 38
Morgan, D.L. 250, 251, 262
Morse, J.M. 116, 176, 181
Moscovici, S. 89
Mruck, K. 462, 472
Mulkay, M. 86, 148
Murphy, E. 50, 51, 54, 62
Murphy, J.A. 499
Murray, M. 264, 286

Nagel, U. 227, 228, 229, 230, 237
Neill, S.H. 46, 418
Neuber, A. 252
Neuman, W.L. 153–4
Nicca, D. 38
Niemann, M. 310, 311
Northway, R. 54

Oakley, A. 74
Ochs, E. 287
O'Connell, D.C. 388, 389, 396
Oerter, R. 214, 239
Oevermann, U. Allert, T. 20, 28, 87, 88, 453, 456
Olesen, V. 79, 93
Onwuegbuzie, A.J. 36

Paavilainen, E. 59
Paechter, C. 134, 331

Struppek, D. 278
Stryker, S. 82

Tahvanainen, M. 230, 231
Tashakkori, A. 35, 38
Taylor, C. 531
Taylor, M. 18
Taylor, S. 62, 106, 134
Teays, W. 342
Teddlie, Ch. 35, 38
Terrill, L. 206
Thomas, W.I. 18, 354
Thomson, R. 131, 134
Thornberg, R. 40, 45
Tindall, C. 18
Toerien, M. 379, 383, 441, 443, 458, 459
Toulmin, S. 22
Trenn, T.J. 76, 148
Tuma, R. 294, 524
Turner, L.A. 36

Ulrich, C.G. 210
Ussher, J. 78, 79

Van Maanen, J. 509, 510–11, 519
Verständig, D. 118, 120, 135, 301, 306, 326, 332, 364, 524

Walter, U. 152, 252
Wästersfors, D. 238
Webb, E.J. 354
Weber, M. 14, 496, 536
Weitzman, E.A. 21, 463, 464, 466

Welch, C. 230, 231
Welsh, E. 462, 463
Wengraf, T. 239
Wernet, A. 20, 42, 379, 454, 459, 530
Wertz, F.J. 59, 380
West, C. 80
Wetherell, M. 70, 86, 379, 446, 447–8, 459, 523
Whyte, W.F. 163–4
Wibowo, S. 214, 239
Wiedemann, P.M. 172
Wiener, C. 398
Wilkinson, S. 79
Williamson, G. 52
Willig, C. 18, 41, 42, 46, 70, 86, 375, 379, 446, 447, 448, 449, 459
Wilson, T.P. 36
Winograd, T. 18, 97
Witzel, A. 202, 223, 224, 225, 226, 240
Wodak, R. 449
Wolcott, H.F. 483, 485, 514
Wolff, S. 85, 159, 160, 166, 301, 353, 356–7, 363, 444, 509, 510, 518, 529
Wright, P.R. 517–18
Wuggenig, U. 336, 337
Wulf, C. 99, 101, 102, 106
Wundt, W. 17

Yardley, L. 494

Zeisel, H. 122
Zimmerman, D.H. 80
Zittoun, T. 121
Znaniecki, F. 18, 174, 354, 497

Subject Index

Figures and Tables are indicated by page numbers printed in bold.

construction of concepts 77
construction of reality 91, 95–6
constructivism 76–8, 97, 535
  and interpretation 98–**9**
  radical 76, 77
  and viability 77
constructivist sociology of science 76
content analysis 378, 379, 429–36
  advantages 435
  coding frame 429–30
  defining research question 430
  defining units 430
  explicative content analysis 434
  limitations 436–7
  step by step procedure 431–**2**
  structuring content analysis 434–5
  summarizing content analysis 431–4, **432**
    rules 432–3
  uses 435
context in language analysis 440
contrasting cases 496–7
conversation analysis 41, 372, 378, 379,
    440–6, 458, 523
  collection building 443
  context 440, 441, 444
  definition 535
  evaluating patterns 443
  individual case analysis 443
  limitations 445–6
  methodological precepts 441–2
  'ordinary' and 'institutional' talk 443
  pattern identification 443
  procedure 442–3
  repair 445
  sequencing 127
  Socio-psychiatric Counseling (case study)
    444
  turns 85, 440, 441, 444, 544
  uses 445
counseling, subjective theory of 89
covert observation 52–3
credibility 487–8, 490
cultural studies 447–8, 535

data analysis 369–82
  aims 369–70
  categorizing 44–5
  coding 44–5, 371, 373
  definition 370–1
  existing data 44
  form and content 370
  forms of data 44, 372
  generalization 371
  in grounded theory 371
  interpretation 375–6
  levels of meaning 370–1

data analysis *cont.*
  methods 376–80
    appropriateness 377, 380–1
    case study 380
    comparison of methods 377, **378–9**
    compatibility with research process
      340, 377
    selection checklist 381–2
  sequential analysis 374–5
  text analysis, goals of 371
  see also data management
data management 371–2
  global analysis 394–5
  indexing data 393–4
  software 394, 464
data triangulation 174, 183
descriptive validity 485
dialectics 163, 535
discourse analysis 41, 70, 372, 378, 379,
    446–50, 458
  definition 536
  and discursive psychology 86–7, 446, 449
  Foucauldian discourse analysis 448–9
  principles and approaches 449–50
  questions to address 447
  Racism in New Zealand (case study) 447–8
  research steps 448–9
disenchantment of the world 14, 536
documentation sheets 387–8
documents 298–9, 353–63
  accessibility 354, 357
  Analysing Documents of Professional Training
    (case study) 358
  analysis: starting point 356–7
  authenticity 355, 356
  constructing a corpus 356
  context 359, 360
  credibility 355, 356
  definition 353
  intertextuality 356, 360
  non-written documents 359
  primary or secondary 355
  purpose and origin 355, 357
  and records 353
  representativeness 355, 356
  selection 355–6
  The Polish Peasant in Europe and America
    (case study) 354–5
  types 353–4
  understanding 357
  Web pages 360–2
    intertextuality 360
    multimedia 361
    non-linearity 360, 361
    sampling 361
  see also film analysis; photographs; texts

e-mail interviews 234–6, 524
  anonymity 235, 236
  reliability 235
elite interviews 230–1, 536
empirical methods 15, 22
episodic interviews 68, 273–80, 536
  episodic and semantic knowledge 273–4
  limitations 280
  Patients' Self-determination in Nursing
      Homes (case study) 278
  problems 278–9
  procedure 275–7
  questions 277–8
  in research process 279
  Technological Change in Everyday Life
      (case study) 275–7
epistemology 26, 536
ethics 48–62
  anonymization 57, 120, 393
  autonomy 51
  avoiding harm to participants 57
  codes of ethics 50–3, 535
  confidentiality 54, 59
  definitions 49
  doing justice to participants 58–9
  duplication of research 53
  informed consent 50, 51, 54–7, 120
  and Internet 120
  need for in research 49, 60–1
  principles 49–50, 50–1
  problems 51–3
  sensitive subjects 59–60
  in triangulation 190
  welfare of participants 54–5
ethics committees 48, 53, 536
ETHNOGRAPH 465, 466
ethnography 42, 44, 127, 296–7,
      319–29, 523
  analysis 330
  assessing reliability 482
  coding 373
  contribution to qualitative methods 322
  definition 536
  features 319–21
  field notes 323–4
  Homeless Adolescents Behavior (case study)
      321
  informed consent 51
  interviews 232–3
  limitations 322
  and other non-verbal data **300–1**
  pragmatic use of methods 322
  reporting 320
  representation 514
  sampling 322
  virtual ethnography 297, 324–9
  writing 510–11, 514, 518

ethnomethodology 40–1, 81, 84–6, 521, 523
  assumptions 85–6
  conversation analysis 41, 85, 86
  definition 536
  discourse analysis 86–7
  ethnomethodological indifference 85
  membership roles 158–9
  studies of work 86
  see also conversation analysis; discourse
      analysis; genre analyis
evaluating theories 489–92
evaluation 34
evidence-based practice 19, 536
existential sociology 158, 159
existing data 44
experimental designs 13
expert interviews 227–30, 537
  conducting 229–30
  forms 228
  technical, process and interpretive
      knowledge 229
  uses 230

failure in research 529
family studies: joint narratives 281
features of qualitative research 14–15
feminism 78–9
field notes 44, 402, 537
  conventions 482
film analysis 342–6
  Alcoholism in Hollywood Movies
      (case study) 343
  Nursing as a Profession in TV Serials (case
      study) 344–5
  realistic and subversive readings 342
  steps in analysis 342–3
  see also photographs; video analysis
focus groups 43, 69, 198, 242–61, 537
  analysis 252, 257–61
    analytic dimensions **258**
    challenges 260
    group dynamics and interaction 258
    identifying patterns 258
    within and between groups 258, 259–60
  beginning 251–2
  characteristics 199–200
  checklist 260–1
  conducting focus groups 251–3
  feedback 253–4
  generating discussion 254
  group discussions 244–5
  group dynamics 256
  group interviews 243
  informality 252
  limitations 253–4, 260
  mediation 243
  member checks 253

focus groups *cont.*
    online 199, 255–7
    in the research process 255–6
    typologies 259
    uses 250–1
focused interviews 211–17
    Adult Interview (case study) 213–14
    depth 213
    forms of questions 212
    limitations 216–17
    problems 215–16
    procedure 211
    range 213
    retrospective inspection 213
    specificity 213
folk psychology 17, 537
FQS (journal) 21, 517

gender inequalities 79
gender studies 79–80
generalization 21, 26, 34, 113–14, 495–8
    analytic induction 497–8
    comparative studies 114
    constant comparative method 496
    and context of research 495
    contrasting cases 496–7
    definition 537
    and demographic dimensions 114
    from cases to theory 496
    general statements 13
    internal and external 495
    minimal/maximal comparison of cases 497–8
    numerical and theoretical 114
    and sampling 496–7
generative questions 537
genre analysis 450–2, 458, 537
German Sociological Association 50
German-language research 527
Germany: phases in history of qualitative research **21**
global analysis 394–5
goal of research 16
'going native' 164, 315–18, 537
grounded theory 40, 42, 378, 379, 522–3, 538
    coding 138, 373, 398, 399, 402–18
        aims 413
        Awareness of Dying and Awareness Contexts 411
        axial 407–8
        axial/theoretical/focused 403
        basic questions for 407
        categories and subcategories 408
        coding families 410, 413, **414**
        coding paradigm **407**–8, 413
        in vivo codes 406, 538

grounded theory *cont.*
        labels 406
        line by line procedure 411–12
        open 403, 404–7
        possible endlessness of options 417
        procedures 403–4, 411–12
        selective 403, 408–9, 413
        substantive codes 413
        theoretical 410–11, 413
        theoretical saturation 403, 544
        Unending Work and Care (case study) 409–10
        versions of coding 403, 414–15
    concepts and generic concepts 404, 406, 408
    data collection 399, 400–1
    field notes 402
    Identity Dilemmas of Chronically Ill Men (case study) 415–16
    limitations 417
    memos 387, 399, 401–2, 530
    methodology 397–9
        versions of 403–4
    priniciple of openness 138
    process of research 137–9
    research questions 399
    sampling 398, 399
    sensitizing concepts 400
    and software 471
    theory development 404
group discussions 43, 223, 244–5, 538
    forms of groups 245
    homogenous and heterogeneous groups 245–6
    limitations 250
    moderation 146–7
      forms of 246
      Group Discussion with Bank Employees (case study) 247
    problems 248–9
    process 247–8
    in the research process 249–50
    Student Dropouts (case study) 245–6
    see also focus groups

hard-to-reach people 13, 164, 196–7
health and ageing, representations of 89
Health Behavior in Social Context (WHO) 27
Health on the Street – Homeless Adolescents (case study) 27–8, 82–3, 150, 153–4, 400
hermeneutic approaches 42, 538
    see also objective hermeneutics; social science hermeneutics
hermeneutic classificatory content analysis 33
history of qualitative research 17–22
    German-speaking areas 20–1
    phases 18
    United States 18–20, **21**
hybridization 525, 538